CW01433229

ISBN 978-1-333-21004-5
PIBN 10473997

1 MONTH OF
FREE
READING

at

www.ForgottenBooks.com

———◆———

By purchasing this book you are eligible for one month membership to ForgottenBooks.com, giving you unlimited access to our entire collection of over 700,000 titles via our web site and mobile apps.

To claim your free month visit:

www.forgottenbooks.com/free473997

English
Français
Deutsche
Italiano
Español
Português

www.forgottenbooks.com

Mythology Photography **Fiction**
Fishing Christianity **Art** Cooking
Essays Buddhism Freemasonry
Medicine **Biology** Music **Ancient
Egypt** Evolution Carpentry Physics
Dance Geology **Mathematics** Fitness
Shakespeare **Folklore** Yoga Marketing
Confidence Immortality Biographies
Poetry **Psychology** Witchcraft
Electronics Chemistry History **Law**
Accounting **Philosophy** Anthropology
Alchemy Drama Quantum Mechanics
Atheism Sexual Health **Ancient History**
Entrepreneurship Languages Sport
Paleontology Needlework Islam
Metaphysics Investment Archaeology
Parenting Statistics Criminology
Motivational

TRANSACTIONS

OF THE

GAELIC SOCIETY OF INVERNESS.

VOL. I.—YEAR 1871-72.

TRANSACTIONS

OF

The Gaelic Society

OF

INVERNESS.

VOL. I.—YEAR 1871-72

Clann nan Gaidheil ri Guaillean a' Cheile.

INVERNESS:

PRINTED FOR THE SOCIETY BY
WILLIAM MACKAY, 14 HIGH STREET.

1872.

CONTENTS.

ERRATA.

Page	23,	line	10	—*For*	éifeached,	*read*	éifeachd.
,,	48,	,,	21	,,	Dh'fheach,	,,	Dh'fheuch.
,,	52,	,,	13	,,	inneal,	,,	ainneal.
,,	56,	,,	8	,,	Comuinn,	,,	Chomuinn.
,,	,,	,,	10	,,	Thi,	,,	Tha.
,,	61,	,,	32	,,	beanneachd,	,,	beannachd.
,,	96,	,,	25.	,,	aeain,	,	acain.
,,	,,	,,	11	,,	son,	,	's an.
,,	,,	,,	18	,,	eaoidh,	,,	caoidh.

Page 52, line 38—*For*   Tri cheud deug le'n dian armachd—
Fir thugad a tha, a chaillich !

Read—Tri cheud deug le'n dian armachd,
'Us lothunn choin aig gach fear—
Fir thugad a tha, a chaillich !

The Gaelic Society of Inverness.

OFFICE-BEARERS FOR YEAR 1872.

CHIEF.
CLUNY MACPHERSON OF CLUNY.

CHIEFTAINS.
THOMAS MACKENZIE. | JOHN MURDOCH.
JOHN MACKINTOSH, M.A.

HON. SECRETARY
W. MACKINNON BANNATYNE, ROYAL ACADEMY.

SECRETARY.
WILLIAM MACKAY, 67 CHURCH STREET.

TREASURER.
JOHN MACDONALD, THE EXCHANGE.

BARD.
ANGUS MACDONALD.

MEMBERS OF COUNCIL.
CHARLES MACKAY. | JAMES FRASER.
DUNCAN MACIVER. | WILLIAM MACKENZIE.
LACHLAN MACBEAN.

BANKERS.
THE CALEDONIAN BANKING COMPANY.

COMUNN GAILIG INBHIR-NIS.

COIMH-DHEALBHADH.

1. 'S e ainm a' Chomuinn "COMUNN GAILIG INBHIR-NIS."

2. 'S e tha an rim a' Chomuinn:—Na buill a dheanamh iomlan s a' Ghàilig; cinneas cànaine, bardachd, agus ciùil na Gàidhealtachd; bardachd, seanachas, sgeulachd, leabhraichean agus sgriobhanna 's a' chànain sin a thearnadh o dhearmad; leabhar-lann a chur suas ann am baile Inbhir-Nis de leabhraichibh agus sgriobhannaibh— ann an cànain sam bith—a bhuineas do chàileachd, ionnsachaidh, eachraidheachd agus sheanachasaibh nan Gàidheal no do thairbhe na Gàidhealtachd; còir agus cliù nan Gàidheal a dhìon; agus na Gàidheil a shoirbheachadh a ghnà ge b'e àit am bi iad.

3. 'S iad a bhitheas 'nam buill, cuideachd a tha 'gabhail suim do rùntaibh a' Chomuinn, agus so mar gheibh iad a staigh:—tairgidh aon bhall an t-iarradair, daingnichidh ball eile an tairgse, agus, aig an ath choinneamh, ma roghnaicheas a' mhor-chuid le crannchur, nithear ball dhith-se no dheth-san cho luath 's a phaidhear an comh-thoirt; cuirear crainn le ponair dhubh agus gheal, ach, gu so bhi dligheach, feumaidh tri buill dheug an crainn a chur. Feudaidh an Comunn urram cheannardan a thoirt do urrad 'us seachd daoine cliùiteach.

4. Pàidhidh ball urramach, 'sa' bhliadhna .	£0	10	6
Ball cumanta	0	5	0
Foghlainte	0	1	0
Agus ni ball-beatha aon chomh-thoirt de	7	7	0

5. 'S a' Cheud-mhios, gach bliadhna, roghnaichear, le crainn, Co-chomhairle a riaghlas gnothuichean a' Chomuinn, 's e sin—aon Cheann, tri Iar-chinn, Cleireach Urramach, Runaire, Ionmhasair, agus còig buill eile—feumaidh iad uile Gàilig a thuigsinn 's a bhruidhinn; agus ni còigear dhuibh coinneamh.

GAELIC SOCIETY OF INVERNESS.

CONSTITUTION.

1. The Society shall be called the "GAELIC SOCIETY OF INVERNESS."

2. The objects of the Society are the perfecting of the Members in the use of the Gaelic language; the cultivation of the language, poetry, and music of the Scottish Highlands; the rescuing from oblivion of Celtic poetry, traditions, legends, books, and manuscripts; the establishing in Inverness of a library to consist of books and manuscripts, in whatever language, bearing upon the genius, the literature, the history, the antiquities, and the material interests of the Highlands and Highland people; the vindication of the rights and character of the Gaelic people; and, generally, the furtherance of their interests whether at home or abroad.

3. The Society shall consist of persons who take a lively interest in its objects, admission to be as follows:—The candidate shall be proposed by one member, seconded by another, balloted for at the next meeting, and if he or she have a majority of votes, and have paid the subscription, be declared a member. The ballot shall be taken with black beans and white; and no election shall be valid unless thirteen members vote. The Society has power to elect distinguished men as Honorary Chieftains to the number of seven.

4. The Annual Subscription shall be, for—

Honorary Members .	.	.	.	. . £0 10 6
Ordinary Members .	.	.	.	. . 0 5 0
Apprentices	.	.	.	. . 0 1 0
And a Life Member shall make one payment of				7 7 0

5. The management of the affairs of the Society shall be entrusted to a Council, chosen annually, by ballot, in the month of January, to consist of a Chief, three Chieftains, an Honorary Secretary, a Treasurer, and five other Members of the Society, all of whom shall understand and speak Gaelic; five to form a quorum.

6. Cumar coinneamhan a' Chomuinn gach seachduin o thoiseach an Deicheamh-mios gu deireadh Mhàirt, agus gach ceithir-la-deug o thoiseach Ghiblein gu deireadh an Naothamh-mios. 'S i a' Ghàilg a labhairear gach oidhche mu'n seach aig a chuid a's lugba.

7. Cuiridh a' Cho-chomhairle là air leth anns an t-Seachdamh-mios air-son Coinneamh Bhliadhnail aig an cumar Co-dheuchainn agus air an toirear duaisean air-son piobaireachd 'us ciùil Ghàidh-ealach eile; anns an fheasgar bithidh co-dheuchainn air leughadh agus aithris Bardachd agus Rosg nuadh agus taghta; an deigh sin cumar Cuirm chuideachdail aig am faigh nithe Gàidhealach rogh-aiun 'san uirghioll, ach gun roinn a dhiùltadh dhaibh-san nach tuig Gàilig. Giùlainear cosdas na co-dheuchainne le trusadh sònraichte a dheanamh agus cuideachadh iarraidh o'n t-sluagh.

8. Cha deanar atharrachadh sam bith air coimh-dhealbhadh a' Chomuinn gun aontachadh dha-thrian de nam bheil de luchd-bruidhinn Gàilig air a' chlar-ainm. Ma's miann atharrachadh a dheanamh a's éiginn sin a chur an céill do gach ball, mios, aig a' chuid a's lugha, roimh'n choinneamh a dh'fheudas an t-atharrachadh a dheanamh. Feudaidh ball nach bi 'a làthair roghnachadh le lamh-àithne.

9. Taghaidh an Comunu Bàrd, Pìobaire, agus Fear-leabhar-lann.

———

Ullaichear gach paipear agus leughadh, agus giùlainear gach deasboireachd le rùn fosgailte, duineil, dùrachdach air-son na fìrinn, agus cuirear gach ni air aghaidh ann an spiorad caomh glan, agus a reir riaghailtean dearbhta.

6. The Society shall hold its meetings weekly from the beginning of October to the end of March, and fortnightly from the beginning of April to the end of September. The business shall be carried on in Gaelic on every alternate night at least.

7. There shall be an Annual Meeting in the month of July, the day to be named by the Committee for the time being, when Competitions for Prizes shall take place in Pipe and other Highland Music. In the evening there shall be Competitions in Reading and Reciting Gaelic Poetry and Prose, both original and select. After which there shall be a Social Meeting, at which Gaelic subjects shall have the preference, but not to such an extent as entirely to preclude participation by persons who do not understand Gaelic. The expenses of the competitions shall be defrayed out of a special fund to which the general public shall be invited to subscribe.

8. It is a fundamental rule of the Society that no part of the constitution shall be altered without the assent of two-thirds of the Gaelic-speaking Members on the roll ; but if an alteration be required, due notice of the same must be given to each member, at least one month before the meeting takes place at which the alteration is proposed to be made. Absent Members may vote by mandates.

9. The Society shall elect a Bard, a Piper, and a Librarian.

———

All Papers and Lectures shall be prepared, and all Discussions carried on, with an honest, earnest, and manful desire for truth; and all proceedings shall be conducted in a pure and gentle spirit, and according to the usually recognised rules.

INTRODUCTION.

THE GAELIC SOCIETY OF INVERNESS may be accepted as more or
less of an embodiment of the sentiment of the Highlands. It is
one of the results of a feeling that Highland interests and ideas
have not had adequate expression in previously existing organisations ; and it is intended at once to stimulate and to give vent, in
its own way, to that public spirit which is awakening in the
country. There was an idea at one time that such diversities as
manifest themselves in the Celt and the Saxon should be smoothed
down so as to obliterate the distinction between the races. Wise
men now think that variety should be cherished in the human
as well as in other species ; and that this variety, even in one
nation, should be a source of strength and not of weakness.
With regard to England, the theory has been laid down that her
force is actually due to the marked variety of races with which
south Britain has always been peopled. In Kent, in Cornwall,
in Norfolk, in Cumberland, &c., it has been said that there
are, and that there have been from time immemorial, and independently even of the Saxon and Norman invasions, distinct types
of men ; and that from these stocks the country has a perennial
supply of that energy, mental and physical, which flows from the
fresh admixture of superior races. Without insisting on the exact
scientific truth of this theory, it has the value of teaching the one
race to look with tolerance, and even with double interest, upon
another, and it ought to go a good way towards extinguishing that
feeling of impatience with which some among us have regarded
the occasional outbursts of nationality which break in upon the
monotony of our trading existence. And this theory or some

other influence has undoubtedly done so. Every spark of Scottish fervour which ventured to show itself above our humble hearths was wont to be made the object of torrents of abuse, the *Times* being the fire-engine-in-chief on the scene of conflagration. If a Highlander or a Lowlander lamenting over the decadence of the clansmen of the North, or at the vanishing of the Gaelic language, had been the premonition of some terrible revolution, the *Scotsman*, published in our own metropolis, could hardly have been more perturbed; and between the indignation and the ridicule thus brought to play upon the sentiments of our people, it is no wonder that some of them shrank from declaring and showing that either Celtic sentiment or patriotic fervour had any existence in their bosoms. Within the last two or three weeks several of our London organs of opinion—the *Times* among them—have signified in no equivocal terms, that it is no longer a crime or an offence for people to make characteristic displays of their nationality; that, in fact, it is rather pleasant than otherwise to behold such displays; and that it is a wholesome sign of people to let it be distinctly understood that they go in for maintaining that type of humanity which happens to be stamped upon themselves. At least, if the *Times, Telegraph*, and others, did not say all this, this and a great deal more may fairly be inferred from their admissions.

There may be other and less philosophic reasons why these amiable things should now be said. It is very questionable if any philosophy ever had anything to do in producing the feeling with which some pro-Saxons regarded the people of the Highlands. At the time when that feeling found the most philosophical—or least absurd—expression, Highland people were in the way of certain powerful parties who professed to be great national economists. The people must be got rid of; but it would not have done to say openly that they must be removed so that the greed of those so-called economists might be satisfied. So a philosophy was invented, and an economic scheme laid down—to be expounded from week to week in such columns as could be prostituted to such purposes—under which the greatest economic blunders and national crimes might be committed, no one making the perpetrators afraid. But now these deeds stand forth in the light of day as crimes and blunders : the desolated glens should now be yielding more beef and mutton, and the expatriated people should be extending the dominion of the plough over the heather. At this hour, steam, at enormous cost, is employed to do the work of reclamation which only human hands can do satisfactorily, and which human beings would have given many years of their lives to be allowed to perform at the time the behests of greed were being enforced against them. The people which at that time were cast out as worthless are now wanted to develop the capabilities of our glens and straths, and the lands which were supposed to be useless are now beginning to be regarded as susceptible of unlimited fertility. So that, in giving ostensible expression to the sentiments of the Highlands, we cherish no antagonism to the Lowlands, but, on the contrary, we act in harmony with the best convictions and in furtherance of the best interests of the South. The cherishing of the sentiments, the traditions, and the characters of our people, will do much to re-inspire them with the energy and the confidence necessary to the manful discharge of the duties which they owe to the rest of the nation as well as to themselves.

The Gaelic Society is further intended to be a medium through which the Highland people may discharge a certain class of duties which they owe to all nations; and the present volume of Transactions, if it is not a large instalment of that duty, is at once an indication of the disposition to pay in full, and an earnest of what remains to be done. The Highlands owe it to the world of letters and philosophy, that whatever the Gaelic language, traditions, legends, poetry, sentiments and philosophy contain which is of value should be preserved by those who know them, and handed over as valuable contributions to the stock of materials out of which human learning must be built up. Whether the Gaelic language is destined to die or not, the above is due from Highlanders; and it is all the more imperative upon them if there be reason to fear that the language will shortly cease to be spoken. The more it is felt that such a calamity is imminent, the more active we should be to rescue from oblivion whatever is liable to perish along with the language. This work is not to be disparaged merely because Highland vanity is liable to show itself. It would be a very churlish thing to reject a man's offered treasure or assistance merely because it pleased himself to make the offer. The offer should be accepted with all the more satisfaction because it left behind, as well as brought with it, a feeling of pleasure, and in the conviction that the service was all the more likely to be genuine, being prompted by a desire for credit, as well as by a disposition to oblige. Besides, that must be a positively bad element of character which would influence one to reject what should be a gain to himself, merely because his acceptance might gratify the giver.

It is an encouragement to know, and a pleasure to record the fact, that although the duty referred to devolves upon Highlanders in general and upon the Gaelic Society in particular, the work has not been neglected. Enough has been done to prove that we possess the materials referred to in rich abundance, and also that these materials are in requisition. For a record of what has already been picked up, and an indication of what may yet be gathered, we need only refer to Mr Campbell of Islay's " Leabhar na Peinne," just out. A great recommendation of " Leabhar na Feinne " is that, besides containing a large quantity of ancient matter never before published, and much valuable information regarding things previously in print, it is such a faithful register of the books which have already been published in the same line, and of the manuscripts which have passed through the author's hands in the course of his researches. This book is valuable as exhibiting the most rigid and ⌠critical care to avoid exaggeration and straining after more than the facts sustain. This will be a defect, no doubt, in the eyes of many ; but even if the author should be found to have carried his caution so far as to shrink from conclusions actually sustained by his own facts and by the facts ascertained by others, the error may well be regarded as both novel and safe. In its own department of Celtic literature, "Leabhar na Feinne " deserves to occupy a position analogous to that occupied by the late lamented Professor O'Curry's " Manuscript Materials of Irish History," a work to which every labourer in this great field is glad to acknowledge his indebtedness, as placing the key, at least, to the most valuable literary antiquities of Ireland in his hand, and saving lives of labour to all future Celtic scholars. Mr Campbell has rendered similar service to those who

would work in the field of Highland literature, and incidentally to
the votaries of Irish, Scandinavian, and even Indian antiquities:
for thus are the language and the very pastimes of the humblest of
our Highland people mixed up with the great and interesting subjects of philology, ethnology, history, and anthropology generally,
and invested with an importance over and above that which they
possess to ourselves as being our own and something of a key and
a stimulus to the minds of our people.   The publication of the
Dean of Lismore's Book was itself an epoch in Celtic literature ;
and every one at all versed in such matters knows that Dr Maclauchlan and Dr Skene, the translator and the editor of that book,
are, like Mr Campbell, institutions in themselves, whose claims on
the world of letters the kindred institution at Inverness will deem
it an honour to rival even in a small degree.

Although there is no real occasion to do so here, beyond that
of gratifying ourselves in acknowledging good work well done, we
cannot refrain from bringing the names of James Macpherson and
a former Lord of Bute before our readers, for the immediate purpose of offering many hearty thanks for the munificence of the
present Marquis of Bute, and for the elegant and scholarly, yet
very unostentatious, service rendered by the Rev. Dr Clerk of Kil-
malie, in bringing out the recent splendid edition of what are still
cherished by thousands as the "Poems of Ossian"—the poems of
the Highland Ossian. ·

From want of a more suitable place in which to mention them
we introduce here two facts which are interesting and pleasing in
connection with the appreciation of the Ossianic Poems, for which
we are so largely indebted to Mr Macpherson.   The first of these
is that Dr White of Waterford, himself a poet and a composer, as
well as an accomplished scholar and popular lecturer, has taken
Comala (Caomh-Mbala) as he found it in Macpherson, and rendered it into admirable verse, and, with lyrics, airs, and pictorial
illustrations, fitted it for representation on the stage as a genuine
Celtic opera, which he calls "The Irish Princess."   In accordance with the idea that the materials of Macpherson's Ossian
were Irish, Dr White says, in his introduction, that he only
"brought home the Irish Princess from her wanderings in the
Highlands."   No one will relish the reply better than Dr White

himself—that if the "Poems of Ossian," aş given by Macpherson, were mere fabrications of his own, some one may appear here-after on a Scottish stage, claiming that he has brought home the "Highland Princess from her wanderings in Innisfail." The great fact lies under the rivalry—that this pathetic episode, like many others in the same category, seizes the genuine Celtic mind, and proves itself native, whether on Irish or on Scottish soil. The fact which follows would justify the addition of "Italian soil" to the broad platform occupied by Ossian. At this present time, there is in the press a magnificent tribute to the Poems of Ossian—twelve graphic and spirited engravings, illustrative of as many scenes, and displaying the physical and mental characteristics of the leading heroes and heroines in Ossian, accompanied by descriptive letterpress. The author is an Italian artist resident in London. Signor Priolo expresses his surprise that the rich mine which he has discovered in Ossian had not been previously worked, and intimates that there is not a page which does not offer most attractive subjects for pictorial illustration. These are the poems which our humble peasantry had the inborn taste to appreciate. Such taste, we opine, is well worthy of being cared for and culti-vated, even though found under a roof of heather ; and the men who preferred such compositions, even to heartless treatises on a false economy, are themselves worthy of being cherished and firmly established in their native land.

Of the papers which follow, it is proper to say that they are not all that were read before the Society. Some were withheld from motives of modesty—the writers not venturing to appear in print. Some were actually lost, and they not the least de-serving of being preserved in type; whilst others, of very great interest, which we might have given in this volume, are held over for our next.

Of the volume as a whole, it may be said to owe its origin in some measure to a strong feeling which exists, that Highland ideas have not hitherto had adequate expression in the press. The idea of a Highland newspaper is still, we believe, entertained by many outside this Society. The proposal to start a Gaelic magazine was before the Society, but while this matter was under the consideration of a committee, "The Gael" returned from his wanderings in Canada and took up his abode in Glasgow. It was felt then that it was but fair and courteous to give Mr Nicolson every chance of reaping abundantly in the field on which he had the penetration and the vigour to enter whilst we were looking about us. But, although another magazine might for a time be a rival, the issue of an occasional volume of our Transactions was an absolute necessity in itself; and with "The Gael" it would be a helpful fellow-worker, coming slowly in the rear. And finally, it was thought that a volume such as this is would be a suitable acknowledgment, on the part of the resident members, of their obligation to those ladies and gentlemen at a distance who gave expression to their patriotism and good taste in becoming members of the Society.

TRANSACTIONS.

The result of numerous private conversations, and some public correspondence, on the subject of a Gaelic Society in Inverness, was that a meeting of gentlemen favourable to the proposal was held on the evening of the 4th of September 1871, in one of the halls of the Association Buildings, Inverness. There were present about thirty-five gentlemen, among whom were Mr Thomas Mackenzie, ex-Rector of the High School; Mr Alex. Dallas, Town-Clerk; Mr John Murdoch, of the Inland Revenue Department; Mr John Mackintosh, M.A., Rector of the Old Academy; Mr Alexander Mackenzie, Clachnacuddin House; Mr John Macdonald, The Exchange; Mr Charles Mackay, Drummond; Mr William Mackenzie and Mr Donald Macleod, Raining's School; Mr Angus Macdonald, Queen Street; Mr Donald Campbell, Bridge Street; Mr Duncan Mackintosh, Bank of Scotland; Mr Robert Macdonald, Gaelic Teacher; Mr Barron, Courier Office; Mr Charles Mackintosh, Commission-Agent; and Mr William Mackay, Writer.

Mr Thomas Mackenzie was moved to the chair, and Mr William Mackay, who had issued circulars calling the meeting, was chosen interim Secretary.

Mr John Murdoch moved that a Gaelic Society be established in Inverness. In so moving, he stated that he had, himself, often felt both surprised and ashamed that until this hour the Highland capital should be without such an institution. He held that, from a regard even for those outside the Highlands, whether Celts or Saxons, there should be in Inverness an organisation of men to whom philologists, archæologists, ethnologists, and the like, could at any time apply for any kind of information bearing upon the language, traditions, poetry, and legendary lore of the Highlands. In the second place, assuming, as some hope and as others fear, that the Gaelic language is destined to die out, there should be a

special effort made to rescue from destruction and oblivion all that
is valuable in the lore now afloat in the Highlands.   That there
are vast stores of valuable matter thus in danger of being lost for
ever, most intelligent Highlanders know ; and clearly Inverness is
the centre into which these stores should be gathered.   It is of
great importance to philology in particular that such an institution
should be established, and such a work of collecting should be
begun, whilst there are large numbers living whose vernacular the
Gaelic is.   He, for example, had always found that the best etymology of a puzzling name was that obtained from a totally unlettered
native peasant—one who did not know a word of English, and very
often one who did not know that he was giving an etymology at
all.   The simple unsophisticated Highland pronunciation of the
word very often preserved the germ of every part of the compound,
and thus carried its own meaning to the Gaelic ear.   Next to this,
and sometimes even before this, was the etymology furnished to
the Gaelic-speaking observer by the object, or the scene itself.
Once travelling in the south of Ireland, the speaker was greatly
amused at the flights of invention to which persons who disregard
this very natural fact sometimes have recourse.   Approaching the
left bank of the river Lee, his companion remarked that they were
just coming to Carrigrohan Castle, " so called after the French De
Rohans."   " Why," said the speaker, " the place tells its own story.
It is the rock overhanging the river, ' carraig air o'ain,' just as plainly
as Carrig on Shannon, or Carrig on Suir."   Balaam's ass did not
speak more plainly than do thousands of places ; but, from not
knowing the language of the country, our learned men are both
deaf and blind to what otherwise might be so clear to them.   In
the third place, we should have books and MSS. bearing upon
everything connected with the language, history, and economics of
the Highlands and Highland people, so that when any one at a
distance wanted to know anything of ourselves or our country,
ancient or modern, he might, with a certainty of being supplied,·
turn towards the Gaelic Society of Inverness for information.   And
he had no doubt that a very great quantity of such valuables could
be·had in a short time.   There were hampers of valuable papers
lying in different parts of the country with scarcely an owner, and
whilst we had no Celtic Library in the Highland capital, valuable
books and MSS. pertaining to our language were treasured in Ireland, in England, in France, in Italy (" Yes," said the chairman,
" in Spain.")   Another thing which pained the speaker was the
slipshod Gaelic often spoken in the streets of Inverness, every third
or fourth word English.   Now he held that our object (with such
an institution as they were that night founding), should be to compare the different local dialects of Gaelic, and with the assistance

afforded by our ancient MSS., erect and polish off what he would call a classic Gaelic speech. This was no mere fancy ; there were evidences that such a speech was at one time recognised in the Highlands, and the actual formation of such a speech in Ireland many centuries back was a simple fact in history. Then there was the less ambitious, but even more obvious object, of members perfecting themselves in the rich and elegant language of their forefathers. Whilst he would not be satisfied with this society being merely a Gaelic class, he would have a Gaelic class to form one of its most vital constituents. He would not enlarge further on the subject, desiring rather to hear the views of others, and he had no doubt many there had valuable suggestions to offer.

Mr Alexander Mackenzie seconded the motion, remarking on the anomaly that when any one wanted to know anything connected with Gaelic literature or tradition, he must apply, not to a body of learned and patriotic men in the Capital of the Highlands, but to a Gaelic, or a Celtic, or a Highland Society in London or New York ! This disgraceful state of things must be at once changed. At the same time he would recommend that the Inverness Gaelic Society should be connected with similar societies elsewhere, not only for literary and scientific purposes, but for the purpose of rendering assistance to young Highlanders seeking their fortunes in other lands. The Society should look after the interests of young men coming from the remote Highlands to Inverness; and when they left Inverness for more distant fields of enterprise, it should give them such directions and introductions as would facilitate their advancement in the lands of their adoption. The fact of their being members of the Inverness Society would be a passport to Gaelic Societies elsewhere. He thought that there were many gentlemen of position in the Highlands and elsewhere who would feel it an honour to be members and patrons of the Society. There was one gentleman in particular, an enthusiastic Highlander, whom he should expect to see a member, and whom he should suggest for patron. He referred to Cluny Macpherson. Then as to the name of the Society, he would hold by the simple " Gaelic Society of Inverness ;" then people would know what was meant. But if you called it the " Celtic Society," or the " Club of True Highlanders," or any other of these farfetched names, he questioned very much if it would not be as great a failure as some of the merely convivial associations which had done so little to better the minds or bodies of their compatriots. Whilst some of these were drinking toddy, the Gaelic Society of London was labouring to raise its race and language from insignificance, and had already, he might say, succeeded in establishing the long desiderated Gaelic Professorship in the University of Edinburgh.

He had great pleasure in seconding the resolution that a Gaelic Society be established in Inverness.

Mr Alexander Dallas, Town-Clerk, had great pleasure in supporting the resolution, not, however, that he agreed with the sentiments expressed on a recent occasion by Cluny Macpherson, who had just been proposed with such deserved compliments as patron of the Society. Cluny said that he would have all the children taught to read and write Gaelic in the schools. Now, whilst he held the distinguished Chief in as high estimation as any one in that meeting, he most decidedly differed with him in that particular. What would be the use of it? It would in no way promote their prosperity in the world; no business was done in Gaelic beyond a few transactions, perhaps, at the Muir of Ord. And who ever heard of accounts kept or rendered in Gaelic? As to the name of the Society, he was favourable to the more general term "Celtic," otherwise it might be supposed that it had no interest in anything beyond the mere maintenance of the language of the Highlanders. Holding by this name, whilst allowing the language to die, we might so labour as to render essential service to philology and archæology generally, by contributing our Gaelic share to the common stock of Celtic lore.

Mr Robert Macdonald was called upon by the Chairman to give his views as an experienced teacher of Gaelic. Mr Macdonald did so by stating that he saw no difficulty in doing business in Gaelic, and he had often seen accounts made out in Gaelic And as to teaching the language, he was engaged at present in teaching Gaelic to a young gentleman who, he had no doubt, would ere long be a distinguished member of the Society—he referred to The Mackintosh of Mackintosh.

Mr Donald Campbell said he could not refrain from stating, in opposition to what Mr Dallas had said, that for his part he would have a great difficulty, indeed, in getting rid of his mother tongue, and he had no desire to do so. On the contrary, he held that so rich, copious, and expressive a language should be preserved for its own sake, and not merely for the sake of the poetry or tradition which might be extant in it.

The Chairman briefly reviewed what had been brought before the meeting, adding that there was nothing peculiarly English in the keeping of accounts, that the very elements of our symbols were as much Gaelic as English, and gave off-hand a formula of a Gaelic account. He hoped that something would be done to save his ears from the jabber of mongrel Gaelic which was becoming a scandal to Inverness. There was, no doubt, reason to fear that the Gaelic would die out as a spoken tongue, but that would not be for a generation or two, and the nearer the catastrophe the more urgent the duty of doing what was contemplated in establishing a Gaelic Society in Inverness.

The resolution was carried with acclamation.

After a good deal of conversational discussion on such matters as the name of the Society, the subscription, corresponding and honorary members, the library, &c., a committee was appointed to draw up a constitution and rules to be submitted for the approval of another meeting.

On the 21st of September the Committee appointed for the purpose—and which consisted of Mr Dallas, Mr Murdoch, Mr John Mackintosh, Mr Charles Mackintosh, Mr John Macdonald, Mr Angus Macdonald, Mr Alexander Mackenzie, Mr Campbell, and Mr William Mackay—submitted a draft constitution. After due consideration and some modification, the constitution, printed on another page, was adopted.

On the 28th a formal incorporation took place, in which those gentlemen who had so far taken part in the proceedings were enrolled as members. A Society of twenty-four members was thus constituted.

On the 5th October a Provisional Committee of Management was appointed, and matters connected with the working of the Society were discussed and cleared up. At the same meeting a sub-committee was appointed to revise the form and terms of the constitution, without any change in the substance.

October 12.—The chief business transacted—making arrangements for the Inaugural Lecture by the Rev. Mr Mackenzie of Kilmorack. On the same occasion Mr Angus Macdonald was appointed Bard to the Society.

INAUGURAL LECTURE.

The Inaugural lecture was delivered on the evening of 19th October, by the Rev. A. D. Mackenzie of the Free Church, Kilmorack, under the presidency of Sir Kenneth S. Mackenzie of Gairloch, Bart., who, in the most handsome manner, set aside several engagements to take the chair. Sir Kenneth was supported by J. F. Campbell, Esq. of Islay ; Duncan Davidson, Esq. of Tulloch ; Hugh Matheson, Esq., London ; Professor White of Waterford, Ireland ; the Revs. A. Macgregor, G. Mackay, D. Sutherland, P. Robertson ; Bailie Simpson ; Jos. Robertson, Esq.,

Northern Counties Fire Office; Thomas Mackenzie, Esq., Broad-stone; A. Dallas, Esq., Town-Clerk, &c.

The large hall of the Association Buildings, in which the meeting was held, was tastefully decorated with a royal stag's head lent by Mr Snowie; drapery of Clan tartans from Clachnacuddin House; and bunches of deers' grass from the *Monadhliath*. There was a large and respectable audience, and every proof was afforded of the interest which was felt in the proceedings.

Sir Kenneth Mackenzie congratulated the meeting on the formation of the Gaelic Society, and referred to its objects—the perfecting of the members in the use of the Gaelic language, the establishment of a library, the preservation of Gaelic manuscripts and literature, &c. He thought their programme set out very fully what the objects of such a society should be, and of all places in the world Inverness was the most suitable for the establishment of a Gaelic library, and the collection of works bearing on Celtic literature. There was no other town in Great Britain where, from a convenient distance, any considerable number of educated people who understood the Gaelic language could be got together. Now that there was some chance of a Gaelic chair being established in the University of Edinburgh, it was very desirable that, in the country, people should have an opportunity of preparing themselves for the University class. Perhaps one of the first results of the formation of the Society would be to excite an interest among the members in that legendary lore which exists among the Gaelic speaking population of the islands and the remote districts of the mainland. Old tales and ballads were disappearing before the spread of the English language, and the changes in popular customs which could not fail to accompany an advancing civilisation. A certain class of these legends was widespread, being common to the whole of Scotland and to Ireland; and though their historical value might be questionable, still, being of great antiquity, they were of much interest and value as giving an insight into the sentiments and feelings of the early people. Another class was more local, affecting particular districts and families; but even these, if thoroughly sifted, might be of value to the historian, as casting a light upon ancient manners and customs. No doubt the Society would endeavour to rescue these old relics from oblivion. And apart from such objects altogether, he thought that even people of unimaginative and realistic mind, for whom pictures of the past had no attraction, would find it to their advantage to be connected with such a Society, at least as long as Gaelic was a spoken language. Gaelic was no doubt a decaying language, and the time must come when it would cease to be generally spoken. He did not know how soon or how late this might be; its existence might be counted by decades or by centuries, but certainly Gaelic as a living tongue would disappear. Still before it went—while it was going—the services of Gaelic speaking pastors and teachers would be required; and it was rather an unfortunate thing in these circumstances that the Gaelic language was gradually being lost hold of by the more educated classes. The Society might, therefore, do some good in a material point of view—not by stopping the advance of English, but by trying to get the educated classes to study Gaelic a little more than they had been doing, and not to forget the language of their ancestors altogether. He would not detain the meeting, because they had come to hear a lecture on a very interesting subject—" The Position of Gaelic and its Value to .the Linguist,"—and he was sure Mr Mackenzie would treat it in a very interesting way.

Mr Mackenzie, who on rising was received with applause, said : —When the gentlemen interested in the formation of the Gaelic Society of Inverness asked me about a fortnight ago to do them the honour of delivering the inaugural lecture, permit me to say, in the outset, that 1 considered the honour as done to me. There are few things indeed which I should consider more complimentary than to be selected to advocate the claims of a language which I have long loved and admired—a language endeared to me by the associations of youth, home, and kindred—a language, moreover, in regard to which I have long entertained a strong and, I trust, intelligent conviction that it has never received from scholars a tithe of the consideration to which it is fairly entitled.

Having agreed, wisely or unwisely, to occupy my present position, the question was, how to render my lecture serviceable to the interests of the Society, and, at the same time, not uninteresting to a general audience. I can only say that it has been my sincere endeavour, with the scanty time and appliances at my disposal, to unite these objects. How far I may have succeeded it is for you to judge.

One of the most formidable difficulties which I anticipate for the Society, at least in the outset, is the *Cui bono ?* " What's the use ?" will be heard on every side, " the language is dying out, and the sooner the better, for it forms a grievous obstacle to the advancement of our Highland people. Besides, all that you may do can avail you little in retarding its decay, or preventing its ultimate extinction." Well, it must be admitted that there is as much truth in this as to make it plausible for the ends for which it is advanced. It is one of the plainest lessons of past history, that two vernacular languages have never kept their ground side by side in any country. One or other has invariably gone down, and it needs no soothsayer to determine in the case before us which

of the two must give way.   In sad and sober truth, the process is
going on before our eyes, and however much some of us may deplore it, we cannot shut our eyes to the fact, that the world will
not be many centuries older when the last speaker of Gaelic shall
be as great a curiosity as was the last Cornish-speaking woman in
the past century.

Now, have we not admitted with sufficient fulness all that can
be said on that side the question?   Have we not put the case
against ourselves as strongly and broadly as the most prejudiced
Saxon or Teuton could desire?   Yes we have, and we can afford
to do it, and still make good our plea.   And now for our reply, or
rather for the heads of it, for we cannot dwell much longer on pre-
liminaries.   First of all, we deny that a knowledge of Gaelic is
any obstacle in the way of a man's advancement, but quite the reverse provided he has English along with it.   It has been one of
my mottoes in dealing with my people—" Get English by all
means, and the more the better, but don't forget your Gaelic."   I
remember an old woman who used to be a hanger-on in our kitchen.
She had a strong dislike to English, and it was truly amusing to
hear her rating the children for speaking English at all—" Shoe
shoe nasty shoe, no shoe ach bròg."   Here was the other extreme.

We might appeal to the present rights of our language as that
which is best understood and most loved by about half a million of
our countrymen, and the only language of by far the greater number of these—its rights to be understood by ministers, doctors,
lawyers, sheriffs, and all such public functionaries.   This was put
very forcibly by Dr Blackie, a week or two ago, in his lecture in
Oban.   It is plain and palpable to any one of common sense.   We
might appeal to the acknowledged excellences of the language itself
—its homogeneousness, in which it seems to me unrivalled, building
up its vocables from its own monosyllabic roots; its descriptiveness;
its antique and picturesque phraseology, which points with sufficient
plainness to a tropical climate as its early home; its stores of
choicest poetry, which in the description of nature can hardly be
excelled; and, finally, its inestimable value as the only exponent of
the topography of a larger area of the world's surface than any
other language of the earth ever occupied.   In a word, such is my
opinion of its value and of its future benefits on this score alone,
that I would regard it as a calamity graver and wider than I need
at present care to express were our old mother to pass into oblivion
before we have extracted from her bosom all that she can now
furnish for its illucidation.

I. But it is time that we should state some of those historical
grounds on which we rest the claims of our language to so high an
antiquity.

1. Let me remark for the benefit of those who may have paid little attention to ethnological questions, that as far back as history guides us we find the Celts occupying an important place in the community of nations. Greek and Roman writers call them by three names, Celtae or Keltae, Galatae, and Galli or Galloi. From Herodotus, usually styled the father of history, born B.C. 484, downward, they are often referred to, and the very terms in which they are referred to can only be explained on the supposition that even then they were being displaced from the wide areas formerly occupied, by successive races from the east, that hotbed of humanity. You find in Strabo, who wrote about the first years of the Christian era, Celts simply, Celtiberians, Celto-Ligurians, Celto-Scythians, Gallo-Grecians. Indeed, to modern ethnologists of a certain stamp, who are determined to over-ride all history to maintain their own pet theories, these references are a sore puzzle. Dr Latham, for instance, is terribly worried with Celts; they crop up about his hands here and there, and the way he takes to get rid of them is somewhat amusing. "Ah, you're here, Mr Celt, are you; yes, it can't be denied; but let me tell you, sir, you are an intruder." Just so, Dr Latham; and what if we can prove that your pet Iberians, Ligurians, and Scythians are themselves the intruders, and that your poor abused Celts have had earlier possession in all these areas. That the Celtic nations are one of the earliest branches of the great Aryan or Indo-European family of nations is now generally admitted by those who are competent to form an opinion.

2. But not only have we evidence of their existence at the very dawn of human history; but we have reason to conclude that they existed as two great branches as early at least as the days of Julius Cæsar. All the test vocables which as yet are available seem to indicate that the Celts consisted of two great branches, speaking then as now distinct languages. You will find this well brought out in a work of very considerable research and ability, "On the Origin of the Gael," published in 1814, by a gentleman of this county, Mr Grant of Corrymony. And yet the names applied to each, Gäel and Gall, their languages Gaelic and Gaulic, together with their adjectives Gäelta and Gallda, though as different in sense as Jew and Gentile, or as Greek and Barbarian, are so similar in sound that it is more than probable that both have sometimes been embraced by ancient writers under the common term Celts, and sometimes mistaken the one for the other.

3. And now let me remark that we have those two races within our own dominions. With the more ancient we are in some respects pretty well acquainted, for they are ourselves; with

the more modern we ought to be better acquainted. In order to avoid circumlocution, and also to avoid the error of regarding them as if always confined to their present circumscribed limits, I have been accustomed to speak of them as the primeval and secondary, or let me rather speak of them as old Celts and later Celts. The former are now represented by the Highlanders of Scotland, the Irish, and the inhabitants of the Isle of Man; the latter by the Kymric, the Cornish, and the Bas Breton or Armoric.

II. And now, turning to the evidence of language, let us endeavour to indicate very cursorily, (1) How the languages of these two races stand toward each other; and (2) How they stand towards Latin and Greek. Taking Gaelic and Kymric as a representative of each of the races, we find a large proportion of words and phrases common to both, and yet with so marked a difference between them as languages, that the speaker of the one is quite unintelligible to the speaker of the other. Take a sample of the agreement in vocables. The word Ass—Gaelic, Asal; Welsh, Assyn. Cock—G. Coileach; W. Ceiliog. Cow—G. Bo or Beathach; W. Bwch. Ravine—G. Beallach; W. Bwlch. Rabbit— G. Coinean; W. Coningen. Man—G. Duine; W. Dyn. Black —G. Dubh; W. Du. Lamb—G. Uan; W. Oen. Goat—G. Gabhar; W. Gafr. Hand—G. Lamb; W. Llhau. Floor—G. Lar; W. Llhaur. Grey—G. Liath; W. Llwyd. Pig—G. Muc; W. Moch. Bull—G. Tarbh; W. Tarw. Fire—G. Teine; W. Tan: House—G. Tigh; W. Ty. I submit a sample of agreement in phrases :—Gander—G. Coileach Geoidh; W. Ceoliog Gwydd. Dead Body—G. Corp marbh; W. Corp marw. Red hand—G. Lamh ruadh; W. Llhau rudd. Big mountain—G. Monadh mor; W. Mynydd mawr. Big ship—G. Long mhor; W. Llong fawr. But while instances of such agreement might be multiplied indefinitely, there are a large number of words which exhibit a fundamental difference. Such as—Eye—Gaelic, Irish, and Manx, Suil; W. Llygad; Cornish, Lagaz; Armoric, Lagat. Sheep—G. I. and M., Caora; W. Dafad; C. Davad; Ar. Danvat. Bone—G. I. and M., Cnamh; W. Asgarn; C. Asgorn; Ar. Asgorn. Flesh—G. I. and M., Feoil; W. Cig; C. Cig; Ar. Cig. Water—G. I. and M. Uisg; W. Duvr; C. Dour; Ar. Dur. I by no means maintain that the three branches of the old Celtic and the three branches of the later hold always together so closely; what I would have you keep in view is that the great *saltus* is found between them as races. Between Gaelic, Irish, and Manx there is but a difference of dialect, and between Welsh, Cornish, and Armoric there is but a difference of dialect; but between any one of the former and any one of the latter there is such a difference as to constitute them distinct languages. Then the article, which occupies a very important place in all the Celtic languages, is so different among the dialects of the old from the article of the later, that, given a few sentences of either, one could be at no loss to which class to assign them. You can see the bearing of this upon the *quæstio vexata*—who were the Picts? This question must now be regarded as confined to the simple inquiry, were they of the old or of the later race? As for a hybrid between the two, I have yet to learn that such has ever existed. You might as well maintain that a sentence could be found bearing such a resemblance to both that you could not say whether it was Greek or Latin. If, therefore, we can discover a sentence or two which can be certified as Pictish, the question then and there will be at rest for ever. For my part, I have no doubt whatever that they formed an earlier immigration of the old race. And if it be true that St Columba could converse with the Picts, as stated by Adamnan in his life, and only needed an interpreter when he preached, this of itself would decide the question.

That we may see the position of our Gaelic, and how little it has been modified by the lapse of a thousand years, let me submit to you some specimens of the Gaelic of the "Book of Deer." I need only say of the book itself that it belonged to the ecclesiastics of the Abbey of Deer in Aberdeen, founded, as one of the Gaelic entries states, by St Columba personally. It consists of a copy of the Gospel of John and part of Luke. But such was the scarcity of parchment in those days, that the practical ecclesiastics turned their New Testament into a cartulary, and recorded on the margin gifts of land made to the Abbey by neighbouring landowners. It was found in the Cambridge University Library, and it has been edited by Dr John Stuart of Edinburgh, author of the "Sculptured Stones of Scotland." It is interesting, as proving beyond doubt that Gaelic was the language of the Buchan district in the ninth century, for it is assigned with considerable confidence to this period, and shows, moreover, how little change has passed over the language since. I shall read the entry referring to the founding of the Abbey :—

" Columcille agus drostan mac Cosrig adalta tangatur ahi marraolsig dia doibh genie abbor doboir, agus bede Cruithne, robo mormaer buchan araginn, acusesse rathaidaig doib ingathraig sain insaere go braith o mormaer acns o thoseg tangatur asaathle sin en Cathraig ele agus dorathan ri Columcille si air fallan do rath de cus dor odloeg aran mormaer bede gonda tobrad da acus nithorad, agus rogab mac da galar iar nere na gleric acus robo marab act mad beg iar sin do chaid in mor: dattao na glerig gon dendaes ernaide leis inmac gon disad slante do acus dorat inadbairt doib ua

cloie intiprat gonic Chlac pette mic garnait, doranset innernaede
agus tanic Slante do. Jarsen dorat, Colum cille do drostran incha-
draig sen agus ros benact acus faracaib imbrether ge be tosad ris na
bod bliena buadhac, tangator deara drostan arscathrin fri Columcille, ralabair Colum Cille bidear anim ohunu imacc."

Collumcille and Drostan, son of Cosraig, his pupil, came from I
(Iona), as God had shewn them unto Abbordoboir; and Bede the
Pict was Mormaer of Buchan before then; and it was he who gave
them that town in freedom for ever, from Mormaer and Toiseach.
They came after that to the other town, and it was pleasing to
Collumcille, because it was full of God's grace, and he asked of the
Mormaer, to wit Bede, that he would give it to him, &c.

There are other extracts, but to them I must not refer at present, further than to remark that we find in them such names as
Domhnull, Ruadri, Mormaer of Mar, Maolpeter nae Dhomhnull,
Gellecallum, son of Domhnull, Maolbrigte mac Cothull; and, but
for other names with which we are not so familiar, you could
fancy yourself among the Highlanders of the present day in Argyle
or Mull.

Now, let us apply this test to English. Chaucer wrote his
Canterbury tales about 1390, or about five centuries later, and yet
we know that to the ordinary English reader they are in a great
measure unintelligible.

And yet with a degree of fixedness in its forms, extending
throughout lengthened periods, which perhaps no other language
can exhibit, it can be shown that Gaelic has undergone very considerable changes. By comparison with the other members of the
Aryian family, and even with the later Celtic, which has in some
instances preserved the more ancient forms, we can demonstrate
such changes as the following:—1, The passing away of initial
consonants, especially in words which begin with two; 2, the passing away of initial b and p; and, 3, the substitution in the middle
and end of words of the aspirate form of consonant, instead of the
natural.

Let us now look somewhat more closely at the connection between Gaelic and Kymric.
1, The first peculiarity that strikes a Gaelic ear on hearing
Welsh is the prevalence of the sound *th*, and that in its two modifications of *th* in the English *this, that,* and *th* in the English *through,*
think. For instance, we say *monadh*, originally *monad*—moor or
mountain; the Welshman says *mynydd* (munuth); and for our
plural monaidhan (moniyun), he says mynyddooedd (munuthoeth).
We say *lamh ruadh* (lav ruă)—red hand; while they say *llaw rudd*

(thlau ruth). Then, owing to the difficulty which some have in pronouncing our aspirate *d* and *g*, which is a deep guttural sound, we ourselves substitute for it *b* aspirate or *v*. And hence arise three forms of the old *ruide*, retained in Robin-*ruide* and ruiteach —the Latin Rubeo, Rubesco, Rufus; while akin to the Welsh Rudd (ruth), you have the Greek ereuthēs, ereutheis, as also eruthros and eruthroō. But not to fritter away our time too much with instances, let me recall your attention to the fact that the sound *th* is unknown in Gaelic, while prevalent in Welsh—that it is unknown in Latin, while very prevalent in Greek. Let me remark also that it is unknown in German, though prevalent in English.

2, The next distinguishing feature which claims our attention is the passing away of initial *s* in Gaelic, to be replaced by *h* in Welsh and its cognate dialects. The student of Latin and Greek cannot fail to notice the prevalence of the same distinction in these languages, *e.g.* Semi hēmi, Sex hex, Septem hepta, Serpo herpō, super huper; and what is very remarkable when we consider the distance of their present areas, the same distinction is found between Sanscrit and Zend. As to this widespread distinction, I shall (1) indicate the explanation which Gaelic furnishes, and which, so far as I know, no other language does; and (2) afterwards notice some further instances.

Every one that knows anything of Gaelic knows this, that every consonant has not only a broad and slender, but a natural and aspirate form. This we have two *v*'s—b aspirate written *bh*, and m aspirate written *mh*. We have also two *h*'s—t aspirate written *th*, and s aspirate written *sh*. In Irish orthography, I am bound to say, this aspiration is more neatly managed by simply placing a dot over the aspirated consonant, thus ḃ=v, ṁ=v, ṫ=h, ṡ=h. Now, let it be observed that the passing of initial consonants from the natural to the aspirate form is so frequent in Gaelic, and under such a variety of conditions, that more than the whole time of this lecture would be needed to discuss this subject alone. I shall, however, indicate in passing a few of those conditions, taking for my illustration the consonant in question (*s*). We say—

1, Duine Sanntach,
    a covetous man.

Bean Shanntach (hauntach),
    a covetous woman.

2, Endach an duine Shanntaich,
    clothes of the covetous man.

Endach na mna Sanntaiche,
    clothes of the covetous woman.

3, A dhuine shanntaich (hauntich),
    O covetous man.

A bhean shanntaich (hauntich),
    O covetous woman.

4, Mo, do, a, shannt (haunt),   Ur, bhur, an, a, sannt,
  My, thy, his, covetousness.   Our, your, their, her, covetousness.
5, Shanntaich—he coveted.   Sanntaichidh—will covet.

With this transition of consonants from their natural to their
aspirate forms (though very perplexing to strangers) the speaker
of Gaelic is quite familiar, for it is a part of the inflexion of his
language. Not only does the initial s, in such cases as the above,
pass into sh-h, but every other consonant is modified less or more.
Yet somehow the speaker of the later Celtic, though to some extent
practising himself corresponding changes, seems to have had a
strong objection to an initial s, and to have substituted its aspirated
form, not only where we should do the same ourselves, but where
the rules of our language demand the consonant in its natural form.
Let us now illustrate this by some instances :—

Salach (Lat. salax),	Shalach ;	W. Halog—Dirty, nasty.
Sannt,	Shannt ;	W. Chwant—Covetousness.
Seabhag,	Sheabhag ;	W. Hebog—Hawk.
Sealg,	Shealg ;	W. Hela—Hunting.
Sealgair,	Shealgair ;	W. Heliwr—Huntsman.
Sean,	Shean ;	W. Hen—Old.
Seanair,	Sheanair ;	W. Hen wr—Grandfather.

Let us now specify a few vocables which obtain, not only in
Gaelic and Welsh, but in Latin and Greek, that we may see how
they follow each other, as pairs—the Latin holding by Gaelic, and
the Greek by the Welsh :—

Sàl ; ·	Lat.	—	W. Hal ;	Gr. Hals	.	. Salt water.
Saluinn ;	„	Sal ;	„ Halen ;	„ Hals	. Salt.
Saillt ;	„	Salsus ;	„ Hallt ;	„ Halizo	. verb. Salt.
Samhuil ;	„	Similis ;	„ Haval ;	„ Homilos	. Like.
Seileach ;	„	Salix ;	„ Healig ;	„ Helika	. Willow.
Sol (old) ;	„	Sol ;	„ Haul ;	„ Helios	. Sun.
Seath ;	„	Sex ;	„ Chevoch ;	„ Hex	. Six.
Sluagh ;	„	—	„ Llwyth ;	„ Laos	. People.
Suaimhneas	Somnus ;		„ Heppian ;	„ Hupnos	. Sleep.

These affinities, some of them to be found in Llhuyd's Archæologia, and others discovered by myself, are but a sample of a large
number equally striking. I have shown you how our ancient
Gaelic solves the problem. If any other language can furnish a
better solution I for one will be ready to accept it; but until I
find a better I must hold by the one I have.

3. I proceed to notice another prominent feature in the relations of Gaelic and Kymric, and which equally holds in the relations of Latin and Greek—the substitution of b and p by the Briton and Grecian for the c and ch of the Gael and Roman. In Gaelic, as many of you know, we ask questions with words that begin with c, *e.g.* co, who; ciod, what; cuin, when. In like manner the Romans, quis or qui, quæ, quod or quid, quando, quare. On the other hand, the Welshman, with his congeners the Celt of Brittany and Cornwall, prefer to ask their questions with words which begin with b and p—as, for instance, pwy, who; pa, what; pa bath, what thing; pa un, which; pan, when. Now, we turn to the Greek, and we find the same adherence to the forms of the later Celtic—Pē, what way; pou, what place; pōs, how; pos-os,-ē,-on, how great. And if you will follow me attentively while I read the following table, you cannot fail to see that this preference of labials on the part of the Kymric and Greek to the palatals of the Gael and Roman extends widely throughout their respective languages. You will find the Latin also, in one or two instances, turning her back, with culpable ingratitude, upon her old mother, and following the fashion of her Greek cousin :—

Gaelic.	Latin.	Welsh.	Greek.	English.
Car, Caraid,	Par,	Par,	—	Pair.
Cas,	Pes and *passus*	—	Pous	Foot, pace.
Caithir,	Quatuor,	Pedwar,	—	Four.
Coc (verb)	Coquo,	Pob,	Piptō,	Cook.
Cochul,	Cucullus,	Cochul,	Peplos,	Veil or cowl.
Corcur,	Purpur,	Porphyr,	Porpura,	Purple.
Cuig,	Quinque,	Pump,	{ Pente, Pemptos }	Five & fifth.
Each,	Equus,	Fr. Eboul,	Ippos,	Horse.
Feasgar,	Vesper,	Gosper,	Hesperos	Evening.

4. Of this class of relations I shall mention but one other. Those who are accustomed to trace the various forms which the same words assume in different languages, may have wondered why the Spaniard should say Espirito for spirit and Escuela for school, and the Frenchman Esprit and Ecole. The key is found in the relations between the Gaelic and Kymric. E. Llhuyd noticed upwards of a century ago that Gaelic words which begin with sc, sg, sp, and st, assume in the later Celtic an initial y before the s. Now, this is manifestly the initial e of the Spanish and French, and the initial i of the Greek; and it is not a little interesting to trace such forms as storaidh, historia, Spain, Hispania,

up through all the ages during which they have so stood, until
we find the key in the hand of our old Celtic mother :

Gaelic.	Latin.	Welsh.		
Sgiath,	Scutum,	Yysgyd,	Eng.	Escutcheon—Shield.
Sgiath-urra?	Armiger,	—		Esquire ⎱ Shield- Squire ⎰ bearer.
Sgoil,	Schola	Ysgol,	Sp. Fr.	Escuela ⎱ Ecole ⎰ School.
Sguab,	Scopa,	Yscob,		Besom.
Spiorad,	Spiritus,	Ysprid,	Sp. Fr.	Espirito ⎱ Spirit. Esprit ⎰
Spain,	Hispania,	Yspaen,	Gr.	Hispania—Spain.
Storaidh, It.	Historia, Storia, ⎱	Ystori,	„	Historia—History.
Spong,	Spongia,	Ysbong,	„	Sponges—Sponge.
Suidh,	Sedeo,	Eistedd,		Sit.

Hitherto I have endeavoured to show you that there is a remarkable affinity between Gaelic and Latin on the one hand, and
Kymric and Greek on the other—an affinity cropping up with
such variety and frequency as to preclude any explanation that
might occur on the ground of coincidence or hap-hazard, and which
shuts us up to the conclusion that, at sometime and somewhere,
there existed a somewhat close connection between the Gael and
the Roman, and between the Gaul and the Greek.

Let us now take up the further question, how do these languages
stand towards each other—I mean the Celtic and the classic—in
point of time ; are they to be regarded as sister languages—as
co-eval, or nearly co-eval, branches of the great Aryian or Indo-
European family ? Such is the common opinion of philologists :
that they are children of a dead mother.   For many years past I
have been unable to fall in with this opinion.   The more I have
investigated the older forms of the Celtic, as discoverable by a
cautious etymology, and from the record of topography—on which
I may have a word to say before I close—the more I feel con-
strained to regard the Celtic languages as vastly older than those
of Greece and Rome.

When of two languages closely related, we maintain that the
one must be older than the other, some are wont to shrug their
shoulders, and to say, well, that must be a matter of opinion, for it
seems a question not easily determined.   And yet with those who
have studied the subject closely it is capable of demonstration.
When I take up certain kinds of sandstone, say for instance a piece
from the Tarradale quarry, and find it studded with nodules of

jasper and quartz, imbedded in a homogeneous matrix of sand, it is surely not without reason that I conclude that those nodules had a separate existence from the matrix in which I find them cemented together; nor when I find those nodules rounded by the action of water, is it without cause that I conclude that this separate existence must have been for a long period. On grounds just as solid and intelligible can we prove the prior existence of a large portion of Greek and Latin by pointing to the rock from which it was hewn. To confine our attention for the present to a comparison of Gaelic and Latin, we find a numerous class of words bearing the same meaning common to both, with only this difference, that the Latin forms carry a terminable syllable for the purpose of declension. Remove this variable termination and you have the Gaelic word, and the Gaelic word corresponding not with modern pronunciation, but with what we know from other sources was the ancient Latin pronunciation. I subjoin a table of Gaelic and Latin synonyms, and I confine myself to words that begin with the letter C, for were I to enumerate all the words which are common I should have to repeat the greater portion of Ainsworth's Latin Dictionary:—

Gaelic.	Latin.	English.
Caile,	Calx, *i.e.* Calc,	Chalk.
Càl,	Caulis, and Gr. Kaulos,	Cabbage, Kail.
Cairbh,	Caro,	Flesh.
Cam, Cham,	Hamus,	Hook.
Cais,	Caseus or Caseum,	Cheese.
Can,	Cano,	Ising, Chant.
Canap,	Canabis,	Hemp.
Caog (squint),	Coccus,	Blind, Sc. Keek.
Cap,	Caput,	Hood.
Capùll	Caballus, Gr. Kaballos,	Horse.
Car, W. Gar,	Carus,	Dear.
Cart,	Cortex,	Bank.
Cart Cart,	Charta,	Paper.
Càs or Cuis,	Causa,	Cause, Case.
Ceangal,	Cingulum, Gr. Ganglion,	Abinding.
Ceart (right),	Certus,	Sure.
Ceil,	Celo,	Conceal.
Ceir,	Cera,	Wax.
Ceisd,	Quæstio,	Question.
Cist,	Cista,	Chest.
Ceithir,	Quatuor,	Four.
Ceud,	Centum,	Hundred.
Ciamh (lock of hair),	Coma,	Hair.

Gaelic.	Latin.	English.
Cill,	Cella,	Cell
Ciod,	Quid or Quod,	What.
Claon,	Inclino, Gr. Klino,	Incline.
Clar (tablet, Cleireach,	Cleriens	Clerk or Cleric.
Cochull,	Cucullus,	Cowl.
Coileach	Gallus,	Cock.
Coille, Choille,	Silva, Gr. Xulon, hule,	Wood.
Com, Tapog. Combe,	Campus,	Plain.
Cord,	Chorda, Gr. Chorde,	Cord.
Corn, Chorn,	Cornu,	Horn.
Corp, Corpura,	Corpus, Corpur,	Body.
Cuid or Codoch,	Quota,	Portion.
Cuileag,	Culex or Culec,	Fly.
Cuing,	Cingo,	Yoke, Bind, Gird.
Creath (Clay),	Creta,	Clay, Chalk.
Cruth (shape),	Creo,	Create.
Cur or Cuir,	Cura,	Care, Hurt.

Look on this picture and on that; consider them attentively; take them as a sample of a resemblance which obtains throughout the compass of both languages; make allowance for the cumbrous orthography of our Scottish Gaelic, which veils its simplicity from the eye of a stranger; and after you have done so I scarcely think you will blame us very much if we claim for it, on this and on other grounds, to be regarded, not as a sister of the Latin, but as its veritable and venerable mother.

I might now proceed to show you that there are many words of which neither Greek nor Latin can furnish us with a satisfactory etymology, but which in their Gaelic forms resolve themselves readily into more simple elements, and that in a way so expressive of the sense as to compel the admission that they are the more ancient representatives. On this field, however inviting, our time will not permit us to enter.

III. The third division of my subject, on which I shall now speak a little, is the bearing of Gaelic on questions of ethnology. It must be admitted by all who have directed attention to this subject, that once we ascend beyond the historical races all is doubt and obscurity. Who can tell us decidedly who were the primeval occupants of any land; and as to the further question, the time when human beings first trode the soil of our own or any land, who can hazard an opinion? Now, if we shall ever be able to speak with thorough confidence on the first of these questions, we shall owe it mainly, I am persuaded, to the topographical record; nay, it may aid us not a little in determining the second. Taken also in conjunction with prehistoric facts, as a guide to their discovery and interpretation, it would seem to me very difficult to over-estimate its value. I venture, therefore, to say, that we have cause to congratulate ourselves and our country on the ordnance survey which is now being carried on by Her Majesty's Government. So much importance do I attach to this survey that I have said it once and again, and say it here anew, that I should consider all the money expended upon it well and wisely laid out were it to serve no other purpose than the preservation of a record which is every day passing into oblivion—a record of Gaelic in by far the oldest form in which it can now be found, a form so old that a considerable number of the words used in it can only be interpreted by a laborious comparison of instances.

Were we to hazard an opinion as to the age of this record, we should be ready to claim for a large proportion of it three thousand years. We should do so on the following grounds :—Besides all the Classic authors, from Homer downwards, who make constant reference to ancient localities, we have three who have written systems of geography as it was known in their own day—Strabo, born 54 B.C., and who died A.D. 54; Ptolemy, a man of great celebrity in his day as an astronomer and geographer, though (alas for fame!) all that is now known of him is—that he was an observer in Alexandria A.D. 139, and that he was alive in A.D. 161; Pliny, a Latin author, who perished A.D. 79 when observing that eruption of Vesuvius by which Pompeii and Herculaneum were overwhelmed. All these authors have described many lands and recorded many names, and we stay not at present to assert how many of those many names of many lands we are prepared to claim as bearing the stamp of Mother Celtica's mint. Our more humble office for the present is to state that they have recorded not a few names that can still be identified in our own country, and when we examine these what do we find? Simple descriptive Gaelic names, with a Latin termination superadded. The merest tyro in topographical Gaelic must be able to identify the following :— Estuary of the Luce, *Aberavanus*—Aber-amhain (avin), river, confluence ; Estuarius *Vararius*—Moray Firth. Here we have the *Farar*, as the Beauly was termed at no very ancient date, down to its mouth. The *Taodunum*, that is, Tagh-dun—Taytown, now Dundee, merely reversing the terms. Avoca or Ovoca is the Oboca of Ptolemy, that is Ob-aga—confluence of water; where the Avon-more and Avonbeg meet. *Eboracum* Evorac, York Aber-ag—confluence of water, that is, of the Foss and Ouse. All the English *Ouses* are altered forms of Uisg—*e.g.*, *Isca* Damniorum, Exeter, and Isca

Silurum—Caer-leon in Monmouth, near the mouth of the Severn.
Then, what are the Avingtons so numerous in England? Simply
our Amhain-dun—River Town.   Then go forth throughout Europe,
and mark the *Eburodunums*—Aber-dun ; *Lugdunums*—Lag-dum—
Bason Town ; *Eburo-magus*—Aber-magh : confluence, meadow ;
Eboralacum—Aber-lag: confluence of bason or hollow.   *Eburovices*,
Eburovices, the same as our own Aber-wick.

Such are a sample of Celtic names as old at least as the Christian
era ; how much older none can say.   We know that the Romans
found our people fired by a patriotism which only the lapse of ages
could have produced ; and if it be true, as I feel assured it is, that
throughout the whole of Europe, without going further for the
present, there is found a substratum of Gaelic topography, then it
follows that Celts must have preceded the present historical races.
In other words, our Gaelic can be traced upwards in its topographic
form to the dawn of history.

I appeal to you, then, if this be not a record worthy of the attention of the Gaelic Society of Inverness, and of every Society in
our land.   I believe we are only awakening to its value; and here
let me bear my cordial testimony to the thorough method and
painstaking labour of the Ordnance service for securing accuracy
in their names.   I can do so from some considerable experience,
having been asked to revise several of their lists.   Even with the
partial progress we have made, the views which it opens up to us
of the ancient condition of our country, and the changes in its flora
and fauna, are extremely interesting.   It speaks of the alder-tree
where it is no longer to be found, the country being drier than
before. · Our Meall na Tuirc and Beallach na muic, speak of the
time when the sow and wild boar were denizens of the country.
It tells us very emphatically that our ancestors when this record
was inscribed were a hunting and pastoral people, for the references
to agriculture are few indeed.   It speaks to us of our ancient bards,
and minstrels, and harpers.   I am not aware of any reference to
pipers.   Our Bail' a Bhaird, Carn a Chlarsair, and Croit an
Fhilidh : Town or holding of the Bard, Cairn of the Harper, and
Croft of the Minstrel—common throughout the Highlands, are
quite in keeping with what we know from other sources as to the
civilisation of our ancestors.

Mr Campbell of Islay, who received a genuine Highland welcome, expressed the very great pleasure he had derived from attending this meeting, and the deep satisfaction which the formation
of such a Society afforded him.   The lecture, he was sure, delighted
and interested them; and for his own part he was both pleased and
instructed by what the learned lecturer had said.   His own name

had been mentioned in connection with the meeting as if he were an authority on antiquities; but his own feeling was that he knew nothing on the subject. He took an interest in old stories—stories which had been voted rubbish by many—and he might be dux in his class, like the little boy who told the minister that he was top, but afterwards let out that the class consisted of "himself and anither lassie." He could hardly say that there was "anither lassie " in the class of collectors of Gaelic stories to which he belonged. There were many advantages in knowing Gaelic. For one thing, Gaelic contained sounds not found in English, just as English contained sounds not found in Gaelic; and any person beginning the study of language with these extra sounds, would find himself greatly aided in his studies. Of this advantage he had lately met with illustrations in the island of Barra, in a case involving a knowledge of Spanish. Then, it was very useful to be able to distinguish sounds in learning foreign languages. Gaelic demands a good ear; and so cultivates an ear to note various niceties of sounds which are apt to escape the notice of those not blessed with the same advantage. Take the three familiar words, " caileag," " cailleag," and " cailleach," master the niceties of pronunciation involved, and you will have some idea of what is here said. Thus, Gaelic, so far from being what some allege, an impediment in the way of men's advancement, would be found a decided aid. The lecturer referred to the interest taken by German *savants* in some of the objects of the Society. The French had actually started a Celtic Society. If the Gaelic Society put itself in communication with these bodies, there might be an interchange of papers which would prove mutually useful. Mr Campbell, after giving several examples of how languages were altered by the substitution of one letter for another, told a number of curious, amusing, and instructive stories, tracing some of them from the western shores of Ross to the eastern plains of India. Thus, these stories, which formed the winter amusements around the peat fires of our Gaelic-speaking Highlanders, were in reality some of the most valuable materials with which our learned men were building up the source of races. All the Celtic languages were derived from one common source ; and he believed that all the languages in Europe sprung from one stock, of which Sanscrit is the oldest known. In concluding, Mr Campbell observed that he had often remarked in the town of Inverness a great gathering of Highlanders for throwing the hammer, putting the stone, dancing, and playing pipes ; but no Society had previously existed for the cultivation of Gaelic literature. He hoped the Gaelic Society would prosper and prove useful.

On the motion of Mr Macgregor, a vote of thanks was passed

to Mr Mackenzie for his excellent lecture; and, on the motion of Mr Murdoch, a similar vote was awarded to Mr Campbell for his very interesting and valuable speech. Mr Dallas moved a vote of thanks to Sir Kenneth for his kindness in taking the chair, and for the efficient manner in which he presided over the meeting. The Chairman, in replying, intimated that letters of apology had been received from Mr Fraser-Mackintosh of Drummond, author of "Antiquarian Notes," and other works; and from Dr Carruthers —in which they expressed their sympathy with the Society, and their regrets at not being able to attend.

Thus terminated the inaugural meeting, which, as to numbers, respectability, intelligence, and enthusiasm, was all that could have been desired, and augured well for the success of the Society.

October 27.—On this occasion the ordinary proceedings were enlivened by Mr Macdonald, the Bard of the Society, reciting the subjoined original lament for Lord Clyde:—

DAN
MU BHAS CHAILEIN CHAIMBEUL TRIATH CHLUAIDH.

Tha airm an laoich fo mheirg 'san tùr;
Chòmhdaich ùir an curaidh treun;
Bhuail air Alaba speach as úr:—
A feachd tròm, tùrsach, 'sileadh dheur.
Mu Ghaisgeach Ghaidheil nan sàr bheairt,
Fo ghlais a bhàis, mar dhùil gun toirt:
Triath na Cluaidh bu bhuadhaich feairt
Ga chaoidh gu tròm, le cridhe goirt.
　Air oidche 's mi 'm laidhe'm shuain,
'S mo smuaintean air luath's na dreig;
Uair agam, 'sa'n sin uam;
Bhruadair mi 'bhi shuas air creig.
Thoir leam gu 'n robh teachd nam 'choir
Fo bhratach bhròin de shròl dubh
Sar mhaighdean mhaiseach, mbòr;
Tiamhaidh, leont'bha ceòl a guth.
Mar dhrillseadh reult, bha gorm shúil;
A glan ghnuis cho geal's an sneachd,
Bha falt donn air sniomh mu 'cùl.
Tiugh chiabha dluth nan iomadh cleachd.
M'a ceann bha clogaid do dh-fhior chruaidh,
Ri barr bha dualach o'n each ghlas;
A laimh dheas chum sleagh na buaidh;
Claidheamh truailte suas ri 'leis.
Sgiath chopach, obair sheòlt',
Le mòrchuis 'na laimh chli.
Luireach mhailleach, greist' le h-òr,
Bu cnomhdach do nighean righ.
Laidh leoghann garg, gu stuama stòlt'
Mar chùithir dhi-moùhair fo reachd
Chuir leth ghuth o beul seòlt
A bheisd fo shamhchair, 's fo thur smachd.
Ghrad phlosg mo chridhe 'nam chòm,
Fo uamhas a's trom gheilt,—
Rinn rosg tlàth o'n ribhinn donn,
Fuadachadh lom air m' oilt.
Chrom mi sios le mòr mheas

'Us dhiosraich mi do threin na mais',
Cia fàth mu 'n robb a h-airm na 'n crios,
Mar shonn ' chum sgrios, a deanamh deas,
Ged 'bha a gnuis mar òigh fo lòn,
No ainnir og 'chuir gaol fo chràdh,
Sheall i rium le plathadh broin,
Measgta le mòralachd is gradh.
Lasaich air mo gheilte 's m' fhiamh
'N uair labhair i 'm briathraibh ciùin:—
　"A Ghaidheil aosda, ghlas do chiabh
Mar cheatharnach a liath le ùin,
Triallaidh tu mar 'rinn do sheors'
Chum talla fuar, reot' a bhàis;
Eisd guth binn na deagh sgeoil,
'Toirt cuireadh gloir ri latha grais.
　Bha agam-sa curaidh treun—
Gun chomhalt fo 'n ghréin 'am beairt:
Ceannard armailt na' mor euchd
Thug buaidh 's gach streup, le ceill thar neart.
Och mo leireadh, beud a leon
Breatuinn comhladh le trom lot:
O'n Bhan-righ 'chum an duil gun treoir—
Uile comhdaicht' le bron-bhrat.
Chaill m' armailt ceannard corr,
Air nàmb 'sa' chomh-strì toradh grath:
Mar dhealan speur na 'n deigh 'san toir,
Rinn cosgairt leointeach latha 'chath.
Air thus nan Gaidheal, 'stiùireadh streup;
Mar fhireun speur, 'an geuraid beachd;
Gaisg' leoghann garg, 'measg bheathach frith,
Cha d' ghéill 'san t-srith, a dh-aindeoin feachd.
Cha chualas ceannard a thug barr
An teas a bhlair air sàr nan euchd:
Misneach fhoirfidh, 'an gleachd nan àr;
Trom acain bais, o chradh nan creuchd.
Do Ghaidheil ghaisgeil, ceannard corr
Am builsgein comhraig, mor na'm beachd;

A' toirt na buaidh 'sa cosnadh gloir,
A dh-aindeoin seol a's morachd feachd.
Mar chogadh Oscar flathail. garg,
'Us Conn 'na fheirg a' dol's an spairn ;
Le Diarmad donn a thuit 's an t-sealg,
'San Sonn a mharbh an Garbh-mac-Stairn.
Gach buaidh 'bha annta sud gu leir,
An neart, an trein, an gleus, 's am múirn—
Bha cliù a Chaimbeulaich dha 'n reir,
Dol thart an éifeachd anns gach tuirn—
Ciùin mar mhaighdeann ghraidh 'san t-sith,
Uasal, siobhalt, min 'am beus ;
Gaisgeil, gargant, crosg 'san t-sri,
Le cumhachd righ 'cur feachd air ghleus.
Fhuair e urram anns gach ceum,
Thaobh barrachd euchd, 'an streup nan lann.
Rinn d' ar rioghachd dion 'n a feum,
Air thoiseach tréiu-fhir Thir nam beann.
'S na h-Innsean thug e buaidh ro mhor,
Le iuil 's le seoltachd 'dol thar neart :
Threoraich e na brataich shroil,
'S a' chonihraig anns bu gloir-mhor beairt.
C' aite 'n cualas sparradh cath
Bu bhuadhaich sgath na Alma dhearg?—
Fuil a's cuirp air beinn 's air srath
Na'm milltean breith, fo 'n laoch na fhearg !
Fhuair o 'n rioghachd meas 'us gloir
Anns gach doigh mar thos-fhear cath :
Dhiol ar Ban-righ mar bu choir

Dha onair oirdhearg 'measg nam flath.
Triath Chluaidh nam fuar shruth,
Mu 'n cualas guth an Oisein bhinn,
A' caoidh nan saoidh, 'ruith dheur gu tiugh,
Bha moralach 'an talla Fhinn,
Ghairmeadh air an uisge 'n sonn
Mar agh nan glonn bu bhonndail coir ;
Cho fad 's a bhuaileas creag an tonn,
S air uachdar fonn 'bhios fas an fheoir.
Chrioch' aich sgeul an ainnir mhoir,
Mu euchdan gloir-mhor an laoich threun ;
Mbosgail mi a m' shuain le bron,
A' sileadh dheoir gu 'm b'fbior an sgeul !
A Ghaidheil Ghlaschu, shliochd nan sonu
A dh'fhuadaicheadh o Thir nam beann,
Da'n dual le coir an sruth 's am fonn :—
Dhuibhse coisrigeam mo rann,
Dhuibhs da'n dealaidh am priomh shar,
'S gach euchd 'thug barr 'rinn Gaidheil riamh
Ri stiuireadh feachd san gleachd nam blair
Bhiodh buaidh na laraich sailt' ri 'ghniomh.
Dearbhaibh gur sibb al nan treun,
Ginealach do reir nan sonn,
A bhuanaich cliu thar sliochd fo 'n ghrein,
'Am blar nam beum 's an streup i an tonn.
Cumaibh cuimhn' air laoch an airm
A ghairmeadh air an abhainn Cluaidh,
'S a' meal e uiram 'theid a sheirm
'S gach linn le toirm ri sgeul a bhuaidh !

Nov. 2.—After the ordinary business was disposed of, the following paper was read by Mr Alexander Mackenzie, on our

LOCAL TOPOGRAPHY.

It may be as well, perhaps, to begin with the name of our own lovely town, Inverness ; or, perhaps, with the ancient name of our country, Albin. "Alb" is the Gaelic for a height or an eminence, and "In" (now obsolete), a country or island. Hence "Albin," the land or island of heights and eminences. Could anything be more descriptive? Then we have "Iarin," Erin, "Iar" being the Gaelic for west—the western island or country. "Sasunn," Saxon, or what we now call English, "Sasuinn," the land of the Saxon. The first part of the word Inverness is undoubtedly from "Inbhear," which is commonly applied to the place where a river empties itself into the sea; but I have no doubt it originally meant and was applied to the land at the confluence, from "In," land, and "Bior," water, called "In-bhior," and easily altered to its present spelling "Inbhear." Ness, the latter part of the word, is of course the name of the river which forms the confluence; but then, what does the Ness derive its name from? You will say, from Loch-Ness; but then Loch-Ness itself? It is generally believed to be from the Gaelic word "Eas," a fall, "Loch-an-eas" being the loch of the cascade or fall. I daresay some gentlemen present may

question this derivation, and I do not say but they may be right.
I believe there are several traditions still extant in Glen-Urquhart
of a celebrated character of the name of Angus Mackay—Gaelic,
"Aonghas Macaoidh." In early times, and even now in some
places, "Aonghas" is pronounced "Naois," and I have seen a
Gaelic story, taken down from a Barra peasant by Mr Carmichael,
in which mention is made of "Loch-Naois," and "Caisteal Naois."
This may be the Gaelic origin of Loch-Ness; but I am more inclined to agree with "Loch-an-eas," at least until we learn more
of the "Naois" theory. I have already expressed my belief that
"Inver" meant originally the land adjoining a confluence, and I
will now add that "Aber," which is pure Gaelic, and not Welsh,
was the name for the confluence itself. "A" or "Ab" was an
old Gaelic word (although now obsolete) for water. Armstrong
points out in his dictionary that "Ab" is Persic for river; Turkish
and Mogul exactly the same; Hebrew "Saab," carry water, from
"Sa," carry, and "Ab," water; Ethiopian "Abbi," wave; Arme-
nian "Ahp," pool; and Persic again "Av" and "Ap," water;
Japanise "Abi," wash with water. "Aber" is made up of this,
"Ab" for water, and "Bior" also water—"Ab-bior," water to
water, or confluence. You will remark the difference between this
and "Inver." The one being originally land to or adjoining
water, the other water to water, or confluence of waters. Armstrong gives the following examples of this word in other languages
—Cornish spelt exactly the same; Hebrew "Heber," to join together; "Haber," a companion; "Heber," a junction; Chaldee,
Syriac, and Ethiopian "Habor," to unite. I suppose I must not
overlook "Clach-na-cuduinn," the meaning of which is quite apparent, namely, "The stone of the tub." There are several kinds
of tubs, and each has its own peculiar name in Gaelic. "Cuduinn"
is the name which applies to that kind of tub or stoup with ears or
lugs, with holes in them, by which it can be carried between two
persons, or through which a stick is passed and carried by two on
their shoulders. This was undoubtedly the kind of tub from which
the celebrated "Clach-na-Cuduinn" derived its name, it being the
one most convenient and always used until the introduction of
waterworks, to carry water from the river. This style of tub is
now quite common in the Highlands, and many's the time when I
was a boy I was tired enough carrying water in it, and would have
been very glad of a "Clach-na-Cuduinn" to rest upon.

Now, I come to Tom-na-hiuraich." "Tom" is the Gaelic for a
knoll or hill, and "Iughrach" is the Gaelic for boat. "Iubhar"
is also the Gaelic for yew tree: Iubharach, "abounding in yew
trees;" hence it may have been the "Hill of the boat-shape," or
the "Hill of the yew-trees." It certainly is a boat-shaped hill,

and I prefer that to the latter derivation. I have heard some speak of it as meaning the " Hill of the Fairies." I do not know any word in the Gaelic signifying fairies that has the remotest similarity to any part of the word—" Sithichean " being the Gaelic for fairies; and although the hill is reported to have been inhabited by the light-feathered tribe, there is nothing in the name to show that they wanted to commemorate the fact in its designation, or they would have called it " Tom-na-Sithichean," and not " Tom-na-hiuraich." " Creag-Phadurig" appears to be Patrick's rock, after St Patrick, I suppose, but I do not think it improbable that it may have been originally " Creag-faireil," meaning, like Cnoc-faireil, in Ross-shire, the rock or hill of the watch. " Clachnaharry" in Gaelic is pronounced exactly what it really was, namely, " Clach-na-h'airidh," or the stone of the watch, or of watchfulness. " Mealfourvonie," is " Meall fuar mhonaidh," the round-topped, cold, or bleak mountain. ·

The Fall of Foyers, usually called in Gaelic " Eas-na-Smuid,' in consequence of the constant vapoury mist it evolves, originally means " Eas Fo-thir," or the fall underground, or under land. This is a literal description of the appearance of the fall as it appeared to people who used always to visit it from the highway, and not from Loch-Ness as is the case now. On their arrival at the top of the fall it appeared to them to dash away underground, or " Fo-thir;" and even when you stand now from the lowest point from which you can view the fall it goes still under you to a considerable depth. The stream *above* the fall is called " Feachlinne" and not "Foyers," and that part of it *below ground* only, or between the fall and Loch-Ness, is called Foyers or Fo-thir. This also gives a true description of the lands and of the " fair house of Foyers," for they all appeared low-lying, under-ground, or " Fo-thir," as approached by visitors in the olden time.

" Culloden," the well-known battle-field, and that district, has been rendered by some to mean "Cuil-fhodair," the bend or hollow of straw. This is like the modern pronunciation, but certainly not descriptive of the district, for I believe it to be one of the worst straw-producing localities in the country. " Cul " means the back, or back-lying district, and "oitir" means a ridge or bank in the sea, a shoal, a promontory or headland, a sand bank. " Cul-oitir " then means the district lying at the back of the shoal, the promontory, headland, or sand bank. Nothing could be more descriptive of the district, and I feel sure this is the correct derivation, for where can you meet with a more extended shoal, sand bank, and promontory than in the neighbourhood .of Culloden? There are many other names in the neighbourhood of Inverness which I might dwell upon, such as the " Merkinch," meaning, I think,

D

"Marg Innis," or the market flat or plain. Drummond—"Druim fhuinn," meaning the land on the height or ridge, &c. ; but I will now carry you to Beauly, and then have a run to Ross-shire.

. There has been considerable controversy about the meaning of the name Beauly. I am not able to enter into the discussion, and, further, I do not think it at all necessary, for it has nothing to do with Celtic topography. Beauly is not the Celtic name of the place, but "Manachain." You never hear a Highlander asking in Gaelic, "C'ait am bheil Beauly?" If he is not acquainted with English he does not know what the term refers to. He will ask you in his own language, "C'ait am bheil a Mhanachain?" This is the Gaelic for "Where is Beauly." "Manach," as most of you know, is the Gaelic for monk, and "Manachain" is the Gaelic for priory or monastery. There was a monastery at Beauly; hence the name of the place in Gaelic topography; and any modern name, such as Beauly, we have nothing to do with. Going further on we come to the Muir of Ord, the market stance. Muir of Ord is an English name, but the Gaelic "Blar dubh," the black or dark muir, gives an exact description of the place.

Dingwall is also English, for "Inbhearfeotharan" (Inverpeffry) is the Celtic, and describes its situation. Then we have the Peffry itself and Strathpeffer—Gaelic, "Feothar" and "Strathfeothar." "Feotharan" means a mountain, valley, or land, adjoining a brook. A perfect description of all this neighbourhood. "Creag an fhithich" is the Raven's Rock. A raven had his nest here yearly until the railway was made. Ben Wyvis is in Gaelic "Beinn fhuathais"—the formidable or gigantic mountain. For instance, you will say in Gaelic, "Nach fuathasach an duine e? Nach fuathasach laidir e? Nach fuathasach fuar e?" (Isn't he a wonderful, or a formidable man? Isn't he awfully strong? Isn't it shockingly cold?) Garve is "Gairbh"—rough or stony. Loch-Luichart is either "Loch-Luichairt"—the loch of the stronghold; or "Loch-luigh-ghoirt"—the loch of bitter herbs, of which there are plenty in the neighbourhood. Kenlochluichart is of course "ceann," or head of the loch. We next come to Achnault. "Achadh" is usually translated field, but this does not convey its whole meaning as originally supplied; "Achadh" not only means a field, but an enclosed field, or rather an enclosed patch of arable land. These patches were here and there throughout the interminable pasture lands of the Highlands, and they had to be enclosed to keep out the sheep, the cattle, and the deer, from the shepherd or manager's small arable croft or farm. Achnault is one of those patches, and is called "Achadh nan Allt" from the number of streamlets which run through this green spot. No passenger on the Skye Railway can help noticing this peculiarity of the place.

Achnasheen, again, is "Achadh na Sine," exactly describing its well-earned reputation for a continual drizzle, above all places on the West Coast, in consequence, no doubt, of so many mountain ranges converging there. The next place you pass on this route is "Luib Mhor," on the Loch-Maree road—the large bend. ("Luib Bheag," or small bend, is on the Lochcarron road.) There is a "public" at "Luib Mhor" still, but it has been done away with at the other some time ago ; but they were both landmarks to the weary traveller, and no doubt he named them from the appearance of the place, and from his discovering in his travels that the one was much longer and larger than the other. The next house on the road was Kenlochewe Inn. This name is pronounced, and means in Gaelic "Ceann-loch-iugh," and is situated, as most of you know, two miles before you reach Loch-Maree.

Loch-Maree is eighteen miles in length, and the river Ewe, which connects it with the Loch-Ewe of the present age, is another mile in length, so that the "Ceann-loch-iugh" of to-day is just twenty-one miles further off than the "Ceann-loch-iugh" of the past. There can be no doubt but Loch-Ewe did come up to Kenlochewe in times gone by. This has been proved geologically by Hugh Miller, and other celebrated geologists, and if further proof be wanted the name of the place is very strong topographical evidence. It is also pretty certain that Loch-Maree is a comparatively modern name for the fresh water loch, and that the whole of Lochewe and Loch-Maree, extending about thirty-three miles, was known by the name Loch-Ewe, and that as late as 150 or 180 years ago. I will now tell you what I think is the Gaelic meaning and origin of Loch-Maree. I think it is generally believed to be called after a Saint Malrube. I do not believe it, nor do I find any connection in spelling or pronunciation with the Gaelic name of the lake. You would have to say "Loch-mal-rub," if it was called after this saint. I have pretty much the same objection to the other origin ascribed to it—namely, "Saint Mary's Loch." This in Gaelic would be pronounced "Loch-Mairidh." I prefer to call it "Loch-ma-Righ," "the king's loch," or the "loch of my king." This corresponds with the Gaelic pronunciation, and it also agrees with local history and tradition. When I was a boy, and living on the West Coast, I used to hear old men relating long tales about the son of a king who lived on "Island Maree." His father, the king, "Macollamh Mor," died while the boy was young, and a conspiracy was got up among his retainers to put the young king to death. His young aunt, Flora, managed to discover the plot ; and on the night that the boy was to be put to death in bed, she managed to get the wife and son of one of the conspirators to occupy the bed always oc-cupied by herself and her young nephew. The ruffians who were

bribed to do the foul deed were satisfied with murdering the oc-
cupiers of the bed, and got their reward.   Flora went off with her
nephew, and brought him up on a pet goat's milk in a cave called
to this day " Uaigh-an-Righ," or the king's cave.   He also built a
stronghold, part of which is still to be seen on Island Maree, and
after many vicissitudes he returned home, was to be executed as a
stranger and a rebel, when his mother, the queen, recognised him
and he was placed on the throne of his forefathers.   There is
another cave called "Toll-an-Righ," or the "king's hole," where
young Ewan Macgobhar was in hiding.   He was called Macgobhar
in consequence of his being fed by the goat, and because Flora did
not wish to have his proper name known, for fear of discovery.
The late Mr Macintyre of Letterewe related this tale to the Ettrick
Shepherd, and you can find it in his prose works under the title of
" Ewan Macgabhar," to which I beg to refer you.   Hogg not
knowing the Gaelic made several mistakes in spelling.   For instance, he spells " Toll-an-Righ" " Toll-au-Kigh," no doubt taking
the "n" and the " R" in his original manuscript for " u" and " K,"
but as he translates it " cave of the king's son," his meaning is clear.
I have no doubt but " Loch-ma-Righ" is the original name for Loch
Maree, in spite of all the fine theories by learned men as to its connection with a saint somebody.   Let them go into the locality and
get the local history of the place, and I think they will adopt this
theory of mine.

Loch-Maree is even now so little above the level of the present
Lochewe that, in my own memory, a stone embankment in the river,
to which the tide almost came up during a very high tide, swelled
or dammed up Loch-Maree, so much that it used to flood the farm of
Tagan, at this end of the lake, and the late Mr Mackenzie objected
to pay any rent until Sir Kenneth Mackenzie had the embankment
taken away.   This allowed the water in the loch to fall to its natural
level, and I question if the fresh-water one is more than 12 or 15
feet above the level of the salt water Loch-Ewe—the name, as I have
already said, by which the whole of the lochs—33 miles in extent
—were originally known.   What, then, is the Gaelic meaning of
Loch-Ewe?   I have never heard the question asked or answered.
In the Gaelic you would spell it " Loch-Iugh."   Then what does
" Iugh" mean?   I believe it was originally " Eugh," and that the
name is " Loch-Eugh," or loch of the calling, or echo.   I am the
more convinced of this as a point on this tide of Talladale, and
exactly opposite Letterewe, is now called " Aird na h-Eugh," and
we have also " Allt na h-Eugh," some miles this side of " Aird
na h-Eugh;" and I believe there is also a " Creag na h-Eugh"
nearer Poolewe, but just now I cannot remember the spot.   When
this was all one lake no person could get over except by a boat.

Even forty years ago, before Telford built the bridge on the river, you could only get over by a ferry-boat when the river was flooded to any degree, and no doubt there would be regular places of calling or "eigheachd," for these boats to fetch people across, as is actually now the case. If you want to get across to Isle of Ewe, you must bawl out until the people on the Island hear you, or light a fire on a particular point. No doubt, in the fearful, deep, and solitary glen, in which Loch-Maree lies, the echo would be loud, and be carried along the whole glen, hence, I believe, the name Loch-Ewe or "Loch-Eugh." I shall be glad to hear a better solution. Gairloch, close to Loch-Ewe, is "Gearr-Loch," or "Loch-Goirid"—short loch. It is short in comparison with all the other West Coast lochs.

It is needless to say that this paper was well received, and gave rise to an interesting discussion, of which, however, we can only give a few notes.

Mr Thomas Mackenzie took exception to the etymology given of *Tom-na-hiuraich*, stating that it was only within the memory of persons not at all old that the letter *f* in the word had been dropped, even in colloquial speech. The hill was resorted to for timber, and it was on account of its timber *(fiodh)* that it was called "Tom-na-fiodhraich." "Tha mi dol an fhiodhrach," was what a person said when going to gather sticks there. In this case the word was very like "Uraich." This was no mere opinion, or far-fetched theory; it was the opinion of an ear and eye-witness. But the "Boat-shaped Hill," and the "Fairy Hill," are not only modern, but recent and ridiculous names. Nothing could better set forth the necessity of the Society doing its duty, and rescuing our topography from the hands of theorists, whilst our language is a living thing in the mouths of unsophisticated people. That Culloden (Cùil-Odair) derives its name from the shoal which forms part of the boundary of the estate he thought exceedingly improbable. He was disposed to class Cùil (or Cill) Oduin with Cill Earnan, Cill Mhoraig, Cill Chuimean. He would not wait to answer the question who was Odin, any more than who was Earnan, or who was Morag. Mr Mackenzie then deprecated the incorrect, un-classical, and misleading spelling introduced into our topography, instancing the displacing of the C by a K; and then, after removing the C from its place in so many words, depriving it of its true value where left. It was sad to hear people giving the sound of S to C, in such words as Cæsar, Cephalonia, Macedonia, words which should be pronounced as if written Kesar, Kephalonia, Makedonia, &c. Then there was the introduction of that queer English letter "Q," into such words as Cuach, making Gleann

Cunich into "Glenquaich!" Our own nineteen Gaelic letters are
quite enough, and the introduction of those other letters, which are
superfluous in English, is a very stupid compliment to our Saxon
neighbours. Our politeness and desire to please do not require us
to adopt their blunders. Then there was the spelling to be seen
in advertisements and shop windows : Skian Dhus for Sgeanan
Dubh ; Sporrans, for Sporanan, &c. This is really neither Gaelic
nor English spelling. We have also such spelling as Balvonie for
Baile-mhonaidh, Balvulin for Baile-mhuilinn, and Balnafettack for
Bail-na-feadaig. And this English invasion goes on, for even lately
we had Dunjardil (a shooting in the district of Stratherrick), now
we have Dunyardil, instead of Dun Dearduil. Dearduil, the
valorous Norseman, a Scandinavian prince, if tradition be true, had
been toppled over the rock into the Faragaig. Pity that the name
of the man who had built such a fort or stronghold should be
changed. If the respected proprietor were made aware of how
much there is in a name, in this case, he would undoubtedly have
the true name restored.

Mr Murdoch remarked that in solving the etymology of our
Highland names, we must not always limit our appeals to Gaelic,
for a great many of them are, beyond all question, Scandinavian,
and utterly unintelligible to the mere Gaelic speaker ; and for his
own part it was not until he had got to the Shetland Isles he was
able to make out the meaning and origin of some names with
which he had been familiar all his days. In the island of Islay,
for instance, there are a very great many names of places out of
which no fair ingenuity could extract a Gaelic meaning. Twenty-
five of those names terminated in *bus*—as Torabus, Persibus,
Eorabus, Eallabus, Carabus, Cullabus, Neribus, Carnabus, Cavila-
bus, Cragabus, Reesibus, Kinabus, Assabus. There is another list
terminating in *stadh* or sta, as Runistadh, Ollistadh, Elistadh,
Tormastadh, Robasadh, Grobasadh. Then there are Sannaig and
Suirnaig, Saligeo and Braigeo, Gruilinn and Gruinnart. In several
of these the Norse elements are quite distinguishable, and the
analysis of one may help to solve the rest. In his young days he
was told that Gruinart meant *Grunnd ard ;* only, unfortunately, it
was a low place with a long, narrow, salt water loch in the bottom
of it. *Ceann traigh Ghruinart* is famous as the name of a Piobaireachd, and the scene of a battle between the Macdonalds and
Macleans. On one occasion he was called upon by a poor woman
in Shetland, who told him she had come from Gruinart. "From
Gruinart?" said he, thinking of the place in Islay. "Yes," said
she, more deliberately, "from Gruina-firth." Gruina is the general
term for a green isle, and we know that "firth" is a bay. And
with Nave Island, in the mouth of Loch Gruinart, Gruinafirth, or

the Green-isle-loch, was an accurately descriptive name. "Sannaig" is really Sandwick; "Saligeo" is the seal-gully; and "Braigeo" is evidently Gaelic and Norse, the brow of the gully or Geo. Of course the Danes and Norwegians gave names to numbers of places all over the North as well when they had settlements. With regard to Culloden itself there was some reason to suppose that it was partly Scandinavian, and made up of Cùil, a neuk, and Odin, one of the Norse deities, sometimes found in the form of *Odair* among our Gaelic-speaking people; and it is very remarkable to what extent this Cùil, or corner, of the country is dotted over with what are called Druidical Circles. The root Cùil, also, is very prevalent in the same locality—as Cuil-earnaidh, Cuil-blair, Cuil-domhaich, Cuil-chuinneag, &c. It was possible that by comparing and considering these various uses of the word, we might arrive at a more satisfactory conclusion than by taking any one application of it by itself. Whilst offering these remarks, he was desirous of expressing the great pleasure with which he listened to the paper, which he characterised as a valuable contribution to the records of the Society.

November 25.—This evening the following paper was read by Mr Murdoch, on

THE CLAN SYSTEM.

It is no uncommon thing to hear and read the Highlanders spoken of as if, in recent times, they had been delivered from the feudal system : the idea being conveyed that the feudal system was that of the clans. I need hardly tell a company of intelligent Highlanders that this is a mistake ; and it is only for the sake of argument that it is necessary for me to say that the feudal system could only be set up on the ruins of the clan system.

It is rather curious that the above blunder is most frequently committed at the very time that the blunderers are trying to make us believe that they are instructing us in politics ; and yet, that the simple truth comes out very frequently when persons put forth no such solemn pretensions. How often do we hear, for instance, of *a feud* between enemies; but of persons who stick closely together and help one another being *clannish*. Here you see the distinction, and even the difference, between the two systems lingering in common speech, after so-called philosophers and designing politicians, had done their utmost to establish a fiction in the public mind. "There was a great feud between such and such

families," meaning, of course, that they hated each other, and were
designing evil against one another. But who requires to be told
that the opposite is meant when it is said " Oh, how clannish these
Highlanders are," meaning, of course, that they help one another,
defend each other, and hold together like a well-regulated family.

And what came out thus in so many words is only what we
know to be contained, and given out by, the one word *clann*. The
clan is really the family from a certain point of view; but it is not
intended to convey the idea of a family in a state of orphanage, or
without a head. To convey that bare idea, it would suffice, I
imagine, to use the word *teadhlach*, simply *a* family. But when
we use the word *clann*, we co-note the relation of the family or
teadhlach to the parent. I may say that the more tender idea of
my own, or his own, children is suggested; and then there arises
in the mind the image or figure of the father or patriarch, looking
down with tender solicitude upon his own children or *clann*, and
the *clann* looking up to him for counsel, for guidance, for instruction, believing in his parental affection, and rendering filial affection
in return.

All this, I say, lingers in our common speech; and if you
wanted to conjure up in the mind the best form and spirit of
society, you could hardly do better than that which is done in the
mind of every intelligent Highlander by the full and fair use of the
word *clann* as applied to a people.

But if you wanted to damage this people, if you wanted to
afford a pretext for breaking in upon this people, society, or family,
you could hardly do better than the Quaker did with the dog, "I
will not kill thee, but call thee mad." Of course, to call the poor
dog mad was to raise every baton in the village against him, and
make sure that some one should kill him. So a good way of
ensuring the breaking up of the clans was to give them a bad
name; and a capital excuse for what had been done in this way
was, to say that theirs was a *feudal* system, or a system of slavery
and of feuds, which ought not to be allowed to exist.

But I must not proceed too rapidly over the ground which lies
before me from this position. As I have said, the *clann* implied
the father; and this is as strong an implication as I can find in the
word, and in the thing which the word represents. And this leads
us to the natural origin of society. It does not matter whether
we go back to the first father and family, or merely to an immi-
grant family; we have the little group established, say, in one of
our glens: the old, sage, and experienced occupying the place of
honour and authority; the young, vigorous, and inexperienced,
ready to run in obedience to that authority, and in conformity to
the wisdom residing there.

But this father must relatively diminish, and ultimately die, leaving an increasing and multiplying family in need of guidance, and requiring some strong cord or influence to keep them still together, and counteract in some measure the centrifugal force of personal selfishness, which would set each member of the larger family to disregard the general good in the eager pursuit of his own gain.

The younger will look up to the elder; and when there are many fathers, the whole community, in quest of one to act the part of father in general to them, will naturally defer to the most fatherly of all these fathers. In the quality of age, the elder brother will, of course, excel, and command the first thought. But more is required than age, although a measure of this is indispensable in him who would rule. I pray you to note this, and bring it with you to the consideration of some things in our ancient Highland polity which have puzzled theorists. It was not because he was old that the natural father was the head of his family, although a measure of age was indispensable—but because he was their father. And he, among the many fathers to whom I have already referred, who possesses the greatest amount of what children look up for in their father, is of right the head of the large family or community of families. The first of these we cannot overlook, viz., blood relationship. This has a hold which is not to be lightly regarded, and which has in all ages been felt, no matter how vigorously individuals and nations have tried to break it. And when I speak of blood relationship, I wish to denote a two-sided relationship. For example, we have not got so far in our descent as to ignore the blood relationship of the head of our community to his people; he must be of the people whom he rules; but he must be still closer, if possible, to the preceding and to the first ruler or father than any one else. In this consanguinity he inherits a potent share of the veneration which, in course of time, gathers around the head of him who has ruled well and long. You will readily understand what a hold this gives to the new ruler. The people feel the force of the two ties—his being flesh of their own flesh, and bone of the bone of him to whom they have been in the habit of looking up. In other words, the fraternal feeling and the filial feeling find ligitimate exercise and use in binding the growing community together. Theories of Government, which go to put the right man in the right place, and yet ignore the force of the feelings to which I have been referring, have generally, if not always, failed in practice. They may succeed in either of two supposititious circumstances—when the entire community has become so Christian as to be thoroughly imbued with that feeling of higher brotherhood which grows out of an absorbing love of Christ;

E

or when men have become so transcendently philosophical as not
to care for their own nearest relatives. The former we are not,
and our fathers were not ; and the latter I hope we never shall be.
The above goes a great way towards accounting for the shortness
of the lives of republics, and for the length of days attained by
very rotten monarchies.

The very fact that my blood relation occupies the seat of
authority in my clan, tribe, or country, gives me a degree of
interest and pride in him which I would not have in another ruler;
and it has often been stated that the idea of a blood relationship to
his chief has in olden times gone to make the poor clansman
cherish the spirit and behaviour of a gentleman ; and I need
hardly say that this relationship had its influence in making the
chief cherish his clan, and devote himself more heartily to its
service. Not to rest so important a point on my authority, or on
your reasoning, I will give what Brown says on the subject in the
" History of the Highland Clans " :—

"The patriarchal system in some of its features exhibited a
strong resemblance to feudalism, yet in others the distinction was
too strongly marked to be for a moment mistaken. The chief was
the hereditary lord of all who were supposed to be descended of
the same stock with himself; the Gothic baron was merely the
hereditary proprietor of a certain tract of land, and as such only
entitled to the service and obedience of those who dwelt on it.
This distinguishing property of the patriarchal system, wherever it
prevailed, was peculiarly remarkable in the case of the Highlanders
of Scotland."

And whilst I am quoting Brown, I wish to direct your particular attention to what he says in the same connection, although
this is not the best place for it :—

" By reason of the similarity already mentioned, the feudal law
was without difficulty introduced into the Highlands in so far as
regarded the tenure of lands ; but in other respects the struggle
between the two systems proved long and doubtful, nor was it
until a very recent period that the feudal law of succession and
marriage came into full operation in the Highlands [mark this],
and displaced that which previously obtained—thus laying a
foundation for those disputes which have since arisen amongst
many of the Highland families respecting chieftainship and succession."—Vol. iv., p. 371.

I want you to note another historical statement of Brown's,
because it contains the testimony of some of our former law-makers
to the superiority of the clan system over that of the feudal
system as a conservator of the subject's liberty :—

" Community of feeling, position, and interest," he says, page

390, "was strengthened by a supposed community of blood, and gave to the Celtic chief a pre-eminent authority which never belonged to the feudal baron. In Wales, in Ireland, and in the Highlands of Scotland, the patriarchal system was universal; whilst opposed to, not identical with, this form was the feudal system of the Saxon invaders. It was long the policy of the Scottish legislature to oppose the feudal power of the barons, and to support that which was exercised by the chiefs: the one was conceived to militate against, and present an obstacle to, the explication and assertion of the royal authority; the other was sought as an ally against usurpations, which were restrained by no ties, and confined within no limits, such as those which at once regulated and abridged the authority of a chief."

With your permission I shall quote another testimony to the same effect. General Stuart of Garth says—"One chief was distinguished from another, not by any additional splendour of dress or equipage; but by being followed by more dependants, and by entertaining a greater number of guests. What the retainers gave from their individual property was spent amongst them in the kindest and most liberal manner. At the castle every individual was made welcome, and was treated according to his station with a degree of courtesy and regard to his feelings unknown in any other country. This condescension, while it raised the clansman in his own estimation, and drew closer the ties between him and his superior, seldom tempted him to use any improper familiarities. He believed himself well-born, and was taught to respect himself in the respect which he showed to his chief; and thus, instead of complaining of the difference of station and fortune, or considering a ready obedience to his chieftain's call as a slavish oppression, he felt convinced that he was supporting his own honour in showing his gratitude and duty to the generous head of his family." "Hence," says Dalrymple, in his Memoirs, "the Highlanders, whom more savage nations called savage, carried in the outward expression of their manners the politeness of courts without their vices, and in their bosom the high point of honour, without its follies." And Mrs Grant of Laggan says—"Nothing can be more erroneous than the prevalent idea that a Highland chief was an ignorant and unprincipled tyrant, who rewarded the abject submission of his followers with relentless cruelty and rigorous oppression." And mark what follows—"If ferocious in disposition, or weak in understanding, he was curbed and directed by the heads of his tribe, who, by inviolable custom, were his standing counsellors, without whose advice no measure of any kind was decided." Numerous examples of the exercise of this counsel might be given. The Clann Choinnich would not allow their chief to pull down the

Castle of Brahan; and the Laird of Glenorchy, more than three hundred years ago, resolved to build a castle on a hill at the side of Loch Tay, and actually laid the foundation, which was to be seen in General Stuart's day, and I do not know but it is still to be seen. The situation was not agreeable to his advisers, who interfered, and caused him to change his plan, and build the Castle of Balloch or Taymouth. In some instances they went the length of deposing their chiefs. One example of this exercise of a very legitimate power is quoted in the case of the Chief Macdonald of Clanranald, and another in the family of Macdonald of Keppoch; and at a later period the pick of the Clan Donnell of Glengarry got up in a body and emigrated to America, the recreant chief appealing to Parliament for power to prevent them from leaving him alone in his glory.

Cæsar observes that "the clannish system was introduced among the Gauls, in ancient times, so as that the most obscure person should not be oppressed by the rich; for each leader was obliged to protect his followers, else he should soon be stripped of his authority." And Logan says—"It is apparent from the construction of Celtic society that a chief could never become despotic. The government was radically democratic"—(Vol. i., page 180); and (page 184) he says—"The connection of the Gaelic chief and his people was not the rule of the strong over the weak: it was maintained by reciprocal advantages and kindnesses. All the members of a clan were connected with each other, and their common safety depended on their united fidelity and co-operation; tyranny and injustice on the part of the chief could not fail to weaken his influence, and, finally, estrange his kindred and his friends."

But I wish you here to notice a remarkable difference between the clan system and the feudal system in regard to primogeniture. You know and see clearly that, from the laird in his mansion to the king on his throne, the succession is not only by descent from father to son, but from father to the eldest son, without any proper regard to the comparative fitness of the different members of the laird's or of the king's family. I need hardly dwell upon the violence which this disregard does to the law of natural affection no less than to the fitness of things. It is not the law of nature that a man should prefer his eldest son to all his other sons; neither is it that the community should have such an overwhelming veneration for the eldest son of their chief as to make them overlook fitness for office, and those lovable elements of character upon which friendship subsists. No; it often happens that the affections of the parent single out the youngest, and that the people show a decided preference for a younger son over an heir-apparent.

Thus, although there are strong laws of nature pointing to *a* son or near relative of a ruler as his successor, there is not any great natural force in the law or custom which is allowed to point to the eldest son as successor. And it is a remarkable thing that in the clan system, notwithstanding the great scope allowed for the exercise of veneration, it was laid down in law and in custom that the succession should not be limited to the eldest son, or to any son of the reigning chief. The best specimen in the best stock was the successor. The chief's family was assumed to be the best stock, and his brother, his son, his nephew—whoever showed himself the best in this stock—was chosen to succeed him. Nor was this in ancient times confined to the Highland clans : we see it in the Scottish and even in the English royal succession. Robertson, in his work called " Scotland under her Early Kings," brings this point out as a recognised principle, and not a mere accident decided by feuds or battles. After mentioning a number of instances in both countries in which the crowns had descended indirectly, and in which the successors had been appointed before-hand, he says— " In Scotland such a system was peculiarly desirable, when the early usage, extending the right of election to the Crown to every member of the royal family, rendered the election of a *Tanist* during the lifetime of the reigning sovereign a matter of absolute necessity, to prevent anarchy and confusion after his decease." Logan confirms this—" The law of Tanistry not only regulated the government of the clans, but determined the succession of the kings of Scotland during the Celtic dynasty, or until 1056, and pervaded the constitution to a much later period." And Dr Macpherson, who mentions that it was not above two hundred years since the custom prevailed in the Highlands, says that it prevailed even among the Saxons; but that it became obsolete before the conquest of Ireland. If possible, Buchanan is still more forcible, not only as to the facts, but as to the wisdom of this system.

Brown, as already quoted, says that the patriarchal system extended over Ireland and Wales, as well as over the Highlands. Spenser complains of it as a hinderance to the consolidation of the feudal power of England in Ireland. In his famous Dialogue on the state of Ireland, Endox asks, " Doth not the parent, in any graunt or conveyance, bind the beyres forever thereunto?" Irenæus answers—" They say no ; for their ancestors had no estates in any their lands, signoryes, or heriditamentes, longer than during their own lives, as they allege, for all the Irish do hold their lands by Tanistrye ; which is, they say, no more than a personal estate for his life-time, that is, Tanistih, by reason that he is admitted thereto by the election of the country." Endox asks—" What is this

that you call Tanistih and Tanistrye? They be terms never heard
of nor known to us.? Iren.—It is a custom among all the Irish,
that presently, after the death of any their chiefs, they do presently assemble themselves to a place generally appointed and
known to them, to chose another in his stead, where they do nominate and elect, for the most part, not the eldest son, nor any of the
children of their lord deceased, but the next to him of blood, that
is, the *eldest and worthiest*, as commonly the next brother to him,
if he have any, or the next cousin-german, or so forth, as any is
elder in that kind or sept; and then next to him they choose the
next of blood to be Tanistih."

He then goes on to describe the ceremony of inauguration,
which is the very same as that gone through at the election of the
Lords of the Isles in Scotland, and embraced this engagement on
the part of the chief—" An oath to preserve all the former ancient
customs of the country inviolate, and to deliver up the succession
peaceably to his Tanistih." Endox asks about the origin of this
strange system, and Irenæus answers—" I have heard that the
beginning and cause of this ordinance amongst the Irish, was
specially for the defence and maintenance of their lands in their
posterity, and for excluding of all innovation and alienation thereof
unto strangers, and especially to the English. For when the
captain died, if the signiory should descend to his child, and he,
perhaps, an infant, another might peradventure step in between, or
thrust him out by strong hand. And to this end the Tanistih is
always ready known, if it should happen the captain suddenly to
die, to defend and keep the teritory from all doubts and dangers.
For which cause the Tanistih hath also a share of the country
allotted to him, and certain cuttings and appendages upon all the
inhabitants under the lord."

All this he refers to the Brehon Laws; and to them I also
would refer, as sending us far back into the early Christian, and
even pagan times, for the original idea of chieftainship. At page
279, vol. ii., of the Brehon Laws, now in course of publication by
a Royal Commission in Dublin, the " Senachus Mor " has this
striking passage—" Every head defends its members, if it be a
goodly head, of good deeds, of good morals, exempt, affluent,
capable. The body of every head is his tribe, for there is no body
without a head. The head of every tribe, according to the people,
should be the man of the tribe who is the most experienced, the
most noble, the most wealthy, the wisest, the most learned, the
most truly popular, the most powerful to oppose, the most steadfast
to sue for profits, and be sued for losses." At page 201 we get a
glimpse of the hereditary element, where it says—" There is a distinction of stock, and of chiefs, that is, a chief who is entitled only

to butter, and seed, and live stock ; an inferior chief, whose father was not a chief." But in page 203 it is said—" The chief of true family, by father and grandfather, is entitled to returns, with all noble rights in general."

You will readily perceive that even with the breadth of basis given to the ruling family by the element of Tanistry, the ties of consanguinity must be getting weaker as the tribe or clan multiplies and extends. Surely, then, it was by no mere accident or chance that the custom of fosterage was established. To me it seems very remarkable as an expedient for bringing the head of the community into a fresh blood connection with the extremities. To borrow an illustration from the vegetable kingdom, it brings before my mind the Banian tree, which, although having a great trunk proper, and numerous primary roots connecting that trunk with the parent earth, sends down fresh props to support its wide-spreading branches, and draw nourishment from a wider area of ground. So the chief, although connected by blood with the whole clan, sends out a son to be nursed in the house of the humble and distant clansman, thus striking a fresh root for his family among his people, and drawing a fresh supply of support from the original source—the body of the people. Nor is that all ; that is only one side of the matter. This nursing, growing, living—this thorough experience in the humbler sphere of the clansman's house, is an important part of the education necessary to a good ruler. It is not merely the knowledge which he acquires of how the other half of the world lives ; there is something more that is very valuable acquired—*sympathy* with the grade of men among whom he has spent his early days. What a corrective will not that same sympathy be of the pride, the arrogance, and the false idea of class superiority which is too apt to have a place in the superior circle to which he returns from the humble home of his fosterfather. Logan says—" The practice of fosterage, by which children were exchanged and brought up, was a curious feature in the system and a most powerful cement to clanship. The son of the chief was given to be reared by some inferior member of society, with whom he lived during the years of pupillarity. The effect of this custom appears to have been astonishing." It is very curious how Logan words the next sentence. You will find that it consists, first, of a statement of facts, and then of a mere opinion, as if he did not happen to have any facts at hand to support it. He says that this custom of fosterage " often prevented feuds." That is the statement of facts. The opinion is that "it seems calculated sometimes to produce feuds." I would be afraid, too, that it would produce feuds. But that would only be an opinion, in support of which I could not produce a morsel of evidence any more than my friend

Logan did. "The attachment of foster-brothers," he says, "was
strong and indissoluble. The Highlanders say, that 'affectionate
to a man is a friend, but a foster-brother is as the life-blood of his
heart.'" And Camden goes to the extravagant length of saying
that "no love in the world is comparable by many degrees to it;"
and Spenser gives a most affecting, though rather gross example,
of the strength of this love in the foster-mother of Murrough
O'Brien. Campion says that five hundred kine and better were
sometimes given by the Irish to procure the nursing of a great
man's child.

The Highland Society's Report on Ossian informs us that Fionn
had no fewer than sixteen foster-brothers. Logan mentions that a
deed of fosterage between Sir Norman Macleod and John Mackenzie,
dated 1645, and written in Gaelic, was in existence in 1830, when
he wrote. Brown but repeats Logan's ideas and quotations in less
felicitous terms.

It is astonishing with what minuteness the Brehon laws go into
this subject of fosterage, taking care that every foster son shall be
fed, clothed, and educated according to certain scales laid down,
fixing the terms, the periods, and the fees; and guarding against
the corruption of the minds, the injury of the bodies, or the
damaging of the interests of foster-children. It is more as a
curiosity than as essential to my present purpose that I give an
extract or two from the "Senachus Mor." Of the raiment, it says
"According to the rank of each man, from the humblest man to
the king, is the clothing of his son. Blay-coloured, and yellow,
and black and white clothes are to be worn by the sons of inferior
grades; red, and green, and brown clothes by the sons of chieftains;
purple and blue by the sons of kings."

Then as to their food. "Leite" is given to them all; but the
flavouring which goes into it is different—salt butter for the sons
of inferior grades, fresh butter for the sons of chieftains, honey for
the sons of kings. Here is another version from Dr O'Donovan,
evidently as the custom got altered—"They are all fed on stirrabout; but the materials of which it is made, and the flavouring
taken with it, vary according to the rank of the parents of the
children. The children of the inferior grades are fed to bare
sufficiency on stirrabout made of oatmeal on butter-milk or water,
and it is taken with stale butter. The sons of the chieftain grades
are fed to satiety on stirrabout made of barleymeal, upon new milk,
taken with fresh butter. The sons of kings are fed on stirrabout,
made of wheaten meal, upon new milk, taken with honey."

Before I proceed any further I must direct your attention to
what I must call, in modern language, a great fact which comes out
of all this. The chiefs and chieftainships, like the kings, were in

in reality public judicial functionaries, chosen, appointed, and supported to administer the laws and customs of their people for the general good. Their appointment depended upon their character and their pedigree ; and the retaining of their offices depended upon their conduct. The full force of the first of these statements will hardly appear until we have gone into the more solid matter of the relation in which chief and people stood to the land ; and this I must leave, I find, for another paper.

Let me note another remarkable thing, viz., that this system embraced the two elements of aristocracy and democracy, forces which, in our day, are regarded as antagonistic and mutually destructive. The chief, as a rule, was an aristocrat by blood and birth at the same time that he was the choice of the people, in the affection developed in them by his character. So far as a superficial reading of history and of tradition conveys, however, chiefs and chieftains (like the kings of the same period), seem to have had their main use in uniting their people for warlike purposes, and in leading them into the ever-recurring fray. Let us give its full force to this reading, merely adding that a very great part of the history of England, no less than that of Scotland, is really taken up with wars, and most of the leading men in other countries at the same period found distinction just as the leaders of the clans did. So that, for the times and the circumstances, the clan system is no worse in that respect than any other system we know of, if it is as bad; and it remains then to be examined, taking into account the principles or the natural laws upon which it was founded, and the possibility of developing and applying those principles in times of science and peace.

Under this system, society was divided into small and manageable communities, composing those who were most conveniently situated for intercourse and co-operation, and who were most powerfully drawn to each other by the first ties which go to bind men together. Nothing, surely, could be better than that, so far as it went. But letting it go further, don't you think that if there were something else required to be done by those communities, beyond defending themselves from their enemies, that it was an admirable arrangement to have them drawn together and organised for purposes of co-operation and mutual improvement? And do you think it a very extravagant supposition to hazard, that if the clan system had been allowed to remain in its integrity and power of growth and adaptation to circumstances, that our poor clansmen would to-day be in their present backward predicament in their own land. I really think not. At present you see there is no head, no union, no organisation. I admit that this want of rural organisation is not peculiar to the Highlands ; but what I want

F

you to note is, that it has come in where an organised union did exist. No doubt many will regard the bare idea of a rural community so organised as Utopian, if not worse. But why should rural unions be deprecated, and municipal unions commended? One of the stock boasts and alleged causes of British freedom is our municipal system of government. Every town finds out that it must enter into an organised union, and that it requires to give the fullest scope for the exercise of the wisdom of its wisest men. Every one admits that our towns could not get on without their local governments; but the scattered, dull, ignorant, rural population is left to gravitate to the lowest level, without any organisation for the purpose of raising it. My idea is, that had the clans been left in their state of natural organisation, they would, in course of time, have got into the way of co-operating for the purposes of improvement in the arts of peace. Thousands of things which are out of the question in their state of isolation would be quite easy for them in their united state. At the present day there are voluntary organisations for such purposes among the farmers of Switzerland; and it is very curious that some of the writers on that system of co-operation which has lately sprung up in England should refer for sanction and example to certain remnants of the clan system which they had discovered in the Highlands at even comparatively recent dates.

Supposing a clan still organised as of yore, with the best man at their head, and the wisest men chosen to guide him with their advice, I should expect, for instance, to find the Tanist becoming versed in every branch of science, and more or less acquainted with every art which was most likely to develop the capabilities of his country, and meet the requirements of his people. Every fresh scrap of minerology, geology, of meteorology, every fresh development of agriculture, of the art of breeding stock, every new feature in railway making and working, should claim his attention; and wheresoever any of these things were to be seen to the best advantage, I should expect to hear of his going there, and bringing home stores of science and volumes of wisdom for the good of his people.

In conclusion, for the present, I wish to take up a strong defensive position founded upon the mass of facts and reasoning, to which *my* few facts and observations can only be regarded as hurriedly referring—that position is, that we, as the descendants and representatives of the clans in these modern times, have no reason, as many ignorant people suppose, to be ashamed of the ancient polity of our race; that, on the contrary, we have reason to be proud of that polity, combining as it did so much sound philosophy with so much that was practically useful in actual life—a system which gave full scope to the best and strongest legitimate impulses in man, and made use of them to bind society together, and lead men on shoulder to shoulder to secure what was for the good and glory of all, a system capable of the most beneficent use even in those enlightened times of ours.

So that, for that part of the matter at any rate, we have no occasion to beg permission to breathe the breath of our own hills, or to think the thoughts of the wise and brave men who went before us. Our forefathers, who established that system of society, left nothing to dishonour their sons. There is too much reason to fear that in our time-serving pusillanimity we may tarnish the good name we inherit from them. They left a noble inheritance in the system of social and political thought which they bequeathed to us; and we shall not be in our duty either to them in the past, or to our fellow-citizens in the present, if we do not make a bold effort to bring some at least of the practical wisdom and profound philosophy which found a place in the clan system, to correct the atheism and the inhumanity which have to so large an extent corrupted thought and life in the present day.

This paper naturally gave rise to a good deal of comment, and some criticism; but most of the objections were founded on facts which the essayist maintained grew out of the feudal system. Every one seemed to feel that the "Land Question" was inseparable from the subject of the paper, and a good deal of discussion which ensued turned upon that connection.

December 21.—Upon this evening the following paper was read by Mr Mackay, the Secretary:—Subject, the Legends of Glen-Urquhart.

SGEULACHDAN GHLINN-URCHUDAINN.

Tha cuid de dhaoine 'am barail nach eil e freagarrach dhuinne a tha beo anns na laithean glice deireannach so, a bhi toirt feart 's am bith air sgeulachdan na laithean a dh'fhalbh. "Cha 'n eil annt' ach faoineachd," ars' iadsan a ta de'n a bheachd so, "agus mar is luaithe a dhi-chuimhnichear iad, 'se is fearr." Tha mi 'n dochas gu'm b'eil iad gle ghaun 'am measg buill a Chomuin Ghailig a tha cho tur chiallach riutha-so; oir tha còir mhor aig sgeulachdan na Gaidhealtachd air ar n-aire, mar a dh'innis Caimbeulach Ile—ùghdar a "bha thall 'sa chunnaic"—dhuinn bho chionn ghoirid. Agus bho'n a tha a chóir sin aig na sgeulachdan oirnn, is e mo dhùrachd, ged is i so a cheud oidhche, nach i an oidhche ma dheireadh a choisrigeas an Comunn dhaibh. Tha sinn 'an so a deanamh

uaill arm a bhi 'nar Gaidheil shean-fhasanta. Cha 'n eil a'dhith oirnn
gu bhi gu buileach sona ach nach eil sinn 'n ar suidhe timchiol
teine mòr moine ann am bothan fail, air oidhche ghaillionnach
gheamhraidh. 'S ann 'an leithid sin a dh'àite a bhiodh e taitneach,
a bhi ag aithris agus ag eisdeachd na seann sgeulachdan ; agus na'n
robh sinn an nochd anns an t-suidheachadh thaitneach sin, cha
chreid mi-fhein nach tigeadh sgail nam baird 's nan sonn, aon uair
fhathast a shealltuinn air an clann gu bàghail tre na neulaibh
dorcha, mar is minic a thainig ann an laithean Oisein ! Ach gus
am bi an Comunn Gàilig 'an comas bothan a thogail dhaibh fhein,
is eiginn dhaibh cuir suas leis an t-seomar a tha baillidhean Inbhirnis toilichte 'thoirt dhaibh. Ach a nise chum na sgeulachdan.

Chunnaic sinn bho 'n oraid a leugh Alasdair Mac-Choinnich
dhuinn bho chionn ghoirid, nach eil sluagh a cordadh a thaobh bun
an fhacail "Loch-Nis." Ma chreideas sibh a cheud sgeul a bheir
mis' an nochd dhuibh, agus is minic a chuala mi ann an Gleann
Urchudainn, cha bhi aobhar ni's mo agaibh a dhol a dh' aona chuid
gu Eas-na-Smuid no gu Naois, air-son ainm an loch.

Bha lath ann anns an robh an gleann mor, a tha 'n diugh fo
uisgeachan Loch-Nis, 'na shrath aluinn naine, air a chuartachadh
air gach toabh le beanntaibh arda, comhduichte le gach crann a
b'aillidh dreach. Bha an gleann fhein sgeadaichte le gach feur
agus lus 'bu mhaisiche na 'cheile ; agus bho cheann gu ceann,
ghluais gu mall, abhainn chiuin anns an d'fhuaireadh gach iasg a
bha chum maith an duine. Ged 'bu lionmhor an sluagh, bha sonas
agus cairdeas 'nam measg. Cha do shanndaich fear bean no bò a
choimhearsnaich, oir bha a bhean 's a bho fhein aig gach fear, agus
bu dileas gach bean agus bu mhaith a chuireadh gach mna cuigeal.
'N uair nach do sharaich an laoch an torc 's a mhagh, sharaich e
am fiadh 's a bheinn ; agus 'n uair nach do sharaich e am fiadh 's
a bheinn, threoraich e a spreidh 'sa chluain ; agus ged a bha an
abhainn a sgoltadh a ghlinne, bha e comasach do 'n bhuachaille air
taobh Shrath-fharagaig oran gaoil a sheinn agus comhradh milis a
dheanamh ann an cluaisean a leannan air taobh Urchudainn.

Air bruach na h-aibhne bha tobair, agus riamh bho'n a bhuail
Dalaidh Mor an Druidh uisge na tobair, bha e ro bhuadhail air na
h-nile tinneas agus creuchd a leigheas. Chuir Dalaidh clach 'am
beul an tobair, agus dh'aithn' e cho luath 's a rachadh uisge 'tharruing, gu'n rachadh a chlach a chuir 'na h-aite fhein—"An lath a
chuireas sibb m'aithn' air chul," ars' es-an, "cuireas am fuaran bhur
tir fo sgrios." Thug an sluagh creideas do dh'fhacal Dhalaidh,
agus bha e 'na reachd 's a ghleann a chlach a chuir am beul an
tobair gach uair a rachadh uisge 'tharruing. Mar sinn chuir latha
scachad latha, agus thug bliadhna a h-aite do bhliadhna.

Ach latha de na laithean dh'fhag bean òg an leanabh a bh'air a h-uchd anns an tigh, agus dh'fhalbh i do'n fhuaran air-son làd huiru. Cha luaith' a thog i a chlach na chual i glaodh gu'n do ghluais an leanabh chum an teine. Thilg i a cudainn 'an so, agus a chlach 'an sud, agus 'na dearbh dheann rinn i air a tigh. Theàruinu i a naoidhean, ach dhi-chuimhnich i facal an Druidh, agus cha do chuir i a chlach 'na h-aite fhein! Dh'eirich an t-uisge, agus bhrùchd e da riridh. Chuir am fuaran thairis agus mheudaicheadh na h-uisgeachan cho mòr, 'o gu'n robh an gleann air a chomhdachadh leo. Thug an sluagh na beanntan orra, a caoidh gu goirt; agus cha robh ach aon ghlaodh ri chluinntinn air feadh na tire; "Tha loch a nis ann!" "Tha loch a nis ann!" Bho sin tha na h-uisgeachan fo'n ainm "Loch-nis" gus an latha'n dingh.

Tha e coltach gu'n robh Dàlaidh na dhruidh ainmeil. Tha seann àit' aoraidh druidheil ann an Urchudainn ris an canar fhathast "Carn Dàlaidh;" agus 'se ainm a bhaile anns am b'eil e "Cartàlaidh."

Tha cuid de dhaoine, tha foghluimte ann an seann eachdraidh ar dùthcha, a smuanachadh gu'r h-ann bho Naois Mac Uisneach, sonn ainmeil a bha beo bho chionn iomadh linn, a tha ainm an loch air a thoir, agus na'm bruidhnichmid gu ceart, nach b'e "Loch-Nis" a theireadh sinn, ach "Loch-Naois." 'S ann air Naois a tha an ath sgeul a dh'ainmicheas mi; ach cha'n ann 'an Urchudainn a chaidh a faighinn. Sgriobh ar caraide, an gaidheal duineil sin Mac Gille-Mhicheil, i bho bhilibh seann duine ann an Eilean Bharra. Tha an sgeula so, (ris an abair sinn Eachdraidh Chlann Uisneach) ro fhada air-son a toir gu buileach, ach bheir mi as-tharruing ghoirid dhuibh, a nochdas an comh-cheangal a th' aicc ri Gleann-Urchudainn. Ach gus an tuig sibb i, feumar innse gu'n robb, roimhe so, duine ann an Eireann, air ainm Golam Cruitire. Cha do gbin beam Gholam cloinn da gus an robh i fada thairis air aois chloinne; ach ma dheireadh, tre eadar-ghuidhe Dhruidh araidh, bha nighean aice air an d' thug Golam agus i fhein Dearduil mar ainm. 'Nuair a dh'fhas Dearduil mor, bha i anabarrach maiseach: "b'i boinne fala bu mhaisiche bha eadar grian agus talamh, agus cha d'rugadh boinne fala riamh 'an Eireann, cho maiseach rithe." Ach fhuair Conachar, Righ Uladh [Ulster] 'na lamhan i, agus chuir e roimhe a pòsadh air ball. Dh'iarr ise latha agus bliadhna dhi-fhein, agus fhuair i iad. Mu'n d' thainig deireadh an latha agus bliadhna, co thainig a shealltuinn air Conachar ach Naois, Aillean, agus Ardan, triuir chlann bhrathair athair, agus laoich a bha ro iomraiteach air fad na tire. Am fear a bu tàire dhiubh, bha e 'na lan ghaisgeach; agus am fear a bu shàra dhiubh, cha robh gaisgeach eile 'an Eireann coimeas ris. Thuit Naois agus Dearduil ann an gaol ri cheile, agus air an aobhar sin bha Conachar feargach 'an aghaidh Naois. "Smaoinich Naois nach robh math dha fuireach na b' fhaide ann an Eireann, leis mar a chuir e Conachar Righ

Uladh, mac bhrathair athair 'na aghaidh a thaobh a bhoirionnaich,
ged nach robh i pòsd' aige, agus thill e air ais do dh' Alba, agus
rainig e Inbhir-Naois [Inverness]. Rinn Naois tigh ri taobh
Uisge Naois, far am marbhadh e am bradan am mach air an
uinneag, agus am fiadh am mach air an dorus, agus bha e fhein
agus Dearduil agus a dha bhrathair a tamh anns an tir so, gus an
d' thainig an t-am Conachar Righ Uladh am boirionnach a
phòsadh, 'an ceann latha agus bliadhna.

Ciod e 'bha Conachar, Righ Uladh, 's an àm ach 'am beachd gu 'n
d' thugadh e mach Dearduil le' chlaidh' agus le lann bho Naois,
i bhi pòsd aige no gun i bhi ; agus ciod e an obair a bh' aige ach
ag ullachadh a chum latha blàir 'us baiteal a thoirt do Naois, agus
a bhean a thoirt bhuaidhe gun taing. Bha e 'an so a smuanachadh
aige fhein, ged a chuireadh e fios air Naois gu ruig Inbhir-Naois,
nach tigeadh e; ach falbhar agus cuirear fios air Fearchar Mac Rò,
agus chuir e mar chumha agus mar gheasan air a dhol gu ruig
Inbhir-Naois agus curadh a thoirt do Naois Mac Uisneach agus do
'bhrathran a thighinn‑chun an luchairt aige-san ; gu 'n robh e 'dol
a thoirt cuirm mhòr shòlasach dha 'chairdean 'us dha luchd sòlais,
agus gu 'n robh e deonach iadsan a bhi 'nam measg. Bha e 'an so
Falbhar Fearchar Mac Rò air a thurus, agus ruigear Tùr Naois
air taobh Loch-nis, agus cuirear 'an ceill a theachdaireachd.
"Mata," arsa Naois, "is cinnteach mise nach ann gu mo chrùnadh
a chuir Conachar fios orm, ach bho 'n a chuir e fios oirnn, theid
sinn ann." "Tha triuir mbae agamsa," arsa Fearchar Mac Rò,
"agus iadsan triuir ghaisgeach, beud 'sam bith a theannas Conachar
ri dheanamh ort, seasaidh iad thu ann am blàir 's am baiteal.
Agus falbhaidh tusa bho 'n chuir ma d' choinneamh e, agus theid
thu chun na cuirm, agus ma nochdas Conachar còirid ruit, noch-
daidh tu còirid dha, agus ma dh' fheuchas e gairge ruit, feuchaidh
tu gairge ris, agus bithidh mo thriuir mhac-sa leat.

Dh' fhalbh Fearchar Mac Rò agus dh' fhalbh comhla ris, Naois,
agus Dearduil, agus Aillean, agus Ardan. Cho luath agus a chaidh
iad air tir 'an Eireann chuir Fearchar Mac Rò fios chun Chonachar,
gu 'n robh na daoine air tighinn."

Ach (gun a bhi 'leantuinn a sgeula ni's faide) bha Conachar 'na
dhuine cealgach ; agus ged a mharbh Naois agus a bhriathrean da
cheud treun ghaisgeach, da cheud lan ghaisgeach agus da cheud
luth ghaisgeach a chuir e 'nan aghaidh, chiadh iad fhein a mharbhadh ma dheireadh le foill. Tha an sgeula 'dunadh mar so :—
"'N uair a bha an t-slochd deas, thilgeadh triuir Chlann Uisneach
ann. Thubhairt Dearduil an uair sin :—

'Teannadh Naois an null,
Leanadh Aillean ri Ardan ;
Nam biodh ciall aig mairbh,
Dheanadh sibh aite dhomhsa !'

Rinn iadsan aite dhi, agus 'n uair a chunnaic ise so, leum i cadar riu do'n t-slochd, agus bha i marbh maille riu ! Dh' òrdaich an droch righ, 'an sin, ise 'thogail as an t-slochd, agus a tilgeil taobh eile an loch a bha ri 'n lamh ; agus rinneadh so, agus dhunadh na sluic. Chinn 'an sin gath giubhais as an uaigh aig Dearduil, agus gath giubhais as an uaigh aig Naois, agus chuir an dà ghath snaim air a cheile os cionn an lochan !"

Cha'n fhiosrach mi gu'm beil mor aithris ann an Urchudainn ma dheighinn Naois, no bhrathran, no Dearduil, ach a mhain gu'r h-ann air Dearduil a tha Dun Dearduil air toabh eile an loch air ainmeachadh, agus gu'm b'eil e coltach gu'r h-ann bho Naois a tha ainm an loch fhein. Chuala sinn 'an so bho chionn ghoirid gu'm b'e sonn Lochlannach a bh'ann an Dearduil, agus gu'n do thilgeadh e leis a chreige a tha nise dol fo 'ainm. Cha'n eil aobhar innse dhuibh nach eil an sgeula sin ceart a tha deanamh laoch duineil cathach dhe Dearduil caomh.

Tha cliu mor air Naois agus a dha brathair agus Dearduil anns a bhardachd Oiseineach, agus 's iad na dain so (ris an can sinn 'sa Ghailig dain Chlann Uisneach) a thug Mac-a'phearson dhuinn 'sa Beurla, fo ainm Dhearduil [Darthula].

Bha Naois na chombach gaisge aig Cuchullain, agus bha iad beo 'an linn Chonachar Mac Nessa Righ Uladh ann an Eireann, a chaochail a reir eachdraidh na duthcha sin air an latha air an deach Criosd a chuir gu bas. Le sin, cha'n e amhain gu'm faidh sinn Naois ann am bardachd na h-Alba, ach tha, mar an ceudna, eliú mor air ann am bardachd na h-Eirinn, agus chunnaic mi dan Eireannach ma dheighinn, anns am b'eil ainm a bhaile anns am b'eil sinn an drasd, a tachairt.

A reir na h-uile coltach bu ro dhoil le Dearduil Tir nam beann. Tha fhathast ri fhaicinn ann an leabhar-lann na'm fir lagha [Advocate's Library] 'an Dun Eideau, seann sgriobhadh Gailig, a chaidh sgriobhadh 'sa bhliadhna 1238, agus anns am b'eil euid de dhain Chlann Uisneach. Tha aon dan ann a rinn Dearduil 'nuair a bha i gabhail a cead de Dh'alba agus i dol gu Eireann cuide ri Naois. Bheir mi rann no dha dhi-so dhuibh gu 's am faic sibb, mar a bha a Ghailig air a sgriobhadh bho chionn corr 'us sea ceud bliadhna, agus an deigh sin bheir mi dha no tri ruinn cadar-theangaichte gu Beurla. 'Se barail *Skene* gur e Gleann Urchaidh 'san Araghaël [Glen-Urquhay], a th'air a chiollachadh le " Glend Urchain " 's an dan so ; ach bho'n 'tha fios againn gu'n robh dluth cheangal aig Dearduil ri Gleann Urchudainn, nach eil e cho farasda 'chreidsinn gu'r h-e sin an Gleann a tha i a caoidh cho gort ?

> Inmain tir an tir ud thoir,
> Alba cona lingantaibh,
> Nocha ticfuinn eisdi ille,
> Mana tisain le Naise.

*   *   *

Mo chen Glend Urchain,
Ba hedh in Glend direach dromchain,
Uallcha feare aoise ma Naise,
An Glend Urchain.

Beloved land that Eastern land,
Alba, with its lakes ;
O, that I might not depart from it,
But I depart with Naois.

*   *   *

Glen Urchain ! O, Glen Urchain !
It was the straight glen of smooth ridges.
Not more joyful was a man of his age
Than Naois in Glen-Urchain.

*   *   *

Beloved is Draighen and its sounding shore,
Beloved the water o'er pure sand.
O, that I might not depart from the East ;
But I go with my beloved !

Sin agaibh a nise beachd Dhearduil air Tir nam Beann, Dh'innis an t-Ollamh ionnsuichte Carruthers, dhuinn o chionn ghoirid, gur ann o chionn beagan bhliadhnachan a thoisich daoine air meas a bhi aca air beanntaibh ard 'us gleanntaibh domhain ar duthcha. Dh'fhe[c]h an t-Ollamh gu soillear gu'n robh iad a cuir oillt gu leoir air na coigrich a thainig a' stigh orra 'n drasd agus a rithist anns na laithean a dh'fhalbh ; ach ciamar a chreideas sinn gun robh iad oillteil do na seann Ghaidheil—sliochd nam beann—nuair 'tha sinn ag eisdeachd ris an laoidh bhinn ud a sruthadh a mach bho bhilibh Dhearduil. Bho rannsachadh a rinn mi bho chionn ghoirid 'am measg bardachd Oisein agus na seann bhaird Ghaidhealach, thainig mi gu creidsinn gu'r h-ann a bha na seann Ghaidheil gle chomasach air aillidheachd coslais ar duthaich fhaicinn agus meas a thoir air ; agus tha mi smuanachadh gu'm biodh e da riridh feumail do dh'fhear a rachadh a thoirt sean[i]chas air a phuno so, a Ghailig ionnsachadh mu'n toisicheadh e. Ach is mithich a bhi tilleadh chum na sgeulachdan.

Ged nach eil mor aithris againn 'an Urchudainn air Naois, tha facal no dha againn ma dheighinn Chonachar—cha'n e Conachar Mac Nessa, tha mi smuanachadh—agus innsidh mi nise dhuibh mar a mharbh e an torc nimhe.

Bha roimhe so ann an Caisteal-na-Sroine (sin Caisteal Urchudainn) duine mor cumhachdach a thainig anall bho Eireann, air an robh Conachar Mac-Aoidh mar ainm. Bha Conachar gaisgeil thair gach gaisgeach 'san tir, agus bha mor thlachd aig anns an t-sealg. Bha cu aige bha ro-mhath 'san t-sealg fbad 'sa bha e og, ach 'n uair a dh'fhas e sean, dh'fhas e cho mor ri damh ! Bha e mar an ceudna cho leisg 'snach rachadh e bho bun an teine. Mar sin chaidh seachd bliadhna 'seachad, ach fad na seachd bliadhna cha'n fhac an Cu mor, tàobh mach an doruis. 'S iomadh uair chaidh iarraidh air Conachar a mharbhadh, agus is minic a dh'iarr e fhein cuir as da; ach na h-uil' nair a bha e dol a dheanamh so, chaidh stad a chuir air le seann bhean a bha 'san tigh "leig leis a chù," ars ise, "tha latha fhein a feitheamh air." Agus fhuair an cù a chead a bhi beò.

Aig ceann na seachd bliadhna chaidh Conachar latha am mach a shealg mar 'bu dual. 'N uair a bha e an deigh an Caisteal fhàgail, sheall e air ais, agus co bha 'tighinn ach an Cù mor, agus e a leum 'sa cleasachd mar a b'abhaist dha an laithean oige! " Am beil thu ann," arsa Conachar, "tha mi meallta mar e so an lath' bha feith- eamh ort l" agus leig e leis a chù a leantuinn.

Anns na laithean sin bha 'n duthaich air a sgiursadh gu cruaidh le torc nimhe a bha a fasachadh nan gleanntan. Bha 'n torc cho tur uamhasach 's nach do thachair duine riamh air a leig e as beò, agus le sin, bha eagall mòr air an laoch bu ghaisgeanta roimhe.

Thòisich Conachar air an t-sealg, ach mu'n deach e fada, co 'tha- inig air 'na làn fhearg, ach an torc nimhe! Dhian Conachar e fhein gu duineil, agus bhuail e an torc mar a bhuaileas sonn a namhad; ach 's beag an lot a rinn a shleagh ann an coluinn na beist.

'An sinn leum an Cù mor air an torc agus sàs anns a cheile chaidh iad. Dh' eirich a ghrian gu a h-airde, agus laidh i a rithist mu'n do sguir a chomhstri gharg, agus bha an talamh dearg le fuil. Mu dheireadh dh'feuch an torc gun robb sgleo a bhais air tighinn air, agus le gnothain 'us beùchdaich a bha oillteil ri chluinntinn thug e suas an deò.

Bheannaich Conachar an Cu mor, a theàrruinn e bho ghlaic a bhàis, agus thug e bòid air a shleagh nach di-chuinicheadh se e gu brath. Ach bha lath' a choin mhòr air teachd, agus le sodan 'us crathadh fheamain ri Conachar, fhuair e bas.

'S ann bho fhacail an t-seana bhean a their sinn fhathast 'sa ghleann "Tha latha fhein a feitheamh air, mar a bh'air Cu mòr Chonachar."

Cha'n fhiosrach mi gu'n deach a sgeulachd so a sgriobhadh riamh roimhe, ach ged nach deach, tha mi fiosrach bho'n ranns- adhadh a rinn mi, nach eil sgeula eile a bhuineas do'n Ghaidheal- tachd a dh'fhag a comharadh cho mor air eachdraidh an Taobh Tuath. Cha d'fhag eadhon Sgeulachd Dhiarrmaid, ged is mor a tha de dh'aithris oirre. A reir beul-aithris a ghlinn againn, b'e Conachar a cheud fhear de Chlann Mhic Aoidh, agus feumaidh e bhi gur e so an sonn a bha 'am beachd mo charaide Mac Choinnich, 'n uair a bha e bruidhinn anns an oraid a dh'ainmich mi, air " Aonghas Mac Aoidh " agus a strith ri " Naois " Mac Aoidh a dheanamh dhe. Tha an t-oran ag radh :—

" Rugadh air a mhuir a cheud fhear
Bho'n do shiollaich Clann Mhic Aoidh,
Conachar mor ruadh, bho'n chuan."

Agus tha fios againn bho sheann eachdraidhean, gu'm b' Urchudainn
creathall Chlann Mhic Aoidh, agus gu'n robh coir ac' air an gleann
sin bho chionn corr is sea ceud bliadhna. Ach thainig atharrachadh cho mor bho sin, agus nach eil ceathrar Mhic Aoidh an diugh ann
an Urchudainn. Reic iad Achamhonaidh (an oighreachd ma dheireadh a sheilbhich iad 'sa ghleann sin) beagan bhliadhnachan 'an
deigh Domhnull Mac Aoidh, an t-oighre aig an àm, agus mo shinn
sheanair-sa, a chuir air fogradh gu>Bardados air-son e cuideachadh
le Prionus Tearlach ann am bliadhna Chuil-fhodair.

Ach cha b'e Clann Mhic Aoidh amháin a shiollaich bho Chonachar. 'Sann bhuaidh a thainig Clann Urchudainn [Urquharts] agus
ghabh iad aium a ghlinne anns an robb e. Thug iad an t-ainm
ceudna air an àite comhnuidh úir ann an siorrachd Rois ; agus mar
a tha Innis-a-Chonachar againne ann an Urchudainn, tha Bad-a-
Chonachar aca-san faisg air Inbhir Górdan. Bha ridir araid ann an
cogaidhean Righ Tearlach agus *Oliver Cromwell* a bha ro dhileas
ann an armailtibh an Righ. B'e so Sir Tomas Urchudainn. An
deigh *Cromwell* baiteal *Worcester* a chosnadh, chaidh Sir Tomas
bochd a ghlacadh, agus fhuair e da bhliadhna 'phriosan. Ach
fad na h-ùine sin cha robb e na thàmh. Chaith a na laithean
dorch' a thainig air a sgriobhadh leabhar a chuir e 'mach fo'n
ainm " The True Pedigree and lineal descent of the most
ancient and honourable family of Urquhart in the house of
Cromarty from the creation of the world until the year of God
1651." A reir an leabhar so b'e Conachar an seathamh ginealach
deug thair an tri fichead bho Adhamh, agus phós e anns a bhliadhna
cuig cheud 's leith cheud 'sa ceathar mu'n d'thainig Criosd. Ach
bheir mi so dhuibh ann am facail Sir Tomas fhein :—

"Upon Philerga he (Daltalon) begot Beltistos. Beltistos
married Thomyris (A.M. 3395, B.C. 554). This Beltistos was
sirnamed Chonchar, for which cause a certain progeny descended
of him is till this hour called the generation of the Ochonchars,
a race truely of great antiquity and renown in the dominion of Ireland. Beltistos founded the Castle of Urquhart above Innernasse,
which being afterwards completed by his posterity, hath ever
since been called the Castle of Uickichonchar" [Mic-a-Chonachair.]

Sin agaibh mar a sgriobh Sir Tomas bho chionn córr 'us da
cheud bliadhna. Ma'n aon am bha duin' eile beo a rinn moran
rannsachadh air seann eachdraidh na h-Alba. B'e so Nisbet, fear a
bha gle churamach nach cuireadh e dad 's am bith air paipeir ach
rud aig am biodh bonn. Tha esan ag radh gu'n d' thainig Conachar
á Eireann—gu thoir dhuibh na fhacail fhein—" In the elevcuth

century . . . . a brother of Ochonchar, who slew the boar, and was predecessor of the Lords Forbes, having in keeping the Castle of Urquhart, took his name from the place."

'S ann bho Chonachar, a rithist, a thainig na Fearbaisich, agus tha iad a creidsinn gu'm b'e fhein da riridh am "fear bathaiseach" a mharbh an torc. 'S ann bhuaidhe 'thainig na Siosalaich, agus innsidh iad dhuinn gum b'e fhein a thug an t- " sith salach " 'n uair a spàr e a shleagh sios amhaich na bèist. Ach gu bhi aithghear, s'ann bho sgeulachd Chonachar a tha ceann na tuirc mar shuaicheantas alg Mac Aoidh, Urchudainn, Fearbaiseach, Siosalach, Ròsach, Innes, agus, tha mi a smuanachadh, an Gordanach agus Mac-antoiseach. Cha'n eil mi a smuanachadh gu'm beil mi 'an so ri faoineachd; oir tha fios againn bho sheann eachdraidhean agus daighneachdan [charters] gu'n robh coir aig na fineachan a dh'ainmich mi air Gleann Urchudainn agus Caisteal Chonachar bho chionn cheudan bhliadhnachan.

'N uair a thoisich mi air so a sgriobhadh, bha mi an rim sgeulachdan a Ghlinne leantuinn bho 'n a cheud te a chuala sibh an nochd, gus an lath' uamhasach sin a thug leithid a dh' atharachadh air cleachdanaibh nan Gaidheil—latha Chuil-fhodair. Ach bha na h-urrad agam ri radh ma dheighinn 'na thug mi, agus nach toir mi dhuibh an nochd ach aon t'eile. Tha i so iongantach air choir 's gu'm faod sinn a filleadh ann am bardachd Oisein. Fhuair mise bho m'athair i, agus dh' ionnsaich es' i bho fhior sheann duine bho chionn leith cheud 's a cuig a bhliadhnachan.

"Thainig a Bhuileardach Ruadh, mathair Righ Lochluinn, do'n Fheinn, a thoirt lethe le foill cuach na geasachd. Bha Fionn agus cnid de dhaoine, a sealg, ach fhuair i Oiseau agus laoich eile ann talla na Feinne. Agus labbar a Chailleach ri Oiseau ag radh.

> Fosgail, fosgail 'laoich long,
> Nan airm fullung faothair ghorm,
> S feuch cuid de d' fhaoildeachd.
> Do chailleach bhoc a thig e caoilte ;
> 'S mise sin a chailleach thruagh,
> 'S fhad a dh'imich mi 's mi buan,
> Cha'n eil an cuigibh na h-Alba,
> No 'n cuig cuigibh na h-Eirinn,
> Aon duine a dhiultadh dhomh fosgladh
> 'Nuair chromuinn mo cheann fo 'dhorus.

> Oisean—Ma dh' imich thusa 'n uigh sin uile,
> 'S biadhtuichean iad ri droch urra ;
> Fuaraichidh do smior, a chaillich,
> Mu'n fosgailear dhuit mo dhorus.

> A Chailleach—'S dona 'n aithne sin a mhic Righ
> ('Us mac Righ 'ga radh ruit),
> 'N uair dhiultadh tu fosgladh do dhorus.

Oisean—Cha dhiultainn dhuit a monadh fiadh,
    Ged bhiodh agad triath do reir ;
    Chuirinn biadh naoidhnear gu d' theach,
    'S biadh feachd leat bho'n Fheinn.

A Chailleach—Cha bhi agam de d' bhiadh feachd,
    Ni mo 's aill leam do shar fhacal,
    B' amhsa leam teas de d' aimhlibh,
    Agus leabaidh mar ri d' ghadhraibh.

Oisean—Gu dearbh cha'n fhaidh thu teas de m'aimhlibh,
    Ni mo gheibh thu leabaidh mar ri m' ghadhraibh !
    Chuirinn gille leat bho'n Fheinn,
    A dh'fhadadh teine dh'aon bheum,
    'Us gill' eile dh'ullaicheadh deadh inneal.

A Chailleach—Cha'n eil mo choiscachd-sa ach mall,
    'S theid an teine sin a crann.

Oisean—Buinig thusa leith taobh chuilinn,
    Cuir geugaibh caol fo d' spuiribh,
    Seid gu caol cruaidh le d'anail,
    'S dean do gharadh ris, a chaillich.

    A chailleach sin bu ghairbh craimh,
    Chuir i guaillean ris a chleith,
    'S bhrisd i na seachd geamhlaibh iaruinn
    Mar nach biodh annt ach seann iallan!

A Chailleach—Tha mi nise stigh 'n 'ur teach,
    'S liubha bhur mairbh no bhur beo,
    'S lionmhor sgolb a bhios 'n ur teach
    Na macan beo a marach !

    Cheangal i iad taobh ri taobh
    'Na bh'eadar an caol san ruith
    'S rug a chailleach air a chuach
    'S thug i gu luath a magh.

Chunnachdas a Chailleach le Fionn, air dha bhi tighinn dha-chaidh bho'n t-sealg:—

Fionn—A chailleach ud a th'air an t-sliabh
    Dha 'm b'eil an ceum cas-ruith garbh dhian,
    Na'n tarladh tu air srath no h-airde
    Bu bhaodhail dhut clann na ceairde.
    Tri cheud deug le'n dian armachd
    Fir thugad a tha, a chaillich !

A Chailleach—Ciod a theireadh tusa ghiulav,
    Nam faguinn-sa iad sin uile
    Eadar chu luath 'us dheadh dhuine?

    Leum a chailleach an t-eas,
    Leum gu garbh bras,
    Thilg i gath nimh' air Fionn,
    A chaidh seachd troimhean 'san fheur uaine,

Thairis air barr a dha ghualainn !
Thilg Fionn a shleagh taobh,
'S bhrisd e cridhe 'na caol druim ;
'S rug Geolach bho'n is i bu luaithe,
Air sliasaid chruaidh na caillich ;
'S rug Caoilte beag nan cuach
Air a claidheamh cruadhach,
'S air a da shleagh.

Bha iad seachd lath' 'us seachd oidhche
A rinn faobha na Caillich,
'Scha d'rug Oisean a bha air dheireadh
Ach air seann chiabhag lia na Caillich.

Oisean—A chaillich, bho'n is e 'm bas e,
Innis dhomhsa ciod e d' aois ?

A Chailleach—Cha'n eil m'aois fhein ri aireamh
Ach tri cheud bhadhn' 'sa dha !

NOTE.—For the sake of those unacquainted with Gaelic, but who take an interest in Celtic matters, I may here mention that I wrote the above curious poem, in 1869, from the recitation of my father, Mr William Mackay, Glen-Urquhart. He learned it, along with other pieces which claim to be Ossianic, from a very old man, at whose fireside he and his companions were wont to spend the winter evenings almost sixty years ago. In January of this year (1872), I sent it to the well-known collector of Gaelic legends, Mr Campbell of Islay, who is at present about to publish a collection of Ossianic ballads, and in reference to it he wrote :—
"The poem which you have been kind enough to send me is called *Duan na Caillich*, and other names. I have a version of it collected by Kennedy last century, and one got by Fletcher about the same time from the MS. in the Advocate's Library. Yours is the third version I have got, and will help in making up a text." When we are told that poems such as those of Ossian could not be preserved for any considerable time without the aid of writing, it is instructive to know that, notwithstanding great changes in the customs of the Highlanders, some noticed in the last century still float orally among them.—W.M.

December 19.—At the meeting this evening, Mr Charles Mackay, Drummond, read the annexed paper :—

BLIADHNA THEARLAICH.

"Is e mo run an nochd beagan inuse dhuibh ma dheighinn nithe a thachair ann am Bliadhna Thearlaich air nach deach fhathast eachdraidh a thoir, ach gidheadh a tha cho firinneach ri facal a chaidh riamh a sgriobhadh. Ann a bhi deanamh so, agus a labhairt mu chliu na muinntir a dh'fhuiling air-son a Phrionns, cha'n iarruinn a bhi fosgladh seann lotan ; ach tha mi ag earbsa gu'n giulan sibh leam ged a their mi nithean cruaidh mu thimchioll iadsan a sharaich cho mor an sluagh sin bho'n d'thainig sinn. Tha e gu tric air inuse dhuinn nach robh anns na Righrean Stiubhartach, ach daoine gun fhiu a bha coma dha'n sluagh, agus a dheanadh ni neo-dhligheach.'s am bith air-son am miann fhein fhaotainn. Gu'n teagamh bha cuid dhiubh a dh'fheuch nach robh moran cogais aca, agus a bhun gu goirt ri sluagh na rioghachd. Ach cha d'rinn iad coire 's am bith 'an aghaidh na Gaidheil. Cha d'thainig teintean na geur-leanmhuinn a stigh air crioch na Gaidhealtachd, ni mo a ghabh na Gaidheil suim dhe na connspoidean a bha cadar na Stiubhartaich agus am parlamaidean ma thimchioll còirean agus cumhachdan an righ. Air an taobh eile cha luaithe a chaidh na Stiubhartaich a chuir de'n chaithir, na dh'aithnich na Gaidheil nach robh na righrean uir gu bhi cho cairdeach riu 's a bha na scaun righrean ; agus ann an uine ghoirid fhuair iad dearbhadh air so ann am mort Ghlinne-comhainn. Le sin, cha robh e ach nadurrach gu'm b'iad na Stiubhartaich, 'nan suilean-sa, na righrean dligheach, agus nach robh anns na Gearmailtich ach an-shealbhadairean gun fhiu; agus 'n uair a thainig am Prionns 'nam measg, thionail iad mu'n cuairt dha, cadar Phrotastanach 'us Phapanach. Tha feadhainn gu coitchionta 'am barail nach d'fhuair am Prionus comhar ach bho Phapanaich; ach tha e soillear gu'n do lean na Gaidheil e gun suim do chreud. Cha mhor gu'n robh duine ann an Urchudainn nach robh 'an toil no'n gniomh air a thaobh agus gidheadh cha robh triuir Phapanaich 'nam measg. Bha toil mhor aig na Gaidheil do 'n t-seann theaghlach rioghail ; agus 's e an toil sin a thug orra an claidheamh a tharruing air-son a Phrionns."

'An so thug Mr Mac-Aoidh cunntas air cruadail a dh'fhuiling na Gaidheil an deigh dhaibh blair Chuil-fhodair a chall ; agus bha euid dhe'na thubhairt e bha iongantach ri chluinntinn a thaobh 's nach deach eachdraidh a thoir riamh air. Ach a chionn 's nach robb na thubhairt e nile sgriobta aige, cha'n eil sinn an comas ach na leanas a thoirt 'an so.

"Beagan uine an deigh latha Chuil-fhodair, chaidh fios a chuir gu muinntir Ghlinn-Urchudainn, na h-uile fear a bh'air taobh Phrionns Thearlaich a thighinn gu Inbhirnis, agus gu'm faigheadh e

protection. B'e so paipeir diona a dhionadh am fear aig am biodh
e bho an-iochdmhorachd na h-airme deirge. Thionail neart na
duthcha aig Baile-macathan, agus 'nam measg bha fear Choire-
mhonaidh, fear Sheoglaidh agus a mbae, oighre Achamhonaidh,
agus Mr Iain Grannd, ministear na sgire. 'N uair a bha iad a
fagail shuas gu thighinn gu Inbhirnis, thainig seana bhean, agus
thubhairt i mar so :—

> " Urchudainn Maith Chrostan,
> Cha bu rosadach thu riamh gus an diugh !
> An taobh ris am beil sibh 'cuir bhur sail
> Gu brath cha chuir sibh clar na h-aodainn ! "

" Bha leithid a bhuaidh aig facail na caillich air na daoine, 's
gu'n do thill fear Choire-mhonaidh agus a chuid a bu mho dhiubh
dhachaidh. Lean cach air an aghaidh gus an d'rainig iad a Bheal-
laidh Mhor, faisg air Abairiachan. Ann an so chuir iad an comhairle cuideachd, agus bha leithid a dhroch bharail aca dhe'n turus
air an robh iad, 's gu'n do thill iad uile ach Granndach Sheoglaidh
's a mhac, Domhnull Mac-Aoidh oighre Achamhonaidh, am ministear, agus naoinear eile. Chaidh iad-san do'n a bhaile, ach an aite
iad *protection* fhaighinn, 's ann a chaidh priosanaich a dheanamh
dhiubh ! Chaidh Seoglaidh 'sa mhac, agus am ministear a chuir
gu *Tilbury Fort*, agus ann an uine ghoirid chaidh 'n ceann a thoir
dhe Seoglaidh, agus fhuair an dithis eile 'chead. Chaidh oighre
Achamhonaidh agus na daoine eile (maille ri tri fichead a thainig a
Gleanna-Moireastuinn air chomharradh meallta), a chuir gu Barbados ; agus cha'n fhac a h-aon dhiubh an dachaidh gu brath ach
Mac-Aoidh agus fear eile. Cha luaithe a chaidh Mac-Aoidh air
tir ann am Barbados na theich e air long gu Jamaica. Ann an
sin rinn e Domhnullach dhe-fhein, agus an deigh dha iomadh
bliadhna a chaithidh ann, thainig e dhachaidh agus phos e.
B'e Domhnull Mac-Aoidh seanair m'athair, agus tha a chiste a
thug e á Jamaica aige-san fhathast ann an Urchudainn."

" Is mor an t-atharrachadh a thug baiteal Chuil-fhodair agus
brùidealachd Chumberland air a Ghaidhealtachd. Rugadh de
chloinn ann an Urchudainn 'sa bhliadhna 1744, 32 ; 'sa bhliadhna
1745, 30 ; 'sa bhliadhna 1746 (bliadhna Chuil-fhodair) 18 ; 'sa
bhliadhna 1747, 12 ; agus 'sa bhliadhna 1748, 26. Tha so a
a feuchainn dhuinn a scapadh uamhasach a chaidh a dheanamh
anus na laithean eitidh sin, ann am measg an fheadhainn a bhiodh,
a posadh 'sa baisteadh, mur d'thainig a chomh-stri mhortach
eadar ri Tearlach agus Deorsa ! Bha an sluagh ni's lionmhora
ann an Gleanntan na Gaidhealtachd roimh latha Chuil-fhodair,
na bha iad riamh na dheigh ; agus bha iad, 'nan doigh fhein, ni's
sona na tha am beagan a th'againn an dingh."

SURVEY OF THE CELTIC LANGUAGES.

February 23, 1872.—A lecture on the above subject was delivered by the Rev. William Ross of Rothesay, Cluny Macpherson, Chief of the Society, presiding. The worthy Chief was received with great applause, and when it was discovered that he was about to open the proceedings in Gaelic, he was greeted with fresh demonstrations of approbation. The Chief spoke as follows :—

Faodaidh mi toiseachadh, am briathran aith-gearr, le bhi cuir an ceill do bhuill a Còmuinn Ghailig, a tha'n so a lathair gu'n robh mor dhoilgheas orm nach robb e 'nam chomas a bhi maille ribh aig 'ur cend choinneamh. Thami anabarrach toillichte a bhi a lathair air an fheasgar so, agus a bhi faicinn aireamh co mhor dhuibh-san cruinn aig am bheil tlachd ann an soirbheachadh "Comuinn Gailig Inbhirnis." Agus tha mi 'galtrum lan dochas gu'n 'sruth mor bhuannachd agus mhisneachd do na Gaidheil o'n Chomuinn, agus gu h-araidh do thaobh craobh sgaoilidh a chanain Gheadhealaich, Tha e ro-thaitneach leam a bhi nis a' toirt fa bhur comhair an t-Urramach Mr Ros á Baile-Bhoid, agus a' gairm air a labhair na h-oraid a ghabh e gu coimhneil os laimh a thoirt air an fheasgair so. Tha mi cinnteach nach ruig mi leas innseadh dhiubh gu'm bheil e 'na ard fhoghlumach anns a chànain Ghaidhealach, agus min-eòlach mu'n dàimh anns an bheil a chànain so a' seasamh ri a dual chàintean. Fèumaidh gu'n teir e mòr thoileachadh dha na h-uile fior Ghaidheal gu'm bheil a leithid a chomunn 'san "Comunn Gailig" air a chuir air chois ann an Ceann-Bhaile na Gaidhealtachd. Cha n-eil teagamh 's am bith agam ann a' soirbheachadh a chomuinn, 'nuair tha agam r'a innseadh dhiubh gu'm facas iomchuidh le ar n-ard-Uachdaran caomh, a Bhan-righinn ordugh a thoirt seachad gu'm biodh a leabhar-sa air eadar-theangachadh chum Gailig, agus tha naill orm gu'n d'earb i sin a dheanamh r'a h-aon do'm chinneadh fèin. Mu'n dean mi suidh dh'iarruinn an cothrom so' ghabhail air mòran taing a thoirt do bhuill rioghlaidh a "Chomuinn Ghailig" air-son an urraim a chuir iad orm ann a bhi ga'm shònrachadh air-son Ceann-suidhe air a bhliadhna so. Cha chùm mi ni's fhaidhe sibb, oir tha mi creidsinn gu'm bheil fadal oirbh gus an cluinn sibb óraid an Urra-maich Mr Ros.

The Chief then introduced Mr Ross, who said that he would call his lecture a SURVEY OF THE CELTIC LANGUAGES, WITH NOTES OF THEIR AFFINITIES TO THE OTHER INDO-EUROPEAN TONGUES.

The following is an outline of the lecture, which was illustrated by specimens of the early Gaelic Manuscript Literature of Scotland, and by diagrams showing the affinities of the Celtic to the other Aryan tongues :—

I.—The place of the Celtic is to be found in the Aryan, and not in the Semitic family of languages—Sir William Jones—Dr Pritchard—" Eastern Origin of the Celtic Nations."

II.—Celtic Languages—Foreign elements, Ecclesiastical and Classical Latin. The Roman Occupation. Immigrations from the Continent. Comparative Vocabularies of Cymric and Gaedhelic. Comparative Grammar.

III.—Celtic Scholarship—Lexicons: Cymric, embracing Breton, Welsh, Cornish; Gaedhelic, embracing Irish, Gaelic, Manx. Grammars—Biographical Notices of Le Gonidec and J. Caspar Zeuss. The Grammatica Celtica : Its Character and Value. Native Scholarship—The Rev. Dr M'Lauchlan, Dr W. F. Skene, Rev. Mr Clark, Mr J. F. Campbell, Professor Blackie. &c.—Welsh, Irish, and Breton Scholars—Our Literature, Oral and Traditional. Manuscripts—Gaelic, Irish, Welsh, Breton. Early Printed Works. Modern Literature.

IV.—Celtic Relationship to the Aryan Tongues : Western—Classical, Teutonic, Slavonic ; Eastern—Indie ; Sanskrit, Persic, &c. Vocabulary and Grammar. The value of the Celtic to the Science of Language. The Study itself, its relations to the Gospel, and bearings upon the welfare of humanity.

Our space will only admit of our giving a brief summary of the lecture, which the author, at the request of the Society, has agreed to publish in full.

I. THE PLACE OF THE CELTIC.

If we cast our eye over a linguistic map of the world, we cannot fail to note that there exists a vast number of languages, and that all of them have certain geographical relations to each other. We are not warranted to conclude that because of their proximity to each other, they are on that account so intimately related as to be one in structure or form—one in the materials of which they are composed, nor yet one in the sense of a common progeny, with diverse lineaments, owning a common parentage. Such a conclusion can only be arrived at on scientific grounds when the science of language shall have attained its majority, and the languages of earth have been analysed and compared. A careful and accurate study of any one form of speech will lead us to see, that although the great bulk of the language may consist of materials of native growth and character, yet a considerable portion is to be traced

H

to the incursion of materials that are of a mixed character—some
bearing marks of a kindred, and some clearly of a foreign extraction. If we extend our inquiries to several languages, we obtain
precisely similar results. The farther we extend our survey the
more likely are we to obtain large and reliable data upon which to
found a safe induction. A tolerably accurate survey of the languages which abound on the face of the earth has led to the discovery of three extensive groups or families of languages, each
family having its own native character, qualities, and genius.
These are the Aryan or Indo-European, the Semitic, and the
Turanian or Allophyllian languages. How far these families are,
if at all, related to each other the future of our science must show.
The question is foreign to our present inquiry. It is enough for
us to know that the Celtic language possesses characteristics
which enable us to fix its place in the Aryan or Indo-European
family. It cannot be without interest to us to inquire how, and
by whom, it was discovered that our language had its legitimate
place among the Aryan tongues. The discovery was not made by
any merely Gaelic or Cymric scholar. Our native scholars, with
one notable exception, the distinguished Edward Lhuyd, the author
of the "Archæologia Brittanica," were busily engaged for many
years in endeavouring to prove an intimate connection between
the Celtic languages and the Semitic family. In the early stages
of philological studies, most linguists laboured long and diligently
to show that their native tongue was the primeval speech, or at all
events closely allied to it. Our Celtic scholars were no exception
to the general rule. It is but just to the memory of Lhuyd, our
first and perhaps greatest Celtic scholar, to observe that in his
"British Etymologicon," he clearly pointed out the affinity between
the Celtic and such Indo-European languages as in his time at-
tracted the attention of learned men. It is possible that an intimate connection may yet be found to subsist between the Aryan
and Semitic families; and if so the Celtic may perform no mean
service to the inquiries that shall issue in this result. The efforts
of our native philologists were at the time, to a large extent, labour
in vain. The discovery that helped to place the Celtic in its right
position was that of the Sanskrit language, which took place in the
year 1808. Previous to that year, it was generally supposed that
there was an absolute distinction in race and language between
the inhabitants of Hindostan and the East, and those of Europe
and the West. In that year the supposed distinction was abolished.
It was discovered that the Sanskrit, though dead for upwards of
two thousand years, was the direct source of all the principal
modern dialects of the Hindoos, while it, moreover, presented the
closest affinities to the language of Persia and the chief languages

of Europe. Sir William Jones, the distinguished founder of the Asiatic Society, was the first to point out the probable connection which might be found to exist between the Celtic and the languages of the East. In a paper contained in the first volume of the "Asiatic Researches" (p. 442), he says, "The Sanskrit language, whatever may be its antiquity, is of a wonderful structure: more perfect than the Greek, more copious than the Latin, and more exquisitely refined than either, yet bearing to both of them a stronger affinity, both in the roots of verbs and in the forms of grammar, than could have been produced by accident; so strong that no philologer could examine all the three without believing them to have sprung from some common source, which, perhaps, no longer exists. There is a similar reason, though not quite so forcible, for supposing that both the Gothic *and the Celtic*, though blended with a different idiom, had the same origin with the Sanskrit. The old Persian may be added to the same family."

The next in order who secured the attention of scholars to a consideration of the question was Dr Pritchard, the celebrated author of a work "On the Varieties of the Human Race." We cannot value too highly the service which he rendered to the Celtic language by the publication in 1832 of his work on "The Eastern Origin of the Celtic Nations." He says—"It will more evidently appear, if I am not mistaken, that from the Celtic dialects a part of the grammatical inflections, and that a very important part, common to the Sanscrit, the Eolic Greek, the Latin, and the Teutonic languages, are capable of an elucidation which they have never yet received." The line of evidence followed by Dr Pritchard, and the materials produced, were of such a character, and in such quantity, as to satisfy the most sceptical that the Celtic must find its place in the numerous cluster of speeches embraced by the Indo-European tongues. The forty years that have elapsed since the publication of his work have only helped to confirm the position he had taken up, and largely to add to the evidence submitted by him. To his labours we are indebted for the first rational and scientific investigation as to the origin, place, and relations of the Celtic languages. The study of the Celtic now received a new impetus, and in the right direction. A singularly clear, comprehensive, and scholarly review of Dr Pritchard's book, by the late Rev. Richard Garnett, of the British Museum, in the British Quarterly Review for September 1836, and valuable articles on the Languages and Dialects of the British Islands, by the same author, in the first and second volumes of the "Proceedings of the Philological Society of London," thoroughly confirmed Dr Pritchard's conclusions, and supplied fresh and valuable materials, which rendered conviction irresistible. "Till lately," says Mr Garnett,

speaking of the Celtic dialects, " they were supposed by various
eminent scholars to form a class apart, and to have no connection
whatever with the great Indo-European stock. This was strongly
asserted by Colonel Vans Kennedy, and also maintained, though
in rather more guarded terms, by Bopp, Pott, and Schlegel. The
researches of Dr Pritchard in the " EasternO rigin of the Celtic
Nations," and of Professor Pictet of Geneva, in his truly able work
" Sur l'Affinite des Langues Celtiques avec le Sanscrit," may be
considered as having settled the question the other way, and as
proving satisfactorily that the assertion of the philologists above
mentioned were those of persons who had never properly investigated the matter, and were consequently incompetent to decide
upon it. The demonstration of Pictet is so complete, that the
German scholars, who had previously denied the connection, now
fully admit it, and several of them have written elaborate treatises
showing more affinities between Celtic and Sanscrit than perhaps
really exist." (Philological Essays, p. 147.) The result of the
publication of the works of Dr Pritchard and Professor Pictet were
of the most satisfactory character, and finally established the position of the Celtic as one of the Aryan tongues. At the same time
it must be conceded, that several very striking coincidences between the Celtic and the Hebrew have been pointed out; while it
is undeniable that the evidence hitherto adduced in support of the
great mass of alleged resemblances is unsatisfactory, and in not a
few instances entirely illusory.

The Celtic language possesses for us not merely a general, but
a special and deep patriotic interest. It was among the first, if
not the very earliest, to part company with its kindred, and to
remove from the ancient fatherland. It was among the first to
furnish names for the beetling cliffs, towering bens, shaded valleys,
flowing streams, winding pathways, and thriving homesteads, of
the continent of Europe—names which may even yet be distinguished as underlying the superficial deposits of Teutonic, Romanic,
and Slavonic designations. Its vocabulary also supplied no small
number of the terms that describe the social relations, and the arts
of husbandry and war. As the parent imparts his lifeblood to his
offspring, and the pioneer the results and value of his discoveries
to his successors, so did the Celtic tribes hand over their treasures
to those who tracked their footsteps and took possession of their
lands and homes. These courageous and numerous tribes formed
the van and centre in the great exodus of the European nations
from their home in the East. They were impinged upon by the
Teutons on the North, by the Greeks and Romans on the South,
while they were pushed forward by the lower Teutonic, Windic,
and Illyric tribes, which took up the rear. The pressure of these

various migrations drove the Celts to the West, and their further advance was for a time stopped by the Atlantic ocean, and their colonisation, by the occupancy of Great Britain and Ireland.

II. THE CELTIC LANGUAGES.

It has been already stated that a careful study of any one language will lead to the discovery of a large number of words of foreign extraction. These are technically called *loan* words. We can in many instances trace historically the successive migrations of large numbers of vocables from foreign tongues into that which is the subject of study. This arises from the intercourse which goes on between various races, nations, and tribes of men. Thus the English language of the present day is a conglomerate, the constituent parts of which are to be traced to the languages of the various races and nationalities with which the paramount influence and unrivalled commercial relations of the English speaking people have brought them into contact. The character of these loan words in any language is in strict accordance with the historical circumstance which led to their introduction. A period of degeneracy and disintegration is manifested by the use of a mongrel speech. This is to no small extent characteristic of the spoken Celtic in various parts of the country. English as the prevailing language of this country, impinges upon and gradually pervades the ancient languages of these islands. In many parts of the Highlands we are not unaccustomed to hear in a Gaelic conversation such words as *scop, sgoil, bata*. These words are clearly aliens. They have not had time to undergo the necessary changes sufficient to disguise them. They are surrounded by the language whence the deposit came, and can therefore be readily identified. But this is merely the illustration of a law that is universal; and, if so, we may expect to find it in operation at earlier and more remote periods in the history of the Celtic languages. Tracing our way backwards, we come to a period when " ministear," " eaglais," " gràs," " aoradh," " aingeal," " abstol," " beannachd," " coron," " eascop," " easbuig," " abbat," " teart," " domhnach," and many such words were new to the language. If foreign, how and whence came they? They were introduced in an age of incipient ecclesiasticism. They are deposits from an earlier period, and from a prevailing language—the language of the Church. We have obtained them directly from Latin, which, as the theological and ecclesiastical language of the period, was in use at and after the introduction of Christianity.

The character and constitution of a language are influenced, not only by the introduction of a new faith, and the labours of the missionary, theologian, and spiritual instructor, but also by political changes, which have taken place through annexation, immigration, and conquest. If we look beyond the introduction of Christianity into our island, we find a period of conquest and occupation by foreigners. We therefore naturally expect that a considerable number of vocables would be brought by them into the languages of the country. These incursions and occupations would naturally affect the topography, the literary and documentary language and court speech, and ultimately, though to a less extent, the vernacular spoken by the mass of the people. The arrival of the Romans in Britain, and their stay for four hundred years in the country, must have influenced the native languages considerably, especially in South Britain, to which their rule was chiefly confined. The remote parts would be affected, if at all, in a much less degree. The English language has been in contact with the Gaelic of Scotland for upwards of twelve centuries. It has told powerfully on the spoken Gaelic along the centre of the country, while the vernacular in Skye and the Hebrides is comparatively unaffected by it at the present day. The well-known historical facts bearing on this question lead us to conclude that, while the Cymric must have been affected by the Latin, both during the period of the Roman occupation and after the introduction of Christianity, the Gaedhelic would be chiefly influenced by the language of the Church.

There are good grounds for supposing the existence at an early period of a Frisian population in this country, while traces of a pre-Celtic occupation, by tribes speaking a language akin to the Finnish of the North, the Basque of the South, and to the basis of the Hungarian of central Europe, are not wholly wanting. These three languages, like the stunted weather-worn remains of a primeval forest, seem to point to a pre-Celtic population in Europe. The subsquent Scandinavian immigrations into our islands are undoubted. Their power is still felt in the topography of the sea coast all round the island, and notably in the North and West Highlands and Outer Hebrides. If they influenced the topography to such an intent, we may reasonably conclude that they left their mark also upon the spoken languages of the country.

After deducting all the vocables bearing traces of foreign lineage, and introduced in the manner already alluded to, we have still left a large residuum, whose character and relations we are called now to consider. The Celtic Language consists of two great branches, the Cymric and Gaedhelic, with several dialects in each. Are these dialects septs of one clan, owning a common, though remote ancestry? If so, how do they stand related to each other? If we fail in tracing their genealogy to a common source, may we not, nevertheless, be able to trace the family likeness in the common offspring?

There can be no difficulty in ascertaining the substantial identity in vocabularly, grammatical structure, and idiom, of the three dialects which compose the Gaedhelic branch, and as little in regard to the unity of the three which make up the varieties of the Cymric branch. The diversities, which serve to constitute the several dialects are capable of being accounted for on historical and circumstantial grounds, while the harmonies are too minute, too important, and too extensive, to admit of any other explanation, than that of real and ultimate identity.

But how do the two great branches, the Cymric and Gaedhelic, stand related to each other ?   How much do they hold in common ?   What are the differences which distinguish them as branches of the one Celtic language ?   To answer these questions fully would exceed our present limits.   A brief summary of the evidence which can be adduced is all that we can now attempt, as showing the remarkable harmonies and peculiar diversities of the two branches.

1. VOCABULARY. They hold much of their vocabulary in common, as the following illustrations clearly show :—

Cymric.		Gaedhelic.	Cymric.		Gaedhelic.
Achar,	Affectionate	Acarra	Drwg	Bad	Droch
Aer	Slaughter	Ar	Dwfn	Deep	Domhain
Afal	An apple	Abhal, ubbal	Duw	God	Dia
Afon	River	Amhuinn	Dwr	Water	Dobhar
Al	A brood	Al	Dyu	Day	Diugh
Amser	Time	Aimser	Efel	Similar	Amhail
Anal	Breath	Anail	Elin	Elbow	Uilinn
Asen	Rib	Aisinn	Enw	A name	Ainm
Au	The liver	Ath	Engyl	Fire	Aingeal
Awr	An hour	Uair	Ffals	Deceitful	Feallsa
Bagud	A cluster	Bagaid	Ffwlach	Refuse	Fuileach
Ballasg	A husk	Blaosg	Gau	A lie	Gò
Bar	Top	Bàrr	Genill	Offspring	Gineal
Bawad	A drowning	Bàthadh	Garw	Rough	Garbh
Bach	Little	Beag	Glan	Clean	Glan
Brawdd	Brother	Brathar	Glas	Green	Glas
Benw	A woman	Bean	Gof	A smith	Gobba
Bu	Kine	Bò	Gre	A flock	Greigh
Burym	Yeast	Beirm	Gwaen	Pang	Goimh
Byl	Brim	Bile	Gwer	Tallow	Geir
Brych	Freckled	Breac	Gwydd	Goose	Geadh
Cad	A battle	Cath	Llafar	Speech	Labhairt
Caib	A mattock	Caibe	Llawn	Full	Làn
Cadair	A seat	Cathair	Llaw	Hand	Lamh
Cam	A step	Ceum	Llo	A calf	Laogh
Cann	Sing	Can	Llom	Bare	Lòm

Cymric.		Gaedhelic.	Cymric.		Gaedhelic.
Carn	A heap	Carn	Llong	A ship	Long
Crwn	Round	Cruinn	Llymnoeth	Naked	Lomnochd
Ci	A dog	Cu	Mad	Good	Math
Cleddyf	A sword	Claidheamh	Mawn	Peat	Mòine
Clust	Ear	Cluas	Mawr	Great	Mòr
Dall	Blind	Dall	Mel	Honey	Mil
Dar	An oak	Darach	Sych	Dry	Seac
Da	Good, right	Deagh	Tarw	Bull	Tarbh
Du	Black	Dubh			

The foregoing list is given as a mere sample, not of harmonies but of identities in both branches. The number might be extended indefinitely. It goes far to show that the great mass of the vocables in the two branches are to be regarded as their common stock or inheritance. From one-half to two-thirds of the words in both languages may be regarded as a fair estimate of their common property. It must not be supposed that all the vocables are of the precise character with the above. Further research will show that each of the branches has its own peculiarities in word formation. Thus we have *p* in Cymric represented by *c* in Gaedhelic, in such words—

Cymric.		Gaedhelic.	Cymric.		Gaedhelic.
Penn,	a head,	ceann.	Pump,	five,	cuig.
Pedwar,	four,	ceathair.	Mab,	son,	mac.

while *h* in Cymric is almost uniformly represented by *s* in Gaedhelic, as—

Cymric.		Cymric.	Cymric.		Gaedhelic.
Hesp,	barren,	seasg.	Hun,	slumber,	suain.
Hallt,	saline,	sailte.	Hwyl,	a sail,	seol.
Heli,	salt water,	saile.	Hèdd,	peace,	sith.
Helig,	willow,	seileach.	Hil,	issue,	siol.
Helu,	possession,	sealbh,	Hir,	weather,	sion.
Hèn,	old,	sean.	Hoedyl,	duration of life,	saoghal.

We have, moreover, *gw* in Cymric represented by *b, m, f, c,* and *g* in Gaedhelic—

Cymric.		Gaedhelic.	Cymric.		Gaedhelic.
Gwann,	meadow,	banaich.	Gwin,	wine,	fion.
Gwall,	wall,	balla.	Gwag,	empty,	caog.
Gwaelaeth,	grief,	mulad.	Gweddi,	supplication,	guidhe
Gwr,	a man,	fear.	Gwden,	a withe,	gad.
Gwrydd,	grass, green,	feur.	Gwasan,	a youth,	gasan.

Other peculiarities, into which we cannot now enter, are illustrated by the following—

Welsh.		Gaedhelic.	Welsh.		Gaedhelic.
Chwaer,	sister,	piuthar.	Llyth,	tribe,	sluagh.
Hael,	liberal,	fial.	Llim,	smooth,	sliom.
Cloch,	bell,	glag.	Llyfn,	smooth,	sleamhuinn
Llath,	rod,	slat.	Llyn	sharp,	liomh.
Tad,	father,	athair.	Mynydd,	mountain,	beinn.

How are we to account for the apparent discrepancy existing between words which at once can be seen to be so closely related to each other? Can any law or principle be found by which those differences can be satisfactorily accounted for? Is it that the *p* in penn, a head, passes into *c* in ceann, or vice versa—that the *b* in mab passes into *c* in mac—that *gw* is represented by *b*, *m*, *c*, *f*, and *g*. The number of illustrations which might be supplied of these changes suffices only as evidence of the fact. These illustrations do not supply a solution of the difficulty. They only show the diversity; they do not account for it. It is too generally supposed that the peculiarity is almost, if not entirely, confined to the Celtic language. This, however, is not the case. It does exist in others, notably in Greek and Latin, and may have been more extensively manifested at an earlier period, and helped to create some of the dialectic differences in other languages. If we take the Greek "hippos," we find the corresponding Latin to be "equus." But this fact, corresponding precisely to what takes place between the Cymric and Gaelic, will not help us directly to a solution. Nor are we much relieved by finding that another form of the Greek word was *hikkos*. The difficulty is but one stage removed, and that brings it only into closer analogy with the Celtic. If, however, we look into another section of the Aryan family, we find the corresponding Sanscrit word to be "açvas," which for fuller illustration might be written açbhas, açphas; we find a combination of letters from which both *hikkos* and *hippos* may be derived. The real solution, therefore, is, not that the labial passes into the guttural, but that both are derivative sounds, collaterally descended from a more complex element capable of producing both. Thus the Latin *bis* corresponds to the Greek *dis*. The diversity is not to be accounted for by supposing that the *b* has passed into *d*, or vice versa. If we go to the Sanscrit we find both of these words represented by *dwis*. We now see that each of the languages has taken the derivative in the precise form best suited to its idiosyncrasy and character. The Greek took the *d*, and the Latin *b*=w. If, again, we take the Gaelic *fion*, Latin *vinum*, Greek *oinos*, we can easily see how the first two are related to each other, but cannot so readily account for the last of the three. Still less can we account for the diversity when we are told that in the Hesychian glosses, *oinos* represents *goinos*. But if we turn to the Cymric, the difficulty is at once solved, for it has preserved in *gwin* the representative of the ancient form whence all the others have sprung. In the Greek *peplos*, Latin *cucullus*, we have a good example of what takes place so regularly in the two branches of the Celtic.

It is too readily taken for granted that the earlier the stage at which we find a language, the more multiplied are its dialects; that the natural tendency of languages is from diversity to uniformity; that dialects are, in the regular order of things, antecedent to language ; and that the great means for lessening the number of dialects is the cultivation of language.   The illustrations given above tend to show that this is but a partial statement of the truth. Dialect infers original unity, which gradually manifests diversity, owing to individual usage, circumstances, and position.   The examples referred to above prove that the earlier the stage at which we find a language the more likely is it to manifest a unity approaching completeness—a unity which enables us to account satisfactorily for dialectic diversity.   It is only when a written language and literature become co-extensive with the individuals making use of them that dialects may be said to disappear, and even then individual peculiarities may not be wholly eradicated. Dialect is disintegration and debris from the primitive rock : written language is the alluvium formed of the select materials resulting from disintegration.   The reverse is a secondary and subsequent process.   The pressure of circumstances which produces the secondary formation, may be of such a character, and the result of such action as shall leave but few remains of valuable materials, whose existence can only be accounted for by tracing their connection to the primitive strata.

The nearer we get to the origin of a language, the more likely we are to find complex elements, which, under the corroding influence of time and circumstances, furnish the simpler sounds which are presented in dialectic peculiarities.   Dialectic characteristics become ultimately so established as to necessitate the change on foreign words introduced into the language, required to bring them into accordance with the established usage.   Thus *pascha*, easter, is in Welsh pasch, but in Gaelic *Caisg.*   The question very naturally occurs, to what principle are we to attribute this departure from complexity to simplicity ?   The principle, if principle it can be called, most generally relied on, as producing the change is that of euphony.   The ear is regarded as the great agent in causing the modifications of the original complex sounds.   But complex sounds are euphonious to the ears of those who habitually make use of them ; the ear must be educated to appreciate the use of the simpler sounds.   This is done through the influence of neighbouring races and tongues, while the exigencies arising from increased communication, demand directness and simplicity. The ear thus trained desires simplicity, and compels the tongue to submit. Euphony is not more the creature of necessity than it is that of fashion. Both causes may have combined to produce the diversities which have been the subject of our consideration.

It would naturally fall to us now to discuss the remarkable system of initial mutations of consonants which distinguishes the Celtic from all the other Aryan tongues; but we cannot enter here upon a minute analysis. The principle of literal mutation as a regular system is peculiar to the Celtic dialects; though the effects of such an aptitude in some of the letters to change their sounds is seen to prevade all languages. But it regulates some of the primary forms of construction in these tongues, as well with respect to syntax as to the composition of words (Dr Pughe). These changes are called *mutation* in Welsh, *eclipsis* in Irish, and in Gaelic *aspiration*. The term *mutation* is not inapplicable to the changes as shown by all the dialects; for the Welsh mutation embraces *aspiration* also, while from the Gaelic of Scotland traces of the eclipse are not wholly eradicated. Persons acquiring the Celtic languages never fail to complain of the continual changes of the consonants. It is no doubt true that "in the changes and variations of these mutables lies a great part of the art and mystery of this very peculiar tongue, the most curious perhaps, and the most delicate for its structures, of any language in the world" (Llewellyn). But the difficulty, though great, is not insurmountable, for the changes are uniformly made with scientific precision; they are all reducible to definite rules, and therefore capable of being accurately acquired. The mutable consonants may, for aid to the memory, be called caPiTals, GaBiDals, and LLiMiRHals, and are thus arranged, with their mutations—

$$
\text{I.}\begin{cases} c, & 1\ g, & 2\ ngh, & 3\ ch, \\ p, & b, & mh, & ph. \\ t, & d, & nh, & th. \end{cases}
\quad
\text{II.}\begin{cases} g, & 1\text{-}2\ ng. \\ b, & f, & m. \\ d, & dd, & n. \end{cases}
\quad
\text{III.}\begin{cases} ll, & 1\ l. \\ m, & f. \\ rh, & r. \end{cases}
$$

The same principles, though with less minuteness, govern the use of the eclipsis and aspiration in Irish and Gaelic.

III. CELTIC SCHOLARSHIP AND LITERATURE.

1. CELTIC SCHOLARSHIP.—In treating of the labours and researches of those who had made the Celtic languages a special subject of study, the lecturer pointed out the principal works in the lexicography and grammar of the Breton, Cornish, Welsh, Irish, and Manx. The first attempt in Gaelic lexicography was

made by Robert Kirke, minister of Balquhidder, in his edition of
the Irish Bible for the use of the Gael of Scotland, and published
in 1690. It was of very modest dimensions, extending only to 5½
pages. The next work was of a more extended and scientific
character, embraced all the dialects, and was composed by our first
great Celtic scholar, Edward Lhuyd—his "Archæologia Brittanica"
was published in 1707. Thirty-four years afterwards, we have the
Gaelic vocabulary of Alexander Macdonald, schoolmaster of Ardnamurchan, and the author of "Aiseiridh na Sean chànain Albannaich." To him succeeded, after an interval of 39 years, William
Shaw, minister of Ardclach, Nairnshire, who published in 1780 a dictionary, which formed also the basis of O'Reilly's Irish Dictionary.
The two Macfarlane's, Robert and Peter, published vocabularies, the
former in 1795, and the latter in 1815. But the first work of
an authoritative character was by Robert Armstrong, schoolmaster
of Kenmore, Perthshire, who devoted time, talents, and industry
to the production of a work which still holds a high place as an
authority among Gaelic scholars. It was published in 1825. The
Highland Society's Dictionary was published in 1828. In addition to the laborious exertions of Ewen Maclachlan of Aberdeen—
the most accomplished Gaelic scholar of his day—this work obtained the services of Dr Macleod of Dundonald, Dr Irvine of
Little Dunkeld, Dr Macdonald of Crieff, and others, and was
completed under the editorial care and supervision of the Rev. Dr
Mackintosh Mackay. Lesser volumes, which were largely compi-
lations from, or abridgments of, the foregoing, were prepared and
published by Dr Macleod and Dr Dewar; by Mr M'Alpine,
schoolmaster, Islay; and a small pocket volume by Mr M'Eachran,
published at Perth. The grammars are well-known, and do not
demand detailed reference. The labours and services of two
foreigners are worthy of special note. These are J. F. M. Le
Gonidec, the author of a grammar and dictionary of the Celto-
Breton, and the celebrated German professor and linguist, J.
Caspar Zeuss, the author of the Grammatica Celtica. Christianity
as well as scholarship owes much to the devoted labours of Le
Gonidec; the former for his invaluable translations of the Holy
Scriptures, and the latter for his linguistic works. Born at Le
Conquet, in Brittany, on September 4th 1775, he was, at the age
of three years, deprived of his mother, abandoned by his father,
and generously adopted by Mr and Mrs de Ker Sauzon. Ere he
was eighteen years of age he became involved in the troubles of
the Revolution in France, and, after a narrow escape for his life,
crossed the Channel, and landed at Penzance in Cornwall. In
1794, after a residence of twelve months in this country, he returned to Brittany, only to be again involved in the civil wars of

the Morbihan and the Cotes-du-Nord. An amnesty granted in 1800 permitted him to retire from civil conflict. It was only now that he began to study scientifically a language which, without any study, he had spoken from his infancy. Henceforward his zeal in that study was intense, and his labours abundant. In 1805 he was admitted a member of the Celtic Academy of Paris, and in 1807, after two years of incessant labour, he published his Celto-Bretonne grammar. His Breton-French and French-Breton dictionaries—the former published in 1821—engaged him for a period of eleven years. Ten years he devoted to the translations of the Scriptures : the New Testament was published in 1821, and the Old Testament shortly before his death, which took place in 1838. The New Testament is justly regarded as the finest translation in the Breton language. The entire edition is said to have been bought in Wales. He was also instrumental in directing the attention of the learned to the manuscript literature of his country, at a time when that literature was almost wholly neglected and lost sight of, and to the true character of his native tongue, in the face of the wildest and most visionary notions regarding its origin and history. All the literary work to which we have referred he accomplished while undergoing the daily toil in other duties necessary for the support of his family, and that without acknowledgment or reward from the State, which, prodigal enough in other matters, could not spend the smallest amount for the encouragement of Celtic literature and the elucidation of the language spoken by a large number of its own subjects.

Professor J. Caspar Zeuss was born, of poor parents, in a Bavarian village, July 22nd, 1806. He enjoyed the advantages of a regular school and college education. At the comparatively early age of 31, he published an elaborate ethnological work upon " The Germans and their Neighbours." In 1840 he was appointed to the Professorship of History in the College of Spire (Speyer), and here he seems to have begun those studies which eventually culminated in his Grammatica Celtica. He had made a thorough study of the Sanscrit, as well as of the Cymric and Gaedhelic languages. In the course of his ordinary historical researches he had become familiar with the great libraries of Europe. In these libraries he discovered parchments of an ancient date, in the classical tongues, with interlinear and marginal annotations and translations into Gaelic. These notes and translations bore the same relations to the original documents that the interlinear marginal notes of a modern student bear to the classical author studied by him. What were these parchments, and how came the Gaedhelic translations there? The early Celtic Church furnished numerous and able missionaries in the 6th and subsequent century, to the continent of

Europe. The condition of the native Churches may be seen in the valuable history of the Early Scottish Church, by the Rev. Dr M'Lauchlan of Edinburgh, in the able monogram on the Culdees by the Rev. Dr Reeves of Armagh, while the condition and cha- raeter of the Continental Culdee Establishments are admirably delineated by the Rev. Dr Ebrard of Erlangen. The missionaries who went out from this country founded several schools of learning and theology on the Continent of Europe. In the course of their studies, they wrote between the lines and on the margin, for their own information and for the use of their pupils, translations into their native Celtic of every difficult word and phrase in the authors perused. In the course of time these institutions, under the sup- remacy of the Church of Rome, became monasteries. The books and MSS. passed, along with the buildings, into the hands of the new proprietors, who revered the Gaelic missionaries, cherished their memories, and preserved those interesting memorials of their life and learning. These memorials are the famous glosses of St Gall, Milan, Wurtzburg, and Bobbio. These are the materials which Zeuss, at the risk of health and life itself, searched for and dis- covered, and by means of which, after thirteen years' patient in- dustry and study, he was able to give to the world—in his Gram- matica Celtica—a masterly analysis of the Celtic as spoken at, and immediately after, the time of the Romans. These were the isolated and often broken fragments by which he re-constructed the one pillar which is his own undying monument, and the ad- miration of the learned world.

Scholars were not slow to take advantage of the hint thrown out by Sir Wm. Jones and of the evidence submitted by Pritchard, but they were slow to admit the whole truth implied in their re- searches. The facts of an intimate connection and close relation- ship between the Celtic and the other Aryan tongues were gener- ally admitted, but the evidence was regarded as insufficient to prove identity, in respect of grammatical structure. There were discrepancies which could not be accounted for. These were point- ed out so early as 1836—four years after the appearance of Dr Pritchard's work. They were three in number :—

1. It was asserted that the Celtic did not harmonise with the other Aryan tongues, in that its substantives, adjectives, and pro- nouns, had no neuter gender, which the other languages possessed.

2. That in regard to the comparative and superlative degrees, the Celtic was wholly wanting in two roots—parallel in significa- tion, cognate in origin, and clearly connected in form—which pre- vailed in the other tongues.

3. That in the Welsh and Breton dialects there were, properly

speaking, no cases, while the few inflections in Gaelic were said to bear no analogy to those of the Indo-European family.

The researches of Zeuss have completely answered all these objections. He discovered that the Celtic had a neuter gender ; that the superlative and comparative not only existed in the old Gaelic, but that they were of the same form with those possessed by the kindred languages ; while in regard to case, he showed that it existed to a much larger extent than was admitted, and was formed upon principles similar to those which governed the formation of the cases in the other branches of the family.

Soon after the completion of his great work, Zeuss sank into a state of exhaustion, and died in 1856. He was not destined to enjoy any of the fruits of his great discoveries and unwearied labours, beyond the satisfaction of having been instrumental in achieving a noble and imperishable work for the language which was the study of his life. For the further study and elucidation of the Celtic, he was successful in laying down a stable and enduring foundation, and no Celtic scholar can now pursue that study without paying a warm tribute to the memory of the German scholar, and without feeling the liveliest gratitude for the noblest gift which any continental author has ever conferred on his race and language.

While paying our tribute of gratitude to a foreign author, for the greatest and most valuble contribution made towards the elucidation of our language, we are not to forget that there are scholars nearer home whose patriotism, genius, and scholarship have won them laurels in the same field. The first attempt at a History of Gaelic Literature was made by Mr John Reid of Glasgow, who published the result of his labours in his " Bibliotheca Scoto-Celtica," in 1832. It is a valuable repertory of information regarding the Gaelic books (with biographical notices of their authors), which had been published up to about this date. To the Rev. Dr M'Lauchlan we are indebted for able and interesting notices of the history and literature of the Scottish Gael, published under the title of " Celtic Gleanings," in 1857, after having previously been delivered as lectures in Edinburgh. This was the first work of the kind bearing on our literature since the publication of the Bibliotheca Scoto-Celtica. The aim of the author was to aid in forming an interested public before which questions appertaining to the Celtic races might be discussed. In that object he thoroughly succeeded, and to that little work, as well as to the History of the Early Scottish Church and the Dean of Lismore's Book, by the same author, added to constant personal effort, no small portion of the interest now taken in Celtic subjects is due. To Dr M'Lauchlan we are also indebted for an admirable, succinct, and clear review of our Gaelic Literature, which appears in the "Scottish Highlands, Highland Clans, &c.," now being published (A. Fullarton & Co., Edinburgh).

To the general reader the history of the early Celtic Church is both interesting and profitable. The simplicity, purity, and earnestness which characterised the early Church, both in worship and doctrine, received a wonderful resurrection at the Reformation. The vital spark which had long lain imbedded in, and was well-nigh extinguished amid the traditions, fictions, and tales of a superstitious and visionary age, was now rekindled, let us hope, never to expire. The remains of an early civilisation, and the reliques of an early and Scriptural worship, abundantly testify to the power of truth in those primitive times, and fill our hearts with gratitude to the learned historian of the " Early Scottish Church." To the linguist and the scholar, it is not less interesting to see the charter chests of the ancient lords of the soil opened, and the dust of centuries brushed away from the parchments, and to find our old language receiving a resurrection in print, through the patience and learning of the transcriber : to see the manuscript collections of former authors and compilers brought down from the shelves of hall and library, where for ages they had lain unperused and unprofitable, and to have them reproduced with a faithfulness that reflects the highest credit on the learning, perseverance, and industry of the scholar who has restored them to our literature, and published them to the world. Such a work we have in the " Dean of Lismore's Book," transcribed, translated, and annotated by the Rev. Dr M'Lauchlan. A worthy coadjutor and fellow-labourer we have in Dr William F. Skene, who writes the introduction to that work, and whose essay on " The Highlanders" first brought him into public notice. He has since edited the " Chronicles of the Picts and Scots" and the " Four Ancient Books of Wales." Another interesting relic of Celtic literature we have in the " Book of Deer," published by the Spalding Club, under the editorship of Dr John Stuart, who obtained the valuable aid of Mr Whitley Stokes, the most accomplished of Irish scholars, and whose " Goidilica" leads us to hope that the mantle of Zeuss has fallen upon a native scholar and linguist. We might here refer to the labours of others who have rendered distinguished service to our literature, such as Mr John F. Campbell of Islay, who has procured for us "The West Highland Tales," and who has now in the press two volumes of our Gaelic heroic ballad poetry ; the Rev. Dr Clerk of Kilmallie, whose magnificent edition of Ossian was lately issued from the press ; Professor Blackie of the Edinburgh University, whose lectures evince his thorough patriotism, as well as his scholarly interest in our language and literature ; Professor

Geddes of Aberdeen, Principal Shairp of St Andrews, and others, whose disinterested services help to revive and extend the interest now manifested on behalf of our mother tongue, and throw light upon the structure and character of the ancient Gaelic.

CELTIC LITERATURE.—We have often to regret that our most distinguished British philologists do not manifest an intimate acquaintance with our language and literature. To this fact it is largely due that we are so constantly met with the statement, "But there is really no literature in the Celtic language." This assertion is said, moreover, to be specially characteristic of the Gaelic of Scotland. There is no doubt abundant ground to wish that our literature were more extensive than it is. The truth in regard to the matter is, that we do possess a literature, which though scanty when compared with the vast treasures existing in modern and in a very few of the most ancient tongues, is nevertheless of the highest value when we take into account its intrinsic worth and character and its bearings on the science of language. It is, moreover, so large as to compare favourably with the literary remains of other aboriginal races. It may be considered large also when we take into account the various hostile influences with which it had to contend, and in the face of which it has been so wonderfully preserved. If it were, as is asserted, small, it would on that account be more easily mastered, and ought therefore to be regarded as specially valuable. The statement, however, is entirely unfounded, and is often the result of ignorance, if not of prejudice. Where, then, is our literature, and of what does it consist? We have already seen that a large portion of the vocabulary of the two great branches of the Celtic may be justly regarded as their common property and inheritance. The same is true to a large extent of their literature. It is notably true of the earlier oral and traditional, and to no small extent of the early manuscript remains in each of the branches. Thus the Welsh and the Breton have an early and common literature, and so have the Irish and the Gaelic. These remains have in some instances undergone changes, and present differences which are to be traced to the natural vicissitudes, circumstances, and historical relations of the race. It is reasonable to suppose that no small portion of our literature must be oral and traditional, the production of bards and seanachies, handed down from generation to generation. Thus we have the Ossianic, and other ballad poetry of ancient times, and the earlier tales and legends of imaginative authors, which have only in recent years been given to the world through the press. We have in addition to this a large and important written literature. These written monuments are of various kinds: 1, The topography of Europe and of our own islands supply us with valuable and extensive materials in this department, and testify to the prevalence in former days of our race and language. 2, We have also the stone monuments engraved by art and man's device, which furnish us with our earlier alphabets, or *Beth-luis-noins.* These stone monuments give us our oldest known forms, and powers of letters and words. Of written stones, the first and earliest in Europe are confessedly Celtic, and consist of the monuments bearing the Ogham marks. Professor Stephens of Denmark, our highest authority on this subject, says " Some three hundred of these pillar stones have been found in Ireland ; about a dozen Ogham blocks have been found in Scotland, and scarcely so many in England and Wales. These Ogham stones are every way so peculiar that they at once strike the antiquarian student. The dispute is still hotly carried on, whether they are heathen or Christian. I cannot conceive how any one can question that this was the most ancient stone row of Celtic civilisation. As far as I know, they have never even once been found in Scandinavia, and could never have been transplanted thence." 3, In regard to manuscripts we are by no means so destitute as is generally supposed. Several hundreds of valuable manuscripts are deposited in the Advocate's Library in Edinburgh, in London, at Oxford and Cambridge, in the treasuries of Trinity College, and in the Museum of the Royal Irish Academy, Dublin. The earlier Scottish and Irish manuscripts are so similar in subject matter, mode of writing, and character, as to lead us to the conclusion that they contain the common literary inheritance of the Gaelic branch of the Celtic race. (See Dr M'Lauchlain's review " In Highlands, Highland Clans, &c.," vol. ii. p. 66-68.)

The following are a few of the oldest and most valuable of our manuscript remains :—

1. " The Book of Deer," parts of which are as old as the ninth century, published by the Spalding Club. It also contains specimens of the eleventh and twelfth centuries.

2. The Exposition of the Tain—supposed to be the oldest Gaelic MSS. extant.

3. " The Albanic Duan," of date about 1050, published in Dr Skene's " Chronicles of the Picts."

4. The " Eethune" MSS. of date 1100.

5. The " Bannatyne," MSS., containing the " Lament of Deirdre," 1208—published in the Appendix to the Highland Society's Report on Ossian, p. 265.

6. " Gaelic Charter" of 1400, published by the Record Commission, National MSS. of Scotland, vol. 11, No. 59. This charter is remarkable in that the language is almost entirely identical with the spoken Gaelic of the present day.

7. The Dean of Lismore's MS., consisting of upwards of 11,000 verses of Gaelic Poetry. This MS. contains poetical pieces from the times of the most ancient bards down to the beginning of the 16th century. The whole of this manuscript, with a few unimportant exceptions, has been transcribed, translated, and annotated by the Rev. Dr M'Lauchlan of Edinburgh, with an introduction by William F. Skene, Esq., LL.D. (published by Messrs Edmonston and Douglas.)

Among the oral and traditional remains of an earlier period, the chief place in public estimation is held by the "Ossian" of James Macpherson, the collections of Gillies, published at Perth in 1786, and of the brothers Hugh and John Maccallum, published at Montrose in 1816, and the admirable collections of the "Popular Tales, &c., of the West Highlands," by John F. Campbell, published in four volumes by Edmonston and Douglas in 1862.

In modern Gaelic literature, the first printed book is the Gaelic translation of John Knox's liturgy, by John Carsewell, Superintendent of the Isles. It was printed in Edinburgh in 1567. Only three copies of it are now known to exist: one perfect copy in the possession of the Duke of Argyle; one imperfect in the British Museum, and one, also imperfect, in the library of the University of Edinburgh. This scarce and valuable relic of our earliest Gaelic printing is now being reproduced under the editorship of Dr M'Lauchlan, and will shortly be published (by Messrs Edmonston and Douglas, of Edinburgh). Detailed information regarding our subsequent Gaelic literature will be found in Reid's "Bibliotheca Scoto-Celtica," M'Lauchlan's "Celtic Gleanings," and "Review of Gaelic Literature," and in Skene's "Introduction to the Dean of Lismore's Book."

The extent and variety of Irish manuscripts are so great that one is almost lost in wonder and admiration. The duty of cataloguing and describing this enormous literature devolved upon a man singularly qualified for the task, the late Professor Eugene O'Curry. With unrivalled powers and capacity for work, and by unwearied patience, he moved through the chaotic mass until, by persevering effort and marvellous success, he brought the whole into shape and order. We have the result of his labours presented to us in his "Lectures on the manuscript materials of Irish History," the second volume of which is eagerly looked for. The principal portions of these manuscripts are "The Ancient Annals," "The Annals of the Four Masters," edited by the late Dr O'Donovan, and published in 1848, "Leabhar na h-Uidhri" of St Ciaran, "Book of Ballymote," "Leabhar Breac," "Book of Lecan," "Yellow Book of Lecan," "Book of Lismore," &c. If to these we add their "Tales," historical and imaginative, martyrologies, festologies, &c., we can easily see what a vast mass of manuscript remains they possess. There are treatises on all the

subjects of human knowledge to which the learned men of the
time directed their attention, as well as detailed information upon
almost every part of ancient Gaelic life. The Irish have also been
wise in their generation, and have not allowed their ancient
documents to lie upon their shelves unperused and unprofitable.
They are anxious that these materials should stimulate the study
of Irish antiquities, and obtain the elucidation they require, by
scholarly and public criticism. With true patriotic feeling they are
accordingly, year by year, sending out from the press, in the most
magnificent and sumptuous manner, lithographed fac-similes of the
literature of their ancient days. "Leabhar na h-Uidhri" was
issued in this manner two years ago, and the first part of the
"Leabhar Breac" is now ready to be put into the hands of the
subscribers. This service to literature and Celtic scholarship
cannot be too highly valued, nor sufficiently rewarded.

The manuscript literature of the Welsh is not less varied, if
somewhat less in extent. The Welsh manuscripts now deposited
in the British Museum amount to 47 volumes of poetry, of
various sizes, containing 4700 pieces, in 16,000 pages, besides
2000 epigrammatic stanzas. There are also in the same collection
53 volumes of prose, in 15,300 pages, containing treatises on
various subjects. The most interesting and valuable portions of
this literature are "The Black Book of Caermarthen," "The Book
of Aneurin," "The Book of Taliessin," and the "Red Book of
Hergest." These have been published under the title of "The
Four Ancient Books of Wales," under the editorship of Dr W. F.
Skene, with a valuable introduction and notes by the editor, and
with English translations by the Rev. D. Silvan Evans, and the
Rev. Robert Williams (Edinburgh, Edmonston & Douglas, 1868).
The Welsh MS. literature is of great extent, and of no ordinary
importance to the historian and philologist. We might have supposed that such an immense mass of valuable literary and historic
materials could not possibly elude the observation of our sovereigns
and statesmen. Scotland and Ireland were so far removed from
Court and from Parliament that there might be some excuse for
inattention to their ancient literature. To the honour of our
beloved Queen, it is to be said that, more than any of her predecessors, she takes a deep interest in our language and literature.
The only prize ever received from Royal hand, so far as we know,
for a contribution to Celtic literature, was bestowed by H.R.H.
the Prince of Wales. But it was no member of the Royal Family
who first brought to light the ancient literary remains of the
Principality of Wales. To a poor peasant boy, Owen Jones, a
native of the Vale of Myvyr, in North Wales, we owe what
neither Government, nor clergy, nor the wealthy lords of broad

acres, cared to supply. From his early years, we are told, that Owen Jones had a singular passion for the ancient treasures of his country's literature. These treasures were scattered over the country, jealously guarded, and difficult of access. The celebrated Edward Lhuyd did his utmost to get access to them, or obtain possession of them, but without effect. Owen Jones resolved to accomplish the feat from which men less brave and less enthusiastic would shrink, and from which other men with true courage had to turn back in dismay. At the age of nineteen he went up to London and got employment in a furrier's shop in Thames Street. For a period of forty years he toiled in business, with one object in view, and at the end of that time his object was accomplished. He had risen in his employment, until the business had become his own, and he had amassed a considerable fortune; but this had been sought by him for one object only—the purpose of his life, the dream of his youth—the giving permanence and publicity to the treasures of his national literature. Gradually he got manuscript after manuscript transcribed, and at last in 1801, jointly with two friends, he brought out, in three large volumes, printed in double columns, his Myvyrian Archæology of Wales. This work is the great repertory of the literature of his nation. The comparative study of languages and literature gains every day more followers, and it has been well said, that no one of these followers, at home or abroad, touches Welsh literature without paying deserved homage to the Denbighshire peasant's name, and without admiring the courage, perseverance, and industry which enabled him to do so much for his country and her literature. (See Arnold's Essay on Celtic Literature.)

IV.—AFFINITIES OF THE CELTIC.

1. VOCABULARY.—After detailing the various theories of Celtic affinity prevalent during last century, the lecturer went on to show that the researches of our great philologists demonstrated the original identity of the Indic, Iranic, Celtic, Romanic, Slavonic, and Teutonic classes of languages. They form together the grand Indo-European system. To the linguist and philologist these languages form but varieties of one and the same primordial speech, spoken by the ancestors of the Aryan tribes. It has been shown by philologists that the vast majority of roots in all the members of the family, including the Celtic, are identical. Excluding those which have been undoubtedly borrowed from obvious natural sounds, and loan words, which are the nomads of language, it is now matter of simple notoriety that the remaining roots are identical in fundamental radical structure. Notwithstanding the

influence of time, the disturbing elements of foreign admixture,
and the peculiarities of the initial mutations and letter changes,
the vocabulary of the Celtic stands in the closest possible relations
to the vocabularies of all the other Aryan languages. It is
no doubt to the peculiarity of the initial mutations, so characteristic of the Celtic, that we owe it that these affinities were
not discovered at a much earlier period in the history of comparative philology. The fact of an internal unity pervading
the Indo-European family may be sufficiently illustrated by the
following table :—

ARYAN LANGUAGES—COMPARATIVE VOCABULARY.

Indic.	Celtic.	Græco-Latin.	Teutonic.	Slavonic.
acvas	each	hippos, equus	ehu (D)	aszwa Li
agnis	eibble, aingeal	ignis aigle	ild D	
avis	oisg davadd ?	ovis ois	awi	awis Li
arv	ar, arbhar, erw	aro, aroo	ariaG., arenD.	aru, L. oriu. R
svann	seinn synin	sono aineo	. . .	zwanu zweniu
sad	suidh	sedeo, hedo	sita, sitzen	sedziu sazu
sadh	sath	satio, ado	sattigen	sotinu
svapnas	suain	hupnos, somnus	schlafen	sopnas
nac, nica	nochd n-oidhche	nox nux	nahts	naktis
namh, namb	neamh	nephos. nubes	naba	nebo
dah	doth	daio		degu
dvar	dorus	thura	daur	durrys
dha	dean	theo	thun	demi
dvac	tigh, teach techu	tectum	taha, decke	taiu, dengiu
tal	talamh	solum, telma	ziele	
it	uidh, aethym	ito, ithuo	iddia, itzt	idu
jan	gin genedlu	geno	keina	gemu
uks	uisge	uo	wasche	ukstu
valg	falbh	helko	walke	welku
ma, mas	mois, meas	metior	mita messe	mezuiu
man	maen ail-mhinn	munio		menk, maniu
miras	muir	mare	marei	mare
mal, mall	muilinn	molo	malwia	malu, meliu
smi	smeid	mediao	schmache	smieiu
pac, pacy	faic	specto	spahe	
laks	leus, leug	lux, luke	lauths, luge	

2. GRAMMAR.—But as has been already said, vocabulary alone
is not regarded as sufficient proof of affinity ; we need, in addition,
the evidence furnished by grammatical structure and idiom.
From the grammatical structure of the languages we are furnished
with seven distinct testimonies, the evidence being at once direct
and cumulative :—1, Phonological, indicative of the powers of
the vowels and consonants. 2, Word formation, illustrating the
use of common terminatives. 3, Declension. 4, Gradation or
comparison. 5, Affinities of the pronouns and numerals. 6,
Affinities in the conjugation. 7, Affinities in syntax. We can

only now refer to one of these evidences, viz., that furnished by the numerals in all the languages, as shown in the subjoined table :

NUMERALS.

Indic.		Celtic.		Græco-Latin.	Teutonic.	Slavonic.
aina	eka	aon	un	hen, uno, oino	aina	odin
dua	dva	da	dau	duo	tva	tva
tri	tri	tri	tri	tri	thri	tri
katvar	chatur	ceithir	petwar	quatuor, tettar	fidvor	cetqr
kankan	panchan	cuig	pimp	quinque pempe	fimf	pyat
ksvaks	shash	se	chwech	sex hex	saihs	sest
saptan	saptan	seachd	saith	septem hepta	sibun	sem
aktu	ashtan	ochd	wyth	octo	ahtau	osm
navan	navan	nao	nau	novem ennea	niun	dewiat
dakan	dasan	deich	deg	decem deka	taihun	desiat

March 14, 1872.—Mr John Macdonald, Exchange, Treasurer to the Society, read the following paper, on

THE HIGHLAND CLEARANCES.

The subject we are called upon to discuss this evening is one which possesses a peculiar interest to us as a Gaelic Society. Although, as an historical fact, the Highland evictions may now be regarded as a thing of the past ; yet they are by no means events soon to be forgotten. In individual life, as well as in national history, incidents sometimes occur, important enough in themselves, but over which the lapse of time may soon bring the shades of oblivion. Among such things we cannot class the Highland clearances. Events which have so completely changed the outward aspect of the North and the social condition of its people, will not and cannot be so easily forgotten, at any rate so long as we are surrounded with their sad and widespread results, and so long as the injustice perpetrated on a peaceable and industrious people is attempted to be justified under the mask of a false political economy.

I am not one of those willing to overlook the misguided policy which effected those clearances by attaching too much importance to solitary instances of apparent good which have arisen out of a glaring evil. In justification of the evictions we are continually reminded that the Highlanders have always been benefited and improved in circumstances when removed from the scenes of their childhood. Wherever such instances occur, everything is made of them to prove the utility of the clearances; but not a word do we ever hear of the thousands of cases of individual and family

suffering caused—the many who on their passage across the seas
found their graves in the deep; others who, having escaped that
fate, were ushered to an end equally sad and untimely by sudden
transition to uncongenial climes; and many more, who, driven
from the healthy air of their hillsides to the unwholesome atmosphere of crowded cities, sank into poverty and ill-health, dying
broken-hearted.   Records of such results as these the approvers of
the clearances would fain efface from the page of history; indeed
that, so far, they may accomplish; but not one of the most solitary
cases of oppression has escaped the eye of

      " Him who sees, with equal eyes, as Lord of all,
        The hero perish and the sparrow fall,"

and according to the unerring operation of His moral government,
the actors in those clearances, and the nation whose laws permitted
them, have even already, and will yet more fully suffer a just and
stern retribution.   It is not my wish in any unseemly manner to
disturb the dust which now covers memories of the past by making
much allusion to the manner in which those clearances were carried
out.   I shall only express my humble yet firm conviction, that the
conduct of those who depopulated our straths and glens, as well as
that of their aiders and abettors, will have yet to undergo a severer
criticism than it has hitherto.   It is only within comparatively recent times that, by means of iucreased travelllng facilities, the vast
circulation of a free press, and other circumstances, that these
northern glens, have become more perfectly known; and just in
proportion as the Highlands, and the history of its people, become
objects of public interest, in the same ratio will an impartial public
opinion stamp with its disapproval that policy which almost extirpated the bravest and yet the most peaceable peasantry which any
country ever possessed.

    I need not remind the Gaelic Society that, even within the last
century, the Highlands have undergone a great change.   Many of
you know from actual observation that things are not now what
they once were.   Wherever you turn you are reminded of the time,
perhaps within your own recollection, when the now still solitudes
of these glens abounded with an active population.   In fact, the
change is everywhere so apparent that it is one of the first things
that strike the attention of the stranger.   Yet, notwithstanding
the silence everywhere reigning, every object met with is eloquent
with a history, not of the present, but of the past: each cairn and
stone, each hill and meadow, has associations pointing to a time
when the surrounding hills echoed the sounds of busy life, the
voices of living men and women; but now, wander whither you
will, you are compelled to join in the lament with which a well-
known friend of the Highlands contemplated the deserted condition

of a strath in Sutherlandshire, which some of you are old enough
to have seen in both aspects—

> " Bonnie Strathnaver, Sutherland's pride,
> Loud is the baa of the sheep on thy side ;
> But the song, and the dance, and the pipe are no more,
> And gone the brave clansmen that trod thy green floor."

Since it is too true, then, that there has been a change, and
that the people are gone which once enlivened those solitudes,
we are surely entitled to ask who they were, and what has become
of them ? Well, as to the first question, although we do not claim for
them to have formed in their time an ideal state of society, and
admitting that, judged by modern standards of excellence, they
might have been deficient in many of the attainments of modern
civilisation ; yet we fearlessly assert, making allowances for the
times in which they lived, and the circumstances by which they
were surrounded, that for honest worth, real virtue, and true manly
nobility, they by far excelled their modern critics. Among
them few or none of those vices were to be met with which disgrace modern society. Their habits of life were simple; and even
in the entire absence of the stringent measures now deemed necessary, protection of life and property were with them comparatively
safe ; mutual confidence and trustworthiness being sufficient sub-
stitutes for the locks and bars of later times. There is another
and very important aspect in which our Highland people of those
days were superior to any section of society now found within the
bounds of the realm. In their living, removed as they were from
the arts and luxuries of modern times, theirs was the full enjoyment of robust health and muscular bodies, which, when acting as
soldiers in defence of their country, often enabled them to turn the
tide of victory on many a battle field. In entire ignorance of
doctors' drugs and dainty dishes, they needed no assistance to
digest their simple fare ; nor would a slight exposure to wind or
rain bring on the horrors of an influenza. The modern tourist, as
he comes to gaze on the silent grandeur of our mountain scenery,
returns to his English friends and tells them of daring feats and
arduous toils, having, after a hard day's work, made the ascent of
this hill and that (tasks which he seldom accomplishes without the
aid of a trustworthy native), hesitating to believe that in days
gone by, in these same solitudes, there lived men who, with perfect
ease, performed the same tasks as mere rambles, and that, too,
often before the breakfast hour. Although, perhaps, somewhat
exaggerated under patriotic impulse, the heroes of Scott existed
not altogether in fancy, for there are tales of the past, with truthful evidence, that tell us of a people who, in their rude crafts,
laughed at the waves which some of us have seen spend their fury

on our western shores. There were men, too, to whom the deep ravines and torrents of our mountain wilds were no impassable barriers; and there were women, also, who could, and frequently did, share the dangers of men, and who, if wanting in the accomplishments of the modern lady, possessed warm hearts and tender sympathies, which prompted to deeds of courage and disinterested devotion (Flora Macdonald, for instance), which only find a parallel in the ancient heroism of Greece and Rome. Such, then, were the people. Let us now inquire what has become of them. The origin of the policy which led to their removal I have no hesitation in tracing to the pride and avarice of human nature, which here, as well as elsewhere, had done its work before the force of an awakened public opinion had time to check it. As a result of the union between England and Scotland, the tide of Scottish wealth and nobility began to drift southward. Our Highland chiefs and lairds, departing from the primitive usage of living among their people, began to make frequent and prolonged visits to the seat and centre of pomp and royalty. Their incomes soon became inadequate to sustain the dissipation of English society, so that it became with them a very serious question as to how those incomes could be increased; and as in all ages "evil communications corrupt good manners," our Scottish lairds became ready converts to the pernicious doctrines of the Saxon-Norman. In connection with Highland clearances, the excuse is often urged, that the people were for their own benefit evicted from bleak moorlands and rugged hill-sides, which hardly afforded them a bare existence. Well, such may have been the primary motive, although it appears to me somewhat incredible; for I find that the carrying out of the same policy has cleared in a similar manner many a broad acre of rich English soil to make room for the extensive pleasure ground and palatial mansion of the Norman. We cannot, then, afford to credit the existence of such benevolent intentions so long as the broad fact stands blazing on the page of history that, in the one case as well as in the other, the rights and welfare of the people have been ruthlessly ignored: the Highland hillside, as well as the English meadow, being sacrificed to the sport and profit of the capitalist.

Let us now examine some of the profit and loss results of these clearances. It is a fact clearly proved by carefully compiled statistics that even the material wealth of the Highlands suffers from the prevalence of deer forests and over-grown sheep-walks. We may have acquired an apparent wealth; the value of land as shown by the rent-rolls may have been considerably increased; but these and many more minor advantages will never compensate our loss, for

" Ill fares that land, to hastening ills a prey,
Where wealth accumulates, but men decay.
Princes and lords may flourish and may fade,
A breath can make them, as a breath hath made ;
But a bold peasantry, a country's pride,
If once destroyed, can never be supplied."

In justification of the evictions we are very properly reminded that emigration is a law of nature ; essential to the welfare of the individual, by bringing into exercise self-energy ; essential to the welfare of the State by relieving it of a surplus population, and opening up of new fields of colonisation. Now in these doctrines we firmly believe, yet with equal conviction that in every well governed country there are natural agencies at work, which, if allowed free scope and encouraged, will always prove effectual in preventing over population, by drawing off the surplus to new and wider spheres of usefulness. Had even limited educational advantages been placed within the people's reach, the Highland people—who were not then, any more than they are now, insensible to bettering their condition—would readily avail themselves of wider and more remunerative spheres of labour ; and certainly no people ever showed greater readiness or aptitude for the work of colonisation than they did. In proof of this need I remind you that at a time when their education and literature were limited to a mere acquaintance with the Bible, catechism, a few theological works, and ballad poetry, there had been from the Highlands a continual exodus of men whose names (notwithstanding all their disadvantages) will be ever associated with what is great and progressive in our country's history. Instead of those clearances, had a few more such facilities been afforded them, the evictions would have been unnecessary, for by a natural process of emigration any surplus population existing would readily remove to other fields of labour. By this process capital, labour, and skill, would accompany each other in suitable proportion ; nor would the tender and kindly tie which ought to bind the emigrant to his native land be rudely severed by his quitting our shores under a real or supposed grievance ; and when his industry abroad is rewarded, he would more frequently return home to spend his accumulated earnings, thus materially benefiting the land of his birth. I ask you were these the circumstances under which we sent out many of our colonists ? On the contrary, in those wholesale clearances the people were forced to emigrate, poor, unprepared, and with encumbrances which quite unfitted them for the arduous toils of colonisation. Need we wonder that, where such emigrants founded and consolidated some of our now rising colonies, the recollection of the circumstances under which they left us will have anything but a tendency to strengthen the friendly tie which ought to bind our country to her colonial family ; and should the time ever arrive in our history when, passing from the present time of her vigour to the decrepitude of old age (which overtakes nations as well as individuals) our nation may have occasion to solicit the assistance of her colonial offspring, in the event of her not then meeting with that ready response anticipated, she will assuredly have to blame the policy which has given many of our colonies such painful histories.

In regard to the increase of wealth and the improved state of things which are pointed out as resulting from those clearances, I am very much of opinion the improvement is more apparent than real. If there is such an increase of wealth, it is by no means shared by the masses of the people. A large proportion of our even now scanty population are poor, many of them, indeed, paupers, supported by forced rates, a species of charity which would ill compare with the generosity which was its substitute in former days. Not only so, but very many of those who hold and occupy the land are in circumstances not very much better. When closely scrutinised, the apparent wealth they enjoy is ficti-tious, furnishing numerous instances of collapse, its owners passing in quick succession through our bankruptcy courts ; or what is much worse, resorting to frauds and actions infinitely more ob-jectionable than the rude but avowed policy of the bold Rob Roy.

Were it my present object to enter into details I think I could, with a certain measure of success, trace many of these evils to the direct influences of the Highland clearances. That they have been a chief source of the pauperism of our northern towns and sea coast villages is as clear as noonday. Families being removed from holdings on which they and their forefathers lived in com-parative comfort, and drifted into towns and villages which afforded them no means of livelihood, naturally, and very soon became public burdens.

It is another important fact worthy of attention, that at this moment, and purely as the result of those clearances, the chief, and I might say the only source of wealth in the Highlands is based on a foundation neither desirable nor permanent. The increased value of land, much of our railway traffic, and circulation of capital, rest on the game laws, and the attraction which the Highland straths and glens on this account present as a sporting play ground. Now, there are many reasons which warrant us to believe that this state of things is not destined to last. We live in an age of rapid progress. Higher and more practical views of life are constantly changing and elevating the habits and pastimes of society ; and if the higher ranks (who are by no means perfect) are to advance in the march of progress at even the same rate as other sections are advancing, is it too much to expect that the time is not far dis-

tant when the sports associated with our moors and forests will be
looked upon as relic pastimes of a less enlightened age. Whether
such a change shall soon take place or not, from the whole tendency
of modern legislation on the subject, it certainly looks as if the
days of the game monopoly were numbered. When this shall take
place, and when, with the sportsman, the large shooting rent will
also disappear, then all interested in the railway enterprises and
entire trade of the North will wish that their revenue and resources rested on the more solid foundation of a thriving, industrious people. That the Highlands are now, and have all along
been, capable of sustaining such a population, is an opinion which
I sincerely entertain. Apart from our ranges of lofty hills and
bleak moorlands we have agricultural resources, if properly developed, capable of maintaining, in industrial comfort, many more
than are now engaged in this department of industry. The fishing
along our sea-coasts, if sufficiently attended to, is of itself a wide
field of industry, which might be made to absorb much idle labour,
and prove to the Highlands a vast source of wealth. Fitted by
nature as a most successful wool-growing district, and with ready
facilities by sea and land of adding to its growth abundant foreign
supplies ; and although, by our distance from the coal-fields, we
cannot command steam on a cheap scale, yet we have pouring
down our hill-sides and traversing our glens abundant water-power,
which might be utilised by its being made to play on the wheels of
busy factories. The prosperity of a people thus busily employed
would place the prosperity of all northern towns on a sound and
permanent basis. Professional and mechanical skill would find
ample employment in providing for their convenience and comfort.
Commerce (more particularly that department of it which is my
own humble sphere) would find safe and ample scope in distri-
buting among them the necessaries of life ; and everything thus
acting together as a harmonised whole, the Celtic people might
yet again not only maintain their position, but even take the lead
in the march of progress ; for we cannot forget that even this had
once been their privilege in a former age, when the light which
shone from the lonely island of Iona diffused among them a measure
of religious life and intelligence nowhere else to be found among
the races of Western Europe.

NOTES ON THE HISTORY OF THE GAEL.

March 28.—The following paper was read by a young Gael,
Mr Lachlan Macbean :—

As a people, we Celts are proverbially proud of our ancestry and
tenacious of our claims to antiquity; and I think justly so, for we
are descended from Gomer, the eldest son of Japhet, who was the
first-born of Noah, the progenitor of the human race; so that the
birthright of the earth is ours. This is certainly a far back origin,
but one for which I have the authority of Josephus, who says that
" Gomer was the father of the nation which was anciently called
Gomerians, and whom the Greeks to-day call Gauls. " Besides
Josephus, Isidore of Seville, Jerome, and many others, bear me out
in this genealogy. Ptolemy speaks of a people who, in his time,
dwelt in Bythinia, of which Galatia was a province, whom he calls
Chomorians, and their chief city Chomora. It is now agreed by all
that the Celts (more properly Kelts) were the aborigines of Europe.
We must conclude their stay in Asia to have been very short, for
Gomer their father is supposed to have been born in the year 2347
B.C., and we learn that Sicyon, a city of Greece, was built before
the year 2000 B.C., only 347 years after the birth of Gomer and
probably during his life. Neither was their stay in Greece of long
continuance, for, probably retiring before the Pelasgi, who were
prevalent in that country before the year 1529, they passed on into
Dalmatia and Italy. Though it is certain that they began to leave
Greece very early, it is not at all improbable that bands of them
continued their westward journey without halting at all in Greece.
The Celtic tongue was spoken in Greece and adjoining parts for
many years until, through the prevailing influence of Pelasgian,
Lelegian, and other languages, it ceased to be spoken excepting in
so far as it is the basis of the Greek tongue. But in Crete and
other provinces it continued as late as the time of Homer and even
that of Herodotus.

The history of the Kelts whilst in Greece is very misty; what
we know of them in Italy is no less so. We read of Pelasgian
colonies, before whom the Gallic element gradually disappears.
About 2000 B.C., a colony of Lydians from Asia Minor came to
Italy, and 300 years after a Pelasgian colony comes from Greece
under Oenatrus. After this the aboriginal Celtic quickly lost
ground, but before its final disappearance it composed in part the
Etruscan, or ancient Italian language, and in conjunction with the
Greek this language became the foundation of the Latin. Our
ancestors now pursued their course into Gaul, whence, in time, as
they multiplied, they spread over Spain, Portugal, Belgium, and the
western parts of Germany. Here for a thousand years their history
is a blank to us : their wars and explorations having nothing to
do with the learned and civilised nations, their record is entirely
forgotten. The next notice we find of the race is by Ezekiel, who
(B.C. 587) threatens to bring them and their allies against the land

of Judah—"Horses and horsemen, all of them clothed with all sorts of armour; even a great company with bucklers and shields, all of them having swords. . . . Gomer and all his bands; the house of Togarmah of the north quarters; and all his bands." It seems most likely, however, that this refers to the Gomerians of Asia Minor and not to those of Gaul. About this time the Gael made an irruption into Italy, under Bellovesus. In this extensive foray they ravaged the whole country throughout the length and breadth of the land, capturing the cattle, exterminating the inhabitants, and finally settling down in the conquered country, which comprised most of Northern Italy. Having thus obtained a footing beyond the Alps successive bands of Celts poured into Italy, each settling farther south than its predecessor. This emigration continued for two or three hundred years, till at length (385 B.C.) a band of Gael fresh from Gaul appeared before the Etruscan city of Clusium, which they besieged. The Roman ambassadors who were sent to negotiate having, contrary to the law of nations, taken part in a sally from the town, Brennus, the Gallic leader, complained to the Roman Senate, but receiving no redress he marched against Rome. 70,000 Romans met him at the Allia, but were cut to pieces; and after feasting and rejoicing over this victory, the Gauls entered Rome and marched peaceably to the Forum; but owing to an outrage committed on one of them, they killed, first the perpetrators of the crime, and then put the city to the sword, leaving none alive, and burning the houses to the ground. The Gauls now divided into two parts, the one continuing their journey, while the other stayed to besiege the Capitol. On receiving a ransom of 1000 pounds of gold they raised the siege and left the territories of Rome.

In the sixth century B.C. a colony of Gael had settled in Pannonia, who (or whose descendants) about this time invaded Greece. Twice they were unsuccessful, but the third expedition, under Brennus II., forced its way through Macedonia. At Delphi they were surprised by the Greeks during a storm and routed. Another division journeyed eastward, and settled in a province thence called Galatia, or Gallo-Græco. In the year 231, the Gael invaded Etruria again and defeated 50,000 men that met them at Clusium. The Romans raised an army of 700,000 infantry and 70,000 cavalry, and after six years ended the war by the victory of Telamo. After an interval of 25 years another Roman war began. Under Hamilcar, the Gael burnt the town of Phœntia; and after a struggle of six years they concluded a peace—a peace of no long continuance, however, for, in 191 B.C., Scipio Nasica defeated the Gael of Italy, and slaughtered the whole colony, leaving none alive but women, old men, and children. Their means of subsistence being thus cut off they crossed the Norsican Alps rather than treat with pitiless enemies or seek sympathy from unfeeling strangers in their own country. Thus ended the last Gallic invasion of Italy. After this the Romans were the invading party, the Gauls acting on the defensive. The history of the Gael in Gaul might be traced down farther, but our business is chiefly with that branch who inhabited Britain, and whose territory is now circumscribed by the boundaries of Caledonia. Though it is well-known that the first inhabitants of Britain or Albion were Celts, it would be a very vain attempt to fix the time of their first settlement in this island. That it must have been very early is clear. Long before the Romans came into Britain, or even into Gaul, Britain was the great stronghold of Druidism, insomuch that priests of Gaul came into this isle to learn the mysteries of that religion, because it was here to be found in its purest and primitive form. The Gauls wandering along the shore of the English Channel would see the white rough cliffs of Albin rising above the waves; some of them would come over and settle here. During the course of years, successive immigrations pouring in on the southern shore of Albin, the primitive Gael would gradually be pushed farther north, until at length they reached the mountains of Caledonia.

It was in the summer of 83 A.D. that the Gael of Caledonia had the first personal acquaintance with the Romans. They had several skirmishes with them that year, which seemed to show them that they had to deal with a courageous and persevering foe. The tribes of Caledonia united into a confederation, of which a chief, named Galgacus by Tacitus, was appointed leader and dictator. Their apprehensions proved not to be groundless, for, next year, Agricola, the Roman commander, left his quarters in Fife and advanced towards the Grampians. The army of the confederation of the southern Gael, numbering 30,000 men, met him at the foot of these mountains. The Romans were 20,000 or 30,000 strong. After a long and bloody battle the Caledonians retired to the mountains, having left 10,000 of their number dead on the field. Obtaining hostages from the Horestians, a southern tribe, Agricola returned to the south.

At this stage it would be a natural query why the Gael of this period were called Caledonians, and their country Caledonia. Buchanan says the word is derived from the great Caledonian forests of birch, hazel, &c., that *calden* is the Gaelic of hazel, and hence the name. Others derive it from Caoill-daoine—men of the woods. The suggestions made with regard to this word are as numerous as they are absurd. Some aspire even to make the Greeks our godfathers, and find the derivation of Caledonia in the Greek *Kaledion*. Had there been a word in the language of the

Caledonians themselves by which they named their country, and having a similar sound with Caledonia, would it not be reasonable to suppose that this was the word Latinised by the Romans and used by them as a designation for the country? The name which the Gael to this day apply to their country is Gaeltachd or Cael-doch (the Celtic pronunciation of G is like our K and the Latin C, so that Gael and Celt, originally the same, are within a "t" of being pronounced alike), and if you soften the doch of the Celt into the Latin donia, you have Caildonia, the country of the Gael or Kelt.

In the year 128 A.D. the Gael were visited by Lollius Urbicus, who built a wall from the Clyde to the Forth. In 183 they broke through this wall, killed their commander, and pillaged the Ro-manised Lowlands; but retired before Ulpius Marcellus. In the beginning of the reign of Severus, the Gael broke into the sub-dued territory again, but were prevailed upon to retire either by the army or the money of Virius Lupus. Another invasion which they made in 207 A.D. so roused the Emperor Severus that he came to Caledonia, determined to conquer and punish the restless enemies of the Empire. As far as conquering was concerned his journey was unsuccessful; he, however, over-ran their country into the far north, without meeting them to bestow the intended pun-ishment. To the empire the results of this excursion to the High-lands were the advantages for the time of its bracing air, the loss of 50,000 Romans, and a treaty of peace. The value of this last item may be learned from the fact that it was scarcely secured when it was broken. The Gael soon showed that neither walls, treaties, nor the august presence of the Roman Emperor were enough to keep them in check, which so enraged that personage that he ordered his son Caracala to renew the war with the utmost severity. Instead of obeying the commands of his late father, that prince entered into a treaty with the Gael, remitting to them the land taken by his father, and yielding up all the forts that he had built in Caledonia. A hundred years pass before we have any notice of the Gael again. At the end of that time the Emperor Constantus Chlorus came to the island to defend his British sub-jects from the incursions of the "Caledonians and other Picts," which he did, and the land had rest for forty years. In 342 A.D. a Caledonian invasion was repulsed by Constans, the son of Con-stantine the Great. About this time the name of the Gael is changed from Caledonians to Picts and Scots; and the Picts are divided into Deucaledones, or Di-caledones, and Vecturiones. The word Picti means in Latin painted—painted men; and every one knows that it was appropriate. Scot was not, and is not, the acknowledged name of the Gael. In Celtic it means contemptible,

and a similar word, *Scuit*, signifies a wanderer.   It seems to have
been given them by their sneering cousins of Pictavia.   A Gael
would think of calling himself a Chinaman as soon as a Scot, if he
knows no language but Gaelic : he calls himself "Gaël," or "Albannach," *i.e.* a Celt or Briton.   Deu-caledones was a northern or
genuine Caledonian.   And Vecturiones (in Gaelic, *Uchdtireans*)
seems to denote inhabitants of the upland country, or of the
Grampians, which are called the ridge of *Uachdtir.*   These two
divisions occupied the east of Scotland, while the Scots dwelt in
Argyle and the west.   In 360 A.D. these divisions of the Gael
formed a treaty to drive the Romans from Britain.   In 364 the
allies, being joined by the Saxons and Atticoats, renewed their
attack on Roman Britain, which they over-ran as far as London,
when Theodosius was sent to repel them.   In 398 and 416 the
war was renewed, but the Romans remained in Britain until the
year 446 A.D., when they left it for ever, leaving the Britons to
the tender mercies of the Gael.   The Britons invited the German
Saxons to help them ; but when the latter came, they formed an
alliance with their enemies, in conjunction with whom they drove
the Britons into the west, to Strathclyde, where for some time
they maintained their nationality and independence.

In 503 a great emigration from Ireland took place.   Though
they spoke a slightly different dialect from the Picts, their language
was mainly and fundamentally the same, as it was well-known
their religion was.   The country which the Scots inhabited now
was the whole west of Scotland, from the midland ridge, called
Drumalbin, to the sea, bounded on the south by the Firth of
Clyde.   For nearly four hundred years these two kingdoms existed
separately, and frequently in hostility to each other.   In the beginning of the fifth century the southern Picts were converted to
Christianity by St Ninian, a British ecclesiastic.   It is thought
that the Scots were Christians before their emigration to Scotland
in 503 A.D., but their great evangelist was Columba, who came to
their country in 563.   It was by him that the northern Picts were
brought over to the true faith : Columba having paid a visit to
Brude, Bridei, or Brudæus, the Pictish king at Inverness, he
succeeded in convincing the king, his court, and finally the people,
of the truth of his doctrines.   This king was engaged in many
wars, especially with his neighbours, the Scots of Dalriad, whose
king he defeated and slew in 557.   St Columba died in 597,
during the reign of Aidan, King of Scots, who was anointed
king by the saint himself.   After several wars by the Picts and
Dalriads, in which the latter generally had the worst, a more
powerful, and, to the Picts, a more disastrous foe appeared in
North Britain, in the Viking, or Norse pirates, who infested the

seas and shores of Northern Europe. The country of the Scots were less inviting to these rovers, or the possessors were more vigorous in repelling invasion, for the Vikings carried on a longer and more determined war against Pictavia. An arduous and bloody struggle ended in the total defeat of the Picts, and the death of their king and many of their chiefs. The eastern kingdom being thus weakened, the ambitious designs of Kenneth Macalpine, the Scottish king, succeeded. By a previous intermarriage of the royal race of both kingdoms, he had a shadow of a title to the Pictish crown, but as the "tanister," or heir-apparent, had been appointed, according to the custom of the Gael, during the life of the previous monarch, it was after a sharp conflict of three years that (843) he obtained his desire. The Picts and Scots being but one race, speaking the same language, amalgamated so readily that in little more than a century afterwards no distinction could be made between them. The Court was now removed from Dunstaffnage, in the country of the Scots, to the Pictish capital. After a war with the Danes, in which the now united Gael were assisted by the Saxons, for some uncertain cause, Caledonia was invaded by their late allies, the Saxons. In return Constantine III. prepared for a gigantic invasion of England. In conjunction with the Britons, Danes, and Welsh, he entered the enemy's territory ; but after sustaining a serious defeat he retired to his own dominions. In 973 the British independence of Strathclyde fell, and was incorporated with the Scottish kingdom.

Ever after the reign of Malcolm Canmore (1057), by the numerous settlements of Saxons and other foreigners, the history of the Scottish government becomes less and less that of the Gael. In his reign the Gaelic was superseded as the Court language by the Saxon, and as far as he dared he introduced Saxon laws, manners, and customs. This state of affairs was sharply counteracted during the brief reign of Donald Bane, the best Scottish king (1093). But on the Scoto-Saxon race resuming the government, the tide of Saxon civilisation and enervating luxury flowed on again. About 1160, the Scots of Galloway, disgusted at the introduction of Saxon manners and the favour shown to Anglo-Norman adventurers, raised a formidable insurrection. Malcolm IV. led his army against them ; but he was twice defeated and driven back. He was successful the third time, and peace was procured. About the same time the Moravians of the Province of Moray rose "in support of their native principles and in defence of their ancient laws." It was not till after a long and fierce struggle that they were suppressed. Some think that at this time the chief families of Moray were transplanted to other parts of the kingdom, and some of the king's foreign protegés placed in their room. Incensed at these intrusions, the Gael of Moray and Ross again took up arms and drove the foreigners from their districts. From 1171 to 1187 the Highlands were in a perpetual commotion. To restore quietness, William, the then king, marched north and encamped at Inverness; but this tour fell short of the intended effect, and from this time local feuds and anti-Saxon rebellions were carried on almost incessantly until the time of Wallace, who is supposed to have been a Celt; and hence his bitter hatred to the English and his popularity with the humbler classes. With few exceptions, the Gael all rallied round the standard of Bruce, though the Lowland barons opposed him; and it was mainly by the assistance of the Highlanders and Islanders that he gained most of his battles, and especially the battle of Bannockburn. In 1411 the petty wars of the Continental Gael were thrown into the shade by a gigantic rebellion or invasion by Lord Macdonald of the Isles, who with 10,000 Hebrideans burst upon the mainland, spreading desolation wheresoever he turned. Having defeated a party of natives, under Angus Dubh Mackay, at Dingwall, Macdonald marched to Inverness, where he was joined by several Highland chiefs. He then marched towards Aberdeen, which he threatened to burn to the ground; but his march was checked at Harlaw by the Earl of Mar. Under the banner of Mar, besides Normans and Southrons, were the Maules, Lesleys, Murrays, and other clans; while Mackintosh, Maclean, and many others, sided with the Island prince. The Lord of the Isles and his Highlanders began by an impetuous charge, but were met with adequate firmness and courage, and when, after fighting for hours, night put an end to the work of death, 900 Highlanders lay dead on the field; while on the other side, the Provost and citizens of Aberdeen, and many men of rank and distinction, had fallen, none surviving but the Earl of Mar and a few soldiers. When the battle was over, Macdonald gathered his men and returned home, without pursuing his course any further, much to the relief of the Lowlanders, who considered this deliverance of greater consequence than even the battle of Bannockburn. This event is celebrated by the well known ballad, the "Battle of Harlaw," itself an interesting item in Celtic literature and history.

> " There was not sin' King Kenneth's days,
>   Sic strange, intestine, cruel strife
> In Scotland seen, as ilk man says—
>   Where monie likelie lost their life;
>   Whilk made divorce tween man and wife,
>   And monie children fatherless.
>   And monie a ane will mourn for aye,
>   The brime battle of the Harlaw."

THE FIRST ANNUAL ASSEMBLY.

In giving an account of this re-union, we shall avail ourselves largely of a report presented to the Society by the Committee to whose management the affair was entrusted. That Committee consisted nominally of all members of the Society residing in Inverness. In terms of a resolution passed at a meeting of the Society on the 2d May last, the first Annual Assembly was held in the Music Hall of our ancient capital on the 11th July, the eve of the Wool Market, and carried through in a manner highly satisfactory not only to the members, but to all who desire to cherish the genuine feelings of Highlanders. It is well, however, to record some of the difficulties which had to be overcome. A drama in which Highlanders were to appear in character was new even in their own capital, and persons otherwise qualified were embarrassed by their own diffidence. Singers, players, and dancers had to be sought for in distant places, and even when they had been engaged, there were casualties to be feared and provided against. The task will be easier, however, another time, and less hazardous, as competent *dramatis personæ* are now known in sufficient numbers, and the diffident will have acquired confidence from the proof which they now possess of their own abilities, and from the marked appreciation with which their performances were received by the large and intelligent assembly which did honour to the occasion. Even some of the Committee had more or less of trepidation. They were going to face prejudices which had been fostered by time and by many-headed power in high places : were they equal to the task of organising a demonstration and aided by genuine Highland feeling and sentiment, which would turn the strong tide—inimical to everything of the kind—which had been flowing northward for more than a hundred years, and which had well-nigh extinguished the Celtic flame in the bosoms of such of our clansmen as had not been swept from their native straths and glens to make room for Southern sheep and Anglo-Norman sportsmen ? After the fact, we do not hesitate to state that they were equal to the task. A programme, rich and varied, was prepared, and if it erred at all, did so in the direction of excess. This, however, was rather fortunate, seeing that the fears as to non-arrivals proved too well founded. But so heartily did every one enter into her own and his own part, that no sign of failure or of difficulty appeared in the execution. But whilst claiming so much for our first Assembly, we do not convey that there are not higher reaches of excellence to be attained on another occasion; such improvements may be made as to give the piquancy of novelty and originality to what will really be a reproduction of the things of other days. What is true to nature, and what affords utterance for the feelings which well up from within a noble people, is always fresh, however old, and the thoughts which crystallise around such feelings are gems of undying worth, even if for a time they suffer neglect under the Vandal influences which greed sets up for its own ends.

With the view of setting forth the advantages of membership, the Committee, in framing the charges, decided to admit all members free. That this was judicious is proved by the fact, that not only did the members add considerably to the receipts by bringing their friends, but considerable additions were made to the Society during the inteıval between the announcement and the holding of the Assembly. We would here give some record of the proceedings. In the main entrance to the hall, Pipe-Major Maclennan and a young pupil of his, Fraser, played together with Corporal Campbell, of the 4th Inverness H.R.V., whilst the Assembly was forming. When the hour for commencing arrived, and the hall seemed occupied by about a thousand people, the pipes were hushed, and our worthy Chief Magistrate, Dr Mackenzie of Eileanach, took the chair, in the unavoidable absence of our first Honorary Chieftain, Sir Kenneth Mackenzie of Gairloch. The Provost was supported by Professor Blackie; Rev. Mr Stewart, Nether-Lochaber; Rev. Mr Macgregor, Inverness; Dr Carruthers; Colonel Macpherson of Cluny; Sheriff Macdonald, late of Stornoway; Bailie Simpson; Mr Dallas, Town-Clerk; Mr Macdonald, Druidaig; Mr Cumming, Allanfearn, &c. The Provost expressed regret that his nephew, Sir Kenneth Mackenzie, who was to have taken the chair, was unavoidably absent, but he could assure them that Sir Kenneth would have been delighted to attend, and would do all he could for the Gaelic Society, or for anything connected with the Highlands. For his own part, too, the Provost said, he was animated by the same spirit; his heart was always in the Highlands, and would most willingly do anything that could promote their welfare. To be sure he was among the youngest members of the Gaelic Society; but his constant engagements might excuse him for being to some extent a defaulter; and besides, it was only a few days ago that he was asked to join the Society. Referring to its objects, he observed that one of them was to keep up the Gaelic language; and he was not sure if that had been the sole object that he could have approved of it so much. He was quite satisfied, however, as to its being an ancient language. What was the meaning of the word Sanscrit but just *seann sgriobhadh*, "old writing?" Then as to the other objects of the Society, such as perfecting the members in the use of the Gaelic tongue;

preserving the poetry, music, and literature of the Highlands; forming a library of books and manuscripts; advancing the interests of the people educationally and otherwise, the Provost expressed cordial approval. Referring in detail to the objects of the Society as laid down in their published constitution, he mentioned an old Gairloch bard who used to sing the hunting of the brown boar of Diarmid, and others of Ossian's poems. Even in the present day a great part of the evenings of the country people was passed in telling old stories round their cottage fires; and perhaps they were just as well employed in this way as if the time were spent at the opera or in the ball-room. It appeared from a short report handed him by the Secretary that the Society was established in September last, and now numbered 120 members; and he hoped the number would be increased very much by the proceedings of that night. He promised to give the Society such support in future as his numerous other engagements would permit, and as an earnest of what he hoped yet to do for so patriotic a body, he presented the Society with a handsome gift, a copy of the Old Testament, one of the first ever printed in the original Gaelic type, and part of which from some cause had been transcribed by an unknown hand, evidently very long ago.

Mr D. Macrae, who came all the way from Lochalsh to help us in our adventure, and who received no previous notice or time for consideration, was called upon to fill the place of another. He may be said to have broken the ice which had formed over so much of what was specifically Gaelic in our midst, by singing *"Failte dhuit, deoch slainte leat,"* which he did in excellent taste and spirit. "Hurrah for the Hielans" was then sung by Mr James Fraser, a well-known local vocalist; so well did he acquit himself that he was recalled, and in reappearing sang, " When the kye come hame." Messrs Smith, Mackintosh, Gordon, and Grant—the two latter from Strathspey—followed up with *Ruidhle Thullachain*, to the music of the great Highland pipes—in which they gave universal satisfaction. The Bard of the Society, Mr Angus Macdonald, then came forward, and gave one of his sententious compositions, the subjoined prize poem, in celebration of the achievements of his compatriots in the Crimea, under the renowned Lord Clyde :—

GAISGE NAN GAIDHEIL ANNS A CHRIMEA.

Canam dan mu euchd nan sonn
' hoisinn cliu le'n glonn thar chach,
Thug anns a Chrimea buaidh.
A dhaindeoin cruadal bhuail nan dail
 Bhagair ar eascaird eitidh, *borb*,
Math-ghamhuinn garg nah-Airde-tuath :
Le foill is foirneart, mar a chleachd,
Umhladh is creach thoirt uainn.

Ghlaodh Breatuinn le sgal buaidh
Gaisgich luath nan tuath bheann,
Armailt bhreacanach nam buagh
Chuireadh namh air ruaig na dheann.
"Tairngibh," deir is, mo chuileanaibh garg,
Ri aghaidh nuar. nan garbh bheisd ;
Reubaidh na leomhainn na'm fearg,
Nan spoltan dearga, siol na ceilg.

Mʌr bu dua*l* da suinn mo ruin,
Dearbhaidh iad an cliu 'sa bhlar ;
Ciosnaichear uamhar fo' smachd ;
Bidh sith is reachd a teachd o's aird.
Shiubhail na fir mheanmueach mhor
Le'm brataich sroil, a' snamh 'sa ghaoth
O'n teicheadh luchd miruin fo gheilt
Le trom oilt, mar bheachain maoth.

  Faic na iuil air thus na feachd.
Dreuchd a chleachd an gaisgeach agh,
Laoch oirdbearg nan treun bheairt,
An Caimbeulach bu neartail laimh.
Curaidh seolta, stolt. gu'n mbeang ;
Cosgarach an shrith na'n lann ;
Fo' mbire-chath le piob nam pong
Cath cheol meadhrach 'thir nam beann

  Fhad sa shiubhlas grian 'sna speur,
Ag eiridh o ear gu iar,
Bidh' cuimhn' air na curaidh chalm,
Rinn aig Alama, a' mor ghniomh.
Tharuing na laochraidh bhras,
Ri sreath mharbhtach, mhiltean dos :
Direadh an uchdaich chas,
Bu lionmhor connspon chaidh gu ch*l*os.
B-oillteil again nan ar   *ŋ̃ʔ·ᵉ·ⁱ'n*
Roimh' lamhach na cuilibhear gleust ;
Sleaghan cruadhach o'm barr,
Torchur an namb ri feur.
Lannan liomhta au duirn dheas,
Nan ceannard bu mhoraich cneas ;
Ga'n tarruing le feirg o'n crics,
Beumach, lotach, geur gu sgrios.

  Mar ghreadh chabrach fo throm fhiamh,
'S gadhair luthmhor dion nan lorg,
Theich na Rusaich fo mhuig,
Am fuil a smuideadh air an leirg !
Na mar sgapas osach dhion,
Ri aghaidh nan sliabh an ceo,
Theich naimhdean air gach 'aòbh,
Na dh'fhaod a dhol as dhiu beo l

Aig Balaclabha bhuail na seoid,
As ur 'sa chomhraig ghàrg,
Dhearbh Cataich mo ruin,
An duchas sa chomhstri gharbh.
Mar sgaoth chuileag o chairbh lobht,
Ag eiridh roimh sgiursadh slait,
Theich borbaich fo' throm gheilt,
Roimh threun-fhir na'm breacan datht.

  Aig daingneachd laidir na mur,
Ri seisdeadh nan tur ard,
B-fhurasd ri fhaicinn's·ɑ uair   *ᵓ∫ a*
Nach d-fhuair sibb ceartas mar chach
Cha bu chothrom an' shrith a bhlair,
Thug don' ghaisridh bas gu'n toirt ;
Ach doinionn, is dumhlachd sian
Eugail, piantan,.plaigh, is goirt.
Mo chreach-a-leir, mar dh-eirich dhuibb ;
Co nach dean ϙaoidh ri'r cas ?   *ℰɑⱱ*
Na gaisgich a b-allail gnuis,
Mar bhruidean a dol gu bas.
Slainte do ar Ban-righ ghraidh ;
'S-don' flaithibh ard, tha'n Glasgho cruinn,
A chumail air chuimhne gu brath,
Biuthas Ghaidheal anns gach linn.
O thus tha riaghladh thar gach sloigh
A Righ mhoir dha buin gach ni,
Cum ris na Gaidheal coir.
'S bi d-uachdran leo air muir, 's air tir.
Eireadh grian le sar ghloir,
A sgapas na sgleo an cein.
Biodh Gaidheal a deanamh reir,
'Stoitt aoraidh do Dhia da reir,
Na'n dion da Morachd, 's da crun,
San cuis an ducha seasamh cruaidh.
Luchd drocb-bheairt a gabhail sgath,
Ri ainm a Ghaidheil a luaidh !

  Gabhadh ar n' uachdarain speis
Do chainnt, 's do bheus an aitim fhiu ;
Ga'n riaghladh le coir, is ceart,
'S do Thriath nam feairt an uile chliu l

Mr C. S. Grant and his aids followed with a selection of Scottish airs, Strathspeys, and reels on the violin, in fine style, and with genuine Celtic feeling.   These stirring appeals to the feelings were followed by an eloquent appeal to the understanding, from that true Highlander, the Rev. Mr Stewart of *Bailechaolais*, known and valued by so many Highlanders as the Nether-Lochaber correspondent of the *Inverness Courier*.   Mr Stewart was greeted with hearty plaudits on rising, and during the following speech was very frequently interrupted with applause.   Mr Stewart said :—

  I am very glad, I assure you, Mr Chairman, to be present here this evening as a spectator of, and so far a participator in, this the first Annual Festival of the Gaelic Society of Inverness.   When Mr Mackay, your excellent Secretary, first wrote to me, with an earnest request that I should be present this evening and give an address, I felt that I should come; but then arose some doubt and perturbation of mind as to what I should speak about—as to the subject-matter of discourse, as we clergymen say.   I was afraid of being called *piobair an aon phuirt*, that is, "the piper with the one tune."   Once on a time, a man down yonder on our West ·

Coast, took it into his head to learn to play the bagpipes; and he did learn to play one tune, a very good tune too, and he played it uncommonly well, as was admitted on all hands; but then he could play none but itself, and he played it so often, so incessantly indeed, that the people of the district got quite disgusted with what was once a favourite " quick-step," and the unlucky amateur soon got to be called in derision "the piper with the one tune," a title that stuck to him till his dying day, and from its pith and point is to this day a proverbial saying among the people. " But surely," my friends may exclaim, "*you* can play more than one tune." Well, yes, no doubt I can ; I have played a good many tunes in my day, as many, perhaps, as most men; but then, you see, for a dozen or more years I have been so constantly playing them in the Nether-Lochaber column of the *Inverness Courier* and elsewhere that it is on such an occasion as this almost impossible to hit on any one worth listening to that you have not heard me play once at least, if not oftener, in times past. Coming down by the steamer this afternoon, a gentleman on board, an American tourist I believe, who intimated his intention of being present this evening, and who, I have no doubt, *is* present, asked me what I was to speak about. "In your continental tour," was my reply, "did you happen to visit Spain?" "I did, Sir," he answered. "While in Spain did you happen to eat of their favourite dish, their 'olla podrida' ?" "No, Sir, I did not," was the response. "In France, then, did you taste their famous 'pot pourri' ?" "Never heard of it, Sir." "Since you have come to Scotland, then," we persisted, " have you ever happened to taste of our 'hotch-potch' ?" " Oh, yes ! " he eagerly exclaimed, "and a capital, first-rate dish it is !" " Well, then," I continued, " my speech this evening will be something of that sort, *de omnibus rebus*, you understand, and very good, and palatable, and heart-sustaining, I promise you, you will find it when the time comes." To nineteen-twentieths of this large assembly, Mr Chairman, I am a stranger. Most of you have very likely heard something of me, and may know me as a literary man whose writings you sometimes read, but very few indeed have ever seen me in the flesh before. I must, therefore, on the present occasion crave the kind indulgence of my unusually large " congregation." And after all, Sir, even if I only give you a dish of hotch-potch, here beside me on the platform is our friend, Professor Blackie, who is ready as he is able, and able as he is ready, to give you such a genuine dish of jolly good Scotch mutton as you have rarely tasted—spiced, too, and seasoned, take my word for it, in such wise as shall make you glad, in gastronomic phrase, to cut and come again. Of Napoleon, not the man of Sedan and Chisleburst, observe, but a very different man—him of Morengo, Auster-

litz, and Jena !—who, by the way, if he had appeared only for one
short week during the recent Franco-Prussia war, would have sent
the Germans hirpling and howling across the Rhine, as was his
wont—Emperor, Moltke, Bismarck, and all, precious quick too,
believe me, and to the tune of " Deil tak' the hin'most." Well,
then, of Napoleon it was said, and said truly, that his personal
presence on a field of battle was equal to a force of 30,000 men ;
and even so the presence of my friend Professor Blackie on such
an occasion as this, is equal to a whole presbytery or synod of
clergy.   I, therefore, gather courage from the presence of such an
ally, and proceed, promising, however, to be as brief as possible,
for your programme is a long and excellent one, and everybody
should have fair-play.   No one, Mr Chairman, could be more
pleased than I was when intimation reached me that such a society
as the Gaelic Society of Inverness had started into existence : it
was much needed, Sir; there was ample room for it ; plenty of
work to do ; and knowing what I know, and seeing what I see
to-night, I am convinced it will really do, as it has unquestionably
undertaken to do, good work—fostering patriotism among the
people, and the study and culture of our magnificent mountain
tongue and literature ; and I am further convinced, Sir, that this
Society will prove not something " born only to die " ; not transi-
tory and evanescent as the aurora borealis, our Northern Lights,
but fixed, steadfast, and abiding, and useful, let me add, Sir, as
the North Pole Star itself.   At first it was intimated to me that
this Society intended to establish a monthly Gaelic periodical,
and I at once consented to give all the help I could to securing
the success of such a praiseworthy venture.   Meantime, however,
another Gaelic magazine, " The Gael," originating in Canada, had
reappeared in sort of second birth in the city of Glasgow.   The
Gaelic Society of Inverness, on finding this to be so, acted, as I
think, with a great deal of good sense and good taste—they determined generously to give way ; to let their own venture,
though almost ripe unto the birth, meantime lie aside, so that "The
Gael " might have every fair-play and every chance of success.   I
hope "The Gael" will be well-conducted, will keep up to the mark ;
and meantime it is only right to say—and I am glad to be able to
say it—it promises well ; its past numbers giving earnest of better
things to come.   But should it be otherwise ; should its teachings
clash with the ecclesiastical or political views of its readers ; should
it in any such sense make itself a party organ, then in that case I
give fair warning—and I wish it to go forth that I say so—that
I shall not fail to use any little influence I may have with the
Gaelic Society of Inverness to induce them to have a periodical of
their own—a free and independent periodical, solely devoted to the

language, literature, and habits of the Gael. I have always observed, Mr Chairman, that on the first starting of "Highland,"
"Celtic," "Ossianic," and kindred societies, literature has a prominent place on their programme, but I have just as constantly
noticed that, through some misadventure or other, it has disappeared in practice—the cut of the kilt and the form of the dance
taking the place of it. I do hope that this will not be the case
with the Gaelic Society of Inverness. That the Society be not
idle in this direction, then, let me suggest that you get up a volume
on the folk-lore of the Highlands, having correspondents throughout the North and West Highlands and Hebrides, and gathering
grist for the common mill from every possible quarter. By folk-
lore—a word of comparatively recent importation into our language
from the German—I mean not the poetry or literature of recent
times ; nor do I mean the antiquities of our country, which is a
big word, having a very wide and comprehensive range indeed ;
but that branch or department of archæology which relates to the
ancient manners, observances, customs, usages, prejudices, pro-
verbs, riddles, incantations, and old stories of the old folk among
the common people. I am convinced that if you only set about it
in right earnest, you can get up a splendid volume on such a subject
—a volume, too, that will be a lasting monument of your diligence as
a Society, and of incalculable use in illustrating the past history of
our country, and doing for the Highlands something like the work
that the brothers Grimm have done for Germany. Many of you
cannot fail to recollect the magnificent passage, one of the finest in
the English language, in which Dr Johnson expresses his feelings
on first setting foot on Icolmkill, just a hundred years ago, wherein
he says, that "whatever makes the past, the distant, or the future
predominate over the present, advances us in the dignity of thinking beings." Now, while I would by no means advise you to
neglect or be indifferent to the present or the future, I would say,
Throw yourselves into the past : that is the field in which it
strikes me you should, at least in the first instance, become earnest
reapers. I have often remarked down yonder with us at Ballachulish, that Ben-Nevis, "monarch of mountains," in the distance,
and the mountains of Appin, Ardgour, and Glencoe around us,
never assume such an air of dignity and grandeur, never such an
aspect of might, and power, and *nearness*, as when in serene repose
they are but faintly, indistinctly, dimly visible in the fast-fading
twilight of a sun that has already set. Throw yourselves into the
past : you have no reason at all to be ashamed of it. No people
in the world can boast of grander memories, of more ennobling
traditions than you. If, down yonder in Lochaber, at fair or
funeral, at *mod* or merry-making, there is any appearance of mis-

conduct, the tumult is instantly quelled when some grey-headed
patriarch arises, and sternly reproves the peace-breakers in these
words—"*Bithibh siobhalt', fhuara'; Ged 'tha sinn bochd, tha sinn
uasal;*" that is—Peace, men! even if we are poor, we are of gentle
blood! If I ask a boy to go a message, I dismiss him with his
instructions and the parting admonition—"*Bi tupaidh 'nis; Cuimh-
nich air nu daoin' o'n d'haurig thu !*"—that is, Be smart now : have
a recollection about you of those from whom you are descended !
and with head erect and flashing eye, the little fellow is off like an
arrow from a bow, and would rather die than under such an in-
centive as *that* not perform his errand to the strictest, minutest
letter of his instructions. I wish you to foster and preserve this
feeling among the people. The more, believe me, you examine
into and ransack the past, the more reason will you have to be
proud of your ancestors. They were, in truth, a grand old race :
moral, I maintain, and high-minded, and brave beyond any other
people of whom I have any knowledge ; and depend upon it that,
having such intercourse with them as I suggest, even at this distant date, will make you happier and better men. Let me conclude, Mr Chairman, with a lyric, the finest, I take it, that has
appeared in our country for full fifty years, the composition of one
whom, while yet a young man, I had the honour to know well,
and whom to know was to love, the late Professor William Ed-
monstoune Aytoun, a colleague of our friend, Professor Blackie, in
the University of Edinburgh, and the son-in-law of the far-famed
" Christopher North " :—

> " Come listen to another song,
>   Should make your heart beat high,
>   Bring crimson to your forehead,
>   And the lustre to your eye :
>   It is a song of olden time,
>   Of days long since gone by,
>   And of a Baron stout and bold
>   As e'er wore sword on thigh
>   Like a brave old Scottish cavalier,
>   All of the olden time!

> " He kept his castle in the North,
>   Hard by the thundering Spey,
>   And a thousand vassals dwelt around,
>   All of his kindred they.
>   And not a man of all that clan
>   Had ever ceased to pray
>   For the Royal race they loved so well,
>   Though exiled far away
>   From the steadfast Scottish cavalier,
>   All of the olden time !

" His father drew the righteous sword
   For Scotland and her claims,
Among the loyal gentlemen
   And chiefs of ancient names,
Who swore to fight or fall beneath
   The standard of King James,
And died at Killiecrankie Pass,
   With the glory of the Græmes :
      Like a true old Scottish cavalier,
      All of the olden time !

" He never owned the foreign rule,
   No master he obeyed,
But kept his clan in peace at home
   From foray and from raid ;
And when they asked him for his oath,
   He touched his glittering blade,
And pointed to his bonnet blue,
   That bore the white cockade :
      Like a leal old Scottish cavalier,
      All of the olden time !

" At length the news ran through the land—
   THE PRINCE had come again !
That night the fiery cross was sped
   O'er mountain and through glen ;
And our old Baron rose in might,
   Like a lion from his den,
And rode away across the hills
   To Charlie and his men :
      With the valiant Scottish cavaliers,
      All of the olden time !

" He was the first that bent the knee,
   When the STANDARD waved abroad ;
He was the first that charged the foe
   On Preston's bloody sod :
And ever, in the van of fight,
   The foremost still he trod,
Until on bleak Culloden's heath
   He gave his soul to God :
      Like a good old Scottish cavalier,
      All of the olden time !

" Oh ! never shall we know again
   A heart so stout and true—
The olden times have passed away,
   And weary are the new :
The fair White Rose has faded
   From the garden where it grew,
And no fond tears save those of heaven,
   The glorious bed bedew
      Of the last old Scottish cavalier,
      All of the olden time !

The rev. gentleman resumed his seat amidst loud and prolonged cheering.

" Ho! mo Mhairi laghach " was then sung by the Misses Mackintosh, supported by Mr William Mackay, our worthy Secretary, and accompanied by Mr Morine on the pianoforte. Each verse was given first in Gaelic and then in English. It is but right to mention here that not only was this the first occasion on which the Misses Mackintosh appeared in public, but, to oblige the Society, they consented to sing without what they considered adequate preparation. Yet we but echo the universal voice when we say that they performed their part to the admiration and delight of all who were privileged to hear them. Of the song, one of the newspaper reports says truly, " Even to English ears the strains were sweet, and the words themselves musical in a high degree." Mr D. Taylor, one of our local vocalists, sustained his high reputation in singing " Prince Charlie's Farewell to Flora Macdonald " ; and one of our young townsmen, Mr A. Mackintosh, closed this, the first part of the programme, with " Gille Calum," with fine effect, to the music of pipes. The great pipes then struck up and discoursed their best under the masterly hand of Pipe-Major Maclennan, followed by Corporal Campbell and Fraser, whilst the assembly were partaking of fruit, cakes, &c.

The second part was opened by Professor Blackie, who most generously came all the way from the south of England to enjoy and help on the proceedings. On presenting himself the learned Professor received quite an ovation, as he so well deserved from a Highland audience, and, during the delivery of his address, was repeatedly interrupted with the most enthusiastic plaudits.

Professor Blackie said—Mr Stewart, in that admirable speech, had done him a great service or disservice—he had given him a good introduction, but at the same time had been guilty of sounding trumpets before him, which the Scripture said should not be done. He was to give them an address. Now, of all sorts and styles of speaking he had ever tried, an address was the most perplexing. If they wanted a sermon he could preach to them—if they wanted a song he could sing to them—if they wanted a lecture he could certainly lecture them—and if they came to hear him on Saturday night he would give them a lecture the length of a Highland sermon, that is an hour and a quarter. But how long an address should be, or what form it should assume, if not hodge-podge, he was very much puzzled to understand. But if ever he delivered an address with pleasure in spite of displeasure, it was on the present occasion. Being a mere south-country Saxon—an alien in blood and language—he certainly should not have been asked unless it were known that he loved the Highlands and the Highland people loved him. And to him the love and esteem of his fellow countrymen were more than all the power of all the politicians, and all the gold of all the millionaires. He would consider it a very high honour to be associated with the Society in this resuscitation of a grand national feeling that had too long lain dormant in this country. It was a very great mistake in past times to neglect our Celtic nationality, and its language, traditions, music, poetry. As Dr Johnson said, the most pleasant view to a Scotchman was the road to England; so the most pleasant view to a Highlandman had long been the road than led to a country which Rob Roy visited sometimes. All very well, but they should not neglect their own nationality. It could never be right to undervalue themselves, to trample upon their own traditions, to cast odium upon their own mother, to neglect the graves of their fathers. But now they made a public profession of something wrong done, and an earnest beginning of a right thing to be accomplished. They were all to blame, Celts and Saxons alike, and he did not know which was most to blame. Not one Highlander in a hundred could read or spell his own language. According to a witty saying, " Gaelic is a language which few can read, and which nobody can spell." Still, he believed the Saxons were more to blame than the Celts. The latter lived in a remote corner, and suffered wrongs of which he would not now speak particularly; while the Saxons were sitting in the comfortable South, having Highlanders to fight their battles at Waterloo and elsewhere, yet despising them, making them the subjects of shallow jests, laughing at them, just as an Englishman laughs at a Scotchman. What a set they were, laughing at one another, instead of engaging in scientific research, and seeking mutual sympathy and philosophical appreciation! Such men as Stewart, Armstrong, Maclauchlan, Mackenzie, and Skene had made a study of Celtic matters, but these were single names; and the philosophy of the Celtic language had been brought out more fully by the Germans than by any Scotchman. The life of Columba, who was an Irish Celt in the days when Scotch and Irish were all one, had been edited, not by a Scotchman, but by an Irishman. The object of the Society was excellent, and the Professor advised them not to despise popular wisdom, or the teaching of the Old Book, for the Comtes and John Stuart Mills, and the rationalism of London papers. The homely wisdom of the people, free from metaphysics and from the crooked ways of politicians, was true and honest, and was always intelligible—and that was more than he could say of the poetry of Robert Browning and many others. It had been said that reading Klopstock's Odes was like eating stones, and he thought the reading of a good deal of modern poetry was like eating thistles and brambles. The neglect of the Gaelic was a loss intellectually, morally, and socially. It belonged to the great family of tongues commonly called the Ayran, and to know

Latin and Greek thoroughly they should read Sanscrit or Gaelic—
no matter which. If people had an interest in old stones, and old
bones, and old urns, surely they should venerate the oldest language
of the human race, still a living language—one rich in illustration,
near to our living sympathies, and of practical interest and importance. The Gaelic language had characteristic peculiarities most interesting in reference to the organisation of human speech, and not
found in Sanscrit, or Latin, or Greek. Some of those peculiarities
opened up quite a new train of thought altogether. It had also
some fine sounds (which the Professor amidst some amusement tried
to bring out, with his hand to his mouth), and it was a great help
to the knowledge of Latin, Greek, German, and other languages.
He had himself traced 500 Greek roots to Gaelic. As an illustration of its affinity with the Greek, he took the well-known word
Clachnacudain, or stone of the tubs. *Clach* was the Gaelic for
stone, and in Homer they would find *laas,* signifying stone—the
initial *c* of the Gaelic being left out, and the *h,* as is not uncommon,
changed into *s.* Then for *cud* they had the Greek equivalent *cvot,*
signifying a round, bulging, hollow thing. But some of those
clever fellows in the South, who knew everything, asked what was
the use of studying a language that had no literature? Now, if
there was not a single book in Gaelic he would study it, because
it was the way to the hearts of the people. Better living men
and women than all the printed books in the world. But Gaelic
had the best kind of literature—the kind of literature that makes
Scotland what it is—the literature of songs, poetry, and national
music. This was of value, not to enable every clever fellow to
talk of all subjects and a few others, but in bringing out all the
noble sentiments of a people's heart, and in cherishing the noblest
memories; this was a literature that would do them more good
than all they could cram at the University of Edinburgh or under
the Education Bill. The greatest evil to them in the South was
that their national music was not made an indispensable part
of the national education. Next to the Bible he placed the
national songs for true, healthy teaching—fresh like the breezy
atmosphere, blooming like heather, rushing like mountain streams;
and making the blood beat in harmony with them. That was
better than clever leading articles. Latin and Greek were all very
well, but a man should be first what God made him, and his duties
were with his own people. Of course they must be fashionable—
that is, go to Italian operas in Edinburgh and London, and force
people to learn Latin and Greek, which they forget soon enough—
but don't learn your own mother tongue, which you suck in with
your mother's milk. People who went away in search of something grand, and did not learn the wisdom and philosophy of com-

mon things, would be shallow fellows to the end of the chapter, though crammed full and fringed round with learning. Touching on the moral and social aspect of his subject, the Professor quoted a saying of Jean Paul Richter, "The way to a woman's heart is through her child; the way to a nation's heart is through its language." And one people could not know another except through their language. The Saxons could certainly not be accused of loving the Celtic people too much. They sung Jacobite songs, but that was a matter of pure sentimentality; and many of them thought and said that the Celts should be stamped out and extirpated. Now, he did not think the Saxons would have spoken in that way if they had known the language of the Celts and their good qualities. They came down to stare at their mountains and glens, but they did not love the Celts, and see that no man turned them out of their glens. He did say that though there was a disease of over-population in some parts of the Highlands, that was no reason why there should be extirpation in any part of them. He spoke of no one personally; but if the country had been depopulated, one cause of that had been that those who held the land did not speak the language, and did not know the hearts of the people, did not care a straw for the people, but felt that they would have no poor-rates when the devils were away. If such thing had been —and he had good reason to suspect that they had—he repeated that the cause was this, that there was no sympathy between the holders of the land and the people who lived upon it; and there would have been more of that sympathy if the landowners had studied the language of a people of whom they ought to have been proud. Well, he had given very good reasons why the Gaelic should be preserved, and he was not bound to give an understanding with them. If they did not sympathise with him and with the Gaelic people, then he was very sorry for them, but thankful also that he was not cursed with the blindness of their intellects or the hardness of their hearts.

The Professor denounced in scathing terms those unpatriotic and time-serving newspaper writers who gave the sanction and the encouragement of their misleading articles to those who have weakened and disgraced the nation by banishing a noble and interesting race from their homes of freedom in the Highlands.

It is scarcely necessary to say that this address fanned and gave wise direction to the flames of Celtic enthusiasm which the previous proceedings had aroused, and gave the sanction of a cultured intellect and an honoured name to sentiments and feelings which many among us had hardly dared to avow until that night. The Professor's address was followed by a selection of airs on the pianoforte by the Misses Mackintosh; the Highland Fling by the four dancers already mentioned; and the "March of the Cameron Men," by Mr James Fraser.

Next came the Rev. Mr Macgregor, our warm-hearted townsman, with one of the most eloquent and pathetic addresses ever uttered in the expressive language of the Gael, in which he spoke. A perfect storm of applause greeted the rev. gentleman, and the delight and enthusiasm went on increasing as the discourse proceeded. Mr Macgregor said—

Ceaduichibh dbomh innseadh dhuibh gu'm bheil e 'na mhòr-thoilinntinn dhomh a bhi'n so an nochd aig a choinneamh so do "Chomunn Gailig Inbhirnis." Tha mi'g a mheas mar shochair nach beag, gu'n tugadh cuireadh dhomh gu bhi'n so. Tha mi duilich, gidheadh, gu'n robh an uine co goirid, agus gu'n tàinig mòran nithe cudthromach eile 'san rathad, air chor 'snach robh comas agam air briathraibh freagarrach a chur a'n altaibh a chéile, chum nan nithe sin a leagadh ris duibh, air am bu mhiann leam labhairt agus léudachach 'n'ur n-éisdeachd a nis. Ach bheir sibh maitheanas domh air son gach teachd-gearr agus neo-iomlanachd a bhitheas, tha eagal orm, tuilleadh's follaiseach anns na nithibh bu mhath leam a thoirt air an aghaidh aig an àm so. Tha'n Comunn airidh air mòr-chliù fhaotuinn air son an dùrachd. an éud, agus an deálasachd, ann a bhi tionaladh, a' dìònadh, agus a' gleidh-eadh gach nì mu chleachdanna, eachdruidh, ceòl, bàrdachd, lùth-chleas, càinnt, dillseachd, gaisge, agus tréubhantas na muinntir sin a dh' àrùicheadh ann an garbhlaichibh, gleanntaibh agus eileanaibh na h-Alba. Tha mòr-dhéigh againn nile air dùthaich ar breith. Cò 'n ar measg nach' eil air a dheacadh le h-aoibhneas-cridhe, an nair a smuainicheas e air "Tir 'nam beann 'nan gleann 'snan gaisgeach ?" Tha na Gaidheil nan sluagh còmharraichte air son liònmhorachd bhuaidhean. agus nithe éugsamhla, trid am bheil iad eadar-dhealuichte, agus air an cur air leth o gach cinneach eile air uachdar na tàlmhuinn. Tha iad 'nan sluagh a bha air an cŭmail fodha, air an sàruchadh agus air an claoidh air iomadh seòl agus dòigh air nach robh iad idir airidh ! Bha iad air an greasadh chum chrìocha cumhann, air am fògradh o ionadaibh agus aois-làraichibh an sìnnsear, air an ruàgadh mar chearcan-coille air na beanntaibh, agus air buntainn riutha air iomadh seòl nach do thoill iad. Gidheadh, faicibh fathasd an dìllseachd agus an deagh-thair-isneachd, an dean agus an deothas chum an ùmhlachd a nochdadh do na h-àrd-chumhachdaibh, o'n Uachdaran air an righ-chaithear, sios chum an rìoghlair a's illse 'na dhrēuchd ! Shuidhich lagh na dùcha seorsa do luchd-faire anns gach baile-beag agus sgiorachd 'nar tir, a ta 'g imeachd gu dìòmhanach o àite gu àite mu'n cùairt, luchd-drēuchd ma seadh, le'n cotaichibh fada gòrm, 's le'm bior-aidibh àrd, agus lc'n slachdanaibh stiàllach-buidhe, a chumail riagh-

ailt a'm measg nan Gaidheal, far nach robh aimhreite riamh gus an
tainig iad fein 'nam measg! Thubhairt mi gu'n robh na Gaidheil
bhochd air an sàruchadh, ach 'siad na nàimhdean a's miosa a bha
riamh aca, nàimhde neochiontach annta fein, na caoraich bhàna,
ainmhidhean a ta féumail gu'n teagamh, ach mo thruaidh! bu dona
air cùl claidheimh iad! Ach dh'aindeoin gach cruaidhchaise a dh'
fhuiling iad, c'àit an robh riamh saighdearan an cosmhuil riu!
Fhad's a bhios iomradh air gaisge agus téuchd ann an eachdraidh,
fhad's a bhios sgēul-aithris air fior-shaighdearachd agus tréubhantas,
bithidh sliochd nam beann ainmeil feadh gach linn air son gach
buaidh-làrach a thug iad a mach anns gach cearnadh do'n t-saoghal!
Co am measg shliochd nan cumhachdach, ann an tir eile fó'n
ghrēin a shamhlaichear riutha? Cha robh e 'nan comas an
cùlaobh a thionndadh aon chuid ri caraid no ri nàmhaid, agus ged
a bhiodh, cha deanadh iad e!—

> " Faigheadh cliu o gach rann-fhear,
> Gu ceolmhor 's gu binn,
> Na fior-shaighdearan Gaidhealach,
> Chaidh arach 'sna glinn ;
> Cuimir, fuasgailte, finealta,
> Slainteil 'sa chom,
> Fearail, ceansgalach, cruadalach,
> Treun agus trom!
> 'S math thig breacan an fheilidh,
> Gu leir do na suinn,
> Osain ghearr air an calpannaibh,
> Tha domhail, geal, cruinn,
> Iteagan dorcha air slios gorm uigheam cheann,
> Sud i eideadh 'nam blar,
> 'S cha b'i 'n te fhada theann.
> 'S ceart a labhras iad canain
> Na h-Alba o chian,
> Mar a bha i aig Fionn,
> 'S aig Oisean gu dian,
> Cha do ghluais chum na tuasaid,
> Is chaoidh iad cha ghluais,
> Gun am bolg-fheadan meur-thollach
> Fuaimneach 'nan cluais—
> Mar so buaidh leis na seoid,
> Ghuineach, gharg, agus bheo,
> Theid do bhuillsgein 'nan naimhdean,
> Mar a' ghaoth dol 'sa cheo ;
> 'S nar fheuch iad an culaobh,
> Do'n dream nach bi leo ;
> Oir cha striochd sliochd nan garbh-chrioch,
> Fhad's bhios annta an deo."

A GHAILIG.

Agus c'áit am bheil càinnt air thalamh a choimeasar ris a Ghailig? Canain a ta binn, blasda, oirdheirc, mar ribhinn gheamnuidh neo-thruaillidh, fhior-ghlan—

> " Cha gheill i do'n Eabhra,
> Do'n Fhrangais no Ghreugais,
> Do Laidin no Bheurla,
> No do chainnt fo na speuran."

Gu robb buaidh le Comunn Gaidhealach a bhaile so, a ta dol gu'n dùlan chum na Gailig a chumail suas, a' Ghailig eireachdail. Mar a thubhairt an t' Urramach Robt. Macgriogair ann a Cill-Mboire.—

> " Bh'aig Adhamh 's aig Eubha,
> Roimh fheum bhi air aithreachas,
> Mu'n do chiontaich iad a'n Eden,
> Gu'n eucail gun smal orra ;
> Air olc mu'n robh iad eolach, ·
> Gun choduch, gun ath orra,
> Do'n pheac' gun bhi ·nan ·traillean,
> 'Sa gharadh gu'n charuchadh.
> Leis na Gaidheal is doimheach
> Facuill choimheach,·
> Sud tha goimheach, guineach dhoibh,
> 'Steach nan obair, 'sa chainnt-thobair,
> Chaoidh cha·togar srath·chainntean ;
> Tha neo-stadach, sguabadh·chladach,
> S'bratach, slatach uile iad; ·
> 'Se'n ruith feadh cach a' cheile,
> An steigh tha 'ga cumail suas—
> A' chanain, a' chanain,
> A' chanain bha'n toiseach i ;
> 'Smar mor-chruaidh-chreugan ladir,
> A tamhsa biodh socaireach ;
> 'M feadh ghleusas slugan cail neach,
> Cha bhas is cha dochunn ,dith ;
> Ach bheir i mach buaidh-larach,
> Feadh ghabhanna 's dhosguinnean.
> 'S lionmhor gaisgeach a ta aice,
> Cumail taic is cothrom rithe,
> Agus caraid, le cruas daraig,
> Dol do'n charraig chogaidh dhi,
> Chum a dionadh anns gach pionadh,
> 'Schum a lionadh dh' fhocullaibh ;
> 'Smar lasair-chath an leirsinn
> Gu leir-sgrios smid dhochaireach."

Tha e taitneach a smuaineachadh gu'm bheil móran ùaislean foghluimte, duchasach, agus geanail, ullamh agus ealamh chum cuideachadh leis a Chomunn so a reir an comais. Tha Tighearna Chlùanaidh, " Mac Mhuirich Mór na brataich," gu cuimear, claidheach, criosach, gu aigeannach, briosgalach, baganta, le bhriathraibh milis, tuigseach, tla, chum an Comunn a neartachadh, agus bha 'gu bhi a'n so an nochd.—

> "An Ridire Coinneach Ghearloch,
>   A ghineadh o na h-armunn,
>   A rachadh sios 'sna blaraibh
>   Leis a Bhrataich, aluinn.
>   A bhuadhachadh 'san araich,
>   'Sa chur nan namh 'nan smur."

Gu cinnteach 's math lionas brathair athar 'aite anns a cha-thair, arduachdaran Inbhirnis, an Leighich Mac Coinnich 'san Eileanach. Gu ma fada slan e gu' bhith stiuradh aig gach cuirm agus coinneamh ann am priomh bhaile na Gaidhealtachd.

Ach cha bheag an t-urram a chuireadh air a Chomunn so, leis an Ard-fhoghlumach "Blackie" a bhi làthair! Fior-theangair, ealamh, deaschainnteach, agus aig am bheil mòr-spéis do'n Ghailig. Tha deagh-fhios aige-san g'm bheil a' Bhéurla thais agus éiglidh, air a deanamh suas, eadar bhun agus bhárr, eadar eárbull agus fheùman do chanainibh eile. Tha mór-mheas aig an duin'-uasal fhileant' agus fhoghluimte so, air.—

> "Homer binn tha deas-bhriathrach,
>   'Sair Virgil mor an t-Eadailteach;
>   Ach 'sann air Oiseau liath nan ceileirean,
>   Bu mhiannach leis 'bhi eolach."

Ach "gach dìleas gu deireadh," c'àit am bheil caraid ni's dèine agus ni's dealasaiche, 'nan t-aodhair cliùiteach "Lochabar Ioch-darach?" Seachduin an deigh seachduin, tha e a' cur a mach a sgriobhanna cumhachdach, a ta 'boisgeadh soluis, cha'n e mhàin air gach eún agus iasg, air gach ainmhidh agus meanbh-bheathach, air gach clach agus creag, air gach luibh agus preas, air gach rionnag agus réult ann an gorm astair nam spéur, ach mar an céudna, air cainnt agus cleachdannaibh nan Gaidheal! Cha'n 'eil sean-fhocal no sean-chleachd, no gniomh saobh-chràbhach, no toimhseachan, no seún, no giseag, o laithibh Ullin agus Oisein, gu ruig an lá an diugh, air nach 'eil e eolach, agus nach 'eil air an teasairginn leis. Saoghal fada agus deagh bheatha dha.—

> "O's gradhach, gur gradhach
>   O's gradhach an duine e;
>   Tha sgeimh is spionnadh cainnte,
>   Anns gach ni a chaidh chumadh leis."

Chùm mi tuilleadh's fada sibh a Chomunn ionmhuinn. Thugaibh maitheanas domh. Gu mo math thèid gach ní leibh, agus gu robh 'ur cáirdean dol a'n lionmhorachd, agus.—

> "Sliochd bhur sliochd is gach sliochd uathasan,
>   Feadh gach linn gu robh sluaghar is mor."

As if it were the lyrical outburst of the spirit in which the patriotic orator had just spoken, next came "An Ribhinn Aluinn,

Eibhinn, og," by Miss Mackay, Glen-Urquhart; Mr D. Mackintosh, Glen-Urquhart, and the Secretary. The song and the singing were not only a delight, but a surprise, and led captive hundreds there who understood not a word ; and the reception was an outburst of applause, which could not be exceeded in its warmth and cordiality. It is to the credit of Miss Mackay that it was only that same evening, and to fill the place of another, that she was impressed into our service. If anything had been wanting at this hour in the evening to dispel the ignorant conceit of some that ours was not a cultivated and artistic system of music, the work was now complete, and every one in that vast assembly raised a voice in attestation. Then came Pipe-Major Maclennan, as if to fill the volumes of applause still further, and filled the hall with one of his noble " Piobaireachds." This was followed by Mr R. Munro, with " My Nannie's awa." Mr W. G. Stewart then gave a most droll and yet characteristic personation of an unsophisticated Highlander on his first experiences of railways, policemen, and other novelties. Mr D. Taylor re-appeared, and gave " Flora Macdonald's Lament," and the four dancers wound up with a Scotch Reel.

This carried us to a very late hour, and although the enjoyment of the proceedings seemed to be unabated, it was deemed advisable to conclude. Votes of thanks were passed, first to the singers, players, and dancers, on the motion of Mr Dallas. Dr Carruthers proposed a vote of thanks to the strangers, and especially Professor Blackie and Mr Stewart, who had come so far to assist at the meeting of the Society; and a vote of thanks to the Chairman was proposed by Professor Blackie. As the Assembly rose to disperse, the note was struck of the National Anthem, rendered into Gaelic for the occasion by our Bard, Mr Angus Macdonald. The surprise was pleasing and the effect grand, as the choir proceeded with—

Dhia gleidh ar Banrigh mhor,
Beatha bhuan da'r Banrigh choir,
 Dhia gleidh 'Bhanrigh.
Thoir buaidh dhi, 'us solas,
Son' agus ro ghlormhor,
Fad' chum riaghladh oirnn' ;
 Dhia gleidh 'Bhanrigh.

A Thighearn ar Dia eirich,
Sgap a naimhdean eitich,
 'Us leig iad sios.
Cuir cli an droch riaghladh ;
Tilg sios an luib dhiabhlaidh
Ar dochas oirre leag :—
 Dhia gleidh 'Bhanrigh.

Do thiodhlaig mhaith thoir dhi,
Doirt oirre pailt gun dith,
 Fad' riaghladh i ;
Ar reachdan dionadh i,
Toirt dhuinn aobhar, gun sgios,
Bhi seinn le'r guth 's ar cridh',
 Dhia gleidh 'Bhanrigh.

With these strains still in their ears the vast assembly dispersed, not only greatly gratified with the entertainment, but with their desire whetted for another of the same. Altogether, we need not hesitate to place upon record, that this, our first Assembly, has been a marked success, whether we have regard to the nature and character of the entertainment to the manner in which it was conducted, to the reception which it met with from those who joined in it, or to that which makes its appearance in the financial statement of the Treasurer.

One of the immediate results of the first Assembly, is a large accession of members. What the ultimate effect of this exhibition of long pent-up feeling will be, it should not be difficult to say. That it will have a salutary effect morally, socially, and commercially on the whole community, we have no manner of doubt. But in order to this being realised to the utmost, the Society must keep firm possession of the vantage ground gained on the 11th July 1872 ; and must use that ground for further achievements. That members will be added is what may be expected from its getting abroad that the Society is a power in the land ; but the realisation of its highest objects will depend not so much upon numbers as upon the cherishing of true and noble Celtic feeling, and upon the manifestation of more or less of the ancient pride of race and ancestry which characterised our forefathers in their best days.

It has long been a low kind of fashion to contemn the Gael and his idiosyncrasies. It is evident already that we have done something to revive an opposite fashion. Since that Assembly numbers who had lost their Gaelic, whether they had mastered the English language or not, have been airing scraps of Gaelic, and ere long kilts and plaids, which have hardly seen the light since the '45, will be brought forth to show on what side the owners stand. So much for the sentiment.

Then, there is the asserting of Gaelic rights ; there is the resisting of Highland wrongs ; there is the duty of taking up the subject of the occupation and cultivation of our Highland glens and straths by Highland people ; there is the setting up of such other industries as are adapted to our capabilities. These things must be kept in view as claiming our sympathetic exertions ere long.

But there are objects to which we would recommend an immediate application of the social force generated by the first Assembly.

First, the formation of a class for the grammatical study of the Gaelic language.

Second, the obtaining of books and manuscripts (which are such preservatives of our ancient spirit), by gift if possible, by purchase if necessary. And towards this there should be a Library Committee appointed.

Third, the collecting of the unwritten lore of our race. For this also a Committee is wanted.

Fourth, we require to open amicable relations with kindred societies in other parts of Scotland, in Ireland, in England, in Wales, and on the Continent.

Fifth, the consideration of a Gaelic Bursary in one of our Universities.

Sixth and finally, we would urge the immediate publication of what we would call our first volume of transactions, embracing the Rev. Mr Mackenzie's inaugural lecture ; Mr Ross's lecture ; Professor Blackie's lecture ; a full report of the Assembly proceedings, and such other materials of permanent value as may be necessary and available to the completion of the work.

LECTURE BY PROFESSOR BLACKIE
ON NATIONALITY.

At an early period in the session, the learned Professor engaged to deliver a lecture for the Society. This he did in the Music Hall on Saturday, the 13th July, on occasion of his visit to attend the first Assembly, Eneas W. Mackintosh, Esq. of Raigmore, M.P., in the chair. The lecturer was also accompanied on the platform by Provost Mackenzie; Mr Waterston, banker; Dr Carruthers; Bailie Mackintosh; Mr Innes, solicitor; Mr Davidson, solicitor; Mr Rose, solicitor; and Mr Mackenzie, Broadstone.

Professor Blackie divided his lecture into several "heads" or parts—first, he would show what is a nation, and the difficulty of creating nationality; second, he would define wherein national greatness consists; and third, refer to our own position, inquiring how far Great Britain has realised the idea of nationality, and pointing out our peculiarities, our dangers, and our duties. That a nation should exist at all seemed at first sight miraculous. The tendency of the individual was to self-assertion; and when there was an infinite number of individuals, it created all sorts of antagonisms, which came into collision and sometimes ended, as among savages, in utter extermination. But how they should come together and act as a whole organic mass, just as one's eyes and arms act in connection with the brain, was one of the most wonderful things in this wonderful world. As illustrating the difficulty of creating nations and keeping them together, he quoted the history of the Hebrews, who were united only during the two reigns of David and Solomon; of the Greeks, who, in consequence of their divisions, fell first before the iron tramp of the Macedonians, and then of the Romans; of our own country, so long a prey to strife and faction; of France, built up out of several dukedoms, and attaining unity by despotism and corruption—a unity that for two hundred years presented a brilliant exterior, but without real concord; and now the result was obvious to the world. True, France had a unity of one kind, but not internal harmony; on the contrary, internal ferment, discontent, and uncertainty. With many elements of hostility existing, what were the forces that tended to

o

unify those diverse tendencies, and to produce nations? First, the
unity of PLACE, a territory well-defined and marked off, as Italy
by the Alps, America and Britain by the sea. And here he remarked that the natural boundaries of kingdoms were not rivers
but mountains; the natural boundaries of France was not the
Rhine, but the Ardennes and the Alsatian mountains. Another
unifying influence was facility of communication. Greece was cut
up into separate geographical pieces with natural bridges between;
Scotland was divided by the bulwark of the Grampians; America
would fall to pieces to-morrow were it not for railway communication, which enabled one thought, one feeling, to pulse through
the whole country. Next was a common LANGUAGE. That was
not essential to make a nation, but it was a great security; or if
not a common language, then some one dominant tongue. The
ready intercourse of soul with soul would facilitate the influence
of master minds, and tend to mould the mass to one type. Next
was a common inheritance of great intellectual and moral tradition;
and then what is called RACE. That was a most difficult thing to
define. He would not now enter into the problem how race was
produced. He did not pretend to know why a Skye terrier was
one thing, and a greyhound another—why a Frenchman was one
thing and a Scotchman another and a very different thing; why
a Celt in Scotland and a Celt in Ireland were different. Language,
education, religion, habit, had much to do with race: a few generations, he believed, would change a German into an Englishman,
or an Englishman into a Frenchman. A common RELIGION was
one of the strongest bonds of nationality. That made the Greeks
act together when nothing else could. As the conception of God
was the only idea that gave a central unity to any system of
thought called a philosophy; so religion, or the system of social beliefs and practices that attached itself to the name of the Supreme
Being in any society of human beings, was the firmest bond of
that unity by virtue of which society existed. A strong central
force was also necessary to prevent the natural tendencies of a
multiplied individualism. The natural tendency of DEMOCRACY
was individualism—every man as good as his neighbour, and perhaps better. MONARCHY was most favourable to unity; democracy
always tended more to resolve society into its original elements.
The mere idea of individual freedom, good in its place, never could
do anything either to create or to conserve society. It was the
idea of the subjection of a part to the whole—an essentially unsel-
fish idea—that made society possible. They knew as a fact that
great nations were always monarchical to begin with. Nations
were made by monarchy and aristocracy. WAR was another
unifying influence. What made the Scottish nationality? Bruce

and Bannockburn, Knox and the Covenanters. War was not mere savagery : war was heroism, war was manhood, war was independence. It united men in common struggles, common hardships, and common triumphs; and the brotherhood of struggle was always stronger than the brotherhood of luxury. If the blood of the martyrs was the seed of the Church, the blood of soldiers and patriots had not less certainly acted as the cement of society. Though he lamented as much as any one the late calamitous and sanguinary war, he was convinced that it would make the German a stronger nation than it could have been otherwise. Every petty State would have asserted itself—the Bavarian would have been a Bavarian, and the Saxon a Saxon; but engaging in a common struggle against the Franks made them Germans. Next, as a unifying force, the Professor mentioned PUBLIC SPIRIT, patriotism —acting for the good of the whole, not for the selfish aggrandise- ment of the individual. Not every man for himself, and for his own shop, or his own trade; but every man acting as part of a great social organisation. Next the lecturer proceeded to show that, to produce a great nation there must not only be central power, but VARIETY. Society was one; but it was composed of a vast number of individuals, and the individualism of these units must not be sacrificed. Society consisted in a free subjection of living individuals, not in the forced common action of the different parts of a vast living machine. Diversity was wealth and beauty, monotony mere meagreness. Strong central power on the one hand; on the other strong local centres of activity and local go- vernment. Excessive CENTRALISATION was the bane of France. And there should be room not only for variety, but for contrast and contrariness, and apparent incompatibility—a union arising out of the combination of things that tend to disunion. The balance of two opposites was perfection—therefore, marriage was the perfection of human nature. The mind of the poet was greater than the mind of another man, because he unites the masculine intellect with the emotion and tenderness of woman. He proposed for acceptance the following proposition—". When all the elements of which society is composed, that is site, population, physical strength, intellectual force, moral nobility, act together under the strong and steady control of all the unifying forces, in such a manner as not to prejudice energetic individualism, and local variety, in this case we have as a product national greatness; and that will be the greatest nation in which these elements are com- bined to the greatest extent, and in the greatest intensity." Now, how far had Great Britain realised the idea of NATIONALITY ? He thought we ought to be thankful to Providence that we had to a greater degree than any nation in history a combination of unify-

ing forces with intense and energetic individualism.   Summing up
our advantages, he spoke of our favourable situation with the sea
around us—that silver streak of which Mr Gladstone was sometimes too fond of speaking—our great physical resources—iron,
coal, &c. ; our climate, favourable for the growth of a good human
animal, with vigour, pluck, coolness, pertinacity—the benefit of a
hereditary monarchy and a manly aristocracy.   If we could throw
these overboard and make a better business of it he should be surprised ; but he would be in Tomnahurich long before that occurred.
Then we had the benefit of a common faith (no doubt with a difficulty in Ireland).   And along with all this, look at the variety in
unity—three peoples in one nation, Scotch, Celtic, English, with
their separate types, language, traditions, and character.   What was
more different than Dr Guthrie, with his strong Scotch character,
and the gentleman with cope, cassock, and bells, in an English
ritualistic church !   He rejoiced in the difference.   He did not
believe in copes and cassocks, but he believed in variety of type
and form in the Church of God; and if certain ladies could not feel
pious except when they knelt on silk cushions and the priest was
decked up in a certain way, by all means let them be indulged.
Then we had an intellectual character full of practical vigour and
sagacity, though, no doubt, in the southern part of the island deficient in subtlety, philosophy, and the power of speculation.   We
had also a character for honour, and truth, and manliness, equalled
by few nations, and assuredly not surpassed by any ; and if in
diplomacy we sometimes came short, it was not always through
ignorance and indifference to matters of foreign policy, but because
we were too honest and two honourable to suspect that we had to
deal with knaves and bullies.   But now to look at our DANGERS
and DUTIES.   In reference to nations as to individuals, nothing
was more dangerous than self-laudation.   If a young lady stood
long at the looking-glass, instead of reading her Bible in the
morning, depend upon it she was a fool—or at any rate she would
not be an honour to herself, and she would not be a beauty long,
because she would not possess a beautiful character.   Well, a great
nation must have a mass of population.   A small State might flame
out for a time, but it could not continue to be a great nation.
Now, our population was not so great in proportion to other European nations as it once was.   Secondly, coal and iron were not
inexhaustible, and besides, they were found elsewhere.   We could
not continue to manufacture for the world, for we were teaching
other nations.   Next, our cohesive forces were being weakened in
several ways, and our harmonies were becoming discords.   The
monarchical idea and principle was being weakened by theoretical
young politicians like Charles Dilke and others of that class.   He

repeated that he did not believe in DEMOCRACY. The United States were an experiment, and one made under peculiar circumstances ; but at any rate, it was one thing to build a new house and another thing to pull down an old one. Then we had a kind of social war between different ranks—very strong antagonisms, which, if carried on, might result in disaster. There were elements of revolution in this country at the present moment. Our moral force—and that was the main thing—was being weakened; and when a nation had lost its character what remained? The Romans became a prey to despotism because they lost their character. He asked them seriously to think whether, at the present moment, we were not undergoing some changes in our old steady, loyal, British character which were not favourable to a healthy moral tone. The love of money, the increase of luxury, the placing of our glory in outward magnificence and splendour— in gas, or steam, or telegraphs—these things had a tendency to put into the back ground, the grand element of moral force. The wealth of a nation consists not in what it has, but in what it is—not in possessions or wealth, but in character and nobility of sentiment. Individualism too strong ; too much eagerness to get on in the world, but not sufficient eagerness for the honour of the nation ; rather peace for our shops than war for our honour—these traits were becoming obvious. He thought we were too much Carthaginians and too little Romans. He wanted to see a noble people, living not for themselves and their families alone, not for mere buying and selling, but for the State to which they belonged. The religious force in the country was being weakened by worldly-mindedness and externalism ; by science without philosophy and divorced from piety. He honoured physical science, but it was a danger when without philosophy, and yet pretending to be philosophical—as if there should be any philosophy in mere microscopes and telescopes! Another danger arose from the increasing gulf between theological orthodoxy leagued with religious bigotry, and the general spirit of modern literature. Our local varieties, our municipal and provincial freedoms, were also in peril of being destroyed by centralisation and London red-tape, so that we who were men here before, with individual lives and hearts, were to be moved like so many chessmen by the authorities up yonder. Look at the Scotch Education Bill; he did not think we had acted nobly regarding it. He considered it a base, shabby, and low Education Bill, utterly unworthy of the ideas we inherited from John Knox and the Confession of Faith—a bill merely to put a smoothing iron on petty religious and church jealousies, but not a bill to elevate the schoolmasters or to elevate education. And now there was another project—to take away the Post-office from Edinburgh. Then they would take away the lawyers perhaps —then perhaps the Universities, and send all our young men to be drilled into Episcopacy at Oxford. He said these things were being done, and we had only to blame ourselves. He once had the honour of being laughed at by *Punch*—as wise men were always laughed at by fools—because he said in Glasgow that the Scotch wanted self-esteem... Now, he repeated, the Scotch did want self-esteem, otherwise they would never allow such things to be done. Take our national MUSIC as an example. He regarded national music and poetry as an noble inheritance of which people ought to be proud. Did they devote themselves to the study of Robert Burns as they ought to do? No—they preferred the Italian opera. What was the opera? A mere magnificent luxury for the ear, but nothing for the understanding and nothing for the heart. He ridiculed false gentility, with its worship of what was foreign and metropolitan. Next to John Knox and the Covenanters, the songs of Robert Burns and a thousand minor singers were the thing we most required. And speaking of the HIGHLANDS, he resumed the strain of his address of Thursday evening, and denounced the extirpation of peasantry from the glens. They would drive away the people and call it improvement. He had known those in the south who would wish to see the whole Highlands turned into one immense Tomnahurich, the Celts buried beneath it, and Saxon palaces piled on the top. This would be a very magnificent, a very selfish, a very despotic, and a very Russian way of governing free men and improving a country. There was a danger of losing that magnificent fellow the Highlander. Could any of the clubs of London turn out such a splendid animal? He wanted as many Highlanders in the Highlands as could be comfortably maintained there. He said there should be no extirpation—except in the way of weeding the turnips; weed but don't exterminate. In this matter proprietors and people had both duties to perform. The duties of a proprietor in the Highlands were quite plain. The wealth of a country does not consist in the number of guineas which found their way with the least amount of trouble into the landlord's pocket, but in the number of well-conditioned people whom, by his superior position in society, he was enabled to cherish, to protect, and to elevate. The landed proprietor was the Bishop of the district in secular matters ; and if he thought his only business was to get his rents paid, to spend them where he would, do what he would with his own, then he did not know his duties, and he was a selfish fellow. Observe, he was not speaking against proprietors generally, but supposing there was such a one in the lot, then these terms applied to him. A landlord, he would suppose, got £1000 from one big farmer, and there were no poor-rates and no trouble about it, and he went and spent that in London at the opera, or at worse places; or spent it in Paris, where it was a gain to France; or in Rome, where it was a gain to the Pope and a loss to us. Would it not be better if the same landlord got £800 or £900 from a number of tenants and spent it among them, than going away with his £1000 and doing with it what he liked? Yes, he might do what he liked according to the letter of the law. The law could not always keep hold of him; but the very constitution of society, and the eternal laws of society, commanded that he should attend to the place where God had placed him, and do his duty there. He (Professor Blackie) hoped they did not suspect he was a democrat; indeed, ever since his famous pugilistic encounter with Ernest Jones he was supposed to be a Tory. But that was not the case; he was not a member of the party who supported Mr Disraeli and passed the late Reform Bill. A Tory he defined as a man who never moves unless he is forced, and then moves too fast. He was neither a Tory nor a democrat, only a thinker, a student, and, in a small way if they pleased, a philosopher. That gave him a certain advantage. His business was to find out truth, to speak truth and justice; and except to do that he would not be there that night. But while he was not a democrat, he would bring in a very democratic kind of measure; he would impose an absentee tax, rewarding those proprietors who stayed at home, and making the fellows who go abroad pay all the poor-rates. Of course he did not object to young ladies going up to London to get husbands—or to the Duke of Argyll and others going, who had business to discharge; what he did object to was the practice of going and squandering money in the dissipation of London and Paris. For himself he was not a proprietor. No doubt he was a feuar, but it was only an acre and three-quarters. He was one of the public; and he considered the public had a duty—not to run after what was foreign, but to cherish self-esteem, to cultivate local independence, to make the most of what we have here. Far fowls had fair feathers—to fools. Let them preserve and maintain their right to *be* themselves. When an Englishman came to Scotland he expected to find a Scotchman—not a second edition of himself, an edition not enlarged and improved, but diminished, dwarfed, and degraded. When he came to Inverness he expected to find a Highlander, and he found him there—(shaking hands with the Provost, amidst loud laughter and cheers). Let them learn a lesson from the wisdom of the unreasoning animals, which were always right because they were always in the hands of God. What animals did unconsciously, let intelligent beings do consciously. Therefore, let the eagle glory in his wings, let the fish glory in his fins, let the hound glory in his swiftness, let the young

man glory in his strength, let the Celt glory in being a Celt, and
the Scotchman in being a Scot.   Otherwise, with all their civilisation, with all their newspapers, their leading and misleading
articles, with all their boasted advance in science, they would be
as flat and as dry as the sands of Brandenburg, as monotonous and
as unsightly as the interminable moors and morasses of Russia,
and as destitute of all vigorous forms of individual vitality as the
Dead Sea.

During the delivery, it is almost needless to say that the learned
lecturer was frequently interrupted by hearty expressions of applause.

The Chairman proposed a vote of thanks to Professor Blackie,
and took occasion to express his sense of the value of philological
studies, and the importance of Gaelic.   He thought that Gaelic
should be made a matter of study, and that a Professorship should
be established; but at the same time that it should be allowed to
die out as a spoken language, and give place to the English tongue.

Professor Blackie wished them distinctly to understand that
he had no desire whatever to foster artificially the Gaelic tongue.
Its natural destiny, like the Cornish, was to die; but while it
existed, he wished it to get fair-play, by being taught in the
schools, and he maintained that English was best taught when
taught in connection with the mother tongue.   He proposed a
vote of thanks to Raigmore for presiding, which was awarded,
and the meeting separated.

MEMBERS OF SOCIETY.

I. LIFE MEMBERS.

Cluny Macpherson of Cluny Macpherson.
Charles Fraser-Mackintosh of Drummond.

II. HONORARY MEMBERS.

Anderson, James, solicitor, Inverness.
Blackie, Professor, Edinburgh University.
Bourke, Professor, President St Jarlath's College, Tuam, Ireland.
Cameron, Captain D. C., Talisker.
Carruthers, Robert, jun., of the " Inverness Courier."
Colvin, John, solicitor, Inverness.
Davidson, Duncan, of Tulloch.
Davidson, Donald, solicitor, Inverness.
Ferguson, Mrs, Earnbank, Bridge of Earn.
Farquharson, Rev. Archibald, Tiree.
Fraser, Andrew, builder, Inverness.
Grant, General Sir Patrick, G.C.B., Muirtown House, Inverness.
Grant, John, timber-merchant, Cardiff, Wales.
Grant, William, Bellevue, Shrewsbury.
Grant, Robert, of Messrs Macdougall & Co., Inverness.
Innes, Charles, solicitor, Inverness.
Macandrew, H. C., Sheriff-Clerk of Inverness-shire.
Macbride. James, Cartbank House, near Glasgow.
Macdonald, Allan, solicitor, Inverness.
Macdonald, F., Druidaig, Lochalsh.
Macdonald, Alexander, Balranald, Uist.
Macdonald, Captain D. P., Ben-Nevis Distillery.
Macdonell, Patrick, Kinchyle, Dores.
Macdougall, Donald, Dunolly Cottage, Inverness.
Mackay, D., Holm Mills, Inverness.
Mackay, Charles, LL.D., Fern Dell Cottage, Boxhill, Surrey.
Mackay, John, Mountfields, Shrewsbury.
Mackay, Neil, Dowlais, Merthyr-Tydfil, Wales.
Mackay, James, Roxburgh, Otago, New Zealand.
Mackay, George F., Roxburgh, Otago, New Zealand.

Mackay, Donald, Gampola, Kandy, Ceylon.
Mackenzie, Sir Kenneth S., of Gairloch, Bart.
Mackenzie, Rev. A. D., Beauly.
Mackenzie, Colonel Hugh, Poyntzfield House, Invergordon.
Mackenzie, John, M.D., Provost of Inverness.
Mackenzie, Major Lyon, of St Martins.
Mackintosh, Eneas W., of Raigmore, M.P.
Mackintosh, Æneas, of Daviot.
Mackintosh, Angus, of Holme.
Mackintosh, Arthus P., Dowlais, Merthyr-Tydfil.
Macmenamin, Daniel, Warrenpoint, Ireland.
Maclennan, Alexander, of Messrs Macdougall & Co., Inverness.
Macpherson, Captain Gordon, of Cluny.
Masson, John, Kindrummond, Dores.
Neaves, The Hon. Lord, LL.D., Edinburgh.
Nicolson, Angus, LL.B., Editor of "The Gael," Glasgow
Ross, Angus, 11 Jane Street, Blythswood Square, Glasgow.
Ross, John Macdonald,   do.   do.   do.
Scott, Roderick, solicitor, Inverness.
Shaw, A. Mackintosh, General Post-Office, London.
Stewart, Charles, of Brin and Dalcrombie, Inverness.
Stoddart, Evan, Burundalla, Sydney, New South Wales.
Sutherland, Alexander, C.E., Cefu, Merthyr-Tydfil.

III. ORDINARY MEMBERS.

Baillie, Bailie Peter, Inverness.
Bannatyne, W. Mackinnon, Royal Academy, Inverness.
Barclay, John, accountant, Inverness.
Black, George, of Thornhill, Inverness.
Blue, William, Stronvar Lodge, Campbeltown.
Cameron, Donald, of Lochiel, M.P.
Cameron, Archibald, Lintmill, Campbeltown.
Campbell, Donald, Bridge Street, Inverness.
Campbell, Alexander, 13 Grant Street, Inverness (deceased).
Campbell, G. J., writer and notary public, Inverness.
Campbell, Angus, Dalintobair, Campbeltown.
Campbell, T. D., Ness Bank, Inverness.
Campbell, William, 68 Castle Street, Inverness.
Carmichael, Alexander A., Lochmaddy, Uist.
Cooper, William, Highland Railway, Inverness.
Dallas, Alexander, Town-Clerk of Inverness.
Darroch, Rev. John, Portree.
Davidson, James, solicitor.
Davidson, Lachlan, banker, Kingussie.

Falconer, Peter, Dempster Gardens, Inverness.
Forsyth, W. B., of " Advertiser," Inverness.
Fraser, Miss, Farraline Villa, North Berwick.
Fraser, A. R., accountant, British Linen Bank, Kingussie.
Fraser, James, C.E., Inverness.
Fraser, James, Church Street, Inverness.
Fraser, Alexander, 16 Union Street, Inverness.
Fraser, Alexander, solicitor, Inverness.
Fraser, William, jeweller, Inverness.
Fraser, William, founder, Inverness.
Fraser, Hugh, Inspector of Poor, Inverness.
Fraser, Huntly, merchant, Inverness.
Fraser, Andrew, upholsterer, Inverness.
Fraser, Alexander, with Messrs Macdougall & Co., Inverness.
Fraser, Simon, banker, Lochcarron.
Gollan, John Gilbert, of Gollanfield.
Grant, Alexander, Church Street, Inverness.
Hood, Miss, 39 Union Street, Inverness.
Hood, Andrew, 39 Union Street, Inverness.
Kennedy, Donald, Drumashie, Inverness.
Macgregor, Rev. Alexander, Inverness.
Macdonald, John, The Exchange, Inverness.
Macdonald, Robert, teacher of Gaelic, Inverness.
Macdonald, Alexander, Newmarket, Inverness.
Macdonald, John, officer of Excise, Lanark.
Macdonald, James, 14 Union Street, Inverness.
Macdonald, Angus, Queen Street, Inverness.
Macdonald, H. J. S., student of Divinity, Grantown.
Macdonald, Andrew L., (ex-Sheriff of the Lews), Inverness.
Macdonald, John D., M.D., Lochcarron.
Macdougall, Donald, Craggan, Grantown.
Macdougall, Archibald, Campbeltown.
Macbean, Bailie Alexander, Inverness.
Macbean, Lachlan, Castle Street, Inverness.
Macbean, John, land-steward, Grantown.
Macaskill, John, Scourie, Lairg.
Macaskill, Donald, Long Row, Campbeltown.
Mackenzie, Thomas, Broadstone Park, Inverness.
Mackenzie, Alexander, Clachnacudain House, Inverness
Mackenzie, William, Bridge Street, Inverness.
Mackenzie, William, Office of " The Gael," Glasgow.
Mackenzie, Alexander, Church Street, Inverness.
Mackenzie, James Hume, bookseller, Inverness.
Mackenzie, Rev. Alexander, Falkland, Fifeshire.
Mackenzie, A., schoolmaster, Maryburgh.

Mackenzie, Donald, 31 High Street, Inverness.
Mackenzie, Alexander, 2 High Street, Inverness.
Mackenzie, Malcolm J., schoolmaster, Lochcarron.
Mackay, Charles, Elmbank Cottage, Culduthel Road, Inverness.
Mackay, Robert, Hamilton Place, Inverness.
Mackay, Charles, coal-merchant, Inverness.
Mackay, Staff-Sergeant George, Royal Artillery, Portsmouth.
Mackay, Alexander, Rose Street, Inverness.
Mackay, David, publisher, Union Street, Inverness.
Mackay, William, bookseller, Inverness.
Mackay, William, 67 Church Street, Inverness.
Mackintosh, Charles, commission-agent, Inverness.
Mackintosh, John, M.A., Drummond, Inverness.
Mackintosh, Duncan, Bank of Scotland, Inverness.
Mackintosh, Peter, Hunt Hall, Inverness.
Mackintosh, Alexander, Drumnadrochit, Glen-Urquhart.
Mackinnon, Charles, Reform Square, Campbeltown.
Mackinlay, Donald, Long Row, Campbeltown.
Macintyre, John, Limecraig, Campbeltown.
Maciver, Duncan, upholsterer, Inverness.
Maciver, Finlay, 72 Church Street, Inverness.
Maciver, Donald, student, Church Street, Inverness.
Maclennan, Alexander, merchant, Bridge Street, Inverness.
Maclennan, Alex., Northern Counties Insurance Office, Inverness.
Maclennan, Ewen, 17 Holmehead Street, Glasgow.
Maclean, Alexander, Lombard Street, Inverness.
Maclean, Archibald, New Quay Head, Campbeltown.
Macleod, Donald, Raining's School, Inverness.
Macleod, Peter, Saddler Street, Campbeltown.
Macleod, Captain Norman, Orbost, Skye.
Macleod, Alexander, Huntly Street, Inverness.
Macmillan, John, 2 High Street, Inverness.
Macneill, Nigel, 84 Argyle Street, Glasgow.
Macphail, Alexander, Drummond, Inverness.
Macphatter, Angus, Lintmill, Campbeltown.
Macpherson, Mrs, Alexandra Villa, Kingussie.
Macpherson, Captain A. F., of Catlodge.
Macraild, A. R., Inspector of Poor, Lochalsh.
Macrae, Rev. Alexander, Bay Head, Stornoway.
Macsporran, Alexander, Saddler Street, Campbeltown.
Matheson, John, Reform Square. Campbeltown.
Murdoch, John, 13 High Street, Inverness.
Munro, James, London House, Inverness.
Munro, John, wine-merchant, Inverness.
Morrison, William, of Birchfield, Inverness.

Noble, John, bookseller, Inverness.
Noble, Andrew, 8 Bridge Street, Inverness.
Noble, Andrew, Academy Street, Inverness.
Noble, Donald, Muirtown Street, Inverness.
Rose, Hugh, solicitor, Inverness.
Ross, James, solicitor, Inverness.
Ross, Donald, Gas Office, Inverness.
Ross, Donald, 39 Union Street, Inverness.
Robertson, Donald, chemist, Fortrose.
Rule, W. Taylor, solicitor, Inverness.
Shaw, Donald, solicitor, Inverness.
Simpson, Bailie Alexander, Inverness.
Smith, Alexander, 8 Bridge Street, Inverness.
Stewart, Rev. Alexander, Nether-Lochaber.
Stewart, John C. G., Clunemore, Glen-Urquhart.
Tulloch, John, Academy Street, Inverness.
Urquhart, Murdo, Inverness.
Watson, David, Long Row, Campbeltown.

DONATIONS MADE TOWARDS THE LIBRARY
DURING YEAR 1871-72.

DONATION.	DONOR.
The Book of the Dean of Lismore, edited by the Rev. Dr Maclauchlan, Edinburgh . . ,	The Editor.
The Early Scottish Church, by the Rev. Dr Maclauchlan	The Author.
Celtic Gleanings, by the Rev. Dr Maclauchlan .	The Author
The Highland Society's Gaelic Dictionary, 2 vols.	Sir Kenneth S. Mackenzie of Gairloch.
Ritson's Annals of the Caledonians, Picts, & Scots, 2 vols.	
Stewart's Sketches of the Character, Manners, and Present State of the Highlanders of Scotland, 2 vols.	..
Skene's Chronicles of the Picts and Scots, &c. . .	
Walker's Economic History of the Hebrides and Highlands of Scotland, 2 vols.	,,
Macleod and Dewar's Gaelic Dictionary	,,
	Colonel H. Mackenzie, Poyntzfield House.
The Poems of Ossian in the Original Gaelic, with a literal translation into Latin, by Robert Macfarlan, M.A. 3 vols.	,,
Dr Smith's Gaelic Antiquities	
Dr Smith's " Sean Dana"	
The Highland Society's Report on the Poems of Ossian	
Dana Oisein Mhic Fhinn	
Orain Nuadh Ghaeleach, &c., le Domhnul Macleoid .	,,
The Gaelic Messenger—1829, 1830	,,
Fingal (Macpherson's first edition)	C. F. Mackintosh of Drummond
Mackenzie's Beauties of Gaelic Poetry . . .	The Rev. Wm. Ross, Rothesay.
Photographs of Gaelic Charter (date 1408), and fac-simile of Portion of Dean of Lismore's MS. . . .	,,
Macfarlan's Choice Collection of Gaelic Poems	Miss Hood, Inverness.
Campbell's Language, Poetry, and Music of the Highland Clans	John Murdoch, Inverness,
Macnicol's Remarks on Johnson's Tour in the Hebrides	
Descriptive and Historical Sketches of Islay, by Mr Murdoch . . , ...	
How best to Cultivate a Small Farm and Garden	
Cameron's History and Tradition of the Isle of Skye .	
Gaelic Messenger	
Letters from the Highlands, or the Famine of 1847	
Bardic Stories of Ireland , ...	
Familiar Illustrations of Scottish Life	
Antiquity of the Gaelic Language	

DONATION.	DONOR.
The Wolf of Badenoch	John Murdoch.
Primitive Christianity in Scotland	..
Livingston's Gaelic Poems, &c.	
Chemistry of Agriculture	
Review of " Eight Days in Islay".	
The Kilchoman People Vindicated	
The Rev. John Darroch's Caraid a' Ghaidheil	
Highland Clearances the Real Cause of Highland Famines	
A Review of the Language of Ireland	
Logan's Concealment of the Scottish Regalia . .	
Lecture on the Life and Times of Hugh Roe O'Donell	
Co-operative Farming	
Sketches of Highland Character	
Something from the Gold Diggings of Sutherland	,,
Campbell's Popular Tales of the Highlands, 4 vols.	Alex. Mackenzie, Inverness.
Eachdraidh a' Phrionnsa, no Bliadhna Thearlaich	,,
Large Old Irish Bible (Partly MS.)	Provost Mackenzie of Inverness.
Archbishop Machale's Irish Translation of the Bible—Genesis to Deuteronomy	Prof. Bourke, Tuam, Ireland.
Archbishop Machale's Moore's Melodies—Gaelic and English	
The Bull "Ineffabilis" in Latin, Gaelic, French, and English	
Professor Bourke's Easy Lessons in Irish . . .	
Professor Bourke's College Irish Grammar . . .	
The Celtic Language and Dialects	,,
Lord Neaves' Helps to the Study of Scoto-Celtic Philology	The Author.
The Apocrypha, translated into Gaelic by the Rev. Alex. Macgregor, Inverness . . . , . .	The Translator.
Collection of Pipe Tunes as verbally taught by the Maccrimmens.	Rev. A. Macgregor.
Dr Stratton's Celtic Origin of Greek and Latin	,,
A collection of Poems, 2 vols.	Duncan Mackintosh, Inverness.
Dain agus Orain le Gilleasbuig Grannda, Bard Ghlinne Morasdainn, 2 copies	Chas. Mackay, Drummond.
Connell's Astronomy (Gaelic)	,,
St. James's Magazine, vol. i.	W. Mackay, bookseller.
Buchanan's History of Scotland (Latin) . . .	William Mackay, 67 Church St.
The Ecclesiastical History of Ireland to the commencement of the thirteenth century . . .	,.
The Catholic Epistles and Gospels, in Breton, Welsh, Gaelic, Manx, &c , by Christoll Ferrier and Charles Waring Saxton, D.D., Ch. Ch., Oxford.	John Mackay, Mountfields, Shrewsbury.
Caledonec Anthology, by Christoll Ferrier, translated into English, by T. Cadivor Wood.	,,

W. MACKAY, PRINTER, HIGH STREET, INVERNESS.

TRANSACTIONS

OF THE

GAELIC SOCIETY OF INVERNESS.

VOL. II.—YEAR 1872-73.

TRANSACTIONS

OF

THE GAELIC SOCIETY

ll'

OF

INVERNESS.

◆•◦•◆

VOL. II.—YEAR 1872-73.

Clann nan Gaidheil ri Guaillean a' Cheile.

INVERNESS:

PRINTED FOR THE SOCIETY BY
THE HIGHLANDER NEWSPAPER PRINTING AND PUBLISHING
COMPANY, LIMITED, 42 CHURCH STREET.

1873.

CONTENTS.

THE
Gaelic Society of Inverness.

OFFICE-BEARERS FOR THE YEAR 1873.

CHIEF.
CLUNY MACPHERSON OF CLUNY MACPHERSON.

CHIEFTAINS.
THOMAS MACKENZIE. | ALEXANDER DALLAS.
ALEXANDER MACKENZIE.

HONORARY SECRETARY.
JOHN MURDOCH.

SECRETARY.
WILLIAM MACKAY, 67 CHURCH STREET.

TREASURER.
DUNCAN MACKINTOSH, BANK OF SCOTLAND.

BARD.
ANGUS MACDONALD.

LIBRARIAN.
LACHLAN MACBEAN.

MEMBERS OF COUNCIL.
CHARLES MACKAY. | G. J. CAMPBELL.
DUNCAN MACIVER. | ALEXANDER M'LEAN.
PETER MACKINTOSH.

BANKERS.
THE CALEDONIAN BANKING COMPANY.

COMUNN GAILIG INBHIRNIS.

CO-SHUIDHEACHADH.

I.

'Se ainm a Chomuinn "Comunn Gailig Inbhirnis."

II.

'Siad rùintean a Chomuinn:—na buill a dheanamh foirfe ann an cleachdadh na Gailig ; cinneas cànaine, bàrdachd, agus ciùil Gaidhealtachd na h-Alba ; bàrdachd, seann-aithrisean, sgeulachdan, leabhraichean agus sgriobhanna Gaidhealach a thearnadh 'o dhìchuimhn'; leabhar-lann a shuidheachadh ann an Inbhirnis de leabhraichibh agus sgriobhannaibh, an cànain sam bith, a bhuineas do chàileachd, fhoghlum, eachdraidheachd, sheanachasaibh agus fhior-thairbhe na Gaidhealtachd agus nan Gaidheal ; còir nan Gaidheal a dhion 's an leas a chuideachadh, an cein 's am fagus.

III.

'Siad a bhitheas nam buill do'n Chomuinn dream a ghabhas suim do a rùintibh, agus a bhitheas air an tairgse agus an tairgse daingnichte aig aon choinneamh, agus' air an roghnachadh le, aig a chuid a 's lugba, tri-cheathramh de na buill a roghnachadh le crannchur aig coinneamh eile.   Air do'n neach a roghnaicheadh an co-thoirt iocadh gheibh e stigh gu aium-chlar nam Ball.

IV.

Bithidh co-thoirt nam ball gu ionmhas a Chomuinn mar a leanas :—

Buill-beatha, aon iocadh de	-	-	-	£7	7	0
Buill-Urramach 'sa bhliadhna	-	-	-	0	10	6
Buill-Chumanta	Do.	-	-	-	0	5	0
Og-bhuill	Do.	-	-	-	0	1	0

GAELIC SOCIETY OF INVERNESS.

CONSTITUTION.

I.

The Society shall be called the "GAELIC SOCIETY OF INVERNESS."

II.

The objects of the Society are :—The perfecting of the members in the use of the Gaelic language ; the cultivation of the language, poetry, and music of the Scottish Highlands; the rescuing from oblivion of Celtic poetry, traditions, legends, books, and manuscripts ; the establishing in Inverness of a Library, to consist of books and manuscripts, in whatever language, bearing upon the genius, literature, history, antiquities, and material interests of the Highlands and Highland people, the vindication of their rights, and the furtherance of their interests, both at home and abroad.

III.

The Society shall consist of persons who take a lively interest in its objects, and who shall be proposed and seconded at one meeting, and elected by at least three-fourths of the members voting by ballot at a subsequent meeting. On payment of the Subscription the person elected shall be admitted to the Roll of Membership.

IV.

The Subscription of members to the funds of the Society shall be as follows :—

Life Members, one payment of -				£7	7	0
Honorary Members, annually	-			0	10	6
Ordinary Members,	Do.	-	-	-	0 5	0
Junior Members,	Do.	-	-	-	0 1	0

V.

Earbar riaghladh gnothuichean a Chomuinn ri Comhairle de da-
bhall-deug, roghnaichte le crannchur an Cend-Mhios gach bliadhna,
agus air a deanamh suas do Cheann-feadhna, tri Iar-chinn-fheadh-
na Cleireach Urramach, Run-chleireach, Ionmhasair, agus cuig
buill eile de'n Chomunn ; feumaidh iad uile a Ghailig a thuigsinn
's a. bhruidhinn, agus feumar cuigear dhiubh airson coinneamh.
Lionar, o am gu am, airson an cadar-uin,' dreuchd sam bith a nithear
falamh re na bliadhna.

VI.

Cumaidh an Comunn coinneamhan gach seachdhuin o thoiseach
an Deicheamh-Mios gu deireadh na Giblein, airson cur air aghaidh
na nithe ainmichte anns an dara Reachd ; feumar seachdnar
airson coinneamh. Aig gach coinneamh mu'n seach bithidh an
oraid no'n deasboireachd agus na labhrar umpa ann an Gailig.

VII.

Cumaidh an Comunn Co-chruinneachadh Bliadhnail anns an
t-Seachdamh-Mios aig am bith Oraidean, leughadhan, aithriseadh
agus seinn an Gailig 's am Beurla, maille ri piobaireachd agus
ceòl Gaidhealach eile. Gheibh nithe Gailig an roimh-urram.

VIII.

Feudaidh an Comunn urrad 'us seachd de na buill, a tha
sonruichte airson am foghlum Gaidhealach, no airson gradh
dùthcha, a thaghadh gu bhi nan Cinn-fheadhna urramach.

IX.

Cha'n atharraichear cnid sam bith de'n cho-shuidheachadh gun
aonta cheathar-chuigeamh do luchd-bruidhinn na Gailig an lathair
aig coinneamh a ghairmeadh airson an aobhar so, air rabhadh mios
aig a chuid a's lugha, agus aig an toir aig a chuid a's gaine fichead
ball an guth. Feumaidh atharrachadh sam bith a thairgear a bhi
daingnichte fo làmh-sgriobhadh aig a chuid a's lugba seachd buill,
agus air a roi-innseadh aig coinneamh chumanta.

X.

Feudaidh an Comunn mion-laghan a dheanamh o am gu am, ach
cha'n fheudar na mion-laghan so a dheanamh, atharrachadh, no
chur am mùtha ach air suidheachadh aig a chuid a 's lugba, da-thrian
de na buill an lathair aig coinneamh chumanta do'n Chomunn, an
deigh rabhadh mios.

XI.

Taghaidh an Comunn Bàrd, Pìobaire agus Fear-leabharlann.

V.

The management of the affairs of the Society shall be entrusted to à Council of Twelve Members, chosen annually by ballot, in the month of January, and consisting of a Chief, three Chieftans, an Honorary Secretary, a Secretary, a Treasurer, and five other Members of the Society, all of whom shall understand and speak Gaelic ; five to be a quorum. Vacancies occurring during the year shall, from time to time, be filled up *ad interim.*

VI.

The Society shall hold weekly meetings from the beginning of October to the end of April, for the furtherance of the objects specified in Article II ; seven to be a quorum. At every alternate meeting the Essay or Debate, and discussion thereon, shall be in Gaelic.

VII.

The Society shall hold an Annual Assembly in the month of July, at which there shall be Pipe and other Highland Music, Singing, Readings, Recitations, and Addresses in Gaelic and English. Gaelic subjects shall have the preference.

VIII.

The Society may elect gentlemen who are distinguished for Celtic Literary attainments or patriotism, and who are members, as Honorary Chieftans, to the number of seven.

IX.

No part of the Constitution shall be altered without the assent of four-fifths of the Gaelic-speaking members present at a meeting specially called for the purpose, on not less than a month's notice, and provided that not less than twenty members vote. Any proposed alteration must be signed by at least seven members, and given notice of at an ordinary meeting. No Rules or Bye-Laws can be enacted, modified, or rescinded, except on the resolution of at least two-thirds of the members present at a Business Meeting of the Society, after a month's notice.

X.

The Society shall annually elect a Bard, a Piper, and a Librarian.

INTRODUCTION

THE Council regret the delay which has taken place in issuing this, the second volume of the Society's Transactions—which is largely owing to the large proportion of Gaelic lore—so much desiderated by the readers of the first volume,—forming its contents. This will be found, however, to have added to the intrinsic value of the work; and the Council are confident the volume will prove worthy to rank with the first, both in value and interest; and they trust it will meet with an equally cordial reception from the members of the Society and from the public.

A large accession to the membership of the Society, and an increase at home and abroad, of societies formed to serve the objects for which the Gaelic Society of Inverness was founded, are some of the results expected to follow this issue.

The Council are glad to find that these objects were to a considerable extent accomplished by the first volume; and the work of organization still goes on. In addition to this, several volumes of Gaelic Poetry, a commodity in which few men of business would but very recently have invested much money, have been published in the interval; and a great variety of music, in one way or another, belonging to the Highlands, or celebrating the praises of the Celt, has been put into circulation. Reference may also be made to the increasing appreciation of Gaelic and Gaelic Literature among other peoples. The "Illustrations of Ossian," mentioned in the previous volume, were soon afterwards published—a splendid tribute to the Gaelic bard and Celtic hero, from the graphic pencil of a son of Italy, and very appropriately seconded by letter-press descriptions from the pen of Mr Murdoch, the Honorary Secretary of this Society. Special mention should be made here of "The Philologic uses of the Celtic Tongue," by Professor Geddes, a work which, though small, has already exerted a large amount of influence on the destiny of the language of the Celt.

Mr C. S. Jerram, an English gentleman and scholar, who has mastered the Gaelic tongue, has given to the world in very acceptable form and style, an English version of *Dan an Deirg* and *Tiomna Ghuill*, a fact which deserves special notice ; and in connection with this, it is also very gratifying to notice that during last session, and previous to the appearance of Mr Jerram's book, a very meritorious English version of *Dan an Derig* was read to the Society by its Librarian, Mr Lachlan M'Bean. The members may possibly have the pleasure of perusing the latter in the next volume of the Transactions. The philological, topographical and other Gaelic papers appearing from time to time in the pages of the *Gael;* and in the Gaelic and Antiquarian departments of the *Highlander* newspaper afford further evidence of an increasing interest in Celtic literature and lore.

Several changes have taken place among the office-bearers since those here given were elected. Among them must be mentioned with regret the resignations of the admirable Secretary and of the Treasurer, both of whom have left the Highland Capital for other spheres of usefulness. It is gratifying to note, however, that the life membership is increasing ; and the Council would earnestly recommend that connection with the Society, to all ardent and patriotic Highlanders who desire to strengthen the foundation of the Society and to increase its usefulness and influence.

The Council would again beg to solicit the attention of the

members to the claims of the Library. Quite an unusual demand for Gaelic books has sprung up, particularly from the colonies ; and unless a special effort be made at once to make the Library what it ought to be, it will ere long become a difficult matter to make satisfactory progress with that important branch of the Society's work.

The practical recognition of Gaelic as a branch of early education in our Highland Schools, and the founding of Gaelic Professorships in our Universities, are two other important objects, deserving some attention from the public, and demanding a special and speedy effort for their accomplishment on the part of the Gaelic Society of Inverness.

TRANSACTIONS.

OCTOBER 3.—Upon Thursday, the 3rd day of October, 1872, the Gaelic Society of Inverness held their first meeting of the second year of their existence, within the Guildry Hall. The evening was devoted to the election of members and other business.

OCTOBER 10.—Upon this evening a debate took place in Gaelic upon the question—"Were the results of the battle of Culloden beneficial to the Highlands?" The discussion was opened by Mr James Fraser, commission agent, who, in an able and interesting address, maintained that the results *were* beneficial to the Highlands. The negative side was opened by Mr Mackay, the secretary, and thereafter a number of those present spoke upon the subject. The discussion was animated, and brought out many interesting incidents of the stirring times of the Forty-five. At the close a show of hands was taken, which was found to be in favour of the negative.

OCTOBER 17.—Upon this evening Mr Murdoch read a paper upon "The Celtic Sympathies of Burns," from which we take the following :—

THE CELTIC SYMPATHIES OF BURNS.

Robert Burns, having been born and brought up among Saxon-speaking Lowlanders, is, of course, claimed and appropriated as a gem in the crown of the chief of races, the mythic Anglo-Saxon! No doubt his mother was an Ayrshire woman. It does not, however, follow that she was a Saxon ; for Ayrshire, until very recently was as Celtic as the neighbouring county of Argyle. The names

B

of the old towns, villages, parishes, and farms are Gaelic; and so
are the names of most of the people—as is the case in Wigtonshire
and the rest of Galloway.   Nay, until within the last two hundred
years, Gaelic was the vernacular of all that country.   So that the
probabilities are in favour of the supposition that even Burns's
mother was a Celt.   Her maiden name, "Brown," falls readily
into the same preponderating scale.   In the Highlands it is common, where it has two origins—the one through a literal translation,
and the other through an accommodating corruption.   The former,
Donn, the Gaelic for the colour *brown*—the other is a corruption
of *Briuinn*, the Gaelic of judges.   Hence many in the Highlands
who are called Brown in English are, in the language of the
country, called *clann a' Bhriuinn*.   The transition in sound from
Briuin to Brown is slight, although in sense the stride is considerable between the colour Brown and the ancient Celtic functionaries
the Briuins.   *Briuin* itself, by the way, as well as the modern Irish
Brehon, is a slight departure in sound, and more in spelling, but
none in sense, from the real old word *Breitheamhna* (judges).
Breith (pronounced nearly brae) is the verb to judge; *Breitheamh*
(pronounced bre-av, or bre-u) is the noun which designates the
official who judges; and *Breitheamhnas* (pronounced bre-anus) is
the name of what the judge does (judgment).   To return : William
Burness, the poet's father, was, we may say, a fugitive member of
a Celtic or Highland Jacobitical clan in the North of Scotland, and
characterised by those qualities which bound the Highlanders to
their country, their clans, their chiefs, and their king, so long as
faith was kept and liberty could be enjoyed; but which, when
these failed, compelled them to betake themselves to other lands.
    So far, then, the Highlanders, from whose fruitful Celtic stem
sprang the imperishable sons and fathers of song—Ossian, Oran,
Ullin, Clan Mhuirich, Clan Chodrum, Mackay, Ross, Macdonald,
MacIntyre, MacNeill, McColl, &c., would seem to have no slight
claim to Coila's Rustic bard.   If this claim be valid, as it certainly
is plausible, it will help to account simply and naturally for his
Highland predilections and sympathies.   The object of his great
love was Mary Campbell, a Highland girl; a circumstance to which
the world is indebted for one of his best and most generally received
songs, "Highland Mary."   This love may, on the one hand, be
traced, in some measure, to the kindred sympathy of Celtic blood ;
or, on the other, be regarded as the origin of that sympathy.   Or,
what is still more probable, this event may have roused to life and
activity those inherited, but hitherto latent, Celtic tendencies and
susceptibilities which ever after manifested themselves under the
slightest stimulation.   So that we may thus say that the Celt and

the Poet were at once awakened by the melody of love, as his muse expresses it in the "Vision":—

> " When youthful Love, warm-blushing strong,
>   Keen-shivering, shot thy nerves along,
>   Those accents, grateful to thy tongue,
>   Th' adoréd name,
>   I taught thee how to pour in song
>   To soothe thy flame."

Now it is not unworthy of notice that these very lines have certain marks of Celtic kinship. "Warm-blushing, strong, keen-shivering," are as if imitations of Ossian or Donnchadh Bàn. But as we cannot call them imitations we must trace them to the same fountain.

Allan Cunningham, after referring to Macpherson's Rant, says, "the genius of the North had an influence over the Poet's musings in other compositions. In 'The Highland Lassie,' the lover complains of want of wealth and of the faithlessness of fortune; but strong in affection, declares—

> ' For her I'll dare the billows' roar,
>   For her I'll trace the distant shore,
>   That Indian wealth may lustre throw
>   Around my Highland Lassie, O ! '

In the 'Northern Lassie,' he utters similar sentiments; and in the 'Braw, braw Lads of Gallawater,' his hand may be traced by the curious in Scottish song." "Stay, my Charmer," if not of Highland extraction, owes its air to the North.

He shews a strong predilection for the ideas, the spirit, the poetry, and the music of the North. In his Highland travels he was quite smitten with the ease, elegance, and sweetness of the society, as well as with the songs and their airs. Of course it was seldom that much of the original richness of the poetry was conveyed to him by a translation, which is but a miserable cribbing, cabining and confining of the Celtic poetic genius, within the bounds of the language of a "nation of shopkeepers." The music, however, took possession of him at once, as strains of liquid language fraught with wealth and melody to every tuneful soul. So thoroughly was this music cast in the same mould with his own poetic muse, that he has several scores of songs to purely Gaelic airs, many of which had not before his day even acquired Lowland names.* Allan Cunningham again says, "I have said that he exhibited early symptoms of Jacobitism : his Highland tours and conversations with the chiefs and the ladies of the North, strengthened a liking which he seems to have inherited from his fathers." And Burns himself says, "By the bye, it is singular enough that the Scottish muses were all Jacobite. I have paid more attention to every description of Scots songs than perhaps anybody living has done, and I do not recollect one single stanza, or even the title of the most trifling Scots air, which has the least panegyrical reference to the families of Nassau or Brunswick, whilst there are hundreds satirizing them. This may be thought no panegyric on the Scots' poets, *but I mean it as such.* For myself, I would always take it as a compliment to have it said, that my heart ran before my head. And surely the gallant though unfortunate House of Stewart, the kings of our fathers for so many heroic ages, is a thing much more interesting than . . . ."

All the above facts, sentiments, and observations go to show the same things—the Celtic constitution and predilections of Burns; and his observations relative to the Scottish muses generally being so Jacobitical, is to the effect that they were eminently Celtic. There were many Celts on the Brunswick side, but certainly all the Scots on the Stuart side may be said to have been Highlanders. So that in saying that the Scottish muses were Jacobitical, he virtually represents them as being Highland too.

And why should it not be added in passing, that even Walter Scott drew no small share of his inspiration from Highland scenes, sentiments, and lore, as well as from this same Jacobitism. Was not Byron's harp strung in the Highlands, and vibrated by the boreal breath of "Dark Lochnagar." Campbell, too, though born in the Lowlands, it was whilst in the Higlands, the home of his fathers, in the retirement of the glens and valleys around Duntroon, listening to the roar of the western waves, as, after a race of a thousand leagues, they forced their way through the gulf of *Coire Bhreachdain,* the beautiful pastoral picture of his retreat, backed by the rugged crags of Scaraba and Alpine heights of Jura, that the

---

*Of the latter are—*An gille dubh, ciarr, dubh; Banarach dhonn a' Chruidh; A' chaora Chróm; Baile 'mhonaidh mhoir; Druimionn dubh; Failte na misg;* "*Gille Morice;*" "*Hee baloo;*" *Latha Raon ruadhraidh; An Gligearum chas; Mòrag; Oran gaoil; Oran an Aoig; Port Ruairidh dhaill; Rinn m'éudail mo mhealladh; Robaidh dona, gòrach; Iain buidhe; Tullochgorm; Coille-Chragaidh.* Besides these, several of his songs are simply to "A Gaelic Air," and to "A Highland Air;" and some to airs whose names would seem to be in a transition state from one language to another.

northern breeze which passed o'er the hills of Morvern and ruins of
Selma, inspired the Celtic bard with the genius of Ossian to sing
the song of liberty in the chivalric spirit of Fingal, king of heroes.

And when Burns wanted the essence of Scottish valour and
warlike power, where did he look for it but among the Highland
hills ! In his "Earnest cry and prayer to the Scottish Representatives," although it is Scotland at large which complains, when he
wants her to assume an attitude of terror to those who would
refuse her demands, it is her Highland phase which he presents :—

> " An' L——d, if ance ye put her til't,
> Her tartan petticoats she'll kilt."

Alas the wearers of the "tartan kilt," who, in time of war have
been the defence of England as well as of Scotland, are in time of
security swept away to make room for sheep and deer.

Here again :—

> " But bring a Scotsman frae his *hill*,
> Clap in his cheek a *Highlan'* gill,
> Say such is royal George's will,
>   An' there's the foe :
> He has na thought but how to kill
>   Twa at a blow."

There is surely *much* in the *little*, that all he wants in the future
life, is "A Highland Welcome."

One of his "Twa Dogs" is called—

> " After a dog in Highland sang,
> Was made lang syne—Lord knows how lang."

This is Cuchulin's *Luath;* and the fact and manner of his introduction show to the careful and competent reader that the bard
had more than a passing acquaintance with the poems of Ossian ;
that he must have learned the Gaelic *pronunciation* of some at
least of the names which figure in Fingal—although Saxon-speaking editors, mispronouncing the dog's name, mangled the passage,
thereby, reflecting but little credit on the versifying powers of
their author, by making *ha'* into *have*, in a vain attempt to rhyme
it with an *English* pronunciation of *l, u, a, t, h !* Burns never
was so hard up for harmonious sounds as to speak or write :—

> " I've often wondered, honest Lua*th*,
> What sort of life poor dogs like *you have*,

with the view of *th* or *ve* being sounded. When he penned that
passage, he knew that *th* in Gaelic was mute, and he finished the
second line accordingly with the broad Scotch, *you ha'*, and not

you have ; thus commending it, as perfect rhyme, to the Gaelic ear
which demanded that it should be read—

> " I've often wondered, honest *Lu-a,*
> What sort of life poor dogs like *you ha'.* "

But from criticism let us come to his "Native Muse," who
counselled him—

> " Thy tuneful flame still careful fan,
> Preserve the dignity of man,
> With soul erect ;
> And trust the universal plan
> Will all protect."

Coila is but a Highland lassie deified, as well in expression as in
costume and proportions :—

> " A hair-brained, sentimental trace
> Was strongly markéd in her face ;
> A wildly-witty rustic grace
> Shone full upon her ;
> Her eye, ev'n turn'd on empty space,
> Beam'd keen wi' humour.
>
> Down flow'd her robe in *tartan* sheen,
> Till half a leg was scrimply seen ;
> And such a leg ! My bonny Jean
> Could only peer it ;
> Sae straight, sae taper, tight, and clean,
> Nane else cam' near it.'

These hurried notes, which are but so many straggling gleams
falling from an unusual point on some of the many glorious traits
which formed the character of Scotia's darling bard, indicate that
whatever may have been the accidents of tongue and birth, the
Poet and the Man were intensely Celtic. But, in thus appearing
less Lowland and more Highland, he only stands higher as the
more perfect Scot.

LECTURE BY THE REV. ALEXANDER MACGREGOR.

Upon the evening of 24th October the Rev. Mr Macgregor,
Inverness, delivered the following Gaelic lecture in the hall of the
Association Buildings, before a large audience. The chair was
occupied by Mr Dallas, town clerk, who introduced the lecturer in
a short but eloquent Gaelic address. Thereafter Mr Macgregor
said :—

Fhir-suidhe Urramaich, a Bhantighearna, agus a Dhaoin'-uailse,
Cénd mìle fàilte,
Air Comunn Gäelig Inbherneis ;
Sŏnas a's àgh,
Soirbheas a's slàinte,
Do Comunr. Gäelig Inbherneis.

Tha dòchas agam gu'm bi sibh bàigheil rium, an nair a tha mi chum dìchioll a dheanamh air an fheasgair so, chum beagan nithe a leigeadh ris duibh a thaobh nan cùisean cudthromach air son an do dhealbhadh an Comunn àluinn a ta nis cruinn anns an talla so. Bha e riamh, agus bithidh e a chaoidh na nì taitneach do na Gaidheil a bhi 'còmhlachadh a' chéile, a' labhairt r'a chéile, agus a' cumail comuinn agus conaltraidh r'a chéile ann an ionad sam bith ; agus cha'n urrainn nach 'eil sin ro thaitneach gu'n teagamh ann an àite mar so, far am bheil sliochd nam beann air an aonachadh ra chéile mar Chomunn dìleas anns a' bhaile so, chum gach ni a bhuineas do'n *Ghaelig*, agus do na *Gäidheil* a chur air an aghaidh, agus a chumail air chuimhne. Tha e, nime sin, 'na aobhar aoibhneis dòmhsa a nis a bhi 'labhairt ruibh, agus a' cur fàilte oirbh 'n 'ur càinnt òirdheirc fein,—càinnt aig nach 'eil coimeas chum smuainte a' chridhe, agus feartan na h-inntinn a leigeadh ris. Tha e sòlasach an comhnuidh, a bhi tachairt ri càirdibh ann an ceàrnadh sam bith de'n t-saoghal ; ach theirinn, gu'n sgàth gu'n eagal, nach 'eil toilinntinn talmhaidh ann ni's mò, na sluagh a bhi 'gabhail còmhnuidh cuideachd ann an càrantas agus gràdh, a' labhairt r'a chéile anns a' chàinnt sin a bha ann o chian, agus a' cuideachadh le chéile mar bhràthaire, a ta air an aonachadh le cleachd, le cainnt, agus le cineadas.

Tha deagh-fhios agam air mo neo-ìomlanachd fein chum na nithe sin bu mbath leam a chur an céill duibh, a dheanamh co soilleir, reidh a's a dh' fhéumadh iad,—ach féumaidh sibb an toil a ghabhail air son a' ghnìomh, agus foighidinn a dheanamh rium rè tamuill bhig. Bu ro mhath leam gu'n cuidicheadh gach tréubh agus fine air feadh na Gaidhealtachd air fad, leis a' Chomunn so a ta air a shuidheachadh ann am baile-cinn so na h-airde-tuatha,— agus gun tigeadh càirdean ann an lionmhorachd o thigh Iain Ghròta a'n Gallthaobh, gu iomallaibh na Gaidhealtachd 'san àirde-deas, agus gu'n seasadh iad gu *deas, dian, tairis,* agus tréubhach air bhur taobh.

Fhir-suidhe urramaich,—Ged a bhithinn-sa cho deas-bhriathrach ris an Olladh Ian Stiùbhart *Blackie*,—no co min-eòlach air cùisibh agus cleachdannaibh na tire ri " Lochabar Iochdarach,"—cha'n 'eil e a'm' chomas, air aon fheasgair mar so, labhairt ach air fior neo-ni de na nithibh éugsamhla sin bu mhiann leis a' Chomunn so a

theasairginn agus a chumail air chùimhne. Tha riaghailtean ùra
rìoghachd air an deàlbhadh,—ìnnleachdan agus ealaidhean eile air
am faotuinn a mach,—laghailtean agus tionnsgnaidhean air an
leigeadh ris anns na lìnntibh fòghluimte so, a ta féumail agus
freagarrach annta fein; ach, tha iad so uile, mar gu'm b'ann, a'
tiodhlacadh, agus a' cur tiugh-fholuchaidh air gach ni air son an
robh na Gaidheil mar chinneadh air an comharrachadh a'm measg
uile chinneacha na talmhuinn. Cha'n 'eil e taitneach gu'm biodh
na nithe sin air an càll; agus le rùn gu'n teasairginn, agus le
deagh-dhùrachd chum an cumail air chùimhne, tha Comunu Gäelig
a' bhaile so air an suidheachadh. Tha na Gaidheil 'nan *sluagh*
comharraichte, tha eachdraigh nan Gaidheal comharraichte, tha
*càinnt, ceòl, cantaireachd, còmhdachadh, cinneadh, cleachdanna,
cruadal,* agus *càirdeas* 'nan Gaidheal, cha'n e mhàin na'n nithe ro
chomharraichte annta fein, ach tha iad 'nan nithe a mheasadh co
cudthromach, co ciatach, agus co càil-ghluasadach, 's gu'n do dhealbhadh iomadh comunn eile, ceart cosmhuil ri Comunn Gaelig
Inbherneis, chum an teasairginn. Tha na buàidhean so gu léir
äiridh air léudachadh orra, gach aon fa soach; ach cha cheadaich
an ùine dhomh labhairt ach air beagan dhiùbh aig an àm. Thugam
fanear, 'san dol a mach,

Na Gaidheil fein.

Co iad? Cia as a thàinig iad? Ciod is cénd-thùs doibh? Ciod
air am bheil fios againn mu'n timchioll a thaobh an stuic agus am
fréum aca? Tha na nithe so uile air an còmhdachadh agus air am
foluchadh le tiugh-dhìomhaireachd agus dorchadas nan céud linn.
Cha *ruig* eachdraidh air ais gu prìomh-thoiseach a' chinnidh so.
Tha lionmhorachd dhaoine fòghluimte ann, a rinn an dìchioll chum
so a rannsachadh a mach,—agus ged a tha iad a' co'-chòrdach,
gu'm bheil na *Gaidheil* agus a *Ghaelig* anabarrach sean, gidheadh,
cha'n 'eil e furasd doibh a' eheart frèumh o'n d'fhàs agus o'n
d'thàinig iad a dheanamh gu soilleir a mach. Air so, chuir an
Granntach, tighearna Choiridhmhonaidh, leabhar ro fhòghluimte a
mach, o chionn thri fichead bliadhna air ais,—leabhar a ta leigeadh
ris mòran nithe ro iongantach mu fhrèumh agus ghinealach nan
Gaidheal. Tha esan a' deanamh mach, mar a ta na h-uiread de
luchd-eachdraidh eile gu'n d'thàinig na Gàidheil a nàll o mhòr-thir
na h-Eorpa, agus gur i a' Ghäelig am prìomh-bhun o'n d'thàinig
a' Ghréugais, an Laidinn, agus cànain eile. Cha'n 'eil teagamh
nach iad na Gàidheil an t-aon sluagh ris na Caledoniich, agus na
Piocaich an sinsearra fein, eadhon na daoine gaisgeil sin a dhìon an
dùthaich agus an saorsa fein, an aghaidh gach ionnsuidh a thugadh
orra le àrmailtibh treun' nan Ròmanach. Bha Alba, no Caledonia

air a h-àiteachadh leis na Piocaich, agus thugadh leòsan ainmean, 'nan càinnt fein, air gach béinn agus baile, loch agus abhainn, agus ionad eile 'san rìoghachd. Uime sin, tha sinn a' faicinn gu ruig an là an dingh, agus dh' àindeoin gach atharrachaidh a rinneadh leis na h-Anglo-Saxons, Lochlunnaich, agus treubhan eile a thug ionnsuidh air Alba, agus a rinn gréim air earrannaibh di,— gu'm bheil iomadh àite anns a' Ghalltachd, agus ann an taobh deas na h-Alba, a' giùlan fathast nan ainmean Gaelig a thugadh dhoibh, o cheann còrr agus da mhile bliadhna air ais, leis na Caledoniich. Tha gach ainm a tha tòiseachadh le Dùn, Bèinn, Monadh, Baile, Craig, Magh, Machair, Ach, Abhinn, Aird, Uachdar, Carn, Blar, Cùl, Drùim, Eas, Gleann, Srath, Innis, Cill, Meall, Tòrr, Cnoc, Tom, Loch, Linn, Póll, Ros, Port, Tuillich, agus mòran eile, a' féuchainn air ball gur ainmean Gäelig iad. Ann an siorramachd Air,—tha Dalbeg, Ballantrae, Auchanleck, Dalry, agus na h-uiread eile,—agus ciod iad sin ach an Dail-bheag, Bail'-an-traigh, Ach-nan-leachd, agus Dail-an-righ ?"

Cuiridh mi a nis beagan an céill mu chainnt nan Gaidheal, eadhon

A' GHAELIG.

Do gach cainnt thugamaid an t-urram do'n Ghaelig. Tha i liath-aosda, gidheadh is lùghmhor, laidir, lùrach i, is fallain, fiachail, fior-ghlan i. Mar òigh gheamnuidh, cha'n aill leatha gnothuch a bhi aico ri nì sam bith a ta truaillidh, no drabasda, no droch-mhuinte. Ann am béul nan laoch, is binn, blasda a fuaim ; agus is tìomhaidh, tròm a guth ann an gearan gach dream a ta fo bhròn ! Air Laidinn, 's air Gréugais bheir i barrachd, agus cha'n fhaighear a leithid 'ga labhairt fo'n ghréin !

Is ceart a thubhairt Ian Griogaireach, am bard, anns na briath-raibh fileanta a leanas :—

Tha 'Ghaelig co luachmhor,
'S nach cuir sinn i suarach ;
Cò nach seasmhadh r'a guallain ?
'Si tha'n còradh nan uaislean,
'Ga labhairt gu'n truailleadh,
Feadh gach àit' anns an gluais iad,
Gu caithreamach, cruaidh, ceolmhor.
Gu caithreamach, &c.

Ged' chaidh a sàruch' 'na triall,
Cha do chaill i a mìagh ;
Tha i fallain o chìan,
Gun ghalar, gun ghiamh,
Buan, farumach, dian,
Gun alladh, gun fhiamh,
Anns gach talamh a dh' iarr eòlas.
Anns gach talamh, &c.

'Si bh' aig Adhamh 'sa ghàradh,
'Si bh' aig Eubha 'ga thàladh,
Gus 'n do mheall i gu bàs e,
'N nair a dh' ith e meas àluinn,
Chaidh a thoirmeasg dhà fhàgail,
'Se dh' fbag sinne 'na'r traillibh,
Ach fhuair sinn ar slànuch' is dòchas.
　　　　　Ach fhuair sinn, &c.

'Nuair a chaidh an saoghal a bhàthadh,
Chaidh a' Ghäelig a theàrnadh,
Si bh' aig Noah 's an àirce,
'S aig gach curaidh a dh' fhàs uaidh,
Fhuair i 'n t-urram gu cràbhadh,
'S cha mhios i gu dànachd,
'S tha i milis a ghabhail òrain.
　　　　　'S tha i milis, &c.

'Si bh' aig Tréunmor an toiseach,
A thog cìs o Righ Lochluinn,
Aig Fionn is aig Toscar,
Aig Cuchullin 's aig Oscar,
'S aig Caoilte nan còs-luath,
A' siubhal aonach, is slochd, is mhòr-bheann.
　　　　　A' siubhal aonach, &c.

'Si bh' aig Conan 's aig Diarmad,
Aig Dubh-Chomar, 's aig Diaran,
Bha i uil' aig na Fiannaibh,
'N àm togail gu fiadhach,
No chasgadh an lotadh,
De fhuil an nàimhdean 'san dian thòrachd.
　　　　　De fhuil an nàimhdean, &c.

Cò thairgeadh dhi mi-mhodh?
'S nach cumadh a'm mìagh i?
Sgur i 'Ghaelig bha sgrìobhte,
Air na clachanna crìche,
Anns gach ionad de'n rìoghachd ;
Ged bha i fuidh mhi-ghean,
Tha i nise a' dìreadh,
S' gu'm mair i gu dilinn,
Mar bha i 's na lìnntibh o thùs ¹
　　　　　Mar bha i, &c.

Mar so mhol am Bard Griogaireach a' Ghaelig, agus feudar a radh m'a thimchioll fein :—

'S urramach, neo-spòrsail,
Ro chòmhnard 'na labhairt e,
'S chuir rogha caoin air còmhradh
Gach Ceòlraidh bha tairis da ;

Tha iomadh ni gu seòlta,
'S gu ceòlmhor air aithris leis ;
'S mòr iongantas nan céndan,
Mu'n ghéurad a thachair da.

O ! 's luachmhor, gur luachmhor,
O ! 's luachmhor a cheileirean,
Gun aon nì annta suarach,
No tual, ach fior eireachdail,
Gu dian iad saoradh Gäelig
O sharuch' 's o dhearasan,
'S cha tearc na facaill àluinn,
O'n bhàs leò chaidh theasairginn.

Saor o dhonas, làn do shonas,
    Air srath, monadh, 's glas thonnan,
Gu'n robh 'm fìrean, riamh nach sireadh
Coingheal lide Shasunnaich ;
Do'n teangaidh bhìnn, bha geamnuidh grìnn,
'N luchairt Suinn nan Ailpaineach ;
'S bha fòs aig Oisean déurach,
A' caoidh na Féinn chaidh thasgadh leis '

A' chànain a' chànain,
A' chànain bha'n toiseach i,
'S mar mhòr-chruaidh-chreagan laidir,
A tàmhsa biodh socaireach ;
'M feadh ghléusas slugan càil neach,
Cha bhàs is cha dochunn di,
Ach bheir i mach buaidh-làrach,
Feadh ghàbhanna 's dhosgannan !

'S lionmhor gaisgeach a ta aice,
'Cumail taic' is cothrom rith',
Agus caraid, le cruas daraig,
'Dol do'n charraid 'chogadh dhi,
Chum a dìonadh anns gach pìanadh,
'S chum a lìonadh dh' fhocalaibh,
'S mar lasair-chatha an léirsinn,
Gu léir-sgrios smid dhochaireach !

REV. ROBERT MACGREGOR, Skye.

Is lìonmhor na daoine fòghluimte agus tuigseach, ann an iomadh rìoghachd, a *bha*, agus a *tha* 'toirt mòr-spéis do'n Ghäelig, agus 'ga rannsachadh a mach mar sheann chanain a ta iongantach a thaobh a fréumhan agus a co'-dhealbhaidh. Cha'n 'eil ùin' agam na daoine sin ainmeachadh an nochd ; ach 'nam measg-san a ta fathasd beò aig am bheil mòr-thlachd do'n Ghaelig, agus an déigh sin, nach urrainn a labhairt, tha an t-Olladh Ian Steuart Blackie, a chual sibh a'n so, o cheann beagan mhìosan air ais. Tha, mar an céudna, an t-Olladh Tomas Stratton, a chuir a mach leabhar beag o cheann da bhliadhna air ais, a' féuchainn gu'm bheil a' Ghäelig 'na bunait do'n Ghréugais, 's do'n Laidinn. A rìs, tha am Prionnsa Louis Lucien Bonaparte, anabarrach déidheil air a' Ghaelig, agus ro fhiosrach air gach meanglan a bhuineas di, mar a ta a' Ghaelig Fhrangach ann am Brittani, agus an Armoric, an Cornish, agus an Cimbric, agus a Ghäelig a ta 'ga labhairt fathasd 'san Odhailt (Wales), 'san Eilein Mhainneanaich, agus ann an Eirinn. Chuir am Prionnsa f'am chomhair-sa an Apocripha eadar-theangachadh chum na Gäelig Albanaich, agus rinn mi mo dhìchoill air sin a dheanamh. Ach a thuilleadh air a' mhuinntir urramaich so uile, tha tlachd mòr aig ar n-ard-Uachdaran a' Bhanrigh fein do'n Ghaelig, mar a ta aice do na Gäidheal, agus do'n Ghäidhealtachd; agus fhuair i a rìs agus a rìs maighstirean-sgoile, chum a' Ghaèlig a theagasg d'a cuid mhac; ach ciod an adhartas a rinn iad nan sgoilearachd Ghäidhealach, cha'n fhios dòmb-sa.

Rinneadh, mar an céudna, dìchioll nach bu bheag, o àm gu h-àm, o chionn da fhichead bliadhna air ais, air luchd-turais beaga, baganta, a chur a mach anns an éididh Ghaidhealach, chum sliochd nam beann a theagasg a thaobh nithe éugsamhla a bhiodh féumail dhoibh; ach mo thruaigh! fhuair fear an déigh fir dhiubh bas. Chaochail iad uile, agus bu laoghach iad! An toiseach ghabh "An Teachdaire Gaidhealach" an t-slighe, agus thug e ruaig air feadh nan garbh-chrioch, ach cha b' fbada gus an deachaidh e a dhìth. A ris, dh' eirich suas "Caraid nan Gaidheal" 'sa bhaile so fein; agus a rìs "Cuairtear nan Gleann," "Fear-tathaich nam beann," agus na h-niread eile, ach chaidh as doibh gu léir, agus b' olc an airidh e. Ach cha d' fhagadh sinn fathast gu'n dòchas, oir dh' éirich o chionn ghoirid "Gäidheal" eile suas ann an Glaschu, a ta 'nis air a thurus, agus s'e dleas'nas a' Chomuinn so, agus gach uile neach eile aig am bheil dualchas agus duchas 'nan cridhe; an aire a thoirt gu'm bi an "Gaidheal" laoghach so air 'eiridinn, agus air a chumail suas .

Air am laimh eile, cha bheag an strìth a rinneadh le muinntir chinneadail air feadh na rìoghachd, chum iad fein aonachadh r'a chéile ann an comunnaibh, gu leas na Gaidhealtachd a chur air aghaidh. Chum na crìche so tha Comunn Gäidhealach ann an Obaireadhain, Cìllribhinn, Dùneidin, Lunnain, Glaschu, 'n-America, agus ann an aitibh eile; agus cha lugba ann an dealas agus deagh-dhùrachd, an leanabh a's òige dhe'n teaghlach aluinn so, "Comunn Gäelig Inbherneis":—

> Glacam an t-àm so chum còmhdachadh,
> Sàr bhuaidhean agus àilleachd a' chòir chomuinn,

Tha eòlach, tuigseach, géur,—lan gliocais agus céill,
Gu'n mhearachd gu léir, ann 'nan seòlannaibh ;
Subhailceach 'nam béus,—ro urramach gu léir,
Gur toilicht' tha mi fein, a bhi còmhladh riu.
Cha'n fhacas riamh 'san tir, aon chonunn bheir dhiubh cis,
'S ceanalt', suairce, sìobhalt', neo-spòrsail iad ;
Mar dhoimain ann an séud, tha na h-òganaich,
Le'm fòghlum, beachd, is reusan, is oirdheirceas ;
'S mar sgathan do ghloin réidh, a' glacadh gathan gréin',
Tha'n cridhe le creidimh thréun, air a stòladh dhoibh.

  Fir dionaidh na Gäelig,
  O gach gàbhadh is éucoir,
  'S on dh' fhàs suas na h-àrmuinn,
  Cha chunnard dhi géilleadh.
  Cha'n ioghna ged tha i,
  Sir éiridh ni's àirde,
  'S gur i bha aig Adhamh
  'Sa ghàradh ri Eubha ;
  'S gur i bha roimh so
  'N talamh 'na h-Eiphit,
  Feadh mhòr-thir na h-Eorpa,
  'Ga labhairt, 's ga h-éisdeachd,
  'S ged 'chaidh' ruagadh air astar,
  Thar na cuantaibh tha farsuing,
  Fhuair i tàmb agus fasgadh
  A'n Albainn 'sa'n Eirinn.
  O'n t-urram, an t-urram,
  An t-urram, do'n chéud chainnt'
  Nach deach' mar chaidh mòran
  Do chàinntibh an éug oirnn ;
  Ma bhios canain air thalamh,
  'Ga labhairt a'm flaitheas,
  Tha mòran 'sa bharail
  Gur Gaelig un té sin !

  Tha nis a' Ghaelig ghrinn
  Anns an rioghachd so,
  Sir thogail suas a cinn,
  'S 'dol an lionmhorachd.
  Ged bha i ionnan 's bàlbh.
  Gun ghuth oirre, no sealbh,
  Cha robh i fathasd màrbh,
  Agus di chuimhnich'.
  Ach fo dheagh gbean gach aoin,
  A frèumhan rim i sgaoil,
  Is dh' éirich i mar chraoibh
  Bha 'na mìn-phreasan.

    Tha uaisle nan Gàll
    Uile foir oirre,

'S ga cumail ann an luach
Agus sporsalachd ;
Seadh, tha na Goill iad féin,
'Toirt aire d'a mor-fheum,
'S bu mhiannach leo gu léir
A bhi eolach oirr'—
A chum gu'm mealar leo,
Gach ionmhas tha 'na coir
'S gu'm faicear air gach seol
Uile bhoidhcheadan.
A' chànain a bha riamh
Feadh bheanntan agus shliabh,
Ban-oighre dhligheach fhior
Chaledonia !
A' chanain a's fearr
Fo na spéuran i,
Chum gach smaoin is ni
'Chur an céill innte.
Làn thorrach i gach am,
Air focail nach 'eil gànn,
Tha gach càinnt eile th'ànn
A' toirt géillidh dhi.
Ach tha i 'nis 'dol suas,
Air bunnchar nach gluais,
Le comhnadh Comuinn uasail,
'S cha tréig iad i.

B' iad sud an Comunu ceanalta,
Bha aineolach air do-bheirt ;
Caoimhneil, fearail, gribheagach,
Làn misniche, gu'n mhor-chùis !
Bu bheothail iad gu deasboireachd,
Co'-pairteachadh gu h-eircachdail
An eòlais le géur spreigeileachd,
Gun easbhuidh, le mor-sheòltachd.
O ! 's mor an spéis a ghabh mi dhiubh,
'Sa chaoidh cha ghabh mi aithreachas,
'S is mor mo dhùil, mar meallar mi,
Gu'm bi sinn tric comhladh !
Cha'n urrainn, is cha'n aithne dhomh,
An cliù a chur an rannaireachd,
'S cha'n innseadh Homer barraichte,
Gach snuadh tha orr, is mor-thlachd ;
No Bhirgil mòr am Feadailteach,
Bàrd urramach gun teagamh e ;
B'e Oiseau liath nan ceileirean,
A mholadh air a choir iad !

Rev. Robt. MacGregor,
Kilmuir, Skye.

Bardachd nan Gaidheal.

Làbhram a nis ré mionaid no dha air bardachd nan Gaidheal. 'Si, feudaidh e bhi, bardachd Oisein, a' bhardachd a's sine a ta againn, agus tha i aillidh gun choimeas.   Tha e air a dheanamh mach gu'm bheil dlùth air sea cénd déug bliadhna o linn Oisein. A réir gach rannsachaidh a rinneadh, fhuair Fionn, athair Oisein bas anns a' bhliadhna 285, agus mharbhadh a mhac Oscar ann am blar fuilteach Ghabhra, bliadhna an déigh sin. Is òirdheirc na dàin a rinneadh le Oisean, agus tha nithe air am filleadh a stigh annta, a ta gu soilleir a' nochdadh an aois aca.   Cha'n 'eil guth annta air aiteachadh an fhearainn, no air tréudaibh, no air cìobair-eachd ; ach tha iad a' cur an céill gach ni mu chogadh, mu thréubh-antas, mu ghaisge, mu'n fhoghaid, mu'n ruaig, agus mu shéilg, a' féuchainn gu'n robh muinntir na linne sin a' teachd beò air sitheann, agus air gach gnè fhiadh-bheathach 'nan còill agus na macharach. Tha mòran ann, aig nach 'eil eòlas no meas air bardachd nan linn sin, a ta 'cumail a mach nach urrainn na dain sin a bhi co sean, a' chionn nach robh iad air an sgrìobhadh sios.   Dh' fheudadh iad an leisgeul cèudna a thoirt an aghaidh na Gàelig fein ; oir ghleidheadh i a mhain mar chanain gun truailleadh o na céud lìnntibh le béul-aithris.   Cha robh leabhraichean, no clòdh-bhualadh ann, ach thainig i 'nùas o'n aithair dh' ionnsuidh a' mhic, ceart mar a thainig dain Ullin, Oisein, agus Orrain, gu ruig an la an dingh.   Cha'n 'eil sin iongantach an uair a chùimhnichear gu'n robh aig gach tréubh, cinneadh, fineadh, agus ceann-feadhna, am baird fein gu bhi 'deachd-adh an cridhe le misnich anns a' chath, agus gu bhi 'g aithris an trèubhantais agus an cliù ann am filidheachd bhìnn agus bhlasda. Bha mar bu ghnath aig gach ceann-cinnidh bard, agus piobair, agus amadan, mar bhùill do-sheachnach 'na theaghlach, agus do na bardaibh agus piòbairibh bha baile saor fearainn air a thoirt o linn gu linn.   An uair a sheas Ian Lòm air baidealaibh Chaisteil Inbher-lòchaidh, ag amharc air a' chath fhuilteach a bha 'ga chur gu h-iosal air an raon am fagus da, thugadh an aghaidh air a' bhard géur-bhriathrach so, a cheann nach do thog e a chlaidheamh 'san teugmhail.   Ghrad-fhreagair e, agus thubhairt e le h-naill 'na dhréuchd—" Na'n rachainn-sa sios do'n chath, agus 'nan cuirteadh gu bàs mi, cò an sin a dh' aithriseadh na gnìomharan éuchdach agus àllail a rinneadh ; agus cò a sheinneadh cliù a' chinnidh ghais-geil a thug a mach a' bhuaidh ? "

B'e Lachlunn Mac Néill Mhic Mhuirich, am bard, no'n Sean-chaidh mu dheireadh a bha aig Cloinn Raonuill.   Thug Lachlunn sgriobhadh ro iongantach seachad ann an Gaelig do dhuin'-uasal da'm b'ainn Ionraic (Henry) Mac Coinnich, a bha 'cruinneachadh nithe mu Oisean, air son Comuinn Gaidhealaich Lunainn. Rin-neadh an sgrìobhadh so ann an Eilean Bharraidh air an 9ᵐʰ la de chéud mhìos an fhogharaidh, 'sa bhliadhna 1800, ann an lathair Ruairidh Mhic Néill, Tighearna Bharraidh, agus mar an céudna, an lathair Dhòmhnuill Mhic Dhòmhnuill, fear Bhaile-Raill, Eoghainn Mhic Dhòmhnuill fear Gheara-sheilich, Eoghainn Mhic Dhomh-nuill, fear Ghriminis, Alasdair Mhic Ghilleain, fear Hosteir, Alas-dair Mhic Neachdail, Ministeir Bheinne-bhaoghla, agus Ailein Mhic Chuinn, Ministeir Uist-a-chinntuath.

Air do'n sgrìobhadh so 'bhi ro fhada, cha cheaduich ùine dhomh ach beagan deth aithris a'n so, agus tha mi' deanamh sin gu fhéuchainn mar bha cùimhne aig na baird air an sinnsear fein gu céudan bliadhnaichibh air ais. Thoisich an sgrìobhadh mar so :—

" Ann an tigh Phadruig Mhic Neachdail a'n Torluim, goirid o o Chaisteal Bhuirghi, ann an Siorramachd Inbherneis, an naothamh la de chéud mhios an fhogair, anns an da fhicheadamh bliadhna agus naoi déug dá aois, thainig Lachlunn Mac Neill, Mhic Lach-luinn, Mhic Néill, Mhic Dhomhnuill, Mhic Lachluinn, Mhic Néill Mhòir, Mhich Lachluinn, Mhic Dhomhnuill, do shloinne chlann Mhuirich, ann an lathair Ruairidh Mhic Néill, Tighearna Bharraidh, a thabhairt a chodaich, mar is fiosrach esan, gur e fein an t-ochdamh glùn-déug o Mhuireach, a bha 'leantuinn teaghlaich Mhic-'ic-Ailein, Ceannard Chloinn Raonuill, mar bhardaibh ; agus o'n am sin gu'n robh fearann Stoileagairi, agus ceithir peighinean do Dhriomasdail aca, mar dhuais bardachd o linn gu linn, feadh chuig ghluin deug, . . . a chumail suas sloinneadh agus seanchas Chloinn-Domb-nuill. Agus bha mar fhiachan orra, 'nuair nach biodh mac aig a' bhard, gu'n tugadh e foghlum do mhac a bhrathar, no dha oighre, chum an coir air an fhearann a ghleidheadh ; agus is ann a reir a' chleachdaidh so, fhuair Niall, athair fein, ionnsachadh gu leughadh, sgriobhadh, eachdraidh, agus bardachd, o Dhomhnull Mac Néill, Mhic Dhomhnuill, brathair athar fein.

Tha cuimhne mhath aige gu robh " Saothair Oisein" sgriobht' air craicneann, ann an gleidhteanas 'athar fein o shinnsiribh ; gu robh cuid dheth na craicnean air an deanamh suas mar leabhraichean, agus cuid eile fuasgailte o cheile, anns an robh cuid do shaothair bhard eile, 'bharrachd air "Saothair Oisein."

Agus mar sin sios. Tha'n sgrìobhadh so aig Lachlunn Mac Mhuirich tuilleadh 's fada, chum a bhi air a léughadh gu léir air an fheasgair so. Féudaidh cuid agaibh smuaineachadh gu'm bheil e 'na nì iongantach, gu'm biodh cùimbu' aig a' bhàrd air àinmean a shinnsear fein, ré na h-uiread de linntibh air ais. Ach cha'n 'eil ach beag neach a rugadh 'san Eilean Sgiathanach, nach slòinn e fein air an dòigh cheudna gu cuig, deich, agus eadhon

tuilleadh linntean air ais. Air do na h-uiread a bhi dhe'n aon
aium, bha'n cleachd so freagarrach, chum cadar-dhealachadh a
dheanamh 'nam measg. Tha e glé chumanta gu'n clùinn sibh
Sgiathanach ag radh ; "Chunnaic mi an dingh Alasdair Mac
Aonghais, Mhic Dhonuill, Mhic Mhurchaidh, Mhic Dhomhnuill,
Mhic Mhurchaidh, Mhic Sheumais, Mhic Alasdair, Mhic Aonghais.
Chunnaic fear eile, Aonghas Mac Alasdair, 'ic Raonuill, 'ic Uisdein,
'ic Cholla, 'ic Dhomhnuill, 'ic Sheumais. Mar so sloinnidh iad an
sinnseara cho luath 'sa ta 'n teangadh comusach air sin a dheanamh.

Ach abram beagan fathasd a thaobh na bardachd. Tha bardachd
ro iongantach a lathair gu ruig an la 'n dingh, a rinneadh le aon de
na bardaibh a dh'ainmicheadh, 'se sin Lachlunn Mor Mac Dhomhnuill Mhic Mhuirich, anns a' bhliadhna 1411. Tha ceithir cheud,
tri fichead agus aon bhliadhna o'n rinneadh a' bhardachd so, ris
an ahrar, "Brosnachadh catha do Dhòmhnull, righ Inuse-Gall, le
Lachlunn Mòr Mac Mhuirich Albanaich," a bhrosnachadh Chloinn
Domhnuill, a bha deich mile ann an aireamh, gu bhi gaisgeil agus
treun, chum baiteal "Harla" a chur, air 25^{la} de Mhios Deirionnach
an t-Samhraidh 'sa' bhliadhna sin. Tha bhardachd so 'na h-ochd
earrannan deug, earrann air son gach litir 'san aibidil Ghaelig, agus
gach earrann a' toiseach dh leis an litir sin.

Cha'n aithris mi a'n so ni sam bith de bhardachd Oisein, air am
bheil moran agaibh eolach. Tha comas a nis aig na Goill fein, air
deagh eolas a ghabhail air na seann danaibh so, air doibh a bhi gu
cothromach air an eadar-theangachadh, leis an Olladh Urramach
Gilleasbuig Cleireach, Aodhair Chillemhaillidh.

Tha seann dan eile ann fathasd air a ghleidheadh a ta gu
h-anabarrach boidheach air a chur r'a cheile, ris an abrar " Mianu
a' Bhaird Aosda." Tha e 'toiseachadh mar so :—

> " O ! caraibh mi ri taobh nan allt,
> A shiubhlas mall le ceumaibh ciuin,
> Fo sgail a' bharraich leag mo cheann,
> 'S bi thus', a ghrian, ro chairdeil rium.
> Gu socair sìn 'san fheur mo thaobh,
> Air bruaich 'nan dìtheau 's nan gaoth tlà,
> 'S mo chas 'ga sliobadh 'sa' bhraon mhaoth,
> 'S e lubadh thairis caoin tro'n bhlar."

Agus mar sin sios. Tha sea earrainnean deug thar fhichead 'san
dan aluinn so ; ach cha 'n 'eil fios ciod an linn anns an robh " Am
Bard Aosda " beo, no c'ait an robh e. Tha cuid a' deanamh mach
gu'm bu Sgiathanach e, agus cuid eile gu'm b' Abrach e. Cha
robh reir coslais, eolas aige air a' Chreidimh Chriosduidh, ged bha
e ann an deigh laithean Oisein, oir tha e 'guidhe air a' ghaoith, a
cheo, no 'anam, a ghiulan gu talla Oisein agus Dhaoil, far an luidh

c

e sios gu brath ri taobh a chruit, a shlige, agus sgeithe a shinnsear.
Thubhairt e :—

> Thig le cairdeas thar a' chuain,
> Osag mhìn a ghluais gu mall ;
> Tog mo cheo air sgiath do luathais,
> Is imich chum an Innis thall !
>
> Biodh cruit a's slige lan rim' shaobh,
> 'San sgiath a dhion mo shinnsear s' chath,
> Fosglaibh-sa talla Oisein 's Dhaoil,
> Thig an oidhch' 's cha bhi 'm Bard air bhrath.
>
> Ach O ! ma'n tig i, seal ma'n triall mo cheo,
> Gu teach nam bard, air Ard-bheinn as nach pill,
> Fair cruit, 's mo shlige dh' ionnsuidh 'n roid,
> An sin, mo chruit, 's mo shlige ghraidh, slan leibh !

Cha cheadaich nine dhomh leudachadh air gach bard, ban-bhard,
filidh, agus fear-dain, a bha aig na Cinn-fheadhna, agus aig na
Fineachaibh Gaidhealach, o cheann ceud no dha bliadhna air ais.
Bha iad ro lionmhor, agus ioma-gnetheach.   Na'm measg so, bha
Mairi Nighean Alasdair Ruaidh, Silis Nighean Mhic Raonuill,
Mac Fhionnlaidh nan da'n, Ian Lom, an Ciaran Mabach, Ian
Dubh Mac Iain Mhic Ailein, an Clarsair Dall, Lachlunn Mac
Thearlaich, Ian Mac Fhearachair Mhic Codruim, Gilleasbuig na
Ciotaig, Alasdair Mac Mhaighstir Alasdair, Dughall Bochannan,
Donnchadh Ban nan Oran, Rob Donn, Ian agus Seumas Mac
Griogair, Uilleam Ros, Eobhan Mac Lachluinn, agus na ficheadan
eile.   Cha choir domb filidh Comunn Gaelic Inbherneis 'fhagail
air deireadh, a thionndaidh chum na Gaelig oran aluinn ar Ban-
righ choir.   Is lionmhor oran, iorram, dan, duan, rann, agus
laoidh a rinneadh leo-san a dh' ainmich mi ; seadh, orain de gach
gne agus cumadh, orain gaoil, orain-molaidh, orain-cogaidh, orain-
buaidhe, orain-treubhantais, orain sgaiteach agus eisgeil, orain
cainidh agus caoidh agus cumhaidh agus broin, orain-luaidhe
agus iomraidh agus buain, marbh-ranna, agus an leithidibh sin.
Tha na fuinn, agus na luinneagan a's boidhiche 'sa' Ghaelig, a
gheibhear ann an cainnt 'sam bith eile.
    Nach boidheach an t-oran a rinneadh le Domhnull Mac Aonghais,
am bard Uisteach ?

> " Mo nighean bhuidh bhan nam falbhadh tu leam, (tri uairean)
> Gu'n ceannaichinn gùn de'n t-sioda dhuit."

C'ait am bheil oran a bheir barrachd air an aon a rinneadh le
Domhnull Caimbeul, a bha 'na chleireach-eaglais aig an Urramach

Mac Aulai, sean-athair a' Mhorair Mhic Aulai, am fear-eachdraidh
cliuiteach a chaochail o cheann bliadhna no dha?

> " Gu mo slan a chith mi
> Mu chailin dileas, donn,
> Air an d' fhas an cuailean reidh,
> 'S air an deise dh' eireadh fonn ;
> 'S i cainnt do bheoil bu bhinn leam,
> 'N nair bhiodh m' inntinn trom ;
> 'S tu thogadh suas mo chridhe,
> 'Nuair bhiodh tu 'bruidhinn rium."

PIOBAIREACHD AGUS CEOL NAN GAIDHEAL.

Is i a' Phiob-mhor inneal-ciuil sonraichte Ghaidheal na h-Alba.
Cha'n 'eil teagamh nach 'eil an t-inneal so anabarrach sean.   Bha i
r'a faotiunn ann an talla an aoibhneis agus na caoidh.   Dheachd a
fuaim na gaisgich chum a' chath', agus chuir i failt' orra 'n am doibh
pilltinn gu beanntaibh am breith.   Bha aig gach ceann-cinnidh a
phiobair fein, agus bha e 'dol maille ris chum gach tuasaid agus
cogaidh.   Bha Clann Mhic Cruimein aig Siol Leoid, Dhunbhegain
mar phiobairean, o iomadh linn air ais, agus bha baile Bhoreraig
aca saor air son sin.   Mar an ceudna, bha Clann Mhic Artair aig
Mac Dhomhnuill nan Eilean, agus Peighinn-ghobhainn aca saor
mar aite comhnuidh.   Bha'n da theaghlach so a' teagasg na Piobaireachd do mhoran eile, a bha 'teachd 'nan ionnsuidh as gach
cearnadh dhe'n Ghaidhealtachd.   Tha eadhon, gu ruig an la 'n
dingh, Piobair aig gach Cath-bhuidheann Gaidhealach, a' dol maille
riu do na blaraibh, agus,

> " Cha do ghluais chum na tuasaid,
> 'S a chaoidh iad cha ghluais,
> Gun am bolg-fheadan meur-thollach,
> Fhuaimneach 'nan cluais."

Tha iomadh gne Phiobaireachd ann.   Tha cuid ann ris an abrar
" Cruinneachadh," cuid eile " Brosnachadh," cuid eile " Cumha,"
cuid eile " Failte," agus cuid eile " Tuireadh " mar a bha a' Phiobaireachd thiamhaidh, mhall, bhronach, bu ghnath bhi 'ga clui-
cheadh aig adhlacadh nam marbh.   Bha duil aig na Gaidheil gu'n
robh a' phiob mar gu'm b'ann a' labhairt bhriathra na Failte, no
an rabhaidh, no an tuiridh, mar a dh' fheudadh a' chuis a bhith.
Mar so, ann an " Cumha Mhic Leoid " bha phiob ag radh :—

> " Cha till, cha till, cha till Mac Cruimean,
> Cha till e gu brath, gu là na cruinne,
> Cha till, cha till, cha till Mac Cruimean,
> Cha till Mac Leoid, 's cha bheo Mac Cruimean."

B 2

Tha "Cumha Mhic an Toisich" air an doigh cheudna. Rinneadh
"Failte" do Uilleam Dubh Mac Coinnich, le Fionnladh Dubh
Mac Rà, 'sa bhliadhna 1715, ris an goirear gu cumanta Failte
Thighearna Sheafoirt." Is piobaireachd ro ghrinn an "Fhailte" so ;
agus bha duil aig Cloinn Choinnich gu'n robh a' phiob a' labhairt,
agus a' gradh :—

> Slan gu'm pill fear 'chinn duibh
> Slan gu'n till fear 'chinn duibh,
> Slan gu'm pill fear 'chinn duibh,
> Slan gu'n till Uilleachan.
>
> Slan gu'n tig, slan gu'n ruig,
> Slan gu'n tig Uilleachan,
> 'S toil leam fein fear 'chinn duibh,
> 'S toil leam fein Uilleachan,
>
> 'S gaisgeach treun Uilleachan,
> Claidheamh geur, 'n laimh 'n fhir-fheill,
> 'S na seoid ag eigheach gu leir,
> 'S trom beuman Uilleachain !

Bha Colladh Mac Dhomhnuill, ris an abradh iad Colladh Ciotach,
'na gaisgeach treun 'na la fein, agus bha piobair aige. Bha Colladh
'na chaisteal fein aig àm araidh, 'ga dhionadh fein mar a dh' fheudadh e ; agus chunnaic am piobair na naimhdean a' tarruing dluth,
agus cha b'fhad gus an d' rinn iad greim air fein, agus air a phiob.
Air da a bhi deonach air a mhaighstir a theasairginn, dh'iarr e
cead piobaireachd a chluicheadh, agus thug iad cead dha. Sheid e
suas, agus chual Colladh 'san Dun a' phiob mar gu'm b'ann ag
radh :—

> " A cholladh, cuir umad, bi ullamh, bi falbh,
> Bi ullamh, bi falbh, bi ullamh, bi falbh,
> A Cholladh, cuir umad, bi ullamh, bi falbh,
> Tha sinne a'n laimh, tha sinne a'n laimh !
>
> Fag an ni, fag an ni, fag an ni,
> Fag an ni, fag an ni, fag an ni,
> Fag an ni, fag an ni, fag an ni,
> Tha sinne a'n laimh, tha sinne a'n laimh !
>
> Ramh is taoman, ramh is taoman,
> Ramh is taoman, ramh is taoman,
> Ramh is taoman, ramh is taoman,
> Tha sinne a'n laimh, tha sinne a'n laimh !
>
> Lamh dhearg, lamh dhearg, lamh dhearg,
> Lamh dhearg, lamh dhearg, lamh dhearg,
> Lamh dhearg, lamh dhearg, lamh dhearg,
> Tha sinne a'n laimh, tha sinne a'n laimh,

'Cholladh, mo ghaol, seachainn an caol,
Seachainn an caol, seachainn an caol,
'Cholladh, mo ghaol, thoir ort a' Mhaol
Buidhinn an ath, buidhinn an ath !

'Cholladh, mo ruin, seachainn an dun
Seachainn an dun, seachainn an dun,
'Cholladh, mo ruin, seachainn an dun,
Tha sinne a'n laimh, tha sinne a'n laimh !

Bha Clann Mhic Cruimein, Dhunbheagain, a' sgriobhadh na piobaireachd sios ann an leabhar, gu bhi 'ga cumail air chuimhne ;
ach cha d' rinn iad sin air an doigh air am bheil ceol 'ga sgriobhadh le muinntir eile a nis. Bha iadsan 'ga dheanamh le focail
bheaga, ghoirid, a bha iad a' cur a'n altaibh a' cheile, chum fuaim
an fheadain, agus na puirt a chiallachadh. Bha e rud eigin cosmhuil ri innleachd an Sol-fa, a ta 'ga gnathachadh 'san am so, ann
an ceol nan Salm. Bha iadsan a' gabhail lionmhorachd fhocal
ghoirid, mar hi, ri, ro, bhi, ha, ra, din, hia, di, rit, hio, dra, ti, re,
dro, tiri, bhia, tara, tetiri, agus mar sin sios. Air an diogh so
chuireadh iad sios piobaireachd " Failte a' Phrionnsa " mar' a
leanas—

AN T-URLAR.

hi o dro hi ri, hi an an in ha rà,
hi o dro hà chin, hà chin hi à chin,
hi o dro hi rì, hi an an in ha rà,
hi o dro hà chin, hà chin hi ì chin,
hi o dro hi ri, hì an an in ha rà,
hi o dro hà chin, hà chin hi à chin,
hi o dro hi rì, hi an an in ha rà,
hi o dro hà chin, hà chin hi ì chin.

SIUBHAL.

hi o dro hi chin, hà chin hà chin,
hi o dro hà chin, hì chin ha chin,
hi o dro hì chin, hà chin hà chin,
hi o dro hà chin, hà chin hì chin,
hi o dro hì chin, hì chin hì chin,
hi o dro hà chin, hì chin hà chin,
hi o dro hì chin, hà chin hà chin,
hi o dro hà chin, ha chin hi chin.

TAOBHDUDH.

hio dro to, hì dro to, hà dro to, hà dro to,
ho dro to, ha dro to, hi dro to, hi à chin.
&c., &c., &c.

EIDEADH AGUS ARMACHD NAN GAIDHEAL.

A thaobh eididh nan Gaidheal, cha ruig mi'leas moran a radh, do brigh gu'm bheil sibh nile eolach oirre. Is eideadh mhaiseach i gun teagamh. Tha "Breacan-an-fheile" 'na thrusgan a ta anabarrach sean, agus a bha air a chleachdadh leis na Gaidheil o na cend linntibh. An toiseach, gidheadh, cha robh an eideadh so, air a deanamh mar a tha i a nis. Bha i an sin, air a deanamh suas de dha shlat deug de bhreacan gun a bhi air a ghearradh idir. Bha 'm breacan so air a shuanadh, no air a phasgadh mu'n cuairt do na guaillibh, agus do'n chom, agus air fhagail an crochadh sios dh' ionnsuidh nan glun. Bha e air a cheangladh mu'n cuairt do'n chom le crios, agus bha e air a dhaingneachadh air a' ghualainn chli le bior, no le braist' airgid, no oir. An deigh sin, ghnathaicheadb an "Fheile-bheag" a bha air a deanamh air leth o'n bhreacan, agus a bha ni's cuimir', sgiobalta na'm breacan air fad, gu'n ghearradh. Tha iomadh dearbhadh againn gu'm bheil an eideadh so anabarrach sean. Thog na Romanaich balla tarsuing air Alba, eadar an amhainn "Forth" agus "Cluaidh," air an tugadh an t-aium "Balla Antonine," an t-Impear Roimheach a chuir suas e. Thogadh am Balla so 'sa bhliadhna 140. An nair a bha an steidh aigo 'ga bhuireachadh suas o cheann beagan bhliadhnaichean air ais, fhuaradh leac air an robh air an gearradh dealbh triuir dhaoine, a bha air an eideadh 'san trusgan Ghaidhealach so. Tha'n leac so air a gleidheadh gu curamach. Tha mar an ceudna, Diodorus Siculus, Tacitus, agus Cæsar, an luchd-eachdraidh Roimheach, a' cur an ceill gu'n robh na Caledoniich air an eideadh le cotaichibh air am breacadh le h-iomadh dath. Fhuaradh iomadh leac eile a ta 'dearbhadh an ni ceudna. Tha aon aig "Dupplin" ann an siorramachd Pheirt, air am bheil Gaidheal air a ghearradh 'san eideadh so, le targaid chruinn, agus le sleagh bhiorach 'na laimh. Tha aon eile a chladhaicheadh a mach aig Dul, ann an Siorramachd Pheirt, air am bheil na fir air an gearradh le sgiathaibh cruinn air an gairdean chli, agus le sporranaibh béine. Tha iomadh dearbhadh eile ann mar an ceudna, air gne, dreach, agus cumadh eididh nan Gaidheal.

'S math 'thig breacan an fheilidh
Gu leir do na suinu,
Osain ghearr air an calpannaibh
Domhail, geal, cruinn,
Iteagan dorcha air slios
Gorm uidheam cheann,
Sud i eideadh nam blar,
'S cha bi an te fhada theann !

REV. ROBERT MACGREGOR, Kilmuir, Skye.

A thaobh armachd nan Gaidheal, tha'n luchd-eachdraidh Romanach, mar a ta Tacitus, a' cur an ceill gu'n do chleachd iad
" Claidhean-mora, fada," le targaidibh beaga, cruinn, agus biodagan.
Air an cosaibh bha osain-ghearra, brogan, no cuarain. An uair a
chuireadh an cath air " Innis Pheirt," an lathair Righ Roibeirt
III. 'sa bhliadhna 1396, le deich thar fhichead Ghaidheal air an
aon taobh, an agaidh dheich thar fhichead air an taobh eile, tha
fear-eachdraidh (Abbot Bower) ag innseadh 'na leabhar, gu'n robb
na Gaidheil air an armadh a mhain le claidhibh, boghannaibh-
saighead, agus tuaghannaibh-catha. Tha e soilleir gu'n robb
armachd an t-sluaigh ghaisgeil so ag atharrachadh gu mor o linn
gu linn, mar a bha innealan ura cogaidh 'gan dealbhadh, agus 'gan
cleachdadh. Ach ge b'e ciod an armachd a laimhsich iad, cha
b' iadsan a thionndaidheadh an cul aon chuid ri caraid, no ri
namhaid !

Ach a thuilleadh air gach ni a dh' ainmicheadh, dh' fheudainn
moran radh mu fhearachas-tighe, cleachdanna-du'chail, inneala-
treabhaidh, buill-acfhuinn, agus airneis nan Gaidheal. Tha na
nithe sin gu leir airidh air beachd a ghabhail diubh, a chionn gu
bheil iad nan nithe a ta air an cleachdadh gu sonraichte leis na
Gaidheil fein, agus moran diubh na'n nithe nach faicear agus nach
faighear, ach am measg an t-sluaigh' chliuitich so. Tha cuid a'n
so a lathair an nochd, aig nach 'eil fios ciod e " Caschrom, Cas-
dhireach, Slachdan, Groideallan, Poit-Uirearaidh, Leachd-ghradain,
Muilean-leth-coise, Muilean-bradh, Bòrd-luaidh, Racan, Plocan
Cisean, Iris, Siomaid, Cliabh, Càineag, Plàt, Sgonnan, Tallan,
Sunnag," agus mar sin sios.

Dh' fheudadh moran a bhi air aithris, mar an ceudna, mu na
Gnàthfhocail, saobh-chrabhadh, giseag, ranntachd, dubh-cheisd,
toimhseachan, taibhsearachd, sugradh, iomairt, agus cluiche, a
gheibhear am measg nan Gäidheal, ach fagaidh mi iad sin, gu bhi
gu soilleir air an lorgadh a mach, agus air an aithris gu h-ullamh,
h-eallamh, deas-chainnteach, leis an Urramach fhoghluimte sin
" Bun-Lochabar ! "

Cha'n inndrinn mi, mar an ceudna, air eachdraidh chianail
shliochd nam beann, a thaobh an doigh air an robb iad air an
ruagadh o aois-larachaibh an sinnsear fein, air an greasadh gu
criochaibh cubhann, agus na miltean diubh air an co'-eigneachadh
gu dol air imirich do dhuchannaibh cein, thar chuanta farsuing
agus ànradhach. Is suarach an dionadh a ni na feidh, na caoraich
bhana, agus na cearcan-coille agus fraoich, an aghaidh an namhaid,
an coimeas ri sliochd nan garbh-chrioch nach do dhiobair riamh !

Ach a thuilleadh air so, cha'n 'eil e 'a'm' chomas an nochd, mar
a bha aon uair a' mhiann orm, cunntas a thoirt air na Fineachaibh

Gäidhealach, agus air gach connsachadh, cogadh, creach, agus blar fuilteach, a bha aca 'nan aimhreitibh an aghaidh a' cheile. Ghabhadh sin moran nine. Bhiodh e taitneach, mar an ceudna, leudachadh air breacannaibh nan Fineachan fa leth, air suaicheantas, gairmibh-catha, brataichibh, agus briathraibh-brosnachaidh gach Fineadh 'sa Ghaidhealtachd. Bha mor-chumlachd aig na Cinnfheadhna anns gach aite, agus air doibh a bhi mar righre beaga thar an luchd-cinnidh, bha comas beatha agus bais aca 'nan laimh. Ach dh' fhalbh na h-amanna deistinneach sin a nis; agus tha e taitneach gu'n d' fhalbh. Am feadh 'sa ta sliochd 'nam beann, 's nan gleann air feadh Gaidhealtachd na h-Alba, co cliuiteach agus cruadalach 'sa bha iad riamh, bha 'n dillseachd agus an treubhantas air an gnathachadh o cheann linntean air ais, cha'n ann ri comhstrith an aghaidh a' cheile, mar is minic a bha iad, ach mar chathbhuidhean gu'n striochdadh, bha iad deas agus dileas, thar tuigse, gu bhi 'dionadh an *saorsa*, an *dù'cha*, 'san *lagh !*

> " 'S iomadh deuchainn a fhuair
> Na fir ardanach, bhras,
> O nach geilleadh dhiubh làmb,
> Is nach tionnd'adh dhiubh cas ;
> 'S o nach feudadh gu'n caochl'adh
> An dualchas 'san cleachd,
> Leis an d'fhagadh gun samhladh
> An sinnseara 'sa ghleachd."

REV. ROBERT MACGREGOR, Kilmuir, Skye.

Cha tug saighdearan ni b' fhearr riamh aghaidh do namhaid. Leò-san sguabadh air falbh an eascairdean as an araich, mar a sguabar am moll le neart na gaoithe. Cha di-chuimhnichear gu brath an gaisge aig "Ticonderago," an treubhantas air la "Fontenoi," am morchruadal 'san Eiphit, agus an dian-thairisneachd anns gach cath sgriosail a chuireadh leo, air mor-thir na Roinu-Eorpa ! O ! cia fearail, cuimear, agus eireachdail iad 'nan eideadh fein ! Cia garg agus colgach, a'n àm dol sios do'n chath ! Cia minic, luath mar na h-iolairean a' dol air iteig chum cobhartaich, a ruith iad air feachd nan namb, agus a chuir iad as doibh gu tur ! Cha'n 'eil e ach 'na fhearas-chuideachd dhoibh an dream a sheasas nan aghaidh a ghearradh as ! Is gann a nochdas iad an treubhantas, ach an nair a tha an cunnard mor, no an namhaid garg agus dalma. An sin comhdaichidh an corruich an talamh lé closaichibh nam marbh, mar a chomhdaicheas corran a' bhuanaiche an t-achadh le sguabaibh ! Fhad 'sa bhios meas air fior-shaighdearachd, cha leagar air dearmad am fearalas air faiche fuilteach "Bhaterlu,"—

'S ann an sud a bha 'ghriobhag,
Le luaidh ghrad, lannaibh biorach,
'S claidhibh sgaiteach 'gan iomairt,
Le dream chalma gun tioma,
Chaidh Siol Alba gu'n ghiorraig,
Anns an t-searbh-chath air mhireadh,
'Creuchdadh chorp is 'gan liodairt,
Is 'gam fagail 'san ionad gun deo!"

REV. ROBERT MACGREGOR, of Kilmuir, Skye.

A nis, beannachd leibh air fad. Cha'n ioghna ged bhiodh uaill
oirbh mar Chomunn, an nair a dh' ainmichear sibh air a Ghäelig!

" Mile beannachd, mile buaidh,
Air Comunn Uaislean mo ruin ;
Cha ghluaisear Breatunn le fiamh,
'S sibhse mar dhion air a cul.
Thog Albainn a ceann le h-uaill ;
Dh' fhuasgladh a' Ghaelig a' snuim :
Tha coir gach saorsainn gu feum,
Aig sliochd Ghaidheal nam beus grinn.
Thig Sonas, is Bliochd, is Maoin,
Fialachd, is Tlus, Faoilt, is Baigh,
Sgaoilidh 'nam miltibh bhur siol,
Mar rainich 'nam fiadh-ghleann fas!"

E. MAC LACHLUINN.

" An là a chìth 's nach fhaic."

_____

On the 14th November the following paper, from Mr A. A.
Carmichael, C.M.S.A.S., Creagory, Benbecula, was read :—

TOIRIOC NA TAINE.

[Seanchaidh Eachann Mac-iosaig (" Eachann Mac Ruaraidh ")
Croitear, Ceannlangabhat, Iocar, Uist a Chinne Deas. Sgriobhta
le Alastair G. Macgillemhicheil, Creagoiridh, Beinn 'a faola, La-
fheill Moire.]

Deilbh agus aobhar na sgeuil.

Bha duin-uasal ann an Eirinn ris an canadh 'ad an Du'altach.
Cha bu tighearna fearainn idir e ; ach bha cnid mhor an t-saoghal
aige agus ionnsachadh math agus e o theaghlach miosail, agus leis a
sin bha aite suidhe aige ann an cuideachd uaillsean. Cha ro eir a
theolach ach aona ghille mic d'am b'ainm Cuchullain. Bha e fhein

agus Iarla Ghlinn-chuilisg comhla anns a' cholaiste agus bha 'ad
nan cairdean 's nan companaich. Bha nighean an Iarla posadh
agus chuir an t-Iarla cuireadh chun na bainnse dh-ionnsuidh an
Du'allaich seachduin roimhe 'n am. Dh-fhalbh an Du'allach agus a
bhean chun na bainnse le'n gillean, 's le'n eich dhiolta. Bha
Cuchullain a' sireadh falbh ach cha leigte leis. 'Nuair a dh-fhalbh
'adsan dh-fhalbh easan as an deoghaidh. Bha ball 'us caman aige
's bha e g-iomain fad fin foineach an la air an rathad. Am biall
na h-oiche an dol fodha na greine rainig 'ad an drochaid mhor bha
dol thun pelios an Iarla. Bha cu eir an drochaid ga gleidheadh 's
cha leigeadh e duine seachad gun phe'eadh. Cha ro airgiod aig
a' ghille. Smaointich e aige fhein gu'm bu tamailteach dha tilleadh
dhachaidh agus chuir e 'm ball eir sorachag agus bhuail e steigh
eir an dala ceann a choin 's a mach eir a cheann eil' e 's chuir e
'n cu na bhuta leis an drochaid.

Sin a' chiad euc a rinn Cuchullain.

Gha' e steigh an bhaile 's chun' e gillean a g-iomain agus thoisich
e air iomain cò-riu. D'uair thainig an oicbe thuirst e ri fear dhe
na gillean bha g-iomain co ris, "Nach ann an seo" ors easan "tha teigh
an Iarla?" "Sann" ors an gille eile ; " De seo do ghnothuchsa
ris ?" "Nach eil beanais (banais) mhor ann ?" "Tha." "B'fhearr
liom gu'n ionnsuiche tu dhomh e." "Cha leig 'ad is teigh thu."
"Tha m' athair 's mo mhathair eir a' bheanais agus fiachaidh mi
an leig."

Bha 'n caisteal eir a lasadh le craoslach chraobhach sholuist.
Gha' e steigh 's gha' miosg na cuideac 's thng e ruith a null 's chaidh
e eadar da ghlun athar.   "An tu tha seo Chuchullain ?" ors
athair, "'S mi" orsa Cuchullain. "Ciamar fhuair thu steigh 's an
cu eir an drochaid ?"   "Mharbh mi 'n cu."

De'art bha ach fear do stiubhartan an Iarla 's an rum agus
falbhar agus innsear dha mhaighstir cainnt Chuchullain. Leum an
t-Iarla nuas. "Co tha seo ors easan a mharbh mo chu eir an
drochaid ?"   Cha tuirst duine diog—bha eagal orra.

Thuirst an Du'altach, "Seo e, tha g-rathain rium gu'n do
mharbh e do chu." "Cha chreid mi sin, gu'm marbhadh giullan beag
mar sin mo chu."   "O ! 's mi mharbh e gu dearbh 's cha chuir
thu gu duin' 's am bith eil' e ach mise" ors Cuchullain. "Bhuil,"
ors an t-Iarla, "feumaidh tu fuireach seac blianna sir an drochaid ga
gleidheadh go 's an tog mise cu ni t-aite, neo pe'idh tu £700
Sasannach dhomh." " An ta pe'idh mise sin eir son mo mhic" ors
an Du'altach ; "ach mu phe'eas cha mhor is fhiach mi fhe' na dheo'-
idh. Ach nam faighinn uine phe'inn sin 's mi fhe' bhi mar bha
mi roimhe."

Dh-eirich Cuchullain na sleasadh agus thuirt e "Cha phaigh thu athair aon sgillin, ach theid mis' thuin na drochaid ga gleidheadh dha, agus fuiridh mi blianna, agus feumaidh easan cearstas a' choin a chumail riumsa."

Bha Cuchullain a sin blianna eir an drochaid. Bha e fuasach eirson sgoil, agus a chuile duine thigeadh chun na drochaid theireadh e ris "Cha leig mi null thu mar toir thu dhomh leasan, agus d'uair thigeadh duin-uasal bheireadh e dha am pé'eadh, agus an leasan cò-ris.

Leis cho dichiollach 'sa bha e ga togail, dh-ionnsuich e mar-seo moran sgoil'. Thainig e sin dachaidh. Bha anns an am sin dh'an t-saoghal colaiste ann un Dun-sgathaich 's an Eileann-Sgitheanach agus cha ro fear ris am b'fhiach fear a ra an rioghac na h-Alba, an Sasunn no an Eirinn nach cuireadh a mhao ga ionnsachadh ann. Cha ro meas eir fear ach fear a gheo'adh ionnsuchadh an Dun-sgathaich. Cha ro sgoil no faolum no math-cbleas nach faight ann, 's cha ro meas eir cleas ach cleas a gheobht' ann. Cha bhiodh Cuchullain beo mar leigt' eir falbh a sgoil Dhun-Sgathaich e, agus leigeadh air falbh e. Bha e naogh blianna an sin. Bha uasal Albannach d'am b'aium Am Feardiag mac Daimbain anns an sgoil ra linn Chuchullain agus be ciad ghaisgeach an t-saoghail e ra linn fhein. Bha'm Feardiag agus Cuchullain a' laidhe 'sa g-eiridh comhla fad nan naogh blianna agus 'ad nan companaich aig a' cheile. 'N am bha 'ad a dealachadh mhionnaich 'ad ga cheile nach cuireadh an dala fear trioblaid eir an fhear eile gu brach. Cha ro sian a dh-ionnsuich an dala fear nach d-ionnsuich am fear eile ach aon cbleas a bh' aig Cuchullain ris an cante an gath-balg. *

Bha gillean aca agus b'iad an da bhrathair an da ghille. 'Se gille na h-Iuraich a b-ainm do ghille 'n Fhirdhiag agus Laochaire Mac Nearst a b'ainm do ghille Chuchullain.

Bha na gillean aca nam *pagechan* aca 's an sgoil agus cha ro 'ad fhein cli. Lean Laochaire Mac Nearst Cuchullain agus Gille na h-Iuraich am Feardiag.

Dh-fhag 'ad Dun-Sgathaich agus thill Cuchullain dachaidh a dh-Eirinn. Thainig Cuchullain agus Laochaire Mac Nearst dhach-aidh gu ruig teigh an Du'altaich an Grianan-math an Eirinn. Bha lechiad agh aig an Du'altach ann an eileann mara agus, de ach rug te aca laogh agus cha ro fios fo thalamh na criosdac cait an d-fhuair e tara. Cha ro dath bh'anu am bogha frois no ann an

---

* Tha'n Seanchaidh ag rath gur h-ann a muigh eir uacar uisge dh-fhcumta an gath-balg a chluich.

iarmailt nan speur no ann an coille-blianain a' chuain nach robh eir
an laogh. Cha bhiodh Cuchullain beo 'se na ghille tapaidh an
deigh tighinn far na drochaid mar h-ainmichte an laogh eir fhein.
Cha ro athair deonach an laogh a thoirt dha bho'n nach bu laogh
boirionn e. "Feumaidh mi fhaighinn. 'S fhearr liom am firionn
seo na deich bhoirionn, agus fhuair en laogh. Cha robb an laogh
ach na laogh ri linn Cuchullain falbh a sgoil an Dun-Sgathaich ach
bha e na tharbh ri linn dha tilleadh as. Cha ro a leithid an
Eirinn ach e fhein. Tha e 'san eachdraidh gu'n cuireadh e marst
eir dhàir le geum an Coig Choigeamh na h-Eirionn. Be'n Donn-
Guaillionn a b'ainm dha.

Thill Cuchullain dachaidh a Ghrian-math an Eirinn agus bhitheadh e fhein 'sa Ghille Laochaire Mac Nearst a' falbh a shealg gu
tao' eile na h-Eirionn. Bha e taghal eir nighinn a Ghairbh Mhic
Stairn, agus theireadh e rithe, "Thig mi'n dingh, 's thig mi 'm
maireach," 's dhianadh e coineamh rithe, agus 'se bun a bh-ann
gu'n do theich i leis. Thug e dhachaidh i gu teigh athar agus
chaidh e eir teigh dha fhein 's bha e fhé' 's ise riarachadh a cheile
gle mhath.

Bu bharuinn eir dala leth Eirinn 's an am boirionnach ris an
canta Maoim a Chruachain agus bu righ eir an leth eile Oiriol
Fhaolamach. Bha 'ad nam bantraichean le cheile. Bhuail an
cairdean 's an comhairleichean eir a dh-rath riu gu'm bu choir
dhaibh posadh 's an cnid a chur ri cheile. Bha fear ionad righ
aicese, mac peathar 'i fhein d'm b-ainm Fearghus Philisteach agus
chuir a Bharuinn a comhairle ris am posadh i Oiriol. "Am bi thu
deonach mise phosagh Oirill?" ors ise. "Bithidh mi" orsa Fearghus
"gle dheonach thu ga phosàdh gu dearbh. Tha uallach trom orm
fhein agus tha mi eirson aotromachadh."

Chuireadh gu posadh 'ad agus phòs Maoim a Chruachain agus
Oiriol Fhaolumach. Am ceann mios no rud-eigin chaidh 'ad gu
butar-scionn 's throd 'ad. Bhuail an dala h-aon eir cur a dh-ailis
eir an t-aon eile gu ro barrac aig eir a chuid an t-saoghal. Thois-
icheadh a seo eir cunntas an stuie agus d'uair chunntadh 's a chuireadh ra cheile 'n stoc bha tarbh aigesan a bharrac oirise. Be
ainm an tairbh, am Binne-bheoch.*

* The reciter says that Binne-bheoch means "the horned beast," and
I think he may be right. In Uist, "binneach," or "beannach," is applied to a horned animal, generally to an animal with high horns. "Caora-
bhinneach," or, more correctly, "Caora-bheannach," is applied to the old
and now nearly extinct Hebridean breed of sheep with four, five, and even
sometimes six horns.

Bhuail a' Bharuin a sin eir feoraich a dh-Fhearghus cait am faighte tarbh a gha'adh eir a Bhinne-bheoch agus a gheo'adh buaidh eir 's nach bitheadh a beo shaoghail aice mar faigheadh.

"Cha 'n 'ainne dhomhse sin" orsa Fearghus "cait am faighear tarbh a gha'as eir, 'sa bheir buaidh eir ach an Donn-guaillionn aig an Du'allach 's a ri fhein cha'n e sin an sugradh dol na dhàil no fhaighinn uaithe. Tha e fhein laidir 's tha mhac ro laidir leomach moralach 's mar faighear le sith e chan fheighear idir le feirg e." "Cha 'n eil duin agam dha 'n fhearr thig a chuis chur an ceil na sibh fhein. Theid sibh a shireadh an tairbh agus bheir sibh leibh tri-diag dha na gillean mora," orsa Bharuinn.

Chaidh Fearghus Philisteach agus tri-diag dha na gillean mor' aig Maoim a Chruachain a shireadh an Donn-ghuaillionn. Rainig 'ad teigh an Du'altaich ma mheadhan la 's chaidh Fearghus is steigh a thalla an Du'altaich. Shir e'n tara as a sheasamh "Tha cabhag orst" ors an Du'allach, "'n ann eir toir teine thainig thu? Dian suidhe 's ga' do sgial."

"Cha dian gos am faigh mi fios ceann mo ghnothuich." "An ta cha 'n ann agams tha sin ri thoirst dhuit ach aig mo Mhac, Cuchullain. Tha e 'sa bheinn sheilg ach bithidh e dhachaidh am bial an anamoich. 'Se do bheatha cò-rium fhein a noc agus fuirich gos an tig Cuchullain o'n t-sheilg." Tha gillean mor' agam, a thug mi liom gus mo chuideacha leis an tara 's cha'n eil e freagrach 'adsan a bhi co-ruinn." Tha saillean gu leoir agamsa 's an cuir sinn eir dhòigh 'ad.

Chuireadh biadh 'us deoch agus aodach leapa gu leoir thun nan gillean mora. Ghabh 'ad an dall daorach. Bha Fearghus agus an Du'altach ag ol 's an teigh mhor gos an tainig Cuchullain dhachaidh am bial na h-oiche.

Chuala Cuchullain roicealac 's an t-sobhal aig athair agus ghabh e null. Thainig e an sin an teigh mhor agus gha' e steigh far an ro athar agus Fearghus a' caitheamh an fheasgair gu cridheil. "Sin fear do ghnothuich" ors an Du'allach ri Fearghus. Thoisich a sin Fearghus eir sireadh an tairbh eir Cuchullain cho milist 's cho seolta 's cho briathrach 'sa b'urradha. "Gheo' thu" ors easan "do dhor 's do airgiod agus cairdeas na Maoim Chruachain agus lamh dheas Oirill." Cha tuirst Cuchullain guth ach dh-eisd e ris. Thionndaidh e chulaobh. "Am faigh mi 'n tarbh?"

"Cha'n eil fiosam nach foigh." Ghrad dh-eirich Fearghus a mach agus thug e 'n sothal eir far an ro na gillean-mora. Lean Cuchullain e. Bha na gillean eir an dalladh leis an daoraich. "An d-fhuair thu'n tara?" ors a chuile fear ria' ri Fearghus.

"Fhuair mi ach cha'n fhaighcadh mo ghillean e." "Am fear

seo 's am fear 'ad eile carson nach faigheadh do ghillean e ?   Mar
faigheadh 'ad a dheoin e bheireadh 'ad a dhaineoin e" orsa chuile
fear riabh. Chuala Cuchullain a' chainnt agus thill e eir ais. Thill
Fearghus eir ais dha'n teigh agus chaidil e fhein agus an Du'allach
's an aon rum.

Chaidh Cuchullain 's chuir e gad eir dorust an t-saothail los
nach faigheadh duine mach agus chuir e'n teigh na theine 's loisg
e ma'n ceann e.

Bha Fearghus agus an Du'allach fada gun chadal ach a seanachas—duine thall 's duine bhos. 'D nair thainig Cuchullain a
steigh 'sa mhaduin thog Fearghus a cheann 's chunnaig e Cuchullain
thall eadar e 's an uinneag.   " Seadh bheil sibh dol bhi cho math
's 'ur gealltanas an dingh ? " orsa Fearghus.

" Tha gu dearbh. Gu deart [de ruid ?] a gheall mi ? "   " Nach do
gheall sibh dhomh an tarbh—an Donn-guaillionn dhomh ? "   " Gu
de 'n gealltanus a rinn mi?   An tuirst mi riut ach nach ro fiosam
nach faigheadh agus tha fiosam an dingh nach faigh thu e.   Na'n
tuga tusa leat cuideaca mhoghail 's docha gu'm faighe tu leat an
tarbh."

Chuir Fearghus nime agus chaidh e mach agus b'e chiad sealladh
a bhuail a shuil an sothal na shineadh agus cnàbhann nan daoin'
aigo eir ghoil nan gual loisgte.   Chaidh e dhachaidh.

" An d-fhuair thu'n tara—an tara Fhearghuis—caite bheil an
tara ? " orsa Mhaoim Chruachain.

" Cha d-fhuair 's ga de chuire' tu cuideac bu mbutha eir falbh
cha'n fhaigheadh 'ad an tara," agus dh-innis e dha'n Bhàrinn 'mar
dh-eirich dha na gillean.

Bhòinicheadh a sin eir a Bharuin agus eir Oiril dol cola rist, 's
chaidh 'ad cola.   Ach mu'n tainig ceann mhios throd iad a rist
agus a rist ma'n Bhinne-bheoch.   Chuir a sin a Mhaoim Chruachain litirichion a mach fad agus farsuinn feadh Albainn, Shasuinn
agus Eirinn, fear 's am bith thigeadh thoirst a mach an Donn
ghuaillionn gu'm bu leis or agus airgiod gu leoir, cairdeas leaghais
na Maoim Chruachain agus lamh dheas Oirill."*

Bha Mhaoim Chruachain na seann chaillich ghrainnde ghlais.

Chuir a sin boirionnach bha mu'n cairst di fhein na ceann litir
a chuir thun an Fhir-diag.

---

* The reciter explains this frequent phrase thus : — He says that
"Cairdeas leaghas na Maoim Chruachain" means the Queen's "healing
friendship" ; and that "Lamh dheas Oirill" means Oiriol's place with herself. To my thinking, "Lamh dheas Oiriol" would signify Oiriol's right-
hand friendship."

Rinn i sin ach cha b' ann gu posadh na dad ach gu cuilm mhor bha i gos a thoirst seachad. Bha brathairean an Fhirdhiag a muigh aig a bhuain agus am Feardiag a spaidsearac mu'n cuairst daibh 's gu'n e dianadh dad nuair a thainig an litir. Shuidh e eir carn faisg eir na buanaichean agus leugh e litir na Maoim Chruachain.

"Tha litir a seo ors easan, a thainig thugam o'n Mhaoim Chruachain ag cur ma 'm choineamh dol a chumail cuilm agus cuideac lethe." "Chuala sinn ma 'n litir sin roimhe. Gos do phosadh!" ors a bhrathair 's e taruinn as. "Deart tha thu g-rath? Ne mise phosadh an t-seann scrait chaillich. Leora cha phosadh ga nam bitheadh eir thalamh na talamhuin ach i fhein a bhoirionnaich. Ach gun teagamh 's am bith feumaidh mi a Bhàruinn a fhreagairst o na chuir i fios orm.

Dh-fhalbh am Feardiag, e fhein agus a ghille, gille na h-Iuraich, agus rainig 'ad pelios Bàruinn Eirinu. Bha là'n sgaoilte rompa. Thoisich ol 'us ceol 'us danns agus gairdeachas 'us greannachas mor ri linn ciad ghaisgeach an t-saoghail tighinn dha'n duthaich.

['S ann dha na fir mbora bha am Feardiag agus dha na fir bheaga Cuchullain.] Chuir a Mhaoim Chruachain ceist ris an Fhear-dhiag. "De 's lagha gha'as tu" ors ise "agus dol a ghleic ri Cuchullain eir faiche-choraig eir da nair 'iag a'm maireach?"

A Mhaoim Chruachain agus a Bharuin Eirinn dhianainse gniomh gaisgich agus euc curaidh a chuire 'tu ma m'choineamh, agus a b'urra mi dhianadh; aah dol a ghleic m' chaomh chompanch Cuchullain rud nach urra 's nach dian mi. Mise dhol a ghleic Cuchullain! 'Ne am fear bha laidhe 'sa g'eiridh nam bhrollach fad nan naogh blianna agus is docha liom na gin dha'm bhrathairen fhé'! Mise dhol a ghleic ri Cuchullain! Ghleacainn fear a ghleacadh ris agus cha chuirinn eir eirson rud 's am bith."

'Thoisich a sin an t-ol agus chuireadh eir 'us eir gus na chuireadh an dall daorach eir a ghaisgeach, am Feardiag, agus thuit e far an ro' e. Cha ro do nearst ann am *pageachun* leibideach Maoim a Chruachain na thogadh as a siod e, agus leigeadh leis laidh far an ro' e agus chuireadh cuirigeann fairis eir. Sgri' a Mhaoim Chruachain litir fhoilleil mhosach an ainm an Fhirdiag gu'n reachadh e ghleac Cuchullain agus chuir i siod na phoca. Aig a bhraiceas an la'ir na mhaireach thuirst ise:

"Seadh Albannaich mbath bheil thu deas deonach do ghealltanas an raoir a chumail dhomh an dingh—dol a ghleic Cuchullain 's an Donn-guaillionn thoirst thugamsa?"

"Ne mise reachadh a ghleac Cuchullain! Fear mo bhithidh
's mo bhrollaich 's mo bhraghaid a tha laidhe 'sa g-eiridh co-rium
fad nan naogh blianna. Bu chruaidh bhiodh a chuis orm d'uair
nach reachainn a ghleac ri fear a ghleacadh ris. Mas ann
eirson seo thug thu cuireadh cuilme dhomhsa cha'n 'eil mi d'cho-
main."

"Seall eir an litir tha d' phoca 's eir a ghealladh thug thu
dhomh."

Chuir am Feardiag a lamh na phoca 's thug e mach an litir
's leugh e i. Chrom e cheann, 'us bhruc a dheoir gu frasach
trom.

Ach mar dhuine 's mar ghaisgeach cha tigeadh e'n cois fhacail,
agus sgri' e litir thun Cuchullain a choinneachadh eir Faiche
choraig eir da nair-iag am maireach. Direach d'uair bha Cuchullain agus Laochaire folbh an bheinn-sheilg co choinnich 's an dorust
'ad ach teacaire an Fhir-dhiag leis an litir.

"Seadh! seadh! Bheil fios agadsa Laochaire de'n litir a fhuair
mise seo?" orsa Cuchullain agus dh-inns e dha.

"Cha'n aona ghnothuch cearst tha eir aire" arsa Laochaire 's
cha teid thu thoirst coinneamh no comhail dha. Na 'm bu ghnoth-
ach cearst a bhitheadh ga dhi thigeadh e lom 'us direach far an ro'
thu cho luath 'sa bhuail a chas fiar Eirinn." "'S docha nach do
bhrist e eir na mionnan a bh' eadaruinn " ors Cuchullain. "O 's
docha nach do bhrist" orsa Laochaire "ach de idir a thug dha
gu'n tighinn lom us direach far an so thu an aite fios a chur orst
gu faiche-choraig?" "'S drochuair," orsa Cuchullain; bheir mi comb-
ail dha co dhin biodh i math no dona.

Choinnich na fir eir Faiche-choraig 's chuir 'ad failte chridheil
eir a cheile. Phog an da bhrathair Laochaire Mac Nearst, agus
Gille na h-Iuraich, a cheile aon nair agus, phog an da ghaisgeach,
Cuchullain agus am Fear-diag, a cheile da uair. Bha 'ad a sin a
spaidsearac a sios 'sa suas agus nan cairdean m'an bha 'ad riabh.
"De na cleasun ris am bith sinn an diugh? ors am Feardiag.
"Cleas 's am bith thogras sibh fhein orsa Cuchullain." "Nach
bith sinn a caitheamh na sleagha an cul na h-eara?" Thug 'ad
treis, mar sin. "Coma liom, ors 'm Fear-diag de'n doigh leibideach shuarach sin, cloinne bige. Ga'amid an t-seann doigh
chearst." "Taing a Ni-math orsa Cuchullain gur tusa bhrist eir
na mionnan 's nach mise."

Lean an ruaig a seo Cuchullain gus na chuireadh a mach eir tao'
eile faiche-choraig e. N'ann a brath am bas a leigeil thugam a tha thu,
ors easan ri Laochaire Mac Nearst? Ruith Laochaire 's chuir e
stad eir a bhial-ath. Thill Cuchullain an torac eir an Fhear-dhiag.

Dh-eubh am Feardiag ri Gille na h-Iuraich ruith a leigeil dha'n bhial-ath 's leig e ruith dha'n t-sruth 's thill am Feardiag an tòrac eir Cuchullain gu tao' eil Faiche-choraig. Leum Laochaire 's rug e eir a bhrathair agus sparr e tarann na chluais ri craoibh. Spion Gille na h-Iuraich a' chraobh as a friamh agus lig e 'n t-ath agus chuir am Feardiag eir Cuchullain. Leum Laochaire agus rug e eir a bhrathair agus spion e 'n ceann as an amhuich aige agas stad e am bial-ath. Bha bhrathair marbh. Bha Cuchullain ris a ghath-bhalg agus cha ro 'n cleas seo idir aig an Fhear-dhiag.

Mharbhadh am Feardiag. Sgriobh Cuchullain a sin litir dh-ionnsuidh na Maoim Chruachain : "Dh-fhairstlich siod orst mar a dh-fhairstlich a chuile h-ionsuidh eile 'thug 'sa bheir thu eir an Donn-guaillionn a thoirst a mach." An ullai-thruis a bh-ann, chuireadh fios eir a Gharbh mac Stairn 'us teigheteas aig eir taobh eile dh-Eirinn.

Thainig e 's chuir a Bharuin failte chridheil chaoimhneil eir agus mar chumba 's mar choineamh eir dol a ghleac Chuchullain chum an tairbh a thoirst a mach. "Gheo thu ors ise or agus airgiod gu leoir, cairdeas leighis na Maoim Chruachain agus lamh dheas Oiril." "Bha mise la dha'n ro' mi" ors an Garbh coir "'s bheirinn tarbh a mach dha'n Mhaoim Chruachain na'm b'urra mi, 's an la eir a bheil an diugh bheirinn diachuin dha n'am b'endar." Bha e sin fad seacuin ga phrapadh (? *prop*) 's ga phripadh (? *bribe*) 's ga bhia'adh aig a Bharuinn. "'S ann a bhrogaicheas mi orm" ors an Garbh "fiach am faic mi mo nighean 's am faigh mi 'n Donn-Guaillionn dha'n Bharuinn." * * * *

Bha Cuchullain a' falbh gu beinn-sheilg la agus chunnaic e 'n Garbh a' tighinn agus thill e dhachaidh le cabhaig. "Nach eil d'athair a tighinn gu faiche-choraig" ors eise r'a mhnaoi. "An ta cha'n aon rud math tha ga dhi. 'S cinnteach gur h-ann eir thoir an tairbh tha e tighinn—tarbh na duibhe!" "De ni sinn?" (Cha ro toil aig Cuchullain dol a mhar'adh a Ghairbh.) "Ni, tilg thusa dhiot do chomhdach, 's leum eir mo chulao an leabaidh 's their mise gur leana mic a chuir mi chun an t-Saoghail thu. Fuinnidh mi bonnach 's cuiridh mi ghreidiol na bhroinn 's bheir mi dha e mar ghreim curaidh."

Thainig an Garbh eir a shnòdan fhein, a' sealltuin thuige 's bh' uaithe. Thainig e steigh 's bheannaich e dha'n teigh 's dh'an teolach.

"Tha ghaoth eir dorust nan laoch," ors casan. "An ta tha," ors ise le guth boc "ach cha bhiodh e mar sin na'n ro' na laoich fhein aig an teigh."

"Gu de dhianadh 'ad 's gu'n ach an aon dorust eir an teigh?"

"Bheireadh 'ad eir an taigh agus chuireadh 'ad tao na gaoith' san fhasga agus tao' an fhasgai 'sa ghaoith." "An ta tha gniomh ghais-geach a sin gu' dearbh agus bha mi fhé' la dha'n ro mi 's dhianainn gniomh gaisgich cuideac ; ach cha duiliom gu'n deanainn sin an la b'fhearr bha mi riabh ach fiacham ris."

Chaidh an Garbh a mach agus sgaoil e 'lambun ri ceann an teighe agus thug e ionsuidh thogail eir agus a shiamh mu'n cuairst, ach cha tug e glidneachadh eir."

Thill e steigh. "Dh-fhairstlich siod orm 's ma riar fhein cha'n ioghnadh géd' a dh-fhairstlicheadh an la b'fhearr bha mi riabh. Ach caite bheil na laoich fhein ?" ". Thà sa bheinn sheilg." "'S gu de tha thus dianadh 's an leabaidh 's do shuil cho beo 's do ghuth cho laidir ?" "Tha mi'n deigh m' asaid 's leana chur chun an t-saoghail." "U 's ciadach an tinneas a th-orst—an tinneas is fhearr na'n t-slainte. De chlann a th'agad ?" "Tha mac." " Cha b'urra bhi b'fhearr. Thatar ag rath riumsa gu'm bi fiaclann aig mic nan gaisgeach d'uair a bheirear 'ad. Fiachair am mac mar an t-athair do mbae-sa." Chuir e mhiar am bial an leainibh 's chaill e barr a mheoir ra linn. "Ud ! ud ! ud ! 's mac mar an t-athair thu gu dearbh. 'S math liom nach mi bhios beo ri linn dhuit tighinn gu ire deich blianna fichead a dh-aois. Ach gu de 'm bonnach mor seo an oir an teine is mutha dha na chunna mi riabh ?" " Cha'n eil ach bonnach a bhios aig na laoich d'uair thig 'ad as a bheinnsheilg." "Theirte laoch rium fhein la dha'n ro mi 's feumaidh mi blas a bhonnaich fhiachain."

Thug e greim as a bhonnach agus chuireadh tri chlaragun a dorust a bheoil. "Ud ! ud a ri ! fhein tha greim curaidh a seo gu dearbh."

"Ach cait a bheil an Donn-guaillionn ?" "Tha e aig a bhuach-aille co-ris a chrodh." " An eirich thu 's an leig thu fhaicinn dhomh cait a bheil an crodh. 'S e sin rud is laogha is cor 'omh dhiana agus dh-eirich i agus sheall i dha an rathad a gha'adh e. Chuir an "leanabh" eir a culaobh cagar na cluais i ga sheoladh rathad fada fiaraidh agus rinn i sin. "Thatar ag rath riumsa" ors an Garbh mac Stairn, 's an dealachadh "gur tu mo nighean—'s tha mi nist a faicinn gur tu."

Sgiobalaich Cuchullain aodach eir agus thar e as, 's bha e aig a chrodh mu'n rainig an Garbh.

"Tilg dhiot a bhuachaille" ors easan "agus thoir dhomhs do chuid aodaich 's cuir thus orst m'aodach-sa 's teich dha'n ghleann ad shios leis an Donn-guaillionn agus ceithir no coig da na mairst." Rinn am buachaille mar a shireadh eir.

Thainig a sin an Garbh 's e na chrŭthail chrăthail, mhor bhodaich. "Seadh a bhuachaille an e siod an Donn-guaillionn," ors eise 's e tothadh ri tarbh bha shios a miosg na tain 's cha ro 'n tarbh, sin fhein cli ga da b' ao-coltach ris an Donn-ghuaillionn e. "'S e" ors am "buachaille." Ghabh an Garbh 'sam "buachaille" sios a choi'ead na taine 's an tairbh, agus mhol 'us mhol an Garbh an tain agus tarbh Chuchullain.

"'Sannathainig mis eirson an tairbh" ors an Garbh "'s tha nám' a bhi folbh leis 's an t-anamoch a tighinn a "bhuachaille!" "Cha bhi'n t-im sin eir an roinn sin, cha leig mise leat an tarbh gos am foigh mi ordan mo mhaighstir 's gos an tig e dhachaidh as a bheinn sheilg." "Cha bhi mi fuireach ris," ors an Garbh 's rug e eir *oiric* eir an tarbh gos a thoirt leis. Leum am "buachaille" 's rug e eir *oiric* eile 'n tairbh 's an tarbh cha leigeadh e leis. Bha 'ad a sin a dràothadh an tairbh o cheile. "Agam fhein a bhios e" theireadh an darna fear; "fiach riut theireadh am fear eile," gos na shrac 'ad an tarabh o cheile o chlar aodain gu bun *urabail.* Chuir am "buachaille" car ma cheann dha'n leth aige fhein 's bhuail e'n Garbh leis 's rinn e bŭta dheth 'sa pholl. "'Usa! bhodaich mhosaich le d' spadaireac a tighinn a chur drăogh eir tarbh mo mhaighstir 's gu'n e fhein aig an teigh gus a thoirst dhuit." Dh-eirich an Garbh 's chrath e'm poll dheth fhein. "Crosam adhol an carrabh a mhaighstir d'uair tha 'm buachaille cho treasa seo" ors easan 's e crathadh a phuill dheth fhein. "Bu cho math liom Cuchullain a bhi am beinu 's a bhi aig baile an la thiginn an rathad. Ach a bhuachaille, bheil cleas 's am bith agadsa bhios Cuchullain a dianadh fiach an dian mi fhein e?" "Tha sin agam, fear na dha." "Siuthad ma tha! dian e," agus bhrosnaich e am "buachaille" gu cleasun Chuchullain a shealltain dha. Gu'm b'e chiad chleas a sheall am "buachaille" dha, trăigh us dorn-gulban * a thomhas thar bearradh creaige.

---

* "Trăigh 'us dorn-gulban" is a trick that used to be practised by boys of old in the Highlands, though probably they are becoming wiser now. A boy stands on the edge of a rock, and places the heel of one foot on the edge, and the heel of the other foot to the toe of that one, and his two closed fists side by side to the point of that toe again. He then leaps backward—if he can. The higher the rock the greater the feat. See *Leabhar Na Feinne,*—

"Thomh'se tu traigh 'us dorn-galban
 Mach o urracagun (a) na dairich (b).
 Mor Chalum, Mor dhugh Chalum,
 Dian laidhe le Moir a Chalum."

An old sarcastic Barra song, levelled at a former factor there, who was famous for his yarns about his own feats of agility and strength.

(a.) "Urrachagun" are the pins to which the halyards of a boat are fastened.

(b.) "Na daraich," the boat, an old name, not now used.—A. A. C.

Ach ga do thomhais am "buachaille" an traigh 's an dorn-gulban
gu sgiolta cha b' ionan sin 's mar a dh-eirich dha'n Gharbh. D'uair
chrom e cheann a dhianadh a chleas chuir am "buachaille"! ghlaic
an cul a amhcha 's thilg e sios leis a chreaig e.

Dh-fhalbh Cuchullain a sin gu dol dhachaidh 's de thachair eir
anns a ghleann ach lorg mhor-mhor duine agus brùit. Bha fhad
agus a liad fhein an lorgan duine bha an deo'aidh na bruit agus mu
dhe'inn lorg na bruit cha 'n 'eil fios de mheudac a bh'anu. Lean
Cuchullain an da lorg mhor a bha seo fiach am faiceadh e de bu 's
ciall daibh. D'uair bha e dol seachad gualain na beinne chunnaic
e duine shios ri taobh an lochain agus tarbh aig eir *oiric*. Smeid
an duine eir agus dh-eubh e ris. Bha eagal eir Cuchullain dol na
choir ach coma co-dhin chaidh e far an ro e.

"Siuthad, cuidich mis" ors am fear mor. "Cha chuidich mi
gos an cluinn mi de's aobhar dhuit mo chuideachadh iarraidh."
"Innsidh mi sin dhuit. Tha mi o chionn sheac blianna toirst
toirioc na taine bho m' bhrathair; ach mu'n tar mi dhol na dail tha
easan agam, 's ga toirst uam. Ach cuidich thusa mi 's bithidh i
againn marbh mu'n tig e agus tha cruach mhor mhoine thallad
eir am bruich sinn i agus bithidh sinn na's treasa gu cath an deigh
a h-ichidh."

Mharbh am fear mor agus Cuchullain an tarbh agus dh-fhadaidh
'ad teine fo'n chruaich mhoine agus chuir 'ad an tarabh eir a muin
ga rosladh. D'uair bha 'an rosladh bruich thoisich 'ad ri icheadh
ach mu'n d' fhuair 'ad ach gle bheag icheadh dheth thainig
brathair an fhir-mhoir eir am muin. Bha chraos fosgailt 's
dhianadh a chridhe 's a ghruthan solust romb bhial. Sheas e ri
tao' thall a bháigh 's shin an da bhrathair eir caitheadh nan sleagh
eir a cheile. Shin Cuchullain ri cuideachadh an fhir mhoir bha eir
a thaobh fhein ach cha tilgeadh [chuireadh] e 'shaighead treasa trian
dha'n astar. Ruith e sin mu chuairst a' bhaigh agus shin e ri
dochan an fhir mhoir o chul (reachadh e steigh fo gho'al), ann an
cul nam bailc. Bha'm fear mor a faireacain tachas ri cul a chas
agus thug e suil far a ghualain agus faicear Cuchullain. Bhuail e
breab eir o thaobh a chuil agus tilgear Cuchullain a null gu tao'
thall a bhaigh agus cait a mhi-sheala a phorst an do stad e ach gu'm
b'ann an *oiric* an tairbh! Ach na fhuair easan a mhialainte
tighinn as a sin cha d'fhuair duine riabh roimhe no na dheo'igh
urrad. Cò-ris mhialaint a fhuair e, bhrist e chlaidh a tighinn as.

Dh-falbh e sin, 's a chlaidh briste na dhorn. Bu tamailteach
leis dol dhachaidh gu'n fhios nach saoileadh bean-an-teighe gur
h-ann a gleac ri h-athair fhein a bhrist e 'n claidh. Thaghail e
sin ann an ceardaich 'san dol seachad fiach am faigheadh e chlaidh
eir a charadh. Bha cheardach lan dhaoine mar a bha chuile

ceardach riabh 's a bhitheas. Shir e eir a ghobha chlaidh a charadh.

"Cha chairich mi 's cha gha' e caradh gos an inns thu ciamar a bhrist thu e no gu de an gniomh gaisgich no an tapadh a rinn thu?" Cuir a mach na daoine mata (bha tamailt eir innseadh an la'ar na'n daoine gur h-ann ri linn dha bi ga thoirst fhein á oiric an tairbh a bhrist e chlaidh). Chuir an gobha mach na daoine. Ach dh-fhalaich nighean mhor mhungach rua leis a gho'a i fhein fo'n bhalg 's bha i g-eisdeac a chuile druideadh seanchais bha eadar a h-athair agus Cuchullain. "Cha'n ann ad' Chu Chullain bha thu 'n uair sin idir ach ad Chu adhriac" ors ise ri linn dhi seanachas Chuchullain a chluinntinn. Siod Cuchullain a mach an dorust leis an tamailt. Cha do sheall e na dheo'igh 's cha d' fhuirich e ri sleagh no claidh. * * * *

Treis an deo'igh seo thainig te do chlann a Challadair far an robb a Mhaoim Chruachain agus thug i comhairle oirre. "O na dh-fhairstlich an Donn-guaillionn eir gaisgich an t-saoghail cuir a nis fios eir reisemeid de bhoirionaich na h-Eirionn agus boirionn-ach 'na sinilear eir an ceann agus thoir la blair 'us baiteil do Chuchullain eir faiche-choraig agus bithidh mi fhein is mo dha phiuthair ga d' chomhnadh."

Rinneadh seo. Chruinnich a Mhaoim Chruchain reisemeid do bhoirionnaich na h-Eirionn agus boirionnach na sinilear (? *seanalair*) eir an ceann agus chuireadh gu faiche choraig ad gu la blair as baiteil a thorist do Chuchullain.

Chuala Cuchullain seo ach cha ro bheag no mhor a dh-umhail aige dhin. Bha e dianadh gu'n cuireadh e fhein agus a ghille ri boirionnaich an t-saoghail. Rinneadh a seo la blair. Chaidh Cuchullain agus a ghille chun a bhial áth. Bha Maoim a Chruach-ain fLein eir ceann a sluaigh.

Bha Cuchullain ga'n leagail nam bŭtaichean a sios lis an t-struth gus an ro e toirst sgrios eir reisemeid an deigh reisemeid. Le teas na h-obrach thug e chlogad far a chinn agus leag e ri thaobh e.

Thionndaidh a Mhaoim Chruachain a sin gu gnua ri Feannag, nigheann a Challadair, agus thuirt i rithe—"Na'nn a brath mo chuid airm leigeil gu bas tha thu an deigh dhuit duais mhor a gha-'ail uam?"

Ghrad leum Feannag an rioc feannaig anns an speur agus thainig i nall 's bhuail i eir seoladh anns an adhar o's cionn Chuchullain. Cha do chuir easan diu dhi—shaoil leis gu'm b'fheannag ghrannda ghlas i. Leig ise sios mionnach glaisein lan puisein eir a cheann ruisgte. Laidh siod eir an ionachain aigesan agus leig e osna ghointe bhais as. Tha mo nearst 's mo leirsin am threigsin, a dheo Laochaire caite bheil thu?" "Ri d' thaobh." "Cuir clach am laimh fiach gu de 'n euc a ni mi." Chuir Laochaire clach na laimh agus shăd Cuchullain a chlach. "Am fac thu ca na bhuail a chlach a Laochaire?" "Bhuail an cul a chinn eir an dobhar-chu 's e eir strabh na fal' eir an ath. "An do mharbh mi e?" "O mharbh gu dearbh; cha'n eil sgrid ann—shaor e na raimh." "Tha sin ag innseadh gu bheil am bas agamsa. Bha e 's an dailgneac gu h-e sin a chiad euc 's an t-euc mu dheireadh a dhianainnse, cu 'mhar'adh. Tog thusa an claidh mor eir mo ghualain agus cuir an t-sleagh mhor fo m' uc. Saoilidh 'ad gu'm bith mi beo 's cha tig 'ad a nall eir an ath. Sinidh tus aiste gu Goll brathair mo mhathar agus innsidh tu dha mar thachair, ach fiach gu'n tiaruin thu do bheatha eir ra linn."

Shin Laochaire mac Nearst a mach agus rainig e'n Fhinn—bha 'ad an Eirinn 's an am. "Seadh a Laochaire, ciamar a dh-fhag thu mo chaomh charaid Cuchullain," orsa Goll. "Bha e diana teigh ur dha fhein d'uair a dh-fhag mis, e." "O! Seadh! seadh! 'n ann mar seo a tha. 'Togaidh an goraiche 'n caisteal 's ga'aidh an gliocaire comhnuidh ann.' Nach math gu'm foghnadh dhasan an seann talla bh' aig an Du'altach athair. Ach bithidh an oige 'san leom fuaighte ri cheile agus sin mar a dh-eirich do Cuchullain 's dha'n teigh ur tha e togail." "U! cha'n 'eil ann ach bothan beag, d'uair a laidheas e eir dhruim direach bithidh a shron 'sa ghath-droma." "Deart a thuirst thu mar sin? 'S ionnan sin 's gu bheil mo chaomh charaid Cuchullain marbh." "Cha tug mise guth eir bas—fhianuis sin orst fhein." "Cha tug thu 'ille mhaith 's tu nach tug. Co eir am bu chruaidhe bas deagh mhaighstir no eir deagh ghille? Ach cha'n am seo gu' fuireach 's Cuchullain na eigin." 'N am bhi dol seachad eir coille bhuain Goll tri ghadun chaola chruaidh agus chuir e siod eir bac ruithe Laochaire. "Seo" ors easan "cum sin gos an lion mis 'ad leis na cinn is docha leat fhein a bhi eir ghad."

Thainig Feannag nigheann a Challadair a nall agus bhuail i eir seoladh o's cionn Chuchullain. Bha i tighinn na bu daine 's na bu daine mar bhios na feannagun grannda'n comhuich gus mu dhireadh na laidh i eir a ghualainn dhios.

"Tha'n t-suil a dunadh 's am bial a gròbadh 's faodaidh luc nan cleas tighinn a nall" orsa Feannag.

Chrom Goll agus Laochaire le Faiche-choraig agus shin 'ad eir arm na Maoim Chruachain as an h-uair. Leig Laochaire ruith leis na gadan tri uairean. Thiondaidh Goll ris gu gnua. Ma bhios ceann a dhi nan tri ghad seo feumaidh do cheann fhein no mo cheann fhein dol eir a ghad ga lionadh. Seo d'uair a leig Laochaire ris do Gholl gun h-ruith a leig leis na gŏid.

Thog 'ad a sin leo corp Chuchullain agus dh-amhlaiceadh e. Tha 'n sgial a mach.

NOTE.—The reciter is 76 years old. He was a joiner by trade, but failing health and sight disabled him from work for some years back. He is a descendant of, and is called after, Hector Macleod, the Uist bard, who so sweetly sung—

> " Moch maduinn Cheitein 's a cheo
> 'Nàm dha'n ghrein togail fo neoil,"

and who rendered good service to many who were out in the '45·

The reciter says he heard "Toirioc Na Taine" 60 years ago from a Ruaraidh Rua Mac Cuithein, a native of North Uist, but who travelled in South Uist as a sort of catechist. This catechiser was a celebrated reciter and *seanchaidh*. He probably knew more ancient Gaelic poetry than any man of his day. The poetry and traditions of the Feinne were his principal themes, and these he always handled with much ability and acceptance to his ever varying yet ever admiring audience.

Mac Cuithein gave much information about Gaelic poetry to Campbell, the author of "Albyn's Authology " (?), and through Campbell's influence, Lord Macdonald, the present young lord's grandfather, gave Mac Cuithein a piece of land rent-free in N. Uist during the remainder of his life. His son is grieve with the Misses Macdonald, Scolpaig, N. Uist, ach cha mhac mar an t-athair e. He has no old lore whatever.

Mac Cuithein, better known as " Ruaraidh Ruadh," died about fifty years ago.

NOTES ON ·"TOIREACHD NA TAINE."

We are indebted for the following valuable Notes on " TOIREACHD NA TAINE" to Standish O'Grady, Esq., M.R.I.A. :—

This story begins with one of that series of feats by Cuchullin which in Irish are known as " Maic-ghnìomhartha Chongculainn," or " Cuchullin's exploits while a boy." In the "Tain Bo Chuailgne," these doings are related round the camp fire to " Meadhbh Chruachna " and her husband Ailill, by Fergus Mac Róich and other warriors of Ulster who were then in the service, having left their own country in the matter of the sons of Uisneach, who had been killed whilst under the protection of Fergus. These exploits are narrated shortly after the setting out of the " Toireacht," in order to prepare Meadhbh of Cruachan and Ailill, and give them to understand what they might expect at Cuchullin's hands. In the Book of Leinster and other MSS., Culann, smith to Conchabhar Mac Neasa, King of Ulster, makes a feast for the latter. The King asks Cuchullin, whose name was at that time Sétanta Beag Mac Sualtaim, to join them. The boy says he will follow later. He does so, and is attacked by a famous " ár-chú " of Culann's outside the fort. Having taken with him his ball (liathroit, as a ball is still called at present,) and " caman " (word still in use, as is also the implement itself,) to beguile the way, he slays the hound as here described. Culann makes a great fuss over his loss, and Setanta having promised not only to get him a up of the same breed, but to act himself as watchdog until the whelp should be "inghníomha," or fit for action ; that wise man Cathbhadh Draoi, who was present, is so delighted with the lad's judgment against himself, that upon the spot he dubs him "Cu Chulainn ; " "Fearr liem m'ainm fein, eadhon Setanta mac Sualtaim," ar an mac beag. "Na h-abair sin, a mhic bhig," ar Cathbhadh Draoi, "oir canfaid fir Eireann agus Alban an ainm sin, agus bhus lan beóil fear Eireann agus Alban de'n ainm sin." Thereupon he adopts the name.

His father's name is written in the Book of Leinster, "Sualtach and Sualtaim." In a good vellum MS., of about 1460, in the British Museum, I find "Sudholtach." (The orthography of this MS. is, however, very affected and uncouth, and evidently of purpose. The scribes of this period, or rather some of them, appear to have amused themselves by altering the spelling of almost every word). In a fine paper copy of the "Tain Bo Chuailgne," written in the County Louth in 1800 from another MS. of 1730, it stands "Subhaltach." When the tale has for so long a period been perpetuated orally, it is quite natural that the name should have glided into one quite similar in sound, but more intelligible to the reciters of the day. Hence we have here "Dubhaltach." This was common as a Christian name in Ireland down to the latter half of the seventeenth century.

There are in Irish two versions of "Coimpert Chongculainn," or Cuchullin's Birth, differing in some respects, but agreeing in this, that Sualtach was his mother's husband, but only nominally his father. The circumstances connected with Cuchullin's birth are flavoured with the supernatural. Sualtach, in the Tain Bo Chuailgne, appears more or less in the light of an old woman, and is treated with scant respect by his hardy stepson, or whatever we may call him. He is eventually killed by Cuchullin's horse, "An Liath Macha"—Macha's Grey— which plays a great part in the Cuchullin cycle of legends. In the Tain Bo Chuailgne Sualtach does not appear much, nor does he fight at all.

We have in Irish no record of the time during which Cuchullin played the watchdog's part.

The "Maic-ghníomhartha" do not speak of his being sent into the "Domhan shoir," but his journey to and sojourn at Scathach's shool of arms in Skye are minutely related in the tale called "Tochmarc Eimhre," or the Wooing of Eimhear (by Cuchullin). In the Irish tales "an Domhan shoir" is often used for Alba.

In Irish the "gilla" or "ara" of Cuchullin is Laogh Mac Rian-ghabhra, a very fine character, who accompanied him in all his doings till death. He never dissuaded him from any enterprise. Among the "Maic-ghníomhartha" is an account of the day upon which Cuchullin first took arms, and first went into a chariot. Arms and chariot had been given to him by Connor, the King, who also lent him one of his charioteers, Iomhar Mac Rianghabhar, a brother to Laogh Mac Rianghabhar. This Iomhar was a man of a different stamp from Laogh, and on Cuchullin's first expedition seeks to dissuade him from killing some deer (which, however, we are not told were pets of Connor's), from ascending a mountain, and from entering the stronghold of the three sons of Neachfa (their mother), &c., &c. Cuchullin acts in spite of him, and of course triumphs. I cannot account for the name Neart. Cuchullin had a great friend, Lughaidh stiabh *n-dearg* (Lughaidh of red stripes), being so marked round neck and waist. He also had a contemporary named Laoghaire, but his cognomen was Buadhach.

In the Irish versions the attendants of Meadhbh's envoy are all called "eachlachs," as are also their equals in all other tales of this and considerably later ages. The "Gallóglach," or, as sometimes written, "Goglaoch," was the heavy, armed soldier of Ireland down to the middle ages, and down to the close of the ·Elizabethan war. He was so called because of the long shirt of mail in which he fought, as well as, perhaps, the great battle-axe which distinguished him from the Ceatharnach (kern, or "light-infantry" man), who borrowed from the Gall, or Scandinavian. The word is always spelt with two *l*'s.

It was Cuchullin that had the "Ga Bulga" (in the Irish version), and Feardiadh calls out to his gille to prevent Laogh's sending it down to the stream to Cuchullin. He succeeds a few times, but eventually Cuchullin gets the "ga," and slays Feardiadh.

The story of the bannock with the griddle inside, and mock-child in bed, is known in Ireland, but not told of Cuchullin. It is sometimes told of Fionn, sometimes of some anonymous Fathach or other, and so on.

With the death of the Feardiadh this tale diverges quite away from the Tain Bo Chuailgne, in which there is nothing answering to what follows. The counsel given to Meadhbh to send for the children of "An Caladair," belongs to the story called "*Brisleach mor Maighe Muirtheimhne*," in which Cuchullin lost his life by practices of magic. During the Tain he fought with and slew one *Calaitin dana* and his twenty-seven sons. Calaitin, however, had left his wife *torrach* when he went to follow the Tain, and she brought forth three sons, and as many daughters. These Meadhbh had educated as sorcerers, with a view to the future punishment of Cuchullin, for whom she had "a stone in her sleeve" ever since the Tain. The story of the Brisleach is very long, occupying 77 closely-written quarto pages in a MS. in the British Museum, in the old hand, and full of contractions.

In the Brisleach, Cuchullin, wounded to death, goes down to the brink of a small loch. "Agus do ghabh Laogh ag ceangal agus ag cornghadh a chneadh agus a chreucht, go rabhadar ag imtheilgean fola, gur ba chaoba cródheargo agus linnte fola foir-dheirge an lochan leathan linn-uaithne uadha ; agus ni fada do bhí amhlaidh sin an nair do chonnairc an dobhar-chu ag 'ol a fbola, agus an uair do chonnairc-sean crú a chuirp ag an g-coin da chaitheamh do ghabh cloch chuige de chiumhais an chalaidh, agus thug urchar do'n dobhar-chein, agus do mharbh i. Beir buaidh agus beannacht, a Chuagain ! ar Laogh ; ni tugadh riamh urchar budh fhearr na sin, agus ni thainic do shaoghal fos, agus dioghail thu fein air fhearaibh Éireann. Truagh sin, a Laoigh ! ar Cuchulainn. Ni mhuirbhfead-sa duine na ainmhidhe d'a eis-si sud go brath ! agus cu an cheud eucht do righne misi ariamh,

agus do tairrngireadh go m-budh chu m'eucht deidheanach." I
quote the above from a MS. of 1712, to show how closely the two
versions agree in this incident. *Dobhar-chu* is an otter. *Dobha*r is
water. In Cormac's Glossary we find "Dobur=uisce. Unde dicitur
dobar-cu ; agus do breth dobar-ci imorro is in Chombreic (*i.e.*, Dobur=
water, whence is named dobar-cu ; and moreover [the name of] dobor-
ci is given it in the Cambrian [Welsh])." Under another head he says,
"Dobur=uisce, unde dicitur dobar-chu. i. dobran." (Modern dobhran=
dobharan. From Stokes's translation of Cormac's Glossary).* The modern Welsh words are "Dwfr," water. "Ci," a dog in composition, "dwfr-
gi," water-dog, otter. Cornish, "dofer-ghi" (the same). Breton, "dour-
gi," and also "ki-dour" (this last "Cu dobhair). "Dobhar-chu" is
obsolete all over Ireland, except in the County Donegal, where
"Dobhar" also enters into the names of places, as "Gaoth-dobhair"
(Anglice, Gweedore ; gaoth=a stream left on the strand by the falling tide). Brother Michael O'Clery (one of the "IV. Masters,"
and himself a Donegal man), in his Glossary of Old Irish Words,
printed at Louvain in 1641, explains "Dobhar-chu" by *madra uisge*,
which is the present name for an otter in Munster and South Leinster.
In Connaught and the West of Ulster and Leinster, it is called
"madadh uisge." In Irish "cu" is feminine, and thus declined :—
"An chu, na con, do'n choin ; Plural, na cointe, or na coin (the
latter the commonest form), na g-con, do na conaibh.
  It looks as if "dobhar-chu" had lost its meaning in the district
where this tale was taken down, and its place supplied by a word of
very similar sound and intelligible to the people of the period, just as
the Norman French Oyez ! Oyez ! (listen ! listen !), by which silence
is proclaimed in an English Court of Justice, has long been transformed
into Oh yes ! Oh yes ! It is evident that "dobhar-chu" is a better
description of an otter than "odhar-chu," for that is not his colour.
So thought the Gaelic bard who sang—

> "Fhuair mi lorg an dobhrain duinn,
>   An dobhrain duinn, an dobhrain duinn !
> Fhuair lorg an dobhrain duinn,
>   'S cha d'fhuair mi lorg mo chóineachain !"

NOVEMBER 21.—We take the following extract from a **paper**
read by Mr. William Mackay, on

THE STUDY OF THE GAELIC LANGUAGE.

> "Sweet tongue of our druids and bards of past ages !
> Sweet tongue of our monarchs, our saints, and our sages !
> Sweet tongue of our heroes and free-born sires !
> When we cease to preserve thee, our glory expires."

---

* *Tobar*, well, remains in use as one form of the ancient word *Dobh-*
ar, water. Also *Dobhran*, a sulky boy ; and *ball-dobhrain*.]

The Gaelic language has in its time encountered many a foe ; but of all those, the Gaelic people has been its most deadly. This seems strange, but it is no less the truth. · We cannot blame any but ourselves for the decay of our national tongue. The blame is often placed upon the shoulders of our Saxon neighbours, but it is as well to lay it at the door of the Hottentot or of the Red Indian—the fault is ours and no other's. In what respect, then, have we Highlanders erred ? Simply in this—that we have neglected the language which Providence gave us to foster and preserve. We may think that we do well if we learn to *speak* Gaelic ; but in the circumstances which now exist, we prove faithless in the trust placed in us as keepers of our language if we do not read, write, and cultivate it. To-day, scholars rejoice in the venerable pages of Greek ˋand Roman authors ; but how much of Greek and Latin would we now have, if the people whose languages these were, were content with the mere ability to speak them ? And in what condition would the English, French, and other modern languages be, were the people who speak them so dead to their responsibilities as we, and our brethren the Kelts of Ireland, are to ours ? The Kelts of Wales hold an honourable position in regard to their language. Although they are hemmed in by the English to a greater extent than either we or the Irish are, it is as difficult to find a Welshman who cannot write Welsh as it is to find a Highlander or an Irishman who *can* write Gaelic. The Welsh language is taught in the Welsh schools ; there are numerous Welsh periodicals, and there is not in Wales a town of any importance without its Welsh newspaper or newspapers. Let us contrast with this flourishing state of matters, the sad state of native literature in the Highlands, and Ireland. Except in a few remote districts, the children in these countries are not taught, or even allowed to speak, their native tongue in school ; and consequently we have an anomaly which does not in any other country exist—people "educated and intelligent," and yet unable to read or write their mother tongue ! But there is another and more painful result of this unnatural system of education ;—there are numerous cases of persons who are able to read English fluently without understanding a sentence of what they read !

As to the Gaelic press, only two Gaelic magazines exist, and there is no Gaelic newspaper.* Our magazines, the *Gael* and the

---

* Since the above was written, *The Highlander* (Inverness), containing a Gaelic department, has been started. The Very Rev. Professor Bourke, of Tuam, Ireland, has also commenced to publish a series of Gaelic lessons, &c., in the columns of the *Tuam News.*

Banner of Truth, are well conducted and merit our best support.
If Highlanders do their duty towards these young periodicals,
Gaelic literature will greatly gain thereby.   There is room for
more such publications, were we Kelts only willing to devote a
very short time to the acquisition of a scholarly knowledge of our
language.   Once able to read Gaelic, there will be no danger of
our being willing to forget it.   The gems hid under its folds are
too precious to admit of their being slighted by any one able to
appreciate them ; and I consider that we commit a crime indeed,
if, through our apathy and neglect, we fail to hand down those
treasures to posterity.   The beauties of our tongue already attract
the notice of the intelligent and unbiassed stranger.   Among the
Germans, French, and English, are enthusiastic Keltic students,
and if we Highlanders do not in this revival become the leaders,
and gather that which Gaelic-speaking people only can gather, we
shall, as I have said, incur a heavy responsibility to posterity.
Low as the Keltic languages are in the estimation of many, they
will yet be deemed as valuable to philology as Greek or Latin.
We may rejoice in the anticipated death of the Keltic, but that
language shall not die.   As a spoken language, at present the
mother-tongue of 5,000,000 of people, we may guarantee to it a
lease of several centuries yet to come ; but after it does, in a good
old age, follow the course of the ancient languages already gone,
and cease to be spoken, it will live in books and in the heads of
the learned.

It is generally taken for granted that Gaelic is a language difficult to learn—impossible to spell ; but had those who are of this
opinion devoted to Gaelic but the hundredth part of the time
which they devoted to English before they became masters of its
orthography, their tale would be very different.   The principles of
Gaelic orthography are few and simple ; and if these principles are
mastered, the language is mastered.   If you speak Gaelic, I assure
you that two months' earnest study—two hours every evening—
will result in your being able to write it.   This is more than can
be said of English.   In a pamphlet by an " Englishman, B.D.,"
the following passage occurs :—" In orthography, Irish "—that is,
Gaelic—" has great superiority over English.   There are easy
rules which insure correctness.   The Welsh claims the same
superiority.   According to Dr Johnson, the Welsh, two hundred
years ago—we must say three hundred—insulted the English for
the instability of their orthography.   They reproach us on the
same ground to this day.   We have in English no fixed principle
of orthography, and it is one of the serious imperfections of our
language.   Mr. Ellis asserts (1), that no Englishman can tell with

certainty how to pronounce any word which he has only seen written ; (2) that no Englishman can tell with certainty how to spell a word which he has only heard spoken and never seen written." Of the principles to which I have referred, I shall here only make mention of that of " broad to broad and narrow to narrow," which in itself is almost a complete key to our orthography.

As members of the Gaelic Society, our duty is to make ourselves perfectly acquainted with our language, as it is written.   As Secretary of the Society, I experience the greatest difficulty in getting members to write Gaelic papers.   This state of matters in the second year of our existence is a slur upon our reputation which must not be allowed to exist.   We must have the language practically and systematically taught to us, either at our ordinary meetings, or at a class specially formed.   Acquaint yourselves with the writing of the language, by corresponding in it.   If there is any one among my young friends here—and it is but charitable to suppose that there is—who has not yet forgot his first love towards some daughter of the mountains, in his native glen, let him correspond with her in the sweet and natural tongue of *Uilleam Ros*.

The subjects of my observations to-night are such as may be discussed ; I therefore conclude.   Permit me to do so in the words of the Rev. Professor Mullin, of Lochrea, Ireland, slightly altered to suit Highlanders.   No Irishman will censure us for the liberty we take in thus adopting unto ourselves the words of an eloquent poem of which the sons of Erin are justly proud. The Kelts of Ireland and the Kelts of Scotland have a common language ; and all differences and quarrels between them over that language are suicidal to their common cause.   Let us hope that the unfortunate jealousies which for so long a time separated the Keltic scholars of Scotland and Ireland are now cast into that oblivion which endeth not—

" Oh, be *Highland*, Highlanders, and rally for the dear old tongue,
Which, as ivy to a ruin, to the dear old land has clung !
Oh, snatch this relic from the wreck, the only and the last,
To show what Albin ought to be, by pointing to the Past ! "

DECEMBER 5th.—There was a paper read this evening, which may be regarded as a sequel to, if not a fragment of the tale, of which so much is given, under the head of " Toirioc na Taine." Throughout the Highlands this paper is known as

LAOIDH NAN CEANN.

[Bho Dhonull Mac-an-t-Saoir,* Aird, Beinn-nam-faothala, Uist,
22na Mart, 1867.   Taken down by
                                          ALEX. A. CARMICHAEL.]

Mharbhadh Cuchullain a' cogadh an aghaidh Maoim a Chruachain. 'Nuair a leonadh e leis a' bhuitsich Feannag nighean a Challadair,
thuirst e r'a ghille, Laoghaire mac Nearst, "A Laoghaire mhic
Neirst, a threin ghaisgich, agus a dheagh sheirbheisich dhilis,
fhuair mis mo bhuille bàis.   Ach cuir thusa 'm sheasamh mi agus
sleagh fo gach achlais agam agus te eile fo m' uc [bhrollach] a chumas
am sheasamh mi am fianuis sluagh Maoim a Chruachain ; agus
cumaidh so Maoim a Chruachain agus a cuid airm gu'n tighinn a
nall eir Ath-Crioch."   Rinn Laoghaire mar a shir a mhaighstir
eir.   "Falbhaidh tu nis a Laoghaire, agus bheir thu fios ga'm
chaomh charaid Connul gu'n do mharbhadh a dhalta (? oide)
Cuchullain."
    Chuir Connul bòidean agus briathran eir fhein gu marbhadh e
neach eir bith a thigeadh a thoirt fios dha eir bas Chuchullain. Bha
fios aig Laoghaire eir a so.
    Rainig Laoghaire taigh Chonnuil agus chaidh e 's taigh. Ghabh
Connul naigheac Chuchullain deth gu suilbhearra — "Seadh a
Laoghaire, ciamar tha mo chaomh charaid Cuchullain ?" orsa Connul. "Tha gu math," orsa Laoghaire. "Tha e 'n trast deigh
taigh ùr a dhianadh."   "Gu de 'n taigh a rinn e mar sin?" orsa
Connul. "Nach bu mbath gu'm fonadh dhàsan' an t-seann aitreamh
aosmhor mhor bha aig a shinnsre ?"   "Rinn teigh anns an fhasan
ur." "Gu de am fasan a fhuair e mar sin ?" "O cha'n eil ann ach
taigh beag.   An nair a laidheas e eir a dhruim-direach eir an urlar
agus a shineas e a chasun buailidh bonn a chas ceann-iocrach, agus
crun a chinn ceann-uacrach, agus barr a shroine droma-mhaide 'n
taighe."   "'S ionnan sin" orsa "Connul agus gu bheil mo chaomh
charaid Cuchullain marbh."   "Cha tug mis iomara eir bas a
Chonnuil," orsa Laoghaire, "fhiannis sin orst fhein, is tu thug
iomara eir a bhas agus cha mhise."

----

* Donald Macintyre, usually called "Do'ul mac Dho'uil 'ic Thearlaich,"
died in 1868. He was a sort of catechist among the Roman Catholic population of Uist and Barra. His lays of Ossian were in more request than his
lays of Rome. The younger people used to tease him much, when he would
break out into great fits of swearing. One of the priests told me that the
Barra people—no saints—complained that he introduced several new oaths
amongst them.   A. A. C.

" O cha tug a laochain 's tu nach tug.   Co leis am bu chruaidhe
bas Chuchullain na leatsa fhein.   Biodhmid a falbh a Laoghaire,"
agus dh-falbh Connul agus Laoghaire.

A chiad choille choinnich Connul chaidh e 's taigh innte agus
bhuain e seac gaid (? *goid*) ura dha'n chaol bu ruighne agus chuir
e siod eir bac ruighe Laoghaire.

Innsidh tu nis dhomhsa a Laoghaire co na daoine bu deise agus
na cairdean bu dilse bha aig Maoim a Chruachain agus a b-fhaide
bh' eir a taobh 'sa chogadh agus cha'n fhag mise ceann eir
amhach (*aca*) gus an lion mi na seac goid so."

Rainig 'ad Ath-Crioch far an tugadh am blar agus fhuair 'ad
Cuchullain na sheasadh ris na sleaghun agus e marbh gun deo,
agus sluagh Maoim a Chruachain thall ma choineamh ga choimhead
agus nach leigeadh an t-eagal leo tighinn a nall na b'fhaisg eir
(gu'n fhios an robh e marbh).

Ghabh Connul a null agus shin e eir sliocadh agus eir seacadh
sluagh Maoim a Chruachain. Ghabh e sios roimh 'n teis meadhoin
's a suas roimh 'n teis meadhoin ; a null eir an tarsuin sa nall eir
an tarsuin, eir an oir, eir am fiaradh agus eir am fad-fhiaradh gus
an robh na seac goid aig Laoghaire lan dha na cinn.   Ach an
deigh sin uile bha tuille namh aig Cuchullain bu mhath le
Laoghaire mbarbhadh agus leig e ruith le fear dha na gaid.
Thoisich Connul as ur agus bha e ga'm bualadh thall 's gan seacadh
a bhos ; ga'n sliocadh shios 's ga'n leagail shuas fad da la agus da
oiche gus na lionadh na gaid a rist.

Dh-falbh a sin Connul agus Laoghaire agus na cinn ac eir a
muin anns na gaid.   Bha 'ad ga'n leon leis an acras agus an am
bhi dol seachad eir aitreabh mhor a bha sin ; fhuair 'ad cuireadh a
staigh gu'n dinnteir.   Nuair a ghabh iad an dinnteir (agus m'
anam fhein bu mbath a thoill 'ad i), thainig 'ad a mach, agus thainig
ainnir aillidh a mach as an deigh oir bu ghaisgeach sgiamhach
Connul.   An trath chunnaig an ainnir na cinn eir na gaid
bhuail i eir faighneac do Chonnul co na cinn a bha ann agus bha
Connul ga freagairst.

An Ainnir—" A Chonnuil shealbhaich nan ceann,
    Is cinnteach mi gu'n dhearg thu t-airm ;
    Na cinn sin a th'agad eir ghad—
    An sloinntear leat eir fad na soinn ?"

  Connul—" A nighean shoirbhearstach nan cach,
    Ainnir og nam bria'ra binn
    An eirig Chochullain nan cleas
    Thugadh (Thogadh ?) liom fo dheas na cinn."

An Ainnir—" Co e an ceann, donn, molach mor
          Is deirge nan ros a ghruaidh ghlan
          A chuir thu thall eir a thaobh cli ?
          A Chonnuil mhoir is ailli dreach."

  Connul—" Maoire foirbhearstach nan each
          Macan le'n creachta gach cuan ;
          Sgar mi dheasan fhein an ceann
          'S ann liom fein a thuit a shluagh."

An Ainnir—" A Chonnuil mhoir le d' ghaisgeadh righ
          Co a (? e) an ceann eil eir dhiol chaich,
          'Fhalt orbhuidh eir dhealra grinn—
          Gu molach sliom mar airgiod nàmh (bàn).

  Connul—" Mac-a(n)-Lŭthaidh o (n) Ros-rua(dh)
          Mac na h-uaille thuit le m' nearst,
          Mo dhoigh ! gur h-e siod fhein a th'ann
          Ard Righ Lochlan nan lann breac."

An Ainnir—" Co an da cheann so th'eir a laimh chli
          Is aille li 's cha'n olc (? mhiosa) an dealbh,
          A Chonnuil mhoir le d' ghaisgeadh righ
          Is cinnteach mi gu'n dhearg thu d' airm."

  Connul—" Cumhal agus Connul cruaidh
          Dist a bhuineadh buaidh 's an léirg [*am feirg* ?]
          Thugadh liom an cinn fo dheas
          Dh-fhag mi an cuirp fo an aon leirg."

An Ainnir—" Co an da cheann so eir a laimh dheis
          A Chonnuil nan cleasun aigh—
          Aon dath eir falta nam fear ?
          O ! 's meirig bean ga bheil am baigh."

  Connul—" Ceann Mhanuis us Mhuinngidh mhoir,
          'S e mo dhoigh gu'r h-eud a th' ann ;
          Aca fhuaradh ceann a' Cboin
          Eir maogh Theamh-righ nan struth seimh."

An Ainnir—" Co a (? e) an ceann a chitheam thall
          'Us fhalt fann gu molach sliom
          A rasg mar fheur 's a dheud mar bhlath
          Is ailli na cach cruth a chinn ? "

  Connul—" Mac mo pheathar o'n Tur-sheimh
          Sgar mi fhein a cheann o chorp;

'S niarach an onair mac righ
Iomachair gu min eir an fhalt."

An Ainnir—" Co na sia cinn a chitheam thall
A chuir thu dhiot eir *a thaobh ma thuath*
Is guirme aogasg 's is caoine rasg
Is duighe falt a Chonnuil chruaigh ? "

Connul—" Seisear bhraithrean a bh' ann
'Siod 'ad thall 's an clab ri gaoith—
Clann Challadair nan cleas
Dream nach robh eir leas mo ghaoil.

" Ceann eir fhichead 's fichead ciad
Gu'n iomaradh eir fear creue no lŏt
Do chlann mhetheun 'us mhaca righ 'un
Thuit an eirig ceann a Chŏin."

" Feannag, agus Annag, agus Mor chiar triuir chlann a
Challadair, a bha g' ionnsachadh na sgoil fhausanac fad sheac
blianna ann an in'arna." SEANACHAIDH.

See this poem in the " Dean's Book," pp. 58 and 41.
See also " Torac na Taine," a tale called in Irish " Tain Bo Chuailgne "
in " Manuscript Material of Irish History," p. 716.

THE ANNUAL SUPPER

Was held on the 26th December, in the Royal Hotel. We give
the report which appeared in the *Inverness Advertiser* :—

There was a large and influential attendance. Mr Fraser-
Mackintosh of Drummond occupied the chair, and the croupiers
were Mr. Dallas, solicitor, and Mr. Murdoch. The company
included—Sheriff Macdonald ; Mr. Colvin, solicitor ; Mr. Alex.
Fraser, solicitor ; Mr. Fraser, C.E. ; Mr. Mackintosh, Bank of
Scotland ; Mr. Barclay, accountant ; Mr. Maclennan, Tartan
Warehouse ; Mr. R. Grant, do. ; Mr. Macdonald, the Exchange,
Treasurer of the Society ; Mr. Duncan Maciver, cabinetmaker ;
Mr. Finlay Maciver, gilder ; Mr. Donald Maciver, student ; Mr.
Charles Mackay, Drummond ; Mr. Alex. Mackay, Rose Street ;

E

Bailie Simpson ; Bailie Macbean ; Bailie Baillie; Mr. Mackenzie,
Clachnacuddin House ; Mr. T. D. Campbell, Church Street ; Mr.
G. J. Campbell, writer; Mr. J. H. Mackenzie, bookseller; Mr.
Mackay, bookseller ; Mr. D. Campbell, draper ; Mr. A. Mac-
kenzie, Church Street ; Mr. A. Macdonald, New Market ; Mr.
Huntly Fraser, merchant; Mr. Angus Macdonald, Bard to the
Society ; Mr. Ross, Gas and Water Co.'s Office ; Mr. Tulloch,
painter : Mr. Kenneth Fraser, writer; Mr. Alex. Fraser, do. ;
Mr. W. B. Forsyth, *Advertiser ;* Mr. Barron, *Courier ;* Mr. W.
Mackay, Secretary to the Society ; Mr. John Munro, wine mer-
chant; Mr. Alex. Grant, Church Street ; Mr. Cumming, Allan-
fearn; Mr. Wm. Mackenzie, Workman's Club Buildings ; Mr. D.
Fraser, Glenelg ; Mr. Wood, *Courier* Office ; Mr. Mackenzie,
teacher, Maryburgh ; Mr. A. Macleod, Huntly Street ; Captain
Mackenzie, Telford Road ; Mr. Logan, Stoneyfield ; Mr. William
Campbell, Castle Street, &c.

After an excellent supper (served up in Mr Christie's best style,
and including a first-class bill of fare) had been done ample justice
to, the Chairman rose and proposed in succession the usual loyal
and patriotic toasts, Captain Robert Grant, 4th I.H.R.V., responding for the volunteers. At the call of the Chair, the Secretary,
Mr William Mackay, then read the following report :—

"At the end of the first year's existence of the Gaelic Society of
Inverness, it may not be out of place to refer to a few particulars
in connection with its founding and constitution. After some
correspondence in the columns of the *Inverness Advertiser* by " U.
M'C.," " Clachnacuddin," "Mealfourvonie," &c., on the subject of
a Gaelic Society in the Capital of the Highlands, an advertisement
appeared in the papers announcing that a meeting of those favourable to the proposal would be held in the Association Buildings,
on the evening of the 4th September 1871. At this meeting it
was formally resolved that a Gaelic Society should be established
in Inverness, and a committee was appointed to frame a constitution. By the 28th of the same month, this committee had their
work finished, and that evening the Society was formally constituted, the number who enrolled themselves as members being
twenty-four. From this date the Society met regularly, and
additions were made from time to time to the membership, until,
at the first annual assembly, held on 12th July last, there were
119 on the roll. This gathering, at which there were about 1,000
present, was a success in every respect, and the immediate result
was a large accession of members. It is now gratifying to report
that at this, the close of our first financial year, there are 182

members on the roll. The Gaelic Society, having objects so thoroughly national and patriotic, ought to be one of our most popular institutions, and in order that it should continue to prosper as it has hitherto done, I would suggest that each member should make it a point to secure at least one new member during the year upon which we are now about to enter—a plan which has been so successfully adopted by a kindred Society, the Inverness, Ross, and Nairn Club.

"Of the work done by the Society, I need not give details, seeing that the first volume of our Transactions is now on the table, and that each member will be presented with a copy in a few days. Suffice it to say that our doings have been as varied in character as the objects of the Society. The lectures and essays delivered, to the date of the assembly in July, will be found in the Transactions, except six papers not published, as explained in the introduction to the volume. The opening lecture of this session was delivered in Gaelic by the Rev. Mr. Macgregor, and up to this date the following papers were read at the ordinary meetings, viz. :— "Toireachd na Taine," an ancient Gaelic legend collected by Mr. Carmichael, Lochmaddy ; "The Study of the Gaelic Language," by the Secretary ; "Laoidh nan Ceann," an ancient Gaelic legend, collected by Mr. Carmichael ; and "The Undeveloped Resources and Capabilities of the Highlands," by Mr. Fraser, C.E. .

"One of the objects of the Society is the formation of a library of books and manuscripts bearing upon the genius, literature, history, antiquities, and material interests of the Highlands and Highland people ; and in connection with this a valuable collection has already been made, principally by donation. A list of the donations is given at the end of the Transactions.

"From the Treasurer's account for the year it appears that the amount of the receipts, including subscriptions and money taken at the public lectures, is £102 18s 6d; the total expenditure, including expenses in connection with the lectures, the publishing of the Transactions, &c., £82 9s 9d ; leaving a balance in favour of the Society of £20 8s 9d.

"It has to be explained that after each member is supplied with a copy of the Transactions there will be over 200 copies in the hands of the Society for sale ; and I may also mention that, as it was decided that the Society's year should close on 31st December, the expenditure extends over fifteen months, while the subscriptions are only for one year.

"A proposal to found a Gaelic bursary in one of our Universities was brought under the consideration of the Council, and they hope

that at an early period the Society will be in a position to carry
this proposal into effect.

" The Council take this opportunity of impressing upon the
members the desirability of a regular attendance at the meetings
of the Society. Seeing that the office-bearers give their onerous
services gratuitously, their work will be materially facilitated if
the members will be prompt in paying their subscriptions, and
otherwise assist in furthering the objects of the Society.

" The present acting Council now retire from office, and at a
meeting to be held early in January, it falls to the Society to
nominate office-bearers for next year. The meeting will be
announced by advertisement, and it is desirable that there should
be a large attendance, as the appointment of office-bearers for the
year is obviously a very important matter."

The Chairman, in rising to propose the toast of the evening,
" Success to the Inverness Gaelic Society," which was received
with enthusiasm, said that before proceeding to read some notes he
had prepared for the occasion, he had a remark to make, suggested
by an observation in the excellent report just read. He referred
to the importance of procuring additional members to the Society.
He undertook to act on that suggestion himself, and he trusted the
other members would do the same, and at least secure one additional member each. He was the more pressed to do this, because
looking at the handsome volume of the Society's Transactions just
published, he felt himself placed in rather a peculiar position.
Only two individuals appeared on the list of life members. One
of these was their excellent President and Chief, Cluny Macpherson,
and the other his humble self. Now, in heraldry a Highland Chief
held the rank of an English Baron, and was entitled to two supporters. As to getting additional members, for his part he undertook to procure the one recommended, so he hoped the company
would exert themselves, for the importance of a Chief depended
upon his following. Another remark he wished to make was with
reference to the two hundred surplus copies of the Society's Transactions. He thought that work would increase their membership,
and that it would be an excellent plan for procuring members were
a circular and copy of the Secretary's report sent out to forty or
fifty of the most influential Highland gentlemen in the north. Mr
Fraser-Mackintosh then proceeded as follows :—Twice happy is
such a society as the present, since it combines two such potent
elements of strength as judgment and enthusiasm. Upon the latter
I need not dwell—it is unquenchable ; but if we carry the former
also, we must attain our ends. Are the ends then we seek, namely,

" The perfecting of the members in the use of the Gaelic language ; the cultivation of the language, poetry, and music of the Scottish Highlands ; the rescuing from oblivion of Celtic poetry, traditions, legends, books, and manuscripts ; the establishing in Inverness of a library, to consist of books and manuscripts, in whatever language, bearing upon the genius, the literature, the history, the antiquities, and the material interests of the Highlands and Highland people ; the vindication of the rights and character of the Gaelic people— and, generally, the furtherance of their interests, whether at home or abroad "—justifiable and necessary? The presence of such an attendance as I now see before me answers in the affirmative. All of us are working men, and in turning for a time from the harassing and anxious exertions of every-day life, could any pursuit or relaxa- tion be more fit than that which, combining judgment with enthusiasm, causes us to investigate the past. In the expressive words of Dr Johnson, " Whatever withdraws us from the power of our senses, whatever makes the past, the distant, or the future predominate over the present, advances us in the dignity of thinking beings." Our views are not aggressive ; they are, on the contrary, defensive and preservative. We are proud of being Highlanders, and of our language ; and jealous of the fame of those who have preceded us. We owe much to Sir Walter Scott for his pictures of the Highlands and Highlanders—in truth, a debt which can never be repaid. Such an expression as "my heart warms at the sight of the tartan," merits, and will have, immortality. But when it is gravely said that he *created* Scotland, and especially the High- lands—while we are forced to admit that such a statement is but the reflex of English opinion—we are called on to deny its truth. These ideas are not confined to the common people, for you will find in works by such an accomplished author as the writer of " The Greatest of the Plantagenets," &c., such a distortion of facts, such a barefaced justification of Edward the First's proceed- ings, as compels any Scotsman of proper feeling indignantly to protest against the language used, the inferences drawn, and the results arrived at. In the matter of our unrivalled scenery, the author of the " Playground of Europe " writes of the Highlands as "a country of dumpy heather-clad hills" In the keeping up of national traits and feeling, and in a minor degree, local aspira- tions, we are broadly and frequently told that being now an integral part of a great empire, we but betray a narrow and petty provincialism. I have yet to learn that men devoted to their country, to its ancient language, to their place of nativity, are thereby generally worse citizens. This field is, however, wide, and I for the present shall confine myself to four points. First, I

shall touch upon the necessity of societies such as ours removing
by every legitimate mode the idea that the Highlands was a barbarous country, and the people little better than savages. Such
charges have been iterated and reiterated. Let them be refuted
and again refuted by facts, as these are gathered from cotemporary
sources and documents of the past. We at once admit that in the
early and middle ages, as they may be termed, of authentic Scottish
history, much shedding of blood, cruelties, and rapine prevailed.
But I ask, were these so peculiar to the Highlands that *they* must
be singled out and held up to reprobation? Were there no Border
feuds? Was there no debateable land, so rife with murder and
bloodshed as to have necessitated the most arbitrary exercise of
power by one of the Scottish Kings? So much for the South of
Scotland. Again, in the north, in the counties of Sutherland and
Caithness, and in the northern isles, I say unhesitatingly that
more purposeless, more sanguine, and more cruel slaughters
occurred among the population of Scandinavian descent than will
be found in the darkest annals of the Highlands, properly so called.
Just let me ask, would any true Highlander—of whom it has been
well said that he is always a gentleman—parade by way of epitaph
his misdeeds upon his tombstone? But what says a Scandinavian
called Donald Mac-Mhorchie-ic-eoin-mhoir of himself? Here it is
—" Donald Mack, here Iyis lo ; vas ill to his frend and var to his
fo, true to his maister in veird and vo. 1623." Why, a dog is
faithful to his master. Again, was it a Highlander who ordered
the head of a man of some status to be instantly struck off because,
in the streets of Inverness more than 300 years ago, the unfortunate took " the crown of the causeway?" The more original
documents are searched out, the more will it be found, as I feel
satisfied from my own researches, that the general character of the
Highlander was peaceful, and the undoubted painful events which
are scattered over history will be traced to the fact that the people
and their immediate masters were driven to desperation by the
grinding encroachments of strangers from the south and west.
The Parliamentary and criminal records which exist containing
such deplorable complaints of the doings of "broken men" in the
Highlands and Islands must be received with caution, now that
we are acquainted with the favouritism and corruption which
surrounded the Court, and sat upon the bench. I do not deny
that these criminal proceedings took place, but I say that many of
them were unjustifiable, and instigated for private ends. If the
Highlanders were, as they have been so often depicted, how is it that
so great a change has taken place within little more than a century ? The instincts, habits, and actings of race can not, and are

not, removed or set aside by Acts of Parliament. We in the Highlands are perhaps the most peaceable, law-abiding people in the
world, and if we wish our posterity to think well of us, as all of
us must do, then it is not only our duty, but we ought to esteem
it our privilege, to rehabilitate our predecessors, by giving them
the justice they have not hitherto received. In reference to our
own peaceful state and immunity from crime of any magnitude,
not merely in the country, but in our northern towns and villages,
is it unjustifiable to notice what has been said a few days ago of
the assizes of the south?—"A succession of murders and minor
outrages has presented a picture of drunken brutality such as might
be more fitly expected in some savage island in the far Pacific,
where the natives have just tasted for the first time the terrible
poison of drink. The northern circuit has been the chief scene of
these horrors, and they tell a shocking story of the state of the
well-paid working classes in the district of which Durham is the
centre." Do I refer to these with satisfaction? No. I merely
wish to remind dwellers in "Merrie England" of the danger of
throwing stones from within glass houses. Second—I shall refer
to the collection and preservation of Gaelic literature of whatever
character. In referring to Gaelic literature, we can never over-
estimate our indebtedness to Macpherson. Before his first appearance, everything connected with the ancient state of the Highlands
was looked on with disfavour, and by many then living in the
Highlands with contempt. It needed, therefore, some strong
stimulant to arouse a counter-spirit of enquiry and defence. This
was presented in the works of Ossian, which as given by Macpherson so startled the public, that two violent currents set in, one in
disparagement and the other in vindication. The enquiries instituted by the Highland Society, and by private parties, had the
great good fortune to bring to light vast masses of song, recitation,
and legend, which otherwise would in all probability have been
lost. We now know pretty well what parts are authentic, and
what Macpherson's own. In justice to Macpherson it may be
admitted that the portions supposed to be his own are equal to the
originals ; and his great poetic genius is undeniable. We, of
course, don't justify his conduct in respect of the famous poems, but
really his reputation, private and political, was so bad, that as concerns the poems, the indirect results having been so important, a
veil, at least by Highlanders, may be drawn over his translations.
Fresh upon the discussions, Dr. Johnson, rough but honest, comes
upon the scene, and were it only for his language in regard to Flora
Macdonald and his reflections upon landing in Iona, we do forgive all
his harsh sayings. He says—" We are now treading that illustri-

ous island which was once the luminary of the Caledonian regions, whence savage clans and roving barbarians derived the benefits of knowledge and the blessings of religion. Far from me, and from my friends, be such frigid philosophy as may conduct us indifferent and unmoved over any ground which has been dignified by wisdom, bravery, or virtue. That man is little to be envied whose patriotism would not gain force upon the plain of Marathon, or whose piety would not grow warmer among the ruins of Iona." Talk of Scotland being destitute of wood. What now-a-days would English railways and collieries do without our Highland timber? What would Johnson say, what would the hundreds of scribblers say, when decrying the antiquity of the Gaelic language, if they had lived to read the "Book of Deer?" This discovery marks a white stone in the history of Gaelic literature. It is neither more nor less than this, that the oldest Scottish document known to exist, is not written in the English language, but in the Gaelic. Aye, and in Gaelic which is readable by ordinary Gaelic students. I observe Professor Innes describes the writing of the Gaelic chronicle as the hand of the 11th century. Others put it earlier, but in any case it now stands as the very first document purely relating to Scotland which exists. The few other documents remaining of that century are in Latin. The antiquity of the language as a written one being thus so satisfactorily established, it would be highly becoming in a Society like ours to search for and print all manuscripts in the language, and to issue in a convenient form new editions of scarce and curious works. Further, all poetry, songs, stories, legends, riddles, incantations, and others should be carefully sought out, collected, and printed. That much in this way has been done, and particularly of late by Campbell of Islay and others is gladly admitted ; but much more can yet be preserved of what still floats about in the Highlands and Islands. And here I would hope and trust that the first volume of our Transactions, so satisfactory in every respect, is but the beginning of a long and useful series. A word of caution, however, is perhaps necessary in the collection of stories. If we are listening to a fairy or other legend, imagination alone is at work, and the more vivid the scenes the better. On the other hand, historical stories must be very carefully sifted, for it is well known that events and persons have become blended, though having in reality no connection with each other. And as for dates, few Highlanders only speaking Gaelic can be relied on for periods prior to Culloden. There are many enquiries, no doubt, of a minor character, but still of interest, which our Society might undertake, serving for "Occasional Papers," as I may call them.

We must not forget to keep in view that the sure mode of permanently and widely enlisting the sympathies and support of Highlanders generally is by *popularising* Gaelic literature, and the past history of the Highlands. It will not do to have learned essays alone, which, to many, and these leal Highlanders too, are as pleasant reading as a dictionary or grammar. Carrying out these views I would suggest such an investigation as the real origin of *Piobaireachd Dhomhnuill Duibh.* If you were to ask nine out of ten, they would doubtless say, of course, it is a tune composed in honour of one of the chiefs of the Camerons. Is Lochiel not *Mac Domhnuill Duibh?* But, notwithstanding, there will be found one man who will say, and perhaps he alone is right, that it was composed in honour of Donald Balloch, at the time of the first battle of Inverlochy. The name of Donald Balloch has had to me from a child something of a charm—as I doubt not it has had to many of you—and I, just in passing, notice that lately, when painfully deciphering an old charter, signed at Inverness in 1446, I was delighted to find the name of Donald Balloch as one of the witnesses, bringing him, as it were, almost bodily before me. Another enquiry might, as I have referred to Inverlochy, be this—Was or was not Montrose actually present at the battle there in 1645? Did he command the royal army, and see Mac-Cailean-Mor sneak off ignominiously in his galley? Most people will say—Yes, he was present; but others will say No: that the battle was a surprise brought on by the wonted impetuosity of the Macdonalds, and that Montrose, who had been in the neighbourhood of Killychumin, did not get back until all was over. Third—The placing of monuments, tablets, or memorials in honour of distinguished Highlanders, or to commemorate great historic events, might well form an important part of the objects of our Society. The name of Flora Macdonald has lately been honoured by a monument which confers the highest credit on the inceptors of the scheme, and those who carried it out; and I must particularly refer to Mackintosh, who lent the influence of an ancient and honoured name; to Mr. Walter Carruthers, who brought the tact, knowledge, and perseverance which have made his paper such a power in the north; to Mr. Alexander Ross, whose massive but chaste design will hand down his name with honour to late generations. Here I cannot help saying of Mr. Ross, that I feel assured the polished citizens of Athens would not have used any artist in the shabby and unfair way those who affect to call their city the Modern Athens have used him! Also, Mr. Forsyth, sculptor, who did his part so well. The name of the Rev. Mr. Macgregor, also a true Highlander, who suggested the memorial forty years

ago, and assisted to carry it out, should not be overlooked. In looking over the list of subscribers, Highland feeling may be seen in
miniature, and although we don't find the name of the two Skye
potentates, we find with pleasure scores of Macdonalds and Macleods giving their shillings and half-crowns. Next, I would speak
of the field of Culloden. The scene of the battle is visited by
hundreds yearly, and from the farthest corners of the earth. That
visitors are disappointed will I think be conceded. What form the
memorial should take it is not for me to say. All I say is that
something ought to be done, and I am aware that Culloden is very
willing that something be done, and to take that leading part
which becomes him. It occurs to me that this is a subject fairly
falling within our province to discuss, and to endeavour in concert
with those interested to carry out. Lastly, we have tablets to
erect in honour of poets such as *Ian Lom* and others. He lived
and had his croft of Clachaig in Brae-Lochaber, "the bard's croft,"
from the time of the Lords of the Isles. His politics were so much
in unison with my own, that before this I should have caused a
monument to be erected at Kilchaoril, where it might be naturally supposed his remains would lie; but the matter has stood
over, as I have read that he was buried in the church of Duthil.
Now, with this locality, or the name of Grant, he could have had
no sympathy whatever. I will be very thankful to receive information on this point, and if the story about Duthil be mythical,
and there be every reason to suppose he was buried with his
kindred, then the picturesque and commanding spot which holds
the remains of so many of the brave men and fair women of the
Brae of Lochaber, shall not want a suitable memorial of the renowned *Ian Lom*. Fourth, I would direct attention to the
importance of encouraging feelings of attachment in Highlanders
to the place of their own or their ancestors' birth. This opens
such wide questions as to prevent more than a passing reference.
We complain that in the past too many have been compulsorily
expatriated. I complain of the great indifference shown by many
who have made fortunes in the south or abroad to the land of their
birth or origin. Unfortunately, land in the Highlands has changed
hands greatly; nay, is changing, and will continue to change.
Who are taking possession of the Highlands? As a rule, we are
safe to reply sportsmen, or business men. The former necessarily
wish as few as possible, and they have no common sympathies.
The latter look to returns for their money, and that, it is well
known, is easier, if not more certain, from large farms and skilled
husbandry. I must not be misunderstood on the matter of sportsmen. Through them rents have quadrupled, whereby the area

of taxation has been so much enlarged, as materially to reduce it. Superior houses have been planted everywhere, good wages are given, and the nature of the occupations evokes rude health to the employed, perpetuated in a vigorous offspring. But notwithstanding, the Highlands can sustain a much larger population than now exists, always, however, if judiciously distributed, taking the climate and locality into account. To do away with sport in a rough and ready manner would be fatal to the Highlands ; but, on the other hand, how much fine arable land, what pretty green spots, where cattle were wont to be herded, what numbers of houses, with occasionally an ash tree or a rowan, to denote that one with a taste above his fellows had there his loved abode, are to be found on large sheep farms ? But the grass of the arable lands is grey from decay ; heather slowly but surely encroaches on the natural pastures ; and not the ruins of cottars' houses, but dismantled walls of the habitations of gentlemen tenants, are found on the possession of a large non-resident sheep farmer. Such places ought again to have their healthy and happy occupants ; the land should again be tilled ; cattle should again abound, and with all this sport could have its fair place and share. Now, it appears to me that as we cannot look for amelioration from the new classes of buyers I have referred to, we can with reasonable assurance of hope look to such an amelioration, if the Highlands were owned chiefly by Highlanders. What I would wish to impress upon every ambitious young Highlander, determined to win fortune, that he ought to keep in view the acquisition of land as his last and ultimate object, and having so acquired it, to do all in his power for its improvement and development, and for the comfort and happiness of the inhabitants. Such as have followed learned professions, engaged in the service of our country, or occupied in trade, and enabled to retire with comfort, should spend as much of the remainder of their days in the Highlands as possible, where their wealth would do good to trade, and their influence be productive of benefit. Now, as an example of what I have been alluding to, take the case of Mr. Matheson, M.P. Is there a better landlord anywhere ? How much has he not done for the North ? Is not his name and reputation such as may be envied by the oldest, proudest, or noblest of our northern houses ? Now when young, let us say when at school at Inverness, and with the world all before him, must he not have often thought that his ancestors had been great Ross-shire proprietors ; were unjustly forfeited at Inverness 400 years ago, and it should be his ambition not only to refound his ancient house, but to extend its borders. We cannot doubt that such feelings and aspirations existed, wafting him on to fortune. Why should not others do the same? Rather is there not every call upon Frasers, Macdonalds, Macleods, Macneills, Macleans, &c., to bestir themselves, re-acquire their old habitations, and inaugurate a new and happier era, when wealth and sympathy would go hand in hand. In furthering such and kindred objects, societies like ours may do much good, and I now ask you to drink prosperity to " The Gaelic Society of Inverness."

A Gaelic song was then sung by Mr. Hugh Rose.

Mr. Dallas proposed the next toast. This duty, he said, is greatly simplified and rendered easier by the very felicitous and lucid manner in which the Chairman has already set forth the objects of such societies as the Gaelic Society of Inverness. My toast is "Kindred Societies"—a very comprehensive style and title of toast as you will presently see, not by the length of my remarks, but by the bare enumeration of societies established and now existing for purposes kindred to our own. Our leading purposes among others are the perfecting of the members in the use of the Gaelic language—the cultivation of the language, poetry, and music of the Scottish Highlands—and the rescuing from oblivion of Celtic poetry, traditions, legends, books and MSS., and also the furtherance of the interests of the Gaelic people whether at home or abroad. The Gaelic language, it is commonly believed, is destined soon to die out as a spoken language. I am inclined to join this belief, and to say for many reasons which I deem cogent, that I think it would not be against the prosperity of the Highlands of Scotland that it should to that extent disappear. It happens that this is'and of Great Britain is a great commercial country; and I think no one will deny that we should all agree upon one common vernacular tongue for the transaction of our common business. We are not sufficiently extensive commercially even to render separate languages in the least necessary for our own internal or home transactions, and the English language is now the language in which all our business is transacted. The stated periodical and most welcome visits of English sportsmen to our Highland glens has tended greatly to the extinction of Gaelic as a spoken language. This,-however, need not in any way interfere with or impede the progress of such societies; but on the contrary, the very fact that a language so interesting as disclosing legendary lore is destined in the course and progress of events to die out as a spoken language is the best reason why such societies should start up for its preservation and proper culture. The kindred societies to whose prosperity I ask you to join me in this toast comprehend no fewer than sixteen separate bodies. But before naming them perhaps you will allow me so far digress as to say that I in common with others regret that we have no ladies present this evening. The ladies must form a part of all such societies as ours. I have no doubt that the different societies whose prosperity you are asked to toast have lady members, and so have we to a limited extent. I have no intention of violating the rules by introducing politics, but whatever may be said of the great question of women suffrage, and whether the concession of that vast privilege to the fair sex would be attended on the one hand with the immense advantages to the human race which its advocates contend for, or on the other with the dire consequences anticipated by some people, I think we will agree here that the co-operation of the silken cords of all society— the bonds that bind men in peace and harmony with each other— would certainly be a most potent auxiliary to such societies as ours and our kindred brethren. Mr. Dallas concluded by enumerating the kindred societies referred to, and asking for a hearty bumper to their health and prosperity. Should any of their members ever come among us here we would receive them with a hearty *céud mìle fàilte.*

After some excellent pipe music, including a beautiful *piobaireachd*, from Pipe-Major Maclennan, the veteran piper of the H.L.I. Militia, who was in attendance, and performed during supper and between the toasts,

Sheriff Macdonald rose and proposed, in the Gaelic language, the toast of "The Gaelic People," which called forth loud cheers.

Mr. Murdoch proposed "Celtic Literature." He said that after the very excellent opening address of the Chairman, and the reference of Mr. Dallas to so many kindred societies engaged in advancing Celtic literature, there was little left for him to say at that late hour. He always felt the awkwardness of the position in which he stood, owing to the attitude taken up by considerable numbers who asserted that there was no Celtic literature at all. He seemed as if he were acting in antagonism where he was only asserting facts, which should be known to all intelligent men. There was neither antagonism nor anything narrowing in setting forth the facts and claims of Celtic literature; we were rather insisting upon contributing our share to the literature of the world, and in our researches we came into friendly contact with our friends in Wales, in the Isle of Man, and in Ireland, which were teeming with valuable materials of this kind. Indeed, Celtic literature was to be found where but very few looked for it; and it was curious to observe the different treatments extended to Macpherson when he laid before the world what were really and ostensibly Celtic poems, and to Tennyson when he brought forth really Celtic poems under an English guise. No one raised a question as to the latter, whilst a regular war arose out of the former. The "Idyls of the King" were not only Celtic in their subject and their incidents, but they were positively Welsh ballads, and so much so, that whole lines, sentences, paragraphs, and even pages, with merely artistic touches, could be traced to Lady G. Fullerton's translations of Welsh into English. Another unexpected quarter in which we found Celtic literature was Buchanan's History of Scotland, composed by a born Celt, from Celtic authorities, and with an intensely Celtic argument. The spirit of the Celtic polity is particularly strong in his arguments on the succession to the throne. It was, perhaps, after all, consistent, first to steal our literature, and then say we had none! There were three famous Gaelic compositions of which it was said:—"*Gach dan gu dan an Deirg; gach sgeul gu sgeul Chonail; agus gach laoidh gu laoidh an amadain mhoir;*" conveying that the standard to which each poem was to be referred was the song of the Red; each story to the story of Connal; and each lay to the lay of the Great Fool. "The Red" was Diarmid O'Duine; of all the great Connals, the one in *the* story was Connal Gulbinu; and the Great Fool was no fool at all. There was no occasion for him to say another word in favour of the toast, unless it were that they should fill their glasses of good Ness water, and drink a bumper to Celtic Literature.

The song "Scotland Yet" was sung in excellent style by Mr. Campbell (of Messrs. Davidson & Scott, solicitors).

Mr. Fraser, C.E., gave the health of "The Provost and Magistrates of Inverness," and in doing so referred to the importance and extent of their duties, discharged without fee or reward, and frequently he believed at the cost of much time and trouble which might have been devoted to their own business. Three bailies had honoured this meeting with their presence, and were members of the Society; but every member of the Council ought to join them, and thereby show a good example to the rest of the community.

Bailie Simpson responded. Any little time or trouble devoted to the affairs of the town by his colleagues and himself was amply repaid by securing the good will of those they represented. He was particularly well pleased to see presiding over the company to-night his old and esteemed friend so long at the Council board, and would for one be delighted if Mr. Fraser-Mackintosh came back among them and gave them a helping hand. They had fought together for a long time in a minority, but the tables were now turned, and the side with which he acted had things now pretty much their own way. He trusted their excellent Chairman to-night would by-and-bye return with honour to the Council where he served so long and faithfully.

"Come under my plaidie," an excellent Gaelic translation, was sung in a hearty and humorous style, at the call of the Chairman, by Mr. Cumming, Allanfearn.

The Chairman then proposed "the Ladies," which, he said, might have more appropriately been given to Mr. Alexander Mackenzie, who had lately been acting as gallant advocate for the sex. He expressed cordial approval of the proposal to have lady members, and their presence at the festive meetings of the Society.

Mr. Fraser, Faillie, gave "the Press," coupled with the local newspapers, which was responded to by Mr. W. B. Forsyth.

The song "Wha'll be King but Chairlie," in Gaelic and English, was sung in capital style by Sheriff Macdonald, after which the Chairman proposed a hearty bumper to the worthy Sheriff's health, and the Sheriff suitably acknowledged the compliment, stating that now he was an enrolled member of the Society he should be only too glad to do all that lay in his power to promote its interests.

Mr. Alex. Mackenzie proposed "the Members of Committee," coupled with their excellent and efficient Secretary, Mr. William Mackay. Next to the toast of the ladies, this was the one he most preferred to give. The great and successful exertions made by the members of the committee in conducting the affairs of this Society, and the perseverance and sound practical sense they invariably exhibited, led to the gratifying position which the Society had now attained. And to the Secretary they were specially indebted for the attention he devoted to their affairs. He had other duties of his own to attend to, and yet without fee or reward he gave much of his time and talents—many of his hours of sleep, it was to be feared—to pushing forward the work of the Society. He trusted the Society would not loose his services, which had been invaluable up to the present and would be so henceforward.

Mr. Mackay, in thanking the company for the honour done him, said he only regretted that he was not able to devote more of his time to the Society's affairs ; but what he had been able to do, had been a pleasure and delight to him—it had brought him many personal friends, whose acquaintance he might never otherwise have formed, and it had brought him into correspondence with some of the most eminent literary men in the country—a circumstance of which he would be proud as long as he lived. He had been greatly helped in the performance of his duties by Mr. Duncan Mackintosh, Bank of Scotland, and but for that gentleman's willing and valuable assistance he could never have undertaken the amount of work that had occasionally to be done.

Bailie Macbean proposed " the Chairman."

The Chairman, in responding, said that he had much pleasure in being present to-night, and when called on to preside over the meeting, though he had much other business to attend to, and his health was not what he would like it to be, he found he really could not refuse, for his sympathies and his heart were with them in this matter.

A Gaelic song was sung by Mr. Charles Mackay, Drummond.

The Chairman rose and proposed " the health of their friends from a distance," to whom the Society were much indebted for their attendance to-night, and for the interest they showed in its affairs. He coupled the toast with Mr. Fraser, a gentleman who had come all the way from Glenelg to be present at this meeting.

Mr. Fraser expressed his thanks for so kindly remembering the strangers from a distance. The best return he could make for this kindness was to state that having already become a member, he promised to secure another one to the Society. He was much gratified by the success of this meeting, and should have great pleasure in circulating all he had seen and heard to-night.

Mr. Dallas proposed "Our Chief, Cluny Macpherson," whom they should be proud of having at their head. Their Chief had delivered the best Gaelic address ever given before the members of this Society. Cluny was not a young man, but he was still a splendid specimen of a Highlander. If he remembered aright, it was of Cluny that Sir Walter Scott wrote in 1825 as the "fine spirited lad" who headed the procession of Highlanders on the occasion of Mons Meg being placed in Edinburgh Castle.

The Chairman said Mr. Dallas was right as to the remark of Sir Walter Scott.

The toast of "the Croupiers" was then proposed by Bailie Simpson, and acknowledged by Mr. Dallas, after which Mr. Alex. Mackenzie proposed "the Absent Members," and in so doing suggested that those members at a distance who were unable to attend the meetings of the Society, might show their interest in its concerns by writing papers, which would be read at their meetings by some other member residing in town—many could write such papers, and would have the pleasure of seeing them in the Society's handsome volume of Transactions.

Messrs. Mackay and Mackintosh then sung together a Gaelic song, and the Chairman proposed that as the hour was late it was about time to part. He said they were exceedingly indebted to the gentlemen who had favoured them with songs, especially Gaelic ones, and who had contributed so much to the harmony of the evening. Before parting they could not do less than tender their acknowledgments to Mr. and Mrs. Christie for the excellent manner in which they had discharged their part of the duties—the attendance having been entirely satisfactory and all the materials supplied most excellent, for which they deserved the company's best thanks.

The meeting then broke up, after singing together at the Chairman's suggestion the bard of the Society's Gaelic translation of the National Anthem.

JANUARY 30, 1874.—On this date Mr. John Murdoch read a paper on

OUR FIRES AND FIRE-SIDES.

The subject which I have chosen is a practical one, and I hope you will consider it seasonable. Even to those in whom the organs of ideality, wonder, and wit are largely developed, this evening devoted to the grosser matters of our Fires and Fire-sides will not, I hope, be a great sacrifice.

I have chosen this subject at the present time, thinking that the exhorbitant price of fuel might induce people to give an amount of attention to the economics of our fires and fire-places which they might decline to do when coals were only at a reasonable price.

No doubt there could be a good deal of poetry and sentiment entwined around the subject. Numbers of beautiful pictures could be conjured up about our ingle-sides, our blazing logs, and our family circles, with their endearing associations and memories; but in one brief hour I can hardly dispose of the mass of matter which I have to lay before you; and in justice to myself, and in mercy to you, I shall not give more time to the subject.

"And," some one asks, "if we are not to have poetry and sentiment around our hearths, what are we to have?"

You shall have a treatise on our Fires, our Fire-places, and our Fuel.

In the first place, I need hardly mention the fact, that no question presses so heavily upon all classes of the community at this moment as that of Fuel does; and if I can do ever so little towards the solution of that question, it is my duty to do so.

F

Hitherto, as a rule, we have applied our fuel as if it had been
an object with us to get it out of the way ; or to burn as much as
possible and get the least possible heat from it.   For example, the
practice of placing the fresh coal on the top of the fire is one of the
most flagrant pieces of waste of which we need be guilty.   A great
deal of the heat of the existing fire is expended in forcing up the
chimney the gas which is distilled from the fresh coal.   Large
volumes of smoke escape up the chimney, or out through the house,
when a fresh supply of coal is put on.   The smoke which we thus
waste is the material out of which, with more scientific con-
trivances, illuminating gas is manufactured.   This smoke escapes,
not only to our own direct and immediate loss, but it becomes a
nuisance to the whole community ; and what should be heating
and lighting our houses, falls in smuts and in flakes of soot upon
our persons, and upon white dresses which are spread or hung out
to dry.   That this is good fuel, you have abundance of proof in
the fact that soot takes fire so readily when it falls back into the
fire-place ; and what we want is an apparatus which will burn it
before it has gone up the chimney at all.   Another proof is often
dsplayed to you in the fire-place when you take time to watch it.
You see a jet of brown smoke escaping from a piece of fresh coal
which has begun to split and crumble with the heat.   Set a taper
to this jet, and it becomes a bright and beautiful flame.   Now,
what is true of these jets of smoke is true of nearly the whole
smoke together ; and one of the practical questions which have
been asked a thousand times is, " How can we best consume our
own smoke, and convert it into heat and light ? "
    There have been a good many contrivances invented for this
purpose, but there have been a good many—no doubt very stupid
—excuses for not departing from the old wasteful way.   The
principle of all of them may be said to be one.   You have a good
example in the paraffin lamp of the present day.   Without the
brass dome and the glass, one-half the gas of the oil would escape
in smoke, and rest in soot upon your ceilings and walls.   But with
the dome, the heat of the existing flame is kept in so as to set fire
to part of that smoke ; and when the glass is added, much even of
what escapes the dome is kindled, and light comes out of darkness.
The same thing is done in those furnaces in which the smoke of
the fresh coal is made to pass closely over the red embers ; or still
better, where this gas is made to pass up, or down, or across, as
the case may be, right through the strong, red fire.   This is the
secret of the whole affair—of consuming your own smoke, and
taking both heat and light out of darkness.
    The thing has been accomplished in thousands of instances, by

simply placing the red fire on the top of the fresh coal. Then, as the gas or smoke escapes from the newly-heated coal, it passes into the overlying fire, is kindled, and becomes fire instead of smoke.

But the waste of fuel in these and in other respects is almost insignificant, as compared with the waste of fire after we have kindled it. The practice of putting our fire places, three sides in the wall, and only one side towards us, is surely very absurd in a country where heat is an object. At a rough estimate, we do not get more than one-fourth of the heat which is thus generated. You have, in fact, fire enough in one stupidly arranged grate or stove to give as much heat to each of three apartments as it at present gives to one, not to speak of the further heating which might be effected with what escapes by the vent.

Every one who has seen the American stoves and ranges in use knows the very small amount of fuel which can be made to do the work of a very large fire in our ordinary ranges. And I have seen a Belgian apparatus which heated five different pans with a fire which you could put into a gallon measure. In Sweden they have carried their economical invention so far as to make one small fire cook half-a-dozen different dishes in such rapid succession as to be done simultaneously. They have a case covered with wadding, so as that it will allow scarcely any of the heat which it receives to escape. There is a cooking pan, or pot, or kettle, which fits exactly into this case. It is charged, say, with so many pounds of mutton to be boiled. It is placed in an opening in the stove, until it has begun to boil. The Swede lifts the heated vessel, and places it in the non-conducting wadding. The potatoes, the pie, the pudding, are in succession brought to the boil in the same manner, and placed in their respective non-conducting cases; and thus you see another way in which one small fire can be made to do three, four, or five times the cooking which we, in our extravagance, would think of making it do !

Instead of letting the heat away into dead walls, we should let it into one or two other rooms, and instead of letting so much heat out at the top of the chimney, make it heat one or two apartments in different storeys. This has actually been done by a clergyman near Dumfries. Then, there is the heating of a whole house by means of hot air pipes, by means of hot water, or by means of steam. The kitchen fire, with any of these, would render any other fire entirely unnecessary in a large house ; and what people would in former years have scouted as un-British, &c., will, in the year 1875, be adopted as eminently practical and necessary, and we will wonder at our own slavish conformity to a wasteful custom.

No doubt it is pleasant to see the flame of our fires, and to watch the faces, of which we have heard so much ; but these, I fancy, must give way to the inevitable, as our pleasant sailing craft gave way to the grinding and champing of the steamboat ; as the pleasant stage coach made way for the iron horse and his train of unpoetical vans ; and as the old system of signals from hill-top to hill-top has been banished by the telegraph.

For my own part, I look forward to the time when these hot air and hot water appliances shall have made our houses ten times more pleasant than they ever were with grates.

Let us have those appliances once in general use, and you will have every new house fitted up with means of delectable cleanliness which will give to every family at home some of the luxuries which cannot at present be enjoyed excepting at the cost of a visit to an establishment like Cluny Hill.

But I must pass from this mere economy in the use of fuel to the subject of how and where we are to get fuel with which to supply the more economical fire-places of the no distant future.

For my part, I do not see any good reason why we, away in the North, or why others away to the West, have waited so long to be taught the use of our peat bogs. I am afraid this waiting was only a matter of silly fashion and prejudice, begotten of a false deference to the denizens of the coal-producing regions of Great Britain. This is no mere flight of fancy ; nor is it a random shaft let fly at another people. It is a well-grounded conviction of mine that in too many things—I do not say in all—we in the Highlands neglect advantages which nature has given us, for no better reason than that the example of utilizing them has not been set in the Lowlands. England and the South of Scotland have their coal beds far down in the bowels of the earth ; we have ours spread out on the face of the earth. Thus, coal has had to be brought up at terrible sacrifices, physical, social, and moral ; in so much, that whole populations have been, to a notorious degree and extent, demoralized, or, as some would say, brutalized—at any rate, degraded—far below the general level of our working classes. Yet, we have stood by lamenting the absence of the coal beds which cost so much, whilst our own coal beds might have been turned to account, in the light of day, and in the balmy breath of heaven. The right way of following the example of England would have been to go to work at the peat which God gave us, as she did at her own coal.

True, we have been cutting peats. But peats are not genteel. They are only fuel for poor, vulgar mountaineers ! We adopted the fire-places, too, of the coal countries, and thus shut ourselves

out from the use of peats.   Our peat-burning neighbours and pro-
genitors had their fires in the middle of the floor, with none of the
heat escaping into dead walls, and not much of it even escaping
by the "lum." They had the full benefit of all they burned.

To this night I have a lively impression. and a grateful recollection of a warning I got at a peat fire in a village inn in the south-
west of Ireland nine years ago.   I had travelled twenty-five Irish
miles on a Bianconi, out-side car, in pelting rain, all the way from
Killarney to Kenmere.   Finishing my business at the latter place,
I set out on a forty-two miles' journey in the evening of the same
day, on another outside car, drawn by a blind horse, as it proved,
and driven by a dozing coachman.   About ten o'clock we came to
a stage at the village of Sneem.   I need not tell you that we were
cold, and stiff, and hungry.   I was shown into a tidy little stall-
like room, to await the tea, the toast, the bacon, and the eggs.   I
did not stay long in my stall.   I made a hurried survey, and
shortly found the kitchen, bright and warm, and comfortable, and
homely, where I readily received a hearty welcome from the inmates,
who sat around the peat fire in the middle of the floor.   I feel as
if some of that warmth were still about me, and the picture of that
pleasant, homely group still hanging up among my mind's furnish-
ings and adornments.   In and around that fire you can get poetry
and philosophy as well as domestic economy, if you choose to hover
about it.   For me, I must leave it, and turn to our own peats and
peat bogs.

There are fourteen years, or more, since I endeavoured to impress
the public with the value of our peat mosses ; and when the country
began in the beginning of last autumn, to feel the pressure of
the coal famine, and when there was reason to think that there
would be some weather to dry peats, I wrote to one of our local
papers on the subject, urging that steps should be taken immediately to cut peats, and have them ready for the winter. Since
then, numbers of others have taken the subject up.

It is far within the mark to say that in the Highlands we have
1,000,000 acres of peat bog, the depth of three feet.   In Ireland
there are over four and a quarter million acres, estimated at an
average depth of eleven feet.

Our own million acres will give nearly five billions of solid
yards ; and if you assume that five yards will yield a ton of dried
peat, compressed peat, or dense peat, as the case may be, we have
one billion of tons of excellent fuel in Scotland, and somewhere
about twelve billions in Ireland.

Now, as to the use of peat, that, as we have seen, is no innovation.   There may, of course, be room for great improvements in

the mode of preparation, both as regards economy in production, and pleasantness and utility in consumption.

There are many processes in which peat, even as at present prepared in the Highlands, is found more serviceable than coal; as in smelting and finishing the best descriptions of iron, and in making malt for distillation. For both of these purposes there has been a considerable traffic in peats ever since I can remember.

The using of our peat mosses would give to our own people the employment and wages which we now pay to others for the mining of coals. It would create traffic for the railways which pass over our mosses—as the Highland, the Dingwall and Skye, and the Sutherland and Caithness. It would lay bare for cultivation vast tracts of country now felt to be needed for the production of straw, hay, and turnips with which to produce more and cheaper beef and mutton.

In regard to the reclamation of land, I remember when Blair Drummond Moss was being reclaimed, and so great was the value attached to the land beneath the peat, that men were employed, and machinery was invented, to remove the peat moss into the river Forth, to be carried down the Firth, and now you will see some of the finest farms and crops in Scotland where, forty years ago, there was nothing but a brown wilderness, fit habitation for nothing but snipe!

I do not know any towns so well situated as Inverness, Nairn and Forres for turning our peat resources to account. I have been on the look-out for available mosses, and I find the finest fields for such an undertaking on the south side of the Highland line, between Dava and Grantown, and Kildrummie Moss, near Nairn.

The peats which come into Inverness are brought a distance of from seven to ten miles in small carts, at a cost which you can readily understand to be enormous. To Forres they could be taken by train from Dava, and thus be less than half the price we pay for them in Inverness.

I know that many persons found coals cheaper than peats, and that coals are used in the heart of peat-producing countries. That is only analogous to the other fact that coals from Newcastle and from Lanark are burnt over the coal mines of Brora and Kilkenny. You can well understand that it would not pay the Durham and Staffordshire farmers to dig for their own use, the coal which lies under their own homesteads. The concentration of trained force and the division of labour make it better for the farmers to stick to their agriculture and for the miners to stick to their mining. If the coalmasters had no better roads to their pits than our farmers have to their mosses, and if they had no regular traffic, they would find the production of coals just as bad, if not worse, than our ordinary citizens find the producing of peats.

With trained hands, with proper implements and machinery, with drying sheds, with good roads, tramways, and railways—all made available for turning our mosses to account—does it not stand to reason that we might have peat fuel at our doors, at least as much cheaper as it is nearer to us than coal.

And what is thus, as I think, so obvious *a priori*, is established by facts gathered from different parts of the Continent of Europe and America.

It is reported that on the Grand Trunk Railway, peat is manufactured in large quantities, at a cost of 9s to 10s per ton, where coals were 40s, and now, in all probability, 45s or perhaps 50s per ton. Peat, there, then, where the manufacture is gone about as it ought to be with us, is not one-fourth the cost of the coal.

Another test. On a train running 177 miles, the coal expenditure was found to be £6. It took £6 3s worth of wood to do the same work; but with peat it was done for £1 10s. There, they use machinery for pulping the peat moss. It is then lifted by another machine which travels over the ground, and spreads the pulp over the grass, heather, and rushes. In this rough way it is left to dry, and afterwards gathered in shapeless masses, and burnt without any further preparation. You will observe, that in this instance, the only improvement consists in the use of machinery. There is evidently no improvement in the finished article.

In Bavaria, there are considerable manufactories of peat, simply cut and prepared as is done already in this country; and the chief use to which the article is applied is that of feeding railway engines.

In the Netherlands, peat, of the ordinary description, is the staple fuel of the country; and during the season people flock in from Hanover, and from the adjacent parts of Germany to work in the mosses, the same as the Irish reapers used to migrate to the English and Scotch harvest, and as the hop-pickers flock to Kent and Farnham.

But in the Netherlands the manufacture of peat has made some progress towards the production of a perfect article of fuel. So it has in Bavaria, in Prussia, in Bohemia, and in France.

There have been two principles attempted to be carried out in this improved manufacture. The one is that of compressing the peat by machinery. This finished article I wish you to remember under the name of "compressed peat." The other principle is that of so preparing and placing the material, that it will become dense

in obedience to the law by which the particles of matter are drawn
to each other. The finished article in this case is called "dense
peat."

Of the first of these, I shall only wait to say, that machinery is
used to tear up the moss, and reduce it as quickly as possible to
dust. This is then placed in a machine, and so driven together by
force, that it comes out in solid cakes, ready for use. I have seen
them, and in form they were very much like as if you cut a large
sausage in discs of about an inch and a-half in thickness.

Attempts have been made to compress the peat in a wet state,
but I do not know that it has been successfully done anywhere.

One of the methods adopted is that of reducing the moss to the
finest pulp, then spreading it out of a certain thickness, and allowing it to dry and solidify of its own accord.

It is a curious thing that this method is simply an improvement
upon what was done by our forefathers when the more tenacious
bogs had been exhausted. I have seen them take the more brittle
strata of the peat, mix the substance with water, and spread it out
on the sward. In the course of a few days, it had acquired a certain degree of solidity, when they entered with their bare feet, and
cut it in long pieces from side to side of the patch. It was then
cut across into lengths of an ordinary peat, and afterwards treated
in every respect as is done with peats cut in the usual way.

Now, in the four northern provinces of Holland, in Branden-
berg, in Gratzen, in Bohemia, and in the French department of
Oise, the old-fashioned principle is being carried out by machinery.
The material is macerated by being put through a machine
somewhat like that used in preparing clay for making bricks.

In some of these places, the macerated mass comes out in two
continuous pieces, which are cut, either by hand or by machinery,
into suitable lengths. The peats are then placed on trays, and laid
out to dry in racks.

At Aibling, in Bavaria, the material is prepared in pretty much
the same way, under the direction of Dr. Herold of Munich ; but
instead of being formed into peats or bricks, it is cut into junks of
about four inches in length. These pieces are placed upon enclined
trays, on which they move, gradually passing from one tray to
another, until at the end of their journey they drop off in dry
balls.

At Gratzen, and at several other places, the pulp is simply
spread out on a prepared surface, and levelled to a certain thickness by means of boards attached to the feet of the workers. In
the course of a day or two, or three, according to the state of the
weather, the stratum is cut, lengthwise and across, into something

the size and shape of bricks. And such is the attraction of the particles that every peat is found in the course of drying to contract and solidify so as to leave a large space between the rows, where there was only a cut to begin with.

When they are sufficiently firm to be handled, they are lifted and placed in racks to dry.

It is to be noticed that in all the instances I have given, the exceptiing Aibling, the drying is done in the open air. Dr. Herold, however, has done what I have no doubt we shall do when we take the matter up—he has erected sheds, so as not only to keep off the rain, but cause a greater draught through the racks.

There is oue fact which I shall mention by way of counterbalancing what a very patriotic gentleman in Ross-shire said a short time ago. Early in the season he went manfully into the peat-cutting; but when the time for carrying them home arrived, he made inquiry, and found that to get at them you had to wade through two hundred yards of water! This "dished" his peatcutting enterprise, and he gave the fact to the world as an evidence of the impossibility of doing anything in the matter. But mark.

In the peat manufacture of M. Colart at Fontaine-sur-Somme, the material is all taken from a marsh under water, from one to two feet in depth. The peat is actually cut under the water. And a German of the name of Brosowsky has invented a machine to be used for the purpose. What would our friend in Ross-shire say to these Frenchmen and Germans? What they would say to him, I presume, would be, to adapt his plans to the requirements of the case, and not to wait till Jupiter dried up the marsh.

Even in the German case, the finished article did not cost more than 6s per ton, including the labour of taking the raw material from under the water.

The cost at Herzfelde was 6s 6d per ton; at Aibling, 12s 2d, but expected to be reduced by Dr. Herold; in America, on the Grand Trunk, 9s to 10s; New England, 8s to 10s; New York, 9s to 10s.

I have said nothing about Box's method, which has been patented, and which has been pretty well ventilated in the press. Besides, there are some points connected with that method of which some of us are not quite sure yet.

I must not, however, pass over the fact, that we can have light as well as heat from peat. I have seen peat gas made, I have seen it burnt, and have seen it tested, and know it to be a fact that it can be made; and it is expected that the suburb of Inchecore, near Dublin, will be lighted with gas made from peat.

Another fact. You will see in this day's *Scotsman* that a com-

G

pany is being formed to manufacture fuel from the bogs of Kerry, in the south-west of Ireland.

And speaking of Ireland, as I should like to so do of Scotland, I must direct attention to the fact that a commission, originated by Mr. Edward Purdon, ex-Lord Mayor of Dublin, and proprietor of *The Irish Farmer's Gazette,* has just returned from the Continent with a large mass of valuable information—not merely in theory or in science—as to what has actually been done in the way of utilizing bogs to yield fuel. To the report published by this commission I am indebted for some of the most telling facts in this paper ; and when we in this country, as well as our friends in Ireland, shall have had the sense to make proper use of our bogs, we shall, if we have the good taste and honesty which ought to characterise us, ascribe a good deal of the result to the patriotism and enterprise of Alderman Purdon, and to the information collected and made public by the other members of the commission.

FEBRUARY 6, 1873.—On this date Mr. William Mackay read a second paper on the Legends of Glen-Urquhart. For the first paper, *see* Transactions, Vol. I., p. 43.

SGEULACHDAN GHLINN-URCHUDAINN.

(An dara earrann.)

'Nuair a leugh mi dhuibh a' cheud earrann de na sgeulachdan so, mu dheireadh na bliadhna 1871, dh' ainmich mi gu'm b'i mo dhùrachd, ged' b'i sud a' chéud oidhche, nach b'i an oidhche mu dheireadh a chuireadh an Comunu air leth airson sgéulachdan na Gaidhealtachd. Bho sin fhuair sinn sgeula no dha bho Alasdar Mac Gillemhicheil, a tha ro-thaitneach. Is mòr am feum a dheanadh sibhse a chaidh àrach ann an Glinn na Gaidhealtachd na'n sgriobhadh sibh gach seann sgéul a chuala sibh 'am bun teintean céilidh bhur n-òige. Tha na sgéulachdan so taitneach ma tha iad faoin ; agus creidibh mise gu'n tig an là anns am bi iad glé mheasail. Cha'n eil cunntas chinnteach againn air moran de chleachdaidhean ar n-aithrichean, agus tha e àraid dhuinn am beagan a th' againn a thionail 'sa ghleidheadh gu cùramach, am fad 'sa tha sinn an comas sin a dheanadh.

Toisichidh mi nis' a rithist air sgeulachdan "Gleann mo chridhe rinn m' arach òg" le sgeula Mhonaidh Mac Righ Lochlainn 'thoir dhuibh.

Mònaidh Mac Righ Lochlainn.

Bho chionn iomadh linn bha Albainn air a sgiursadh gu cruaidh le na Lochlannaich—daoine borb a thainig a nall à Lochlann a thogail creach 'sa ghabhail seilbh ann an tir a' Ghaidheil. Bh Mònaidh, Mac Righ Lochlainn, na laoch calm, agus b'e miann a chridhe cogadh a dheanadh an aghaidh nan Gaidheal, agus cliù a chosnadh ann an righeachd 'athar. Anns a' bheachd so thionail e buidheann mhath dhe flathaibh òga Lochlainn, agus ghabh esan agus iadsa an cuan, chum seoladh gu Albainn. Bha piuthair aig Mònaidh aig an robh mòr ghaol dha, agus sheòl ise maille ris. Thainig na Lochlannaich air tir ann an Araghaidheal, agus air ball thòisich iad air cuir fàs 'us losgadh. Dh'eirich na Gaidheil an guaillean a chéile, agus chuir iad an ruaig air Mònaidh agus a chuid daoine. Rinn na Lochlannaich air an cuid long, ach bha na Gaidheal rompa; agus b'fhéudar dhaibh tilleadh gu tuath agus na longan fhagail air an culaobh. Theich iad tre Ghleann mor na h-Alba, agus lean a' chuid bu ghaisgeanda dhe na Gaidheil gus an d' thainig iad gu Gleann-Urchudainn. Ann an so—air Craig Mhònaidh—rinn na Lochlannaich seasamh chruaidh an aghaidh nan Gaidheal. Ach dhlùthaich Sliochd nam Beann orra, agus chaidh cath a chuir air Dail-a'-Mhònaidh anns an d'theach cuir as dha neart nan Lochlannach. Theich Mònaidh suas an Gleann le 'phiuthair, ach chaidh chuir gu bas ann an Coire-Mhònaidh, 'us e gu dicheallach ga 'dian-sa. Dh' adhlaic sluagh a' Ghlinn e ann an Uaigh Mhònaidh 'sa Choire agus ghabh iad gu caoimhneil ris a' bhoirionnach. Bha i beò maille riu fad iomadh la, agus fhuair i bas 'nam measg. Tha àite cumhang fasgathach eadar da sgorr ann an Craig Mhònadh ris an abarar fhathast Leabaidh nighean an Righ; agus 's iomadh sìneadh Sàbaid a rinn mi innte. 'Nuair a tha mi 'n sin tha Srath àluinn Urchudainn gu leir fo mo chomhar, agus dhomsa cha'n 'eil sealladh eile fo'n ghréin coimeas ris air feasgar Dòmhnaich samhraidh !

Domhnul Breac 's na Piochdaich.

Tha 'n sgeula so air a toir bho Bheurla fhir de phaipearan naigheachd a' bhaile so (*Inverness Courier*, July 2, 1868). Mar a tha sgeula Mhònaidh, tha i cuir solus air ainmean nan aite 'tha tachairt innte :—

Rinn Domhnul Breac, righ Dhail-an-righ, a chaidh chrùnadh ann an Dun-Stathanais 's a bhliadhna 637, cogadh an aghaidh nam Piochdach, no na Cruithne Tuath, agus dh' fhalbh e le móran sluaigh chum 's gu'n glacadh e lùchairt righ nam Piochdach—

Caisteal Spioradail, aig Ceann an ear Loch Nis. Air a shlighe thainig e gu Caisteal-na-Sròine (Caisteal Urchudainn) agus thug e ionnsuidh air a ghlacadh. Ach cha robh e farasda so a dheanadh, agus air do Domhnul 'chluinntinn gu'n robh armachd mhor de Phiochdaich a tarruing dluth air, dh'fhàg e an caisteal, agus chaidh e 'nan coinneamh-sa; agus chaidh baiteal a chuir aig Dochnalurg anns an d' fhuair e buaidh. Ach 's ann a thog so na Piochdaich nile, agus b'fheudar dha Domhnul tilleadh gu Urchudainn a rithist. Chaidh blàr fuilteach eile 'chuir aig Poll a' Ghaoir fo Chraig Mhonaidh, agus a rithist bhuadhaich Domhnul. Faisg air Poll a' Ghaoir tha aite ris an canar Blar na Geilt far an do chuir buidh-eann de dh-armachd Dhomhnuil eagal mor air euid de dh-armachd nam Piochdach. Tha glaic eile so, faisg air Tigh Bhaile-macathan, ris an canar Lag nan Cuspairean. Ged a chaill na Piochdaich am blar an dara nair cha do chaill iad am misneachd; agus thill Domhnul thairis air a' Mhonadh Leumnach, seachad buin Mheall-nafuarmhonaidh, gu Gleanna Moireastuin. Aig an Dìg Odhar, 'sa Ghleann so, chaidh baiteal eile chuir, agus an ruaig a chuir air Domhnul Breac. B'fheudar dha a' chasan a ghabhail, 's a chuid bu mhò dhe 'shluagh fhagail marbh air a bhlàr.

Tha baiteal Ghlinne-Moireastuin air ainmeachadh ann an Eachd-raidh Thighearnach (Annals of Tighearnach) a tha 'g innse gu'n do thachair e 's a bhliadhna 638.

An Gobhainn Mòr.

Bha roimhe so duine àraidh ann an Polla-Mhàili ris an canadh sluagh "an Gobhainn Mor." Bha seachd mic aig a' Ghobhainn, agus bha e fhein 'sa chuid mac cho maith air inneil airm a dhean-adh ri duine a bhuail riamh ord air innean. Gu h-àraidh bha cliù orra air son na claidheambean fuar-iarunn a rinn iad. Bha na claidheamhean so air an deanadh gun teine idir, le teas a chuir 's an iarunn le buillean nan ord; agus bha meas mor aig na Gai-dheil orra a thaobh 's gu'n do lean buaidh mhor iad. Cha'n e a mhain gu'n robh cliu air a' Ghobhainn Mhor mar ghobhainn, ach 's mor an cliu a bh' air fhein 's a sheachd mac mar laoich.

Bha crodh aig a' Ghobhainn ann am Polla-Mhàili a bha air leth briagh, ach ann an uine ghoirid dh' fhàs iad cho bochd 's gu'n gann a dh'éireadh iad 's a bhathaich; 's a dh' aindeoin na gheibh-eadh iad ri ithe cha ghabhadh iad coltach ni b'fhearr. Faisg air Polla-Mhàili tha Tòrr-na-sith, torran boidheach a bha, ann an laithean a' ghobhainn, 'na aite comhnuidh aig na sithichean. Tha iad a cuir air a ghobhainn gu'n robh sithich na leannan aige ged a bha 'bhean beo. La air an robh e fhein 'us ise 'sa choille, dh'-innis i dha gu'n do ghoid na sithichean an crodh briagh, agus gu'm

b'iad *croth sìth* a bha nise 'sa bhathaich. Ann am fearg mhor rinn
an gobhainn air a' bhathaich agus thoisich e air a' chrodh le's an
tuadh. Ach ann am priobadh na suil thug iadsa an cinn a na
bualaidhean agus mach as a bhathaich ghabh iad. Rinn an gobhainn greim crua.dh air earbull na ba 'bheir dheireadh, agus lean e
rithe gus an d' thàinig iad gu Carn-an-Rath ann am Beinn a'-Ghar-
bhlaich, faisg air Achadh-na-ba-baine. Dh' fhosgail an Carn agus
chaidh an' crodh a stigh; agus ma chaidh, lean an Gobhainn gus
an d' thainig e gu seòmar àluinn anns an robh gach ni bu luachmhor' na cheile; agus chaidh iarraidh air an ni bu docha leis ainmeachadh 's gu'm faidheadh e e. Ann an oisinn uaigneach de'n
t-seomar bha loth bheag pheallagach air an cuala an Gobhainn a'
leannan sith a bruidhinn mar an loth a b'fhearr' 's an righeachd;
agus thubhairt e gu'n gabhadh e an loth. " Fiacall a bial d'iom-
paidh," orsa na sithichean, oir dh'aithnich iad gu'n d'fhuair e comhairle mhaith; ach thug iad an loth dha, le aithne gu'n a cuir 'an
cairt gu brath, oir fhad 'sa chumadh e ann an crann i nach biodh
loth eile 'san tir a threabhadh rithe—

Threabhadh i Achadh-nam-bo,
'S an Lurga-mhor bho cheann gu ceann;
Mar sin 's an Gortan-ceapagach
Mu'n leigeadh i as an crann!

Bha'n loth pheallagach iomadh la aig a' Ghobhainn Mhor, agus
b'fheumail i dha-fhein 's dha muinntir na duthcha gu léir. Ach
ma dheireadh chaidh lòban a chuir oirre a dh' innearadh; agus
riamh an deigh sin cha robh i ni bu treise na loth eile.

Bha seachd mac a' ghobhainn a cadal anns an t-sabhal air Cnoc
ris an abarar fhathast Torran nan Gillean. Bha nighean a Ghobhainn posda aig fear air an robh Gille Phadruig Gobha mar ainm.
Anns na laithean sin thachair dha Camshronach duine 'mharbhadh
ann an Loch-Abair; agus theich' e gu Urchudainn, far an d'fhuair
e obair ann an ceardaich a' Ghobhainn Mhor. Chuala Mac Dhomhnuil Duibh gu'n robh am mortair 's a Ghleann, agus chuir e daoine
a dheanadh greim air. 'N uair a chuala 'n Gobhainn gu'n d'
thainig na h-Abairich, thug e air an duine air an robh iad an toir
'fhalt agus fhiasag a ghearradh. Thainig na h-Abairich 'na cheàrdaich
a dh'thaighneachd air son an duine, a bha aig an àm buaileadh an
uird. " Buail an t-ord, a Ghille mhaol," ars' an Gobhainn—
Bhuail an Gille maol an t-ord mar fhior ghobhainn; agus cha
d'aithnich na daoine e. Thill iad dhachaidh agus dh'innis iad nach
do theach an turus leo. Greis an deigh so fhuair Mac Dhomhnuil
Duibh a mach gu'm b'e am fear air an robh e 'n toir a bha da
riridh 'sa Ghille mhaol, agus lasadh 'fhearg an aghaidh a ghobhainn

agus sluagh a' Ghlinne; agus chuir e roimhe sgiùrsadh a thoir orra! Thainig e fhein agus moran sluaigh, agus ghlac iad Caisteal Urchudainn. Bha 'an so an duthaich fo 'chasan, ach an gobhainn 'sa chuid mac, agus cha robh chridh' aige feuchainn riuth-sa le sàbaid; agus smuainich e gu'n gabhadh e doigh eile. Chuir e fios air Gille Phadruig Gobha, cliamhuinn a' ghobhainn, agus gheall e dha na'm faigheadh e seòl air an gobhainn 's a mhic a chuir gu bas, gu'm faigheadh e talamh a ghobhainn ann an Pollamhàili. "Tagh buidheann dhe na fir is tapaidh a th' agad," orsa Gille' Phadruig Gobha, "agus leanadh iad mise am meadhon na h-oidhche 'nochd." Mar sin a bha, agus dh' fhag an Gille agus na h-Abara-ich an Caisteal am meadhon oidhche, agus rinn iad air an t-sabhal 's an robb mic a' ghabLainn, a smuaineachadh na'm faigheadh iad cuir as daibh-se, gu'm biodh e farasda 'n seann ghobhainn a chuir gu bàs. Sheas cnid diubh aig dorus an t-sabhail, agus chaidh an corr a stigh agus bhuail iad air na gillean. Dh' fhiach na gillean ri faidhinn mach, ach mar a bha iad dol thairis air starsuinn an doruis, bha na h-Abaraich cuir nan eanchuinn asta le cabair. 'N nair a bha 'n obair so aig an t-sabbal bha bean a' ghobhainn a faicinn bruadar gu'n robb muc mhor dhubh, 'us cuain chuilein aice, a bùrach fo clach-bhuinn an tigh. Chunnaig i am bruadar so tri uairean; agus 'an sin dhuisg i an Ghobhainn, 'us thug i air a dhol gus an t-sabhal a dh' fhaicinn ciamar a bha na gillean. Thug an Gobhainn an claidheamh mor aige leis, agus air dha tighinn gus an t-sabhal agus na h-Abaraich fhaicinn, thoisich e orra. Theich iadsa, agus lean esa, a marbhadh air na h-nile beum! Bha e a deanamh gu cruaidh air a chliamhuinn, agus 'nuair a chunnaic an gealtara sin so, thoisich e air eigheachd "'s mi fhein a th' ann! 's mi fhein a th'ann!" "Tha fios agam gu'n tu fhein a th'ann," fhreagar an Gobhainn. Ma dheireadh rug an Gobhainn air a chliamhuinn air dhaibh bhi dol thairis air allt ris an abarar fhath-ast "Allt Gille Phadruig Gobhà;" agus ghearr e a chluais de. 'Sin litir agad, ars esa a bheir thu dha Mac Dhomhnuil Duibh, agus innis dha gu'm bi mise aig mo bhiadh-maidne am màrach cuide ris. An sin thill e gus an t-sabhal, agus fhuair e a chuid mac marbh, ach am fear a b' òige. Chaidh druim an fhir so a bhristeadh, agus riamh an deigh sin, chaidh e fo'n ainm "an Gobba Cròm."

Ghabh an Gobhainn Mor bàs a mhic cho mor gu cridhe, 's gun do chaochail e 'an ùine ghoirid. An deigh a bhàs, chuir an Gobba Crom a chuid acainn air srathar Ghaidhealach air muin each, agus dh'ìh g e Urchudainn, ag radh gu'n stadadh e far am bristeadh an t-srathar. Cha do bhrist an t-srathar gus an d' rainig e Peart. Anns a' bhaile sin thog e ceardaich, agus tha muintear Urchud-

airin a cumail a mach gu'm b'e an "Gobha Crom" a bha 's an
t-săbaid fhuilteach a bh'eadar Clann Dhaibhidh 's Clann Chatain
an lathair an Righ, air Innis Pheairt, 'sa bhliadhna 1396.

Tha feadhainn gus an la 'n diugh ann an Urchudainn a tha
creidsinn gur h-ann dhe sliochd a Ghobhainn mhor a tha iad, agus
tha e air a radh gur h-ann bhò 'n a Ghille Mhaol a thainig Clann
Ic 'Ille Mhaoil a tha 's a Ghleann.

CREACH INNSE BHRAOIN.

Thainig roimhe so bean bhochd a mhuinntir Braidh Loch-Abair
gu tigh Granndach Sheoglaidh ann an Gleann Urchudainn, agus
dh' iarr i cead tàmh fad na h-oidhche. Fhuair i leabaidh, ach 'n
nair dh'eirich bean an tigh 'sa mhaduinn, fhuair i am mach gu'n
d' thug a bhean bhochd leanamh gille chum an t-saoghail 'san oidhche. Chaidh leabaidh 'us biadh a chumail rithe gus an robb i 'n
comas am baile fhagail, agus 'ñuair a dh' fhalbh i, chùm fear
Sheoglaidh an leanamh, agus thog e suas e mar a mhae fhein. Dh'
fhàs an gille mòr, agus air dha faighinn a mach gur h-ann dhe
Clann 'Ic Uaraig (Kennedy) 'an Loch-Abair a bha e, thoisich e air
taobh mor a chumail ri na h-Abaraich a bha 'cleachdadh creachan
a thogail ann an Urchudainn. Ma dheireadh dh'fhas cuisean cho
teth eadar e fhein 'us gillean oga na duthcha, 's gu'n d' fhag e an
Gleann agus chaidh e gu duthaich a mhathar. Ann an Loch-Abair
cha robh an Gille Dubh (oir b'e sin an t-ainm a bh' aig sluagh air) fada
ga dheanamh fhein iomraideach ann an togail chreach ; agus ann an
ùine ghearr smuainich e fhein agus Clann 'Ic Uaraig gu'n rachadh
iad 's gu'n togadh iad crodh Urchudainn. Ghabh iad am monadh
gu Seoglaidh, agus 'nuair a thainig iad gus an aite sin bha na
daoine anns a mhonadh huain na mòine. Thionail iad crodh
Inuse Bhraoin gun bhacadh, ach cha do bhean iad dha crodh Sheoglaidh, agus thill iad gun dàil do'n mhonadh. Cho luath 'sa bha iad
an comas, chruinnich prasgan dhe daoine Bhraighe Urchudainn,
aig Seoglaidh ; ach a chionn 's nach ro iad idir cho lionmhor ri
Clann 'Ic Uaraig, dhiult fear Sheoglaidh dhol air toir na creach.
"Theid mise ann," arsa bean Sheoglaidh, "oir tha e coltach gu'm
feum na mnathan an claidheamh a ghabhail, 's gu'm feud na daoine
tamh aig a' bhaile cuir a chuigeal!" Ghabh fear Sheoglaidh
tàmailt ri so, agus dh'fhalbh e le 'dhaoine an deigh a' Ghille
Dhuibh. Thainig iad air na h-Abaraich anns a' Choire Bhuidhe ;
agus thug an Ghille Dubh an crodh air ais dha fear Sheoglaidh
gu'n fhacal feargach eadar riutha. Thill daoine Urchudainn leis a
chrodh. 'Nuair a bha iad da no tri a cheudan slat bho na h-
Abaraich dh'eirich çearr eadar riutha agus iadsan, agus thog fear
dhiubh a ghunna ,ri 'shuil agus loisg e oirre. Shaoil le Clann 'Ic

Uaraig gur h-ann orra fhein 'chaidh losgadh, agus loisg iad air ais.
Mar sin thoisich baiteal a lean gus an do thuit fear Sheoglaidh
agus a chuid bu mho de dhaoine, oir cha robh ann ach beagan
diubh.   Cha'n e a mhain gu'n do ghlac an Gille Dubh rithist an
crodh a bh'aige, ach thill e agus thog e crodh Sheoglaidh.   Bha
bean Sheoglaidh tròm 's an àm, agus ghuidh' i air truas a ghabhail
ri, agus i 'sa staid 'san robh i.   Ach 'se am freagar a fhuair i—
"ma tha thu tròm, beir searrach !" agus dh'fhalbh na h-Abaraich
le cnid cruidh.   Thog muinntir Urchudainn cuirn anns a' Choire
Bhuidh air an d' thug iad Cuirn Marbh Dhaoine mar aium.   Tha
iad 'an sin gus an la 'n dingh.

'Nuair a thainig a h-ùine bha mac aig bean Sheoglaidh; agus 'n
nair a dh' fhas e mòr, b'e mianu a chridhe creach Innse Bhraoin
agus bas 'athar a dhialladh air a' Ghille Dhubh.   Anns an inntinn
sin ghabh e turus gu Braigh Loch-Abair, agus dh' fhaighnichd e
air son tigh an duine sin.   Fhuair e an tigh, agus an Gille Dubh
'na bhraisiche duine aig taobh an teine.   Chaidh an dithis 'an
còmhradh a' cheile, agus bho sgeula gu sgeula thainig iad gu Creach
Innse Bhraoin.   An deigh do'n Ghille Dhubh an sgeula aithris,
dh' innis Fear òg Sheogla'dh dha, gu'n d' thainig a nise àm an
diallaidh.   " Co thusa," ars' an Gille Dubh.   " 'S mise," fhreagar
an t-oganach, " an searrach a bha 'am broinn bean Sheoglaidh la
creach Innse Bhraoin ;" agus le na facail sin sparr e a sgian
dubh 'an cridh' a' Ghille Dhuibh gu 'bun ! 'An sin ghabh e a
chasan, agus cha do stad e gus an robh e fo dhruim Tigh Sheoglaidh.

FEBRUARY 17.—On this evening, Mr G. J. Campbell read the
following

REMARKS ON SCOTTISH GAELIC LITERATURE,

by Mr Nigel M'Neill :—

It is proposed in this paper to give some of the leading characteristics of Scottish Gaelic Literature, with special observations on
the compositions known as the Poems of Ossian.

Gaelic literature has never been properly, because never dispas-
sionately, estimated.   All attempts to bring its worth into relief
may be arranged into three classes.   The mere chroniclers of the
number of Gaelic books, their dates of publication, &c. ; Reid, the
author of the " Bibliotheca Scoto-Celtica," may be taken as the

representative of this first class. The fulsome undiscerning enthu-
siasts who cultivated a fixed determination to find in the Celtic
language and in its literature the germs, or rather the great
originals of the languages and literature of the greatest countries,
ancient and modern ; Lachlan MacLean, the author of a "History
of the Celtic Language," and Wm. Livingstone, the bard, author of
the "Vindication of the Celtic Character," may be taken as the
representatives of this second class. The unfriendly critics, the
traducers of the Celt and all his belongings, who habitually spoke
of himself and of all his literary pretensions with contempt, and
whose darling political idea had been the extirpation of the Celt,
who was looked on as a rival and an alien " in blood and speech ; "
Dr Samuel Johnson, and all the roaring young lions of anti-Celtic
prejudices downwards represent this third class. The first class
have supplied us with an excellent guide to the materials necessary
for a critical account of our literature ; the second, by their un-
regulated enthusiasm and wild exaggerations, have brought our
literature into contempt, furnishing with matter of ridicule the
third class, whose great aim had been to sneer everything Celtic
into utter oblivion. The writings of these three classes themselves
constitute a large amount of literature of a doubtful cast. They
have, however, all helped much to clear the ground for the critical,
impartial historian, who, it is hoped, will soon make his appearance.

There is besides a fourth class in germ, some of whose efforts
assumed a correct critical direction. Among the few representatives of this class, the best trained mind for the appreciation of the
true, the beautiful, and the good in Gaelic literature, was that of
the late Rev. Thomas Pattison, author of "The Gaelic Bards." In
this work we have indications everywhere of aesthetic tastes of a
high order, which, had their possessor been spared, would have won
him fame equal with that of his fellow-students and literary contemporaries, Mr Buchanan the poet, and Mr Black the novelist.
The early death of Mr Pattison has been a great loss to English
letters, as well as unfortunate to the interests of the Celtic race.
There is another who has done Herculean service to the cause of
Gaelic literature, and who is deserving of a tribute of great respect
as a critic for his biographical and critical notices of the bards—
Mr Mackenzie, the author of "The Beauties of Gaelic Poetry."
He, however, leans slightly to the failings of the second class referred to, whose enthusiasm, effervescence, and undiscerning
laudations too truly indicate the unsubdued and untoned character
of their high intellectual gifts. There are also many interesting
critical observations in the " Celtic Gleanings " and " Review of

II

Celtic Literature," by the Rev. Dr Thomas Maclauchlan, who has done otherwise very extensive service. MacPherson, earlier, in his introduction to the translations, and in his numerous notes, left us some remarks on Ossianic Literature.

After premising thus what the critics have done for our literature, let us refer to some of its leading characteristics. And in doing so, we must speak of what *is not*, as much as of what exists —of the literary elements absent in our literature that the attention of the nascent Celtic poets may be, if possible, directed to their proper development.

Let us examine, first, then, whether Celtic literature presents all the features which other great bodies of literature possess. A comparison of our literature with those—though we must acknowledge that the institution of comparison on account of many circumstances is scarcely fair to the Highlander—will evince at once the absence of two or three features in ours of outstanding prominence ; these we may call negative characteristics. They are the epic and the dramatic features. To these may be added the comic or serio-comic element in literature. For we have no burlesque writers unless the witty poems of MacCodrum, the Uist bard, and some snatches of Rob Donn be considered representative of this feature.

With regard to the epic feature, the dictum of sneering Celts and Saxon ill-wishers, that we have no epic, can not be gainsaid. The pretensions of Fingal and Temora, as from the hands of MacPherson, to the character of epics are quite hollow, and can not bear in that character the scrutiny of the keen appreciative reader of Virgil, Danté, or Milton. Those pretended epics of Ossian are epic only in name and length. They are essentially balladic ; and there can be no hesitation in affirming that the ballad was the first and original form. A number of ballads on the subject of Fingal strung together with the episodes of the trying situations and slaying of beautiful women thrown in between, made up Fingal ; and the same process was adopted in the manufacture of the other epics. The world would have relished them equally much, and more so, had James MacPherson presented them in their own innocent primeval simplicity, and not draped them imitatively in the unwieldy and unnatural garb of less spirited people. Nor on referring to the works of other poets since the days of Ossian can we be relieved by the discovery of an epic. Some of the poems of Mac Mhaighstir Alastair and of Livingstone are pretty long ; the longest of Macdonald's, the "Birlin," is, however, only about 600 lines, and the longest of Livingstone's between 900 and 1,000. It is quite evident that, without referring to the nature of the poems at all, there can be no comparison between such and the 10,000 or 11,000 lines of the "Paradise Lost."

This result, the absence of epics in Gaelic literature, forces us to observe that there seems to have been for ages back a rooted aversion in the Celtic mind to undertake the accomplishment of any great design. It can not be said that the conditions of success in epic composition are wanting in the case of the Celtic mind, although it is a fact that hitherto the poetical works of the Celt do not exhibit literary epic patience and epic perseverance. In other spheres Celtic patience and perseverance are truly extraordinary. With his brilliant exploits, his mighty military achievements; with his successful defence of his mountains for thousands of years, and with the hitherto undimmed brightness of his surpassing energies—with all these before us in their epic pristine splendour, as well as in their glorious successes, we cannot help according to the Celt the possession of the eternal conditions of epic success. These are patience, perseverance, with an inherent love for measure which must characterise the doer of great deeds requiring years for their accomplishment. Even in matters of every-day life, the Celt exhibits these qualities. How few there are of Southern or Lowland extraction who would work or make a pleasant living of it in the hard rocky, or barren nooks into which some of our Celtic brethren have been oppressed, with the gloomy, rainy clouds above, and an equally uninviting soft soil beneath? How few they are who would live thus with Celtic perseverance? They have frequently tried it alongside the derided Celt, and been as frequently found wanting. But, above all, where could you find people who would endure so patiently, so unrepiningly, the long-continued infliction of wrongs, and the cruel wresting away from them of their hereditary rights? (This ignominious patience must soon come to an end.)

The Celt's possession of Epic perseverance in other spheres convinces us that the Celtic mind is capable of undertaking and accomplishing literary Epic designs, whenever, or wherever the congenial circumstances exist. The age, the man, and the circumstances, will come together.

With regard to the Dramatic feature of Literature, though we have neither Tragedies nor Comedies, our Literature is not destitute of Dramatic forms. We have what may be called Dramatic poems. But it must be admitted that we have no regular Tragedies nor Comedies. Theatres were never in vogue with the Celt; hard, real, terrible life was in too close proximity to his experience to allow of mimic representations. To him, the snow-wreathed mountain and the misty glen, with its hundred mistier corries and foaming cataracts, were a theatre grander far than the finest temples made with human hands.   True it is, however, that elements tragic enough,—appallingly tragic—surrounded the life of our ancestors, though they never assumed a regular, literary, dramatic form.   Many a pleasant, social entertainment also they had in the halls of Kings, of Princes, and of Chiefs, with the sounds of the harp and the songs of the bards in full harmony with the gentle, lovely voices of lovelier *òighean*.   At such feasts ballads narrative of many a mighty achievement, by many a mighty hero, were recited by the bards amidst the applauses of royalty and of chiefs of military renown.   It never occurred to the bards that there might be amusement in mimicking such scenes.   They lived amidst enough of real tears, real tragic life, without having recourse to artificial imitation.   The people were too peripatetic and predatory in their habits to permit of stage culture.   Their life was too real, too earnest, to render it desirable ; and with their military haste, their brilliant feats of war, their martial expeditions, and the deep-flown pleasures of their social being, stage representations could not seem otherwise than flat, stale, and unprofitable :—therefore the absence of this kind of literature in Gaelic letters.   And if the Celt had no artificial theatre it need not be said that none of the immorality that follows such corrupted him.

We have confined our remarks to the poetical department, because hitherto we have scarcely any other department.   Those of Philosophy, History, etc., are, with trifling exceptions, blank. Somewhat akin to the poetic is our Taleologic Literature, repre- sented by "The Popular Tales of the Western Highlands," which is of great value from an historical point of view.

Space will not permit to say much regarding the positive charac- teristics of Scottish Gaelic literature : these, however, are *practically* known and felt by most Celts.   The first that strikes us, in looking at his literature, is the great passion for poetry shown by the Celt wherever he is.   He has given his first and only love to poetry. All the admiration, the enthusiasm, the sympathy, the love, and passion of the lover, he has bestowed on poetry, The poetical genius, like a sort of universal inspiration, seized the soul of the whole race, until it became a race of love, sentiment, and emotion. The mental attitudes favourable to profound reflection and to philosophy, with its subtle analysis of the intellect, were not much cultivated since the days of Abaris, the hyperborean philosopher from Iona, who paid a visit to the Grecian philosophers of the Porch.   The cooler calculations of reason were considered tame compared with lays of patriotism, love, and military deeds, or with the sweet bursts of bardic song. And, while the Celt's great passion is poetry, in that field, again, it would seem that descriptive poetry is the kind he most relishes and cultivates. Indeed, it would appear that the Celtic genius is descriptive, tinged, or rather, relieved, with the presence of emotion and sentiment. The language itself, on account of its highly descriptive nature, has contributed much to this characteristic of Gaelic poetry. This descriptive character of the language suggests another leading characteristic, whose presence furnishes the spell —the natural magic—of Gaelic poetry—the element of sensuous imagery. This element of sensuous imagery, fed by the highly emotional nature of the Celt, constitutes the deeply poetical character of Gaelic song.

The next leading characteristic is love. This poetical element has been, by the Gaelic bards as by those of other countries, very energetically, but, at the same time, with great purity of thought and expression, developed. It is the leading theme, the first inspirer of the lays of the most of the minor worshippers of the muse. In connection with this exhibition of feeling, the sad, melancholy retiring spirit of the Celt has very fully revealed itself. There is the same symbolic cry, the same tears over the world slipping away from his grasp, which he wails over the coyness or loss of his deeply-loved mistress.

Now may be introduced, very appropriately, and by suggestion, the highly elegiac character of Gaelic poetry. The *cumha*, or elegy, was never inattentive to the good qualities of the departed. It was a species of composition sadder than the tomb itself. Its wail was so piercing, its sorrow so heartrending, and its regret so enduring, through bardic influence, that, occasions arising naturally in succession, as well as on the path of the tragic, warlike life of the Celt, it preserved and cultivated a spirit of sadness and proximity to the grave which shed its gloom over the whole race.

The satiric element was not developed to any considerable extent. The greatest satirist was *Iain Lom. Rob Donn, Mac Mhaighstir Alastair*, and *Duncan Bàn* have also written good satires.

Before referring to Gaelic hymns we may remark that the Highlands have produced, in proportion to the population, a larger amount of first-class popular lyrical poetry than any people on the face of the earth ; and these compositions, though the production of simple, unlearned individuals, in many cases, showing finish, taste, and elegance of a high order.

With regard to our Gaelic Hymns it may be truly said that we have one hymn-writer, Dugald Buchanan, that has never yet been

surpassed by any hymn-poet, of any country, ancient or modern.
The great characteristic of our hymns is their devotional and
evangelical tone.   A heterodox mist, or even an unscriptural or
doubtful expression is never met with.   They have, however, one
great fault in common—their length, which renders them more
like spiritual poems than like hymns.   The same fault characterizes
all the popular songs of the Celts.   The singing of 50 or 100 stanzas
with our ancestors seemed a very common, and quite a feasible
thing.

Considering the region of the world where it has been produced,
the amount of good Gaelic poetry, even in print, is truly immense ;
and claims thorough critical investigation at the hands of those
who are able and anxious to show the outside world the treasures
and rich qualities of the Celtic genius of which we all feel so justly
proud.

Ossian's Poems being our greatest works,—"the source of our
fame,"—claim particular reference in a paper on Scottish Gaelic
Literature.

The Ossianic compositions, ushered into the world by the clever
and ingenious James Macpherson, are the only Gaelic literary
works which have received anything like an adequate amount of
intelligent criticism.   They were at first criticised unreasonably,
fiercely, and crucially,—were investigated in a deadly process in
which all merit might almost be expected to evaporate into its
native heaven.   The result was that they came out " gold of the
seventh refining."   Then their genius, pure, ancient, and sublime
as their native hills and skies was universally acknowledged.
It appeared on the scene of letters, British and Continental,
decked out for the admiration of the whole world, in the garb of
Celtic primitive belief and manners.   It brought men face to face,
as it were, with a bygone age, whose men and women, though
fifteen centuries distant in respect to people's ever-varying manners,
were still felt in their high-toned morality, their chivalry, and
their tenderness in all relations of being, to be wonderfully akin to
the best and noblest echoes of modern times.   This genius of
ghosts and sadness, surrounded by the snowy wreaths of its native
hills, the wandering mists of its native valleys, in full accord with
the deep shadows and gloomy clouds of its native skies, presented
to the imaginations of men fresh phenomena so unearthly and fascinating that the whole world gazed in rapture.   This genius again
uttered a cry peculiar and piercing, but still highly human—a cry
unheard since the age of the Titans.   It reached the heart of all
the young poets in Europe, and it chimed harmoniously over that
lava-stream of melancholy which overflows for a season the whole

soul of youth. Goethe, Byron, and Lamartine felt and acknowledged the potent force of the spell. Thus, the sublime, melancholy,
and magic strain of the Celtic bard of Cona affected all the literature
of modern Europe.

It does not matter exceedingly whether you hold James Mac-
Pherson of 1760, or the son of Fingal of 360, the author; the
spirit is felt, in the case of either view, to be ancient and Celtic.
There can be no doubt regarding the existence of Ossianic poems
and ballads for ages before MacPherson ; and it is equally beyond
disputation that MacPherson, even supposing his whole work is
not a translation, has, to a certain extent, utilized such ballads and
poems. In any case, the marrow of the work must be acknowledged to be Ossianic. And Macpherson, while we cannot help
condemning the *form* or *shape* in which he sent forth those grand
compositions of byegone ages,—the absurdity of his working into
the impossible consistency of Epics materials which would be more
relished in their primeval balladic garb,—deserves the gratitude of
Celts as well as the homage of the discerning, for bringing, as has
been already referred to, "this soul of the Celtic genius in contact
with the soul of the nations of modern Europe." There can be no
hesitation in pronouncing James MacPherson, whether translator
or author, of the works going under Ossian's name, a genius, equal
in some of the most necessary qualifications of the poet, to the
great half-mythical Ossian himself. MacPherson was a poet of no
mean order ; and he has left to our language, and to our literature,
what might otherwise be lost, a priceless legacy—the one great
work, of which we have a true and worthy reason to feel proud.
For Ossian alone is our one mighty work, which even the most
enthusiastic writers on Celtic matters could venture to compare
with the great and finished productions of other nations.

Reading the poems of Ossian and those of any of the modern
Gaelic poets—*Mac Mhaighstir Alastair* for example—we feel at
once that we breathe the air of different regions, or live in the
atmosphere of the influences of different ages ; while it is equally
true that we discern at the same time between them and the
common herd of versifiers a vast interval in the range of their
poetical conceptions and imaginations. The minds of both were
nurtured by the same poetical elements, the same influences and
scenic images ; but the spirit of their poetry is widely different.
Both breathe a spirit that speaks of "the land of the mountain
and the flood"—"tìr nam beann, nan gleann, 's nan gaisgeach"—
but the echoes that convey to us the notes of their voices—their
deep utterances of the soul—their cries of the human—from the
fairy land of fancy and passion, are far unlike. The inspiration

of both is that of the great Bens, the mysterious-seeming valleys, rendered here and there unearthly vocal by the gurgling tones of some stream and those of deep crying unto deep. And considering that the language of the two poets is the same, that they lived in the same country, that the source of their poetical pictures and representations was the same, one would suppose that the resemblance between the two would be very striking in these instances. Such, however, is not the case. MacDonald is wild, picturesque, and gorgeous, presenting ever the dread realities of nature, and loves to picture her coarser characteristics more than her qualities of tenderness; while Ossian also is wild, but sublime, imaginative, and ever pure and refined in his conceptions; MacDonald's poetry glows with sensuous imagery, luxuriance of thought, and voluptuousness of feeling, partaking more of the earthly, animal, and material portions of creation; while Ossian's continually moves us with his magnanimity of thought, his regular, sustained, and solemn grandeur, and his exhibitions of tenderness and generous valour,—thus moving in the higher regions of human conception and feeling in a glow of aerial magnificence and moral loftiness,—thus his genius ever soaring to the contemplation of what is ethereal, heavenly, pure, and spiritual, and never descending to depicture what is low, common, or altogether earthly. The music of Mac Donald is wild, spirited, and irregular, and his verses occasionally harsh; while that of Ossian is subdued, soft, and mellifluous, and his cadences ever harmonious. Mac Donald, in the accomplishment of his more elaborate efforts, gives many indications of spasmodic tendencies; while the most majestic designs of Ossian are finished with the ease and freedom of one who is conscious of strength sufficient to complete successfully the greatest undertaking. In intensity and fiery vehemence of thought and expression MacDonald will yield to none; but he wants the condensity and dramatic terseness of Ossian. But for occasional signs of spasm and feeble appendages of phrases to finish a verse or to make the rhyme orthodox, the "Birlin," notwithstanding MacDonald's dramatic inferiority, would be equal in most respects to any of Ossian's poems of the same length. The force of thought and energy of poetical ardour with which he

> " Hurls the Birlin through the cold glens,
>   Loudly snoring,"

is truly absorbing; and if not equal, certainly not much inferior to anything of the kind we have read. We may here give a description of morning from the " Birlin " (Mr. Pattison's translation), and compare it with Ossian's master touches on the same subject. It may serve to illustrate the difference between Ossian's conceptions of common phenomena and those of other Highland bards.

> "The sun had opened golden yellow,
>   From his case,
> Though still the sky wore dark and drumly
>   A scarr'd and frowning face ;
> Then troubled, tawny, dense, dun-bellied,
>   Scowling and sea-blue ;
> Every dye that's in the tartan
>   O'er it grew.
> Far away to the wild westward
>   Grim it lowered,
> Where rain-charg'd clouds on thick squalls wandering
>   Loomed and towered."

This vigorous and striking representation is very descriptive of a Hebridean morn in spring ; and though his descriptions of nature are generally more extended than Ossian's, he never flags. "Where rain-charg'd clouds on thick squalls wandering loomed and towered" is very majestic. We get from Ossian in general but a verse on morning, a subject that suffers such exquisite pains too frequently in the crucifying hands of minor poets, rhymers, and versifiers. . Such as,

> "Dh' eirich maduinn air innis nan stuadh."

Morn brightened on the isle of waves.

Ossian is so rich in resources of poetical *talk* that he merely suggests the general vital point, and, like Milton, leaves you to infer the necessary existence of particulars. He does not give life-size portraits of the same subject every time it occurs in his poems ; he brings all his mental energies *once* into operation and then makes a successful attempt, such as the following Address to the Sun or Morning, and does not afterwards endeavour to picture from another point of view which might perhaps not be so faithful to nature and to his own conceptions of things. It is somewhat long, but its beautiful imagery and its poetical entirety would be defaced by witholding a single verse of it :—

> "Son of the Young Morn ! that glancest
>   O'er the hills of the east with thy gold-yellow hair,
> How gay on the wild thou advancest
>   Where the streams laugh as onward they fare ;

And the trees yet bedewed by the shower,
  Elastic their light branches raise,
While the melodists sweet they embower
  Hail thee at once with their lays.

But where is the dim night duskily gliding
  On her eagle wings from thy face?
Where now is darkness abiding?
  In what cave do bright stars end their race—
When fast, on their faded steps bending,
  Like a hunter you rush through the sky
Up those lone lofty mountains ascending,
  While down yon far summits they fly?

Pleasant thy path is, Great Lustre, wide-gleaming,
  Dispelling the storm with thy rays;
And graceful thy gold ringlets streaming
  As wont, in the westering blaze.
Thee the blind mist of night ne'er deceiveth,
  Nor sends from the right course astray;
The strong tempest, all ocean that grieveth,
  Can ne'er make thee bend from thy way.

At the call of the wild morn, appearing,
  Thy festal face wakens up bright,
The shade from all dark places clearing,
  But the bard's eye that ne'er sees thy light."

We shall quote one other picture of morning by MacDonald from the opening stanzas of his "Sugar Brook," where the unrestrained vehemence and gorgeousness of the Birlin give place to simple truthful delineations. Like Cowper he descends very much in this delicious poem to particularities of portraiture; and his minute picturing contrasts powerfully with the dramatic vividness and graphic vastness of Ossian's imagery.

  " Passing by the Sugar Brook,
      In fragrant morn of May;
  When, like bright shining rosaries,
      The dew on green grass lay;
  I heard the robin's treble,
      Deep Richard's bass awake;
  And the shy and blue-winged cuckoo,
      Shout ‐' goo goo' in the brake

> The thrush there threw its steam off,
>   Upon a stake alone ;
> And the brown wren so blithesome,
>   Had music of its own ;
> The linnet with a jealous bend
>   Tuned up his choicest string ;
> The blackcock he was croaking,
>   The hen did hoarsely sing."

Ossian gives us *all* the poetry of this in four lines; and that in such choice language and with such forcible clearness and expressive vividness that you could not wish a single word added, while you are satisfied to perfection with what you have. We quote these lines in the original ; they are given already above in the second half of the first stanza in the translation.

> Tha croinn uaine ro' dhrùchd nam fras,
> Ag éiridh gu bras a' d' chomhdhail,
> A's filidh bhinn nan coillte fàs
> A' cur fàilt' ort gu moch le'n òran.

The exquisite and faultless melody, the aerial silentness of music that pervades these lines, have a mysterious and most striking effect on the soul.

In the glowing and adequate depicturing of magnificent objects Ossian is unapproached. His muse is essentially sublime and imaginative ; while that of many of the succeeding famous bards is mainly made up of emotional sweetness, or tame, spasmodic, but splendid delineations, richness of diction, or an endless glow of melodious words. Dugald Buchanan is perhaps the only modern poet that possesses much sublimity ; many verses of his minor pieces, and nearly the whole of his Day of Judgment, are dramatically vivid and very sublime. In the fine ethereal spirit that pervades his poetry Ossian is not unlike Hogg. Indeed, the resemblance between the two is in many respects well traceable. But the poet among the Celtic modern bards between whom and Ossian is the most perfect resemblance is William Livingstone. Except in the absolute difference which the civilization of many centuries creates between them in the manner and garb in which each delivers himself of his " all-comprehending idea " or message, and which the transformation through which the spirit of Antiquity passes ere it appears in modern times renders necessarily discernible, Livingstone is in all other instances truly Ossianic, both by the nature of his genius and by the form in which he has given expression to it. We forbear here to touch on their points of likeness.

Ossian is not the poet of a particular clan, tribe, or race ; he is the general interpreter of humanity at large, and the special painter of the time, life, habits, and achievements, of those brave warlike people who first occupied the plains of Europe, and who form the substratum of the populations of most European nations. He lived at a time when the world was going through a mighty metamor- phoses, when tribes were beginning to assume a national cast, and nations an individuality, and were preparing to run the race sketched out to them by Destiny, the path of each bounded by a particular boundary or limit of sea, stream, mountain, or valley, and were throwing aside all the encumbrances of superseded cus- toms and laws that might clog their progress or defeat their designs. The language of the blind old bard of Cona began to show signs of confusion into many dialects, and was already no more in several countries after other languages had been based upon it, as the mother dies and leaves the house to her daughters. The Feinn— his own peculiar people—appeared in immortal brilliance crowned with the laurels of deathless warlike heroism on the stage of the world and now disappeared from the scene—fading together like a sun-gleam in wintry weather hastening over the wide heath of Lena. Now as he muses on the departure of his kindred heroes and hunters and on the loneliness of his own state, led by the white-armed Malvina, the betrothed of his fallen son Oscar, he seeks their former haunts and breathes, as he rests in the well- known shades, the pathetic lamentation "the last of my race !"

Na Gàidheil gu bràth!

SECOND ANNUAL ASSEMBLY.

THE SECOND ASSEMBLY was held on the evening of Thursday, the 10th of July, in the Music Hall. We take our report of the proceedings from the local papers. *The Highlander* of 12th July introduces the proceedings thus :—

Many will inquire what is the meaning of the "second" annual assembly of the Gaelic Society in the capital of a Gaelic speaking province, and wonder if the Gaelic Society of Inverness is only an infant entering upon its second year. The question is certainly pertinent, and the wonder natural. We know that there are now in Inverness numbers of persons who are ashamed to confess that the Gaelic Society only came into being sometime in the year 1871. Perhaps it would not be very far wrong to say of those who are thus ashamed, there are some who would have been more or less ashamed to have joined such a society a year and a-half ago. So strong was the anti-Celtic idea in Inverness a very short time ago that both Celts and Saxons put their heads together to denounce the movement as retrograde, impertinent, fantastic, and all the rest of it; and a large amount of small wit was expended in the vain attempt to make one of the most natural and healthy movements ever started in Inverness, ridiculous. One of the most ludicrous things imaginable was to see and hear men, who had never managed to get rid of a strong Highland accent themselves, fancying that they were transfixing a member of the Gaelic Society with a keen arrow when mimicking his Gaelic accent. They reminded one of the gallant Major O'Dowd, who swore in the strongest accent of Roscommon, that the greatest misfortune that ever befel him was being born in Ireland! These are among the most deplorable signs that, whether conquered or not, the men who exhibit them possess the souls of a subjugated people, and are uncomfortable at the prospect of being expected to act the part of free men. It is to be born in mind, in extenuation of this craven conduct, that many influences have been at work to make the people of Inverness actually believe that their only chance of getting on in commerce, and getting up in society, lay in disowning their race, and becoming as quickly as possible transformed into so many Cockneys. The wonder really now is that Inverness did not occupy a large extent of space in those works now-a-days devoted to the elucidation of the subject of the transmutation of species.

Instead of that, Inverness is a striking example of the persistency with which one type of humanity holds its place as well as its form; and the existence of the Gaelic Society, and the results which it already exhibits, are striking facts with which to carry to the minds of the dullest a conviction of a truth which had well nigh been stamped out under the feet of recreant Celts themselves. No doubt Saxons had something to do with this recreant action; but we have little, if any, right to blame them for it. They asserted their ideas and their power, and they made their mark in our midst. If the Celt had been equally faithful to the idea entrusted to him, the Saxon would have coalesced with him, and helped him upwards and onwards according to the genius of the race. There is always an advantage in having two good pure, vigorous races in close neighbourhood, so long as they both know how to respect themselves and one another. The evil is when the one is not satisfied unless it lords it over the other; the still greater evil when the one invites the other to do this lording over it. What we want is to see the Saxon treated with generous hospitality by the Celt, and the Celt all the time maintaining the bearing of the free man on his own heath. The Saxon who cannot bear this is unworthy of his race; and the Celt who is not up to this measure of manliness should have on a brass collar, with a legible inscription inviting every man that passes to kick him.

There is nothing more galling to this class of men, than to see a proper exhibition of manliness. It is a reflection upon them; and we have some curious accounts of the mean and cowardly shifts they resort to for the purpose of gratifying their spite. We know of cotteries at this moment, who, from day to day and from week to week, congregate like so many yellow flies, or so many meaner creatures, to scrape, and nip, and pinch in the security of their insignificance, at those who are trying to put fresh life into the body politic, and give proper, expansive effect to the constitution handed down to us by our fathers. The idea of anything being done by our community which ensures vitality and originality is to them an offence. They are only fit to live upon weak constitutions; and the signs of vigour are a terror to parasites.

There is good reason to believe that the Gaelic Society has, in less than two years, outlived the greater part of this annoyance. In this triumph, every other local and congenial movement has more or less of encouragement. Those who frowned on the struggling cause will smile upon it when it is in the ascendant. The spirit in which the Society originated is developed and strengthened to enter into other movements; and the day is not far distant, we hope, when the most sceptical in our midst will be able to trace to the Gaelic Society a large accession of social, moral, commercial, and political power in the Highlands.

It is in this light we have always regarded the Society; and we hope the Council will always keep before them the idea of its being not merely an organization for getting up a successful display of Highland sentiment, but a great power fraught with every kind of good which should favour the enlargement of the souls of living men. Let the Society cultivate the spirit in which it originated, and it will prove the most valuable institution of which Inverness can boast.

The success of the first assembly as a mere exhibition of revived Celticism was such as to cause a fresh current of life to pass through the Highland capital—a current which many felt, but few understood. We have no doubt the present assembly will add to the force of that current, and give a fresh impetus to that active life which has been showing itself in our midst of late.

As we raise our head from writing these words the streets are becoming thronged with wool buyers and sellers. The trains from the north bring the wealthy farmers from Sutherland and Easter Ross, and the stalwart men of Kintail, Strathglass, Lochcarron, Lochbroom, and the western isles. The steamers have brought the Lochaber men, and men all the way from Lorn and Appin, from Glenorchy and Ardnamurchan. The trains from the east and south bring them from Athol, from Badenoch, Strathspey, Speyside, Strathdon, and Glenlivat, and all the way from the southern borders. And a good display they make. Physically, it would be very difficult to say where one could go for another muster of men to match. Tall, stout, ruddy with health, and with all well put on—some in broadcloth, some in tweed, and not a few in the dress of the country, displaying the well-formed limbs of mountaineers. Everywhere are to be seen evidences of prosperity, as if, indeed, the country were positively bursting with plenty, for these men are the very personifications of well-to-do-ness.

But as we are viewing the countrymen parading Union Street, our ear is pierced by the sound of *Piobaireachd.* At the entrance to the Music Hall there is a veteran piper with silver locks, accompanied by a younger man, playing in perfect harmony "The Marchioness of Tullibardine." This is a characteristic invitation to the assembly of the Gaelic Society of which we have been speaking. Numbers are passing in. Desirous of witnessing, on our first visit to the Highlands, a really characteristic social "gathering of the clans," as well as being commissioned to report the proceedings, we enter a large hall, capable of holding about a thousand people, and find it rapidly filling. The sound of the great Highland pipe comes rolling up the staircase, and after all seems to fill the hall with strains which send the mind back to "the days of the years that are past," when pipers and minstrels, bards and harpers, were essential constituents of a chief's establishment; and when "clansmen brave" and numerous, too, mustered in their now deserted glens to defend their rights and maintain the ' honour of their race. We are aware that there is an affected delicacy of ear to which the sound of the national instrument is assumed to be harsh. We plead guilty to the charge of feeling that there are no strains which delight our ears more than those of the pipes when well played. The prejudice against the pipes—for prejudice and nothing else we call it—is founded on the performances of persons who should be sentenced to a month on the tread-mill for daring to touch the noble instrument. As we think over these things the measure is changed, and "Mount Stuart" comes up in musical billows, and falls upon the ear with delightful effect. In come the members of assembly, some in the Garb of old

Gaul, but, sad to say, far more in the garb of modern England. Just as the pipes are turned to the march of "The Celtic Society," .

Duncan Davidson, Esq., of Tulloch, mounts the platform and takes the chair.　Along with him are.—The Rev. Alexander MacGregor; Charles Mackay, LL.D.; Revs. Alex. Stewart, Nether Lochaber; Dr Murray Mitchell, Robson, and D. Sutherland; G. J. Campbell, Esq.; Bailies Simpson and MacBean; Alex. Dallas, Esq., Town Clerk; Chas. Innes and Alex. Fraser, Esq., solicitors; John Mackenzie, Esq., Provost of Inverness; Provost Lyon MacKenzie; Sheriffs Macdonald and Blair; Dr Carruthers; Osgood Mackenzie, Esq.; Captain Chisholm, Glassburn; John Murdoch, Esq., of *The Highlander.*　In the Hall we observed— W. Mundell, Esq., Inverlaul; A. Macdonald, Esq., solicitor, and Misses Macdonald; Dr Macnee; Mr Mackenzie, Broadstone Park; Mr Menzies, Millarton; Mr John Mundell, Scalascaig; Mr D. Shaw, Leys; Mr Macdonald, live stock agent; Mr Mackenzie, Maryburgh; Dr Macdonald; Mr D. Cameron, Union Street; Mr Macdonald, Tormore; Mr Fraser, Banker, Lochcarron; Mr Mackenzie Caledonian Bank; Mr L. Davidson, Kingussie; Miss Wakeman; Mr Angus Ross, Wool Broker, Glasgow; Mr Murray, Inverness; Mr Mackenzie, Bookseller; Mrs and Miss Murdoch, Tomatin Cottage; Mr A. Mackenzie, Church Street; Mr Davidson Solicitor; Mr Fraser, Union Street, &c.

The platform was adorned with stags' heads, and draped with tartans from Clachnacudain House.

Mr A. Stewart was then introduced, and gave, with fine effect, *An Gaidheal, am measg nan Gall.*　It is true a large number present did not understand a word of what was sung, but the influence of the very sound was felt even by them, and the Gaelic speaking portion of the audience were quite electrified, so much so that he was called back and gave some verses of another Gaelic song in praise of Lord Clyde.

Mr J. Fraser then gave "The McGregor's Gathering," which he sang in his well-known style of excellence, accompanied by Miss McLearnan on the pianoforte.　Both were cordially greeted by the audience, who would fain have had them back.

This was followed by a dance.　Messrs Gordon, Smith, Macpherson, and Stewart, danced *Ruidhle Thullachain* with great spirit, to the music of the pipes.　Many would have had a repetition of the treat, but time and order forbade.

The choir was then called upon, when the Misses Mactavish, Fraser, Barclay, and Mackay, together with Messrs Wm. Mackay, D. Mackintosh, Jas. Cameron, and J. Mackenzie appeared, and gave forth in rich and heart-reaching strains the plaintive song of

Fear a' Bhata, Miss McLearnan presiding at the piano. The effect of this pure stream of mountain melody on the hundreds of mountaineers present was striking, and all yielded to the influence. The singing was admirable, and the accompaniment most effective.

The Rev. Alexander M'Gregor was then called upon, and received with loud and long continued cheers; and the eloquent address which follows elicited repeated cheers from those who understood the language in which it was spoken :—

Fhir suidhe Urramaich agus ionmhuinn,—Cha bheag an sòlas do'n Chomunn so,—agus is mòr gun teagamh an toilinntinn do gach àrd agus iosal a tha 'làthair a'n so air an fheasgair so, gu'm bheil Ceann-Cinnidh cho cliùiteach, comharraichte; Uachdaran cho bàigheil, truacanta, agus Gaidheal cho càirdeal, ceanalta ri Tighearna Chluainidh 'na Ard riaghladair air an ceann. Mar a thubhairt am bàrd :—

> "Sàr cheànnard air sluagh curannt 'thu,
> Leis an doirteadh fuil 'sa' bhlàr;
> Bhiodh cuimhneach, ciallach, faiceallach,
> Neo-lapach anns an spàirn;
> Bhiodh reubach, fuilteach, faobharach
> 'Sa' chaonaig ris an namb,
> 'S bu tréunail colg nan gaisgeach aig',
> 'Toirt euchd nan arm thar chaich l"

Cha'n 'e mhain, Fhir-suidhe Urramaich, gu'm bheil mòr-spèis aige-san do na Gaidheil, agus d'an duthaich, d'an cleachdannaibh, agus d'an canain oirdheirc, ach tha e fein comusach air a' chanain sin a labhairt 'na fior-ghloinead, air comhradh a dheanamh ìnnte ri dhillsibh fein, agus air gach nile mhaise agus mor bhuaidh a bhuineas do chainnt Oisein agua Fhìnn a thuigsinn agus a thoirt gu soilleir fa'near. Agus a ris, a thaobh éididh aosda nan Gaidheal, c'ait am faighear am measg nan sonn air fad aon uasal eile do'm fearr an tìg am breacan 'san fhéile, na do Thighearna Chluainidh; seadh, a' bhonnaid bhinneach, le ite an fhireoin mhoir ag éiridh gu h-àrd, agus le osain ghearra air a chalpannaibh geal crùinn? Tha na cinn-fheadna Ghaidhealach gun teagamh fathast 'nan uaislean urramach, agus air iomadh buaidh cliù-thoilltinneach, aah mo thruaigh? co 'nam measgan gu léir aig am bheil cumhachd a' Ghaidhlig a labhairt? Co 'nam measgsan air fad nach 'eil gu tur aineolach air cainnt nam beann chum comhradh a dheanamh ìnnte, ach esan na aonar a ta 'cur urraim air " Comunn Gailig Inbhirneis," le suidhe a dheanamh co tlachdmhor 'na chaithir-riaghlaidh os an ceann? Gu ma fada beo Tighearna

K

Cluainidh, agus gu robb sliochd a shliochd-san a' giùlan a dheagh-
ainm-san agus a ehliù sios, lìnntean gun aireamh r'a teachd l
(Amen! and applause).

Fhir-suidhe Urramaich, dhealbhadh agus shuidhicheadh an
Comunn so chum leas nan Gaidheal a chur air aghaidh, agus chum
an cainnt agus an cleachdanna a chumail air chuimhne re linnte
r'a teachd. Cha'n 'eil ni bhuineas doibh, no gaisge a rinn iad, no
cruaidh-chàs a dh'fhuiling iad, nach miannach leis a' Chomunn so
a rannsachadh a mach chum an cliu! Cha'n 'eil teagamh idir,
nach e mor-dhurachd a Chomuinn gach dìchioll, éug-samhail a
dheanamh, gach strith agus saothair a chleachdadh, agus gach maith
'nan comas, a chur air aghaidh, air son an luchd-du'cha fein athleasachadh a thaobh nithe aimsireil, modhannail, agus spioradail!
Ged nach 'eil annam-sa ach duine beag, aodhar bochd ann am inbh
iosail, aig nach' eil ach neoni a'm' chomas, gidheadh, is taitneach
leam fhaicinn gu'm bheil aig mo luchd-du'cha fein cairdean a ta
dealaidh, dileas, agus dian, agus leis a'm micnn gu'n soirbhicheadh
gach ni leo? *(Applause).*

Tha duilichinn orm, gidheadh, (mar a tha air gach neach a tha
eolach air uile-bhuaidhibh urramach nan Gaidheal), gu'm hheil
élgin air a cur air aireamh co mor diubh tir am breith fhagail, gu
dol thar chuanta fad agus farsuing dh'ionnsuidh dhuchanna céin.
Mo thruaigh! 'S i'n èigin fein a dheanadh so! S i'n éigin fein a
spionadh air falbh á gleanntaibh an eolais, iadsan ris am bheil iad
air an taghadh le mile ceangal co dluth, 's cho tean 'sa ta an iadh-
shlat ris na craobhaibh aosda! Cha'n 'eil comas air, ach, tha e
cianail, muladach, gu'm biodh neart na du'cha, agus iadsan a bha
riamh cluiteach chum an righ, agus an tir, agus an saorsa a
theasairginn à laimh nan namh, air am fogradh air falbh do
chearnaibh coimheach. Cha'n ann an dingh no'n dé a thachair so,
ach bha e dol air aghaidh o cheann ficheadan bliadhna air ais.
Tha fios aig na h-nile nach 'eil sluagh air an talamh aig am bheil
barrachd spéis, agus teas-ghràidh do dhuthaich am breith na th'aig
na Gaidheil—*(applause)*—agus is ni mulagach e gur éigin doibh
a fagail. An uair a dh'aidicheas na h-nile nach robh riamh sluagh
ann, a bha ni bu chliuitiche, mheasaile ghaisgeile, agus chairdeil'
no na Gaidheil, is duilich nach tugadh cothrom doibh am beo-
shlainte fein fhaotuinn ann an tir an roimh-aithrichean! Ghreasadh
iad chum chriochan cumhann, agus chuireadh am fearann aca fo na
caoraich bhàna! Ochan! mo thruaigh! chithear a' chaora mhor,
mhin, bhan, ach gann ann an uile sgiorachdaibh na h-Alba, le a
gnnis gheal, aoidheil, agus le a tròm-rusg air a druim, chithear i ag
ionaltradh ann an aois-laraichibh nan tighean sin anns an d'
aruicheadh iomadh curaidh calma, tréun, agus is cianail an

sealladh e! Aig a' cheart am so tha moran a' cur rompa dol air imirich do dhuchannaibh fad as. Tha dochas againn uile gu'n eirich gu math dhoibh, agus gu'n soirbhich gach ni ris an cuir iad an lamh, leo. Tha müinntir nan Garbh-chrioch 'nan daoine glice, tuigseach, agus deagh-bheusach, agus 'nan daoine a bha riamh air an cleachdadh ri mor-chruadal, agus cruaidh-shaothair! Cha'n 'eil teagamh nach 'eil iad air gach seol freagarrach air son nan du'channan sin 'dh'ionnsuidh a'm bheil iad a cur rompa dol, agus dh'ionnsuidh an deachaidh na miltean diubh o chean leth-cheud bliadhna air ais.—Ach an nair a tha chuis mar sin, nach 'eil e ni's freagarraich' gu,m biodh iad air an aruchadh, agus air an gleidh-eadh 's na gleanntaibh, 's na h-eileanaibh, agus 's na garbh-chriochaibh sin far an d'rugadh iad? Nach mor an call iad do'n Rioghachd Bhreatunnaich, an nair a dh'fhagas iad i? Nach cunnartach am briseadh a nithear le'n imirich-san air neart-cogaidh na rioghachd! Tha e cinnteach, gidheadh, gu'm bheil na Gaidheil a tha dol null air fairge, le'n teaghlaichibh, a' deanamh ni a bhios chum buannachd dhoibh fein aig a cheann thall, o'n tha cothrom agus ceartas air a dhiultadh dhoibh ann an tir an roimh-aithrichean. Leis an imirich sin ni iad solar air son an sliochd rè linntean r'a teachd. A réir coslais, bithidh an sliochdsan céndan bliadhna an deigh so, a' sealbhachadh bheannachdan a' phailteis, na sithe, agus na saorsa, an uair a bhios "SEANN ALBAINN A' CHLUARAIN," air tuiteam, feudaidh e bhi, gu neoni! (*Applause*).

A reir coslais, bithidh a' Ghaidhlig ghrinn againn fein ga labhairt, agus 'ga searmonachadh a'n America, 'n Australia, ann an California, agus ann an cearnaibh iomallach eile dhe'n t-saoghal, an nair nach cluinnear aon lide dhi ann an Gaidhealtachd na h-Alba. Feumar a chuimhneachadh gu'n robh rioghachdan agus cumhachdan talmhaidh, dh' aindeoin am meud, am maise, agus an greadhnachais, ag eiridh agus a' tuiteam anns gach linn o'n chruthachadh a nuas gu ruig an la an diugh. Chaidh iad sin seachad, cosmhuil ri sgiamh an t-saoghail, agus cha'n 'eil aobhar againn a chomh-dhunadh nach lean an Rioghachd Bhreatunnach nair eigin air slighe chaich! Feudaidh an t-am a' teachd anns an tilgear a laghanna air chul, anns an lughdaichear a cumhachd, agus ans am briscar a co'dhealbhadh 'na bhloighdibh! Feudaidh so uile tachairt do dhuthaich-breith na muinntir sin a dh'fhag i, agus a ta 'ga fagail, an uair a bhios an sliochd-san a' soirbheachadh, agus a' dol a'n lionmhorachd ann an duchannaibh cein, agus a' labhairt cainnt lurach an roimh-aithrichean fein 'na h-uile oirdheirceas agus mhaise, mar a bha i aig Fionn agus aig Oiseau o chian! (*Applause*).

Ach do bhrigh gur atharraichean so nach fhaic sinne agus nach 'eil sinn idir ag irraidh fhaicinn, tha e ceart agus freagarrach gu'm biodh eachdraidh nan Gaidheal, an cleachdanna, an treubhantas, agus an iomadh buaidh urramach air an gleidheadh air chuimhne, agus air an teasairginn o dhol a'm mugha! *(Applause)*.

'Si durachd "Comuinn Gailig" a' bhaile so, agus gach Comuinn Gaidhealach eile, a dhol gu'n dulan chum so uile a dheanamh. Tha iad a' gnàthachadh gach innleachd chum gach fiosrachadh fhaotuinn mu na nithe so, agus cha diobair iad a'm fad is beo iad. Air an doigh cheudna 'se durachd mhoran de mhaithibh na rioghachd, o'n Bhanrigh choir air an righ-chaithir, an ni ceudna a chur air aghaidh. 'S e so durachd cridhe mhoran eile de dhaoinibh cumhachdach agus foghluimte 'nar tir fein—seadh, daoine de gach inbh, dreuchd, agus staid, gaisgich chalma, foghlu- maich ionnsuichte teallsanaich sgrudail, ollamhain de gach gne, ollamhain-diadhaidh, ollamhain-leigheis, ollamhain-lagha, agus an leithide sin, a' dol a'm boinn r'a cheile chum gach ni air am beil fiamh na Gaidhlig a theasairginn, agus a chumail suas. 'S e an ni ceudna durachd cridhe nan daoine dealaidh sin, a tha 'cur a mach au "ARD-ALBANNAICH" anns a' "GHAIDHEIL" ann an Glaschu, agus na h-uiread eile. 'Se so durachd "BUN-LOCHABAIR," co ealanta, deas-chainnteach an comhnuidh *(Applause)*.

Tha aobhar gairdeachais aig nile chairdibh nan Gaidheal, gu'm bheil na h-uiread de na Goill fein aig am bheil speis-cridhe do shliochd nam beann, leis an Ard Theagasgair *Blackie* air an ceann! Uime sin, mar a thubairt a' Bhan-Bhard, Mairi Nic Eallair :—

Dean a dhuthaich nan treun,
Iollach eibhneis as ur ;
Chualas nuallan 'nam piob,
A'n tigh riomhach nan tur
Is t'uaislean 'nan cendan,
Gu h-eudmhor tighinn cruinn,
'Chumail suas na cainnt bhuadhar
Bha dual do na suinn !

Chruinnich bantighearnan min-gheal
'Nan side is 'san srol ;
'S iad a' boisgeadh le seudaibh,
Mar reultan 's na neoil ;
A'm maise 'san ailleas,
'Toirt barr air a' cheile,
'S an gaol air a' Ghaidhlig,
Ga gnath chur an ceill.

The rev. gentleman resumed his seat amid the most **deafening** applause.

Miss Fraser then came forward and sang in fine style, "O l for the bloom of my own native heather." Miss Fraser is well known to be an accomplished vocalist, and it is enough to say that she did herself justice on this occasion, and greatly delighted her large auditory.

Mr. W. G. Stewart, a well-known and most obliging member of various useful societies in Inverness, came forward and recited in finished style, and with most grotesque effect, TURUS EACHAINN DO PHAISLEY.

Mr. Smith made his appearance again, and performed *Gille Calum*, to the music of the pipes. This he did in dashing style, and yet with freedom and grace, and greatly to the delight of the spectators.

This closed the first part of the evening's proceedings.

Pipe-Major M'Lennan then undertook to fill an interval with the sound of the pipes. This he began by playing *Chumh an aona mhic.* This fine *piobaireachd* greatly delighted those versed in such matters, and all seemed to appreciate the wonderful manipulation of the performer. Then there were the dignity, the elegance, and the gracefulness of the whole combination of pipe and piper, which made quite a favourable impression even on those who could only appreciate what they saw. After the *piobaireachd*, he was joined by Messrs Macdonald and Fraser, and all three struck up *Piobaireachd Dhomhnuill Duibh.* In this way the ear was filled during the interval with measured and harmonized sounds, and those assembled moved about, some going out, whilst others stood about in clusters congratulating one another on the success of the re-union, and the treat they were enjoying.

Dr. Charles Mackay, who was received with loud applause, said that being a Highlander so far as he could trace his descent, and not having a single drop of Saxon blood in his veins, he stood there with a feeling of shame that he could not speak the language of his ancestors. He was sorry that the eloquent speech of Mr. Macgregor was not intelligible to him, but the sonorous beauty of the mere sounds was striking even to his ears, and put him in mind of the old lady in England who said that Mesopotamia was a blessed word; it filled her with emotions of delight only to hear it pronounced. *(Laughter and applause.)* Something of the same kind filled his mind on hearing the Gaelic spoken. He did happen to have studied that venerable speech so as to know something of its methods, its structure, and its beauties, and he envied his reverend friend the power of speaking it so well; but not being able to use the language of his ancestors, he must just address them in plain Saxon English :—in what he might call the language

of the comparatively modern interlopers upon the sacred soil of the
Highlands. *(Applause.)* He was glad to discover proofs every
day that there was a revival not only in this country and in Ireland, but in England and on the Continent of Europe, of the study of
the venerable tongue of the Gael. In this department of philology
the Germans were far ahead of all the rest of Europe, and had
published ten times as many works upon the subject as ever were
published in Scotland, or within the limits of the British Islands.
The Germans knew more about the language than people here,
even than those who spoke it fluently. For his own part a con-
scientious course of study had convinced him that Gaelic lay at
the root not only of the vernacular and colloquial English, but of
French, Spanish, Italian, Latin, and Greek. A correspondent of
a paper published in Inverness had lately discovered (and newspaper correspondents discovered everything now-a-days) that
twenty years ago he had been unwise enough to assert that the
music and poetry of Scotland were almost wholly confined to the
Lowlands. The charge was no sooner made than he pleaded
guilty to it, but he would urge in extenuation the offence was
committed in ignorance, for he had not at that time studied the
language of the Highlands. But he was older and wiser now—or
if not wiser, he might be allowed to say he was less foolish, and
had discovered that the Highlands did not compare disad-
vantageously with the Lowlands, either in music or in poetry. It
was of the Celtic nature to be poetical. The greatest poet of
Scotland, perhaps the greatest of his kind that any country had
produced, Robert Burns, though claimed by the lowlands, was in
reality a Celt by birth, descent, and name. The original name of
his family was Burness, which every Highlander knew to signify
the fall or cascade of the burn. Ayrshire, where he was born, was
the most Celtic of Lowland counties, all its rivers, valleys, and
mountains, farms and estates, having Gaelic names. The pure
Anglo-Saxons had never produced a very great poet. The hills
and rivers of South-England had never inspired a rural bard of
any note to celebrate their beauties or sing their praises; but in
Scotland—both Lowland and Highland—there was not a stream
flowing, a lake shining, or a mountain rearing its summit to the
clouds, that had not been celebrated in immortal verse. Scotland
had been called the

> " Land of brown heath and shaggy wood,
>   Land of the mountain and the flood,"

but other lands had also brown heath and shaggy wood. Scotland
had been called the land of cakes, but there were cakes, and good

cakes, too, in other countries. Scotland had also been called the land of brave men and bonnie lasses, but there were brave men and bonnie lasses in other countries, only not perhaps in equal numbers. *(Laughter and applause.)* Scotland, with mere justice, might be called pre-eminently the land of music and of song, in these respects, perhaps, surpassing every country in the world. To this it was indebted for its large Celtic element. The greatest of poets—Shakespeare himself—notwithstanding his Anglo-Saxon name—might be claimed as partially, if not wholly, of Celtic blood. He was born in Warwickshire, the very heart and centre of England, in which the Saxon invaders had never wholly displaced the original Celtic inhabitants. Shakespeare had wandered on the banks of the Avon, a river with a Gaelic name; and had meditated or sported in the leafy recesses of the forest of Arden, a name that also was purely Gaelic. The songs of the Anglo-Saxons were neither abundant nor beautiful. Ben Jonson wrote beautiful songs, but he was a Scotchman and a Celt. Thomas Campbell wrote some of the finest songs in the English language, but he also was a Scotchman and a Celt. Thomas Moore wrote some of the finest lyrics ever printed in English, but he, too, was a Celt and an Irishman. All the Celtic races were lovers of song, and were stirred and excited by song to an extent that often surprised the more impassive Anglo-Saxons and Germans. Just now in Paris they could not find a song with which to receive the Shah of Persia. If they struck up the Marseillaise, the Communists and Red Republicans would take fire. If they struck up "Partant pour la Syrie" the Bonapartists would be encouraged to hope for the restoration of the Empire; and if they had recourse to La Parisienne, the inspired strain would be held to excite the Orleanists to make an effort for the Crown. Song did not stir the sober English in this fashion. In fact the only two songs which were truly national to the south of the Tweed were "Rule Britannia," written by James Thomson, a Scotchman; and "God Save the Queen," originally "God save the King," of which the author was unknown, which it was originally treason to sing, because it was written by a Jacobite in favour of the Stuarts, whom the author wished to "send" back victorious over the House of Hanover. But this was a wide subject, on which time would not allow him to enlarge. In conclusion he would only say that he had very great pleasure indeed in being present at such a large gathering assembled for such a purpose, and in meeting so many old friends in Inverness. *(Cheers.)*

Mr. Sim was then introduced and gave, with great taste and sweetness, "Bonnie Scotland," the accompaniment by Miss

M'Learnan. Admirably the two acquitted themselves, and the large audience greeted the performance with every sign of appreciation.

The four dancers made their appearance again, and did the Highland Fling to the great delight of the audience. This was followed by one of the gems of the whole evening's performances.

The choir sang *Air faillirin Illirin Uillirin O !* with great spirit and in fine taste. Miss M'Learnan again presiding at the pianoforte; and the audience seemingly ready to bound off their seats in response to the stirring and melodious strains of the singers, who seemed to have their audience spell-bound.

Rev. Mr. Stewart, Nether-Lochaber, was the next speaker, and was received with applause. He commenced by observing that if in getting up at two o'clock that morning, and galloping across Drumochter, the backbone of Scotland, through mist and small rain and cloud, and coming an equal distance by train in a smoking carriage—if in doing all this to be present there was any merit or any virtue, then, in the words of the song written by his eminent friend on the left, he might say they ought to " Cheer, boys, cheer." *(Laughter and applause.)* Some might think it a very easy thing to speak at a meeting like that, before so many people, but he wished they would only come and try it. He had felt a considerable amount of mental perturbation all day at the thought of it, and notwithstanding the pleasant colloquy of Davie, the driver of the coach, and the kind attentions of the guard of the train, and his reception by his friends in Inverness, he still felt in a considerable state of mental flurry. Give him a good goose quill and a large folio, and he might undertake to write something, but to make a speech before such an audience was a very different matter indeed. However, since he came into the hall, and met so many kind friends, he felt that with their warm sympathies he might get on better than he expected—in fact, the hand-shaking which he had gone through was enough to make him feel as if he had suffered from rheumatism for the last twelve months. *(Laughter and applause.)* He was also very fortunate in having the support of Mac Dòmhnull Dhu, their member of Parliament. *(Applause.)* And with all these encouragements, he thought he might well cock his beaver. *(Applause.)* I assure you, continued Mr. Stewart, that I am not a little proud, as well as pleased, to be present here this evening at this the second annual festival of the now world-renowned Gaelic Society of Inverness. I say world-renowned advisedly, for you have no idea how deep and heart-felt an interest is taken in all your sayings and doings by our leal-hearted countrymen in all the British colonies, and in every

foreign country wherein, for the time being, a son of the mountain
may be resident. All the way from Moulmain in Burmah; from
Canton and other cities of China; from the Indian Presidencies;
from the Mauritius; from the Cape; from all parts of Australia
and New Zealand; from the Canadas and the United States; from
Buenos Ayres, Demerara, and the West Indian Islands; from all
these places I have, since our last year's assembly, had letters, and
in almost all of them there was more or less reference to the Gaelic
Society of Inverness. Our countrymen abroad were delighted to find
that we were at last alive to our own dignity and interests as a
nation at home, and proud that we had at length got the right
thing in the right place—a Gaelic Society, destined, I do believe,
to be the best conducted and most influential thing of the kind in
the kingdom—a Gaelic Society in the Capital of the Highlands,
the pride and gem of the north! On appearing before you last
year, I at once and unhesitatingly predicted that your meeting was
to be a success—and a decided success it proved. To suppose for
a moment anything else regarding this year's festival, would be
simply an insult—an insult to the programme I hold in my hand,
to the array of talent around me on this platform, to the large
and enthusiastic assemblage before me, and to Cluny Macpherson,
your distinguished and excellent president, whose very name is
synonymous with all that is high-minded, and chivalrous, and
Celtic, and kindly. Nothing could be more satisfactory than the
rapidity with which your Society has attained to its present
eminence. Born, if I may so put it, to-day, to-morrow it had
attained a robust and healthy manhood, It reminds me of an
ancient Fingalian *sgeulachd* ·that I wrote down a short time ago
from the recitation of an old Glencoe man. The story goes on to
tell how a certain Fingalian chief had a son born to him as it were
to-day, which son, to the surprise of every one, was on the morrow
morning a full-grown warrior, of gigantic proportions, taking his
part in a battle that was fought against the Danes, and laying
about him like a very Achilles, performing prodigies of valour.
(*Laughter.*) His miraculous growth is accounted for in the
sgeulachd by the fact that his nurse, "a wise woman," had,
immediately after his birth, bathed him *thrice* in the waters of an
enchanted well, at the bottom of which lay coiled the serpent of
wisdom, and valour, and strength. Somewhat similar seems to me
to have been the progress of this Society, a childhood, as it were,
of but a single day, followed by a vigorous manhood, in its quickness of growth unexampled, perhaps, in the history of such
institutions. It is a well-known phrase, of such meaning in the
hunting-field—as you, Lochiel, know—that "blood tells," and

Celtic blood, pure and uncontaminated, is, I believe, at the bottom
of all this success. (*Applause.*)   Your volume of "Transactions,"
for 1871-72 is a wonderfully good book, of which you have every
reason to be proud.   Outwardly, small and unpretentious, quite
becoming a Society yet in its infancy, it is inwardly as full of good
matter as a freshly laid egg is of meat.   The inaugural address by
the Rev. Mr. Mackenzie, Kilmorack ; Professor Blackie's lecture
on "Nationality" ; the Rev. Mr. Macgregor's Festival address—
Mr. Macgregor, who writes Gaelic with all the elegance and force
with which Cicero wrote Latin, and all the homeliness and care
with which Addison wrote English, always illustrating his remarks
with snatches of Gaelic song, a habit characteristic of Scott, and
which lends such a charm to his inimitable romances—why, sir,
any one of these articles possesses sufficient vivacity and buoyancy
in itself to float a much more ponderous and bulkier book than the
Transactions of the Gaelic Society of Inverness. (*Applause.*) And
here let me say a single word on behalf of the clergy.   There was
for a time, sir, in this country, a foolish prejudice against what was
called literary clergymen ; if they were to write at all, it must be
only tracts and sermons, and if they were to speak, it must be only
from the pulpit, or on the floor of kirk-sessions, presbyteries,
synods, and general assemblies.   This prejudice, however—the
existence of which was very much owing to the clergy themselves
—has, I am happy to say, been knocked on the head, and long
since consigned to the limbo of all the stupidities.   The clergy now
take their fair share in every good work out of the pulpit, and,
extra ecclesiam, beyond the walls of the church as well as within,
and your "Transactions" shows how capable they are of aiding in
the furtherance of the noble and patriotic work which you, as a
Society, have solemnly declared it to be your mission to foster and
encourage.   In a note to one of his novels—"Waverley," I think
—Sir Walter Scott tells a very good story of a worthy old lady
who kept an hostelry at Greenlaw, in Berwickshire.   One day a
gentleman, well advanced in life, and three younger men, entered
the old lady's inn, and with a good deal of high-handedness and
fuss, ordered their dinner.   The dinner was duly served and eaten,
and some of the old claret discussed, and the bill called for and
paid ; but the old lady did not think much of her guests.   Their
reserved and haughty bearing disgusted her, and she felt, above
all, insulted by the fact that she was not offered a glass of her own
wine as she laid it on the table, as was the habit of the period.
When about to leave the house the old gentleman said, "You
probably do not know, my good woman, whom you have entertained to-day.   Your hostel, I'll be bound to say, has rarely, if ever

before, been honoured with four such guests." The old lady could'nt see it. "You must know, then," continued the gentleman, "that I am a 'placed' minister of the Kirk of Scotland, incumbent of such and such a parish, and these are my three sons, all of them 'placed' ministers of the Kirk of Scotland too! Now tell me, Luckie, have you ever in your life entertained such a company before?" The old lady, who by this time began to understand who her colloquist was, and remembered hearing that neither he nor his sons were at all popular as preachers, bluntly replied, "Indeed, sir, I canna say that ever I had such a party in my house before, except once, in the forty-five, when I had a Hieland piper here, with *his* sons, all Hieland pipers ; *and deil a spring they could play among them.*" (*Loud laughter.*) Now sir, in the Society's volume of "Transactions" you will find the names of some four or five clergymen, each of whom has proved that he can play a spring, and to some purpose, and with reverence be it said, without unduly "drawing the long bow" either. (*Loud applause.*) I might add more, but will not detain you seeing that our time is limited. (*Applause.*)

As a compliment to Lochiel, Mr James Fraser sang the "March of the Cameron Men," which he rendered very effectively, and for which he was loudly cheered.

Lochiel, who was received with hearty cheers, said—If my worthy friend on the left, (Mr Stewart), one so able and fluent in speech, and so ready with his pen, expressed his diffidence in addressing you, and that, too, after having his thoughts directed to the subject the whole day, and enjoying the solace of the guards by coach and railway, what must be my feelings, called on as I am in this most unexpected manner, to speak on a subject before so many people more able to give utterance to their sentiments upon it—sentiments, however, in which I fully sympathise and share? (*Applause.*) But if I have not been so fortunate as to secure the ear of the guard of the coach, or the guard of the train, I have, without saying anything disrespectful of those two worthy persons, enjoyed the greater honour and pleasure of travelling, though without knowing it, in the same carriage with Dr. Charles Mackay! (*Applause.*) I had the great privilege and satisfaction of being able to compare with him certain roots of the Gaelic language with which I was unacquainted, other roots of the Sanscrit with which I was still more unacquainted, and passed in this way a most agreeable couple of hours. It was with great pleasure I arrived just in time to hear his able and interesting speech on behalf of the Society with which we are all connected, and to which we wish well. (*Applause.*) The immediate object

I have in rising is to ask you to tender your best thanks to the other gentlemen who have spoken—Mr. Macgregor, Dr. Charles Mackay, and Mr. Stewart. Mr. Macgregor spoke, I am sure, with an eloquence and feeling that did honour to his head and heart, and Mr. Stewart is known to the end of the world for his writings in the *Inverness Courier*—not only for his learned discussions of Celtic subjects, but for the enthusiastic and heartfelt interest which he takes in everything that conduces to the maintenance and extension of our ancient language and literature. (*Applause.*) I grieve to say—and I say it most sincerely—that unfortunately I am not a Gaelic scholar myself. I feel I deserve to be hooted out of this hall for not knowing the language. At the same time I am bound to say that there is no one here who feels more strongly or more sincerely and deeply the advantages of Gaelic literature to the rising generation of this country, or who would regret more to see it banished from the studies of our national schools. (*Applause.*) I believe there is no better way of appealing to the heart of a child, than through the medium of its mother tongue, and no better way either of appealing to its intellect and reaching it with those subjects which constitute education, than through the instrumentality of the language which the child knows better than any other, and through which it loves to learn. (*Applause.*) I have no sympathy, whatever, with those utilitarian doctrinaires who tell us that because the Gaelic language is confined to a portion of this country, therefore it is a hindrance and an incumbrance to our progress. I feel when I speak to a Highland lad, a crofter's son, or a gillie, that he has the advantage over me, in that he speaks two languages perfectly, while I speak only one perfectly. (*Applause.*) And although I cannot pretend to great enthusiasm for a language which I cannot speak, I do profess to have an enthusiastic love of the Highlands. I feel it more every time I come from the south, and my only regret at present is, that after two days I must turn my back upon these beautiful Highlands. (*Cheers.*) I shall say no more, except to thank Mr. Fraser for the way in which he has sung that heart-stirring song, "The March of the Cameron men," a song which did apparently touch every one of you most deeply, and which touched myself more than any one else. (*Applause.*)

The motion was seconded and carried amid great cheers.

This was followed by a reel, which the previous four performers danced in fine style, sending much of their own active energy into the spectators.

Dr. Carruthers then moved a vote of thanks to the Chairman, which was carried with great applause, and a vote of thanks to the musicians and artists, moved by the Rev. A. Stewart, concluded the proceedings.

The choir then sang *Dhia gleidh Bhanrigh.*

The Company dispersed, the pipers playing "Good night and joy be wi' you a'."

So closed the second assembly of the Inverness Gaelic Society, and we feel sure that we did not say too much when we anticipated that it would be another bound upward on the part of the Society. The Council, the Committee, the Secretary, and all who have had any hand in getting up this rare national reunion, deserve the hearty thanks, not only of those who were present to enjoy the treat, but of the tens of thousands scattered over the world, who rejoice at the evident revival of Highland feeling and spirit in the land of the Gael, of which the Gaelic Society in its numbers, in its earnest work, and in its recreations, is so good an example.

"ON LETTERS."

As the integral representatives of intelligible articulation in speech, and a brief comparison of Gaelic with English in relation to them.

BY

ALEXANDER HALLEY, M.D., F.G.S.

Ball-beatha de Chomuinn Gailig Inbhir-nis agus Londuin.

The history of *letters* is one of the most pertinent topics in discussing the *development* or *formation of language*; but it is not possible, in the very limited time that can be allotted to any *one* paper, at the meetings of a society, to enter at all fully upon many points of interest connected with the theme. I will therefore, crave your permission to limit myself to a few remarks bearing on the subject rather as "nuclei" for *consideration*, than as dogmatic or absolute propositions.

When men first attempted to fix and to exhibit the sounds of language appreciably and definitely to the eye, they drew *pictures of objects to indicate them*, either directly or symbolically. This system is known under the name of "Hieroglyphics;" to this day, many letters still extant, own their origin to some such symbolic root or sign. For example, the first letter of our alphabet—the capital A called in Hebrew "Aleph," which means an *ox*, is a symbolical representation of the head of the animal with two horns and ears.

The letter M, too, which in Hebrew is called "Mem," and means *water*, represents the wave of water in motion.

I need hardly allude to the well known fact that in many languages, especially in the natural or primitive ones, the "onomatopœia" or formation of names, has close reference to some characteristic *sound* or other peculiarity, of the object named ; in the Gaelic language, this is particularly marked. The name of the *cow*, "bo," a *sheep* "Caor," a *horse* " Each, " a *calf* " Laogh " and many others which I need not *indicate* to a *Celtic* audience ; all bear most distinct resemblance to the natural cry of the various animals, *provided* the letters are *naturally* and *properly* pronounced.

Again, as with the Chinese, the object pictured may stand not only for itself, but for other objects with a similar name—*e.g.*, a picture of a *Yew Tree*, might represent *itself*, or the pronoun *you* or a *Ewe*, a sheep ; a "Pear," might represent the *fruit*, or a *pair*, or the verb *to pare*, to cut.

The most perfect, simple, and useful form of signs, however, used to indicate the sounds of the *voice* in *speech*, probably developed itself gradually into the so-called "Alphabet" from many sources and forms of definition, and after many periods of change. Yet it is not improbable, that at some future age, when *space* and *time* come to be regarded even more tangibly and jealously than at present, a *more compact and yet not less distinct* system of *articulate sound-pictures* may be introduced and generally adopted instead of our present alphabetical writing.

Phonetic Shorthand now so commonly used and so necessary where rapid and yet correct reporting of the speeches of our political and social orators has to be accomplished, is a great step in this direction, which only wants full development and teaching *for common practice* ; and it is to be regretted that it is not introduced, into the ordinary curriculum of our public schools.

The principles that ought to apply to representative characters or *letters* may be thus briefly stated.

1st—that *every* elementary articulate sound should be represented by a corresponding character or *letter*.

2nd—that each letter, or combination of letters, should indicate only *one* special and definite sound.

3rd—that *no more* letters should be employed than are necessary to exhibit *every* individual sound.

If it were otherwise, the *written* picture of the language would *not* be a correct or adequate representation of the *spoken* language, or speech.

Now the perfectness of a speech depends, in the first place, upon the precision with which the integral sounds of articulation in letters, can be fully enunciated and represented.

It is not to be supposed that in the *primary* attempts to *systematise*, that this principle would be correctly or uniformly attained, but by careful observation, the laws governing and applicable to the development of determinate articulate Letter-sounds, would *eventually* be fully discerned—hence certain fixed and determinate sounds came to be represented by determinate signs, called "letters." The number of these letters' varies in different languages, and the "alphabet" so called, did not assume its present form, until practical use had *eliminated* the *serviceable*, as well as the *useless* sounds and signs. There is reason to believe that it originated in Phœnicia, and thence passed into Greece and Rome.

The form generally used in Britain as well as by other nations of Western Europe, about the end of the *Sixth* century, was the Roman, or what has been called the *Hibernian*, having been taught by the missionaries from the schools and colleges of Ireland and Iona ; and it was not until the *Eleventh* century that the present form, more or less, was adopted into English.

In the *Gaelic* language the *Beth-Luis-nion*, so-called as was the Greek *Alpha-Beta* from the names of the first letters of the *Letter-muster*, consists of *eighteen letters*, including the euphonic aspirate *H*, which however initiates *no* Gaelic word, and was formerly represented by a simple point or dot, its chief use being to modify the sound and value of letters, by affixture and combination with them.

Arranged according to the Roman method, the letters in use in the Gaelic language are *A*, B, C, D, *E*, F, G, H, *I* L, M, N, *O*, P, R, S, T, *U* ; *eighteen in all.*

In the *English* orthography, besides, there are J, K, Q, V, W, X, Y, Z ; *eight more*, making *twenty-six altogether.*

These letters are divided into vowels and consonants.

The *vowels* make *simple, open, perfect sounds of themselves.*

The *consonants*, articulations or joints, require to be *joined to a vowel*, in order to produce *their* sounds.

The organs involved in the formation of Voice and Speech, consist of—

The Lungs, or bellows.

The Windpipe, or nosle, conducting the air from the Lungs.

The Larynx, or vocal apparatus at the top of the Windpipe.

The Buccal or Oral reverberating cavity, bounded by the precincts of the Pharynx, Palate, Cheeks, Lips, and Tongue, and capable *at will*, of infinitely varying and modulating the sounds emitted in speech.

The *Vowels* usually defined and specified, are five in number— viz., *a. e. i. o. u.*

In *Gaelic* they are but *imperfectly* represented by these *five*; there should in fact be *six*, for there *are* six perfectly distinct simple vowel-sounds, as I will endeavour to show as we proceed.

These articulate sounds are produced by the action and modulation of the muscles and tissues of the *mouth, tongue, and palate*, combined with the *efflux* of the *voice*. They are, however, *otherwise*, independant of the *Larynx*, which is alone concerned in the formation of the voice.

For the clearer comprehension of the mode of formation of the vowels and of the position of the mouth, &c., in their enunciation, and on Horace's principle that

> "What's heard more slowly stirs the mind
> Than what by trusty eyes we find." *

I beg to draw your attention to the following rough diagrams of sections of the Mouth, Tongue, Palate, and Fauces—*i.e.*, of the organs connected with the production of articulation. Varieties in the position of which, when acted upon, by the articulate breath or voice, produce the Vowels and Consonants.

If we note carefully the bearings and forms of the organs in the utterance of the *Vowels*, it will be perceived that in their *Normal* sounds they *advance from behind forwards in the mouth.*

The first vowel *à* (pronounced like *ă* in *făr*, or in *făther*, in English, or in *ărd*, high, in Gaelic), is produced at the back of the palate, opening the mouth rather fully, slightly raising the arches of the palate, whilst the median portion of the tongue is depressed, or rendered slightly concave, allowing the articulate breath or voice to exhale from the Larynx.

The next vowel sound, although distinct, has no *single letter-symbol* to represent or distinguish it. It is indicated in Gaelic, by the dipthong *ao* (ao) sounded as in *caol, caor*, &c., and is produced a little in advance of the above *à*; the posterior arches of the palate rise still more; the root of the tongue also rises slightly, —its median portion however is not affected, but the anterior portion or point advances, the mouth or cheeks being slightly more compressed.

These two, form the first, natural couple of *Broad* vowels.

Next come *E* and *I*, the couple of small vowels.

E normally, is pronounced as *e* in *there*, English, or in the Gaelic *è* (he). It is produced by advancing the tongue and lower jaw slightly, bringing the front of the tongue into distinct but slight contact with the inner surface or back of the lower teeth, at

---

* " Segnius irritant animos demissa per aures
   Quam quæ sunt oculis subjecta fidelibus."

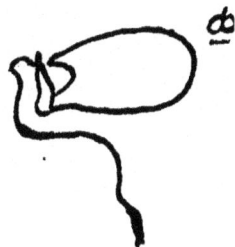

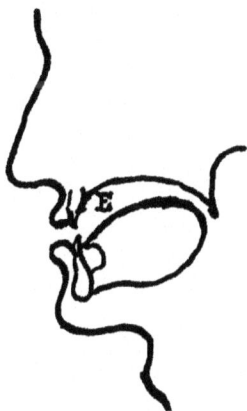

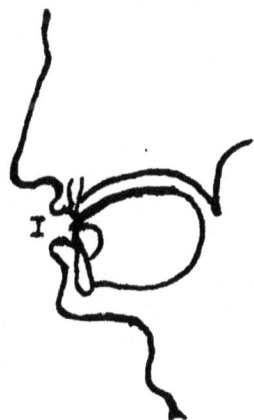

the same time closing the jaws a little, so that the free edges of the teeth are about ⅜ths of an inch apart.

I normally is pronounced like double *e* in *see* in English, or as in *mìn* (smooth) in Gaelic. It is produced by still further compressing the mouth or jaw; the lower jaw being raised and projected slightly forward and closed a little, so that the edges of the front teeth are only about a quarter of an inch apart; the margins of the upper surface of the tongue coming in contact with the teeth of the upper jaw, and are slightly protruded so as nearly to fill up the space between the upper and lower teeth.

Last come *O* and *U* the second couple of broad vowels.

O is the only vowel nominally sounded in English, as in the word "open," or as in "tom" (a knoll or hillock) in Gaelic. To produce it, the jaws separate so that the front teeth are about ¾ths of an inch apart,—retracting and depressing the point of the tongue.—the lips (especially the under one, which is the more mobile), are projected and concentrated, the lower lip rising for the purpose, the perfection of the sound being emitted from the Horatian " ore rotundo " or rounded opening of the mouth about ⅜ths of an inch in diameter.

U has normally the sound of double *O* in "moon," in English, or as in " ùr " (fresh) in Gaelic, and is produced by still farther contraction and projection of the lips, and raising and projecting the lower jaw—concentrating both lips, so that the opening surrounded by them is little more than ¼th of an inch in diameter.

Having thus given the normal distinctive sounds, and the mode of their production in the specific vowels it is proper to state that the vowel sounds are susceptible of infinite variety, and run into one another by a continuous gradation. Each has certain variations or sounds both as to quantity — *i. e.,* "time," which may be long or short, and as to accent—*i. e.* tune, which may be sharp or flat. These variations aid the euphony, or serve the purpose of giving a different meaning to the word by its sound. To some extent these variations are distinguished by accents, placed over the letters.

We now turn to the Consonants, and with the exception of *C* which is always pronounced hard, like the Greek *K,* and a few others, they have in Gaelic mostly the same force as in English. J, K, Q, V, W, X, Y, Z, in English, are wanting in Gaelic, but, *B* and *M,* by aspiration (*bh* and *mh*) in the beginning and middle of words, both sound like *V,* hence the one sometimes occurs in lieu of the other, and some words are spelt indifferently with either.

As just stated *C* was the sound of *K* but when aspirated *Ch* is pronounced like the Greek *X (chi).*

M

Dh and *gh* before the small vowels, in the beginning and middle of words, have the power of *Y* guttural; before the broad vowels they have a guttural quasi *G* sound; when sounded at the end of a word, they have a sound like " ugh "; all of these gutturals are peculiar.

Fh is always silent.

In general in Gaelic any letter coming before *H*, is silent.

S loses its sound after *T*; and before the small vowel (*e* or *i*) is pronounced like *sh*.

T sounds usually more like *D* in English, but with the small vowels it has the sound of *ch* in English.

Ph sounds like *F*, but is used to shew the radix of its word.

All the consonants have their sound changed by being *aspirated*, and the effect is different on different consonants.

No consonants are written double in Gaelic, except *L*, *N*, *R*.

These are the chief points of distinction between the power and sound of the consonants in Gaelic and in English. I may remark however, that Stewart (in his Grammar, second edition, page 18, note) says, " It is certain that the natural sound of *D* aspirated is that of *th* in *thou*; as the natural sound of *t* aspirated is that of *th* in *think*. This articulation from whatever cause, has not been admitted into the Gaelic, either Scottish or Irish; although it is used in the kindred dialects of Cornwall and Wales."

From what has been stated, it is evident that the chief use of the vowels is to represent the vocal sounds of speech, whilst the consonants represent its articulations or joints—hence their name. The vowels are continually varying, from diversity of tone or dialect in different districts. But the articulations or consonants are less subject to variations. The reason of this, is that the different modifications of the vowel sounds effected by easy, facile or minute changes, in the conformation of the organs uttering them; whilst those of the articulations are produced by more distinct and operose inflections of these organs.

It follows from this that the vowel sounds usually admitted are uttered with ease, in whatever situation they occur, for the same organs are employed for all; but as in forming the consonants or articulations, different organs act, a degree of difficulty is apt to arise in shifting from one articulation to another, when, as in certain words, they do not easily coalesce, and thus, for the sake of easing the pronunciation and to get rid of discordant sounds, a gradual alteration in the mode of spelling is prone to occur.

Hence it is found that the changes that occur in the articulations, spring from a cause more urgent and constant in its nature, as well as more uniform in its operation, than those which occur with the vowels, in which, a cause more local and temporary in its nature, as well as variable in its operations, acts.

If this idea or theory be correct, it ought to follow that in all polished tongues, an agreement should be found among the irregularities which occur to the articulations. That is not so marked in those which affect the vowel sounds.

As it appears then, that the vowel sounds in speech are constantly varying in the mouths of different speakers, from causes which either elude our search or are of trivial import, it would therefore be a vain attempt to make writing follow exactly all these minute variations, and although it may thus happen, that the same vowel-sound may be represented in some instances by different letters and *vice-versa*—different vowel-sounds by the same letters—yet this disagreement between speech and writing, must be tolerated, for the sake of preserving uniformity where alone it can exist, viz.—in the written language.

Again, if it appear that the variations from established analogy which are made in the articulations are less frequent, and proceed from obvious and cogent causes, ought not these variations to be exhibited in writing, for the very sake of preserving the general correspondence betweeen the *written* and *spoken* language, which must manifestly be maintained.

One exception, however, from this principle seems allowable, in the case of quiescent consonants, where these are requisite to point out the derivation of vocables on the radicals of declinable words ; but even here, the exception should be very limited, as in many instances the roots are easily discovered without any such index in the *written* any more than in the *spoken* language.

As before stated, it is one of the fundamental or settled principles in Orthography, " that *each letter* or combination of letters in the written language, should always denote *one and the same* sound." Yet in actual practice this rule is not strictly applicable, for, almost every one of the letters represent more than *one* sound ; yet it must be remembered, that there is an evident *affinity* between the several sounds of the same letter, and it will be readily admitted that less confusion and inconvenience follow from representing a few kindred sounds by the same letter, than would occur were the characters multiplied, so that each separate sound had its own appropriate letter.

As an example of departure from the principle above named, let me notice that in the case of the liquid consonants *L, N, R*, the distinction in Gaelic between the plain and aspirated state, is not signified in writing,—in both states the consonant is written in one way. This appears to be a mistake—analogy, the laws of inflection, and correctness, all require that this anomaly should cease to exist. In the vocative singular, and genitive and vocative plural of indefinite nouns, these letters assume their *attenuated* sounds and ought to be *aspirated*; so also in the aspirated cases of the adjective; again after the possessive pronoun *à* (his), and in the past tense and infinitive of verbs (*Forbes's Grammar*, page 10). If these letters were aspirated like the others (by affixing the letter *H*), the errors in reading and the ambiguities in Syntax would be done away with.

The 2*nd* principle of Orthography, "that each letter or combination of letters, should indicate only *one* special sound" is seldom violated in the Gaelic language. The sound of *ao* (*ao*—my second broad vowel) is sometimes represented by *a* alone, or by *o* alone; *dh* and *gh* final, have analogous sounds; *bh* and *mh* as before remarked, both sound *V* and are interchangeable; and *C* final, is sometimes sounded as *chd*; but these are the chief deviations from the rule.

The 3*rd* Rule of Orthography, viz.—"that no more letters ought to be employed than are necessary to represent the special sounds" —is one that is characteristically broken by all the polished or cultured tongues. In the English language the superabundance of letters is a frequent cause of perplexity—much increased by the *uncertainty of pronunciation* in those not redundant; as a single example, the combination *ough* varies in a remarkable way, as— *thorough, plough, enough, cough*, &c., &c.

G and *J* and *Y* in English are often transposed. Thus the English word *gate* from the saxon *geat* is called *yatt* in the upper parts of Yorkshire, and *yett* in the Lowland districts of Scotland.

J and *Y* are modifications of the vowel *I* articulated or turned into a consonant—the *J* being an importation from the French.

Q is a Latin redundancy, amply represented by *cu*, just as *X* can be by *ecs*.

In regard to Orthography, it has been remarked that "our utterance is warped the moment we set ourselves to observe and examine or note it;" and that "Orthography is always in the rear of pronunciation." Both of these dicta are true; but the standard that certainly determines Orthography is the *Press*. Hence, since the invention of Printing in the 15TH Century, the variations of spelling are comparatively small and insignificant.

In Gaelic, quiescent letters, both vowels and consonants, are not unfrequent; yet, although they have no sound themselves, they are not always without influence in pronunciation, as they often determine the sound of other letters. Most—if not all—of the quiescent vowels seem to have been introduced for this purpose, determining the broad or small sound of the adjoining consonants. Now, a consonant has its broad sound both when *preceded* and when *followed* by a broad vowel; in like manner it has its *small* sound, both when preceded and when followed by a small vowel. If a consonant were preceded by a broad vowel, and followed by a small vowel, or *vice versa*, it might be doubtful whether the consonant should be pronounced with its *broad* or with its *small* sound. Hence the rule of Gaelic Orthography, "*Leathan ri leathan 'us caol ri caol*"—broad to broad, and small to small; *i.e.*—that in polysyllables the last vowel of one syllable, and the first vowel of the next syllable, must be of the same quality.

"It is owing to the rigid observance of this rule, that so many diphthongs appear where the sound is expressed by a single vowel —and that the *homologous* vowels—when used in their quiescent capacity are interchanged or written indiscriminately for each other. The former cause loads most of the words in the language with superfluous vowels; from the latter, the orthography of many words appears unsettled and arbitrary." Both of these points may be considered as *blemishes* in the fair character of the Gaelic language, and the question may fairly be asked, whether this rule ought not in many cases to be set aside?

"The labials *b*, *m*, *f*, *p*, whether aspirated or not, have no distinction of broad and small sound. It cannot therefore be necessary to employ vowels, either prefixed or postfixed to indicate their sound; thus *abuaich* (ripe), *gabhaidh* (will take), *chromainn* (I would bow), *ciomaich* (captives), are written with a broad vowel in the second syllable, corresponding according to the rule, with the broad vowel in the first syllable, yet the letters *abich*, *gabhidh*, *chrominn*, *ciomich*, fully exhibit the sound!

"The prepositive syllable *im* when followed by a small vowel, is written *im* as in *imlich* (lick), *imcheist* (perplexity)—but when the first vowel of the following syllable is broad, it is the practice to insert an *o* before the *m* as in *iomlan* (complete), *iomghaoth* (a whirlwind), *iomluasj* (agitation), yet the inserted *o* serves no purpose in respect to the derivation, inflection, or pronunciation!

"The absurdity of the universal application of this rule, appears unequivocally in words derived from other languages; from the Latin words *imago*, *templum*, *liber*, are formed the Gaelic *iomhaidh*, *teampull*, *leabhar*. Nothing but a servile observance of the rule could have suggested the insertion of a broad vowel in the first syllable of these words, where it serves neither to guide the pronunciation, nor to indicate the derivation.

"Another instance in which the observance of this rule seems unnecessary, is when two syllables of a word are separated by a quiescent consonant:—thus in *gleidheadh* (keeping), *itheadh* (eating), *buidheann* (a company), *dligheach* (lawful), the aspirated consonants in the middle are altogether quiescent; the vocal sound of the second syllable is expressed by the last vowel—why then write a small vowel in the second syllable?

"But there are still other cases in which the rule might be safely laid aside.

"Many of the inflections of nouns and verbs are formed by adding one or more syllables to the root. The first consonant of the root must always be considered as belonging to the radical part—not to the adjective termination—the sound of that consonant whether broad or small, is determined by the quality of the vowel which precedes it in the same syllable, not by the quality of that which follows it in the next syllable. It seems therefore unnecessary to employ any more vowels in the adjected syllable, than what are sufficient to represent its own vocal sound. Yet the rule under consideration has been applied to the orthography of the oblique cases and tenses, and a supernumerary vowel is thrown into the termination, whenever that is requisite to preserve the qualitative co-relation with the next vowel in the preceding syllable. Thus in forming the nominative and dative plural of many nouns, the syllables *an* and *ibh* are added to the singular, and these letters fully express the true sounds of these terminations; if the last vowel of the nominative singular is broad, *an* alone is added to form the nominative plural, *e.g.*, *lamh-an* (hands), *cluas-an* (ears); but if the last vowel be small, an *e* is thrown into the termination, as in *suil-ean* (eyes), *sroinean* (noses). Now if it be observed, that in the two last examples, the small sound of the *l* and *n* in the root is determined by the *preceding* small vowel *i* with which they are necessarily connected in *one* syllable, and that the letters *an* fully represent the sound of the termination, it becomes evident that the *e* added in the last syllable is altogether superfluous and embarrassing.

"So, in forming the *dative* plural—if the last vowel of the root be small—*ibh* is added; *e.g.* *suilibh, sroinibh*. But, if it be broad the termination is written *aibh*, as *lamh-aibh, cluas-aibh* but the *a* here is totally useless.

"These remarks apply with equal force to the tenses of verbs, *e.g.* *creid-idh* (will believe), *stad-aidh* (will stop), *chreid-inn* (I would believe), *stad-ainn* (I would stop), *creid-ean* (let me believe), *stad-ain* (let me stop), creid-ibh (believe ye), *stad-aibh* (stop ye).

"The same observations may be further applied to derivative words formed by adding to their primitives the syllables—*ach*, *achd, ag, an, ail, as*—in all of which *e* has been uselessly introduced when the last vowel of the preceding syllable is small ; as *sauntach* (covetous), *toil-each* (willing), *naomh-achd* (holiness), *doimhn-eachd* (depth), *sruth-an* (a rivulet), *coul-ean* (a whelp) ; *cuach-ag* (a little cup), *cail-eag* (a lassie), *frarr-ail* (manly), *caird-eil* (friendly), *ceart-as* (justice), *caird-eas* (friendship)."

The foregoing remarks appear sufficient to establish the following general conclusions.

That in all cases in which a vowel serves neither to exhibit the vowel-sound, nor to modify the articulation of the syllable to which it belongs, it may be reckoned as nothing better than a useless encumbrance, and should be expunged.

There seems therefore, much reason for simplifying the present system of Gaelic orthography and pronunciation, by the rejection of a considerable number of quiescent vowels.

The pith of these latter observations, is drawn in a great measure from the admirable remarks made by the late Dr. Stewart, in his excellent grammar. Upwards of sixty years have elapsed since the publication of his second edition, yet no result has followed from the statement of his *cogent* opinion. Have I then taken too great a liberty in thus prominently bringing forward *his* great authority, and in using the fact as a powerful argument in favour of the foundation of a *Professorial Chair of Gaelic and the Kindred Celtic* at one or more of our great Scottish Universities, the very purpose and object of which, would be the study and teaching of the noble and venerable language—the correction of errors and abuses of orthography and style—and a renovation of its purity and vigour? Is it not the duty of all true Celts to further this cause to their utmost? Is there no rich Celt—no Highlander with *means,* as well as the *heart*—to found and endow such a Chair and Professorship? If not, "*mo naire* !"

In conclusion, I feel that there are many other points of interest connected with this national topic, upon which I have not ventured to touch; but, if by the remarks I have made and brought before your notice, I happily rouse the zeal of many of you, far better able than myself to lubricate the subject, my attempt will not have been in vain. In homely vernacular then, I will simply say to you all- -

"*Biannachd l'ibh.*"

MEMBERS OF SOCIETY

I. LIFE MEMBERS.

Cluny Macpherson of Cluny Macpherson.
Fraser-Mackintosh, Charles, of Drummond, M.P.
Halley, Alexander, M.D., 16 Harley Street, London.
Mackenzie, Sir Kenneth S, of Gairloch, Bart.

II. HONORARY MEMBERS.

Anderson, James, Solicitor, Inverness.
Blackie, Professor John Stuart, Edinburgh University.
Bourke, Very Rev. Canon, Pres. St. Jarlath's College, Tuam, Ireland.
Cameron, Captain D. C., Talisker.
Campbell, George Murray, Gampola, Ceylon.
Chisholm, Captain A. MacRae, Glassburn, Strathglass.
Colvin, John, Solicitor, Inverness.
Davidson, Duncan, of Tulloch, Ross-shire.
Davidson, Donald, Solicitor, Inverness.
Duff, George S., Sanquhar House, Forres.
Farquharson, Rev. Archibald, Tiree.
Ferguson, Mrs., Earnbank, Bridge of Earn.
Fraser, Huntly, Merchant, Inverness.
Grant, John, Cardiff, Wales.
Grant, General Sir Patrick, G.C.B., &c., Muirtown House,
    Inverness.
Grant, Robert, of Messrs. Macdougall & Co., Inverness.
Grant, William, Bellevue, Shrewsbury.
Innes, Charles, Solicitor, Inverness.
Macandrew, H. C., Sheriff Clerk of Inverness-shire.
Macdonald, Alexander, Balranald, Uist.
Macdonald, Allan, Solicitor, Inverness.
Macdonald, Andrew, Solicitor, Inverness.
Macdonald, Captain D. P., Ben-Nevis Distillery.
Macdonell, Patrick, Kinchyle, Dores.
Mackay, Donald, of Nicol & Co., Holm Mills, Inverness.
Mackay, Donald, Gampola, Kandy, Ceylon.
Mackay, Donald, 267 South Displainer Street, Chicago.

Mackay, George F., Roxburgh, Otago, New Zealand.
Mackay, James, Roxburgh, Otago, New Zealand.
Mackay, John, C.E., Mountsfield, Shrewsbury.
Mackay, John, of Ben-Reay, near Montreal.
Mackay, John Stuart, 267 South Displainer Street, Chicago.
Mackay, Neil, Dowlais, Merthyr-Tydvil, Wales.
Mackenzie, Rev. A.D., Free Church, Kilmorack.
Mackenzie, Major Colin Lyon, of St Martins, Provost of Inverness.
Mackenzie, Colonel Hugh, Poyntzfield House, Invergordon.
Mackenzie, John, M.D., of Eileanach, Inverness.
Mackenzie, Osgood H., of Inverewe, Poolewe.
Mackintosh, Æneas W., of·Raigmore, M.P.
Mackintosh, P. A., Clutton, Somersetshire.
Maclean, Rev. John, Free Church, Stratherrick.
Maclennan, Alexander, of Messrs. Macdougall & Co., Inverness.
Macpherson, Captain Gordon, of Cluny.
Menzies, John, Caledonian Hotel, Inverness.
Neaves, The Hon. Lord, L.L.D., Edinburgh.
Nicolson, Angus, L.L.B., Editor of *The Gael*, Glasgow.
Ross, Rev. William, Rothesay.
Scott, Roderick, Solicitor, Inverness.
Seafield, The Right Hon. the Earl of, Castle Grant.
Shaw, A. Mackintosh, Secretary's Office, General Post Office, London.
Stewart, Charles, of Brin and Dalcrombie, Inverness.
Stoddart, Evan, Burundalla, Sydney, Australia.
Sutherland, Alexander, Taff Brae Cottage, Cefn, Merthyr-Tydvil.
Sutherland-Walker, Evan Charles, of Skibo.

III. ORDINARY MEMBERS.

Alison, James Mackenzie, Redcastle.
Baillie, Bailie Peter, Inverness.
Bannatyne, W. Mackinnon, Royal Academy, Inverness.
Barclay, John, Accountant, 67 Church Street, Inverness.
Black, George, Brewer, Inverness.
Brownlie, Alexander, Rector, Raining School, Inverness.
Cameron, Archibald, Auchafarick, Muasdale, Kintyre.
Cameron, Colin, Polmaily, Glen-Urquhart.
Cameron, Donald, of Lochiel, M.P.
Campbell, Donald, Draper, Bridge Street, Inverness.
Campbell, George J., Writer and N.P., Union Street, Inverness.
Campbell, Fraser, of Fraser & Campbell, High Street, Inverness.
Campbell, T. D., of Cumming & Campbell, Ness Bank, Inverness.

N

Carmichael, Alexander A., Excise Officer, Lochmaddy, Uist.
Charleson, Hector, Church Street, Inverness.
Charleson, Kenneth, Highland Club, Inverness.
Cook, Alexander, Glen-Urquhart.
Couper, William, 5 Huntly Place, Inverness.
Cullen, James M'C., 63 Stevenson Street, Calton, Glasgow.
Dallas, Alexander, Town Clerk, Inverness.
Davidson, James, Solicitor, Inverness.
Davidson, Lachlan, Banker, Kingussie.
Falconer, Peter, Plasterer, Inverness.
Forbes, Dr. George Fiddes, of the Bombay Army, Viewfield
    House, Inverness.
Forsyth, Ebenezer, *Inverness Advertiser* Office, Inverness.
Forsyth, W. B., of *The Inverness Advertiser*, Inverness.
Fraser, A. R., British Linen Company's Bank, Kingussie.
Fraser, Alexander, Drummond Estate Office, Union Street,
    Inverness.
Fraser, Alexander, Solicitor, Inverness.
Fraser, Andrew, Builder, Inverness.
Fraser, Andrew, Cabinetmaker, Union Street, Inverness.
Fraser, D., Glenelg.
Fraser, Donald, Solicitor, 9 Castle Street, Inverness.
Fraser, Hugh, Inspector of Poor, Inverness.
Fraser, James, of Fraser & MacTavish, Lombard Street, Inverness.
Fraser, James, C.E., Inverness.
Fraser, James, Mauld, Strathglass.
Fraser, James, Manufacturer, 41 North Albion St., Glasgow.
Fraser, Kenneth, Writer, 67 Church St., Inverness.
Fraser, Miss, Farraline Villa, North Berwick.
Fraser, Simon, Banker, Lochcarron.
Fraser, William, Jeweller, High Street, Inverness.
Fraser, William, Iron Founder, Inverness.
Fraser, William, Glenconon, Skye.
Galloway, George, Chemist, Inverness.
Garden, Archibald, Thornbush, Inverness.
Gollan, John Gilbert, of Gollanfield, 56 Lansdowne Road, London.
Hood, Andrew, Commercial Traveller, 39 Union Street, Inverness.
Hood, Miss, 39 Union Street, Inverness.
Keith, Charles, Bookseller, Inverness.
Kennedy, Donald, Farmer, Drumashie, Dores.
Kennedy, Neil, Kishorn, Lochcarron.
Macbean, Bailie Alexander, Inverness.
Macculloch, Duncan, Teacher, 55 Castle St., Inverness.
Macdonald, Alexander, Messenger at Arms, Inverness.

Macdonald, Alex., Flesher, New Market, Inverness.
Macdonald, Angus, Queen Street, Inverness.
Macdonald, Andrew L., Sheriff, Telford Street, Inverness.
Macdonald, Colin, Draper, High Street, Inverness.
Madonald, Finlay, Druidaig, Kintail.
Macdonald, James, clerk, National Bank of Scotland, Inverness.
Macdonald, John, Merchant, Exchange, Inverness.
Macdonald, John, Excise Office, Lanark.
Macdonald, Robert, 48 Telford Road, Inverness.
Macdonald, William, M.D., Inverness.
Macdougall, Donald, Craggan, Grantown.
Macgregor, Donald, 42 Glassford Street, Glasgow.
Macgregor, Rev. Malcolm, F. C. Manse, Ferrintosh.
MacIver, Donald, Student of Aberdeen University, Church Street,
    Inverness.
MacIver, Duncan, Cabinetmaker, Church Street, Inverness.
MacIver, Finlay, Carver, 72 Church Street, Inverness.
Mackay, Alex., Carpenter, 32 Rose Street, Inverness.
Mackay, Charles, Builder, Culduthel Road, Inverness.
Mackay, David, Publisher, 33 Bridge Street, Inverness.
Mackay, George, Royal Artillery, Gun Wharf Barracks, Ports-
    mouth.
Mackay, Robert, Merchant, Hamilton Place, Inverness.
Mackay, William, Writer, with Messrs. Gibson-Craig, Dalziel, &
    Brodies, W.S., Edinburgh.
Mackay, William, Bookseller, High Street, Inverness.
Mackenzie, Alexander, Clothier, 2 High Street, Inverness.
Mackenzie, Alexander, Grocer, 22 Church Street, Inverness.
Mackenzie, A. C., Teacher, Maryburgh, Dingwall.
Mackenzie, E. G., Solicitor, Inverness.
Mackenzie, C. D., 102 Linthorpe Road, Middlesbro' on Tees.
Mackenzie, Donald, Grocer, 31 High Street, Inverness.
Mackenzie, Finlay Matheson, 208 Stirling Road, Glasgow.
Mackenzie, Hector, Gollanfield House, Fort George.
Mackenzie, Hector, 54 Telford Road, Inverness.
Mackenzie, Hugh, Bookbinder, Inverness.
Mackenzie, Captain John, 62 Telford Road, Inverness.
Mackenzie, James H., Bookseller, High Street, Inverness.
Mackenzie, Malcolm J., Teacher, Parish School, Lochcarron.
Mackenzie, Thomas, late of High School, Broadstone Park,
    Inverness.
Mackenzie, William, 17 Telford Road, Inverness.
Mackenzie, William, Draper, 10 Bridge Street, Inverness.
Mackinnon, Charles, Back Street, Campbeltown, Argyle.

Mackintosh, Charles, Commission Agent, Church Street, Inverness.
Mackintosh, Donald, The Hotel, Glenelg.
Mackintosh, Duncan, Bank of Scotland, Oban.
Mackintosh, Ewen, Roy Bridge Hotel, by Kingussie.
Mackintosh, John, Divinity Student, Mauld, Strathglass.
Mackintosh, Lachlan, Milton of Farr, Daviot.
Mackintosh, Peter, Draper's Assistant, Hunt Hall, Inverness.
Maclachlan, Duncan, Publisher, 64 South Bridge, Edinburgh.
Maclean, Alexander, of Black, M'Lean & Co., Lombard Street, Inverness.
Maclennan, Alexander, Clerk, N. C. Fire Office, Inverness.
Maclennan, Ewen, 45 High Street, Inverness.
Maclennan, Kenneth, Clothier, 14 Museum Street, Ipswich.
Macleod, Alexander, Grocer, Huntly Street, Inverness.
Macmillan, John, 2 High Street, Inverness.
Macneil, Nigel, 84 Argyle Street, Glasgow.
Macphail, Alex., Farmer, Cullaird, Dores.
Macphater, Angus, Lintmill of Campbeltown, Argyle.
Macpherson, Col. A. F., of Catlodge, Waverley Hotel, Inverness.
Macpherson, Pryse, 2 Hill Street, Richmond, Surrey.
Macpherson, Mrs Sarah, Alexandra Villa, Kingussie.
Macrae, Rev. Alex., Free Church Manse, Strathpeffer.
Macrae, Rev. Angus, Glen-Urquhart.
Macrae, Donald, High School, Inverness.
Macrae, Duncan, Braintraith, Lochalsh.
Macrae, Duncan A., Fernaig, Lochalsh.
Macrae, R., Postmaster, Beauly.
Macraild, A. R., Inspector of Poor, Lochalsh.
Menzies, Duncan, Millarton, Inverness.
Mundell, John, Scallisaig, Glenelg.
Munro, James, London House, Inverness.
Munro, John, Wine Merchant, Inverness.
Murdoch, John, Editor of *The Highlander*, Inverness.
Murray, William, Chief Constable, The Castle, Inverness.
Noble, Donald, Baker, Muirtown Street, Inverness.
Noble, John, Bookseller, Castle Street, Inverness.
Rose, A. Macgregor, Divinity Student, 15 College Bounds, Old Aberdeen.
Rose, Hugh, Solicitor, Inverness.
Ross, Alexander, Architect, Inverness.
Ross, James, Shipowner, Portland Place, Inverness.
Ross, John, Auctioneer, Inverness.
Ross, Jonathan, Draper, 4 High Street, Inverness.
Rule, William Taylor, Solicitor, Inverness.

Shaw, Donald, Solicitor, Inverness.
Simpson, Bailie Alexander, Inverness.
Sinclair, Duncan, Teacher, Parish School, Lochalsh.
Sinclair, Roderick, 15 High Street, Inverness.
Stewart, Colin S., Dingwall.
Sutherland, Rev. A. C., Strathbraan, Perthshire.
Tulloch, John, Painter, Academy Street, Inverness.
White, John, 93 North Frederick Street, Glasgow.
Wilson, George, S.S.C., 14 Hill Street, Edinburgh.

IV. APPRENTICES, or JUNIOR MEMBERS.

Macbean, Lachlan, Draper's Assistant, 6 Castle Street, Inverness.
Macaskill, D., with D. Watson, Long Row, Campbeltown, Argyle.
Macdonald, Murdoch, with Mac Iver & Co., Church Street, Inverness.
Mackenzie, Alex., 17 Telford Road, Inverness.
Maclennan, Donald, 15 Innes Street, Inverness.
Macpherson, Wm., with Mac Iver & Co., Church Street, Inverness.
Noble, Andrew, Assistant Grocer, 9 Bridge Street, Inverness.
Ross, Donald, 39 Union Street, Inverness.
Smith, Alex., Assistant Grocer, 9 Bridge Street, Inverness.
Thomson, Robert, The Grocery, High Street, Inverness.
Watson, David, with D. Watson, Long Row, Campbeltown, Argyle.

Highlander Newspaper and Printing and Publishing Company, Limited, Inverness.

TRANSACTIONS

OF THE

GAELIC SOCIETY OF INVERNESS.

VOLS. III. AND IV.,

1873-4 & 1874-5.

a Celt

TRANSACTIONS

OF

THE GAELIC SOCIETY

OF

INVERNESS.

VOLUMES III. AND IV.,

YEARS 1873-4 & 1874-5.

𝕮lann nan 𝕲aidheil ri 𝕲uaillean a' 𝕮heile.

INVERNESS:

PUBLISHED FOR THE GAELIC SOCIETY OF INVERNESS,
BY JOHN NOBLE, JAMES H. MACKENZIE, AND WILLIAM MACKAY,
BOOKSELLERS, AND
BY MACLACHLAN AND STEWART, EDINBURGH.

1 8 7 5

31256

PRINTED AT THE COURIER OFFICE, INVERNESS.

CONTENTS.

———◦◦⦂✕⦂◦◦———

1 8 7 3 - 7 4.

PAGE

The Gaelic Society of Inverness.

OFFICE-BEARERS.

YEAR 1874.

CHIEF.
ir Kenneth S. Mackenzie of Gairloch, Bart.

CHIEFTAINS.
Thomas Mackenzie, Broadstone Park
Sheriff Macdonald, Telford Street
John Murdoch, Highlander.

HONORARY SECRETARY.
orge James Campbell, writer, Church Street

SECRETARY.
Donald Macrae, High School, ad interim.

TREASURER.
James Fraser, C.E., Castle Street

COUNCIL.
Charles Mackay, Culduthel Road
John Macdonald, Exchange
Jonathan Ross, 4 High Street
W. Mackinnon Bannatyne, Royal Academy
D. Macrae, Charles Street

LIBRARIAN.
Lachlan Macbean, Castle Street

BARD.
Angus Macdonald

PIPER.
Pipe-Major Alexander Maclennan

YEAR 1875.

CHIEF.
C. Fraser-Mackintosh, Esq. of Drummond, M

CHIEFTAINS.
Sheriff Macdonald, Telford Street
Charles Mackay, Culduthel Road
Dr F. M. Mackenzie, 54 Church Street

HONORARY SECRETARY.
George James Campbell, writer, Church Stre

SECRETARY.
Alex. Mackenzie, auctioneer, 57 Church Stre

TREASURER.
Councillor John Noble, 12 Castle Street

COUNCIL.
John Macdonald, The Exchange
Donald Campbell, draper, Bridge Street
Donald Macrae, High School
William Mackenzie, Free Press
James H. Mackenzie, bookseller, High Str

LIBRARIAN.
Lachlan Macbean

BARD.
Vacant.

PIPER.
Pipe-Major Alexander Maclennan

BANKERS.
The Caledonian Banking Company

COMUNN GAILIG INBHIR-NIS.

CO-SHUIDHEACHADH.

1. 'S e aium a Chomuinn "COMUNN GAILIG INBHIR-NIS."

2. 'S e tha an rùn a' Chomuinn:—Na buill a dheanamh iomlan s a' Ghàilig; cinneas Cànaine, Bardachd, agus Ciùil na Gàidhealtachd; Bardachd, Seanachas, Sgeulachd, Leabhraichean agus Sgriobhanna 's a' chànain sin a thearnadh o dhearmad; Leabhar-lann a chur suas ann am baile Inbhir-Nis de leabhraichibh agus sgriobhannaibh— ann an cànain sam bith—a bhuineas do Chàileachd, Ionnsachaidh, Eachdraidheachd agus Sheanachasaibh nan Gàidheal no do thairbhe na Gàidhealtachd; còir agus cliù nan Gàidheal a dhìon; agus na Gàidheil a shoirbheachadh a ghuà ge b'e àit am bi iad.

3. 'S iad a bhitheas 'nam buill, cuideachd a tha 'gabhail suim do rùntaibh a' Chomuinn, agus so mar gheibh iad a staigh:—Tairgidh aon bhall an t-iarradair, daingnichidh ball eile an tairgse, agus, aig an ath choinneamh, ma roghnaicheas a' mhor-chuid le crannchur, nithear ball dhith-se no dheth-san cho luath 's a phaidhear an comh-thoirt; cuirear crainn le ponair dhubh agus gheal, ach, gu so bhi dligheach, feumaidh tri buill dheug an crainn a chur. Feudaidh an Comunn Urram Cheannardan a thiort do urrad 'us seachd daoine cliùiteach.

4. Pàidhidh ball urramach, 'sa' bhliadhna   .£0 10 6
   Ball cumnta 0 5 0
   Foghlainte 0 1 0
   Agus ni ball-beatha aon chomh-thoirt de   . 7 7 0

5. 'S a' Cheud-mhios, gach bliadhna, roghnaichear, le crainn, Co-chomhairle a riaghlas gnothuichean a' Chomuinn, 's e sin—aon Cheann, tri Iar-chinn, Cleireach Urramach, Runaire, Ionmhasair, agus còig buill eile—feumaidh iad nile Gàilig a thuigsinn 's a bhruidhinn; agus ni còigear dhiubh coinneamh.

GAELIC SOCIETY OF INVERNESS.

CONSTITUTION.

1. The Society shall be called the "GAELIC SOCIETY OF INVERNESS."

2. The objects of the Society are the perfecting of the Members in the use of the Gaelic language; the cultivation of the language, poetry, and music of the Scottish Highlands; the rescuing from oblivion of Celtic poetry, traditions, legends, books, and manuscripts; the establishing in Inverness of a library, to consist of books and manuscripts, in whatever language, bearing upon the genius, the literature, the history, the antiquities, and the material interests of the Highlands and Highland people; the vindication of the rights and character of the Gaelic people; and, generally, the furtherance of their interests whether at home or abroad.

3. The Society shall consist of persons who take a lively interest in its objects, admission to be as follows:—The candidate shall be proposed by one member, seconded by another, balloted for at the next meeting, and if he or she have a majority of votes, and have paid the subscription, be declared a member. The ballot shall be taken with black beans and white; and no election shall be valid unless thirteen members vote. The Society has power to elect distinguished men as Honorary Chieftains to the number of seven.

4. The Annual Subscription shall be, for—

	£	s	d
Honorary Members . .	£0	10	6
Ordinary Members . .	0	5	0
Apprentices . . .	0	1	0
A Life Member shall make one payment of	7	7	0

5. The management of the affairs of the Society shall be entrusted to a Council, chosen annually, by ballot, in the month of January, to consist of a Chief, three Chieftains, an Honorary Secretary, a Treasurer, and five other Members of the Society, all of whom shall understand and speak Gaelic; five to form a quorum.

6. Cumar coinneamhan a' Chomuinn gach seachduin o thoiseach an Deicheamh mios gu deireadh Mhàirt, agus gach ceithir-la-deug o thoiseach Ghiblein gu deireadh an Naothamh-mios. 'S i a' Ghàilig a labhairear gach oidhche mu'n seach aig a chuid a's lugba.

7. Cuiridh a' Cho-chomhairle là air leth anns an t-Seachdamh-mios air-son Coinneamh Bhliadhnail aig an cumar Co-dheuchainn agus air an toirear duaisean air-son Piobaireachd 'us ciùil Ghàidh-ealach eile; anns an fheasgar bithidh co-dheuchainn air Leughadh agus aithris Bardachd agus Rosg nuadh agus taghta; an deigh sin cumar Cuirm chuideachdail aig am faigh nithe Gàidhealach rogh-ainu 'san uirghioll, ach gun roinn a dhiùltadh dhaibh-san nach tuig Càilig. Giùlainear cosdas na co-dheuchainne le trusadh sònraichte a dheanamh agus cuideachadh iarraidh o'n t-sluagh.

8. Cha deanar atharrachadh sam bith air coimh-dhealbhadh a' Chomuinn gun aontachadh dha-thrian de nam bheil de luchd-bruidhinn Gàilig air a' chlar-ainm. Ma's miann atharrachadh a dheanamh a's èiginn sin a chur an cèill do gach ball, mios, aig a' chuid a's lugha, roimh'n choinneamh a dh'fheudas an t-atharrathadh a dheanamh. Feudaigh ball nach bi 'a làthair roghnachadh le lamh-àithne.

9. Taghaidh an Comunn Bàrd, Pìobaire, agus Fear-leabhar-lann.

Ullaichear gach Paipear agus Leughadh, agus giùlainear gach Deasboireachd le rùn fosgailte, duineil, dùrachdach air-son na fìrinn, agus cuirear gach ni air aghaidh ann an spiorad caomh glan, agus a reir riaghailtean dearbhta.

6. The Society shall hold its meetings weekly from the beginning of October to the end of March, and fortnightly from the beginning of April to the end of September. The business shall be carried on in Gaelic on every alternate night at least.

7. There shall be an Annual Meeting in the month of July, the day to be named by the Committee for the time being, when Competitions for Prizes shall take place in Pipe and other Highland Music. In the evening there shall be Competitions in Reading and Reciting Gaelic Poetry and Prose, both original and select. After which there will be a Social Meeting, at which Gaelic subjects shall have the preference, but not to such an extent as entirely to preclude participation by persons who do not understand Gaelic. The expenses of the competitions shall be defrayed out of a special fund to which the general public shall be invited to subscribe.

8. It is a fundamental rule of the Society that no part of the Constitution shall be altered without the assent of two-thirds of the Gaelic-speaking Members on the roll; but if an alteration be required, due notice of the same must be given to each member, at least one month before the meeting takes place at which the altertion is proposed to be made. Absent Members may vote by mandates.

9. The Society shall elect a Bard, a Piper, and a Librarian.

All Papers and Lectures shall be prepared, and all Discussions carried on, with an honest, earnest, and manful desire for truth; and all proceedings shall be conducted in a pure and gentle spirit, and according to the usually recognised rules.

INTRODUCTION.

———o-›;•;o‹o———

In introducing the Society's Transactions to the members at this period, we have to express regret for the delay which has taken place. Various reasons may be given, among others the unavoidable changes which have taken place among the office-bearers of the Society. We, however, have not been idle for the last two years, as will be seen from perusal of this volume, which embraces the Transactions up to date. The most important subjects of all to Highlanders and to the Celt generally, in which the Gaelic Society has taken an active interest during that time, are the establishment of a Celtic Professorship in one of our Scottish Universities, and the teaching of Gaelic in Highland Schools. What we have already done, and are still doing, will be seen in these Transactions, but we think it proper in this Introduction to give a short history of what has been done by others as well as by ourselves, to bring about the present feeling in favour, and we might say, the assured success of the movement for the institution of the Celtic Chair. The Gaelic Society of London stands out pre-eminently among all others for its exertions in this cause, and that single-handed, for nearly half-a-century. It is impossible to give the history of the movement, without according considerable space to the doings of that Society on this particular subject, while they were equally energetic in all movements calculated to benefit the Celt, his language, and literature. James Logan, who was at one time (1835-1838) Secretary to the Highland Society of London, says, in a preface to the book-list of the Gaelic Society (1840), that "the name of the first coterie was the *Gaelic Society*. The Society rapidly increased in numbers and respectability. One of their first acts was to obtain the repeal, in 1782, of the repugnant law which made it felony for a Highlander to wear his native dress." After the American War several officers joined the Society, and considering "Gaelic Society" too circumscribed a designation, that of " Highland Society" was adopted.

Although in the original constitution of the Highland Society, one of the objects was the founding of a Professorship in one of the Scottish Universities, the Lowland element became too powerful, and the Celtic sentiments of the Society consequently became comparatively enfeebled. In 1808 the "Gaelic Society" was again resuscitated, through the exertions of Rev. Duncan Robertson, a gentleman to whom also belongs the credit of instituting a fund, amounting to £4000, for the support of a Gaelic preacher in London. In 1816, however, the title of Gaelic Society was again overwhelmed, by the good-natured inclination of the members, allowing gentlemen other than Gaelic-speaking members to attend their meetings. Members from all parts of Scotland were admitted, and by their influence the name was again altered, this time to that of " The Club of True Highlanders." The minority, anxious to have concourse with their fellow-natives, afterwards succeeded in re-establishing their old Society, under the classical title of " The Sons of Morven." Although the name was changed, the Gaelic language was used " in the conversation of all the meetings." Some of the members of the Highland Society joined this body—notably, General Stewart of Garth, 78th Highlanders ; General Sir Alan Cameron of Erracht, 79th Highlanders; and General John Macdonald of Dalchoisnie. Among other names are found—Donald Mackinnon, M.D.; Murdo Young, an Invernessian, and subsequently proprietor of the *Sun* newspaper; Dr Andw. Robertson, &c. This coterie pursued a course more decidedly of a literary nature than its predecessors or contemporaries—-subjects of Highland interest being regularly debated. Prizes were awarded among the members for the best essays on Celtic subjects. They collected a number of valuable books, papers, and MSS., which were unfortunately destroyed, along with their minutes, by a fire which burnt the premises. This catastrophe caused the suspension for a time of the regular meetings of the "Sons." A remnant of them, however, kept it from extinction, among whom were Mr Wm. Menzies, musical manager to Nathaniel Gow, and Lewis Macdougal. To these two gentlemen are we indebted for the re-institution of the present Gaelic Society of London, in 1830. They met for fifteen years in the British Coffee-house, Cockspur Street. Their principal object was "to accustom the members to the language, poetry, music, and dress of Caledonia." In 1840 "the Society accumulated 260 volumes of books on various subjects, and in several languages; forty-five essays have been read; besides these the library contains an unique collection of tracts and pamphlets on the state of feeling during the disturbances of 1715 and '45." The library also contains a copy of petition prepared by the Gaelic Society, in favour of the institution of a Professor in the University of *Aberdeen*, for the teaching of the Celtic languages, and presented to the House of Commons in 1835. In 1839 the Society presented another petition for the same object, but withdrawing the selection of Aberdeen. The second petition was taken charge of by Mr Campbell of Islay, M.P. for Argyllshire, W. A. Mackinnon, M.P. for Rye, and Sir George Sinclair, Bart., M.P. for Caithness. On its presentation, the Chancellor of the Exchequer, Mr Spring Rice, took exception to its being received, for the reason that "petitions praying for grants of money were inadmissible." The following afternoon Mr Campbell obtained the consent of the Chancellor to receive a deputation of the petitioners on the subject of their rejected petition. The deputation consisted of Mr Jas. Stewart, Albemarle Street; Mr Wm. Menzies, Golden Square; and Mr John Cameron Macphee, the present President of the Gaelic Society of London. The Chancellor was particularly struck with astonishment when told that the ministers of Highland parishes received no training in the language in which they expounded the Scriptures to the people, except what they knew of it from reading or general conversation. He then suggested (addressing himself to Mr Campbell of Islay), that Highlanders should give an earnest of their desire for establishing a Celtic Chair by subscribing to a fund for that purpose, after which the Treasury would consider the alternative of granting an equal sum to that subscribed. This alternative appeared too much for these Celtic pioneers, and the subject was for a time given up. In 1840 the Earl of Aboyne became Patron of the Society, and was taught Gaelic for five or six years by D. Macpherson, one of the members. In 1847 the Society took steps and collected subscriptions to alleviate the distress brought about by the famine in Ireland and the Western Highlands. A ball given in Willis's Rooms alone producing £500, after paying all expenses. Captain Lamont, R.N., was treasurer of this fund, and John Cameron Macphee, hon. secretary.

The Scottish fetes at Holland Park, patronised daily by the Queen, the Prince Consort, and the aristocracy, were supported by the Gaelic Society. Its representatives, Wm. Menzies and John Cameron Macphee, were appointed judges of the competitions.

The Gaelic Society never lost sight of the Celtic Professorship, and in 1869, at one of their monthly meetings, the subject was brought forward, when a committee was nominated to investigate what had been done, and what could be done, to awaken the nation for the removal of this stigma on the language of so considerable a portion of the population of Scotland. A proposition was submitted by P. H. Cameron, then English Secretary for the Society, and now "S.S.C." in Edinburgh, and by the Gaelic Secretary, J. C. Macphee, to address circulars to all the ministers of Highland parishes and of other denominations throughout the Highlands, asking their views on the desirability of establishing a Celtic Professorship in one of the Scottish Universities, and to what extent Gaelic was preached in their respective parishes. The Society adopted the proposal. The circulars, dated 10th December 1869, with forms of reply, were prepared, and despatched (prepaid there and back). The first reply was from the Free Church Manse of Campbelltown, dated 11th January 1870, and signed "John L. Maclean." The circulars were returned in most cases, with detailed information, and the result showed that out of 3395 places of worship of all denominations in Scotland, 461 had Gaelic services once-a-day in the following proportions :—Established Church, 235; Free Church, 166; Catholic Chapels, 36; Baptists, 12; Episcopalians, 9; Congregationalists, 3.

At a general meeting of the Society, held on the third Tuesday of January 1870, further steps were taken to agitate the removal of this flagrant indifference exhibited towards the cherished language of our Highland countrymen. Aware that some of the objects for which the Highland Society of London was instituted were the "preservation of the Gaelic language," and "to establish a Professor of Gaelic in one or more of the Universities of Scotland," one of the first proposals made at this meeting was to instruct the Secretaries "to draw the attention of the Court of Directors of the Highland Society to the desirability of instituting the Professorship for Gaelic, and suggesting a joint committee of the two Societies (the Highland and the Gaelic), to co-operate for the accomplishment *now* of this too long deferred act of justice to the language." To this communication Sir Patrick Colquhoun, the honorary secretary, replied, under date 3d April 1870:—

"Dear Sirs,—There being no quorum of the Highland Society (the 8th March), the consideration of the Gaelic Professorship question was postponed. This need not, however, prevent your proceeding *independently* of the Highland Society."

This reply was not calculated to cheer the smaller but far more patriotic Society, nor was it likely to inspire confidence in the sincerity of ultimate co-operation. At a future meeting it was decided to institute systematic proceedings in the press, and through other public channels, to aid the attainment of this, one of the articles of faith of the Gaelic Society. A consultation at this juncture, with the editor of the *London Scotsman*, resulted in the determination to make arrangements to get together such gentlemen as could be influenced, and thus ventilate the subject through members of the London daily press. Three articles appeared soon after on the subject in the *London Scotsman*, from the pen of Professor Blackie. Some time afterwards the following circular, dated 3d May 1870, was received by the Society from Professor Macgregor :—

" Extract from the minutes of meeting of the General Council of the University of Edinburgh, of date 19th April 1870. The Council remitted to the following committee to report on the question of establishing a Chair of Celtic Literature.
(Signed) " THOMAS GILBERT,
" Secretary of General Council."

The Gaelic Society of London supplied the Committee told off by the University Council with their tabulated statement, and all the other valuable information in their possession. In the month of November 1870, Mr Alexander Mackenzie, now Secretary of this Society, read a paper before the Inverness Literary Institute, on the Gaelic Professorship. In the paper he referred to the work done by the Gaelic Society of London for the establishment of a Chair for teaching the Celtic language in one of the Scottish Universities, the desirability, and even the necessity, of having such a Chair established, and concluded by suggesting that a Gaelic Society should be established in Inverness, having for its objects the preservation and cultivation of the Gaelic language and literature, and by which many other interesting subjects closely connected with the Highlands might receive some amount of attention. The suggestion was laughed at by some, and warmly supported by others. The paper afterwards appeared in the "Inverness Advertiser" and in the "London Scotsman." For a time, the subject of establishing this Society was not pushed, but it was not lost sight of.

In the spring of the following year, a letter appeared in the correspondence column of the "Inverness Advertiser," signed " U'. M'C.," proposing the establishment of a " Celtic Debating Society" in Inverness. Replies were written by " F. D. G.," " J. M'G.," " Caberfeidh, Ross-shire," " Meallfuarvonie," and " Clachnacudain," all enthusiastic in support of the proposal in favour of having some Celtic Society in our midst. Who the writer "F. D. G." was we have never learned. "U'. M'C." were the Gaelic initials of William Mackenzie, now Inverness representative of the "Aberdeen Free Press;" "J. M'G." was John Macgillivray, Tain; "Caberfeidh" was Mr A. C. Mackenzie, schoolmaster, Maryburgh; "Meallfuarvonie" was Mr William Mackay, now solicitor in Inverness; and "Clachnacudain" was Mr Alexander Mackenzie, the present secretary of the Society. It may be remarked that "Meallfuarvonie" and "U'. M'C." also held that office.

In the autumn of 1871 the Society was established, under most auspicious circumstances, for particulars of which we refer our readers to the first volume of Transactions issued by the Society. Shortly after this, Celtic Societies were established in Oban, Tobermory, Greenock, Glasgow, Aberdeen, and other places, and those previously in existence received an *impetus*, and exhibited an energy and activity in the good cause previously unknown. In 1871 Mr Angus Nicolson brought over his "Gael" from Canada; the "Highlander" made his appearance in the Highland Capital in 1873; *Bratach Na Firrinn* followed. The "Highland Pioneer" appeared two months ago. "Celtic columns" were started in several North-country newspapers, and a feeling was produced which made the tiny rivulet first set forth by the Gaelic Society of London gradually gather volume strong enough to carry before it all previous obstructions in a roaring torrent of "liberal culture," but which was at an earlier stage in some quarters gracefully designated "negative Highland bigotry."

On the 14th of October 1874, Professor Blackie delivered his lecture on the Celtic Professorship, under the auspices of our Society, in the Music Hall, Inverness. The result is already well known, and surprised no one more than the redoubted Professor himself. "Blackie! Celtic Chair! Success!" express more than we could write in a volume.

Among the societies which have not only exerted themselves to procure subscriptions from the public and individual members, but which have subscribed liberally out of their own funds, we may mention the Glasgow Celtic Society, the Greenock Highland

Society, Dundee Celtic Society, Royal Celtic Society of Edinburgh, Skye Association of Glasgow, Highland Literary Association of Glasgow, Glasgow Sutherland Association, Lorne Ossianic Society, Highland Society of London, Inverness, Ross, and Nairn Club, the Highlanders of Birmingham and of Burrow-in-Furness, our own Society, and others. The Gaelic Society of London has organised a London committee, and are now actively engaged collecting subscriptions.

In concluding these introductory remarks, we would request that members at a distance would send us on papers to be read at the meetings of the Society and for publication in our next volume of Transactions, especially would we urge upon members to supply us with the folk-lore of their district, and with papers and MSS. bearing upon the genius, literature, history, and antiquities of the Celt at home and abroad. We crave the indulgence of our readers for many errors and shortcomings, many of them in consequence of the rapidity with which the volume was hurried through the press.

Inverness, 28th June 1875.

TRANSACTIONS.

15TH JULY 1873.

At this meeting (the first of the session) it was unanimously agreed to ask Tulloch to preside at Dr Mackay's lecture, to be delivered on the following Monday. James Fraser, C.E., was elected Treasurer *ad interim*, in room of Mr Mackintosh, who was leaving Inverness for Oban. A large number of new members were elected, including the Earl of Seafield.

19TH JULY 1873.

A special meeting was held in the Music Hall, to hear a lecture from CHAS. MACKAY, LL.D., on

"THE SCOTCH IN AMERICA."

Duncan Davidson of Tulloch occupied the chair, supported by Dr Carruthers and Thomas Mackenzie, Esq., Broadstone Park. There were also present—The Rev. Alexander Macgregor, M.A.; Bailie Simpson; Alex. Mackenzie, Clachnacudain House; D. Maciver, Chas. Mackay; Æneas Mackintosh, Dalmigavie; Councillor Rose; G. J. Campbell, &c., &c. We give the following condensed report of the lecture.

Dr Mackay said—In speaking upon the subject of America, I speak from personal experience, extending over a period of nearly four years. It is calculated that there are ten millions of Scotch men and women in the world—Highlanders and Lowlanders; and that perhaps not less than four, and not more than five millions live at home in their own beautiful and romantic land. The Scotch are scattered all over the earth where there is liberty, wealth, and honour to be gained—(Hear, hear)—whether it be at the point of the sword or nip of the bayonet. By perseverance and hard work—by head or hand—wherever they go, they prosper. They are not contented with a humble place or station in life, if a higher one is in their reach. Much has been said about their national character, and more perhaps of its effects. Both friends and foes have been led to admit that although the Scotchman is a firm antagonist, he is a dear friend, and that whatever he has to do he does it with all his might. The Scotch are welcome and popular in every part of the world where they go. If any unpopularity exists against them anywhere, it is in England. It was raised in the past century, when Lord Bute rendered his countrymen very unpopular in that country. During the examination of the trade outrages at Sheffield last year, Mr Kinnaird, member for Perth, asked one of the witnesses—a great employer of labour—whether he had any Scotchmen in his employ. "No," said the witness, "I will not have one about me." All the committee laughed at Mr Kinnaird, who, however, asked the witness another question: "Have you any objection to Scotchmen?" "Yes, I have a very great objection to them." "Will you please tell the committee what the objection is?" "Well, it is this. If I get a Scotchman in my employ, he will be either my employer or partner before I know where I am." (Laughter.) This explanation was very satisfactory to Mr Kinnaird. Long before the distress of '45, the Scotch had found their way abroad, some being compelled to do so by poverty, and some for the mere sake of ambition and adventure. It was the unfortunate Charles I. that first sent the people out of the land in any considerable numbers—at a time when Scotch manhood and Scotch womanhood was surrounded by glaring difficulties on every hand. They were compelled to go anywhere where land could be got and an honest living obtained. Emigration was resorted to in more modern days by the Highland poor, but emigration has been more advantageous to them than was perhaps expected. The hill-sides and glens in many parts of Scotland that could once send forth 1000 or more men to war in the hour of danger, are now almost desolate. They have sought honour in other climes. Sent adrift as they were to make way for Nimrods and hunters, they sought in other countries what they were not allowed at home. It was at this time that some of our bravest and best men emigrated. Some went to New Zealand, some to Australia and other colonies, and large numbers to America, and they all found new homes and new friends away from their mother country. A striking instance

of this was shown to me in one of the largest cities in Canada. I
was invited to dine with a wealthy gentleman of my own name.
There were present on that occasion 120 other Scotchmen, and
most of them wore the Highland dress. My host had a piper
behind the chair playing the old familiar strains of the pipes. The
gentleman told me, in the course of the evening, that his father
was a poor cottar in Sutherlandshire. "My mother," said he,
"was turned out upon the moor on a dark cold night, and upon
that moor I was born." My friend's family afterwards went to
America, and my friend became a "dry" merchant, or as you
would say in Scotland, a draper. I said to him, seeing that his
position had so improved, "Well, I suppose you do not bear any
grudge against the people by whose agency your family were
turned upon the moor." "No," he replied, "I cannot say that I
bear them any grudge, but at the same time I cannot say that I
forgive them. If my position has improved, it is by my own
perseverance, and not by their good deeds or through their agency."
In every great city of Canada—Toronto, Kingstown, Montreal,
New Brunswick, St John's Nova Scotia, and in almost every town
and village, you will find many Scotchmen; in fact, in the large
towns they are almost as numerous as in Edinburgh and Inverness. You will see a Highland name staring you in the face in any
or every direction. If you ask for the principal merchant or principal banker, you will be almost sure to find that he's a Scotchman;
and no matter in what part of the world your fellow-countrymen may be cast, they keep up the old manners and customs of
their mother country. They never forget the good old times of
"Auld lang syne;" they never forget the old songs they sung,
the old tunes they played, nor the old reels and dances of Scotland.
There is one day in the year which seems more dear than any other
day to the Scotchman in all parts, and that is the 25th of January.
It may be asked why that day is more dear than any other. It is
because it is the anniversary of the birthday of Robert Burns.
(Applause.) In every city in the Union of Canada there is a
Burns Club. No name—not Bruce, Wallace, nor even Sir Walter
Scott —is so dear to Scotchmen abroad as that of Burns. (Hear,
hear.) Scott might have been greater than Burns, but never so
much beloved. They look upon Scott as having a rather aristo-
cratic tendency, but Burns was loved for his defects, absolute
independence and firmness, for he maintained that what was his
own was his own in all places, and carried out this principle
through life. Burns always wrote with spirit and feeling. It is
a common saying, when anything had been bought cheap, that it

is bought at the price of an old song, to which it might be replied,
"Cheap, is an old song cheap? What is the value of the old song,
'A man's a man for a' that?'" (Hear, hear, and applause.) This
has urged thousands on to independence. Well, as I was about
to say, on the 25th of January the Burns Clubs in the United
States of America and Canada meet to give a toast to Scotland's
humble poet, with patriotic fervour. These clubs send messages
of greeting along the wire desiring each other to drink to the
immortal memory of him whose aim was to teach the poor poverty-
stricken man to hold his own against all encroachers, and remember that in all circumstances, though he might be "down in the
world," "a man's a man for a' that." (Hear, hear.) The Scotch
find in Burns a representative of their own character. If Burns
had been utterly unblemished, pure, and with a high station, it is
possible his countrymen would not love him as they do. Read the
"Bard's Epitaph":

> Is there a man whose judgment clear,
> Can others teach the course to steer,
> Yet runs himself life's mad career,
>   Wild as the wave;
> Here pause, and through the starting tear,
>   Survey this grave.
>
> The poor inhabitant below,
> Was quick to learn and wise to know,
> And keenly felt the friendly glow,
>   And softer flame;
> But thoughtless follies laid him low,
>   And stained his name.
>
> Reader, attend,—whether thy soul
> Soar fancy's flights beyond the pole,
> Or darkling grubs this earthly hole,
>   In low pursuit;
> Know, prudent, cautious self-control
>   Is wisdom's root.

The Scotch are noted in America for what Americans truly
call their "grip." They hold fast what they get, and never relax
anything they put their hands to. There is another thing which
endears the Scotch to American politicians. The Irish politicians
are not looked up to in America, for when they vote, they vote
altogether, according to the instructions of their spiritual advisers.

All parties try to get the Irish vote, but at the same time they hate it. The way to get at the Irish heart is to abuse England. But the Scotch never give them any such trouble. They do not vote in the "lump," but each Scotchman votes for himself, and nothing that Americans say against England, either with regard to the "Alabama" or anything else, can weigh in his judgmeni. He must be satisfied in his own mind, and then he goes in for the truth, and that only. The Scotch, especially in Canada, take the Gaelic with them. They have Gaelic newspapers, which have a large circulation—larger, perhaps, than any Gaelic newspaper at home. They have Gaelic preachers. In fact, there is one part of Canada which might be called the new Scotland; and it is a Scotchman who is now at the head of the Canadian Government —John Macdonald. * (Applause.) The lecturer then described at some length the able manner in which the Scotch pilots took the place of the Indians, and their ability as statesmen, merchants, and workmen. He referred to the love of Scotland which seemed to dwell in the minds of not only Scotchmen in America, but Americans themselves.

He strongly recommended Canada to the attention of emigrants. That country could take a million, two millions, or ten millions of people, if we only had them to spare, and they would find scope and return for their energies. He thought he was only doing his duty in pointing out the advantages of emigration to the new Dominion—not the emigration of clerks or shopmen, or of those who wanted to be fine ladies and gentlemen, but of those who had strong hands and backs, and could plough the land. Referring to the threats of the United States, during the "Alabama" dispute, the lecturer said their armies might over-run Canada, but they would find it a very difficult thing to hold; in fact, they would soon be glad to get rid of it. Chatting at a dinner party in New York, he said to an American, who was boasting of what the States would do, " Canada has a defence on the other side of the Rocky Mountains. If the States were to annex Canada, perhaps Great Britain would find means to annex California." A gentleman, who heard the remark, turned round and said—" Sir, I am the Governor of California." " I hope," said Dr Mackay, " I have not offended you." " Offended me," he replied, " you have greatly delighted me. We in California are too far off from the Atlantic side of the United States. We must become independent some day, and if we become independent through the help of Great Britain, all I can say is we shall be very much obliged to her." But feelings of irritation as between England—he begged pardon,

* At the date of publication it is another Scotchman, Mr Mackenzie.

between Great Britain—(Applause)—and the United States had
calmed down, and he did not think this or the next generation
would see a war between the two countries.   The strong Conser-
vative influence of Scotchmen in American politics would always
incline the American Government to seek peace and amity with
the old country.   Mr Reverdy Johnson, late United States Minister to the British Court, deplored to him that he was not a Scotchman, and thought he would insert the letter *t* into his name just
to claim the connection.   (Laughter.)   Mr Seward was also proud
of his Scotch descent, and the same feeling was universal in the
South.   When they could find time to leave their pursuits, the
greatest delight of these men was to visit the land of Scott and
Burns; and the hotel-keepers of Edinburgh and other places would
gladly admit that Americans were their best customers.   The late
Jefferson Davis—of whom even his opponents would say " he was
an American, and he fought like an American "---(Applause)—
travelled with the lecturer through a great part of Scotland, and
was familiar with the history and traditions of every place they
came to.   He knew every song that had been written on Yarrow,
and he could repeat all Sir Walter Scott's Lady of the Lake.   Coming
to Killiecrankie, and looking at it with the eye of a soldier, he
said, " Your namesake, General Mackay, was a great fool to fight
the Highlanders at such a place as that;" and coming to Culloden
he said, " What fools the Highlanders were to fight the English
at such a place as that."   When here, it was his pleasure to call
himself not Davis but Mactavish.   (Laughter.)   He was, he said,
of Welsh descent, but then the Welsh and the Highlanders were
both Celts.   Talking about the war, the lecturer said to him—and
he did not think in repeating this he was committing any breach
of faith—"Mr Davis, why did you not abolish slavery?   Why
did you refuse to yield, and so cast away all sympathy from you ?"
" I am an enemy to slavery," he said, " I always was, but I had
no more power to abolish slavery than you had.   The Confederate
States of America were each sovereign, and no one State had
power in any other.   If any State by its own Assembly had
chosen to abolish slavery, it was welcome to do so, and I should
have been glad.   But, as chief of the whole Confederation, I had
no power whatever.   Slavery," he said, " has been abolished, and
for my part I am glad of it.   I wish it had been abolished a little
more carefully, because I am afraid the negroes will suffer from
the suddenness of the act; but they are a good people, and with a
little patience they will become good citizens.   The dearest friend
I had was one who had been my own slave.   He is ninety-eight
years of age, and the poor man has been weeping much about me.

He said, 'I had but two friends in the world, the Lord Jesus and
Massa Jeff. They have put Massa Jeff in prison, and I have no
friend now but the Lord Jesus.' That man, though free, would
not accept his freedom," added Mr Davis. "He considered that
he belonged to me, and as long as I have a crust to share with him
he shall share it." (Applause.)

Votes of thanks both to the lecturer and chairman were
awarded by acclamation.

31ST JULY 1873.

At this meeting the Society received, with regret, an intimation from their excellent Secretary, Mr William Mackay, of his
intention to resign office on an early date, in consequence of his
leaving Inverness for an appointment in Edinburgh. The following report of the Annual Assembly, held on the 10th instant in
the Music Hall, was read, approved, and ordered to be engrossed
in the minutes of the Society :—

" The Special Committee appointed by the Council to carry out
the arrangements for the Second Annual Assembly of the Gaelic
Society, have much pleasure in reporting that the assembly was
in every sense a decided success. The large Music Hall was full,
the music, vocal and instrumental, was of a very high order, and
the Committee wish to record their grateful appreciation of the
services rendered to the Society by the performers, who so handsomely came forward and gave their services gratuitously, especially the young ladies, also to the dancers, and speakers. They
also wish to congratulate the Society on the excellent reports given
by the local press of the whole proceedings, and recommended that
the *Highlander's* introduction to the Report, and its report of the
Rev. A. Macgregor's address, be printed in the volume of Transactions for (1872-73), and that the other addresses, being more
fully reported, be printed from the *Inverness Courier.* It is
evident that the Annual Assembly of the Society has now become
an event which every true-hearted Highlander will look forward
to, in future years, and the Society must keep in view the necessity of making it yearly more attractive. The Committee regret
that many friends from the West, who intended to be present, did
not arrive in Inverness in time, owing to an accident on the Skye
Railway. As already stated, the press did its work so well, that
it is quite unnecessary to give a fuller report here.

(Signed) " ALEX. MACKENZIE,
Convener of Assembly Committee."

24TH SEPTEMBER 1873.

At this meeting, in accordance with previous notice, Mr Wm. Mackay resigned his office as Secretary. The Society unanimously expressed their regret at the loss of so valuable an official, and adopted, by acclamation, a recommendation of Council, that the Society present Mr Mackay "with a small acknowledgment and token of the warm regards which are entertained towards him by the Society." A Committee was also appointed "to draw up a resolution, to be engrossed in the minutes, expressing their views and feelings on the subject" of Mr Mackay's resignation and his past services to the Society.

2D OCTOBER 1873.

Mr William Mackenzie, 17 Telford Road, was unanimously elected Secretary *ad interim*.

9TH JULY 1873.

At this meeting, after several members were elected, Mr JOHN MURDOCH, of the *Highlander*, read a paper on "Charter Rights to the Land."

16TH OCTOBER 1873.

The Society authorised the Council to select and appoint a properly qualified gentleman to teach a grammatical knowledge of the Gaelic language, and to add some Gaelic grammars to its Library. After which, Mr WILLIAM MACKENZIE, the Secretary, read a paper, which produced considerable discussion, on the character of Mac' ic Alastair, "the last *real* chief of Glengarry." Mr Mackenzie declined to give any of his papers for publication.

23D OCTOBER 1873.

This evening a paper was read by the Secretary (Mr MACKENZIE) on "Ossian's Poems," in which he argued strongly against their authenticity. A long discussion ensued, and the general opinion of the members was against that of the essayist.

5TH NOVEMBER 1873.

The following lecture was delivered by the Rev. ARCHIBALD FARQUHARSON, of Tyree, in the Association Buildings, Castle Street, on

" HIGHLANDERS AT HOME AND ABROAD,"

including a plea for teaching Gaelic in our national schools :—

Mr Farquharson introduced himself "as true-hearted a Gael as ever was looked upon." He mentioned several grievances his countrymen had to put up with, and ridiculed the idea of men calling themselves Highlanders, and wearing the Highland dress, while they knew not a word of the Gaelic language. " I would have the wives, when they see such going about amongst them, to take out the gridiron, and to ring with it, crying aloud ' Ye great hypocrites, off, off with that kilt, on with the breeks,' le gleangai- saieh na greidil ag eigheach ' a chealgar' mhor dhiot, dhiot a' feile, umad a bhriogais."

" These grievances are nothing compared with the treatment which our language receives in our schools, where, with very few exceptions, it is completely laid aside. We might bear with those which I have already mentioned as comparative trifles, although somewhat irritating to our temper, and aware that others are led astray by them; but this we cannot treat so. It is a grievance that reaches the quick, that pierces our very souls, causing us to lose the life-blood of our existence, and which aims at our total extinction as a race. Yes, it makes our heart's blood boil within us with indignation, on account of the disgrace, the cruelty, and the injustice done to us. There are not many races of people on the face of the earth who are greater slaves than the Gaels are by their schools; and were it not that their chiefs have forsaken them, by renouncing their language, they would not put up with it; and I trust that the time has come when they will manifest that they can put up with it no longer.

> ' Now's the day, and now's the hour,
> See the front o' battle lour,
> See approach proud Edward's power—
> Chains and slavery !

> ' Wha will be a traitor knave ?
> Wha can fill a coward's grave ?
> Wha sae base as be a slave ?
> Let him turn an' flee !

'Wha for Scotland's king and law
 Freedom's sword will strongly draw ?
 Freeman stand or freeman fa',
   Let him follow me!

'By oppression's woes and pains !
 By your sons in servile chains !
 We will drain our dearest veins,
   But they shall be free !

'Lay the proud usurpers low !
 Tyrants fall in every foe !
 Liberty's in every blow !
   Let us do or die !'

There is a Scotch man for you. What a grasp ? What a powerful hold has he taken of his countrymen ? Can the polished
Englishman, with his artificial English, ever come up to that ?
Never, never. The power of the whole piece arises from the artless
simplicity of the language, which is peculiar to the Broad Scotch
and the Gaelic, and which the superfine English cannot imitate.

   " In pleading for my countrymen and their language, I cannot
do so without giving sore thrusts to the schoolmasters. I do not
hate them ; any wounds that I shall inflict shall be the wounds of
a friend. They are not to be blamed, as I will show afterwards.
It would appear, then, that proud Edward has a successor in that
system of education in our schools. It is a common saying, that
the schoolmaster is abroad ; yes, he is abroad through the whole
extent of our native country ' with chains and slavery.' He is
there as a traitor to his countrymen. He is not intentionally so ;
neither is he suspected of any evil design. He is generally looked
upon as their true friend, whose object is to make them great
scholars ; but the less he is suspected and the more highly he is
esteemed, the more dangerous he is, because he is betraying them,
I do not say slyly or deceitfully, but quietly and peaceably, into
the hands of a foreign power ; certainly nothing has a greater
power over any people than language.

   " At one period Scotland to a certain extent was under the
power of Englishmen ; but in those days of darkness their souls
were never conquered, they remained Scotchmen at heart, determined with the first opportunity to throw off the yoke ; that opportunity presented itself at Bannockburn, when they showed that
they would rather die on the spot than remain under their power.
Now, I ask you, my countrymen, do you think that those Gaels

who fought at that decisive battle, when forty thousand Scotchmen put to flight one hundred thousand Englishmen with great slaughter? Do you think that they, with their onward, determined, irresistible rush, sword in hand, decided the fate of the day as much as anything else? Do you think that these men would be willing to renounce their own language, and to receive the Englishman's in its place? I am certain they would not, that they would rather die on the spot than do it. And what would they think of many of their posterity were they to see how fashionable and Englified they are become, so much so as actually to be ashamed of their native language. They would be horrified at the sight—would be ashamed to own them as their descendants.

"Whenever our children enter school, they are made slaves by the alphabet that is forced upon them, which is not suited to the Broad Scotch, and not at all to the Gaelic. Our vowels are à è i ò ù (pronounced as oo, in moon). I pass by o, because it is the humble and obedient subject of both languages, and take up the other four. These vowel sounds are essential to the Gaelic, there is not a single instance in which they have the sounds of a e i u (as in English). The alphabet taught in our schools is not essential even to the English. The short and the long sound of a as we have it in at, that, far, farther, fall, call, I am certain are more frequent in the English than the sound of a as we have it in care, wave. The same may be said of e as we have it in test, send, tell; and of i as we have it in it, is, him, bid. The long sound of u is no exception. Come away and say your lesson. What's the name of that letter? à; it is not so, with a slash from the slave-master's whip, it is a. What's that? it is è; it is not è, with another slash, it is e. What's that again? it is ì; it is not ì, with a third slash, it is i. What's that? it is oo; it is not oo, with a fourth slash, it is u. Mata (weeping) 'se à agus è agus i agus oo a theagasg mo mhathair fhein domh (it was à and è and ì and oo that my own mother taught me.) I care not what your mother taught you, this is what I teach you, and you must obey, otherwise you will feel the consequences.

"The sound of a is formed by placing e before it, as tearnadh, to save; sometimes in the sound of ei, as gleidh, teach, in safe keeping; also in the sound of e, when used as the first personal masculine pronoun, as è, he; 'sè, it is he; b'è, it was he. The sound of i is formed by placing a before i, as baigh, kindness; traigh, shore. The sound of long u is formed by placing i before u, as cliu, fame; iul, guidance.

"As Mr Campbell of Islay said, that there are sounds in the

English which are not in the Gaelic. I have done my utmost to
search them out, and could only find one vowel sound, namely, the
short sound of u, as we have it in up, must thrust, which is short
and abrupt like the Englishman himself. There are sounds of
consonants which we have not: mp, as in trumpet; mph, as in
triumph; nce, as in ounce, renounce; also th, as in that with.
Now, listen to all these sounds, and you will find them all without
the least melody. But we have many sounds which are not in the
English at all, and which are full of melody, such as ceann, head;
gleann, glen; doigh, manner; cloimh, wool; fadheoidh, finally;
seol, guide; ecol, song; eigh, cry; spreidh, cattle of any kind;
fuar, cold; shuas, up; and when the i is added to the ua, it makes
a sweet sound, as buaidh, victory; fuaim, sound. The short sound
of u, as we pronounce it in duine, man; fulang, suffering. Also, the
sound of ia is as we have it in fial, generous; criosduigh, christian;
sgiath, wing. This sound is frequently heard from birds, and
from the chanter of the bagpipe. But the sublimest sound that is
listened to is the sound of ao, as we have it in glaodh, cry. None
but the true Gael can utter this sound; it is their shiboleth. It
resembles the sound of a large trumpet, and of distant thunder.
It comes with power and authority, and has a greatness and a
majesty in it that no other sound has. Let any man say—the
world, the human race, the Redeemer, and how weak and insignificant these sounds are, compared with an saoghal, an cinne
daoine, am Fear-saoraidh. The very sound of these words conveys
the idea of vastness, greatness. How tame the word wind compared with gaoth. Listen to the wind blowing upon a window,
or upon large trees surrounding the house, and nothing could
express that sound better than to say gaoth, gao ao aoth. This is
a sound that is heard in a rocky glen in the time of a flood, the
rocks resounding to the water roar. It is the sound of the Atlantic
waves, as they are heard in a calm evening in the island of Tiree,
beating upon its rocks and sandy beaches with the sound of
thunder. Nothing could express that noise better than the very
name they give to it, Gaoirich a chuain, the roaring ocean, gao ao
aoirich. The voice of the Son of God is as the sound of many
waters-

Mar thuil nan gleann tha fuaim a ghuth.
Like flood of glens His voice divine.

That voice has an echo in the Gaelic language, but not in the
English. This is the sound heard from the big drone of the Highland bagpipe, and also from noble stags in autumn, gh, gh, ghao

aoth. It is when he begins to look out for his sweethearts that his voice is heard saying, gh, gh, ghaoil, love, dear. Where i is added to the ao it makes a sound as sweet and as full of melody as any that can be listened to, as aoidh affability; caoimhneas, kindness.

"Now, I ask you, my countrymen, are you willing that a language so sweet, so expressive, so natural, so stirring to the soul, so calculated to warm the heart, and to set you a singing with its melody and music; the language of your forefathers, the language of your hearts, and which has made us what we are, such a warm-hearted race, should be driven from our country by our very schools.

"The English alphabet is not only forced upon them like slaves, but they are also forced to read a language they know nothing about, which is the most stupid, the most absurd, and the most irrational mode that could be; their cwn judgment will be of no avail to them to put us to keep them right. They are treated as if they were mere reading machines or speaking parrots. They speak and understand a language of their own which is completely laid aside, and not even made a medium for acquiring the knowledge of the English. I am quite confident that their own language ought first to be taught them. I challenge any man to prove that it ought not, convinced that no man will accept the challenge but one who has some moral or mental defect about him. Their own language ought certainly to be first taught them, beginning with the Gaelic alphabet, and when they could read the four Gospels tolerably well, to commence at once with the English alphabet; and then, as reading and writing went along, to translate every word into Gaelic, aided to do so by one another as well as by the teacher. This mode of teaching would give a stimulus in our schools such as does not at present exist. The little folks would become big in their own eyes when they found that they could master the Sassunnach's hard sayings, and convey an impression to their minds that their object was to master the English, and not to become slaves to it by renouncing their own language. They would resemble a hive of bees in a fine summer day. The hum of the busy bees would be heard amongst them. W-h-i-t-e, white, geal; s-t-r-o-n-g, strong, laidir; s-w-i-f-t, swift. De Ghaelig a th' air swift? Luath, swift, luath. S-h-a-l-l-o-w, shallow. De Ghaelig th' air shallow? Cha'n'eil fhios 'am. Master, if you please, give me the Gaelic for shallow? Tàna, shallow, tàna. I-n-f-i-n-i-t-e, infinite. De Ghaelig th' air infinite? Cha'n'eil fhios 'am. Master, if you please, give me the Gaelic of infinite? Neo-chrioch-nach gun toabh thall aige.   There is the master's voice ringing through the whole house, and the young ears listening attentively to it.

" Reading a language they do not understand has a very bad effect upon children.   It leaves the mind indolent and lazy; they do not put themselves to any trouble to endeavour to ascertain the meaning of what they read; whereas, were they taught to translate as they went along, whenever a word they did not understand presented itself to their minds, they would have no rest until they would master it by finding out its meaning.   And I am pretty certain that were the Gaelic-speaking children thus to be taught, that by the time they would reach the age of fourteen years, they would be as far advanced, if not farther, than those who have no Gaelic at all; so that, instead of the Gaelic being their misfortune, it would be the very reverse.   It would, with the exception of Welshmen (were they aware of it), place them on an eminence above any in Great Britain, not only as scholars, but as having the best languages for the soul and for the understanding.   And should they enter college, they would actually leave others behind them, because, in the first place, they acquired the habit of translating in their youth, which would make translating from dead languages comparatively easy; and in the second place, they would derive great aid from their knowledge of the Gaelic.   If Professor Blackie has found 500 Greek roots in the Gaelic, what aid would they derive from it in studying that language ? and they would find equally as much aid in studying Latin, and even Hebrew. There is no doubt that the Gaelic is one of the oldest of the spoken languages on earth, and consequently must be of great advantage for acquiring the knowledge of other languages.

" Were educated Germans to visit our country, and see the treatment which the Gaelic receives in our schools, they would say that we are not only great slaves, but great fools also, because it is a known fact that the Gaelic is the language which many of them first study.   They, the greatest scholars in the world, are picking up these pearls which scholars amongst us are trampling, like swine, under their feet.

" It is one of the most extraordinary, and the most unaccountable, facts that has ever been presented to my mind, and which makes me blush for my country, not only the almost total exclusion of the Gaelic, the native language, from our schools, but the place which that dry, dead Latin has found in them.   Is it not a fact that all the schoolmasters must not only teach Latin, but that the most of them do actually teach it, and that many of them cannot even speak the Gaelic. I suppose for one lesson taught in the Gaelic, that there are thirty in the Latin. Mo chreach! mo chreach! 'n do chaill iad an ciall? Alas! alas! have they lost their reason? Certain am I, that the less the English-language is Latinised the better, and that, if anything more than another has made skeletons of many of our young men, undermined their constitutions, ruined their health, and brought them to an early grave, it has been the study of dead Latin. Would the glorious Redeemer, would the Apostle Paul, approve of such a mode of training for the ministry? Others may, but I cannot believe it. I am convinced that nearly the one-third of those who go from the Highlands to college suffer in their health. Now, I am certain that Latin is extensively taught in this fashionable town; that boys are well drilled through the Latin rudiments here, and that young Misses are taught French, too; but it does not raise the blush of shame on their faces for not studying the native language of their country, because it is not fashionable to do so; but it is quite in the fashion to study Latin and French. Whether are the children or the parents to be blamed? Certainly the parents. They are for bringing up their children quite in the fashion, which I declare is one of the devil's straight roads to hell. Of all the nations on earth there is nothing dearer to them than their native language, and are the Gaels the only people that do not seem to care for it? Shall they with their eyes open allow their schools to banish it entirely out of the country? For as certain as two and two make four, three and three six, the Gaelic will cease to exist unless taught in the schools.

"Had the brave Poles renounced their own and received the language of the Russians in its stead, their slavery would be complete. The Hebrews, seventy-five in number, entered Egypt, where they remained 400 years. During the latter part of that time they were in bondage to Pharoah and his taskmasters, but although their bodies were in bondage, their souls were comparatively free. They took their language along with them, held it fast, and left Egypt in full possession of it, free men. Had Pharoah succeeded in bringing them under the power of the Egyptian, to the total exclusion of their own language, their subjugation would be complete.

"The existence of all the nations of the earth depends upon their maintaining their own language; it is their life blood as a nation. Losing their language, their nationality would come to an end. Now, it is evident that our language has made us a race distinct from others, so that we have a nationality of our own. When-

ever, therefore, we lose our language we cease to exist. Were an
Englishman to be asked—What countryman are you?—he would
hold up his head without a blush, and say, I am an Englishman,
sir.   Were a Scotchman asked the same, with a head equally as
high, he would answer—I am a Scotchman, sir.   But were a Gael
to be asked the question, with a head equally as high as either, he
would boldly reply—I am a Scotch Gael, sir.   Now I am certain
that were the question put to many in the Highlands, that they
would be at a loss for an answer.   They do not look upon themselves as belonging either to the Lowland Scotch or to the English.
I suppose they would be disposed to look upon themselves as
Scottish Highlanders.   I tell you, gentlemen, that you are mistaken, that it is a delusion that exists only in your own brains.
Your nationality is not a reality, you have excluded yourselves
from the Scottish Gaels by renouncing their language.

"Another grievance which we feel, and it is a painful one,
namely, the manner in which the great body of our landed proprietors and chieftains have renounced our native language.   The
consequence is that the English is now the respectable, the genteel,
the fashionable language of society.   The whole united power of
rank, and wealth, and fashion is arrayed against us, which carries
everything before it like an irresistible current.   It is easy to
conceive how empty, weak, silly minds are carried away by the
stream; wishing to appear genteel, they are for soaring so very
high in the regions of fashion, so as to look down upon the Gaelic
and those who speak it as vulgar, to gratify the pride and the
vanity of their minds.   Such I despise in my very heart; I cannot find language strong enough to express my contempt for them.

"Now, I ask, 'Whether have our landlords and noblemen
ascended or descended in the scale of true greatness?   Has the
present race more manly dignity about them than their forefathers
had when they spoke the language of their country?'   I am
certain they have not.   Take, for example, the present Lochiel,
the Chief of the Camerons (and I have no feelings but those of
respect towards that nobleman).   Although an M.P., is he a greater
man than his forefathers were?   Has he a voice of power like
them?   Do his words pass like electricity through the whole House
of Commons, as their words passed through their whole clan?   Has
the present a key to the hearts and the affections of the Cameron
men?   Is he exalted as a king there like them?   His voice
would be equally as powerful, and I am certain would command
more respect even in the House of Commons, were it known there
that he could address his clansmen in the language of their hearts.

"At one time they were the men of the people, standing with them on a common level, speaking their language, sympathising with them in their difficulties, counselling them in their straits, frowning upon them for their misconduct, and settling their quarrels. But now they are so far removed from them as if they were not the same race of beings at all ; so far removed that they seldom see them, and never speak to them but in a foreign tongue ; only they feel that they exist, when some of them are unmercifully driven from their homes—when their rents are raised, and when they have to pay them. There is not a class of people on earth capable of showing greater attachment to their landlords than the Gaels, were they properly treated. They have shown, in times past, that they would shed the last drop of blood in their defence.

"Many of our nobility and landed proprietors, in their efforts to vie with Englishmen in their luxuries and extravagances, is what has brought on this painful state of things; which has ruined many of them, and the reason why so much of our native country has passed into the hands of foreigners. I could almost weep for the miseries which several of them are bringing upon themselves and their countrymen, by the foolish gratification of their pride and vanity. I believe that during the last fifty or sixty years, the incomes of most of them have not only been doubled but trebled, and still many of them are as poor as ever. I fear that an awful day of retribution is coming, and will certainly overtake them, unless they change their mode of living. Certainly nothing can add more to the happiness of a landlord than to be the father of a grateful tenantry, whose praise is on all their lips—who is aware that his name is a household word, which is never mentioned but with respect. How very different from the happiness of that man, which arises from spending abroad that money which has been squeezed from them with reluctance. In the one case, they sincerely wish their landlord a long life ; but, in the other, a speedy removal by death. Poor, indeed, would be the state of my soul at this moment, had I reason to believe that many of my fellow-creatures longed for my death.

"There is still a more awful grievance that we have to complain of as men, and especially as Christians, namely, that our children are not taught to read the Word of God in their mother tongue. I question if the one-sixth of the Gaelic-speaking population of our country can do so ; and the few who can read it, it is not our public schools they have to thank, but the Sabbath schools, and their own efforts. I am told that the whole county of Suther-

2

land is disgracefully behind in this respect, that very few can read
their mother tongue at all. It would appear that that county is
riding post haste to England, spurred on by factors, and on by
schoolmasters and ministers acquiescing. Are the brave Sutherlandshire men to renounce all connection with the Gaels ?

"Words were used in the hearing of some present, the most
shocking to my mind that ever I read. The question was put,
'What would be the use of it ?' (that is, the children to be taught
to read and write the Gaelic in the schools)—'it would in no way
promote their prosperity in the world.' Is the individual who put
that question a Christian? Does he believe in the great realities
of Christianity?—that children have immortal souls?—that there
is a great God above them?—that they are hastening to an eternal
world of misery or of happiness?—and that that God has given a
revelation of His mercy, through Christ, to teach them the only
way of escaping misery and securing happiness ? Would it be of
no use to children to be taught to read that revelation in their
own language ? Certainly nothing could be of greater importance.
Is prospering in the world the chief end of man ? Certainly not,
but to glorify God, and to enjoy him for ever ? Would it be of no
use to read the rule which God hath given for their direction in
that respect? Who will dare say, not ? Worldly prosperity without this would be their greatest snare and curse.

"I ask—Were our schoolmasters, and those who have the
management of our schools, true Christians, what would be the
first thing they would teach our children? Certainly to read the
history of the great author of Christianity, as contained in the
four Gospels, in their native tongue. I defy any man to give a
different answer ; any man that pretends to be a Christian can
give no other answer. I feel myself standing upon a rock as firm
as that rock upon which Edinburgh Castle is built; and standing
upon that rock, I pass a sentence of condemnation against our
schools. Yea, I go a little farther, standing upon that rock, Christianity, against which the gates of hell shall not prevail, I denounce those schools, where the Gaelic is the language spoken by
the people, and where it is not taught, as the schools of Antichrist;
and I defy any man to contradict or to overturn the statement.
I go a little farther still, and charge those schoolmasters, and their
patrons, who do not teach the children to read the Word of God
in their own language, with the awful crime of withholding the
lamp of life from them, which is God's greatest gift to a lost world.

"It is a most extraordinary fact, that our ministers in the
Highlands—and many of them such eminent men for piety,

zeal, and talent—never raised their united voices against the schools for excluding the Gaelic. The only reason that can be assigned for it is the known fact that most of them brought up their families without a word of the Gaelic taught them, so that they could not consistently open their lips against the schools for excluding it, seeing that they excluded it from their own families.

"Several noblemen and gentlemen of intelligence, and a high degree of learning, have spoken their minds freely before this Society, stating that the Gaelic, as a spoken language, is destined soon to disappear before the advancing English. Considering the changes that have taken place in many parts of the Highlands during the last thirty years, the conclusion to which they have come is quite correct. But I am not sure that any have attempted to give the reasons before this Society, why the Gaelic is losing ground. Now, what reasons can be given ? It cannot be said that it has lost its hold of the hearts of the people. I am certain that it has still a hold of the affections of those who know it properly, such as the English never can, and never shall have, What, then, are those reasons that can be given ? Because the united power of rank, and wealth, and fashion, is arrayed against it. Is there not a feeling spreading amongst a certain class, that it is low and vulgar to speak it ? It would be equally vulgar in a young woman to wear her own, without false hair ! Vulgar to speak the Gaelic ! 'N dream a tha 'g a shaoilsinn, 's e stamaig balgair tha aca. I pity the poor deluded creatures who think so. Another, and the principal reason, is because it is not taught in the schools. Why is it not taught ? Can any proper reasons be brought forward ? I would like to hear them. I am certain, were I to do so, I would have the largest mark for firing at that ever I had. Is it in justice and compassion to our youth that it is not taught ? Certainly not. Is it for their benefit either for the present or the future life ? I am certain not. Both, especially the latter, are kept entirely out of sight So that those great men who wound our feelings, who grieve and vex our souls, by telling us that the language of our hearts is destined soon to disappear, and to vanish for ever—it would be much more to their honour were they to unite together in devising means for its revival, for its being taught in the schools, and in that respect setting a good example before others, giving us the weight of their influence, and of their names.

"It is a very easy thing for those who comparatively know very little of our language, to speculate, to reason, and to endeavour to show us, in apparent kindness, that it would be greatly to our advantage were we to renounce our own, and to choose the prevailing language of the country. We would spit in the face such a kindness—kick it from us, and look upon it as the greatest cruelty. Those who are disposed to treat us in that way, are ignorant of us; they do not enter into our feelings; they have no sympathy for us; they think of us as if we were no men at all—without the hearts, the souls, the feelings of men; as if we had no history, no associations, no songs, nothing at all to make us feel proud of the race of men we have descended from. They think of us as if it was as easy for us to renounce our own, and to receive another language, as to change a suit of clothes; not considering that before we can change our language, we would require to change our nature.

"There are some men, like the Editor of an Elgin paper, in his review of the pamphlet that I published, who think that the great use of the Gaelic is in its dead state, to be brought into the dissecting room of great scholars, there to be dissected and examined. There is one thing evident, however, that should they ever have my venerable mother in that state, they shall not notice the tears of gratitude and kindness dropping from her mild eyes; and neither shall they feel the warmth of the pulse-beating heart. Such unfeeling, such cruel monsters, deserve the treatment which some belonging to this very town met with in their efforts to bring a dead body to their dissecting room, and had I no other spirit but that of the Gael, I am certain that I would be disposed to apply it.

"It is true that the Gaelic will not come up to the English as an instrument in the hands of great scholars, for informing the minds and convincing the judgment of the better educated class—the one-fifth of the population does not reach that advanced education that will make them capable of appreciating a learned discourse in English; but as a language for the great mass of the people who understand it, and on ordinary subjects, it surpasses the English. The English is a language for the intellect, the Gaelic for the soul and its affections. The English, as it abounds so much with hard consonants, is clearer and more distinct in its sounds, and, consequently, more capable of being apprehended by the ear; but, in proportion as it becomes clear and distinct, in the same proportion is it cold and grating to the ear, and, of course, awanting in melody. I love the Gaelic and the Broad Scotch, there is an artless simplicity about them which I cannot but love. The Gaelic is as natural to the Gael, and his native language to the Scotchman, as bleating and lowing are natural to sheep and oxen.. I cannot love the artificial English, although I were to be cut in pieces. I could not do it. I see the handiwork of the great scholar in every sentence of it. Being artificial, it has a bad effect upon those who receive it, it makes them artificial likewise. It separates them from the rest of the community, raising them high above their heads, looking down upon them and their language as vulgar. Both parties are injured; the one by their pride and vain conceit, the other by a feeling of discontent, because they are despised.

" Were there a colony of those who spoke nothing but pure English, and who knew nothing else, it would be natural for them to speak it, it would be their native language ; they would speak it without pride, or vanity, or fashion. But even in that case their language would be cold; and they could not be called a warm-hearted people. Besides, it would have no melody. Certainly, compared with the Gaelic and the Broad Scotch, it has no melody. I affirm it. It is true that it may be set off and adorned with artificial melody. What is the difference between natural and artificial melody ? Natural melody is the appropriate melody with which a piece is sung which has true melody inherent in itself, and artificial melody is that with which a piece is sung that is destitute of real melody. In the former case the mind is influenced by what is sung, the music giving additional force and power to it ; but in the latter case the mind is more influenced by the sound of the music than by what is sung. I may explain this by two young females ; the one has, I do not call it a bonny face, but a very agreeable expression of countenance ; the other has not. Were the former to be neatly and plainly dressed, her dress would give additional charms to her, but in looking at her you would not think of the dress at all, but of the charms of the young woman. But although the other were adorned in the highest style of fashion, with flowers and brocades, and chains of gold, and glittering jewels, in looking at her you would not think of the charms of the young woman, for charms she had none, your mind would be altogether occupied with what was artificial about her, with what did not belong to her, and not with what she was in herself. Both the natural and the artificial melody elevate the mind, the one by what is sung, and the other by the grand sound of the music. There is real melody in ' Scots wha hae,' which is natural and appropriate, which gives additional power and force to the sentiment of the piece. In singing it the mind is not occupied with the sound, but with proud Edward, his chains and slavery— Scotia's King and law—the horrors of slavery—the blessing of liberty, and a fixed determination to act. Artificial melody, although it pleases and raises the mind, is but a great delusion— it does not move men off their seats—it is but a blast of empty air. But natural melody has a power and is a reality, which sets men a-thinking, a-resolving, and acting. Artificial melody is one of the great delusions of the age.

"But before I conclude, I must do justice to the schoolmasters. We cannot blame them, they are a very respectable class of men. They are acting like their predecessors, and like one another; besides, they are to a certain extent under the control of others. Neither can we altogether blame those who have the management of our schools; they are also a most respectable class of society, who are also acting like their predecessors. Where, then, shall we lay the blame? We must lay it at the door of old long standing custom, which is more agreeable than to blame any men. Should that culprit be brought to the bar and found guilty, he has no conscience; should he be disgraced, he has no sense of shame; and should he even be kicked about like a foot-ball, he has no feeling of pain. I am not very sure, however, that some of those whom he influenced may not complain. It is not a very agreeable thing to renounce old habits. But who are they whom we ought to endeavour to influence? The public generally, and those who have the management of our schools in particular. Let no one say it is a vain attempt, they are not so dull as the knowes, not so unmanageable as the raging sea, and the winds and rains of heaven. 'Cha n'eil iad cho dur ris na cnuic, cho do-cheannsaichte ris a mhuir bhuairte, no ri siantan nan speur.' They are rational men, capable of being reasoned with—intelligent men capable of perceiving what would be a benefit to their countrymen; besides, many of them are native Gaels. But before they will listen to us, we must show them that we are unanimous—that we are sincere and in real earnest, and that we have the welfare of our countrymen at heart for time and eternity."

We extract the following from the Gaelic portion of the lecture:—

"A mhuinntir mo dhuthcha, an ceadaich sibb do aon aig am bheil mor speis duibh labhairt ruibh a thaobh na canain sin o'n d'fhuair sinn ar n-aimn, a labhair ar n-athraichean, agus a dh'fhag iad 'nan daoine cho blath-chridheach, agus cho ceolmhor? Nach uamhasach maslach dhuinn mar a tha ar canain air a cuir gu tur

air chul ann an sgoiltean ar duthcha ? 'Nuair a theid ar cloinn
do'n sgoil, 's iad leabhraichean nach tuig iad ach gann aon fhocal
diubh a theid a chuir 'nan laimh, agus an aite a' chanain a tha iad
a tuigsinn 's a labhairt bhi air a deanamh na meadhon chum
ruitheachd air a' Bheurla 's ann a tha i ga cuir gu tur air chul—
obair cho neo-thurail, 's cho michiallach 's a b' urrainn a bhi. Tha
fios agam cionnas a bha cuisean do m' thaobh fein, 'n nair a chaidh
mi do'n sgoil aig aois chuig bliadhna. Cha d'fhuair mi aon leasan
's a' Ghailig ; cha robh facal de na bha sinn a' leughadh air eadar-
theangachadh, air chor 's ged a bha mi comasach air leughadh, air
litreachadh, air sgriobhadh, 's rud-eigin a dheanamh air cunntas, 's
air *Grammar*, 's gann a bha mi tuigsinn aon fhocal. 'Se sud an
t-oileanachadh truagh a fhuair mise, 's tha mi fiosrachadh dhibhse
cionnas a bha cuisean do 'r taobhsa. Nach eil e dearbhta gar h-i
'r canain fein bu choir a theagasg dhuibh an tuiseach. . . .

"Tha 'maighstir-sgoile coltach ri banarach a bhiodh a' beathachadh da laogh, laogh Gallta's laogh Gaidheag Gaidhealach. Tha
'darna laimh 's a' ghogan ga chumail ris an laogh ghallda, 's slat 's
an laimh eile. Tha 'n laogh mor gallda 'sa bhus fo chobhar, a'
crathadh earbaill ; san laogh eile seang 's an deireadh's caol 's an
amhaich, agus balg mor air mar mhàla piob, cha'n ann lan de'n
bhainne ach lan gaoithe 's ged a bheir an truaghan bochd oidheirp
air a bhus a chuir san t-soitheach gheibh e sguidse de'n t-slait.
Cha'n'eil fodha ach a theanga chuir a mach a dh'imlich a bheoil, a
miannachadh an ni nach fhaigh e. 'S cha 'n e a mhain sin ach 's
ann a bhios a bheisd mhor, purradh a' chreutair bbig, ni a tha toirt
mor riarachadh do'n bhanaraich ; ach coma leibhse ma'm faigheadh
an creutair beag a dhiol mar am fear eile, cha'n e amhain gun
rachadh e gu guineach 'na charamh, ach chuireadh e'n teicheadh
air a' bhoganach mhor ghallda mar an ceudna.

"Tha 'm maighstir-sgoile mar an ceudna coltach ri ciobair
bhiodh a' beathachadh cuig ciad caora, da chiad gu leth dhiubh
maol-cheannach ban, 'n da chiad gu leth eile, dubh-cheannach
adharcach. Tha na maol-cheannaich ann am paircean, 's fiar aca
gu ruig an suilean, 's na dubh cheannaich ann an sliabh monaidh
—gu crotach seang air an casan a' sior chriomadh, neo-chomasach
air an cuirp a lionadh. ' Tha na maol-cheannaich 'ri fhaicinn tric
'n an laidhe, an ceann an togail ag cnamh an cire, mar gu'm biodh
iad a' toirt taing do'n chiobair. Ma bheir na dubh-cheannaich
bhochd oidhirp air leum a stigh do na paircean, tha cu a' chiobair
a thiota 'g an ionnsuidh, 's tha iad cho cleachdta ris 's gu'n teich
iad air falbh le fead, 'nuair nach caraich cach. 'S cha 'n e sin
a mhain, ach thainig a chloimh a steach a'm measg nan dubh-

cheannach mar an ceudna, 's chitear aon 'g a rubadh fein ri bun
craoibh, aon eile ri cloich, ri creag, no ii bruaich; aon a' sgriob-
adh a slinnean le 'cas deiridh, h-aon eile 'spionadh na h-olainn le
fiaclan, 's h-aon eile 'tachas a droma le barr a h-adhairce. Tha na
h-uile a tha gam faicinn aon sgeulach ann a bhi gradh 'Cha seas
na dubh cheannaich—cha chuir iad an geamhradh seachad—
gheibh iad gu cinnteach am bas—cha n'eil feum bhi 'gan cumail
ni's fhaide.' 'Se sin an cainnt, gun bhi toirt feainear an t-aobhair
airson nach seas iad. Tha cuid 'n'ur measg a' gearan air Gailig a
bhaile so; 'm bheil sin 'na iongantas? nach eil dearmad air a
dheanamh oirre? 'Sann a tha i mar gun tigeadh a chloimh a
steach 'nam measg. Cha 'n'eil gearan air a dheanamh air Beurla
a'bhaile; C'arson? A chionn 's gu'm bheil an *Grammar* Beurla
air a theagasg 's na sgoiltean.

"Tha mi a nise feoraich dhibh, 'm bheil sibh a' saoilsinn gur
coir a' Ghailig bhi air a cumail suas le bhi air a teagasg 's na
sgoiltean? Air cho cinnteach 's a ni dha 'sa dha ceithir, ni tri
'sa tri sia, cho cinnteach sin, cha seas a Ghailig gun bhi air a
teagasg 'sna sgoiltean. Si so mata an fhreagra bheir sibh seachad:
's bheir sibh seachad e le'r n-uile chridhe mas fior Ghadheil sibh.
'Le 'r n-nile chridhe tha sinn ag radh, feumaidh! feumaidh!!
feumaidh!!!'

"Theid mata an fhuaim a mach le luathas a' Mhictalla o
phriomh bhaile na Ghaidhealtachd, agus se a' chiad chomunn a
ruigeas e 'Comunn Oiseanach Lathuirn,' Grad fhreagraidh an
comunn sin e mar na seana Ghaidheil, creagan cruaidh an Obain
ag eigheach gu sgairteil, 'Feumaidh! feumaidh!! feumaidh!!!'
O sin theid e do Ghrianaig leis an luathas cheudna, a ni Gaidheil
Ghrianaig a mhosgladh chum an fhuaim cheudna, 'Feumaidh!
feumaidh!! feumaidh!!!' a thogail le h-iolaich ait. A thiota
ruigidh e baile mor Ghlaschu, agus cha luaithe a ruigeas se e na
bhios stair-ir-ir-ich ann a thaobh lionmhorachd nan comunn. Na
h-uile comunn a th' ann le aon inntinn togaidh iad an guth ag
eigheach, 'Feumaidh! feumaidh!! feumaidh!!!' Ni an fhuaim
gun dail leth cheann Mhic Phail 'Mhuile nam mor bhearn,' a
bhualadh a 'm baile Dhuneidin a ni e fein is a cho-Ghaidheil a
mhosgladh gus an eigh a thogail, 'Feumaidh! feumaidh!! feumaidh!!!' Agus anns a' cheart am 's am bi Mac Phail 'sa chuideachd air an dúisgeadh. Duisgear suas Commun Lunnainn agus
mend an aoibhnis cha ghabh cuir a'n ceill a'n fhuaim thaitneach a
thainig 'g an ionnsuidh o thir an duthchais agus an sinnsearachd.
'Siad na briathran is ait a labhair iad riamh agus is mo tha tighinn
a reir an naduir, bhi 'g eigheach:

" Oir feumaidh ! feumaidh ! ! feumaidh ! ! !
A' Ghailig 'bhi ga leughadh
'S na sgoiltean mar a' Bheurla
'S e ni is eiginn tachairt e.

" Theid an fhuaim mhor bho Ghaidheil Lunnainn a dh' ionnsuidh na h' aird an iar tre *Wales,* agus mar fhuaim tairneanaich
a' faotainn freagraidh Pharuig a'n Eirinnn 's an dol seachad, agus
le luathas a Mhictalla a null do Cheap Breatuinn, *Nova Scotia,*
Gleanngarradh 's Canada uachdrach, a' dusgadh nan Gaidheal le
h-iolach 's le caithream gu bhi 'g eigheach le'n uile chridhe : ' Feumaidh ! feumaidh ! ! feumaidh ! ! !' Ath-phillidh an fhuaim air a
h-ais, cha 'n e mhain á America, ach mar an ceudna a Lunnainn,
Duneidin, Glaschu, 's Grianaig—

" 'S gach beinn is creag is sgairnich :
Tha 'n Gaidhealtachd na h-Alba
Ni uile 'n cur gu stairirich
'S crith-thalmhainn 'g an creanachadh.

air choir 's gum bi luchairtean nan daoine mora, taighean nam
Ministearan 's na Maighstirean-sgoile air an creanachadh ann an
leithid de dhoigh, 's gun teich iad a mach le h-eagal. Bios an
fhuaim ud *'feumaidh ! feumaidh !! feumaidh !!!'* a'n uachdair na
h-uile ge b'ois leis, 's gur h-eiginn daibh striochdadh :—

" Dhoibh 's eiginn striochd' is geilleadh,
Do 'n fhuaim ud feumaidh, feumaidh,
Air neo na Gaidheal eiridh
Ri guaillibh cheil' gu bagarach.

"A' boideachadh gu laidir
Nach bi ni 's fhaid nan traillean,
Ri dimeas air an canain
'S luchd riaghl 's gach ait ri tarcuis oirr'.

13TH NOVEMBER 1873.

Mr ALEXANDER MACKENZIE, journeyman tailor, Telford Road,
read a paper in Gaelic on " Baird Ghaidhealach an latha 'n diugh."
A lively discussion took place during which the Secretary suggested that the Society take steps to encourage the bards of the
present day, by offering prizes for the best poems, and by instituting a Gaelic poetical competition. Several members were then
elected.

19TH NOVEMBER 1873.

"THE GAEL IN THE FAR WEST."

This evening the Rev. Dr MASSON, of Edinburgh, lectured in the Association Hall, the subject being "The Gael in Canada." Provost Lyon-Mackenzie occupied the chair.—

"From his cradle-land, thousands of years ago, in the dim, primeval East, the progress of the Gael has long been westward—by slow and hard-won stages, ever westward. And in the West—far out in that mysterious, ever-sounding Atlantic—Ossian and his heroes sought their heaven. In that same West, across the same western main, mysterious no more, but bridged by steam and telegraph, the Gael of our day has found his rest.

"Through many ages, like the pious Æneas, *multum ille jactatus et terris et alto.* Over nearly half the earth's circumference he has left his footprints. On many a fair isle of the Mediterranean ; among the temples of Greece and the vineyards of Spain ; on the banks of the Rhone and the Po ; around the head waters of the Danube and the Rhine ; and down the beautiful Seine, he has left the indelible mark of his progress. And on the Cams and the Avons of Merry England as well as by the side of many a Lowland 'dun' and 'ben' in Southern Scotland, he tarried just long enough to write his name, and then moved on. Rest for his weary feet, through all these long ages of ceaseless migration, there was none. And truly his last estate, behind the Grampian ramparts, at least since fighting times have ceased and the chiefs have learned to rent their lands on 'commercial principles,' has been worse far than the first.

"But now all that is a thing of the past : and, under the bright skies of the New Dominion, the Gael of Caledonia has found, at last, a settled home. Beside the crystal waters of the mighty St Lawrence, and the dark torrent of the Ottawa ; on the Thames, the Grand River, and the Saugeen, on the fertile shores of Huron, Erie, and Ontario ; as well as, 1000 miles nearer Scotland, though still 3000 miles away, in the fair isle of Prince Edward, on the golden arm of Cape Breton, and among the pinewoods of Nova Scotia, he has found a sure abiding place for his children's children. The land is his own, and, in token of perpetual possession, in his own land he has buried his dead ; and there is little fear that failing crops, or lack of bread, or rising rent, or stern, unsympathetic Southern factor, as so oft in Scotland, will ever come to him again with a hard, imperious 'move on.'

" At what time the emigration from the Scottish Highlands to America first took definite proportions, I shall not undertake to say. But there can be no doubt that long ere the close of last century very large bodies of emigrants, from all parts of the Highlands, had already settled in the Far West. Indeed, the emigration at this early period was so extensive as to cause serious concern among the proprietors. The 'clearings,' or forced emigration of later times, had not then been dreamt of; but, on the contrary, the proprietors and the magnates of the Highland Society were using their utmost endeavours to discourage, and, forcibly prevent, the emigration of the Highlanders. You will find a curious proof of this in the Third Report of the Highland Society on emigration (page 4.) You will see, *e.g.*, how two men, by name Maclean and Maclellan, in Barra, were threatened with a legal prosecution for 'enticing the people to emigrate to America.' Among other charges, it was alleged that, while 'conversing with the people at a place of religious worship, they said that the Highlanders in America were not troubled with landlords or factors, but that all the people were happy and on an equal footing, that they had the blessings of the Gospel, and peace in the midst of plenty, and no threatening for rent at Martinmas.' 'Such,' indignantly, exclaims the Report, 'such is the train of sentiments, such the seditious discontents preached by the emigrant traders;' and then it goes on to argue 'that when this traffic draws into its service the preaching of sedition, and even,' tremendous climax, ' the calumniating of landlords and factors, . . . there was at common law full power vested in the magistrate to restrain and punish such irregularities.' One reason why the proprietors at that early period were so hostile to the emigration of their people was evidently that the emigrants were men of substance, for the complaint continually turns up in the Report, that they were ' carrying away the capital of the country;' and one ship is mentioned in which, to the bitter mortification of the landlords, the emigrants had thus carried away with them a sum of not less than £1500.

"In these early times an emigration party from a Highland district would naturally go out together; and together they would settle down as neighbours in the new world, while new arrivals from the native district would naturally join the old neighbours or blood relations who had preceded them. Thus certain districts in the Highlands came to have their corresponding special settlements in America, traces of which may still be found more or less prominently among the people. Let me here present to you very

shortly the results of my inquiries an this interesting topic.
Perthshire, and more especially Breadalbane, as well as Badenoch
and Strathspey, were chiefly represented, near the end of last century, in the State of New York; and you will still find families
not a few representing the old emigrants from these parts of Scotland on the Delaware, Mohawk, and Connecticut Rivers. The
people of Inverness settled chiefly in Georgia. The people of
Argyll and its islands, of Skye also, and the Long Island, and the
opposite coasts of Ross and Sutherland, betook themselves to
North Carolina, where they formed the large settlement of Fayette-
ville. This colony is celebrated in the history of America for its
loyalty to the British Crown and its sore misfortunes in the war
of independence. Many of these loyal Highlanders removed to
Canada rather than live under the Republic. Still, the Carolina
Highlanders formed a large and distinctly Gaelic settlement up to
very recent times. Mr Duncan Stewart, of Detroit, informed me
that he visited them as recently as 1860, when he found them
occupying 'four counties back off' the Cape Fear River.' He
then found amongst them large congregations of masters and their
slaves, who regularly worshipped in the Gaelic language. General
Wigfall, of the Confederate army, also told me that all through the
late lamented civil war 'twixt North and South, he had a regiment
of the Carolina Highlanders in his command—'brave, gallant
soldiers, of whom you might well be proud,' but, he added, with a
tear in his eagle eye, 'they were sadly cut up in the war.'
Flora Macdonald, he told me with pride, once lived with her kinsmen in Carolina. Her house, and many personal relics of the
heroine, some being relics also of Prince Charlie, had often been
shown to him. But Gaelic is now no longer preached in this
famous Highland settlement; nor, indeed, anywhere else that I
could hear of in the United States, save in one church at Elmira,
100 miles west of Chicago.

"The real home, I had almost said the only home, in these later
times, of the Gael in the Far West is Canada; and in Canada from
January to August of last year it was my good fortune to be his
guest. All that time I lived among Gaelic-speaking people of the
Dominion as one of themselves, travelling amongst them nearly
6000 miles on Canadian soil; and if the short sketches I am now
to present to you, of what thus I saw with my own eyes among
your kinsmen in the Far West, will give you but a tithe of the
pleasure I have in recalling the experiences of that memorable sojourn, I shall feel that I have not addressed you in vain.

"Let me say, once for all, that in these eight months I heard more Gaelic, and met more Gaelic men, in Canada, than in the previous twenty years at home   From Chicago to Cape Breton in one direction ; and, in the other, from the Georgian Bay to Lake Erie, and from Lake Simco to Lake Ontario ; in the great valley of the Ottawa ; here and there also among the French of Quebec; and all through the wide maritime provinces of Nova Scotia, Prince Edward's Island, and New Brunswick, I was never, though often preaching most days of the week, without a Gaelic congregation ; and, wherever I have been, the tale was still of out-lying Gaelic congregations which I had not time to visit.   Some I heard of, as, for example, the descendants of an Inverness-shire regiment of Frasers disbanded in Quebec at the close of the American War, who spoke Gaelic, French, and Indian, but not a word of English. Alike in the cities, in the older rural settlements, and in the backwoods, congregations almost invariably exceeding 400, and sometimes exceeding 1000, everywhere met me to worship God in the Gaelic language.   The very names of places were redolent of the heather—in the land where, alas ! the tenderest care has never yet been able to make the heather grow—Fingal, Glencoe, Glengarry, Inverness, Tobermory, St Kilda, Iona, Lochiel, Lochaber, and the rest !

"My first contact with the Gael of Canada was at Kingston, a pleasant, stone-built city, at the foot of Lake Ontario, and once our chief military station in the West.   I had just entered the Dominion from the State of New York, crossing the lake on the ice ; and who, think you, was my first-foot on the threshold of this Gaelic enterprise ?   He was a Gael : truly a Gael of Gaels, whose name is not less known and respected in Canada, than it is remembered and revered in the West Highlands of Scotland.   My 'first-foot' was none other than the Celtic bard, Evan Maccoll !   He was one of the Custom-house officers who searched my baggage on entering the Dominion ; and it will rejoice you to hear that though, like Burns, our Gaelic poet is a gauger, he is universally respected as a patriotic, and in every way an exemplary citizen of his adopted country.

"In trade and commercial activity, Kingston has fallen behind her old rival, Toronto, and could never compare with Montreal ; but, besides the prestige and academic culture of a university, her society can boast some of the best blood of our old Highland families— Macphersons, Hamiltons, Grants, Frasers, Macraes, and Mackays, mostly descendants of British officers, who, when stationed in the garrison, became attached to the place, and made it their home.

"While waiting in this pleasant city for a few days to adjust the programme of my mission, we had two Gaelic meetings which, though not numerously attended, were full of interest. To me they were indeed the beginning of an experience entirely new. For the first time in my life, I could feel what it is to be far from many home and dear ones ; and the aged people around had not for long years worshipped in the dear old mother tongue. If the truth be told, we all fairly broke down together ; and the silent hand-shaking, and the tearful eyes at the close of our little service were more eloquent by far than the sermon. The singing had a strange softening effect on us all. It was so like 'singing the songs of Zion in a strange land.' We did not sing that psalm. I could not venture to give it out. But, indeed, it was in all our thoughts, as with faltering voice, and many a quivering, broken note, the wail arose—

> " Mar thogras fiadh nan sruthan uisg',
>   Le buradh ard gu geur;
>   Mar sin tha m' anam plosgartaich,
>   Ag eigheachd riutsa, Dhe.

> " Tha tart air m' anam 'n geall air Dia,
>   'N geall air an Dia ta beo:
>   O cuin a thig 's a nochdar mi
>   Am fianuis Dhia na gloir ?

Or this—

> " 'N sin thubhairt mi, is truagh nach robb
>   Sgiath colmain agam nis !
>   'N sin theichinn as ag itealaich,
>   Is gheibhinn tamh is fois.

"One of the strangest incidents of these, my first Gaelic services in Canada, was the presence among the worshippers of a large family of coloured people—father, mother, and grown-up daughters, all dark as Erebus. It reminded me of a kind letter, on the eve of leaving Scotland, I had from Dr Norman Macleod, in reference to the Highlanders of North Carolina, of whom I have just made mention as worshipping regularly, themselves and their slaves, in the Gaelic language. You can well conceive the strange mingled feelings with which I looked on these dark African faces, so full of deep emotion, as we sang the praises of Jehovah, and worshipped His great name in the old Gaelic tongue.

" But I must not linger o'er thy pleasant scenes, fair, hospitable Kingston : so to thee farewell ! And, ladies and gentlemen of the Celtic Society, as I bid you a momentary good night at the door

of this magnificent railway carriage—the Pulman's palace sleeping
car—in the night train westward, permit me to skip the wondrous
incidents of this wondrous journey, 300 miles by rail and sleigh,
and in a new chapter let me introduce you to the first real work
of my mission.

" This was on the banks of the pleasant Saugeen, a river very
much larger than the Clyde. It enters the north-east angle of
Lake Huron a little to the south of the opening from that great
fresh-water sea into the Georgian Bay, and in an indefinite sort of
way gives its name to a district about 30 miles square, now thickly
peopled. This district for four weeks was to be my parish. Judge
then of my surprise to find that here, 5000 miles from Scotland,
Gaelic was the common speech of the people. Three out of every
four men you met, spoke the language with ease and purity.
Some of these Gaels of the Far West were Canadian born, having
hived off in quest of cheaper land and elbow room, from the older
settlements further east ; many were emigrants from Mull and
Kintyre, with a sprinkling also from all parts of the Scottish
Highlands. One little colony I found, at a place called Elderslie,
who were almost to a man from Colonsay. They were living a
sort of simple patriarchal life, under the mild rule of three pious
elders, bearing the West Highland names of Bell, Blue, and Mac-
fayden. Everywhere the guest of the people, and constantly moving about among them and living with them as one of themselves,
with as little reserve on their side as my own, I had abundant
opportunity of acquainting myself with their condition ; and as
Saugeen may be taken as a specimen of the vast Huron tract from
Godrich to Collingwood, it both will save time and otherwise be
of advantage, if I give you here, with some minuteness, my impressions of the district.

" But seventeen years had passed since the people entered this
wide district by the 'blaze line.' What a change these seventeen
years had wrought ! For the first few years, as you can well imagine,
the life of the hardy pioneers was one of toil and many privations.
One noble-looking old Highlander, from Strathspey, told me that
for nine weeks he wrought on in the forest solitudes without ever
seeing a white man's face. And it was quite a common thing for
a man in these times to carry a bag of wheat a distance of twenty
miles on his back to the nearest grist mill, and then, in the same
way, carry back the flour to feed his family. Most of the early
settlers, also, carried with them into the forest no other capital
than the strength of their own strong arms. And even, when
with sore toil they had cleared and got under crop a considerable

breadth of land, they had no sure market for their produce; while for the small loans from some Jewish usurer, with which they bought a few animals to stock their farms, they had to pay 12 to 25 per cent. But now, in seventeen brief years, all was changed! Everywhere, along the best of roads—main roads and cross roads—it was an unbroken succession of 200 acre lots, all closely adjoining, each with its comfortable homestead, and more than half cleared. And every six miles there is the comfortable schoolhouse, with its band of romping, well-clad children. My friend from Strathspey has his 200 acres all cleared, save what of the bush he must now reserve for firewood and shelter; his farm is heavily stocked; he has money in the bank; his house is comfortably furnished; with his comely daughters and well-built, strong-limbed sons (hard working women and men, but in dress and education ladies and gentlemen), he drives to church on Sunday in a handsome sleigh or waggonette, according to the season, drawn by a magnificent team of fast-trotting greys. And many have prospered as he has; while there be few that lag far behind him. Thus, where seventeen years ago the psalm of the pious Highland pioneer wakened up the echoes of the forest primeval, you have now the well-built churches of but too many denominations, and, side by side with the still surviving wigwam of the Indian, you have all the comforts of the Saut Market everywhere at hand. Five miles from the house which was my headquarters all these four weeks, you have, on one side, the rising town of Port-Elgin, with its three churches, two doctors, two large hotels, and shops where you can buy anything from a needle to an anchor, or from a cake of scented soap to a drift of herring nets; and nine miles on the other side you have Paisley, which boasts, besides the conveniences above specified, two flourishing woollen factories. Port-Elgin has a good harbour on Lake Huron. For this reason, next to Southampton at the mouth of the river, and Kincardine further South, it is the great centre of the district for the export of wheat. In February, therefore, when I was on the Saugeen, the town was thronged with farmers who, proudly independent of roads and bridges, were sleighing their produce to market by tracks smooth as our city tramways, and straight as a bee-line. At that time Port-Elgin was full of wheat. The granaries, indeed, had overflowed into the churches; for it is a fact that one church at least had been converted into a temporary granary till the opening of navigation in the spring. And when I speak of a granary, you are not to picture to yourselves a series of lofts with ventilating windows on either side, and a man with a wooden shovel continually turning over a thin layer of grain to prevent its moulding. The air in Canada is so dry that a granary may be described as a vast, solid bin, full of grain, 'choke full' from floor to ceiling. Two facts will suffice to give you an idea of the wondrous exuberance of the soil. The first crop of wheat gathered by my Speyside friend from his fresh cleared ground was sixty bushels to the acre; and ever since he has been taking yearly crops of wheat from the soil without any manure! Unfortunately, being but a winter visitor, I could only guess the genial character of the summer from the magnificent preserves of grape, peach, and tomato, which were everywhere set before me. What a change from the wholesome frugal products of ' Caledonia, stern and wild !' What a change, indeed, from the same place itself eighteen years ago! Then : nought but the trackless forest on every side; now : the best of roads to the doors of hundreds of comfortable settlers, and several times a-day, this summer for the first time, a well-equipped railway train speeding its rapid career through fields of golden grain !

" The home of the Gael in his native glen—too often miserably uncomfortable, if not also unhealthy, and sometimes sorely stricken with poverty—is a picture well known to most of us. Let me sketch lightly his home in the Far West. Even in Saugeen the old log shanty has now all but disappeared. The smart brick villa, so familiar to me a month or two later in the older settlements of Ontario, is not yet common in Saugeen ; but the comfortable and picturesque ' frame house' meets you everywhere. Now, the main characteristic of the frame house is that it is built of sawn timber. Given this essential condition, and you can have it in what form, size, or style you please. In Saugeen it is usually an unpretending erection of some 40 feet by 25, a storey and a-half or two storeys high, with a verandah and overhanging eaves for its only artificial ornaments. I say ' artificial ornaments,' for, when summer comes, the vine, the hop, and a hundred native creepers, rising from the brightness of the gay surrounding garden, adorn it with a beauty surpassing that of any or of all the orders of architecture. Let me sketch for you the winter interior of such a home. Its chief room is the large, airy, well-lighted kitchen, whose centrepiece is a handsome cooking stove on the middle of the floor, its black, polished stove-pipe piercing the ceiling and warming the room above. The principal ornaments of a Canadian kitchen are the plentiful festoons of dried apples and other good things which hang on its pure white walls. The cellar underneath, opening by a trap-door in the floor, through which the busy house-

3

wife often appears and disappears like the good fairy in an old play, is also characteristic. Next to the kitchen in importance, and opening from it, is the family eating-room; opening from which again is the nicely decorated parlour, where, in all the luxury of a real Canadian rocking-chair, before a fire of real Canadian rock maple, I oft in these four weeks spent the hours in pensive day-dreams of home, and family, and far-off friends. And then there were the two or three bedrooms up the creaking open wooden stair, carpetted with pretty home-wrought rugs of quaint primitive patchwork, and the sheets and curtains purely white, as only Canadian snows can bleach. Nor can I forget the 'bacon room,' through which, at the head of the stair, I entered my pleasant bedroom. Laugh, gentle friends, if you will; but of that room I cherish warm feelings of respect, and indeed a sort of reverent affection. It looked so comfortable like; it was so grateful and substantial an emblem of the happy change my countrymen had made from the poverty and intermittent famine of twenty years ago in the Highlands, as nightly I passed through it with my coal oil lamp, and marked its goodly array of fragrant hams, sides of bacon, and other cured meats. And, moreover, it was so truly Christian-like, always to observe another bare nail, where good things used to hang, after the visit of some unfortunate brother or sister, who, from accident or disease, was no more a breadwinner—such, for example, as poor Widow M'K., or the one-handed man, with the pretty little girl ever gambolling in and out of the sleigh, in loving horse play with the comfortable rozinante which carried father and child on the beaten round from farm to farm. God bless you, worthy Neil Cairns, best of hosts; you had aye a warm heart towards all distressed and unfortunate ones; and gude be wi' ye, Mrs Neil, his frugal spouse, if withal a wee thing stern and crusty in the rind, yet soft and sweet within as thine own Spitzbergen apples. I will not soon forget the memorable weeks spent beneath your hospitable roof, our reverent morning and evening worship, our pleasant meals, our visits to the sick, our christenings, our pleasant teas and prayer-meetings with the neighbours, our visits to the cows, and to that wonderful black mare, heavy in foal, and therefore to be driven with tender consideration; your patient endeavours to teach my awkward hands the woodcraft mysteries of the axe while chopping the daily firewood; and above all, the delicate, gentle instinct, with which ye saw and humoured the home-sick mood that loved to sit alone in the old rocking chair, with book in hand, but in thought and fancy far, far away!

"But more important even than the dwelling-house on a Canadian farm is the huge barn, which serves for stack-yard, granary, stable, byre, and sheep-cot all in one. This, and a hundred objects more, rise before me as I write, all claiming a place in my picture; the handsome C.P. Church at Port Elgin, where, the church proper falling into a state of arrested development, the congregation made themselves comfortable down stairs in the "basement," or, as we would say, in the cellar; and the fine, well-finished church at Paisley, which one night we had to enter through ten feet of fresh drifted snow; and the church which is in thine house, O venerable elder B——, where, during the service, you roasted me in the place of honour next the stove, but in the evening turned me out into the sleigh, with no better apology for buffalo than a poor miserable bed-cover!

"Fain would I here depict you one and all; but this rapid sketch of the Saugeen kirk, my own church in a special sense all these four weeks, must suffice.

"Drive up with me, then, to the church. It is a clear frosty morning, and the dry crisp snow chirps gently, like the winter song of our own homely robin, under the glancing runners of the sleigh. Round three sides of the church-lot the horses, many of them still in the sleigh, are drawn up facing us, like the three sides of a hollow square. On the fourth side, along the road, and clustering round the door, the congregation awaits the minister. The church is all of wood, almost new, and not yet painted. We enter through a spacious doorway, under a handsome tower, which forms the vestibule, and thence into the body of the church. Right and left, as you enter, is a large roaring stove : opposite, the platform or pulpit; and the whole length of the church, from the stoves at the door to either side of the pulpit, and about seven feet above the floor, the two long lines of stove pipe which there bend up at a right angle and pierce the roof. As the pulpit is elevated about two feet from the floor, the preacher stands up with his head literally between two fires. If he be a 'basswood man,' the caloric thus fiercely radiated from a fiery stove pipe over either ear may stimulate his brain to some advantage; and, possibly, the apparatus may be designed to produce that effect. But, for my own part, I would not recommend its use in the churches or lecture rooms of this country. In the precentor's seat before me sits the trusty elder, Cairns, another tuneful singer by his side; and, as they stand up and lead the praise-offering of the congregation, if their music has not all the grace and delicate light and shade of a well-trained city choir, they at least stood there before God and his people, a visible picture of most Christian harmony; adjacent

arms twined lovingly round each other's waist, and outside arms
stretched at full length, and held well up, to grasp the one psalm-
book from which together they sing. And they sang; and we all
sang, with all our might; sang without restraint, as God gave us
voices; sang as men that would say, 'While I have breath I will
sing praises to my God;' sang this noble psalm—

> 'Good unto all men is the Lord,
> O'er all his works his mercy is.'

Or this other, in the sweet mother tongue—

> 'O thigibh agus faicibh nis
> Gur maith 's gur milis Dia;
> Am fear sin 's bannaicht e gu beachd
> A dhearbas as an Triath.'

The parting with these kind Christian friends was no small trial
to me, and it issued in a catastrophe. The people wished to send
me on to Paisley, where I was to preach in the evening; but a
pious man of that place, an estimable tailor, whose wife had once
been a member of my church in Edinburgh, came over for the
purpose, and claimed the honour as his due. There was no
denying the real kindness which prompted this act of courtesy to
his wife's old minister; yet, with all my heart I wished that he
had stayed at home; for the first glance made it evident that,
however expert with the measuring tape, he certainly was not at
home with the ribbons. His horse, moreover, a tall, raw-boned,
vicious-looking brute, was borrowed from one customer, the sleigh
from a second, the harness from a third; and the three an egregious
and almost laughable misfit. It will not, therefore, surprise you
to hear that less than a mile from Saugeen church I was pitched
head foremost into a huge snow-wreath, crushing into a pancake,
beneath my aching ribs, a hard leather hat-box with its precious
contents. Fortunately, the effects, real and apparent, were not
much other than as if I had been pitched into a heap of flour; and,
the break-down notwithstanding, I was able to keep my evening
engagement.

"My next 'circuit' was 150 miles further south, on the
Thames, a navigable river running parallel to the northern shore
of Lake Erie, and near it, though entering Lake St Clair. At
Glencoe, Dunwich, Chatham, London, Fingal, and Oneida, we had
large gatherings of the Gael. The settlements here were older
than at Saugeen: the towns were much larger; and in town and
country the houses and churches were more largely built of brick.

"The chief difference to me was that, the season being now more advanced, I had to exchange the pleasant sleigh for the cumbersome high-wheeled buggy.

"Leaving the Thames, and preaching in Gaelic by the way at Hamilton; at Niagara, where our Gaelic psalmody was 'organed by the thund'ring cataract;' and at Toronto, a journey of 300 miles brought me to our next large group of Gaelic congregations on the shores of Lake Simco. Chiefs and patriarchs among the Highlanders of this fertile region, had long been, by universal consent, Colonel Cameron of Beaverton, and his three brothers— cadets of the noble family of Lochiel. Alas! that to-day the last of these noble brothers lies cold in an exile's grave, far from the ashes of his fathers. Long the pillar of our large Gaelic congregation at Thora, at the time of my visit he lay on what he knew to be his death-bed. The brothers were excellent farmers, as well as men of taste and enterprise; and their lands would compare favourably with the 'home farms' of our aristocracy.

"In our congregation at Eldon, in this district, I found a few of the North Carolina Highlanders, who twenty years ago came north to join a fresh arrival of cousins from Argyll. One of them was our Gaelic precentor. Among them also was a coloured woman of whom the following anecdote will bear to be repeated. The little slave girl grew up among our countrymen at Eldon without ever seeing a person of her own colour; and if ever she examined her face in a glass, like him in the Scripture, 'she straightway went her way, forgetting what manner of person she was.' By and bye, when the country was opened up by steamers from the Georgian Bay into the lake, she one day happened to see a coloured man on the quay at Beaverton, at which dread apparition she ran home trembling with fear, and gasped out, 'Chunaic mi duine, lethid a dhuinne! Bha e cho dubh; agus chuir a do dh' fheagal orm 's gun d'fhas mi cho bann ri mo leine!'

"Back again by Toronto, to meet an old pupil, an energetic and singularly successful Black Islesman, who, hearing of me at Hamilton, and following me thence to the Ontarian capital, only to find that I had just left for the north, telegraphed me to meet him ' *anywhere* in Canada,' my journey lay once more through dear old Kingston, and thence round by Lanark, a distance of full 400 miles, to Ottawa, the political capital of the Dominion. Here, in a large Gaelic congregation, on a week-day evening, I met seven first cousins of my own, who left the Highlands twenty-five years ago with only the blessing and example of eminently pious parents for their whole worldly estate. They are all men of substance

and influence in the land of their adoption; and they told me of
many more from our native district who had prospered as they
had done. 'In fact,' said one of them, 'any man can do it, if only
he is industrious, honest, and, like me, a teetotaller.' Down the
valley of the grand, dark-rolling Ottawa—a day's sail, varied by
one or two short bits of railway to skirt the rapids—brought me
to Montreal, that city of merchant princes—merchants of whom
some of the most princely are Highlanders, and were among the
800 who, in the mother tongue, worshipped with me in the beautiful church of St Andrew.

"Crossing the St Lawrence at Lachine, a little above the
awful rapids of that name, I had a few days of quiet rest with
dear old friends from the Black Isle, in the old Scotch settlement
of Beechridge. A day in the old church-yard of the settlement
(fifty years in Canada look as old as five hundred in Scotland)
was literally a meditation among the tombs. Many of the young
men of Beechridge have gone West, and not a few of the old people
have followed. But the church-yard is full of the beautiful white
marble tombstones of Highlanders who have gone to their long
home. Some of these snow-white tombstones had a text, and
some a verse, and some a pious epitaph. In this and other respects they differed, as even tombstones will; but in one thing
they all were one—these three words, pointing homewards even in
death, as the exiled Israelite in his prayers turned ever to Jerusa-
lem: 'A native of'—Stewarts, Finlaysons, Mathiesons, Morrisons,
Macraes, Mackenzies, Macleods—'a native of Glenelg;' 'a native
of Kintail;' 'a native of Gairloch;' 'a native of Kilmuir, Isle
of Skye.'

"About this time there befell me one night an adventure
which, for the moment, was a little embarrassing. The good lady
whose guest I was occupied a beautiful, well-appointed mansion.
But somehow, though it was summer, the stove-pipe from my
bedroom to the chamber adjoining had been left in its place; and
as it did not quite fill the aperture by which it pierced the partition, you could hear distinctly—and for that matter I suppose you
could also *see*—from the one room into the other. Thus it became
painfully evident to me, soon after retiring to rest, that side by
side with my bed, on the other side of the thin partition, there
was another bed. And a most crazy bed it must truly have been,
and its occupant the most restless of mortals. For such a creaking and a ceaseless tossing to and fro I never heard before. Still,
after some time, I slept the deep, sound sleep of the weary. But
at midnight I was suddenly roused up with successive bursts of

violent unnatural coughing. It was a thousand times worse than if the adjoining room had been turned into the whooping-cough ward of a children's hospital. Such coughing surely was never heard before. Yes, thought I, it must be my dear old friend, and she's being suffocated. To start up in bed and hastily whisper through the aperture, 'I've my medicines; shall I bring you something?' was at once my thought and act. 'Oh, yes, and be quick!' I fancied I could make out through the spasmodic, suffocating *cynanché* of my dear distressed friend. To strike a light, jump into my trousers, and snatch the fitting medicament, was the work of a moment, and I darted into the corridor, when, pausing an instant to see my way, I found that the coughing had entirely ceased. All was still as the grave. But again—what on earth can it mean?—that strange, suppressed gurgling sound? Good heavens! can it be that my worthy friend is in *articulo mortis?* Bah! it's but the smothered giggling of some frivolous joker bent on having a rise out of the parson. So I turned on my heel, and half-angry, half-amused, I laid me down again and slept on without further adventure or disturbance till the sun was high in the firmament.

"On the back of the railway guide-books, and on the green cover of the *Gael*, there is a standing advertisement which says.—

'When you are in the Highlands, visit Macdougall's?'

"Gentlemen of the Celtic Society, when you are in Canada, visit Glengarry. This was the advice everywhere given me in the West: if you would see the Canadian Gael at his best; if you would carry back to Scotland any just idea of our great Gaelic communion gatherings in the open air; if you would hear the ceiste opened up in a style worthy of your own 'men' of 40 years ago—then visit the Gaelic congregations of Glengarry. And yet Glengarry, the oldest, largest, and most purely Celtic of all the Highland colonies in the great province of Ontario, I did not visit. At one time it was the miscarriage of a telegram, at another the burning of a large passenger steamer on the St Lawrence, that gave me this great disappointment; and engagements made for me in the maritime provinces, 800 miles further East, put it out of my power to make a third attempt; the Gaelic adage notwithstanding, 'air an trieamh uar bheira chailleach buaidh.'

"Before asking you, however, to accompany me to the maritime provinces, let me pause here for a moment, and give you one or two examples of the great prosperity to which in the West our countrymen have attained. As an example, then, of the high general level of comfort, as independent owners of the land they cultivate, easily reached by men who at home could never hope to rise above the condition of crofters or day labourers, take this picture. It is from a congregation of Highlanders to which I preached in the school-house of Oneida, near Fingal. Before me sat a venerable man, who, five-and-thirty years before, left the shores of Lochfyne, with the price of an old boat for all his capital. On one hand sat his three sons, their wives, and children; on the other his daughter, her husband, their children, and their children's children; each the free owner of 200 acres of rich cleared land. Half-an-hour would suffice to gather them all around the old man's hearth. As examples of great mercantile success, take the Hon. J—— W——, an Inveraray gentleman, the leading man of the forest city. Three years ago he paid off principal and interest of a heavy failure, which was the only reward of his previous mercantile efforts in Glasgow. He is now one of the most influential men in the Dominion. Or take the Hon. J—— Mack——, one of the richest, and certainly the most liberal, of the merchant princes of Montreal. On proper occasions he is not ashamed to tell of the day, when a barefooted, friendless boy, he turned with a heavy heart from the smoking ruins of his grandfather's cottage at Kildonan. And from many brilliant examples of the success of our countrymen in the arena of political conflict, take just these two names—the Hon. Archibald Mackellar, another Argyllshire man, and every inch a Highlander, the Minister of Public Works; and the Hon. Alexander Mackenzie, a Perthshire man, from the confluence of the Tay and the Tummel, to whom, as Premier of Canada, has been entrusted by Providence the noble work of consolidating the new Dominion, and moulding the destinies of an empire wider and mightier than it ever entered into the dreams of the great Napoleon to rule over.

" These honoured names are but a sample of the way in which the Gael everywhere takes his place in the first rank of professions and of public life. Yet, after all, the great prize of the country, whether to Gael or Saxon, is the land—your own land, free for ever to your children's children—your own land, gloriously independent of factor, landlord, or superior. You remember how our semi-Celtic Professor Blackie has right nobly sung—

> ' If I had land, as I have none,
>   The people round me I would gather,
>   And every lad I'd call my son,
>   And every lass would call me father.'

Buoyant and versatile enthusiast as he is, I fear the poet-professor is now too old to launch his bark on the Atlantic; and, after a ten days' sail, put his theory in practice on the rich virgin soil of Ontario. But to the chivalrous young men of this Celtic Society, I say deliberately that I do not know an enterprise, in this prosaic nineteenth century, that holds out so many solid, and yet nobly captivating inducements.

"But, now, farewell, Ontario! and, ladies and gentlemen, a glimpse or two in conclusion—skipping the 800 miles between—of the Gael in the maritime provinces. Only a glimpse; for, though we must despatch him in a few short paragraphs, he is at once more numerous, and far more the ideal Gael of our romance, than his ambitious enterprising brother in Western Ontario—far more unsophisticated, more pious and contemplative, and, with many creditable exceptions, immeasurably more the simple counterpart of his unenterprising brother in Ross-shire and the Isles, forty years ago. In some parts of Cape Breton, for example, which, though as mountainous and picturesque as Assynt and Skye, is full of coal, iron, and other precious mineral, you will find the people to this day, even in dress, very much the same as they were in the Highlands when I was a child, and long before some of you were born. The high-crowned, white muslin mutch, the kertch and black silk handkerchief for head-dress; the scarlet cloak; the guidman and guidwife slowly ambling their way to market, mounted on the same palfrey, perhaps a bag in front, balanced over the horse's neck, with a jar of butter in either end; the spinning-wheel and domestic loom; the same unskilled primitive agriculture, aiming only at so much hay and other provender as will keep the stock alive through the winter, and at the sale of the summer's butter, and a stirk or two in the autumn. All this, though in a worldly point of view far behind the enterprise of exuberant, energetic Ontario, has yet a charm and fascination of its own, on which, did your time permit, I would gladly dwell. For, indeed, the Gael of these maritime provinces, happy, and lacking for nothing, as if in his old home his old enemy the factor had laid him down with the seven sleepers of Ephesus, leads a sort of primitive Arcadian life, which, in many respects, is very beautiful. And, moreover, if he has gained something in comfort, intelligence, and independence, he has assuredly lost nothing of the devoutness and keen religious sensibility which he carried with him from Skye and Barra and the lone straths of Sutherland.

"The largest settlements of these simple-minded people are to be found in Cape Breton, Pictou County, and Prince Edward's

Island. Fully the half of them are Catholics—*na h-Uistich 's na Barraich*, as they are still called—but the Catholics have always lived on good terms with their Protestant neighbours and countrymen. Hitherto their common Highland blood has proved thicker than holy water.

"My eight weeks work among our large and numerous Gaelic congregations in these parts, consisting mainly of sacramental services, was one unbroken round of religious excitement, of which, even had there been time, this is not the place to speak in detail.

"A sketch or two, from notes taken at the time, may, however, give you a fresher picture of the people than anything I can now, by an effort of memory, condense into the few remaining pages which must close this lecture.

"Take, then, as an example of many, this sketch of a communion Sunday in Cape Breton. We kept it in a sweet, bosky dell, Broadcove by name, that nestles in a pleasant glen of the grassy Mabow Hills. Unhappily the day was very wet. But, as I entered the tent, the gaze of full 1200 people, from the slopes rising gently around in the form of an amphitheatre, converged on the spot where I stood. What a sight: grandsires of eighty winters and the youth of scarce twelve summers; strong men in their prime and graceful maidens in their teens; here a clump of old men, head bare of bonnet and protecting locks, each leaning on his staff, eager for the word of life; and there a line of aged women, mutch covered with handkerchief, and the black shawl, with one hand held up to the angle of the mouth, as they rocked to and fro, and wept with deep emotion; their thoughts, doubtless, busy with 'the light of other days' of high communion, and with precious memories of Maighstir Lachlan, and the Kennedies, and the great Macdonald of Ferrintosh.

"For five long hours that multitude sat upon the soaking sward, as if glued to it. For the first two hours it rained incessantly, yet every male had his head uncovered. We had four tables: and to serve the last of them was the most trying duty of all my ministry. The refrain of the few simple words I spoke was, 'Behold the Lamb of God!' and, as I spoke, the feelings of many seemed to master them; a swell of agitation heaved the bosoms of the communicants, and their inmost hearts seemed to gaze through the streaming eyes. Awe crept over me as I looked from face to face; and, as the words rose to my lips, a new light of quickening spiritual insight kindled up the wail of the Psalmist —'As the hart panteth after the water brooks, so panteth my soul after Thee, O God.' Oh! what a rebuke to the growing *dilettantism* of our fashionable churches in Scotland, and to its petulant, affected cry of 'twenty-five minutes sharp.'

"Or take again this picture of an ordinary Sunday in fair Prince Edward's Island, the garden of Eastern Canada. The way from the manse to the church is through a grove of grand old trees, which the people, with a good taste too rare in Canada, have spared from the axe; and, as we walked up the forest aisles, the over-arching branches closed over us like the roof of some mighty cathedral. We passed upwards of 200 carriages in the wood, and this prepared us for the great congregation which overflowed the church and gathered around the building; windows and doors being all thrown open, not less for the convenience of those outside than to give air to the crowded multitude within. The reverence and wrapt attention of this large congregation all through the service, and the hearty fervour with which they joined in the old-fashioned Gaelic psalmody, carried me back to the days of my boyhood, thirty years ago, when with the multitude I sang the same psalms in the Burn of Ferrintosh.

"As the last extract from my note-book, take this notice of a brave, leal-hearted Highland clergyman, a native of Rannoch, the late Rev. Donald Macdonald of Prince Edward's Island. For forty years this truly apostolic man lived only for his people, knowing no home and drawing no stipend, but living among his flock as one of themselves, and taking such things as they gave him. His published remains show him to have been a man of learning and vigorous intellect; and the present state of his churches, after years of comparative neglect and discouragement, show what a true leader of men, and what powers of energy and wise organisation lie under his fair white monument at Orwell Church. He built his seventeen churches without extraneous aid, and he organised and ministered to them without one brother's help or counsel; yet, though thus labouring single-handed, he peremptorily set his face against lay preaching; and to this day lay preaching is sternly discountenanced by the great body of his followers. They have still, as ordered by Mr Macdonald, a large staff of elders, who hold regular meetings on Lord's-days and week-days for prayer and reading of the Word. As a people they are peculiar for a wondrous gift of prayer, and they are mighty in the Scriptures. Some of them, I doubt not, could preach with power. But with every inducement to take up with lay preaching, and a widely-prevailing example of it around them on every side, preaching without regular Church orders is a thing hitherto unknown among the seventeen churches of the Macdonaldites, most of them practically

vacant since their founder's death. I know not whether this
strong repugnance be founded, as probably it is, on their views of
Scripture truth.   But they have one reason, which to them is
almost as valid as Scripture authority, ' *he* forbade it.'   That the
Macdonaldites are ' a peculiar people,' they themselves would be
the last to deny; and of certain physical manifestations cherished
among them as indicating 'a work of the Holy Spirit, I shall not
venture to express an opinion; but it cannot be denied that they
are, as a people, peculiar for good works, and that they maintain
a high standard of morality.

    " Besides some tractates in controversial theology, Mr Mac-
donald wrote for his people a volume of ' Hymns and Sacred
Songs,' in Gaelic and English, which is highly esteemed among the
Highlanders of Eastern Canada.   By order of the author, these
sacred songs are not allowed to be sung in what he calls the
' solemn' worship of God.   They are used only in certain intervals
of the long and highly-exciting service of his churches, when the
congregation, coming down from the mount, and resolving itself,
as it were, into a ' committee of the whole,' is occupied with exer-
cises strictly religious, but still by them counted less sacred than
'solemn' worship.   In these intervals of much-needed relaxation
from overstrained spiritual tension, the ' sacred songs' are sung by
the people with unstinted zest and spirit, to such airs as ' Blaw
wastlin' winds' and 'The Banks of the Dee ;' after which the congregation reverts to ' solemn' worship, only to be again speedily
absorbed in wrapt lofty contemplation, or swayed and tossed with
wave on wave of intense excitement.

    " Let me now close this lecture with two quotations from the
'Sacred Songs,' simply observing that the fine, sparkling scintilla-
tions of ' holy commination' in the last of them is to be set down
to a famous ecclesiastical controversy, being, in fact, the Voluntary
conflict of our own day, between Mr Macdonald and the great Anti-
burgher, another Highlander, of whom and of his great missionary
work, controversy notwithstanding, we may all be proud, Dr James
Macgregor, of Pictou :—

  ' Air laith'reachd Iehobhah bhi seinn tha e taitneach,
    Do dhream a fhuair eolas 'us fiosrachadh geur,
    A dh' fhiosraich a bhaigh 'us a ghradh 'us a fhreasdal,
    Gan lionadh le solas 's a tiormach' gach deur.
    Tha fas air a ghras doibh, le danachd a chreideamh,
    Mar dhruchd a tha tla agus blath air an fheasgar ;
    Cha 'n eil brigh ann an ni' ach le lath' reachd gun teagamh,
    Tha toradh a lath' reachd air 'fhagail na dheigh.'

'Dh' eirich Solus 'us aigh oirn,
Dh' eirich Iosa ar Slanuighear on uaigh,
Dh' eirich Grian agus gloir oirn,
Dh' eirich Criosda na mhorachd le buaidh,
Dh' eirich latha na slaint' oiru,
Dh' eirich Prionnsa na sith o gach truaigh,
Dh' eirich Ceannard ar slainte,
Dh' eirich Teachaire grasmhor da shluaigh.

'Siubhlaidh nise na sgailean,
Siubhlaidh dorchadas bais agus truaigh,
Siubhlaidh ceannairc 'us naimhdeas,
Siubhlaidh peacadh gu brath o do shluagh,
Siubhlaidh *teagasg neo-ghrasmhor,*
Siubhlaidh *mealtarachd ghraisgeil gu luath,*
Siubhlaidh cumhachd a namhaid,
Siubhlaidh *teachdairean Shatain gu truaigh.'* "

27TH NOVEMBER 1873.

The Secretary read, as proxy, a paper by ALEXANDER HALLEY, Esq., M.D., F.G., London, and a life member of the Society, on "Letters as the integral representative of intelligible articulation in language, and a brief comparison of Gaelic as a natural tongue, with English as a cultured artificial speech." This learned and interesting paper will be found at page 109 of Volume II. of the Society's Transactions, wherein it was printed by a resolution of the Society.

11TH DECEMBER 1873.

This meeting was devoted to the arrangements for the Annual Supper to come off in January.

18TH DECEMBER 1873.

A letter was received from George Murray Campbell, Esq., Gampola, enclosing a cheque of £5 as a donation to the Society. Mr William Mackenzie, the *ad interim* Secretary, gave notice of his intention to resign office, in consequence of his leaving Inverness, and a committee was appointed to select a suitable Secretary.

13TH JANUARY 1874.

A special meeting of the Society was held within the Caledonian Hotel, for the purpose of electing Alexander Fraser, Esq., Drummond Estate Office, as a life member of the Society, which was done, on the motion of Mr Murdoch, with acclamation, after which the members adjourned to partake of the

SECOND ANNUAL SUPPER OF THE SOCIETY,

under the presidency of CLUNY MACPHERSON of Cluny, Chief of the Society. Sir Kenneth S. Mackenzie, Bart. of Gairloch, and Sheriff Macdonald, late of Stornoway, were croupiers.

On the right of the Chief were—Captain Chisholm, Glassburn; Major Donald Davidson, and Bailie Davidson. On the left the Chief was supported by Colonel J. F. Macpherson and Bailie Simpson. Sir Kenneth was supported by Councillor A. Mackenzie, and A. Mackintosh, Esq. of Dalmigavie, J.P.; and Sheriff Macdonald was supported by Messrs Davidson, Scott, and Ross, solicitors. There were also present—Mr Noble, Castle Street; Dr Macnee; Mr A. Fraser, writer; Mr Fraser, Mauld; Mr H. Mackintosh, Castle Street; Mr J. Macdonald, of Macdonald Brothers, Union Street; Captain Grant; Mr Macrae, High School; Captain Mackenzie, Telford Road; Messrs Tulloch, painter; Peter Falconer, plasterer; Maclennan, of Macdougall & Co.; R. Grant, do.; Barclay, accountant; Huntly Fraser, merchant; Mackay, Dempster Gardens; Macleod, grocer, Huntly Street; Garden, Mackintosh Estate Office; Maclean, coal-merchant; W. Macdonald, plasterer; Rev. Mr Wright, congregational minister; Whyte, photographer; W. Mackenzie, Club Buildings; Sinclair, tailor; J. S. Mackay, Chicago; W. Fraser, Glasgow; John Macdonald, Exchange; Maciver, cabinetmaker; J. Fraser, C.E.; D. Campbell, draper; Couper, Highland Railway; J. Murdoch, hon. secretary of the Society; Kay, Drummond Street; Kenneth Fraser, writer; Young, Royal Academy; W. Macdonald, Maryhall, &c., &c.

As the company was assembling, and during the dinner, Pipe Major Maclennan, Piper to the Society, played some of his finest *Piobaireachd* and quick steps, to the great delight of his Celtic hearers. After dinner,

The Chief gave the toast of "The Queen" in Gaelic—'S e mo dhleasanas agus mo dhurachd a nis iarraidh oirbh 'ur cuachan a lionadh agus deoch slainte na Ban-righ ol. Tha mise cinnteach gu'm beil sibh uile gle thoilichtè sin a dheanadh, oir 's math is airidh i air. Tha i na ban-uachdran mhath, agus a bhar air a sin

tha speis mhor aicè air na Gaidheil agus air a Ghaidhealtachd;
agus tha i a cur seachad moran dé a h-uin' nar measg. Air an
taobh eile, tha fios agamsa gu'm beil moran urram aicè dha na
Gaidheil. Tha iad mar so ann an run math ri cheile. 'S math is
airidh ise air speis agus gean math a cnid sluaigh, agus 's math is
airidh iadsan air uachdaran math mar tha ise. So ma tha, Deoch
slainte Ban-righ Shasuinn, Albainn, Eirinn, agus nan Innsinn, an
ear 's an iar. Cha neil Righ, no Ban-righ eil' anns an t-shaoghal
aig am bheil a leithid do dh-fharsuinneachd, no aig am beil sluagh
cho dileas. Olamaid mar sin a deadh dheoch slainte. Bha e 'na
aobhar gairdeachas dhuinn gun d' thainig i n'ar measg an uridh,
agus gun deach i fad an rathaid a' Ceann-a-ghiubhasich gu Inbhir-
lochaidh, gun ghille-ruith gun chas-luath, gun each gun fheachd,
ach aon ghille a's aon mharcaiche, direach mar gu'm bi bean tighearna no ceile ceann-cinnidh, leigeil fhaicinn an earbsa tha aicè a's
na Gaidheil. This speech was greeted from time to time with loud
and hearty applause, and the toast was drunk in the most enthusiastic manner.

The Chief then gave " Prionnsa agus Bana-phrionnsa na Coim-
reich, Mor-fhear nan Eilean, agus a h-uile h-aon eill de'n teaghlach
Rioghail." This also was drunk with great enthusiasm. The
Chief said—Tha duilichinn orm gu'm feum mi nis a Ghaidhlig a
chur air chul agus tionndadh gus a Bheurla.

The Chairman called for a bumper to the Army, Navy, and
Reserve Forces. (Applause.) He could not help alluding to the
unpleasant war in which we are at present engaged. It was very
unfortunate that her Majesty's troops should be engaged in fighting
savages. However, such things would happen; and when any
insult was offered to the British Crown, the skill and prowess of
our army must be felt by any people who dared to offer the insult.
(Applause.) He trusted the Ashantees would get a lesson which
would prevent their attempting anything of the kind in future.
He hoped they would excuse him speaking feelingly on this
matter, considering that he had a son engaged in the war—
(Applause)—and who was now with that gallant regiment, the 42d
Highlanders, as senior major. (Applause) He was quite sure
that the three regiments now on their way against the Ashantees
would soon bring the war to an end. These regiments were the
23d Fusiliers, a battalion of the Rifle Brigade, and the 42d Highlanders. They were now landed, and were on their advance to the
Prah, and he was sure they would soon return with fresh laurels.
(Applause.) Without introducing politics, he might say that
many soldiers seemed to have a dislike to the present army system;

but Mr Cardwell, the War Secretary, had acted in the most wonderfully liberal manner, and had done everything he possibly could do for the troops on service. (Applause.) Everything had been provided for them—clothing supposed to be suitable for the climate, a liberal commissariat, and, in short, the men had received the greatest attention and encouragement that men could receive. (Applause.) On their arrival, instead of being landed in a swampy country and bad climate, they had been sent to sea to be kept healthy. The soldiers' wives who remained at home got each sixpence a-day, and every child also received an allowance. That was the way to encourage soldiers—(Applause)—and if Government went on in this way, they might depend upon it the British Crown would have cordial defenders, and would stand for generations to come. (Applause.) In giving the toast, he could not help alluding to his own Volunteers. He had the honour of commanding the Inverness-shire Volunteers now for nearly fourteen years. (Applause.) During that time, he was proud to say, he had hardly ever had a difference of opinion with an officer or man. They had all done their duty in the most cordial manner, and his command had been a most agreeable one. He must also allude to the loss the regiment had recently sustained in the retirement of the Adjutant. In him they had lost their right-hand man, and one who was an efficient officer in every possible way. However, after a certain time of life, they must all retire. He supposed he would have to retire himself one of these days. ("No, no.") He might also mention that he had been successful in getting the Commander-in-chief to appoint a very efficient man as Adjutant— a clansman of his own, though not a relation. (Applause.) This officer had served for ten or twelve years as Adjutant of the 93d, and was now a Captain of the service, which rank he would retain in his new position. His name was Captain Fitzroy Macpherson (called after Lord Fitzroy Somerset), and he hoped he would be here one of these days to take the place of Captain Fraser. (Applause.)

The toast was acknowledged by Colonel Macpherson of Cat-lodge on behalf of the army, and by Captain Grant on behalf of the volunteers.

Mr Whyte sang "Ta Phairsan."

The Chief said Mr Murdoch, Honorary Secretary of the Society, would read the annual report.

Mr Murdoch, on rising, said he had received several letters expressing regret that the writers could not be present—from Mr Fraser-Mackintosh, Professor Blackie, Mr Charles Innes, Sir

Patrick Grant; Raigmore; Major Grant, Glen-Urquhart; Mr Macgregor Rose, Aberdeen; Mr Osgood H. Mackenzie, Inverewe; and Mr Angus Mackintosh of Holme. He then said that the worst part of his report was the fact that the presenting of it devolved upon himself.

"Since the first annual supper last year, the Society had lost the invaluable services of Mr William Mackay, the first secretary, by the removal of that gentleman from the Highland to the Scottish capital. That was a very serious loss to the Society, and a matter of personal regret to the members. The Society had the good fortune to secure the services of Mr William Mackenzie, one of the best Gaelic scholars of the day, and one of the most enthusiastic of Celts, but just as the arrangements for the supper were becoming most urgent, the Secretary was prostrated by sickness; and thus the Honorary Secretary, whose head and hands were previously too fully occupied, had to step into the breach, which he now so inadequately occupies.

"At the end of the first year of the Society's existence, the membership stood thus—Life members, 2; honorary members, 53; ordinary, 127. The two life members were—Cluny Macpherson, the worthy Chief of the Society, and Charles Fraser-Mackintosh, Esq. of Drummond. Since then the Society has had the honour and satisfaction of adding the names of Sir Kenneth S. Mackenzie of Gairloch, Bart., one of the Honorary Chieftains; Dr Halley, F.G.S., 16 Harley Street, London; and Mr Alexander Fraser, accountant, 16 Union Street, Inverness, to the list of life members. So that now the membership stands thus—Life members, 5; honorary members, 67; ordinary, 180; total, 252; being an increase of 70 on last year—125 resident and 127 non-resident.

"Of these there are 25 Mackenzies; 21 Frasers; 17 Mackays; 17 Macdonalds; 14 Mackintoshes; 9 Rosses; 7 Macphersons, including a lady member; 6 Campbells; 6 Grants; and 6 Macraes, and so forth. The Council would earnestly impress upon each member the propriety of introducing a new member, and thus increase the numbers present of his own clan on the list.

"The receipts during the past year were £102. 18s. 6d. Expenditure, £82. 9s. 6d. Balance, £20. 8s. 9d. At the present date we stand—Receipts, £122. 8s. 8d. Expenditure, £113. 17s. 9d. Balance, £52. 17s.

"In men and money the Society has made decided progress during the year. But the Society has to consider how it serves the purposes of its existence. Towards perfecting the members in the use of the Gaelic language, it is satisfactory to know that a

4

Gaelic class has been formed by Mr Lachlan Macbean, the librarian of the Society, and it is to be hoped that the members will
give Mr Macbean all the assistance and encouragement which he
deserves. Numbers of old and young should flock to this class,
and prove that they are worthy of the name which they bear.
Towards preserving the poetry, traditions, &c., of the Highlands,
the Society has sent another volume of Transactions to press, which,
it is believed, will be deemed equal, if not superior, to the first
volume of Transactions. Besides the magnificent address delivered
from the chair at last annual supper, that volume will be found to
contain papers on a variety of subjects, such as 'Torreachd na
Taine,' being the Hebridean version of the famous 'Tain Bo
Chuailgne'—one of the most ancient of Irish tales, and purporting
to be an account of events which occurred in the first century of
the Christian era. For the purpose of making this paper all the
more instructive and suggestive, the hon. secretary placed it in the
hands of Mr Standish O'Grady, M.R.I.A., one of the leading
archæologists of the day. Mr O'Grady has kindly gone over the
whole of our paper, and enriched our volume vastly with his notes.
In the volume will also be found a sequel to that tale, 'Laodh nan
Ceann.' There are also papers on 'The Study of the Gaelic
Language,' on 'Gaelic Literature,' &c.; and there is a profound
scientific paper on 'Letters,' with a most interesting comparison
of Gaelic and English in relation to them, by Dr Halley, illustrated by diagrams.

"And referring to the speech of Mr C. Fraser-Mackintosh, one
of the things which the Chairman at our last annual supper
regretted, was the want of a monumental stone over the grave of
Ian Lom. That want has been supplied, and that, too, very much
through the exertions and munificence of Mr Fraser-Mackintosh.

"It was hoped that this volume would be in the hands of
members by this time; but there has been much time lost in the
correcting of proofs which had been sent to places, sometimes to
which a letter may be 14 days on the way. It should also be
stated that in terms of a resolution, no name is to appear in the
printed list at the end of the volume against which there is a
blank in the column for last year's subscription. The printer has
been calling for that list for more than a month; and the Treasurer
has been indefatigable in his endeavours to have the blanks filled
up. This is a matter which the members have in their hands;
but they must place it in the hands of the Treasurer, Mr James
Fraser.

"Of the first volume of Transactions there are sixty copies in the hands of the booksellers, and one in the library. To the library there have been 35 volumes added during the year. But still there are only 110 volumes in all; and that, it must be confessed, is not a library in keeping with the pretensions or actual membership of this Society. The Council would again urge upon the members and friends who have books, MSS., and the like, bearing upon the object of the Society, the desirableness of making contributions, in kind or otherwise, towards the library. It is a fact, that great numbers of books which should be found in the library of the Society, are being rapidly bought by book collectors in the South; and unless an effort is made very speedily to supply your library, it will have to be furnished, not from the Highlands so much as from English and Irish repositories, and at double the price which would buy them in our own province to-day.

"With regard to the meetings of the Society, the Committee would urge upon the members the necessity of attending in greater numbers. These meetings are of very great importance, not only to the Society and to Celtic literature, but to the material prosperity of the Highlands. If Highlanders do not show their appreciation of, and their zeal for, those objects which are specifically their own —as their language, their sentiments, their traditions, and their literature—what will the powers that be say, but that the Celt must pass away from the face of his own land, and make way for a race which shows a greater, though perhaps a grosser, appreciation of its own importance. Meetings are held every Thursday evening in the Guildry Hall; and if any one is deterred from attending by the fear that the proceedings are not full of interest, he is greatly mistaken. At least it can be safely said, that if they are not interesting, it is his own fault not to make them all that they should be.

"The present Council retires now, and there will be a meeting advertised shortly, to elect a new Council, when a large attendance is now earnestly requested."

The Chief—I think the best thing we can do now is to drink the health of our kind Secretary, Mr Murdoch, and thank him for the trouble he has taken in the affairs of the Society. (Cheers.)

The toast was drunk, and Mr Murdoch remarked that the drinking of his health was not in the programme. He, however, thanked Cluny for proposing it, and the croupiers and gentlemen present for drinking it so heartily. (Applause.)

The Chief then proposed, "Success to the Gaelic Society of Inverness," saying—Bliadhna mhath ur dhuibh a luchd Comuinn

Gailig Inbhir-nis. Tha e toirt moran toilinntinn dho' a bhi 'n ur measg a nochd, agus a bhi ann am shuidh mar cheann air a chomunn agus air a chuideachd mhor so de dh-fhior Gaidheil. Tha mi ro thoilichte a chluintinn gu'm bheil an communn so a soirbheachadh agus a deanamh math le bhi cur na Gaidhlig air h-aghaidh, agus le bhi gabhail curam de 'n bhardachd agus de na scriobhannaibh, na sgeulachdan, agus nan eachdraidhean a tha a measg luchd labhairt na Gaidhlig. Tha duilichinn ro mhor orm nach eil e air a chur mar fhiachaibh anns na sgoilean 's a Ghaidhealteachd, Gaidhlig a theagasg. Tha e gle dhuilich leam a'rath gu'm bheil moran pharanntan a tha an aghaidh an cuid cloinne bhidh ag ionnsachadh na Gaidhlig, a leigil as am beachd gu'r ann le bhi eolach air an canain fhein as urrain doibh canainean agus nithé eil ionnsachadh. Tha ministearan agus maighistearan-sgoilè ann an iomadh aite, cur an aghaidh na cloinne bhi ag ionnsachadh Gaidhlig. Ach cho fad 's bha e ann am chomas a dheanadh, bha mise cumail suas teagasg na Gaidhlig anns na sgoilean. 'S gann gu'm bheil guth agam anns na sgoilean a nis, leis na riaghailtean ur a tha an deigh eiridh 'nar measg. Ach tha guth agam a measg luchd a chomuinn so, agus tha mi a togail mo ghuth le m' uile dhurachd, agus a guidhè soirbheachadh math agus moran tapadh don chomunn, agus do na h-nile ball a bhuineas da, agus gu mu mor a math a ni sibh.

Mr Macrae of the High School, then sang very sweetly *Mairi Laghach*, and was greatly applauded.

Mr John Macdonald being called upon, said—The toast which it is my privilege to propose is one in which I am quite sure you will all heartily join. When I propose " Prosperity to the Highlands and Highland People," you will at once see that the toast conveys a wish which I am sure is the earnest wish of every one here, and a wish that will find an echo in the hearts of the thousands of our scattered countrymen, whether at home or abroad, who feel an interest in the welfare of our Society, and who all retain ties of warm attachment to their native glens. It is a remarkable and yet truly satisfactory fact, that while we are here heartily wishing prosperity to the Highlands, we are at this moment surrounded with numerous indications that the Highlands are really on the verge of a practical era of prosperity. When comparing the extensive commerce, gigantic enterprises, and busy industries of the south, with the scale on which things move in those quieter northern regions, one feels creeping over him a feeling of discontentment; but when the matter is more closely looked at, this feeling at once vanishes, giving place to

opposite feelings of thankfulness with our lot. If in the Highlands our trade is not extensive, or our industries numerous,
there is at least this true of them, that they have about them the
vigour and enthusiasm of youth. In the southern and larger
centres of population everything seems wrought up to the highest
pitch, so that it requires really an extraordinary power of wealth
or genius to strike out a new path, or bring existing industries
to a higher stage of development. Happily with us in the Highlands it is different. Our industries and enterprises, such as they
are, are in the bud, and have before them a wide field for development. Our railway system, for instance, is not yet completed;
and yet so far as it goes it has created wealth and awakened
dormant energies. We have also indications that the Highlands
also possess mineral wealth, as may be seen from the coal operations now going on at Brora. I need not refer to our fisheries,
facilities for woollen manufacture, and various other industries yet
undeveloped. I have said enough to point out that there actually
exists fair prospects of progress and prosperity. But, Mr Chairman,
we can conceive of much prosperity and accumulation of wealth
throughout the Highlands without the great body of the people
reaping the full benefit. Such a state of things would not satisfy
the wish of the toast. We want not only the Highlands to
prosper, but also the Highland people. Now, sir, in the prosperity of the people there are, or at least ought to be, two
elements at work. First, the people on their part cultivating
habits of industry, self-reliance, and independence. I fear I am
correct in saying it is peculiar to the Highland character, especially
at home, to cringe too much to everything, presenting a shadowy
appearance of superiority. They lack, on the whole, that which
the artizan population of our large towns exhibit perhaps too
much of, a proper estimate of their own worth, and a readiness to
demand from those disposed to overlook it, a fair recognition of
their rights and services. But, sir, in the matter of the prosperity
of the people there is another element to be considered. They
are placed in and surrounded by circumstances beyond their
control; and while they do their part, it devolves upon other
responsible parties to adjust these circumstances to their wants
and welfare, by furnishing them with a securer tenancy and more
abundant labour. I do not mean that kind of employment that
is associated with sport or amusement, but real productive labour.
Much more of this sort than we at present have would go a good
way to realise the wish of our toast, "Prosperity to the Highlands
and Highland People."

The Chief then requested Mr Fraser of Mauld to give a song.
Regarding the songs of Iain Macmhurchaidh, Mr Fraser told an
anecdote, showing the origin of the song which Iain composed in
honour of the gentleman who sent a messenger after him with a
bottle of whisky.   The song—"Ho-ro gu'm b'eibhinn leam," was
sung well, and received with great applause.

Sir Kenneth Mackenzie, in giving the "Members of Parliament for the Northern Counties and Burghs," said he might not
know all these gentlemen, or might not have attended to their
Parliamentary career, but he was sure that any body of gentlemen
who had been elected by the free votes of Highlanders must be
very good fellows indeed. (Laughter and applause.) He wished,
however, very much that some of them would occasionally show
themselves in this company, though he had no right to blame
them, because he himself had not the pleasure of being present at
any of their gatherings since he presided at their inaugural meeting. (Applause.) Still, he thought it would be a good thing to
attend, and to enter into those feelings which meetings like this
tended to foster. (Applause.) He had no doubt, for his own
part, that it was well to encourage that ancestral pride which
induced people to emulate the virtues and noble characters of
their ancestors. Of course, faults might be found with that pride,
but nothing, he believed, tended more to ennoble people than the
feeling that they had a right to be noble. (Applause.) *Noblesse
oblige*, as the French say ; and Dr Guthrie, in his autobiography,
lately published, told that though he could not prove himself to
be a descendant from the Covenanting Guthries, yet the mere
thought that he belonged to that stock had a remarkable influence
on his whole public life. (Applause.) So he would be very glad
to see some of our northern members there occasionally, and to
see them more imbued with the feeling that they were Highlanders ; but, so far as he knew, they all discharged their Parliamentary duties very well, and he hoped they would long retain'
their seats.   (Laughter and cheers.)

Mr Rose, solicitor, proposed "The Magistrates and Town
Council of Inverness." He observed that this was a toast which
ought to be drunk with great enthusiasm by those present. The
Magistrates and Town Council of Inverness are a body well qualified to rule over their own affairs—(Laughter)—and they took
good care that the chariot did not drive too fast. (Laughter.)
The present Council were able to discuss their own matters, to
take care of the business of the town, to dispense justice on every
hand—(Hear, hear)—and to watch and preserve the public rights.

That was what they wanted. No men should go into office for the sake of being a Bailie or a Councillor, but should have the public good alone in view. With regard to Celtic matters, which more immediately concerned those assembled, he need not tell them that the Magistrates and Town Council of Inverness had always done everything in their power to preserve the literature, habits, and customs of the Gael. The burgh of Inverness had been a refuge for all classes, from the King downwards. It had been a harbour of refuge for many a good old chief who had been in trouble, and he was told that even Prince Charlie, although it is not very well known where he rested—and it is as well it is not—found refuge in Inverness. (Cheers.) The burgh of Inverness was a very ancient one, and for the past three centuries its municipal authorities had been very noted. It had stood forth boldly as a royal burgh, and its charter was very ancient. They had an excellent Town-Clerk at present, who was a good chronologist, and he kept them well posted up in matters of dates, &c. (Hear, hear, and laughter.) With this toast he begged to couple the name of Bailie Davidson. (Applause.)

Bailie Davidson responded.

Mr Charles Mackay was then called upon to propose a toast to the "Highland Regiments." He said—I need not recount the many deeds of valour performed by our Highland regiments since the time of the dashing exploits at Fontenoy till the present day (when we are gratified to learn of their arrival on an African shore, where they are certain to do their duty.) We know the 42d is the father of Highland regiments, or we may say the first and the last. The spontaneous spirit in which the Highland regiments were raised is remarkable. The Fraser Highlanders (who did so much service in America) were raised to the number of over 2000 by their chief and chieftains in a few weeks. Others were raised with equal despatch, as the 79th, the 78th, and the 92d. In Lord Macleod's, now the 71st regiment, I will always feel an interest, as my father was born in it, and his father fought and bled with it on the plains of Buenos Ayres, at the Cape, &c. In the memorable retreat from Salamanca to Corunna, it is worthy of note that it was six of the 42d that carried their beloved commander (Sir J. Moore) off the field. We know what these Highland regiments did in restoring the forfeited estates to their proper owners, although we lament that some of their successors have so soon forgotten it. But we are glad that there are chiefs who still hold by their people. Of this we have good examples at this table. It is often said that the martial spirit has degenerated in the Highland people. Those who say so know nothing of Highland character. They may know a little of Highland statistics. Of the martial spirit of Highlanders we have ample proof from the number of volunteers who joined the 42d from the 79th the other week for the Gold Coast, among them two acquaintances from my own native Glen-Urquhart. This is what would be expected from *Reisamaid Alainn an Earaichd.* I believe there is at the present time a gallant officer from the War Office on a tour in the Highlands, inquiring into the alleged scarcity of recruits for the Highland regiments. It is to be hoped he will meet with the people to give him the proper information. Where I last heard of him was at Oban. It would be well if, ere he leaves that quarter, he crossed the Sound of Mull to the shores of Lochaline, where, in the tumbled homesteads and desolated fields, he will be told in silent, but unmistakeable language, one of the great causes of the scarcity of recruits. He will also find there greater enemies to Highland regiments than they ever met on the battlefield. If, however, he moves northward to the territory of one of our excellent Croupiers, he will find people as thick as midges, and that of the best material for Highland regiments, although we know that in recruiting they would be the better of Sir Kenneth at their head. I will conclude, then, by proposing the toast of "The Highland Regiments."

This toast was coupled with the name of Captain Chisholm of Glassburn, but the Chief responded, thanking them for drinking to the "Highland Regiments." For several years he had led the 42d, and his brother had also led the same gallant regiment. He (Cluny) at present had a son in the same regiment, who had gone with it to the Gold Coast. He had another son in the 93d Regiment. He hoped that some day one of these sons would command the 42d, and the other the 93d. This was his highest ambition. Although he said it himself, he thought they would be the right men in the right places. (Great applause.) Nothing could be more gratifying to him than to know that Highland regiments, when called upon, no matter what part of the world they had to go to, were always ready and willing to do their duty. The 42d, as they had heard, had now arrived on the Gold Coast, and he was in hopes that the men of his regiment would do that duty which was expected of them. He thought that the reason so few recruits were found was that wages at home were so high, and that there was not sufficient inducement offered to those that might be inclined to go. The same blood ran through their veins now as in days of old, and if sufficient were offered, he believed they were ready to go. (Cheers.) In conclusion, he thanked those present for the manner in which they had drunk to the "Highland Regiments."

Sheriff Macdonald then gave a Gaelic song.

Councillor Davidson then proposed "Prosperity to the Trade and Town of Inverness" in a very appropriate manner.

Councillor Falconer briefly replied to this toast in suitable terms.

Councillor A. Mackenzie, Clachnacudain House, said that he felt himself quite incompetent to do anything like justice to the toast handed to him, for he could lay no claim to any special knowledge of the subject. Before, however, saying a few words to the toast, he would perhaps be allowed to express his gratification at the great success of this meeting under such happy auspices; having, as they had, the great honour of Cluny Macpherson's services, the Chief of the Society, as Chairman on this occasion, and of Sir Kenneth Mackenzie, his own chief, and Sheriff Macdonald, as Croupiers. He was glad to say that he had the honour of proposing Cluny as Chief of the Society, and of proposing or seconding —he forgot which—Sir Kenneth as first Honorary Chieftain. The manner in which both acted this evening, and the interest they have always taken in the proceedings of the Society, proved that they had made an excellent choice, and he felt quite sure that all round the table would bear him out in this opinion. (Applause.) He would also say; in fact he felt that he was getting quite egotistical —(Laughter)—that he believed he was the first who suggested the idea of having a Gaelic Society in Inverness—first to Mr Murdoch, and afterwards to many others, some of whom quite ridiculed and pooh-poohed the idea; but now matters have so much changed, that hardly any one who could lay the slightest claim to respectability but was a member of the Gaelic Society. (Laughter.) But to come to the subject of his toast, "The Clergy of all Denominations." No one had a greater respect for them than he had. They held a position in which they wielded, or at least ought to wield an immense power; but he felt, with some of the ablest of themselves, that many of them were not keeping pace with the times. Although they had the peculiar advantage of talking any amount of good sense, or the reverse, without a chance of refutation by their audience, men of great ability and intellectual power, here and in other countries, were raising many difficulties in the present day, and our ministers were shutting their eyes to them. But how could clergymen be expected to grapple with and successfully refute these difficulties, when there were so many other claims upon them of a different nature. There was hardly a baptism, a funeral, or a marriage, a dinner, tea, or any description of party, but ministers were supposed to grace with their presence, thus wasting the time necessary to prepare able discourses, and cope successfully with the errors of the age. He was glad, however, to have made the acquaintance of a clergyman present, who evidently kept himself well posted up in the literature of the day, and who did not shrink from grappling with the difficulties referred to, and that with considerable ability. He proposed "The Clergy of all Denominations," coupled with the name of his friend, the Rev. Mr Wright.

Rev. Mr Wright, in responding, said it was, of course, not expected that he should endorse all the sentiments expressed by Councillor Mackenzie in regard to religious matters, and as he did not anticipate that any remarks which he might at present make would tend much to modify his opinions in relation to these, he would meantime leave him to his own private judgment. (Laughter and applause.) Referring to the special topic of the evening, he said it had been his privilege to come into pretty close contact with two gentlemen thoroughly enthusiastic on the subject of the Gaelic language and literature, the one was Professor Blackie of Edinburgh, whose name ought ever to be respected by every true Highlander, for his zeal in behalf of the mother tongue, and the other was Monsieur Terrien of Paris, who, in conjunction with Dr Saxon of Oxford, had published a work in four different dialects of Gaelic, viz., Scotch, Welsh, Irish, and French. The latter gentleman used often to assert that in the province of France to which he belonged the Gaelic language was highly appreciated, and looked upon as an indispensable accomplishment by those who laid claim to polite learning, and on this account it was even more cultivated there than in many parts of Scotland. (Applause.)

Mr Murdoch gave "The Non-resident Members of the Society." He observed that in reading the report he made the discovery that there were now 125 members of the Society resident in Inverness, and 127 non-resident. They were largely indebted to the non-residents for the funds of the Society, and for much influence used in their behalf. The resident members were inside, and the non-resident members were outside the tent, and acted as stays to support it. They had members in nearly all parts of the world, and with this toast he would couple the name of a gentleman from Chicago now present—Mr Mackay. (Loud and prolonged cheers.)

Mr Mackay, in responding, spoke of the Celtic feeling which prevailed in the city in which he resided. They had now formed a Celtic Association, and were keeping up their Celtic manners and customs much better than is being done in many parts of the Highlands. They did all they could to keep up their language and games. They often had a game of shinty, and sometimes had a Highland fling. (Cheers.) The Chief of the Association belonged to the clan of which the Chairman to-night was Chief, namely, the Macpherson. (Great applause.) So that in that respect the Chicago Association and the Inverness Gaelic Society were on the same footing. (Applause.) When he left Chicago, the Association numbered 50 members, and by this time he expected it would number 100. He thanked this Society for the kind reception it had given him.

Dr Macnee then gave " The Bench and Bar," to which Sheriff Macdonald and Mr James Davidson replied. Mr G. J. Campbell gave " Kindred Societies," acknowledged by Mr K. Fraser, secretary of the Literary Institute ; Mr Huntly Fraser gave "The Press," to which Mr Barron replied.

Sheriff Macdonald gave " The Health of the Chairman," and in replying, Cluny stated that he was proud of being Chief of the Gaelic Society. What he could do was but little, but that little was always at their service; and he would continue doing everything he could for the Gaelic language and the Highlands of Scotland. (Applause.) He had now been Chief for two years, and with all deference, he submitted that some one else should now be appointed, and some one who was more accessible than he was. Cluny concluded by remarking, in Gaelic, that he would do everything, so long as in our midst, to keep up the Celt. (Applause.)

Mr Alex. Ross proposed " The Croupiers," and Sir Kenneth, in reply (alluding to the previous toast of the Clergy), said he had been told that he was the chaplain * of the Society. (Laughter.) Now, Mr Mackenzie had said that ministers had, or ought to have, an influence; and he would add that if they wished to improve the Highlands, there was no way in which it could be done better than by raising the class from which ministers were drawn. He remembered saying at the opening meeting of this Society, that one of its objects should be to excite the interest of the upper classes in the language of their forefathers, inducing them to retain that language, or acquire it if lost. Because, when the cultivated classes lost their interest in it, the leaven which leavens society ceased to influence the mass of the people; and it was one of the most unfortunate things in regard to a dying language, when

* Referring to a paragraph in a newspaper, calling him honorary chaplain, instead of honorary chieftain.

the upper classes lost the use of it, and the uneducated classes came to be in a worse condition than in an earlier stage of civilisation, when there was an element of refinement among them. It was an undoubted fact, that the clergy at this moment had a great influence in the Highlands; and although there were persons present of different persuasions, he thought they would all admit that the Free Church was the Church that influenced the great mass of Highlanders. There were Catholics in Mar, Lochaber, the Long Island, and Strathglass, and Episcopalians in Appin; but the people generally belonged to the Free Church, and if they wanted to influence the mass, it was through the clergy of the Free Church they could do it. (Applause.) Now, it was an unfortunate thing, and generally admitted, that the clergy of the Free Church—he believed it was the same in the Established Church—were not rising in intellect and social rank—(Laughter) —that there was rather a falling off in that—that the clergy were drawn not so much from the manse as from the cottar's house; and though he knew a number of clergy, very excellent, godly men, and very superior, considering the station from which they had risen, he thought it was not advantageous, as a rule, to draw the clergy from the lower, uneducated classes. (Hear, hear, and applause.) They did not start with that advantage in life which their sons would start with. There had been a talk of instituting bursaries for the advancement of Gaelic-speaking students. He did not see why they should not start a bursary or have a special subscription—he would himself contribute to it—a bursary for theological students sprung from parents of education—whose parents had been ministers, or who themselves had taken a degree in arts. That would tend to encourage the introduction of a superior class of clergymen. He wished to say nothing against the present ministers. He knew they were excellent men, but he thought their sons would be, in many cases, superior to themselves if they took to the ministry. He was sorry they did not take to it more frequently, and he would be glad if this Society offered them some encouragement.

Mr Grant, Tartan Warehouse, proposed the "Retiring Council of the Society." Mr Couper gave the "Host and Hostess," and the Chairman then wished the company good night. During the evening a number of capital songs were given by Mr Whyte, Sheriff Macdonald, Mr Kay, Mr Fraser, Mauld; Mr Macrae, High School; and Mr Couper; and the evening was altogether of an extremely pleasant character.

15TH JANUARY 1874.

At this meeting it was decided that a secretary be appointed in future at a salary. It was reported to the Society that Mr Lachlan Macbean, the librarian, had commenced a Gaelic class, and the meeting expressed its hearty approval of Mr Macbean's action, and passed a unanimous vote of thanks to him for the same, after which several gentlemen were nominated for office-bearers for 1874.

There was no business of importance at the meeting held on the 22d January.

29TH JANUARY 1874.

This being the annual meeting for the election of office-bearers, after several accounts were passed and ordered to be paid, the meeting proceeded to ballot for office-bearers. The result will be found in the second part of this volume, referring to 1874-75. A vote of thanks was accorded to the retiring office-bearers for their services during the past year. Thereafter, the meeting unanimously "resolved to record in the minutes a special vote of thanks to the late secretary, Mr William Mackenzie, who, on the resignation of Mr William Mackay, in September last, cheerfully undertook, and since, with the greatest enthusiasm and acceptance to the Society, performed the duties of secretary."

12TH FEBRUARY 1874.

A letter was received from Sir Kenneth S. Mackenzie of Gairloch, Bart., thanking the Society for the honour conferred on him by being elected Chief of the Society for the current year, after which Mr DONALD MACRAE, High School, read a paper on

"THE STATE OF EDUCATION IN THE WESTERN HIGHLANDS,"

from which we make the following extracts :

"The subject that I have chosen for this paper is one that at the present time attracts a good deal of attention from all who take an interest in the subject of Scottish education. There are several reasons why the educational condition of the Highlands takes up so much more public attention than some of the more favoured localities. Among these reasons are the geographical peculiarities of the country, the poverty of the inhabitants generally, the difference in language, and the sparseness of the population in many districts. Intersected as the country is by straits, estuaries, and bridgeless rivers, it is very difficult to devise a scheme that can be sufficient to educate all the people.

"At the commencement of the present century the population was more generally distributed over the country than it now is. Then might be seen thickly-populated glens, the habitations of a happy tenantry, who, had they appreciated, could easily have afforded to provide the benefits of education for their children. They did not, however, feel the want of instruction. They were in a manner a people by themselves, and did not mix much with their more advanced fellow-countrymen in the south and east. They lived by the produce of their lands, and cherished an ardent attachment to the owners of the soil, who owned not only the towering hills and picturesque glens, but also the hearts of their tenantry.

"This state of patriarchal happiness (if such we can now call it) was not, however, destined to continue. The owners of the land were beginning to discover that Cheviot sheep and red-deer would be more remunerative than kilted men, and then began that heartless system of Highland clearances, about which so much has been said and written. These smiling vales were depopulated, and the people forced to seek a home elsewhere. A few of the more adventursome spirits sought a home and a market for their labour in the colonies, while others crowded to the manufacturing and mining districts of the Lowlands. But far the greater number merely removed to the various fishing hamlets which stud the coast, and there try to eke out a precarious subsistence by fishing during part of the year, and when this fails them they emigrate to the South in search of employment as labourers. When thus forced to mix more with the rest of their fellow-countrymen, they begin to feel the want of education. This they do to a much larger extent than those whose mother tongue is English. They feel their want of English very much, and they know that the only way by which they can attain this knowledge is to take advantage of whatever English schools may be placed within their reach. It is always a great object with an illiterate Highlander to enable his children to read their Bibles, and communicate with one another by writing. They keenly feel the inconvenience of having to let another person know what they wish to communicate to their friends, or, as one of themselves expresses it, 'It is a hardship to have your tongue in another man's cheek.'

"The district that I include under the general term of 'Western Highlands,' includes the parishes comprised within the bounds of the Synods of Argyll and Glenelg, and those within the Presbytery of Tongue, with the parish of Assynt, which belongs to the Presbytery of Dornoch.   The district extends from Loch Long in the south, round the West Coast to the boundary between Sutherland and Caithness on the Pentland Firth.   It includes also all the Hebrides, from Islay in the south to Lewis in the north.   When I mention either of the counties included in the district, I wish the Society to understand that any statement I may make regarding them will apply only to the West Coast parishes in each case.

[An Act was passed in 1803 making further provision for education in the West Highlands and Islands.]

" The supplementary schools established under the Act of 1861 are known as side-schools.   This provision was never very largely taken advantage of, and there is not much cause to regret it, when we consider that the heritors were not bound to provide accommodation, and that the salaries would be necessarily small.

" When Parliamentary churches were built in remote divisions of the larger parishes, Parliamentary schools were built in connection with each.   These differ from side-schools in the source of their salary, those for Parliamentary schools being derived from a Parliamentary grant.

" The various associations at work in these necessitous districts are—

(1.) " The oldest of these is the ' Society for Propagating Christian Knowledge,' which was established in 1709 for the purpose of supplying education in the remote districts of Scotland, especially in the Highlands and Islands.   If some of the landowners could be induced to assist in building schools, the usefulness of this Association is capable of much extension.   It differs from all the other associations, in having permanent funds instead of being dependent on annual subscriptions as all the others are.

(2.) " The next agency established was the ' Society for the support of Gaelic Schools,' which was instituted in 1812.   The object of the Society was to supply circulating schools for the teaching of Gaelic reading in such places as could not be overtaken by the Society for Propagating Christian Knowledge.   Of late, the directors passed a resolution, authorising instruction in English where it is required.

" These schools are very much appreciated by the people.   Not only children, but also adults, come a long distance to attend them. In the island of Benbecula, the Society's report states that they had the old man of sixty and the young man of thirty learning the same elementary lesson. In Lochs, in Lews, there were no less than nine mothers attending and acquiring the same lessons as their own children. Of the pupils of another school in the same parish, one was the mother of a family, of whom three were sitting round her, and acquiring the same acquaintance with the rudiments of language. In the quarterly report of one of the teachers occurs the following passage :—' I may mention to you that I have attending the school here nine married women, and one of them is 61 years of age; herself and her daughters, and daughter's children, are at school. There are other two of them 51 and 49 years of age.' These are startling statements, and show sufficiently, I think, what an earnest desire for instruction exists among the inhabitants of these remote corners of the land. These schools are a great blessing to these necessitous districts, not only in affording the means of instruction to the young; but in many cases the teachers carry on the missionary work of their district, when far removed, as many of them are, from any church. They are generally chosen with reference rather to their personal piety than to their literary acquirements, and their attention has been directed to the diffusion of religious as well as secular knowledge. The instruction given in Gaelic stimulates the people to seek the acquirement of English, and the late Rev. Dr Mackay, of Harris, in his evidence before the Commissioners, says that Gaelic should be taught in the schools, but exclusively Gaelic schools will not satisfy the people.

"The General Assembly scheme of the Church of Scotland was originated in the year 1825, mainly with the view of supplying elementary instruction in the Hebrides, which was much required at the time. General Assembly schools are now, however, to be found throughout the whole of Scotland, though the most of them are still in the Highlands. In order to provide a supply of suitable teachers for the Highland districts, they afforded much encouragement to young men possessing a knowledge of Gaelic; such of these Highland students as were not qualified to pass the examination for admission to the Normal Schools, and consequently got no scholarships, were put on what was called the General Assembly Free List, and received a sum generally equal in value to the ordinary scholarships. By this means a number of young men were trained, who were appointed to schools in the Highlands, where a knowledge of Gaelic is absolutely necessary in the teacher.

"A great impetus was given to education in the Highlands as

well as elsewhere by the Disruption in 1843.   The Free Church
was anxious to maintain a school in connection with each congregation.   The leaders of the Church were at the time impelled to
this course by the necessity for making provision for all the
teachers of Parochial, Society, and General Assembly schools who
joined them, and had consequently to resign their situations.
Much has been said against the placing of these schools in close
proximity to existing ones, but this has not been done to a large
extent in the Western Highlands, except in the case of large
villages.   It is a very rare thing to find a Free Church congregational school within a mile of the parish school.   There was room
enough for all the schools that could be established.   It can easily
be understood, that when a teacher ceased to be connected with a
school at the Disruption, he would be anxious, as far as possible, to
retain his connection with his former pupils, whose parents had a
common cause with himself.   Hence, that in some cases the new
schools were set up so near the old ones.   In some cases the
people supported the Free Church schools so much that the General
Assembly and Society for Propagating Christian Knowledge with-
drew their schools altogether.

"The 'Edinburgh Free Church Ladies' Association for the
Religious Improvement of the Western Highlands and Islands'
was founded in 1850.   Its objects are twofold, to establish and
assist schools in Highland districts, and to assist promising young
men in prosecuting their studies for the ministry.   The teachers
nearly all go to college in winter, and leave the school under sub-
stitutes.   So that during the school-going period of the year they
cannot be but indifferently conducted.   Notwithstanding these
disadvantages, Mr Nicholson reports them to be, as a rule, pretty
well taught, and but a few really bad.   Ministers and other
gentlemen interested in education visit these schools, and some of
their reports are very gratifying.   In 1868 they were visited by
the Earl of Cavan ; Principal Lumsden, Aberdeen; Dr Maclauchlan, Edinburgh ; Rev. Lewis Irving, Falkirk ; Rev. D.
Sutherland, Inverness ; Rev. Mr Mackay, Lybster ; Dr Gibson,
Glasgow ; and several of the local clergymen.   One of the latter
was accompanied by the Editor of the *Inverness Courier*, who gave
the following account of it in his issue of the 9th April 1868 :—

"'Excellent schools have been established in all parts of Kintail and Lochalsh, one of which we had the pleasure of seeing at
work.   It is probably one of the smallest on the estate; the
children belonged to various classes, some of them in easy circum-

5

stances, and others very poor; but they appeared to be all exceedingly well taught, and the teacher evidently took a pride in his
work.   In another column will be found the reports of various
school examinations in the Highlands; they are all most favourable; so much so that one hardly knows how much of the lauda-
tion to believe; and if we were told that in an out-of-the-way
place like Ardelve (Sallachy), occupied almost entirely by Gaelic-
speaking labourers and crofters, there was a really good school, we
should have been somewhat sceptical on the point.   But having
seen it in operation, our testimony, whatever it may be worth, is
very favourable.'

"This reference to schools in the Highlands is gratifying from a
gentleman of such standing as the editor of the *Inverness Courier.*
The school in question, I consider a fair specimen of the Ladies'
Schools.   The class of children there, in my opinion, are in better
circumstances than in many other districts occupied by the Association.   In many other schools I know, more advanced scholars
can be met with; but I have no doubt the school will be equal to
the rest in that respect through time, as it is one of the newest
schools.
"The Glasgow Free Church Ladies' Association was formed
in 1852, with objects similar to the Edinburgh one."

19TH FEBRUARY 1874.

This evening the following paper, from the Rev. JOHN MAC-
PHERSON, Lairg, entitled—

"ORIGIN OF THE INDO-EUROPEAN LANGUAGES & THEIR AFFINITY TO THE SHEMITIC CLASS,"

Was read by the Honorary Secretary:—

"Man, as he originally came from the hand of God, his Maker,
was endowed with the gift of language.   He had occasion for the
early exercise of this gift in the Garden of Eden in his giving
'names to all cattle, and to the fowl of the air, and to every beast
of the field, and in giving expression to his gratitude in the reception of her who had been created that she might be a help-meet for
him.'
"The language thus immediately given to Adam, and spoken
by our first parents in the Garden of Eden, was the only language

spoken by their posterity during a period of upwards of one thousand seven hundred years. At the time of the building of the Tower of Babel, we are told that 'the whole earth was of one language and of one speech.'

"What the primeval tongue of the human race may have been has formed the subject of much discussion among men of learning. According to some, the primeval tongue has been lost, and it is now impossible to determine to which of the existing classes of languages it made the greatest approximation. According to others, if the primitive language of mankind was not the Hebrew, it was probably a language of the same (that is, of the Shemitic) class.

"The fact of the Hebrew tongue having been made the medium through which the oldest writings on record, the Old Testament Scriptures, have been transmitted to us, *cœteris paribus*, gives it a preferable claim to the distinction of its being regarded as the primeval tongue. We have strong presumptive evidence in favour of its originality, from the proper names contained in the Book of Genesis, and through the Pentateuch. Such names as Adam and Eve, Cain and Abel, Japheth and Peleg, are there given to those who are so called, because of some notable event in their individual history, or some prominent feature in their character; and the reasons assigned for their being so named are expressly connected with the etymological roots from which those proper names have been derived, which roots unquestionably are pure Hebrew. Thus, *e.g.*, Cain, *possession*, so called by his mother, is from a Hebrew root that signifies *to get, to possess*, Gen. iv. 1; and Peleg or Phaleg, *division*, is taken from a corresponding root, which signifies *to divide*, 'And unto Eber were born two sons: the name of the one was Peleg, for in his days was the earth divided,' chap. x. 25.

"The way in which this notable fact is accounted for by those who do not admit the reality of any particular connection between the Japhetic or Indo-European languages and the Shemitic, is by making the highly improbable conjecture that in these parts of the sacred narrative Moses, the inspired penman, has given us a mere translation of the original. This, as the learned Walton observes in his Prolegomena, is an unreasonable conjecture, utterly destitute of historical analogy.

"Those who were engaged in the building of the Tower at the time of the confusion of language were 'the children of men,' as distinguished from 'the sons of God.' 'That Noah himself and all the godly,' says Dr Owen, 'abstained from that insane project, the sacred Scripture has indicated. Those who undertook that wicked enterprise were " the children of men." These are opposed to " the sons of God," or to those who were pious and feared God. For " the sons of God," from the days of Enos, both before and after the flood, were pious men, adhering to the theology of Adam, and to divine worship. " The children of men were deserters and apostates." '

" It does not appear, therefore, that the primeval language underwent any change in the family of Shem in the line of Arphaxad, Salah, Eber, and Peleg. They seem to have still remained inhabitants of the vale of Shinar. 'And their dwelling was from Mesha, as thou goest into Sephar, a mount of the east.' Hence it is called the Jews' language. Isaiah xxxvi., 11. Out of the same country went forth Terah and Abraham, who were descendants of Eber, Chaldea being situated in the land of Shinar.

" We may reasonably assume that, in the case of ' the children of men,' the confusion of tongues was brought about at this remarkable era, not by the introduction of languages radically new, but as the words of the Scripture narrative appear to signify, by means of a supernatural change wrought upon the minds of the builders, so that they could no longer distinctly remember the words and idioms of their former language, or understand one another's speech. ' Because the Lord did there confound the language of all the earth.'

" In the classification of languages the Shemite class comprises the following branches :—

    1. The Hebrew Branch.
    2. The Syriac Branch.
    3. The Median Branch.
    4. The Himyaritic Branch.
    5. The Arabic Branch.
    6. The Abyssinian Branch.

" Of all the languages having their origin, either immediately or more remotely, in the confusion of tongues, and at the era of the subsequent dispersion of the families of the sons of Noah, the most important by far is the class denominated the Japhetic or the Indo-European. This class includes the following branches :—

    1. The Medo-Persian Branch.
    2. The Teutonic Branch.
    3. The Sanscrit Branch.

4. The Greco-Latin Branch.
5. The Sclavonic Branch.
6. The Celtic Branch, comprising—

CYMRIC LANGUAGES, viz.:—	GAELIC LANGUAGES, viz.:—
Welsh.	Irish.
Cornish	Scotch.
Breton or Armorican.	Manx.

"These languages, the Indo-European, having been compar d one with another, are found to have so many characteristics in common as to leave no doubt of their belonging to the same class, and of their having sprung from one common original. This is shown among others, with much ability, by Professor Bopp, of Berlin, in his Comparative Grammar of the Sanscrit, Zend, Greek, Latin, Lithuanian, Gothic, German, and Sclavonic languages. 'No one, perhaps, now doubts any longer,' he says, 'regarding the original identity of the above-mentioned languages.' 'Even so early as in my system of conjugation, the establishment of a connection of languages was not so much a final object with me as the means of penetrating into the secrets of lingual development, since languages which were originally one, but during thousands of years have been guided by their own individual destiny, mutually clear up and complete one another, inasmuch as one in this place, another in that, has preserved the original organization in a more healthy and sound condition.'

"The argument in support of the common origin of the Indo-European tongues, founded partly on the fact of a large number of kindred words, bearing a close resemblance, being met with in the various languages of the class to which they belong, may also be legitimately employed in comparing this class of languages with the Shemitic. It will not be denied that there is a multitude of words in the one class bearing a close resemblance to kindred words in the other. As an explanation of this, it is not enough to be told that a correspondency so observable and so extensive may have been brought about accidentally. The only rational way to account for this fact is by supposing that both classes of languages had a common origin, or that the one class has been derived from the other.

"But the main difficulty in connecting the Aryan or Indo-European with the Shemitic class consists in the difference of their grammatical structure. How the one class, on the whole, can be so complex and elaborate in its grammatical system, and the other so simple, is the principal philological problem that requires to be solved. The only answer, perhaps, that can be given to this inquiry, sufficient to account for so extensive a similarity in the vocabulary, together with a difference so wide in the grammatical forms of those classes respectively, is to be found in the preceding theory regarding the origin of a diversity of tongues. The change wrought on the minds of those designated 'the children of men,' so that they could no longer understand one another's speech, or distinctly remember their former language, would no doubt continue after their occupation of the different regions assigned to them, 'every one after his tongue, after their families, in their nations.' Supposing that, in the case of the families of the dispersion, the influence by which the new languages then introduced were made to differ from their common original in their vocabulary, to be continuous in its effects, we have no reason to wonder at our finding a somewhat corresponding change in the grammatical forms of those languages.

" In tracing out the origin of the Indo-European tongues, and the relation in which they stand to those of the Shemitic class, the Celtic language appears to afford peculiar advantages. So different is this branch in some of its characteristics from its kindred languages of the Eastern stem, that several eminent philologists refused to assign it a place among the languages of the Indo-European class.

" As the result of able investigation, on the part of men who have made comparative philology their study, we have reason to think that the Celtic has its appropriate place among the Japhetic languages. But we believe at the same time in its having a real systematic connection with the languages that belong to the Shemitic stock.

" A proper exhibition of this affinity would require a lengthened investigation. For the present, taking the Hebrew as a representative of the one class, and the Celtic as a representative of the other, we shall only notice the following particulars :—

" 1. In the Hebrew language there is no neuter. The only genders are the masculine and the feminine. These likewise are the only two genders in Gaelic.

" 2. The noun in Hebrew for the most part comes before its appropriate adjective. The case is the same in the Gaelic language.

" 3. In Hebrew the verb generally comes before its nominative. It is the same in the Gaelic.

" 4. In the Hebrew verb, strictly speaking, there is no present tense. The only tenses are the preterite and the future. It is so likewise in Gaelic. For the formation of the present tense an auxiliary verb is required.

" These are a few of the many coincidences that might be ad

duced, and what has been stated in connection with the Scoto-Gaelic might generally be maintained in regard to the other dialects of the Celtic.

" We are aware that the views above indicated regarding the relation in which the Indo-European languages stand to those of the Shemitic class are not according to the prevailing theory, but it cannot be said with propriety, that therefore they are not scientific. We know, moreover, that the most eminent for their philological attainments will not readily aver that success in this direction is hopeless. Much encouragement to the prosecution of inquiries on the principles of this very theory was given by that great theologian and eminent scholar, the late Dr Duncan of Edinburgh."

26TH FEBRUARY 1874.

The Honorary Secretary read the following paper, contributed by Dr THOMAS MACLAUCHLAN, Edinburgh, entitled

"NOTICES OF BRITTANY."

" On the west coast of France, between latitude $47\frac{1}{2}$ deg. and 49 deg., and projecting into the Atlantic Ocean, not unlike Cornwall on the opposite island of Great Britain, lies the district of France called in French Bretagne, and by us Brittany. The country is divided into three large departments. To the northeast lies that of the Côtes de Nord, the Northern Coasts, a French name. To the west lies the department of Finisterre, a mixed French and Latin name. A portion of this department is called in the native language, Cornwaille, identical with the British Cornwall right opposite. And the third is called the Morbihan, a Celtic name meaning the Little Sea, from *mor*, the sea; and *bihan*, the Welsh *fechan*, and the Gaelic *beagan*, ' little.' This region is occupied by a population of about 800,000, who speak a Celtic tongue called, both by the French and by the natives, Breton.

" The oldest notices we have of Brittany are from Julius Cæsar. From no nation in ancient Gaul did he receive a resistance more resolute than from the Veneti. They were a people accustomed to the sea, who brought large and well-manned fleets to meet the incursions of their invaders. This name suggests an interesting and important historical inference. It has long been a question whether the inhabitants of Brittany were not a colony from Britain, driven over by the later Roman or the Saxon invaders,

The solution of the question may be found, among others, in the very word referred to. The Roman name, Veneti, is a new adaptation of the Breton Guened, a term found to this day in Vannes, the name of the chief city in the Morbihan. The word is a Breton word, derived from 'Guen,' the Breton word for *fair*, a term found in the Welsh, 'gwen,' and the Gaelic 'fionn,' *white*. From this it appears that the Breton tongue was not only spoken in the days of Cæsar, but existed in the topography of the country, a sufficient reply to an assertion as baseless as the one which, on authority of similar value, would derive the population of Scotland from Ireland. Such emigrations were highly popular among historical writers at a period not far distant, however at variance with what common-sense and historical fact suggest with regard to the peopling of countries. The Bretons held Brittany in the days of Julius Cæsar.

"Cæsar's account of these ancient Celts is full of interest. He tells us that the Veneti had more influence than any of the countries on the whole sea-coast, because they had a great many ships with which they were accustomed to sail to Britain, and consequently excelled all the other Gauls in their knowledge of nautical affairs. The Celts have been accused of not being seamen, which, with all other excellencies, has been claimed for the Saxon; yet at this present time the chief nursery for the navy of France is found among the Celts of Brittany. The ships of these people were large, and heavier than those of the Romans, and so high in the sides that the latter could not with effect cast their spears into them. They were overcome by means of a weapon to which they were strangers—a sharpened hook, which cut their leathern sails away from the masts. Their towns were built upon points of land projecting into the sea, which rendered their storming difficult; and upon danger becoming imminent, the inhabitants were able to retire with all their effects to some neighbouring town. They thus were able long to resist the assaults of the Romans, who had never met a braver or more stubborn foe.

"In modern times the most remarkable thing about the Breton population is their religious zeal. They are supporters of the Church of Rome, and in no part of France has that Church supporters so fervent. The churches are large, handsome, and well attended. A church filled at six o'clock every morning by the working population of a small town who congregate there, without any priest or service, to begin the day with prayer, is a remarkable spectacle, and one which speaks much for the religious earnestness of the people. In addition to this, the country is studded with crosses. Several Calvaires, or representations of the crucifixion—some of them, as that of Pluhastel, near Brest, very famous—exist; while figures of our Lord, both on the cross and with the wounded body in other attitudes, are used to stimulate the religious affections of the people. Nor is the country without its martyrs and its martyrdoms. Near to Vannes is the ' Champs de Martyrs,' where 5000 women and children were shot down in cold blood by the soldiers of the first French Revolution—the wives, and sisters, and children of the men who had fought for the Bourbons, and who, in doing so, believed that they were fighting for their religion. Our history records the meetings of our Covenanters for religious worship on the desolate moors and barren heaths of our land; the history of Brittany records similar meetings of men of a different creed on a no less desolate and barren ocean. Christian worship was forbidden by revolutionary and infidel France. The Christian Bretons, with the ministers of their religion, put to sea at night, and far out on the bosom of the ocean, by the light of a few twinkling lamps, they celebrated the services of their religion. We do not acquiesce in their religious views, but we can the no less admire the firmness and constancy which made them hold, at every cost, by what they held to be pure and true. A generalisation of the facts connected with Celtic religious history brings out with marked relief the strong religious feelings of the race. Usually ethnologists have divided them into two great branches, which are denominated severally with most accuracy the Gaelic and the Cymric branch. The religious condition of each of these is remarkable and suggestive. Among the divisions which constitute the Gael, one section, embracing the Scottish Highlanders and the Manx, are among the most earnestly Protestant population in the world; the other section, composed of the native Irish, are just as devoted to the Church of Rome. The same classification is found among the Cymric. Nowhere will a more earnestly Protestant population be found than in Wales, nowhere will a more earnestly Roman Catholic population be found than in Brittany. Their respective religious history shows how firm is the hold which religious ideas and principles take of the Celtic mind, and with what warmth and devotedness the Celts range themselves on the side which they choose among religious bodies.

"One of the first objects which visitors have to encounter in travelling through Brittany, is the language of the people. It is soon found that while a number of them, especially in the towns, speak French, the body of the people speak a language totally distinct.   And the first feature of the language, as in other languages with which we are brought into contact, is its accent. On listening closely to Bretons speaking French, and then suddenly turning to Breton, it appears as if there were little or no change of accent.   When a Highlander passes from speaking Gaelic to speaking English, he carries his accent usually along with him, and that accent appears foreign to the latter.   When the Breton carries his accent into the speaking of French, it appears as natural to the latter language as to his own, so much so that a stranger to both languages could not tell by the accent which it was he spoke.   A warrantable inference from this fact is, that it is the Breton which has communicated its peculiar accent to the French.   The language itself has retired to a corner of the Empire, but its accent remains behind, despite of Roman and later influences from beyond the Rhine.   The same fact appears in our own country.   The accent of the English in the several districts which border the Highlands, is the peculiar accent of the Gaelic which has retired.   The English of the West of Scotland is distinguished by the Gaelic accent of Argyllshire and the West generally.   A stranger to both English and Gaelic could not tell by the accent of an Ayrshire peasant whether he spoke Gaelic or English.   This statement is the result of close and continuous observation, and the writer is well assured that, in the study of accent as distinguished by words, a field of inquiry is opened up which, cautiously and skilfully cultivated, will yield important results in the interests of historical truth.   It is a subject of inquiry on which no man need enter who has not a sensitive musical ear, and has not made himself familiar with musical modulations.

"The Breton language belongs to the Cymric branch of the Celtic tongues.   It is rather a remarkable thing that both the great branches of which these are composed divide themselves into three subordinate sections—the Gaelic into Scotch Gaelic, Irish, and Manx; and the Cymric into Welsh, Cornish, and Breton, all these being confined to the United Kingdom except the Breton. The closest affinities of the Breton are with the ancient Cornish. We have heard it said that a Highlander could understand a Breton speak ; stories have been told of Highland soldiers conversing with Bretons during the wars of this country with France. The thing is a pure delusion, or else both languages, or one of them at least, must have undergone wonderful changes in a short period.   The fact is, a Welshman cannot understand a Breton, and it is very doubtful whether an ancient Cornishman could, except pretty much as a Highlander does a native Irishman.   Yet the

Breton language has affinities with the Gaelic, and in some cases approaches nearer to it than to the Welsh. For instance, *a good man* is in Welsh 'dyn da,' in Breton it is 'dyn mad,' in which latter there is a very near approach to the Gaelic 'duine maith.' This is but an instance of several that might be given. It is clear, however, that the Breton does not hold himself to be Gaelic, for the name which the Breton applies to French to this day is Gallec. If a Breton wishes to ask you whether you speak French, he asks you whether you speak Gallec. This is sufficient to prove that, in the estimation of the ancient inhabitants of France, the French is not of Teutonic extraction, notwithstanding all that Pinkerton said of the origin of the race who spoke it.

" In writing their language the Bretons use the Roman letters, and all those that compose the English alphabet are in use save the w—strange contrast to the Welsh, in which no letter is in more common use than the w, used as a vowel. The Breton undergoes those changes in the initial articulations of words characteristic of the Celtic tongues, and called by Gaelic grammarians 'aspiration.' These, as in Gaelic, sometimes indicate gender—thus, 'un den mad' is *a good man,* 'ur voes vad' is *a good woman,* where the *m* passes into *v,* just as in Gaelic. These changes in the Bretons are called by French writers 'adoucissement,' or softening, a very expressive term, and more comprehensive than our 'aspiration.' In these mutations, for the letters subject to them are called mutable, the letters c k and q pass into g, which becomes softened further into h; p passes into b, which softens into f and v; t has its corresponding d, softening into z; and m makes one change into v. These mutations differ from those which the corresponding letters undergo in Gaelic, but the principle which regulates them is the same. The length of this lecture does not admit of my giving you the corresponding mutations in Welsh, but they are very similar to the Breton. The vowels have generally the same sound as in French. The use of the z gives a peculiar character to the whole spoken language, just like the ll in Welsh. A stranger can hardly conceive to what an extent that particular articulation affects the whole character of spoken Welsh, although it may be found among ourselves, for the writer has the belief that the broad l of the Lothians, so marked in the way in which the word *lady* and similar words are pronounced in this city, is a remnant of the ancient British l, and has come down from the time when the Pictish Britons spoke their language in this very place. The z which gives a sort of buzzing sound to their language, is equally characteristic of the speech of the Bretons,

" As in the other Celtic tongues, the Breton has but one article, the definite, but this article assumes many shapes for euphony's sake, being found as en, er, el, the first of these corresponding to the Gaelic *an*. It differs from the Gaelic article in having no masculine or feminine form, and in being the same in the plural as in the singular number. In Gaelic we have a masculine and feminine form, most distinctly in the genitive, and frequently in the nominative, as 'an duine,' 'a bhean,' although our grammarians ignore the latter as a separate form, by attaching an apostrophe to it. The Bretons make more use than the Gael of the numeral 'un,' *one*, which comes to stand for the indefinite article.

" As in the other Celtic tongues, nouns have two genders, the masculine and feminine. The numeral *two* has a remarkable influence, for it is by the use of it that the gender of a noun is distinguished. In Gaelic it is decided by the form of the succeeding adjective, in Breton by that of the preceding dual numeral. The *two* has the masculine form *deu* and the feminine form diüe. If, in speaking, a noun takes *deu*, it is masculine, as 'deu zen' *two men;* or diüe, it is feminine, as 'diüe vam,' *two mothers*. This can only be decided by the ear, as no fixed rules can be given for distinguishing the gender beyond those of somewhat general application. In the case of adjectives, the gender is indicated almost precisely as in Gaelic, by what we call aspiration in the case of the mutable consonants. Thus, *a strong man* is 'un den bras,' *a strong woman* 'urvoes vras.' The identity of grammatical form is remarkable.

" The Breton plural is formed like the Welsh. The normal method is by the addition of ' en.' As 'aval,' *an apple*, 'avalen,' *apples*; 'amser,' *time*, 'amseren,' *times;* 'tu,' *a side*, 'tuien,' *sides*. But the exceptions, if they should be called such, are numerous, as a large class taking *ion;* thus, 'bugul,' a shepherd, 'bugulion,' *shepherds;* 'mevul,' *a servant*, 'mevulion,' *servants;* others take 'ed,' as 'magueres,' *a nurse*, 'magueresed,' *nurses;* 'avocad,' *an advocate*, 'avocadéd,' *advocates;* 'oen,' *a lamb*, 'cenéd,' *lambs*. Some plurals are abbreviations of the singular, a somewhat anomalous form, as 'piren,' *a pear*, 'pir,' *pears;* 'quelionen,' *a fly*, 'quelion,' *flies;* other forms exist, but most of them follow closely the analogies of the Celtic tongues. There is hardly one of these plural forms whose analogue may not be found in the Welsh and Gaelic.

" The Breton verb appears to the learner inextricably complex, and would almost lead us to believe of the language, what some Welshman said of his own, that he would defy any man but a

Welshman to learn it. The Breton verb, however, suffers in this respect from being presented to us alongside that of the French, which is made use of to represent its power. It would be somewhat easier for us if its power were elucidated by means of the English verb. As presented to us by French grammarians, we find that the verb *to be*, ' bout,' has seven different conjugations. There is the simple form, there is the form representing the use of the French *que*, there is the negative form, there is the form used before an adjective, there is the impersonal form, represented in French by *il y a*, there is the form after conjunctions, and 8th, there is the unimpersonal form after ' mar,' *if.* All these forms include all the tenses. Other verbs, however, are satisfied with two or three modes of conjugation. The Breton, unlike the Gaelic and the Welsh, and like the Irish, has a present tense. ' Gobèr' is the word for *to make*, no doubt the same word with the Gaelic ' obair,' *work*, ' ag obair' being the Gaelic participle *working*. The present tense of the verb ' gober' is ' hra,' ' me hra,' *I do*. There is a curious analogy here with the Gaelic. One Gaelic word for ' res,' ' a thing,' is ' ni.' The representative of ' I do,' being the future in Gaelic, is ' ni.' The Breton word for ' a thing' is ' dra,' and *I do* is ' hra.' This last word is obviously the Gaelic ' rud,' and both are clearly related to the Latin ' res.' But the curious thing is how in both languages the word representing *an object* passes into the form of a verb, and becomes the representative of the action which calls the object into existence. The Breton, again, differs from the Gaelic, the Irish, and the Welsh, in having a verb to represent the English *have*. In the latter languages this idea of possession is represented as in Latin, when *est mihi* has the power of *habeo*. The Gaelic has the representative of *habeo*, ' gabh,' but it means *to take*, and not *to have;* in Welsh, ' cafael' represents the gentler idea of *to get*. But in Breton the ' tha agam,' or *I have* of the Gael, is expressed by the verb ' en dout,' *to have*. Being an irregular verb, *I have* is ' me més.' The Breton verb further differs from the Gaelic in having, like the Latin, the infinitive as the root. This part of the verb has three distinct terminations—' ein,' as in the Gaelic ' faicinn,' ' saoilsinn,' ' mealltainn ;' ' at,' the Gaelic 'adh,' as in ' bualadh,' 'magadh;' and ' al,' as in the Gaelic ' faghail,' ' gabhail.' But in whatever form it is, it is the root of the verb, and not the present, as in Irish, or the imperative, as in Gaelic. But without continuing this sketch of Breton grammar further, it will be found that, while the language has its own peculiarities, it is essentially one of our Celtic tongues, resembling most closely the Cymric and the Cornish, but having numerous analogies not found in them with the Gaelic.

" The language follows the general course of the Cymric branch of the Celtic languages in its peculiar articulations. Gu uniformly stands for the Gaelic f. The word 'guen,' referred to already, synonymous with the Welsh 'gwen,' stands for the Gaelic 'fionn,' translated *fair*. It is interesting to find how uniformly the Romans represented this sound by their f or v. The 'guenned' of the Breton became the Roman 'venetia,' a peculiarity pervading their whole nomenclature in Gaul and Britain. It was thus that the Guortigern of the Bretons became the Roman Vortigern ; p and c interchange between Breton and Gaelic, as is the case with the Welsh—thus the Breton 'pilme,' stands for the Gaelic 'co,' *who;* as the Breton 'petra' for the Gaelic 'ciod,' *what;* the Breton 'piar' and 'pedair,' for the Gaelic 'ceithir,' *four*, and so forth. In like manner the Breton h stands for the Gaelic s—thus the Breton 'halar,' represents the Gaelic 'salann,' *salt;* the Breton 'hael,' *the sun*, represents the Gaelic 'solus,' *light;* and the Breton 'halogi,' *to defile*, the Gaelic 'salachadh.' In like manner h and f interchange, as may be readily understood in the case of the aspirate and the digamma. There are several other such interchanges, in which for the most part the Breton and the Welsh occupy the same ground. In no class of languages is this change of initial articulations in the same words so marked as in the Celtic, nor can it anywhere else be studied so well. The dialects are all living but one, and they are so near each other in point of locality that the scholar can find little difficulty in making them a subject of inquiry. They teach us the process by which languages having the same origin do gradually diverge more and more from each other.

" The written literature in which this language is treasured up is somewhat more limited than that of your own Gaelic. In prose it is pretty much confined to the Bible, recently translated, and the service book of the Roman Catholic Church, with other religious works. The priesthood are the warm friends of this ancient tongue, notwithstanding the opposition of the French Government. All that the latter can do to suppress it they do, even going so far as to forbid its use in schools. There are parties in Scotland who would not allow a word of Gaelic to be taught if they could help it. Of ancient writings Zeuss refers to chartularies of Breton monasteries so far back as 1162, in which the language is found written, especially so far as its proper names are concerned. He refers also to a life of St Monna or Monnita, the mother of St David, written previous to the 12th century, and edited recently by a well known Breton scholar, M. Legonnidec. Latterly the collection of Breton poetry by the Count de Villemarqué is too well known to require much notice here. It is a remarkable work, and well worth the attention of the Celtic scholar. The whole style of the poetry, and the music which accompanies it, are purely Celtic, and wonderfully like what was common but a few years ago among the Gael of Scotland. A dictionary, two grammars, and vocabularies of the language exist, and are sufficiently accessible to such as understand French. Specimens of the language may here not be uninteresting. *The world* is 'er bed,' the Welsh 'byd,' and the Gaelic 'bith;' *heaven* is 'en nean,' the Gaelic 'neamhan;' *the sun* is ' en hiaul; *the moon* 'el loer;' *day* is 'en dé;' *night* 'en noz;' *a church* is 'en ilis;' *a town* 'ur guer;' *how are you?* 'ha hiu zon gáillard?' *I am glad to see you,* 'joé, bras e mès doh hiu cùélèt;' *where were you yesterday ?* ' mèn é hoèh-hui bet dèh?' *At Vannes, at Mr ——'s, who arrived from Rennes to see his father.* 'E gùénèd, è ty en entru—pehani e arihué a ruan a huélèt é dad.'

" It will be seen, in examining the structure of the modern Breton, that it has borrowed largely from the French. Half the verbs of the language are French, while a large proportion of the nouns are from the same source. It is at the same time true that the French is largely a debtor to the Breton. Much of its grammar is Celtic, in nothing more clearly so than in the use of the double negative. The *ne pas* of the French is just the *ne quet*, and sometimes the *ne pas,* of the Breton; while innumerable vocables still in use among the French are remnants still existing, invested with a new life, of the ancient language of Gaul.

" The monuments of Brittany are among the most interesting relics in the world. They have been divided into Christian, Roman, and Druidic. It is with the latter that I intend to deal for a little. It has been estimated that there are ninety localities in the Morbihan alone where remains exist of the ancient Armoricans. These are found of various kinds. There is the menhir, or *high stone,* often standing alone, and frequently in groups, variously arranged; then there is the dolmen, or *table stone* (from ' dol,' *a table,* and ' maen,' *a stone),* consisting of a large stone laid horizontally upon other stones standing erect. These dolmens are sometimes exposed to view ; at others, deep in the heart of a tumulus. The tumuli are themselves remarkable relics, rising, as they do, to a height of thirty or forty feet from the surface, and covering half-an-acre of ground, the whole being obviously constructed by the hand of man. Other structures are found, thought by some writers to be remains of heathen altars, but so defaced that their condition is accounted for by the supposition that, being peculiarly sacred among the heathen, they were objects of peculiar animosity to the early Christians. Let it not be imagined that the Reformers were the only iconoclasts. The places and objects dedicated to an abandoned worship are ever objects of marked aversion to the supporters of a succeeding faith, more especially so long as the memory of the former lives in the public mind. Christianity itself was iconoclastic everywhere in its earlier stages, and not without reason, if we allow our forefathers the right which we challenge of judging for ourselves.

"Perhaps the most satisfactory way of presenting you with a view of some of these Celtic remains, is by giving you a short account of a personal visit last June to some of those at Carnac and the neighbourhood, the most remarkable in all Brittany. Two lines of road lead the traveller from Auray, an important town in the Morbihan, towards the great collection of Celtic monuments to the south—the one goes nearly southerly to Carnac and the neighbouring villages, the other south-east, towards Locmariaquer and Gavr-Innis. I and the friends who accompanied me devoted a day to each. On the western route, to the north of the village of Plouharnel, we saw the first specimens of dolmens, but passed them hurriedly, in order to reach the group of three to the west of the village. Here, in a heathery heap, these remarkable structures appear. They are not buried, although some antiquaries are of opinion that in all similar cases the covering tumuli have worn away. But as they exist now, the dolmens of Plouharnel are perfectly exposed to view. The three are placed close to each other, the long passages by which they were entered facing the south. In the middle one this passage is 33 feet long, with an opening of about four feet square. This passage leads to a chamber of about 12 feet by 9, formed of 13 upright granite stones, placed all round, with masonry in some places filling up the interstices. Above are immense covering stones, moved or placed there by a power, the nature of which at the period it is difficult to conceive. The height within is about six feet. The northern dolmen is about a foot lower, with the peculiarity of having a small side chamber, and the southern is upon a smaller scale altogether. Although much of the mind that all these structures are sepulchral, two of these look as if they had been human habitations at one time. They were vividly brought to my recollection as I penetrated a Pict's house the other day in Sutherland, which extended thirty feet under ground. Nor can one forget, in exploring them, although on a grander scale, the recesses of the Egyptian Pyramids.

"To the east of Plouharnel lies Carnac, with the greatest wonder of all. Here one comes on a great heathery plain, covered with lines or *alignments*, as the French call them, of huge grey stones extending over acres of it. These stones stand from about eight to ten feet high, and at a distance of 25 to 30 feet each way. There are no less than 1200 of them in eleven distinct lines, and hundreds have fallen and been carried away. Perhaps in no spot in the world is the human mind more deeply impressed than amidst this array of monoliths so huge, so grey, so still, the relics of an age two thousand years gone by; and so utterly unchanged by the lapse of ages, that if unmeddled with by the hand of man, and free from the influence of great natural convulsions, they are likely to be as unchanged at the end of 2000 years more. As one surveys them, the questions arise, how came they there, and why? The first question was answered to me very simply by a Breton boy. Once upon a time the holy St Anthony was chased by a Roman army (the anachronism of making St Anthony and a Roman army contemporaneous matters nothing). For a time the Saint fled, but at last he reached the sea, and could flee no further. Shut out from every other hope, he turned and cursed his pursuers; the curse was effectual, for the Roman soldiers were in a moment converted into stone. And here they stand in the gigantic lines of Carnac, monuments of the power of St Anthony. Close beside this array of monoliths stands Mont St Michael, a great tumulus, with a chapel on its summit. Here the Government of the Department have, with great skill and care (and too much cannot be said in favour of what the French authorities are everywhere doing in this direction), succeeded in penetrating, and at the end of a long passage have succeeded in laying open, an enclosure in the form of a dolmen, which, when opened, contained human bones and cinders. The stones, of which the sides of this structure were formed, were not placed perpendicularly, but were laid horizontally; and the bones, instead of being found on the floor, were found laid on the ledges of the stones which formed the walls of the sepulchre. It is a wonderful cavity, suggestive in a measure, too, of the esteem in which the bones there laid were held, and perhaps affording a key to the object of the whole relics at Carnac, which may be a group of what was once 2000 separate monuments in memory of one man or more. If so, there does not exist in the world another such memorial of the illustrious dead. Such monuments leave considerable room for the belief that the men who lived in those early days to which their erection may be traced, were truly giants; and yet Joceline of Furness, in his account of the life of St Kentigern, shows how such monoliths were erected by men of ordinary stature in the earliest years of the Christian Church in Scotland. 6

"A few miles to the east of Carnac lies Locmariaquer, and on the other side of the Morbihan or the inland sea, which gives its name to the department, lies Gavr-Innis or Goat Island, both of them famous as possessing remarkable ancient remains. Locmariaquer is surrounded with dolmens, and has one remarkable tumulus. The description of the dolmens of Plouharnel may suffice for those here, but they have one peculiarity, that many of them have no figures carved on the stones. There are carvings at Maen-né-lud, but a Celt carved upon the covering stone of what is called 'Table des Marchands' is one of the most remarkable specimens of the stonecarver's art to be witnessed anywhere. The tumulus to the south of Locmariaquer is in many respects like that of Mont St Michael. The side stones of the cavity are laid horizontally, and besides bones and cinders, jewels and several other curiosities of jet and malachite, were found strewed on the floor when the tumulus was first laid open. Diamond and other rings were cast into the grave of the late Lord Palmerston in Westminster Abbey. What should hinder the ancient Celt from paying similar honours to the remains of the distinguished dead of his day. So-called barbarism and civilisation are not always so far apart as modern vanity would prompt us to assume. Here too are carvings on the inner faces of the stones of a very curious character. But of all the tumuli of Brittany none can be compared to Gavr-Innis. If the greatness of the person interred is to be judged of by the extent and variety of the carvings on the stones which form the enclosed dolmen of the tumulus, none was so great as he whose dust was laid here. The tumulus itself is like a little hill as seen from the sea, and yet every spadeful that composes it was carried there by human labour. Every stone here is inscribed, and all of them, both in the long entrance passage and in the body of the cavity, are placed erect. On one of these granite masses three projections exist like the handle of a stone pitcher placed horizontally. According to our Breton guide, people were in use of getting married here, the parties to the union inserting their hands and joining them within these openings. But of all marriage chambers this must have been the most dismal, and very little observation is sufficient to show that these curious projections must have served some other purpose. I examined closely the carvings upon this and all the other inscribed dolmens I saw, and although prepared to allow the difficulty of interpreting them aright, the impression made upon me was that there is not one of them that does not more or less distinctly represent some warlike instrument. We know that in later times, as may be seen in the burying-ground of Oran at Iona, and other places in the Western Highlands, the rank of the dead is often represented by carving on their grave-stones their weapons and their dogs, with the game which they pursued. Might not the ancient Bretons, by their inscriptions of celts and other weapons on the monuments of their dead, repre-sent thereby also the warlike character and fame of the men who rested beneath or within them. This view is at least consistent with what we know of the customs of the Celtic race.

" In Brittany I picked up, among other fly-leaves, a printed copy of an old Breton poem called ' Ann hini goz, hag ann hini iouank,' or *the old woman and the young;* interpreted to mean in Breton, 'Breiz ha Bro-chall,' *Brittany and France.* The poem must be of the 13th or 14th century at the latest, and gives ex-pression to the strong feelings of national rivalry between the two countries and peoples. No Irishman ever felt a hostility more bitter towards England than did the Breton of that day, as ex-pressed in these verses, towards France. The object of the poet is to show the superior attractions of the old woman, by which he means his native Brittany. Any one acquainted with the modern native poetry of Ireland, where Ireland is represented as a fair, soft youth, or highly attractive young lady, who has been sorely used by a cruel and unsparing enemy, will understand the nature of the allegory. But it is to a note by the editor of the poem that I desire to direct attention. It is to the effect ' that this ancient poem, now printed for the first time, represents senti-ments of national rivalry which, thanks to God, have now ceased to exist.' The French have succeeded in governing the Celtic races under their control, and in amalgamating them with the general population of the empire in a way not attained to by the Saxon Government of England. One cannot but contrast the large cities, the well-peopled villages, the fruitful fields and abun-dant orchards of Brittany with the matchless misery of Celtic Ireland and the desolations of the Scottish Highlands. No colonies of Bretons are found filling, with an expatriated popula-tion, the forests and prairies of America ; but they will be found a cheerful, prosperous, and loyal people, still occupying their own beloved land, and contributing largely by their industry and naval skill to the strength and prosperity of the French empire. I must own to a very large amount of sadness in passing within a couple of months from the fertility of Brittany to the desolations of Sutherland and many portions of the Outer Hebrides. Whence is this ? Is the Anglo-Saxon a less skilful governor of foreign races than the Frenchman ? Is he more destitute of sympathy with other nations than his own ? Let this be as it may, disloyal

Ireland and the largely desolated Highlands would seem to form
a striking comment on his capacity for governing or amalgamating
other races.   Wales would no doubt seem to argue the other way,
for no population in the empire is more prosperous than the Celtic
population of that principality; so with the Gaelic Celts of Man,
who, however, have been allowed to govern themselves.   But the
present condition of Brittany speaks loudly in favour of the
French method of government, among what is largely a foreign
population to the mass of the French people ; although the
Bretons would probably say that they were the foreigners, as we
might of the Anglo-Saxon."

The paper was highly appreciated by the meeting, and it was
resolved to record " a special vote of thanks to Dr Maclauchlan
for his interesting and learned paper."

5TH MARCH 1874.

Mr CHARLES MACKAY read a very interesting paper in Gaelic,
" Air Chuairt an Lochaber."   We were unable to procure it in
time for insertion in its proper place.

12TH MARCH 1874.

At this meeting Mr LACHLAN MACBEAN read the following
English metrical version of

"DAN AN DEIRG"—DARGO.

PART FIRST.

See Dargo* in the gloomy grove alone,
And listening to the forest's dreary moan ;
Crimina's† ghost see on the mist appear,
While on Scoorelda‡ rest the timid deer.
5 No hunter now the heath-clad mountain tries,
On Dargo and his dog deep sorrow lies,
And with thy story I am filled with woe,
Adown my cheeks the tears incessant flow.

* Dargo (Dearg)—the red, or red-haired man.
† Crimina (Cridh-min)—tender-hearted.
‡ Scoorelda (Sgur-eilde)—the ridge of roes.

On yon glad day brave Cuval* heard the strains
10 Of music with his people on the plain,
  (Though 'neath the grassy meadows of the roe
  To-day the hero, fierce in wrath, lies low.   .
  Beneath the mossy stones is now his bed,
  In shelter of the aged oak tree's shade).
15 With eyes half closed, and face in attitude
  Of listening, leaning on their spears, they stood.
  The King and Innisfail's† prowess and might,
  When swept they both th' embattled field of fight,
  The bard sang, when a ship was noticed near,
20 That to the cloud-girt coast was seen to steer.
  " Yon is the ship of Innisfail, and high
  See his crantara‡ raised against the sky.
  Swift o'er the white crests of the billows press,
  To help the monarch who is in distress."
25 And from the south strong swept the stormy gales,
  Rough wrestling with our tall and white-rigged sails,
  When dark descending night to meet us poured,
  Upon the sea of waves that round us roared,
  " Why should we thus upon the sea be tossed,
30 When that cool island, with its creeky coast,
  To meet us spreads its shield as to invite
  Us to its shelter from the stormy night ?
  Like a bent bow its circling arms compress'd,
  And peaceful as my love's soft-heaving breast,
35 Beneath its wing then let us spend the night,
  It is the joyful place of visions bright."
  And from her rock we heard the owl's lone cry,
  And from a cave a mournful voice reply.
  Said Cuval, " 'Tis the voice of Dargo's ghost,
40 Dargo, who in the billowy sea was lost,
  When we returned from woody Lochlin's§ shore,
  Driven helplessly the stormy blast before.
  Among the clouds the waves upheaved their brows,
  Mountains of spray upon the ocean rose,
45 And the grey briny billows of the deep
  Were rolled from west to east with ceaseless sweep.

    * Cuval (Caomh-mhal)—mild or kindly brow.
    † Innis-fail—the isle of the Falans ; Ireland.
‡ Cranntara— the muster-sign, or Fiery Cross. (See *Lady of the Lake,*
           canto iii.)
    § Lochlin (Lochlainn)—Scandinavia.

O Dargo, when ascending on our sail,
Weak was the thong to which thou clung'st, and frail.
Morven,* thou never shalt again behold,
50 The waves sport with thy wandering hair of gold !
Great is the loss, O storm ! wrought by thy might.
Bear him, ye spirits, to your cloudy height.
Our voice," brave Cuval said, "they did not hear.
Sad is thy place, my hero, cold and drear !
55 Ye hostile ghosts ! from Lochlin, land of trees,
Who followed us across the stormy seas,
If 'tis by you that he is here confined,
You can't prevail though many be combined.
For Trenmor† comes with fury, and in wrath,
60 Like thistles he shall sweep you from his path,
Incumbent on his shield shall Dargo rise
In triumph to the children of the skies.
Let thy melodious voice be heard aloud,
O Ullin,‡ by the heroes of the cloud,
65 They know thy voice, they oft have heard thy lay,
Tell them that Trenmor comes without delay."

"O ! may thy soul have joy and bliss for aye,
　　Be thy lone stay 'mong rocks or gloomy caves,
　O ! sad are we that thou art far away,
70　　With Lochlin's ghosts upon the stormy waves !

If 'tis the warring of the cloudy throng,
　　Or their hard thongs by which thou art opprest,
Great Trenmor comes with lithely blades, and strong,
　　Tough shields, by whom they shall be quick dispersed.

75　As the crisp withered foliage is blown
　　By desert winds from oak trees hoar and grey,
So driven by him their power shall be strewn,
　　Then may thy soul have joy and bliss for aye !"

" Thy words are wonderful, and strange to me,
80 It never, Bard of Cuval, used to be,
The wont of heroes of thy house and race
To leave a friend in danger or distress."

---

* Morven (Mòr-bheinn)—the land of great mountains ; the Highlands.
† Trenmor (Treun-mòr)—tall and mighty ; the father of Cuval, and
　　　　　　　grandfather of Fingal.
‡ Ullin—Cuval's bard.

The voice of Dargo, Gyalcos* quickly knew,
And as he used when o'er the plain he flew,
85 He whined and barked with glad response, and o'er
The surging waves he hastened to the shore.
Like arrow glistened from the bending yew,
His feet scarce skimmed their crests as o'er he flew.
More joy than when behind the roe be pressed,
90 He showed for Dargo, leaping on his breast.
There was beheld their eager joy displayed,
Seen by the light the stars dim glimmering shed;
'Twas like the meeting of old friends of yore,
That chance to meet upon a distant shore.
95 And Dargo had our ships forgotten quite,
So great his joy, so ardent his delight;
But faithful Gyalcos led him by the hand,
To meet our coming on the sloping strand.
" And dost thou live, O Dargo, who wert lost,
100 In the wild sea on which our barque was tossed,
'Tis wonderful that thou art safe restored,
From roaring death by whom thou wert devoured."
" By bursting waves upheld and driven, 1 lay
Through that benumbing night, till morning day.
105 Seven weary moons, and each to me a year,
Have waxed, and waned, and passed upon me here.
'Mid tuneful strains I passed the whole day long,
Listening to murmuring waves and birds of song.
At night through gloomy, ghostly nooks 1 crept,
110 And treacherous stole on seabirds where they slept.
Slow o'er this gloomy place revolves the sun,
And tardy is the moon her course to run.
Was it not strange, King Cuval, that while here
Each weary month was longer than a year?—
115 But what is this that causes you such woe?
I see your bursting tears in silence flow.
Are they awakened by my saddening tale?
Alas ! you have a sadder to bewail !
Oh ! is my love Crimora† now no more?
120 My loving bride ! in sorrow I deplore
Thy death, since floating on the dusky clouds,
That glided round the moon in eddying crowds,

* Gyalcos (Geal-chos)—white-footed ; Dargo's dog.
† Crimora (Cridh-mòr)—large-hearted ; Dargo's first wife.

I saw thy form; she looking down surveyed,
Through showers, the sea's calm face before her spread,
125 In many changing aspects she was viewed,
Her waving, shining locks, with tears bedewed.
I knew my love's fair form, and understood
The cause ere she had risen from the flood.
O, pity me, Crimora! Wilt thou go,
130 And leave me here in solitude and woe?
Fair virgin sprites surround her, whose soft notes
Moaned like the breeze on which the dry leaf floats,
Hushed is the song of birds, unheard the roar
Of waves while on mine ear their voices pour.
135   ' Come with us, Crimora, with joy,
      To the hall of blest maidens on high;
    Where Soolmault* and Trenmor enjoy
      The aerial chase of the sky.'
And sad were heard her sobs and heavy sighs,
140 As, turning, she looked back with mournful eyes.
The music ceased, the vision disappears,
And I am left all lonely and in tears.
As on the shore an only, lonely wave,
Heard by the mariner within his cave,
145 So, thus forsaking me, was my love's sigh,
Like hunter's dream, when wakened by the cry.
I shouted after them, but 'twas in vain—
Bootless as water on the level plain.
Like a thin cloud of smoke in forest wide,
150 On my lone cliff they left me to abide.
My loud lament from early morning's light
Continued to the darkness of the night.
Crimora! when shall I see thee again?
While I have life I shall have grief and pain.
155 Through wildering mists my soul roams for my bride,
But tell me how my fair, my loved one died."

    " When the dark tale was given to thy bride,
In sad and silent grief three days she sighed,
Upon the fourth she to the seashore sped,
160 We found herself there in her husband's stead.
Like winter snow upon the level wide,
Like the white swans o'er Lanna's wave that glide,

---

* Soolmault (Suil-malld')—gentle-eyed; the wife of Trenmor.

She by the maidens of her love was found,
Who gathered from their mountain streams around.
165 With their soft hands they wipe away the tear,
With their soft sighs blow back the flowing hair.
Of stones and green sods from the sea-beach torn,
Thy wife's last dwelling-place we sadly form.
Oh! many a one sobbed cheerlessly that day;
170 Gentle, but sad, the grief that on us lay,
Like the weird sound that rises soft and slow,
When on the reeds of Lego breezes blow.
Pleasant her fame, and sweet I thought her praise,
It were my choice, my most desired always.
175 But see ! what light is this in Innisfail that glows,
And from the dire crantara this way shows ?
Re-set your sails, resume your oars again,
Impel our ship across the heaving main."
Before our faithful mountain wind we glide,
180 And fast to aid its force our oars we plied,
Against the towering waves they strain and bend,
While all expectant for the strife attend.
Upon his target Dargo's elbow leaned,
While down its face his tears unceasing streamed.
185 " Silent and gloomy I see Dargo there,
Ullin of chords, dispel the hero's care."

CULTCHA.

In Trenmor's time that chief of shields of yore,
Young Cultcha chased the deer by Aetcha's* shore;
By him the antlered mountain oxen fell,
190 And his loud shout re-echoed from each dell.
Her love returning home Minvela† spied,
And in her fragile skiff to meet him hied,
But cruel hostile blasts unpitying blew,
And in the deep her hapless barque o'erthrew.
195 Brave Cultcha coming, heard her wailing cry,
" My love! my love! O help me, or I die!"
But the dark pall of night shut out the day,
And gradually her voice decayed away.
Like murmur of a distant gurgling stream,
200 Her languid dying cries to Cultcha seem,

* Aetcha (Eite)—now Loch Etive.
† Minvela (Mln-bheul)—soft-voiced; the wife of Cultcha.

Amid the breakers' strife at dawn of day,
Upon the shore the young bride's body lay:
And there he raised the stone upon her tomb,
Near the sad brook beneath the forest's gloom.
205 And well the hunter knows the silent glade,
And loves to 'scape the heat within its shade.
And Cultcha, ceaselessly and comfortless,
The livelong day through Aetcha's forest strays;
And through the lonesome night is heard his cry,
210 From which the startled seafowl frightened fly.
But Trenmor struck his shield a warstroke strong,
And gladly to his side brave Cultcha sprung ;
And aye, as for his deeds he heard his praise,
His joy returned and he resumed the chase.

215 " The hero, I remember," Dargo said,
" Like memory of a pleasant dream that's fled,
At Aetcha, when he used my youth to steer,
And used to wet her tombstone with his tear.
' Why Cultcha dost thou thus lament and fret?
220 Why are thy aged locks with sorrow wet?'
Cultcha would answer this with streaming eyes,
' Because beneath this turf my loved one lies.'
' Cultcha wilt thou prepare for me a bow?'
' Beneath this sod my love lies cold and low!
225 O! choose this place, thy resting place to be,
When tired of wandering on the sultry lea.'
And Cultcha, thy request I grant always,
And oft thy praise is mentioned in my lays,
O ! if my fame so long as thine should last,
230 And with my love I to yon cloud were passed !"
" I know full well that it shall last for e'er,"
Said Cuval, who in speech was mild and fair.
" But who are these with shields and bold array,
Thus take the light of the first watch of day?"
235 'Tis Lochlin's host, if I can see them well,
With their fierce force surrounding Innisfail.
The King looks from a lattice-window high,
On us, his faithful allies, rests his eye.
Like misty clouds he sees us through his tears,
240 The tears evanish, and our fleet appears.
His gladness glistens in his tearful eyes,
" King Cuval and his ships are near," he cries.

" See Lochlin's people down to meet us pour,
And like a wild ox Armor comes before,
245 On Erin's shore, though haughty now his hands,
I freed them once from firm-bound captive bands.
Let every one resume his sharp grey brand,
And bind it on his thigh, then leap to land;
Let each remember his own bravery,
250 And the famed feats of Feinan* chivalry!
Before thee, thy broad shield, O Dargo, spread!
And draw, O Curril, thy white gleaming blade!
O Conell ! shake on high thy spear of might,
And Ullin! sing the war song for the fight."
255 We met with Lochlin then, nor to our weal,
For firm and fast they stood before our steel,
Like the proud oak on Myalmor's† height that grows,
That bends not to the roughest blast that blows.
But seeing that our force did not prevail,
260 Soon rushing to our aid came Innisfail,
And then was Lochlin scattered far and wide,
And every living branch upon him died.
Armor and Innisfail met in the crowd,
And meeting, glorious was their bearing proud.
265 The King's good spear the giant's breast at length
Pierced through, despite his targe's solid strength.
Then Lochlin wept, and wept too Innisfail;
And all the Feine there joined in the wail,
And sang his bard with trembling voice of woe,
270 When thus he saw his chieftain lying low.

ARMOR'S LAMENT.

Like giant oak tree in the valley was thy height;
Thy swiftness as the mountain eagle's fearless flight;
Like Lodda's‡ wrath, when roused to fury, was thy might;
Incurable thy blade as Lego's vap'rous blight !
275 Ah! soon, too soon, has been thy journey to thy clouds;
Too young, our hero, hast thou fallen, too early died.
Who shall inform the aged that thou art no more?
Or who can now console or comfort thy young bride?

* Feinan, from Feine (Pron. Fainyae)—the Celts of Morven. Written
also Finns, Feinn, Fenians, or Fingalians.
† Myalmor (Meall-mòr)—a large hill.
‡ Lodda—supposed to be Odin, a Scandinavian deity.

I see thy father bent beneath his load of years,
280 Still vainly hoping to espy thy coming sail,
His trembling hand infirm, he leans upon his spear,
His bald and hoary head like aspen in the gale.
Each floating cloud deceives his dark and dazed eyes,
He fondly fancies that thy coming boat he spies;
285 A flitting sunbeam now across his features flies,
" I see the boat!" he gladly to the young ones cries.
The little children gaze across the ocean wide,
They see the floating mist on the horizon glide,
He shakes his grey and aged head with bitter throe,
290 His sigh is sad, his downcast face is full of woe.
    I see the fair Crimina smiling in her charms,
Expecting on the shore thy coming steps to meet,
And dreaming, in her sleep her rosy lips thee greet,
In ecstacy embracing thee with joyful arms.
295 Ah me ! vain is thy dream, thou young and loving bride;
Ne'er shalt thou see thy noble hero's visage more!
Far, far from home thy love has fallen, and wounded, died.
In Innisfail his beauty is all stained with gore!
Ah! thou, Crimina, from thy sleep shalt wake, and then
300 Thou shalt discover that thy idle dream was vain.
But when shall he awake from his drear slumber?   When
Shall end the grave's quiet sleep? thy hero rise again!
    The angry clang of shields, the bark of baying hounds,
      Within his narrow house of clay he shall not hear;
305   And still despite of hunting or of battle sounds,
      Beneath the plain the hero sleeps for e'er.
Ye children of the plain! ye need not for him stay,
He shall not hear the peaceful voice of morning gay.
Ye children of the spears! your trust in him ne'er lay,
310 The battle shout shall never wake him now for aye!
    Now with the hero's soul may joy and blessing be,
      Fierce was his fury when engaged in field of fight,
Of Lochlin King supreme, head of its tribes was he,
      In many a well-fought battle has he shown his might.
315 Like giant oak tree in the valley was thy height,
Thy swiftness as the mountain eagle's fearless flight,
Like Lodda's wrath, when roused to fury, was thy might,
Incurable thy blade as Lego's vap'rous blight!

We finished his last narrow dwelling place,
320 His people o'er the waves their way retrace,

The voices of their songs seemed sickening wails,
And to our ken sad moved their silent sails.
Like whistling mountain breezes seemed their woe,
In desert vales through moaning reeds that blow,
325 When sighs the wind through grasses of the tomb,
And solemn night reigns round in silent gloom.

Part Second.

Like beam of brightness on my soul, the lore
And legends come of times that are no more.
Like beams of brightness on a dreary plain,
While all around the shades of darkness reign.
5 But sorrow still is near to happiness,
The shadows of the clouds the brightness chase,
They overtake them on the mountain height,
And vanquished are the rays of love and light.
Thus, like a light on which the shades prevail,
10 Upon my soul comes Dargo's plaintive tale.
Like giant Armor in the fight, my soul
Is like a sail o'er which fierce tempests roll.

In the grey hall of generous Innisfail,
As was our wont we spent the night; the shell
15 And song went round with sociality,
Nor lacked we wonted hospitality.
But ever and anon a dismal wail
Comes to our ear upon the rising gale.
Ullin and Soolva* searched the place around,
20 Crimina on the hero's grave was found.
Where fell her Armor in the strife of blades,
She also fell beneath the branch's shades;
But to his grave she crept by night, and made,
Intent to rise no more, her lonely bed.
25 We raised and bore her back with tenderness,
And with our sighs replied to her distress.
To Innisfail's glad house she was conveyed,
Cheerless and sad by this the night was made.
Ullin at length his frame of music caught,
30 And soft, with melody and sweetness fraught,
Amid the sounding of the strings he sought,
With gentle finger, every soothing note.

* Soolva (Suil-mhath)—sharp-sighted,

MORGLAN AND MINONA.

Who is he thus from misty clouds descends?
Adown the moaning winds his grief he send ,
35 O deep is in his side the woesome tear!
O dark beside him looms the airy deer!
Yon is the ghost of Morglan,* lord supreme
Of distant Sliglas,† land of many a stream.
With Sora's daughter, maid of graceful frame,
40 His loving bride, to Morven's hills he came;
Fearless he went our moorland heights to roam,
Leaving Minona‡ by herself at home.
Dark mists descended with the cloudy night,
Loud roared each stream, and shrieked each wandering
45 The young bride raised her eyes to the hill-side,   [sprite.
And through the mist a deer she dimly spied.
She drew the string with well-directed art,
In the youth's breast was found the fatal dart!
We laid the hero in a mountain tomb,
50 With dart and antlers in his narrow home.
To lay her 'neath his sod Minona yearned,
But to her home in sorrow she returned;
Heavy her melancholy on her pressed,
Till by the stream of years it was effaced.
55 With Sora's daughters now she's of good cheer,
Unless at times her rising grief they hear.
Who is he thus from misty clouds descends?
Adown the moaning wind his grief he sends,
O! deep is in his side the woesome tear,
60 O! dark beside him looms the airy deer.

"Methinks the day has brightened clear and grey"
Said Cuval, generous and kind alway.
"Take, Ullin, thy good ship and bear away,
To her own land the stranger maid convey,
65 And may she yet shine like the moon when seen,
Gazing from nightly clouds calm and serene."
"O Cuval! may a thousand blessings rest
On thee, the help and stay of the distressed,
But what would I do in my land again
70 Where everything would but augment my pain?

---

* Morglan—tall and handsome.
† Sliglas (Sli'-ghlas)—the green mountain. ‡ Minona (Min-fhonn)—melodious.

Where every grove, ravine, and waterfall,
My lover's wounded bosom would recall.
'Twere better far with thine own maids to go,
Great is the love and gentleness they show.
75 And so the youths that once I would disdain
My eyes shall never more behold again;
If one of them should ask, ' Where is thy Armor dear ?'
Their conversation I will never hear."
    So we brought back with us Crimina, and
80 We gave to Dargo her smooth tender hand;
But kind and courteous though our maidens were,
Oft was she sad with them, and in despair.
Each mountain cascade heard her grievous wail;
Short was her day, and sorrowful her tale.

85 And on a day while hunting Lana's deer,
White-rigged and masted ships were noticed near.
'Twas thought that it was mustered Lochlin come
To bring by force the fair Crimina home.
'Twas then mean Conan said, " I do not care
90 For strife, unless I know for what I dare.
So first investigate with care, and find
How leans to usward now the woman's mind.
Let us her husband's garments redly dye,
In wild boar's blood upon the mountain high.
95 Then bring his seeming lifeless corpse, and see
If aught of truth in her affection be."
We listened then, but sore repented have,
To the advice that luckless Conan gave ;
We felled the savage and ferocious boar
100 Within the thickset forest near the shore.
" Keep him for me," the mean-souled Conan said,
" And off him by my hand shall be his head."
We covered Dargo with the clotted gore,
And, raised upon our backs, the hero bore.
105 Heavy and sad, O King ! our slow strains were,
As, bearing him, we to his love repair.
Conan ran forward with the wild boar's hide
(For he was always prone to ill), and cried,
" The boar that tore thy spouse fell by my blade,
110 When his own spear broke in the lonely glade."
Crimina heard the fabricated tale,
And saw her Dargo deathlike all and pale;

She grew like ice in winter on the tops
Of Mora,* of the hard and barren slopes.
115 Thus, motionless, a little while she stayed,
Then took an instrument in hand and played.
She softened every heart, nor did we yet
Dargo to stir upon his arm permit.
Like the swan's voice in dying agony,
120 Or like the other's notes that round her cry,
Calling their ghosts from cloudy lakes to come,
That on the wind's wing they might bear her home;
Such the lament Crimina sang and played,
Thus with her Dargo stretched beside her laid.

CRIMINA'S LAMENT.

125 Ye spirits from the cloudy lakes on high,
Bend down to bring your Dargo to the sky.
Ye virgins of the brave! come from above,
Come from your hall with new robes for my love!
Why, Dargo, were our hearts so interlaced,
130 So closely intertwined within our breast?
And why thus from me wert thou pluckt away
While I am left in anguish and dismay?
Like two flowers we, that laugh with dew, full gay,
Beside the rock, beneath the sun's warm ray,
135 Having no root except the one alone
On which the two flowers have so sweetly grown.
For the fair flowerets Cona's † maidens cared,
Beauteous to them they seemed, and blithe they fared.
They were respected by the light hinds too,
140 But one of them the boar ferocious slew.
O! heavy, heavy, and with drooping head,
Is the weak plant that is not yet decayed,
Like a dried leaf that in the sun did fade;
O happy were it now if I were dead!
145 And there has crept upon me endless night,
Sudden has sunk my sun in darksome blight,
Early on Morven brilliant was her sheen,
But late unfortunate her course has been.
If thou, the sun of my prosperity
150 Hast left me, I shall ever cheerless be.

* Mora—the great mountain.
†_Cona—weeping; Glencoe.

Alas ! if Dargo from his slumber drear
Wake not, a dark cloud is his wife for e'er.
Pale is thy visage and thy heart is still,
Thy foot lacks strength, thine arm lacks nerve and skill.
155 Ah! dumb is now thy mouth melodious,
Ah! sad am I, my love, to see thee thus;
Thy cheeks once glowing ruddy, changed are,
Thou of the mighty deeds in every war!
Inactive as the hills on which it leapt,
160 Is now the foot that nimble deer outstript!
More dear was Dargo than aught 'neath the sky,
My father sad or mother mild, their eye
Is aye to sea, and oft is heard their cry,
But I would rather with my love to die!
165 And I have followed thee o'er vale and sea,
In the dark pit I'd lie content with thee;
O! let death come, or savage boar to tear,
Or else my state to-night is sad and drear.
Last night for us upon the moor a bed
170 Was in the mountain of thy hunting spread.
Nor shall a sep'rate couch to-night be made,
Nor torn from Dargo shall my corpse be laid!
Descend, ye manes of the cloudy sky!
From warriors' halls of hospitality.
175 Upon your mist's grey wings descending fly,
Nor hesitate to take my mist on high!
Within the heroes' halls, ye virgins fair!
Crimiua's robes of mist weave and prepare,
But Dargo's flowing mantle I prefer;
180 In thy skirts, Dargo, let me be for e'er!"

And now her voice forsaking her we hear,
We see her fingers weak and stiff appear.
We lifted Dargo, but it was too late,
Breathless and dead the fair Crimina sate!
185 The harp fell from her hand, in the lament,
Departing with the song her spirit went.
The hero laid her in the shore, beside
Crimora fair, his former loving bride.
In the same spot he has prepared and placed,
190 The stone beneath which he himself shall rest.

And twice ten summers have come round again,
And twice ten winters with their cold since then,

7

While Dargo has been in his grotto drear,
No sound but strains of sorrow will he hear.
195 And oft I sing to him at noontide here,
Crimina on her bright mist hovering near.
See Dargo in the gloomy grove alone,
And listening to the forest's dismal moan!

NOTES TO DARGO.

PART FIRST.

LINE 1.

' And the melancholy fir trees
    Waved their dark green fans above him,
    Waved their purple cones above him,
    Sighing with him to console him,
Mingling with his lamentation their complaining, their lamenting."
                                                    Longfellow.

LINE 25.

" Now from the sight of land our galleys move,
    With only seas around and skies above ;
    When o'er our heads descends a burst of rain,
    And night with sable clouds involves the main.
    The ruffling winds the foamy billows raise,
    The scattered fleet is forced to several ways."—*Æn.* iii.

LINE 33.

" The land lies open to the raging east,
    Then, bending like a bow, with rocks compressed,
    Shuts out the storms."—*Æn.* iii.

LINE 75.

" Like the leaves of the forest when autumn hath blown,
    That host on the morrow lay withered and strewn."—*Byron.*

LINE 121.

" And sudden through the shades of night appears—
Appears no more Creüsa nor my wife,
But a pale spectre larger than the life."—*Æn.* ii.

LINE 195.

" And the desolate Hiawatha,
Far away amid the forest—
Miles away among the mountains,
Heard that sudden cry of anguish ;
Heard the voice of Minnehaha,
Calling to him in the darkness,
Hiawatha ! Hiawatha !"—*Longfellow.*

LINE 257.

" As when the winds their airy quarrel try,
Justling from every quarter of the sky,
This way and that, the mountain oak they bend;
His leaves they scatter, and his branches rend ;
Unmoved the royal plant their fury mocks,
Or shaken, clings more firmly to the rocks."
Dryden's Virgil.

LINE 279.

" Day after day,
Sad on the jutting eminence he sits,
And views the main that ever toils below ;
Still fondly forming on the furthest edge,
Where the round aether mixes with the waves;
Ships, dim-discovered dropping from the clouds."
—*Thomson.*

" I climb the highest cliff; I hear the sound
Of dashing waves ; I gaze around,
But not a speck can my long-straining eye,
A shadow o'er the tossing waste descry,
That I might weep tears of delight, and say,
'It is the barge that bore my child away.'
I linger on the desert rock alone,
Heartless, and cry for thee, my son ! my son !"
W. L. Bowley.

LINE 291.

" Tears of the widower, when he sees
A late lost form that sleep reveals,
And moves his doubtful arms, and feels
Her place is empty, fall like these."—*Tennyson.*
See also Canticles iii. 1.

PART SECOND.

LINE 1.

" This memory brightens o'er the past,
    As when the sun, concealed
Behind some cloud that near us hangs,
    Shines on a distant field."—*Longfellow.*

LINE 49.

" They laid within his peaceful bed,
    Close by the Indian chieftain's head,
His bows and arrows, and they said,
    That he had found new hunting grounds."

See also Æneid vi., 312; Odyss. viii., 11; Ezek. xxxii., 27.

LINE 144.

" Wailed and wept the sad Nokomis,
    ' O that I were dead !' she murmured,
    ' O that I were dead as thou art !' "—*Longfellow.*

Mr Macbean received the thanks of the meeting, and his translation was considered highly creditable to him.

19TH MARCH 1874.

There was little business of any importance at this meeting, with the exception of the election of several members. The meeting unanimously agreed that Messrs Maclauchlan & Stewart, Edinburgh, be named as the publishers in Edinburgh on Volume II. of the Transactions, which resolution, by some mistake, has not been carried out.

26TH MARCH 1874.

Mr DONALD MACRAE read a Gaelic paper, entitled "Sgeul-achdan Lochaillse," with specimens of Gaelic poetic composition. Mr Macrae declines to give it for publication,

2D APRIL 1874.

After some formal business was disposed of, it was unanimously and with acclamation agreed "that the Society congratulate Cluny Macpherson of Cluny Macpherson, the late and first Chief of the Society, on the distinguished conduct of his gallant son, Major Duncan Macpherson, younger of Cluny, in leading the 42d Royal Highlanders victorious through the battle of Amoaful, on the Gold Coast, notwithstanding that he was twice wounded during that action; and further express great satisfaction at learning that he has now safely returned home, and that the Queen has raised him to the position of Lieutenant-Colonel and Commander of the Bath, in acknowledgment of his distinguished services." The Honorary Secretary was instructed to forward a copy of the resolution to Cluny, and to get it engrossed in the minutes.

10TH APRIL 1874.

The Rev. A. C. SUTHERLAND, Strathbran, Perthshire, read the following paper before the Society, on

THE POETRY OF DUGALD BUCHANAN, THE RANNACH BARD.

"In the following paper, which you have done me the honour of permitting to submit to you, I intend to confine myself to some remarks on the poetry of Buchanan, though his life and prose writings are worthy of serious attention. His autobiography, though of limited range, and occupied chiefly with the mental confusion, disorder, doubt, and struggles through which he passed into inward strength and peace, is a very able composition. The same spirit runs through it as that which informs the *confessions* of Augustine, though, of course, we need not expect a mind nurtured amid the simple associations of a Highland peasant to stand face to face with all the profound questions which agitated and developed the intellect of one carefully trained in all the arts and learning of the mighty civilisations of Greece and Rome, while at the same time in bondage to some of their most degrading vices. Buchanan's mind bore much and suffered much ere it attained to that inward harmony which he so exquisitely describes in his poem called the "Hero," and to a mind in sympathy with him,

his description of the path he trod to it is helpful and instructive
in the highest degree.   It is no disparagement to say that the
African bishop will be more helpful to the man whom culture,
learning, and society have brought into contact with facts, with
conclusions of which ordinary men are, to the increase of their
happiness, comparatively ignorant.   Buchanan, Bunyan, and
Augustine may have travelled by different paths, one seeing more,
another less, but they have all found their resting-place in a firm
grasp of the eternal, as the fountain of what is good and nothing
but good.

"Buchanan never writes verse merely that he may produce
what is artistic and beautiful in form and sentiment.   Probably
he would have regarded it as trifling, or worse, to use his pen in
ministering to the sense of the beautiful, or in creating an appreciation of it, as popularly understood.   The remark that poets
have learned in suffering what they teach in song, has all the
familiarity of a proverb.   But it is none the less true for that.
Every true poet draws on his own experience for the materials
which he fashions into forms of abiding beauty and imperishable
influence.   We are sure that Buchanan's poetry is an expression
of the character of his own mind and heart.   And yet, we must
so far qualify that sentence, by adding that he has not transfused
into his poetry that part of his life which he was enabled to throw
off.   That he considered entirely inartistic, inharmonious, fit to be
forgotten, or only to be remembered as a warning to men, and by
no means to be glorified by the art of the poet.   Had poets
generally been of that view, Plato would not have banished them
from the ideal commonwealth which he sketched for the benefit
of his race.   There can be little doubt that Buchanan too, at one
period of his career, was on the verge of joining hands with those
who lend their genius to the service of licentiousness, whom,
doubtless, he could have rivalled on their own field.

"All the poetry of Buchanan which remains is of a purely
religious character.   At the time when the great English critic
was oracularly declaring that the verities of religion were incapable of poetic treatment, there was a simple Highlander, quietly
composing poems, which, of themselves, would have upset the
strange view, otherwise sufficiently absurd.   But in all justice, we
must say that many, very many, both of Gaelic and English
poets, who have attempted to embody religious sentiments in
poetic forms, have, by their weak efforts, exposed themselves, un-
armed, to the attacks of those who would exclude religion from
the sphere of the imagination.   All good poetry, in the highest

sense, deals with, and appeals to, what is universal and common to all men. No doubt poets there are who deal with thoughts, emotions, passions, which many men are not in conscious possession' of, but the blame may rest not with the poet, but with the reader, much of whose nature may be dormant, under the cold of ignorance, prejudice, and self-interest. Poetry is the outcome of man's dissatisfaction with the mere vulgar appearances around him, and of the desire to make the show of things conform to his own conception of what they ought to be. Still, while things as they are are not sufficient to fill the capacities of our nature, we must not, in our search for poetry, cut ourselves adrift from the appearances of nature, either in the informing mind within, or in those things which appeal to our senses from without. Rather, every fact must be regarded as suggesting something more than meets the eye. Poetry, by its own vitality, blends the inward and the outward into unity and sympathy. Thought, feeling, adoration, passion, desire, seem to have their counterpart and interpretation in earth, and sky, and sea. Poetry is thought, but not the thought that is squared and shaped by the cold chisel of pure intellect, that is science. Poetry is thought fused into awe, joy, anger, hope, fear, love. On the other hand, poetry cannot dissociate itself from the deepest thinking, else it becomes the crackling thorns that blaze up and die.

"The careful student of Buchanan will, I think, find the quality of universality in him. His principles in his poetry are those which find an echo in the heart and mind of humanity. Buchanan himself had decided and well-defined views in religion and politics, had his mind made up as to the right and the wrong in ecclesiastical polity, as well as in the relations of high and low, of rulers and ruled; but in his poetry he seeks not to make men Romanists, or Episcopalians, or Presbyterians, or Independents, but Christians. He strives to lay bare in naked beauty and simplicity the true, the good, and the beautiful, in order that men may drink at their breasts and be blessed. Nor does he hesitate to give poetic shape to the infinite evil—if shape that can have which shape has none—so that men may see and escape. There are critics in the present day who say, that every poem is vitiated that reminds men of the infinite issues of wickedness. Robert Buchanan thinks that in the progress of man the hell described in "Paradise Lost" will, as a dangerous leak, cause that great poem sink in the stream of time. What human nature may be in the future, we cannot say, but we know that all the mighty poets of the past have felt that retribution has its roots deep down in the soul of man. Homer could not get rid of it with all his Grecian love of the sunny beautiful, any more than could the Scandinavian sagas, who sang under the shadows of ice mountains; or the great Puritan, who lost his eyes fighting for human freedom and intellectual and moral culture. Buchanan, too, declares, with fearful power, that there comes a time in the history of the wicked when punishment, not reformation, will be their experience. Still, as a genuine poet, he deals out that punishment, not to those who may offend a rubric, or hold certain ecclesiastical views regarding bishop or presbyter, or who may have certain theories of the universe, or give certain explanations of God's ways to man, but to those who violate the distinctly-expressed commands of God, whether revealed in the nature of man or more clearly in Jesus Christ. Thus punishment with our poet is not arbitrary, but natural, and will be sanctioned at least even by the sufferer's own conscience. With him the final cry of despair comes not from a Calvinist or Arminian as such, but from him who spurns the Son of God, as the embodiment of all blessing in a life mean, sensual, greedy, unmerciful, and tyrannical. The doctrine of the continuity in immortality of the present nature, according to its character, is powerfully illustrated by Buchanan in these graphic and penetrating words.—

> ' Ged bheirinn sibh gu rioghachd mo ghlòir,
> Mar mhucan steach gu seomar righ,
> 'Ur nadur neoghlan bhiodh ga chràdh,
> Le'r miannaibh bàsachadh chion bidh.'

"It is frequently charged upon the Celt, that in religion as in other matters, emotion, inward feeling in the shape of awe, adoration, undefined reverence, are more eagerly sought, and consequently more honoured, than the practice of the simple external virtues, of which feeling should be the ministers and fountains. Whether this accusation holds good generally, or whether it applies more particularly to the more recent manifestations of the religious life among us, this is not the time to inquire. One thing we are sure of, that a representative religious teacher like Buchanan never allows that any fulness of inward life can dispense with the duties of every-day life, with mercy, truth, industry, generosity, self-control. The unworthy man who is excluded from the kingdom is not the man of blunt, homely feeling, incapable of ecstatic rapture and exalted emotion, but the man who locks up for himself the gold God gave him for the

general good, who shuts his ear to the cry of the poor, who en-
trenches his heart behind a cold inhumanity, who permits the
naked to shiver unclothed, who lessens not his increasing flock by
a single kid to satisfy the orphan's want. Indeed, one who reads
carefully Buchanan's *Day of Judgment*, with his mind full of the
prejudices or truths regarding the place of honour given by the
Celt to inward experience and minute self-analysis, cannot fail to
be astonished how small a place these occupy in that great poem.
There, at least, mental experience is of no value, except in so far
as it blossoms into truth, purity, and love. We cannot, however,
pause to illustrate these statements in detail. We shall merely
refer to the indignation into which the muse of Buchanan is
stirred in the presence of pride and oppression. The lowest deep
is reserved for these. The poet's charity for men in general becomes the sublime growl of a lion as it confronts the chief who
fleeces but tends not his people.

> 'An robh thu ro chruaidh,
> A' feannadh do thuàth,
> 'S a' tanach an gruaidh le màl;
> Le h-agartas geur,
> A glacadh an spréidh,
> 'S am bochdainn ag eigheach dail?

> 'Gun chridhe aig na daoine,
> Bha air lomadh le h-aois,
> Le 'n claigeannan maola truagh;
> Bhi seasamh a' d' chòir,
> Gun bhoineid 'nan dòrn,
> Ge d' tholladh gaoth reota an cluas.

> 'Thu nise do thràill,
> Gun urram a' d' dhàil,
> Gun ghearsonn, gun mhàl, gun mhod:
> Mor mholadh do'n bhàs,
> A chasgair thu trà,
> 'S nach d' fhuilig do straíe fo'n fhòid '

"There is the ring of the old claymore charge in these lines.
I think, with all impartiality, they are superior to Burns's lines on
the same subject, beginning—

> 'Poor tenant bodies lack o' cash,' &c.

"It is not often that death is praised; but we do not, under the circumstances, grudge it the vote of thanks which the poet so fervently awards it. Perhaps it is but fair that I should allude to the lines immediately following those I have quoted above, for they deal out severe justice to spiritual guides who act as unfeeling stepmothers to their charges, not heeding though the fox might tear, if the wool, all they cared for, were but safe. These are not the words to be spoken to a people who are supposed ignorantly to depute their intellects to a priest as such, unless he has that commanding power which men must acknowledge and follow.

"We have been looking at our poet in connection with his poetic handling of the universal principles of morality and vice, of religion and its opposite, in their profound issues of happiness and ruin. Was Buchanan capable of touching his lyre with a lighter finger? It can be shown that though his heart was given to the serious muse, yet he could, if he so chose, have rivalled, on their own ground, those who lent their power to what ministers to the tender and the convivial. Has not genius been described as vast general capacity applied to a particular subject, but capable of dealing with any. It has been alleged that there cannot be a good song from which wine and love are excluded. Some exquisite lyrics, on both these themes, are scattered up and down amid our shorter Gaelic poems, from the days when Màiri Nighean Alastar Ruaidh tapped her mull, drank her wine, and sang its praise. Of course I don't refer to songs which encourage vice and brutality, but those that embody pleasures that are regarded as innocent. On such subjects Buchanan touches in an incidental and illustrative manner only. What he says of them are the mere sparks that fly from the heated metal he is beating into poetic form. Listen to his description of the drunkard—

> ' No am fear thu bha pòit,
>   Gu tric 's an taigh òsd,
> 'S tu cridheil ag òl an dràm,
>   Nach iarradh dhut féin,
>   De fhlaitheanas Dé,
> Ach beirm a bhi 'g eiridh a' d' cheann?

> ' Nach iarradh tu ceol,
>   Ach mionnan mu'n bhòrd,
> Is feuchainn co 'n dorn bu chruaidh :
>   Mar bho no mar each,
>   Gun tuigse, gun bheachd,
> Is tu bruchdadh 's a sgeith mu'n chuaich.'

" The first of these stanzas clearly reveals the fact that the poet could embellish conviviality with the charms of poetry. The second, in its strong realistic imagery, paints excess in all its moral and physical loathsomeness, and makes us thankful that its author was not permitted to use his power in casting an attractive witchery of poetic grace over such hideousness; and so disguising, and therefore making more dangerous, the poison of the debauchee's cup.

" By a touch of his pen, Buchanan gives us another glimpse into his wealth of lyric faculty, as a famous painter once proved his mastery over his art by drawing, with one sweep of his pencil, a circle which, when tested by unerring compasses, was found to be mathematically correct. Is not the verse I am to quote, a beautiful little lyric circle, completed at a stroke, yet revealing a cunning, a native art, which, if it took the trouble, could fill the largest canvass with every form, and colour, and shade, for which we praise the graces ?

> ' 'M bu mhaighdean deas, thu,
> Bha sgìamhach a' d' ghnuis,
> 'S deagh shuidheach a' d' shuil da reir ?
> Le do mhaise mar lion,
> A' rìbeadh mu chridhe,
> Gach òganach chì'dh tu fein ?'

" Enamoured of this fair creation, the poet hurls his anathema against death for robbing it of the enchanting beauty which rains sweet influence. But, as already stated, Buchanan had more serious work in view than to be the interpreter of what is merely playful and brilliant in the nature of man. He chooses to apply his imagination to other departments of our common humanity— to the lofty and ennobling in religion and duty. In so doing, he plays with all the emotions we are susceptible of, awakening admiration, terror, sympathy, love, awe, for the purpose of disentangling men from all that stands between them and the realization of the perfect ideal that underlies all humanity.

" The genuine poet can never lose sight of human nature. He may, to the unthinking, do so when he casts his plummet into the dark depths of the supernatural; but as the anchor which holds its grip many fathoms down is visibly bound to the ship above, so the true bard never detaches his imagination from the facts, the feelings, the joys, the woes, the hopes, and the despair of the human spirit. This is eminently true of Buchanan. In his noble poem the *Day of Judgment,* Scripture, nature, human experience are laid under contribution to illustrate the awful circumstances and the mighty issues of immortal life standing in the presence of the tribunal of absolute righteousness. The Roman critic instructs poets to deal with materials equal to their genius, and to guard against the folly of laying upon their shoulders a burden they are unable to sustain. Buchanan has in this poem bent his energies to a gigantic task, and the way in which he has carried it through unmistakeably reveals surpassing poetic strength. The poem begins almost with prosaic simplicity. This in itself is a high merit, for no fire that is to burn with power and effect puts forth at the outset all its force of heat and light. First comes the gentle curling smoke, then the brilliant blaze. In the same true artistic spirit our poet, like the setting sun, softens his splendour before he parts with his readers. The excited feelings awakened by the overpowering incidents of the poem are gradually toned down, by gentle expostulation with those who foresee not the evil day, and by soothing words of hope to all who, through the Son of God, are seeking a life with its root, not in sense, but in the invisible God. I cannot find the heart to analyse this poem in a critical spirit, not because of a lurking suspicion that it would be found wanting when rigidly tested, but because it is of a nature more fitted for deep meditation than for public discussion. We have already indicated that it belongs to no party, no sect, no school of theology in particular, unless, indeed, those who believe in salvation by Jesus Christ, and the eternal issues of good and evil are to be so designated. Direct description, dialogue, soliloquy, the outpourings of hope and ruin, are here pressed together into a splendid unity. We have no space for copious extracts. As an illustration of the felicity of Buchanan's descriptions take the following verse, in which the effect of the advent of the Judge on the stars is set forth :—

> ' Bidh iad air uideal ann san spéur,
> Mar mheas air géig ri ànradh garbh,
> Tuiteam mar bhraonaibh dh' uisge dhì,
> 'S an gloir mar shuilean duine marbh.'

" That last line has always seemed to me singularly powerful. Nature is dissolving, and the splendour of the heavens assumes the ghastly hue of a dead man's eye. One thing is noticeable amid these sublime musings, and it is this, that the poet assists us to realise his conceptions by images drawn from ordinary experience. Generally this is done with beauty, dignity, and suggestive aptness, e.g., the parting of the cloud through which the Judge passes is the opening of the King's chamber-door. The flash of the Divine eye is like the lightning; the lightnings themselves wait upon their Lord with the eagerness of the obedient dog waiting to be set free for duty from its leash, &c. It is doing the poet injustice to be detaching his imagery from its setting, and to be forcing them into the associations of another language. We must not conceal the fact, that now and then the image degrades the thought; as when the rising of the dead is compared to the agitation of an ant-hill, or when the eternally lost are represented as fastened on rocks of fire, like limpets; or when the shrinking of the blue curtain of the sky in the all-devouring element is likened to the curling of thin bark on the living coal. The thought here is, of course, taken from Scripture; but the imagery sinks, in its anxiety to be definite, to the level of the mean, the too familiar, and even the coarse, in a manner for which revelation is in no way responsible. It is but fair to add that there are but one or two unsightly shrubs in a glorious garden of beauty and fruitfulness.

"It may be profitable now to follow our bard into poetic fields, where we shall find it easier to hold our footing, and keep our way without being lost in wandering mazes. Here, too, it will be easier for us to measure the poet by the standard which determines the value of other Celtic poets, especially of those who may practically be regarded as his contemporaries. None of Buchanan's contemporaries, so far as known to me, essayed the soaring wing of the 'Day of Judgment,' though the attempt has been common enough in other languages, from the time of that singularly lofty and impressive Latin hymn, 'Dies Irae,' down to its imitation by Scott, in the lines beginning 'That day of wrath, that dreadful day,' &c. The poetry of Buchanan's day was chiefly lyrical and satirical, varied with elaborate descriptions of set themes taken from nature or human life. Much of the former too gave expression to itself in Jacobite songs, and in virulent personal attacks, often offensive to common civility. Buchanan, both by his religion and his politics, was excluded from exercising his genius in that line. On the other hand, the aim of his life—the religious elevation of his countrymen — compelled his muse to make his descriptions the handmaid of religious truth. But we have descriptions of set themes, common to the other poets, from Buchanan's pen. We may detach these for the moment from the instruction which is elaborated out of them in so ingenious, and yet so natural a manner. Take, as an example, that exquisite and

highly-finished poem, entitled *An Geamhradh*. The description of
the literal winter occupies about a third of the poem. Here we
have an opportunity of bringing Buchanan face to face with other
bards well known to fame. Macdonald, Maccodrum, Rob Donn,
Macintyre, have all attempted to give poetic expression to the
associations and circumstances of the changing seasons. It seems
as if they could not feel their laurels secure until their muse paid
homage to these diversified divisions of time. That was a fortunate circumstance, for it forced the bard to look on facts outside
of his fancy, without doing harm to the informing power within,
which interprets and harmonises the appearances of nature in
accordance with its own principles and laws.

"In helping us to see poetically the changes of the world
around us, I venture to say, after due deliberation and comparison, that no bard of the last century is superior to Buchanan.
Would that in this, as in other respects, he had been more liberal
to posterity with the fruit of his gifts. In describing nature, the
Gaelic poets I refer to are too often the victims of a vicious con-
ventionality, with its consequent weak style and puerile conceits.
True poetic insight and warm natural expression are not wanting,
nay, found in abundance, for genius will assert its right in spite of
the restraints of a false taste. But the evil I mention is undeniable. Macdonald, for example, begins his poem on wonder by
telling us very accurately, I suppose, that the king of the planets
(i.e., the sun), came to the sign of Cancer on Wednesday, and
will soon be in the winter solstice. Taurus, Capricorn, Gemini,
have due attention paid to them. The citizens of the sky no
longer sing vespers or matins. This may be learned, but it is
very unpoetic; for such allusions may interest the understanding, but they touch no feeling. Will it be believed that the author
of *Morag, Birlinn Chlann Raonuil,* permits himself to liken the
heather, with its blossom and golden dust, to the powdered and
oiled wig ! The sun, too, is the valet which makes the heather
trim and neat, with its powder and oil! Then there is that
absurd and ostentatious stringing together of long epithets, *e.g.*—

'A mios cratanach, casadach, lòm,
     Churraiceach, chasagach, lachdunn a's dhonn,"

&c., for six lines more in the chain.

"I am aware that some admire this sort of writing, as showing
a command of words. Doubtless, it does that, but for poetry
there is as much in the command of the juggler over his muscles.
The end of the faculty in both cases is simply to make us stare

with astonishment at clever tricks. Something of a similar style of writing is found, I believe, in some Grecian hymns of the second century, when the ancient poetry was in its decrepitude. From this mode of writing Buchanan is singularly free. He preferred to knit his words together as a living tissue, rather than string them loosely, as a savage his barbaric pearls. Besides all this, Buchanan escapes the minute realism which marks too much Gaelic descriptive poetry. Instead of elaborate detail, we get clear firm lines, which seize and make living the object to be presented, in a way which cannot but gratify our sympathies and emotions. Winter spreads his wings between us and the sun, his cold breath steals the soul of the flower, he strips the trees, and chokes the music of the brooks, he is the merciless foe of those who provided not against his coming, but deals kindly with the prudent. Imagery of this kind go to the heart, and the poet who uses it compels us for ever to see nature in the colours he has clothed it with. After we read Burns's poem to the 'Daisy,' we cannot help somehow transferring our own feelings to the lowly and modest flower. Unlocked-for misfortune and the daisy are inseparably associated, and Buchanan has bound in the same human chain old age and winter. Nature is thus made to minister to man in his aspiration after perfection, and to rebuke him in his levity, his sin, his meanness, or despondency. Listen to this description of old age, in terms furnished by the desolating power of winter:—

> 'An aois a tha n toir ort,
> Bheir i leon ort nach saoil thu;
> Air do shùilean bheir ceathach,
> Is treabhaidh si t aodan;
> Bheir i crith reodh mun ghruaig,
> Is neul uain an aoig leis,
> Is cha tig aiteamh na griàn ort,
> Bheir an liàth reodh a chaoidh dhiot.'

"I must not, however, follow this subject further.

"Before closing, will you allow me add a sentence regarding that remarkable poem entitled the *Skull*. The subject does not seem a very promising one for poetic treatment. Repulsive as it appears, yet Buchanan arrays it in the richest imagery, and gathers around it fascinating ideas. It would have astonished an ancient Greek beyond measure, with whom the happiness and perfection of his nature was limited to the life that now is, to be told that a poet had sung of a hideous skull carelessly flung from the loathsome grave. Yet so it is, and Buchanan has, among

other things in the poem, softened the hard features of death with
the halo of a glorious hope in the case of the worthy, but has
intensified its horror and degradation for those who allowed the
brute in their nature to triumph. There is in this poem the
same wonderful command of appropriate phrase and impressive
imagery, the whole flowing as sweetly as the gentle stream. It is
remarkable that the introduction to this poem corresponds in idea
very much with the scene of Hamlet and the gravediggers, though,
of course, Buchanan is too grave to jest and pun, like the philosophic prince, in connection with the emblems of man's mortality.
It is probable enough that Buchanan read the tragedy of Hamlet,
in which speculations are started regarding those great questions
which ever press men hard for a solution, and which Buchanan,
too, looked steadily in the face. We know that Hume quoted
Shakespeare to the poet, doubtless well aware that the quotation
would be thoroughly appreciated. Assuming, then, that the idea
of our poet's description of a skull was taken from Hamlet, that
will so far detract from his originality. But a perusal of the poem,
and of the scene in the play already referred to, will at once show
that all Buchanan could have borrowed leaves untouched his
absolute originality of treatment and form. Indeed, Shakespeare
himself is not original, if the fact of a poet getting the idea of his
work from another destroys his claim to originality. Hamlet and
Buchanan speak of various persons to whom the skull might once
belong, and for whose ends, good or bad, it was the willing servant,
and moralise each in his own way on the base uses to which we
may return. There is, however, a cynicism, and possibly a de-
spairing scepticism, in the one, which gave way in the other to a
tender melancholy, and to a faith that the house which 'lasts till
doomsday' does not imprison the essence of humanity. Buchanan
does not dwell on what is disgusting in death—though that fact
is not concealed—with the same glee as the Prince of Denmark.
He paints the grave rather as robbing us of the grace, the attractions, the faculties, the senses, the energies of life, than as con-
verting us to the vile clay, as Hamlet does, that might stop a
hole to keep the wind away. For example—

> ' Gun àille gun dreach,
>   Gun aithne gun bheachd;
>   Air duine theid seaeh na dhail,
>   Gun fhiacail na dheud,
>   No teanga na bheul,
>   No slugan a ghleusas càil.'

"You observe that that graphic description deals entirely in negatives. We think of the varied endowments of man's senses, of his intellect, social capacities, and physical beauty, as having passed away. What dissolution directly produces is less minutely depicted, though from the moral and religious aim of the poem the subject is not ignored. This last way of looking at the grave is introduced with great effect in connection with the death of the brutal and the sensual, as we may see in the lines which remind us of their doom. To the glutton it is said—

> ' Tha nise do bhrù
> Da 'n robh thu a lùb',
> De ghaineamh 's do dh'ùir gle làn,
> Is do dheudach air glas',
> Mu d theangaidh gun bhlas,
> Fo gheimhleachadh prais a bhais.'

"This quotation gives us also a very good example of the habit of the poet in referring to the grave in figures taken from the character, profession, or general circumstances of the person to whom the skull may be supposed to belong. Is it a physician's, then his skill failed him at the last, and the enemy he fought so long at last made him prisoner. Is it a general's, then his sword, too, had its edge turned, and his last battle was a defeat, &c. This sort of writing runs through the poem to a degree which makes it almost a mannerism, though, be it remembered, a mannerism which makes the poem very easily remembered, and which is a great auxiliary to the didactic intention of the poem. With his usual poetic feeling, Buchanan parts not with his subject, so full of what we do not like to contemplate, until it becomes transmuted with hope into the forerunner of perfect beauty.—

> ' Oir deasaichidh Dia,
> Do mhaise mar ghrian,
> Bhiodh ag eiridh o sgiath nam beann;
> Cur fradharc ro gheur
> 'S na suilean so féin,
> 'S iad a dealradh mar reulta a' d' cheann.'

"The clear eye of hope sees that ghastly socket filled once again with an eye still more radiant than the old, those hideous angles and hollows clothed with a more translucent beauty, and that bare forehead beaming with a mightier intelligence than it

8

ever knew before, if the present debasement was preceded by a life of truth, self-denial, and conformity to the Son of God.

"From what has been already so imperfectly said, I think you will allow that Buchanan deserves a close and sympathetic study from every ingenious member of the Gaelic Society. We are so taken up in the present day with the antiquities of our language, as to be in danger of overlooking what appeals in it to other faculties than the historical or philological. These last are, of course, to be exercised and trained into all fulness and exactness; but let them not, like a mighty tree, overshadow and kill, by drawing all the nourishment and appropriating all the sunshine to themselves, the love of poetry for its own sake, of beautiful and heroic sentiments which help to ameliorate the hard niggardliness of nature where that exists, and to impart still greater fruitfulness to what is already good.

"I think a young Celt thrown into the whirling excitement of our modern life, in which the aim of most men is not to cultivate into full activity the powers and feelings of their nature as rational creatures, but rather to surpass everybody else in material splendour and power. Civilisation with such is not the culture of the true, the good, and the beautiful, with success; but display, mechanical power, and enormous balances. That spirit is to be honoured in its own place, but it must not over-ride what is due to man as a living soul needing angel's food. Buchanan teaches, in songs of magical grace, that no external advancement can bring us fulness and roundness of life, for the royal pillow bears sighs no less than the straw one of the peasant. Nor shall we reach the end of our being by the mere energy of the intellect, the very expansion of which is often the inlet to intensified bitterness. Such energy is the energy of the lamb which has lost its mother, and goes about bleating, repulsed, and wounded at every turn, among those that care not for its wants. In our poet we have an instructor who, with exquisite grace, insinuates into our bosoms all the elements fitted to keep our humanity fresh, strong, and sweet amid all in life's struggle that tend to wither and dwarf its nature. In an age when the glory of the battle-field was the dazzling idol adored, Buchanan sang that men may win battles and not be heroes. He told them, in words still more needed in a time of more selfish personal pursuits, that the hero is the man who sets out on the path of life, in a true spirit, without fear, conquering the cowardice that makes us slaves to what is base, who shrinks not from death itself, and who encounters with a great and glad heart what Providence brings across his path.

Much of this would be grateful to the ears of a warlike people, but to be told that after all a man's great battle has to be fought on the field of his own heart, would not be so welcome. If what our critics say of us be true, that we need more patient, steady endurance to make our natural quickness of practical avail in life, no better antidote to our weakness, and no greater help to our strength, can be found than in incorporating Bùchanan's poems into our very life. He would have us to be heroes, capable of all the self-mastery, all the abstinence from passions, all the endurance in misfortune of the old stoic, softened and refined by a harmonious development of our entire manhood, and, as the crown and flower of all, permeated with the life of Christ—the living impulse that bursts through and throws off our old husk.

"Thus we shall not only have the dash which carries us through a splendid charge, the vivacity that creates and enjoys what is graceful and charming, but have, in addition, the mind firm as adamant, and equally patient, so that defeat shall not be despair and collapse, but the occasion of a severer discipline, in which order shall regulate enthusiasm, and enthusiasm shall inspire order with vitality. Buchanan will help us to measure ourselves not by what we possess, but by what we are; to cultivate charity toward all men; to be fearless and independent; but, above all, to be ready to sacrifice every interest at the command of duty, which, with him, was the will of God. He will do this, too, in a style not harsh and crabbed, but musical as the lute of Appollo, where no crude surfeit reigns, at once fitted to ravish the heart, to gratify the imagination, and to satisfy the intellect, except where these are vitiated or debased. In the words of Ben Johnson, a rare poet needs rare friends."

A hearty vote of thanks was accorded to Mr Sutherland; after which a letter was read from Cluny, thanking the Society for the resolution passed at their last meeting.

16TH APRIL 1874.

At this meeting it was unanimously agreed to suspend Rule III., and dispense with a ballot, when Alexander Forbes, Esq., San Francisco, was unanimously elected a life member of the Society, after which Mr D. MACCULLOCH read a paper, entitled "Rambles in the Highlands." It has already appeared in a local paper, and it is therefore unnecessary to reproduce it here.

23d APRIL 1874.

The following paper, from Mr JOHN MACDONALD, of the Excise, Lanark, entitled

"AM FEUM A TA AIR AON DOIGH SUIDHICT', AITHNICHTE, AIR SGRIOBHADH NA GAILIGE,"

was read by the Hon. Secretary.

"A dhaoin' uasail, tha eagal orm gu 'n saoil sibh mi ro dhàn' ann a bhi cuir òraid Ghàilig do bhur n-ionnsuidh o'n Ghalldachd, agus tha eagal orm nach mòr a shaoileas sibh dhi 'nuair a chluinneas sibh i. Na'm bithinn math air Gàilig a sgrìobhadh cha bhiodh e idir doilich dhomh mòran innseadh mu 'n chearn so, fada gu deas mar a tha mi, a bhiodh ro thaitneach do Ghàidheil a chluinntinn. Tha againn comharraidhean lionmhòr, neo-mhearachdach, gu 'n robh an dùthaich so aon uair air a h-àiteachadh le Gaìdheil. Gu h-àraidh air taobh shuas amhainn Chluaidh tha ainmean nan àiteachan a' cuir an céill cho cinnteach gu 'm bu Ghàidheil sluagh na tir aon nair, agus a tha dol fodha na gréine air chùl nam beann a' cuir an céill gu 'm bheil an oidhich' a' tarruing dlùth. Ann an sgìre *Lesmahagow*, mu thiomchioll leth mbile o *Lanark*, ach air taobh eile Chluaidh, tha chuid a's mò do ainmean nam bailtean air an sgrìobhadh agus air an labhairt cho Gàidhealach 's ged a bhiodh iad ri taobh Loch-Nis. Faodar muinntir a chluinntinn gach là a bruidhinn mu Auchlochan, Auchnòtrach, Auchinbeg, Auchmeddan (meadhou), Auchenleck (lag), Auchtool (t-shabhaill), Auchinstilloch, Ardoch, Corramore, Craigenrig (righ), Carngour, Glaickhead.

"Anns an sgìre so tha seann Chaisteil Chraignethan mu 'n do sgrìobh *Walter Scott* ann an 'Old Mortality' fodh an ainm 'Tillie tudlem.' Anns na sgìrean mu 'n cuairt tha againn—Drumalbin, Balgray (greidh), Glentaggart, Glendouran, Glendorch, Glencaple, Glenochar, Strancleugh, Liscleugh, Duneaton, agus mòran tuilleadh. Ma theid sinn thairis air crioch shiorraichd *Lanark* gu *Dumfries*, gheibh sinn, Clachleith, Glenbuie, Glensalloch, Glenrae, Glengaber, agus an leithidibh sin. Is tric mise feòrach do na Goill ciod e seadh agus brìgh nan ainmean so, agus cionnus a thugadh leithid a dh-'ainmean do nà h-àitean. Ach cha 'n aithne dhoibhsan. Ni mò a's aithne dhoibh no thuigeas iad an t-aoibhneas a tha na h-ainmean so air uairibh a' cuir ormsa, no na smuaintean muladach, tùrsach, trom, a tha air uairibh a' taiseachadh mo chridhe 'n uair a dh-imicheas mi thairis no seachad air na h-àitean ud, far am bheil an Gaìdheal an duigh na choigreach.—

'Tha clann nan treun air dol a dhìth,
Is muinntir eil' air teachd do'r tìr.'

"D'fhaodainn mòran innseadh mu 'Chluaidh chaoin,' mu 'Chluaidh nan sruth sèimh,' mu 'Chluaidh nam bruach.' 'S maith a b'aithne do Bhàrd mhilis Shelma an amhainn mhòr, mhaiseach, a tha dol seachad sios fodh *Lanark*. Is trio a choinnich a ghaisgaich agus 'oighean mu bruach, agus is tric, aig an là 'n dingh, a chithear fleasgaichean 's an leannan ri taobh a sruth. Is iomadh seann chaisteal, liath, briste, air a bruachan a tha 'g aithris 'sgeul air àm o aois.' Tha Easan Chluaidh iomraiteach airson an àilleachd 's an greadhnachas, agus chithear 's an t-shamhradh luchd-turuis as gach cearn a' tighiun 'g am faicinn. Is maith a dh-ainmich na Gàidheal an Eas mheadhonach, 'Eas a' Choire.'

"D'fhaodainn innseadh mu 'Tintoc,'—an Tein-chuoc, an cnoc a's àird' anns a chearn so. Chithear air là soillear o mhullach, an dùthaich mu 'n cuairt air son mòran mhìltean. Is iomadh aite-dion Gàidhealach (*British hill-fort*) agus campa Romanach a chithear o mhullach. Ann an àm cogaidh agus cunnairt b'iomadh sùil a bha ri fair' air an Tein-chnoc, agus bu tric a dhears an 'gath' gu lasrach, boillsgeach, air a mhullach, a' tabhairt rabhadh gu 'n robh an namhad a' tarruing am fagus. Mar sin thionail na Gàidheil an gaisgaich gu cuir an aghaidh nan Romanach, mar sin chum na Romanaich am feachdan air am faicill an aghaidh nan Gàidheil, agus mar sin is tric a thugadh rabhadh do dh-Albainn gu 'n robh na Sasunnaich chiocrach a' tighinn a rithist a thabhairt ionnsuidh air a slugadh.

"D-fhaodainn innseadh mu gach gniomh treubhach, gaisgeil a rinn *Wallace* treun ann an *Lanark*; mu na h-àitean folaich a bh'aig ann an Creagan *Chartland*, agus aig Eas a' Choire; mu 'n iomhaigh shnaighte mhòr a tha air a cuir suas dha aig ceann eaglais *Lanark*, a tha muinntir a' bhaile air là àraidh gach bliadhna a' sgeadachadh le breacan, le blathan, le barradh chraobhan beithe, agus le rainneach, mar chuimhneachan air na rinn agus na d'fhuiling e airson a bhaile 's a dhuthaich.

"D'fhaodainn innseadh mu thigh ainmeil, gaisgeil an Douglas, a bha cho comharraichte re iomadh linn do eachdraidh Alba. Tha 'm fearann 's an Caisteal dlùth air *Lanark*. Tha an t-aium air a labhairt an dingh le sluagh an àite cho Gàidhealach 's a bha e cheud là chualadh 's a bhlàr an glaodh, 'Seall-tibh an Dùbh-ghlas.'

"Bu taitneach innseadh mar fhuair na Cumhnantaich (*Covenanters*) gu tric fasgadh o 'n luchd-geur-leanmhuinn ann an còsan dorcha Chreagan Chorrach *Chartland,* dlùth air a bhaile; mar a chum iad iomadh coinneamh dhiomhair ann an doimhneachd uaigneach sgoltaidh uamharra nan creag sin—am Mactalla a' tabhairt fianuis leis an earail dhìleas agus leis an urnuigh dhùrachd-ach, agus torman an uillt a' co-sheirm ri fonn bronach nan Sailm.

" D'fhaodainn tionndaidh gu eachdraidh sgriobht' an àite agus innseadh mar a shuidh daoine glic a bhaile so ann an comhairle mu thiomchioll dà cheud bliadhna roimhe so, agus a thug iad geur àithn' agus òrdugh gu 'n rachadh gach diol-deirce, gach Eirionnach, agus gach *Gàidheal,* a sgiursadh agus fhuadach as a bhaile; mar a chum muinntir *Charluke,* 'san ath sgìrè, là taingealachd air son gu'n do chaill na Gàidheil blàr Chuilfhodar, ach feumaidh mi sguir. Ge taitneach 'sgeul nan laithean a d'fhalbh,' cha 'n fhaodar dearmad a dheanamh air na laithean a tha làthair, agus neo-chomasach mar a tha mi, gun leabhraichean, gun ùine, 's fheudar laimh a thabhairt air a cheann-teagaisg.

" Is e tha mhiann orm a chuir fodh chomhair a Chomuinn, am feum a tha air aon doigh suidhicht', aithnichte, air sgrìobhadh na Gàilige. Cha 'n eil a rùn orm, ni mo tha mi comasach, air ceistean cruaidhe, foghlumaichte a rannsachadh no shocrachadh, no air riaghailtean sonraichte a chuir sios air son an doìgh sgrìobhaidh a's fearr a fhreagras do chomh-dheilbh na cànaine. Is e tha mhàin a rùn orm beagan bheachdan agus smuaintean mu'n chuis a chuir, gu ro ghoirid, fodh bhur comhair, agus a leigeil leibhs', ann bhur gliocas, a chùis a rannsachadh, agus breith a thabhairt co dhiù is fhiach i deadh-aire agus geur-bheachd no nach fhiach.

" Cha ruig mi leas innseadh dhuibh nach robh aig sgoilearan roimh so aon dòigh suidhichte air sgrìobhadh na Gàilige. Mo chreach gu 'm bheil na dearbhaidhean tuilleadh a's lionmhòr. Mar a thubhairt ' Alpein Og,' o chionn ghoirid, bha 'n doigh sgrìobhaidh cho caochlaidheach ri breithnachaidhean an luchd-sgrìobhaidh. Ma choimeaseas sibh leabhraichean Gàilig a chaidh chuir a mach an Inbhirnis, an Glascho, 's an Dùneidin, shaoileadh sibh nach deach riaghailt a chuir sios riamh chum sgrìobhaidh na Gàilige a theagasg, ach gu 'n robh gach aon air fhàgail gu saors' a thoil, gu dheanamh mar a bha ceart 'na shuilean fein. Tha leabhraichean òrain agus laoidhean air an cuir a mach is gann is urrainnear a leughadh na thuigsinn; co dhiù is e coire nan sgrìobhadairean no nan clo-bhualadairean cha 'neil fhìos agam, theagamh gu 'm bheil iad àraou ciontach. Tha againn fathast ann ar measg beagan do sgoilearan Gàilig, ach tearc mar a ta iad cha chord iad mu 'n doigh a's fearr air sgrìobhadh na cànaino. Cha chord Maclauchlinn, Clerk, no Camshroin; cha chord luchd-sgrìo-

bhaidh an 'Ard-Albannaich,' a 'Ghàidheal,' no na 'Brataich'; seadh
—ach na innsibh e ann an Gat—chithear eadhon mòr iomadach
anns an leabhar a chaidh a chuir a mach le Comunn Gàilig Inbhirnis   Cha 'n eil e idir doilich a thuigsinn cionnas a tha leithid
do dh-eadar-dhealachadh am measg luchd-sgrìobhaidh.   Cha d'
fhuair iad 'nan 'òige foghlum, agus ionnsachadh o leabhraichean
freagarrach no a reir riaghailtean suidhichte, agus cha 'n eil e idir
iongantach gu 'm bheil muinntir a' leantuinn an dòigh sin a dh'
ionnsaich iad 'nan òige anns a chearn do 'n duthaich 's an d'fhuair
iad an àrach, agus is e 'nam beachdsan an dòigh a's fearr.   Ma
chumas sinn ann ar n-aire cho bochd 's a bha 'n luchd teagaisg,
agus cho beag 's a bha 'm foghluim a fhuair Sgoilearan Gàilig
'nan òige, is ann a bhitheas iongantas oirnn cho maith 's a tha
luchd-sgrìobhaidh na Gàilig' a' cordadh.   Is e mo bharail gu 'm
faodar sin a ràdh mu Eirinn mar an ceudna ; oir ma d' fheuch
Tomas O'Neill Russell ni sam bith anns na nithibh a sgrìobh e
ann san Ard-Albannach o chionn ghoirid, is e cho beag 's a tha da-
rireadh a dh-atharrachadh eadar Gàilig Albannach agus Eirionnach.   Leugh mi 'n ait 'air chor-eiginn nach mòr nach tuigeadh
Gàidheil Albannach agus Eirionnach gach focal a labhradh iad ri
cheile ; agus cha robh e idir doilich dhomhsa comhradh a chumail
ri Eirionnaich a thachair orm.   Ach faicibh an t-atharrachadh
mòr a tha eadar ar dòighean sgrìobhaidh.

   " Ma ghabbas sinn ann an cearn sam bith do Shasuinn leud
dùthcha cho farsuinn ris a Ghàidhealtachd, gheibh sinn a cheart
uibhir, mar fhaigh na 's mo, do dh-atharrachadh am measg luchd-
labhairt na Beurla.   Ach 'n an sgrìobhaidhean cha 'n fhaicear dad
do dh-atharrachadh do bhrìgh gu 'm bheil aca aon seòl suidhichte,
aithnichte, a tha iad a' leantuinn.   Tha fios agaibh ciod a rinn
Addison, Johnson, agus an leithidibh sin air son na Beurla ; cionnas a thug iad a stigh dòigh sgrìobhaidh a chaidh a leantuinn gu
mòr mar riaghailt agus mar eiseamplair a nuas o 'n àm sin ; agus
cionnas is ann a reir seòl sgrìobhaidh sgoilearan comharraichte
mar sin a nithear deuchainn a chuir agus breith a thabhairt air
sgrìobhaidhean muinntir eile.

   " D'fheòraichinn ma ta, nach eil sgrìobhaidhean idir againn a
d'fhaodar a chuir sios mar riaghailt agus mar eiseamplair do luchd-
sgrìobhaidh na Gàilige?   Nach eil am measg uil' ionnsachaidh nan
Gàidheil sgrìobhadh poncail agus coimhlionta gu leòir gu bhi 'na
riaghailt shuidhichte leis an deanar deuchainn a chuir agus breith
a thabhairt air sgoilearan Gàilig?   Is e mo bharail sa gu 'm bheil
againn a leithid a riaghailt agus a dh-eiseamplair :—Gu 'm bheil
againn anns a Bhìobull Ghàilig, a dh'aindeoin beagan mhearachdan

suarach, cha 'n e mhàin dòigh sgrìobhaidh eheart, ghlan, shnasmhor, ghrinn, a thaitneas ris, agus a thuigeas, gach Gàidheal,
ach mar an ceudna an seòl sgrìobhaidh a's fearr a fhreagras do
chomh-dheilbh na cànaine. Ma tha e mar so, is e am Bìobull
na sgriobtuirean do na Gàidheil ann an seadh dà-fhillte, raighailt
an caithe-beatha, agus riaghailt agus eiseamplair an sgriobhaidh.
B' aoibhneach leam an là fhaicinn anns am biodh sgoilearan
Gàilig a leantuinn an seòl sgrìobhaidh a th' againn anns a'
Bhìobull. Leanadh ann an Dàin Oisein, mar air an cuir a
mach an Dùneidin anns a bhliadhna 1818, le gle bheag atharrachadh, an dòigh sgrìobhaidh a th' againn 'sa Bhìobull. Tha
againn mar an ceudna ann an sgrìobhaidhean Thormoid Mhic-
Leòid anns an 'Teachdaire Ghaidhealach' agus ann an 'Cuairtear
nan Gleann', seòl sgrìobhaidh a tha araon ro cheart agus phoncail, ro
shnasmhor, agus ro ghrinn, ma chuireas sinn a leth-taobh beagan
fhocail agus dhòighean-labhairt a bhuineas gu h-àraidh do 'n Earra-
Ghàidheal. Tha nàir' orm innseadh nach do leugh mi Dàin Oisein
mar air an cuir a mach le Dr Clerk, ach tha mi làn chinnteach gu
'm bheil dòigh sgrìobhaidh fear deasachaidh 'Charaid nan Gàidheil,'
grinn, glan, agus ceart. Chi sibh nime sin nach e cion riaghailt
agus eiseamplair is aobhar do 'n eadar-dhealachadh sin, am measg
luchd-sgrìobhaidh na Gàilige, air son am maith a d'fhaodas Gàidheil
caoidh agus gearan a dheanamh. Cha 'n eil teagamh sam bith agam
nach mòr an cron agus an call a rinn e do 'n chànain, gur iomadh
aon a chum e o ionnsachadh cainnt a shinnseara, agus gur iomadh
leabhar agus sgrìobhadh Gàilig air an do chum e muinntir aineolach.

"Tha sibh a faicinn nach eil againn aon dòigh suidhichte air
sgrìobhadh na Gàilige, ged a tha againn, a reir mo bharail-sa, riaghailt eheart, phoncail, agus eiseamplair glan, grinn, a dh' fhaodas
sinn a leantuinn. Ciod e ma ta brìgh na cùise? Nach e gur
mithich ionnsuidh chruaidh, dhìchiollach a thabhairt air sgrìobhadh
na Cànaine athleasachadh. Agus a chionn nach eil againn fear-
teagaisg ann an aon air bith do Ard-sgoilibh Alba, co dha a's fearr
a thig sin a dheanamh, no co a's comasaich air a dheanamh, no
Comunn Gàilig Baile mòr na Gàidhealtachd, air am bheil a rùn
a Ghàilig a chuir air a h-aghaidh, agus 'bàrdachd, seanachas,
sgeulachd, leabhraichean, agus sgrìobhana, 's a chànain sin a
thearnadh o dhearmad?' Do bhrigh an coimhcheangal dlùth a tha
eadar sibb agus a Ghàidhealtachd, buinidh dhuibh an toiseach a
ghabhail, agus bithidh aig Comuinn Gàilig Inbhirnis, ughdarras
agus cumhachd anns a chùis nach biodh aig Comunn sam bith eil,
aon chuid an Glascho, an Dùneidin, no 'n Lunnuin. Gabhaibh ma
ta na sgrìobhaidhean a's fearr agus a's comhlionta 's an chànain,

mar stéidh agus mar bhonn, mar riaghailt agus mar eiseamplair, agus cuiribh an cèill gu'm bheil a rùn oirbh fein sgrìobhadh a rèir an dòigh sin, agus gu'n tabhair sibh breith air sgoilearan Gàilig a rèir an riaghailt sin. Cha 'n e sin a mhàin ach gairmibh air gach Comunn Gàilig anns an tìr chum ar còmhnadh agus ar cuideachadh le'n comhairle agus le'm maoin, ann a bhi cuir a mach clò-bhualadh athleasichte, saor, do bhàrdachd agus sgrìobhaidhean eile nan Gàidheil. Deanaibh sin a reir dòigh sgrìobhaidh grinn, glan, a Bhiobull Ghàilig, agus tha mise meallta mar bi an luchd-leughaidh lionmhòr anns gach cearn de'n t-shaoghail. Leagaibh sios stéidh agus bonn suidhichte, a ghabhar agus a dh'aithnichear le luchd-sgrìobhaidh na Gàilige mar riaghailt agus mar eiseamplair, agus cuiribh sibh mar sin air aghaidh cìnneas na Gàilige, coisnidh sibh dhuibh fein deadh ghean nan Gàidheil, maille ri cliù agus meas gach sluaigh, agus saoraibh sibh Baile mòr na Gàidhealtachd o 'n tàmailt ud is tric a thilgear air—nach d'rinn e dad riamh air son leas no cinneas na Gailige.

The meeting expressed strong approval of the writer's suggestion, that the orthography of the Gaelic edition of the Bible should be the basis of Gaelic orthography in general. The Society instructed the Hon. Secretary to convey their thanks to Mr Macdonald for his paper.

7TH MAY 1874.

At this meeting the Committee, appointed at a previous meeting, to procure a Secretary at a salary, reported that Mr Hector Maclean, Islay, declined the office, and they recommended that Mr Donald Macrae, High School, be appointed. The recommendation was adopted; Mr Macrae was unanimously elected Secretary, and being present, accepted office.

The meeting thereafter remitted to the Council to make the necessary arrangements for the Annual Assembly.

6TH JULY 1874.

Several members were elected, and, on the recommendation of the Annual Assembly Committee, it was decided (and as it proved unwisely) to postpone the meeting from the Thursday evening of the Inverness Wool Market to the week of the Highland and Agricultural Society's Show,

The meetings of 22d and 24th July were taken up with further arrangements for the

ANNUAL ASSEMBLY,

which was held in the Northern Meeting Rooms, on Tuesday evening, the 28th July 1874. We take the following report of the proceedings from the "Highlander" newspaper:—

"The third Annual Assembly of this Society was held in the Northern Meeting Rooms, Inverness, on Tuesday evening, when there was a fair attendance. We regret that the demands on our space otherwise render it impossible for us to give that full and fervent account of the proceedings which the importance and native character of the Society and its proceedings would indicate as proper from us. Sheriff Macdonald, one of the Chieftains of the Society, occupied the chair. The Chairman was supported by the Rev. Alexander Macgregor, M.A.; Captain Chisholm, Glassburn; Rev. Mr Wright, Congregational Minister; Robert Carruthers, Esq., LL.D., "Inverness Courier;" Alex. Macdonald, Esq., Balranald; Mr Jolly, Her Majesty's Inspector of Schools; Mr John Murdoch, of the "Highlander." Amongst others present were Capt. Rose; G. J. Campbell, Esq.; Bailie Macbean; James Fraser, Esq., C.E.; Captain Stewart, Bialid; — Cameron, Esq., Strone; Donald Davidson, Esq.; David Rose, Esq., Ceylon; James Ross, Esq., solicitor, &c., &c.

"The Chairman rose with diffidence to address the meeting, as it was only the evening before that he was informed of the honour intended for him in asking him to preside at the Assembly, and he had only a short time before got a programme of the order of procedure put into his hands. It was under these disadvantages that he came before them, and he therefore craved their indulgence for a short time. To begin with, the objects of the Society were decidedly patriotic, and by no means exclusively confined to the cultivation of the Gaelic language, nor to interfere with the Gaelic-speaking people from learning the modern and commercial languages. To show this, he would take the liberty of reading the following paragraph from the rules of the Society :—

"'The objects of the Society are—The perfecting the members in the use of the Gaelic language ; the cultivation of the language, poetry, and music of the Scottish Highlands; the rescuing from oblivion of Celtic poetry, traditions, legends, books and manuscripts; the establishing in Inverness of a Library, to consist of books and manuscripts, in whatever language, bearing upon the genius, literature, history, antiquities, and material interests of the Highlands and Highland people ; the vindication of their rights, and the furtherance of their interests, both at home and abroad.'

" The Highland and Agricultural Society of Scotland, now holding its show at their doors, began on a very small scale, although now it included all Scotland in its operations. He held its motto, *semper armis nunc et industria,* 'always foremost in valour, now foremost in industry,' to apply aptly to their Society. He held in his hand the second volume of the Society's Transactions—which would soon be in the hands of the members—from which it would be seen that the number of members was yearly increasing, amounting at present to 261. That number, however, did not adequately represent the number of members, because these numbers were made out before the Transactions of the Society were sent to the printer, and a considerable number had been added to the membership since then. The funds were also prosperous, the Society holding, independently of debt, from £70 to £80. He recommended the members to take a lively interest in increasing the membership. Let each member take a pride in trying to bring in other members year after year. In that way the numbers would increase, and they might be very soon in a position to effect the teaching of Gaelic in their cottages, schools, and colleges, which had been in view for some time past. He hoped that the Society's membership would increase like a snow-ball, and that every successive year would in its roll bring large accessions to the roll of members. From the names of the parties on the programme, the evening's meeting promised to be a success, and he sincerely hoped it would. (Applause.)

" Rev. A. Macgregor, M.A., who was received with several rounds of applause, spoke as follows:—

" Fbir-suidhe Urramaich, a' Bhantighearnan, agus A 'Dhaoinuaillse gu leir, Cha bheag an t aobhar taingeileachd a th'againn gu'm bheil bliadhna eile air toirt a cuairt agus gu'm bheil sinn air ar caomh bheil nadh fathast ann an tir nam beo, agus, gu'm bheil Comunn Gaelig Inbherneis a' fas ann an cumhachd,—a' dol ann am farsuingeachd' agus a' cosnadh durachd agus deagh-gbean nan urramach anns gach aite air feadh na Gaidhealtachd air fad. Tha so ro thaitneach gu'n teagamh, agus is leoir e chum gach anam aig am bheil fuil nan Gaidheal a ruith 'na chuislibh a lionadh le

gairdeachas. Is leoir e chum gach fior-dhuine aig am bheil spéis
da dhuthaich fein, a dheachdadh gu bhi 'guidhe le uile chridhe fein
mar a leanas :—

"Gu robh buaidh leis a' Chomunn ud,
Cho seasmhach, saor, somalta;
Gu'n cuirt' na miltean comain orr',
Le dol gu'n dail a'm boinn riu.

B'e sud an Comunn ceanalta,
Tha uasal, ard, eireachdail,
Co iad a theid an coimeas riu,
'N uil' bhailtibh mor na rioghachd?

Tha Ghaelig ghrinn 'ga labhairt leo,
'S gu'n agh is gu'n agartas;
A'm measg a' cheil a' tagaradh,
Gach cuis is cleachd mu'n Ghaidhealtachd.

A'm Baile-cinn na Siorramachd,
'S riaghailteach iad a' cruinneachadh;
'N sin thig gu luath na h-nile fear,
'Chur urraim air a' mhor-shluagh.

Air Clach-na-Cudainn chuireadh leo
A'n t-urram is a'm mor-mheas;
A thoill a' Chlach o'n h-uile neach
'Ni 'dhleas'nas mar is coir da!   ·

Co cruaidh 'sa 'Chlach gu'n charrachadh,
Nach brisear leis an ord i,
Co dian ri sin 'tha tairisneachd
Na Cuideachd aluinn, coir so!

An Comunn curant', ceanalta,
'S maiseach agus geanail iad;
Tha feartan 's buaidhean 'leanachd riu,
Nach treig iad 'm feadh is beo iad.

Tha uaislean ard a' cuideach leo,
'S Cinn-fheadhna 'teachd le mor-ghean;
'S gach Fin, a's Treibh; a's Ceannard treun,
A' dol mar aon 'gan comhnadh!

Tha Cluanaidh mor 'nam bras-bhuillean,
Gu h-aiginnsach 'gan seoladh;
'Na chanain bhinn is bhlasda, ghrinn,
'A Ghaelig aosda, oirdheirc,

'S Lochiall nan euchd is caidreach e,
Is Coinneachd Ridir Ghearrloch ;
Is Traith na Tullaich aiginneach,
Is Blackie tla 'nam ban-chiabh !

Gu leir le h-eud is daimheileachd,
Is laidir, tairis, dian iad ;
A'n cairdeas is a'n caoimhnealas,
Cha d' thug 's cha toirear buaidh orr' !

Gu robb rath leis a' Chomunn ud,
Seasmhach, suilbhear, coimhlionta ;
Fearail, fialaidh, solaireach,
Co 'mholas mar bu choir iad ?

"Seadh, 'Co 'mholas mar bu choir iad ? Chan'neil teagamh
agam nach dean an t-Ard-Albanach a dhichioll air clach dhiong-
mholta a chur ann an carn-cuimhne Comuinn Gaelig Inbherneis;
agus nach dean e spairn chruaidh le' bhonait 's le bhreacan-an-
fheile, chum an deagh-chliu a chur a'm fad 'sam farsuingeachd.
Ach 'Co 'mholas mar bu choir iad?' Cha'n fhurasd r'a fhaotuinn
fear-dan, no filidh, no bard, 'n 'ar la 's nar linn fein, aig am bheil
cumhachd uilo bhuaidean Gaildhead a leigeadh ris mar a thoill iad.
Nochd iad an dillseachd agus an gaisge fein anns gach rioghachd
fo'n ghrein, agus cha'n fhurasd an euchdan anns gach cath agus
teugmhail a chur an ceill mar bu choir !—Bu chliuiteach, druigh-
teach, cruaidh chainnteach Ian Lom, agus an Ciaran Mabach, Ian
Mac Fhearchuir Mhic Chodruim, Donnuchadh Ban, Rob Donn,
agus sgaoth gu'n aireamh eile a dheachd na Ceolraidhean ann am
mor-thomhas ; ach an deigh sin cha bhiodh an ceileirean ach diblidh,
fann chum gaisge shliochd nam beann aithris mar a thoill iad. Is
ceart a dh' fheudadh an luchd dan gu leir a radh :—

"Dhiult na Ceolraidh an combradh binn,
Is cliu nan treun cha'n eirich leinn;
Is lannan boisgeil, cruaidh nan saoidh,
'S nam flath 'nam feirg, cha seinn sinn chaoidh.

"Ach dh' aindeoin gach saruchaidh agus cruaidhchas a ta iad
a fulang—dh' aindeoin mar a ta iad air an ruagadh 'mar na
cearcan-coille air na beanntaibh'—an deigh sin nile, cha do chaill
iad fathasd am misneach, no'n cruadal, no'n curantachd. Is iad
nach do chaill—Cha'n 'eil ach beagan mhiosan o'n nochd na feachdan Gaidhealach an treubhantas, agus an dian-thairisneachd 'san
Roinn-Africa, far an do chuir iad an ruaig air na h-Ashanteich,
agus far an d'rinn 'Am Freiceadan Dubh' gu h-araidh teuchd do
chur an ceill !

"Ghrad chuir iad smuid ri Camassi,
Bha'm baile gu leir 'na lasair;
'S mar nead chonnspeach thuit e 'na smal,
Gach cabar is clach dheth gu lar!

Ochan! Righ Coffi Calcalli,
Bu mhealltach, fealltach am ball e!
Ach fhuair e na thoill e gu cruaidh,
Le gaisg' nach dean briathran a luaidh!

"Cha saruich mi bhuir foighidinn le bhi 'labhairt a' bheag
tuilleadh aig an am.—Thubhairt mi ni's leoir, air do fhios cinnteach a bhi agam gu'm bheil deagh run aig maithibh na tire do
Chomunn Gaelig Inbherneis. Ach tha Comunn eile a ta air ainmeachadh air ar luchd-duthcha,—comunn eile a ta mor agus cumhachdach, agus tha e 'sa bhaile anns na laithibh so. 'Se so Comunu
Gaidhealach na h-Alba,—agus cha'n 'eil teagamh nach 'eil e ann
an dluth-dhaimh ruinne. Is mor agus is cosdail an t-ullachadh a
rinn an Comuun so, leis an aitreabh-fiodha a thog e a'm fochair a'
bhaile, chum gu'm biodh spreidh de gach gne gu follaiseach air
an nochdadh, seadh, crodh, caoraich, eich, mucan, torcan,
cearcan, agus gach ainmhidh 'nar duthaich a ta 'feumail do mbao
an duine. Ach, a thuilleadh air sin, tha gach ball agus ac fhuinn
tuathnachais, a fhuair innleachd an duine a mach, air an nochdadh
an sin:—inneala gu miorbhuileach air an co'-dhealbhadh,—agus
ceart co miorbhuileach air an gluasad le gaoith, le teine, le
uisge, le h-aile, no le toit! Chithear an sin oibrichean chear-
dail de gach seorsa, mar a ta oibrichean-creadha,—oibrichean-gloine,
—oibrichean-lin, oibrichean-snaidhte, oibrichean-uairdeadair,
oibrichean-chuidhleachan, agus mar sin sios. Chithear ann,
innealan air son gach gne ealaidh agus ceairde,—agus geochail
gu'n aireamh nach ceadaich uine dhomh fiu an ainmeachadh. Is
mor, cumhachdach, agus cudthromach an Comunn so. Se Bun
Lochabair fein le' bhriathraibh soilleir, bandaidh, reidh, a loig-
eadh ris air choir e. Ach mor agus lionmhor 's mar a ta na cuspairean a ta aig an ard-chomunn so 'san amharo, cha'n ionnann na
nithe a ta 'san amharc aig 'Comunn Gaelig Inbherneis,'—oir 'se
durachd a' Chomuinn sin gach modh, seol, gnath, agus cleachd,—
gach buaidh, gne, feart, agus cail a bhuineadh riamh do na Gaidheil a thoirt air an aghaidh, agus a chumail air chuimhne.—

"O! gu mo fad an Comunn beo,
Is gu mo farsuing mor an reachd;
'S gu robh beannachd an Ti a's Aird',—
'Nan cois gu brath, 'nan gniomh' s'nan cleachd!

" Rev. Mr Wright, Congregational minister, after a few introductory remarks, proceeded to give the audience some words of advice with regard to Ossian and his poems. It was somewhat humiliating, he said, to find that in some parts of France and Germany, there were men better acquainted with the times, style, and characteristics of Ossian's poetry than they in the Highlands of Scotland were. They looked upon Ossian as their true poet, and in order that he should be properly understood and appreciated, it was necessary that they should give their literature and his poetry a free and full chance and scope. In Ossian they found the true characteristics which mark the poet. The humdrum of life was oftentimes hard to bear, and they were often willing to go away from society to get to nature. Then they were glad to get a man true to his nature, and the nature by which they were surrounded. Such an one they found in Ossian, whose imagery and the scenes by which he was surrounded, made them feel it was good that they had been born on the earth. They need not expect in Ossian the refinement and polish found in the productions of the highest English poets, who being reared and educated in the quietude of English life, wrote in a similar strain to their surroundings. So Ossian, surrounded by those grand old mountains and hills, whose ears heard the sounds of those mountain streams, wrote in a rough, rugged style, but in a style which spoke with force to them as Scotchmen. Ossian had been styled the Homer of Scotland, lacking truly the vivacity of Homer, but having all the *esprite* which is characteristic of Highlandmen—which had carried them to the heights of Alma and to Coomassie. In Ossian they would find matter to suit all tastes. Among the young the poems of love would be appreciated, while those of a martial spirit should read of the sons of Fingal. He came there simply to show his sympathy with the movement, and to ask them to give the Society a fair chance. (Applause.)

" During the evening the following ladies and gentlemen contributed towards the success of the Assembly in a manner which was evidently highly pleasing to the audience. Pipe-Major Maclennan played 'Failte an t-Siosalach,' 'Captain Campbell's March,' &c., ' Cumha an aon mhic,' and 'The Cameron's Farewell to Gibraltar.' Mr A. Stewart sang ' Air faillirin, illirin, uillirin, O,' and 'Oran Chaptean Huistean.' Mr James Fraser sang 'John Grumlie,' ' Come under my plaidie,' and 'It fell upon a Martinmas time.' Mr W. G. Stuart recited ' Fionnladh Piobaire,' 'Turus Eachain gu Paisley,' and ' Clan nan Gaidheil ri guaillean a' cheile.' Miss Flora Matheson sang ' Failte dhuit, deoch slainte leat,' and ' Ho

ro mo nighean donn bhoidheach.' Professor Morine rendered
Gaelic airs on the pianoforte. Mr Sim sang 'Mary of Argyll,'
and 'My native land.' Mr D. Wilson sang 'Oran do'n Fhrei-
ceadan Dubh,' and, along with Mr Macrae, 'Ho! mo Mhairi
laghach.'

"Mr Jolly, H.M.'s Inspector of Schools, in moving a vote of
thanks to Sheriff Macdonald for presiding over the meeting, said
it was only the Sheriff's love for the cause the Society had in view
which induced him to come forward that evening. He (Mr Jolly)
was only sorry that the meeting was not more largely attended to
enjoy such a pleasant evening's entertainment. He hoped they
would carry forth with them the ideas contained in the grand old
songs and music they had that night listened to, and that the
result of the evening's proceedings would be that they would take
greater interest in the Society, which should command their best
attention, and, at the same time, show what they could do in in-
vestigating the great philological link which the Gaelic language
supplied, which was now for the first time demanding and receiving from scholars and others who appreciate the study of philology
the attention which it deserved. (Applause.)

The proceedings were then brought to a close by the playing
of Dhia Gleidh Bhanrigh (God save the Queen) on the pianoforte.

[We regret to have to state that the assembly was not the
triumphant success which we should have desired. The presence
of the magnates of the Highland Society in Inverness; the hospitality due to the strangers attending the show; the rain, hail, and
thunder, during part of the day; and, no doubt, the deviation from
the eve of the Wool Fair for holding the Assembly, all conspired to
keep the people from attending. Still the true spirit pervaded the
proceedings; and the members present were animated by the hope,
the zeal, and the determination, which should sustain Clann nan
Gaidheal ri guaillean a cheile!]

TRANSACTIONS, 1874-75.

The first meeting of Session 1874-75 was held within the
GUILDRY HALL on Tuesday evening, the 1st September 1874.
There was no paper read. Complaints were made as to the delay
in printing Volume II. of the Society's Transactions, and the Publishing Committee was requested to report progress.

10TH SEPTEMBER 1874.

At this meeting Mr Mackenzie, Bank Lane, presented the
Society with a handsomely bound copy of his publication of the
"Airs and Melodies of the Highlands and Islands of Scotland,"
by the late Captain Fraser of Knockie. A vote of thanks was
accorded to Mr Mackenzie for his elegant and valuable donation
to the Library.

14TH OCTOBER 1874.

This evening a lecture was delivered by Professor BLACKIE,
of Edinburgh, on "The Teaching of Gaelic in Highland Schools,
and in the Universities." Charles Fraser-Mackintosh, Esq. of
Drummond, M.P., occupied the chair; supported by Sir Kenneth
S. Mackenzie, Bart., of Gairloch, Honorary Chieftain; Alexander
Dallas, Esq.; Thomas Mackenzie, Esq., Broadstone Park; and
John Murdoch, Esq.—Chieftains; Dr Carruthers; Sheriffs Blair
and Macdonald; Bailies Macbean and Davidson; the Rev. Messrs
A. Macgregor, Dawson, and Wright; Angus Mackintosh, Esq. of
Holme; James Anderson, Esq., solicitor, &c., &c.

9

We take the following report, being the best, from the *Aberdeen Free Press*:

"PROFESSOR BLACKIE ON THE TEACHING OF GAELIC IN SCHOOLS & UNIVERSITIES.

" Mr Fraser-Mackintosh having introduced the learned lecturer,

"Professor BLACKIE, who was received with loud and continued applause, began his lecture by referring to how he, a Saxon, without a drop of Celtic blood in his veins, stood before them that evening to speak on the subject of Gaelic education. People were now beginning to see that our Scottish Universities were running in a rut. Sometime ago a representation was made that a professorship should be established in the University of Edinburgh, not of Gaelic alone, but of all the Celtic dialects. Several took an interest in this movement, and among others on the committee were Lord Neaves and Cluny Macpherson. Knowing the extreme difficulty of moving the Scotch people, and the extreme practicality of the Scotch intellect, the committee resolved to adopt some measures to bring them to their duty, and there he was in the North among them that evening. The office of convener of this committee was put upon him, and he was therefore determined to do something. He was there claiming their support. A great number of people were rather the better of being told what they should do; they did not always object to do it; but still they had to be told. For the past ten or twelve years he happened to live in the Highlands, and he sang songs there too! Yes, Highland songs, along the running waters, and under the shadows of the fragrant birch. There he learned to weep with those that wept, and to mourn with those that mourned. He had taken up the question of the Highland clearances; he often barked on that question, and gave an occasional bite. He then went on to speak of the Celtic language and literature. This was the moment to state the question. If there was to be a representation of the Celtic language and literature in our Universities, this was the moment—it was now or never; and said the Professor—

' There is a tide in the affairs of men,
    Which taken at the flood leads on to fortune,' &c.

There was a grand organisation up in London and Edinburgh, but those fellows did not know anything about your requirements;

and if you allowed them to get the mastery, what would be the
case ? Speaking of the character and position of the Gaelic language in Great Britain, he said that Gaelic was a branch of one of
the great Aryan languages that emigrated from the high grounds
of Central Asia to Middle and Western Europe, and had, for at
least three thousand years, been spoken by a people of fine qualities and marked character, but which, from its peculiar circumstances, had never been able to assert for itself any prominent
place as an organ of literary expression. Gaelic was an old and
venerable language—he would not say the mother of Latin and
Greek ; but he would say the sister, or, if they preferred it, the
brother. (Laughter.) Speaking of the literature of the Gaelic
language, he said that not to speak of Ossian, we had the Lismore
Book of Ballads, and also ' Mordubh,' a poem in the style of
Macpherson's ' Ossian.' Speaking of the Education Code, and the
duties of School Boards, he said it was their duty to support this
language on grounds of patriotism, religion, and sentiment. The
Gaelic language was neglected, and that by the very people who
spoke it. This neglect of the language was not to be attributed
to the Highland Celt alone. The Lowlander did likewise. He
also forgot his native Scotch music, and ran after Italian and
German novelties, which, whatever their excellencies may be, are
not the national element which a Scottish soul should love. For
the neglect of the Gaelic language there were several reasons, such
as that ' Far away birds had fair feathers;' then there was the
novelty of a foreign tongue; and people who wished to be genteel
considered Gaelic vulgar; and lastly, there was the question of interest—a very Scotch question—What was the use of the Gaelic
language ? He would answer that by another question—What
was the meaning of ' use'? That would puzzle them. The question
was often asked—Would a knowledge of Gaelic help one to get on
in the world ? Of course, that meant this world. (Loud laughter.)
People often gave out in a nasal tone the words—

' Here lies the body of Alexander Macpherson,
   Who was a very extraordinary person.'

But that had nothing to do with Gaelic, and getting on in
the world. It was said often there was no practical advantage to
be got by a knowledge of Gaelic. But whatever the practical
uses, Gaelic was rooted in the affections of the people, and, as the
mother tongue, maintained its hold like an old tree, holding with
many fangs to the soil, and required a force greater than the Duke

of Sutherland's steam engines to tear it up. Notwithstanding all this neglect, it has maintained, and will maintain, a stronghold within the *garbh chrioch*, or rough boundaries, where it has its home. Gaelic was the language of religious life in the Highlands; and they knew that religion was the most radical thing in human nature, and the most closely connected with the noblest expression of the popular life. If there was no Gaelic preaching, Gaelic would die out; but as, being the mother tongue, it would have a welcome in the hearts of all people who had a heart; but God knew there were many people without a heart at all. There was less Irish preaching than Gaelic preaching, and on that account he would predict that Irish would die a hundred years before Gaelic. A few minds of superior patriotism or enthusiasm recognised the value of the mother tongue as an instrument of moral and intellectual training. He referred to such men as Mr Campbell of Islay, who hunted up all the old women, and old sailors, and old tailors and tinkers, for old stories. He would also refer to the father of the late Dr Norman Macleod, who was popularly and deservedly known as ' *Caraid nan Gaidheal.*' He was, as Sir Robert Peel said, a model clergyman, a perfectly polished gentleman, and a true Highlander. It has been well said that if that man's heart had come out of his bosom it would be found dressed in a kilt. Again reverting to the Gaelic language, he said that the existence of a peculiar language justified the existence of a peculiar people—of a peculiar type of man, of peculiar traditions, manners, and customs; and to obliterate a language was to erase the memory of the past and to wipe out a peculiar type of men from the face of the earth. Our nationality was in a measure couched up in our Highland Gatherings and Northern Meeting. There were seen the kilt, the plaid, the bagpipe, the dirk, the hose, and exhibition of muscle, but no brain. From this he went on to speak of the Education Act, which he condemned as ignoring the Gaelic language. Some people maintained that the language was harsh, was difficult to acquire, and was barbarous. This he totally denied. If the Education Department wanted Gaelic books, from the poetry of Duncan Ban Macintyre he would make a book which would have a better moral effect on the youthful Highland intellect than any of their English schoolbooks. (Loud applause.) Well, Gaelic was old, but he had no reason to believe that Gaelic was the language of the prayer-book by which Adam and Eve were married in Paradise. (Laughter.) This was said by a great poet of their own— Alastair Macdonald, *Mac Mhaighstir Alastair*—but it was calculated to do more harm than good to the cause of Gaelic. A know-

ledge of Gaelic strengthened a knowledge of English; and men
who did not know a word of Gaelic were not entitled to pronounce
the language as being barbarous, or anything else. Some people
said that a knowledge of Gaelic hindered a knowledge of English.
He wondered if a knowledge of Latin and Greek had the same
effect in the Lowland schools. Here he read a letter from Colonel
Gardyne of Glenforsa, which was to the effect that the Colonel,
and his father before him, took an interest in the teaching of
Gaelic in Highland schools, and that they always found that the
pupil who could best read the Gaelic language was the best English
scholar also. Gaelic, it was said, was an extremely difficult language, and its acquirement demanded more time and labour than
most languages. No language was difficult to persons who im-
bibed it with their mother's milk. There is no difficulty in Gaelic.
He would, indeed, come to the conclusion that man was a very
lazy, a very stupid, and a very cowardly animal. He (the Professor) would not condescend to learn an easy language. What if
a man was to pride himself on mountain-scaling, he would not be
satisfied with getting to the top of Tomnahurich; he would take
Ben-Nevis. The prevalence of *ch* was the only difficult thing
about Gaelic; and as for *ch*, everybody in the world except John
Bull could pronounce it. It was not his knowledge of Gaelic, but
his want of English, that prevented any Highlander from getting
on in the world. There was a difficulty in finding teachers in the
Highlands able to give instruction in Gaelic. The best teachers
could only teach English, Latin, or French, and, it might be, a
little Greek. These were all masks for ignorance —an apology for
laziness. There was no reason whatever why an elementary
teacher in the Highlands should know Latin and Greek; it was
only learned superstition. (Laughter.) They should teach Gaelic,
English, music, drawing, and botany. For the teaching of Gaelic
in schools, he would lay down the following rules :—1: Wherever
the majority of the people hear with preference Gaelic sermons,
they ought to be able to read a Gaelic Bible, and the reading of
Gaelic ought to be taught in the school. 2. Prizes and distinc-
tions ought always to be given for the recitation of Gaelic poems
and the singing of Gaelic songs in Gaelic schools. 3. Where the
Gaelic-speaking population form only a small minority in Highland
schools, Gaelic ought not to be taught as a regular part of school
business; but special prizes ought to be offered to those who, in
a voluntary way, attain excellence in Gaelic reading and recitation,
by private study and extra scholastic appliance. 4. The Education Board, in selecting schoolmasters for Highland parishes, should
give a decided preference to such teachers as can show a grammati-

cal knowledge of the Gaelic language, and an increase of salary
should be given to all teachers who make a dexterous use of the
mother tongue in the teaching of English and Latin, or in the
encouragement of correct Gaelic reading and recitation.   The
learned Professor then went on to speak of Gaelic in the University.
He strongly argued for a Chair there, both for training teachers
and preachers, and cultivating the language in its philosophical
aspect.   But the great Scotch question, Will it pay? unfortunately intruded here.   If it did pay, good and well; if it didn't,
that was the reason why it should be established.   He himself
had offered £50 towards this end.   If we cannot get great names
to lead us as they ought to do, let us not neglect what Dr Chal-
mers said of the power of littles.   Let us agitate the clans and
county gatherings and associations, and let us appeal to the prosperous Celt abroad.   Why not follow the example of the Roman
Catholic clergy of the middle ages and of the Free Church clergy
of the present day?   Let us teach old Celtic leaders and gentlemen to make wise wills, for which purpose there were plenty of
lawyers in Inverness and elsewhere.   And then, in conclusion, he
said—If the Celtic soul amongst you is dead; if you have ceased to
believe in yourselves; if you are willing to be snuffed out by a
pair of Saxon snuffers; if you wish to be strangled by London and
Edinburgh ' red tape;' if you wish to be absorbed into the big
body of the beef-eating, grouse-shooting, deer-stalking, and salmon-
fishing Brahma, called John Bull—in that case I can do nothing
for you.   You can't steal from a man who is willing to have his
pockets picked.   To those who refuse to be helped there is no help
possible.   The Professor then resumed his seat amid thundering
applause.

    " Dr Carruthers proposed a vote of thanks to the Professor for
his interesting lecture; and said that though the Education Code
did not prescribe, it did not forbid the teaching of Gaelic in the
national schools.

    " Sir Kenneth Mackenzie seconded.   Speaking of Gaelic in
schools, he said that though no mention was made of Gaelic in the
Education Code, inspectors were instructed to test the knowledge
of the pupils by making them translate the words into Gaelic.
He only wished they were all as Highlanders imbued with the
enthusiasm which animates Professor Blackie.   If they were, a
Gaelic Professorship could easily be established.

    " Professor Blackie said that inspectors knew nothing of Gaelic,
and would only be showing their own ignorance in asking the
pupils to translate words into it.

    " Sheriff Blair proposed a vote of thanks to the Chairman for presiding, and remarked that during the late election canvass he was sure Mr Fraser-Mackintosh found Gaelic of great use to him.

" Mr Fraser-Mackintosh said that he found Gaelic of advantage to him not only during the late canvass but throughout the progress of his life. He hoped that School Boards would look after the interests of the Gaelic language, and see that it was taught in schools in all districts in which it was the language of the people. In regard to the Gaelic Chair, any proposal in connection with it would have his most cordial support. Invernessians would be failing in their duty if they did not contribute speedily to the object Professor Blackie had in view—an object he hoped would receive all manner of success.

" At this stage the Professor was stimulated to such a pitch of enthusiasm that he arose and took the Chairman cordially by the hands to congratulate him."

29th OCTOBER 1874.

Several gentlemen were nominated members of the Society.

11TH NOVEMBER 1874.

The Secretary, Mr DONALD MACRAE, read a paper on the " Gaelic Language," showing the influence it exercised upon the topography of Gaul, and the place it must have held in that province previous to the invasion by Julius Cæsar; its relation to Latin and English; and its philologic, social, and economic uses. In the debate which followed, the duty of having the Gaelic language taught in Highland Schools, as a special subject, was advanced, and it was proposed that this question should be the subject for discussion at the next meeting, with a view to the Society taking proper steps towards having this important part of its duties carried into effect.

It was unanimously resolved to convey the thanks of the Society to Charles Innes, Esq., for the manner in which he conducted the defence of the so-called Bernera " Rioters," and for giving such publicity to the whole proceedings. After which, the gentlemen previously nominated were duly elected members of the Society.

19TH NOVEMBER 1874.

The question of teaching Gaelic in Highland Schools was fully discussed, when it was found that the national system of education, in its present form, is not adequate to meet the educational wants of the Highland parishes; that the Gaelic School Society has done much for the Highlands, and deserves the support of Highlanders; that it was the teaching of Gaelic in these schools that rendered them so successful above other supplementary systems of education; and that the Gaelic Society of Inverness, and kindred societies throughout the world, have done their own cause, and that of the Highlands, a decided wrong, in so far allowing the Gaelic language to be treated with indifference by the Legislature. On the motion of the Secretary, the resolution (which will be found embodied in the circular sent to the School Boards) was unanimously carried. "The Society resolved that the best steps to carry this resolution into effect should form the subject for discussion at next meeting." Several gentlemen were nominated members.

26TH NOVEMBER 1874.

After discussing the resolution passed at last meeting, the Secretary was requested to prepare a letter to be inserted in the newspapers, with the resolution passed at last meeting on the subject of teaching Gaelic in Highland schools. It was also agreed to urge upon the Legislature and the School Boards to make provision for teaching children in Gaelic-speaking districts through the medium of their native language; and the Secretary was requested to prepare a circular address to kindred Societies and School Boards, asking their support in favour of this movement. The members nominated at last meeting were thereafter elected.

7TH JANUARY 1875.

The Secretary produced draft letter and circular, which was approved, and ordered to be sent to the newspapers, and to the School Boards throughout the Highlands. The circular was as follows:—

"GAELIC TEACHING IN HIGHLAND SCHOOLS.

"Sir,—The Gaelic Society of Inverness, having for some time past fully considered the subject of teaching Gaelic in Highland Schools, passed the following resolution at a meeting held on the 19th of November—'That the national system of education does not, and cannot, supply the educational wants of the Highlands and Islands of Scotland, however thoroughly it may be carried out; that it is proved by the experience of generations that a knowledge of Gaelic, instead of being a hindrance to the acquirement of, and progress in, English, greatly facilitates instruction in the English language—no method of teaching languages being so successful as that of double translation; and that the new Act should make special provision for the teaching of Gaelic in the schools of Gaelic-speaking districts as an independent subject of instruction.'

"At a later meeting the Society discussed the best course to take for carrying this resolution into effect; and in furtherance of this object I have been directed to forward the above resolution for the consideration and co-operation of your Board, and beg to subjoin the following remarks :—

"The question whether Gaelic should have a place in the Revised Code of Education as a subject of school instruction in Gaelic-speaking districts, has been duly considered and answered in the affirmative by the most competent authorities; and in fact the reception given to the Celtic Chair scheme warrants this conclusion without further proof. University education is expected to begin exactly where school education ends. But where are we (the Highlanders) to find students qualified to take advantage of the Celtic Chair unless Gaelic be taught in our Highland schools?

"There are many strong reasons why Gaelic should be taught. In the case of the numerous Gaelic-speaking districts, is there anything more irrational than trying to give a child a thorough and rapid training in English without the use of the language with which only he is acquainted? The method of teaching languages by double translation is universally adopted, except in this case of English in the Highlands; and why *it* is an exception has never been explained. This grievance—or mistake—is worthy of the attention of most, if not of all, of our Highland School Boards.

"In the case of Gaelic-speaking children, whose education will be limited to three or four years, the mistake of neglecting their native tongue must be still more injurious. On leaving school they will be found to have acquired a very imperfect knowledge of English, which will avail them little in a commercial, or any other point of view; and of their native tongue they have not been allowed to acquire any grammatical knowledge whatsoever, and cannot even read the Bible with intelligence. With due attention to both languages, the result would be much more satisfactory. It has been found from experience that even incidental lessons in their mother tongue—and, indeed, incidental attendance at school —for not more than three or four years, have enabled children of very ordinary capacity to master the Gaelic, so far, at least, as reading the Bible is concerned.

"Much might be said as to whether Gaelic ought to receive the same attention in places where it is only partially spoken. But I forbear going into this part of the subject at present.

"The philological importance of the Gaelic language is so well known and admitted by those who have paid the matter any attention, that others may take this for granted, although it were certainly better, and more profitable, to *know*, than to believe from hearsay.

"It is very gratifying to observe, from advertisements in the newspapers, that *some* School Boards in the Highlands are alive to the fact that Gaelic-speaking teachers are more suitable for their schools than those who are ignorant of the language of the place; but unfortunately, many Boards have shown their indifference to, if not their contempt for, this view of the question. By united effort and co-operation, Highland School Boards and Highland societies throughout the country may do much to get the question properly settled by legislation, although as individual bodies the most influential of them can effect but little for a cause so purely local. The press, generally speaking, is favourable to our views; and by its influence, and through it, we can, at least, examine into the merits of the case. Highland School Boards may rest assured that the teaching of Gaelic will in their case prove more profitable than that of Latin or Greek, socially, philologically, and financially. Financially, because if Gaelic were allowed the place assigned to Latin and Greek, the number of Highland pupils who would pass the examinations would be much greater, and the aggregate amount of grant consequently increased, with corresponding benefit to pupils, teachers, and ratepayers.

"The Education Act as it now stands, suggests that school inspectors allow a pupil to express himself in Gaelic in the event of a difficulty of explaining in English any passage in the English reading lesson, warranting the assertion that more is not granted by the Act, simply because more was not demanded by those concerned. We ourselves, therefore, may be blamed for this defect in the Act; and with ourselves also rests the responsibility of its amendment.—I am, &c., "Don. Macrae,

"Secretary, Gaelic Society of Inverness.

"High School, Inverness, 9th January 1875."

Alexander Mackintosh Shaw, Esq., London, at this meeting, presented the Society, through the Secretary, with a copy of his work "The Clan Battle of Perth."

ANNUAL SUPPER.

The members of the Society held their Annual Supper on Wednesday evening, in the Station Hotel. The chair was taken at eight o'clock by Sir Kenneth Mackenzie of Gairloch, Bart., Chief of the Society, supported on the right and left by Provost Lyon-Mackenzie; Sheriff Macdonald, late of Stornoway; and the Rev. Mr Macgregor, Inverness. The Croupiers were Cluny Macpherson of Cluny, and Captain Macra Chisholm of Glassburn, supported by Mr Mackintosh of Holme; Colonel Macpherson, Inverness; and Mr Jolly, Inspector of Schools. Among the company were:—Bailie Baillie; Bailie John Davidson; Dr Macnee; Mr Dallas, Town-Clerk; Mr G. G. Allan, Caledonian Bank; Mr Andrew Macdonald, solicitor; Mr Menzies, Caledonian Hotel; Dr F. M. Mackenzie, Church Street; Rev. Mr Macgregor, Ferrintosh; Councillor John Noble; Mr James Fraser, C.E.; Mr A. Fraser, writer; Mr W. B. Forsyth, of the Advertiser; Mr Ellis, builder; Councillor Donald Macdonald; Mr D. R. Ross, Gas and Water Company's Office; Mr John Macdonald, Exchange; Capt. Mackenzie, Telford Road; Councillor Peter Falconer; Mr John D. Shaw, Union Street; Mr G. J. Campbell, writer; Mr Alex. Macleod, Huntly Street; Mr Fraser, Tomnahurich Street; Mr Fraser, Castle Street; Mr Macdonald, live stock agent; Mr Mackintosh, Post-office Buildings; Mr John Murdoch, Inverness; Mr Kenneth Fraser, writer; Mr Mackenzie, bookseller; Mr Sinclair, tailor, High Street; Mr Charles Mackay, contractor, Drummond; Mr Macrae, High School (secretary); Mr A. Mackenzie, wine-merchant, Church Street; Mr Macfarquhar, sheriff-clerk-depute; Mr Campbell, draper, Bridge Street; Mr Maciver, Church Street; Messrs Barron and Bain of the Courier; Mr Mackenzie, Free Press; Mr Duncan, Highlander, &c.

Grace was said in Gaelic by the Rev. Mr Macgregor, after which an excellent and substantial supper, served up in the best style, was done ample justice to by the company. The following was the printed bill of fare:—

" SUIPEIR NAN GAIDHEAL.

" *Tha i toiseach le brigh*—Sugh mhaigheach, no chreamh.

" *A leantail le taobh-shoithchean grinn*—Eoin fhraoich 'chion nan cnamh; Feoil chaorach mion-ghearrt; 'S taigeis a thaitneas ri suinn.

" *Tha uill ann gu saibhir*—Feoil roist is feoil bhruich; 'S cinn

nam mult Gaidhealach 'n am bianu; Tha turcaich 's eoin ghreight
ann; Slios chrochte na muic; Is slias'dean nam mult, mar 'o
chian.

"*Nithean milis air dhealbh*—Marag phlumbais nan Gall; Is
ubhlan 'an sligeachan taois; Sugh mheasan is caithan; Gach fuin-
teach is pithean; Is aran is caise maraon."

Pipe-Major Maclennan played appropriate airs in the ante-
room during supper, and in the intervals between the toasts.

The Chairman kept up the traditions of the Society by proposing the health of the Queen in Gaelic, as follows—A Thighearna Chluanidh agus a dhaoine uailse, Tha e na chleachdadh
gu'n toir am fear a tha 's a chathair so Deoch slainnte na
Ban-Righ, ann an Gaidhlig.   Chan eil mise ro mhath air a
Ghaidhlig, ach cha ruig an deoch-slainnte so a leas moran bruid-
binn, gu sonraichte ann an lathair a Chomuinn so.   Bha na
Gaidheil riamh dileas ri an Uachdarainn, agus cha ro Righ na
Ban-Righ ann riamh a bha cho mor an run nan Gaidheal ris a
cheann a th' againn aig an am so air an duthaich.   So, ma tha,
" Deoch slainnte na Ban-Righ."   (Applause.)

After the other loyal and patriotic toasts were disposed of,

The Chairman called for a bumper to the toast of the evening
—" Success to the Gaelic Society of Inverness."   (Loud cheers.)
Though this toast, he said, is one which must evidently commend
itself to us, members of the Society, the question may not un-
naturally occur to outsiders whether the objects we aim at are
worthy of support, and whether we have endeavoured to carry
them out in a manner to deserve success.   Now, briefly, it may
be said that the objects of the Society are—(1.) The preservation
of the unwritten history, poetry, and legends of the Scottish Celt,
which have thus far been handed down by tradition; and (2)
the promotion generally of the interests of the present generation
of the Gaelic-speaking race.   There can be no question that these
are patriotic subjects well worthy of entertainment by this or any
other society—(Applause)—and the only point, therefore, for consideration is whether the Gaelic Society of Inverness has fulfilled
its aim.   It is a proverbial saying that unless you aim high, you
hit low, and that nothing great or noble would ever be done unless
the aim were something above and beyond the mark which may
be reasonably attained.   But I must confess for myself, that looking at the programme of the Gaelic Society, at the outset of its
career, I had very little hope of its being able to advance, to any
appreciable extent, the interests of the existing generation of

Highlanders. In this part of its programme it seemed to be aiming so much too high. There may be instances of oppression or expatriation, but how is a society like this to fight the oppressor or expatriator even if the case is proved against him? And then there are always two sides to a story, and exaggeration on both sides whenever a large amount of feeling is imported into the case. It seemed to me that the Gaelic Society was more likely, in dealing with the misfortunes of Highlanders, to get into trouble itself than to do them any good; but I am glad to say that no such event has occurred, and that, on the other hand, circumstances have arisen in connection with our new Education Act, which have opened to the Society a path of usefulness I had not foreseen, and of which, I am glad to understand, it is now availing itself. (Applause.) The Education Act of 1872, though it recognised to a certain extent the peculiar character of the Highlands, took no notice of the language of its people. Children who knew no word of English were to be put through an educational drill intended for those who knew no word of Gaelic, and it is impossible not to feel that the results of such a system, among a purely Gaelic-speaking population, must be extremely unsatisfactory. Mr John Stuart Mill tells us, in his Autobiography, that he could read Greek at five years old, and did not remember the time when he began to learn it; but, though Highlanders are naturally very intelligent, it cannot be pretended that they all have such very remarkable intellects as Mr Mill possessed. (Laughter and applause.) It stands to reason, in the case of a vast majority of children, that if their education is to be addressed to their intelligence, and not to their memory alone, it must at the outset be conducted through the medium of the language with which they are familiar, otherwise you offer education in the letter but not in the spirit; a dead education, unproductive of fruits, as indeed many of us know a vast amount of the education given in the Highlands at the present day is. (Hear, hear.) Now the Society has very properly taken this matter up, and I most sincerely trust that the efforts it makes, directly and indirectly, may be crowned with success. If so, it cannot be said that its existence has been in vain. In securing the aid of Professor Blackie, and inducing him to lecture here on this question, the Society did much to influence the opinion of persons interested in education, who had, perhaps, abandoned themselves too readily to an acceptance of the existing order of things. That there has been an awakening on the subject, I am glad to think. The letters in the *Scotsman* from Machaon and Messrs Macquarrie and Mackinnon contain most valuable argu-

ments in favour of the recognition of Gaelic by the Education
Department, and the fact that these letters have been so largely
copied into other papers, shows the subject to be one that has
acquired a general interest. Professor Blackie's remark, that the
devotions of Highlanders were always conducted in Gaelic, has
also led many religious-minded people to feel that a Gaelic-speaking
person, unable to read his Gaelic Bible, has been educated, if educated at all, very much without religion; and as secularism meets
with no favour in the Highlands, we now find that on religious
grounds many good people are anxious to co-operate in the endeavour to secure the introduction of Gaelic teaching to our schools.
I have, indeed, heard it argued that any Gaelic-speaking person
who had been taught to read English, would be able to pick up
sufficient knowledge of Gaelic reading to render his Bible intelligible to him. But who of us would have his children taught Latin
and Greek, or other foreign tongues, and allow them to pick up
English for themselves? Yet, that would be comparatively reasonable. The education of children who are taught Latin and
Greek, and modern languages, is carried on for a much longer
time than that of the majority of children who attend our parish
schools; the higher education they receive enables them to apply
themselves with greater intelligence to any special branch it may
be necessary for them to acquire. But a child who leaves school
with a mere smattering of education in a foreign language has
practically received no education at all, and is rarely fit to apply
himself to the study of the literature of his mother tongue. (Applause.) This very day I met a man who was a candidate for an
office in my county. He came to speak to me, and said he had sent
in an application. I asked if it was in his own handwriting. 'No,'
he said, 'it is a long time since I left school, and I don't think I can
write very well.' (Laughter.) That was just a specimen how a little
learning was soon forgotten. The impediment to the introduction
of Gaelic into our schools consists in this, that the schools are supported partly by the ratepayers and partly by a grant given by
Government; the greater the grant from the Education Department, the less the burden on the ratepayers, and as that burden is
in any case very heavy, every effort is naturally made to satisfy
the conditions prescribed by the Education Department, and to
secure the full amount of its grant. I feel sure, from what has
been told me by persons experienced in the matter, that in a five
years' course of education, a child who knows no English loses
nothing by first learning to read Gaelic, his subsequent progress
being so much more rapid; and what is required is that this

fact should be borne in upon the Education Department, so as to induce them to recognise Gaelic in the Code and in the standards to which the teaching in public schools must necessarily conform. I do hope that this Society will not cease from its efforts to obtain this boon from the Education Department till rewarded with success. (Applause.) I have seen it stated that in the Gaelic schools where children begin by learning Gaelic they never make any progress in English afterwards. But the fact is, that the Gaelic schools—which were very excellent institutions in their way—did not at first teach English. At present they do teach a certain amount, but their educational apparatus is so very limited that the absence of progress in the children is to me no proof whatever against the commencing with the teaching of Gaelic. (Applause.) And with reference to the introduction of Gaelic into the national system of education, I cannot pass over the exertions that have been made by Professor Blackie to secure the foundation of a Chair of Celtic Literature in the University of Edinburgh In his lecture under the auspices of this Society, he explained very fully the value of such a Chair, and he has since then collected a large sum of money towards its foundation. A few years ago it might have been difficult to get up an interest in his proposal in this community; for Inverness, though occupying a central position in the Highlands, has not been a Gaelic-speaking town for a long time, certainly not since the date of Captain Burt's letters, now nearly a century and a-half ago. But yesterday a meeting on behalf of Professor Blackie's scheme was held in Inverness, and what support it then obtained I attribute to some extent to the indirect influence which this Society asserts by its very existence, and to the more or less interest which its creation has excited in Celtic antiquities and literature. (Applause.) I fear we have not done much as yet in storing up and giving to the world the unwritten poetry and legends of the Celt. To do this successfully, it would be necessary that the Society were considerably strengthened. We have two classes of members, ordinary and honorary; the first, the working bees, who pay just a sufficient subscription to cover the expense of the ordinary meetings; the second, supposed, I presume, to contribute the funds necessary for the Society's publications. At least, I do not know on what other footing the distinction between the two classes of members is made. Now, I think that every ordinary member should be taken bound to produce some work, and when a collection of manuscripts worthy of publication were got together, then a canvass should be made to increase the number of ordinary members. In such case, funds would no doubt be forthcoming to pay for the editing and publication of so interesting a volume. But the first thing to insist on is, that every ordinary member shall once, within a certain cycle of time, produce, either by himself or deputy, some specimen of Gaelic literature worthy of being recorded, preference over original compositions being always given to those that time had stamped with its approval. (Applause.) If our Society has not yet fulfilled all its aims, there is no ground for despair that it may not yet do so. In the direction in which I expected it would hit wide of the mark, it has found a very proper nail to hammer at, which I hope it will continue to hit on the head till driven home. The Society has done less than I expected in adding to the written literature of the Highlands, but its work is yet before it, and it is, as I have said, by its mere existence, exciting a certain interest in Gaelic remains. Without depreciating what has already been done—for we are as yet but a young Society—I look forward to greater exertions on the part of individual members in the future, to a more strenuous endeavour to carry out the objects of their Association, so that the Society may fulfill its entire mission, and both deserve and obtain that success to which I now call on you to drink. (Loud cheers.)

The Secretary, Mr Donald Macrae, was then called upon to read the report. Before doing so he stated he had received letters of apology from Mr Charles Fraser-Mackintosh, M.P.; Raigmore; Tulloch; Dr Mackenzie of Eileanach; Dr Carruthers; Mr Macandrew; and Bailie Simpson; expressing regret that they could not be present, and gratulations on the rising fortunes of the Gaelic cause. Mr Macrae then read the report, which was frequently applauded, as follows:—

"It is necessary in this, the third annual report of the Gaelic Society of Inverness, merely to mention a few facts sufficient to show the actual position of the Society at this moment. In the previous reports we have an account of its origin and aims. The work done at the ordinary weekly meetings of the Society during the past year was more than usually confined to the discussion of questions referring particularly to the objects of the Society, and of social importance; such as the social and philological advantages to be derived from the study of Gaelic and of Celtic literature; the subject of Celtic professorships; the teaching of Gaelic in our Highland schools, and kindred subjects.

"With regard to the teaching of Gaelic in our Highland schools, your Council have brought the matter before the public generally

through the press; and have taken steps to induce School Boards
to have Gaelic taught in the schools under their management; and
from the manner in which the Gaelic language is rising in public
estimation, there can be no doubt but School Boards and the
Legislature will ere long do what is necessary towards placing the
mother-tongue of our people in that place on the Education Code
to which it is entitled.

" Regarding the Celtic Chair, your Council have the satisfaction to report that the movement, which was inaugurated by the
lecture of Professor Blackie in the Music Hall, Inverness, on 14th
October 1874, under the auspices of this society, has made most
satisfactory progress. Already, the learned and enthusiastic Convener of the University Committee which has charge of this business in Edinburgh, is in possession of above £2000, fully one-fifth
of the sum required. The society has reason to be proud of the
action taken by the Glasgow Skye Association, which, over and
above the sum of £15, the surplus after defraying the expenses of
the soiree, subscribed there and then the sum of £239. The Inverness, Ross, and Nairn Club, Edinburgh, gave £50 out of its
funds. The Glasgow Highland Association is getting up a concert
in furtherance of the object; kindred bodies are preparing to
follow these examples, which may be regarded in some measure, at
least, as the fruits of the labours of the premier Gaelic Society,
resident in the Highland Capital. The revival of the spirit of the
Celt, as indicated by the formation of such a society in Inverness
could not fail to produce a beneficial effect on the minds of Highlanders from home; and the facts mentioned are to the point.

" The Council would also recommend that these noble deeds
on the part of other bodies, be followed by our subscribing a handsome sum to the same object. The funds are in a flourishing condition, £58. 15s. 5d. being to our credit in the bank.

" The number of members admitted into the Society since its
formation in 1871, up to this time, is 268, including 18 members
chosen last year; but after deducting resignations, deaths, and
those who have allowed their subscriptions to fall into arrear, the
number of efficient members is 225. Six are life members :—
Cluny Macpherson of Cluny Macpherson; Charles Fraser-Mackintosh, Esq. of Drummond, M.P.; Sir Kenneth S. Mackenzie of
Gairloch, Bart., the present Chief; Mr Alexander Fraser, writer,
Church Street, Inverness; Mr Alexander Forbes, 143 West
Regent Street, Glasgow; and Dr Halley, London. There are 58
honorary, 146 ordinary, and 15 junior members. About one-half
of the members are non-resident. The Society has a valuable

10

book-case, and about 120 volumes. Among those received this year are six copies of 'Munro's Gaelic Primer,' procured for a Gaelic class in connection with the Society, and conducted by Mr Lachlan Macbean, the Librarian; copy of 'Carswell's Gaelic Prayer Book;' the 'Airs and Melodies of the Highlands and Islands of Scotland, by Captain Fraser of Knockie,' from the publisher, Mr Hugh Mackenzie, Inverness; a copy of 'Turner's Collection of Gaelic Songs,' and 'The Clan Battle of Perth,' from the author, Mr Mackintosh Shaw, London, &c. The Librarian complains that the library does not receive the support it deserves, and suggests that any members having old Gaelic books lying on their shelves should hand a few over to the Society.

"Before closing the report, your Council express regret that the ordinary meetings are not better attended, and trust that the current year will show an improvement. The now acting Council retires, and office-bearers for the current year will be elected this month, at a meeting called for the purpose."

Sheriff Macdonald moved the adoption of the report, which was agreed to with applause; and he followed up by proposing the health of the Secretary, Mr Macrae, which was cordially responded to, Mr Macrae briefly returning thanks.

The Provost, Magistrates, and Town Council of Inverness, was proposed by Cluny in a neat and spirited Gaelic speech, which was repeatedly applauded. He said :—A Ridire, Choinnich Mhic-Choinnich, Iar-chinn, agus a dhaoin uailse, bu mbath leam an deoch slainnte so a thoirt duibh 's a Ghaidhlig, mar bu choir a dheanadh ann am priomh bhaile na Gaidhealtachd, agus aig suipeir a Cho-muinn Ghaidhlig, ach tha eagal orm gainne mo Ghaidhlig a leigeadh ris an lathair nan deadh sgoilearan Gaidhlig a tha 'n so. Tha an t-urramach Mr Mac-Grigair an so; agus mo charaide Mr Mac-Mhuirich, leis am bheil ni agamsa r' a shocrachadh. Tha mise saoilsinn gum bheil mis a 'm cheann cinnidh agus tha easan a deanadh a mach gu 'm bheil e fhein. Nis tha mise toileach an t-urram a thoirt dha. Tha mise eolach air Inbhirnis leth-cheud bliadhna, agus s' e mo bharail nach robh nithean riamh na b-fhearr air an riaghladh na tha iad aig an am so; agus 's mor an toilinn-tinn a th' agamsa bhi faicinn mar a tha am baile soirbheachadh le an stiureadh. Agus cha 'n urrainn dhomh gun a radh gum bheil ac ann an so am baile agus a choimhearsnachd is boidhche 's aithne dhomhsa anns an duthaich gu leir. A bharrachd air sin, tha Pro-aist a bhaile, agus na h-urrad do 'n luchd riaghlaidh eile ann an so a nochd a toirt an cuideachd agus solus an gnnis do'n Chomuinn Ghaidhlig a tha deanadh na h-urrad air son math agus cliu na

Gaidhealteachd. Ach cha'n fheud mi bhi g 'ur cumail. So " Deoch-slainnte a Phroaiste agus luchd riaghlaidh Baile Inbhirnis." (Great applause.)

Provost Lyon-Mackenzie, though not understanding what Cluny had said, knew from the enthusiastic way in which the toast was received that great justice had been done to the subject. He sincerely thanked Cluny and them on behalf of his fellow Magistrates, and expressed the delight they always had in seeing Cluny and Sir Kenneth among them. (Applause.)

Mr James Fraser, C.E., proposed the Non-Resident Members, whose good services to the Society were so patent that they did not require any lengthened commendation from him. Among those were included Sir Kenneth Mackenzie, Cluny, and others not within visiting distance of Inverness. This section is very widely spread over Scotland, England, Wales, Ireland, Canada, United States, New Zealand, Australia, and Ceylon, and very often those furthest away were heard from sooner than those at the end of the town. Those members supported the Society with literary and monetary contributions, for the former of which he need only refer to the " Transactions" of the Society. (Applause.)

Mr Murdoch, of the Highlander, proposed " Education in the Highlands," congratulating himself and the meeting on the fact that the Chairman had so admirably anticipated what he intended to say. There were just two or three points which he would mention, but not enlarge on. The Chairman's reference to the Society's neglect of the material interests of Highlanders was only apparent; for he held that in bringing Gaelic and its valuable un-written literature into public favour, the first and best thing was being done to re-inspire our people with the self-respect and self-confidence which were necessary to that enterprise on which so much of their physical well-being depended. Depend upon it, there was nothing more deadly in its effects on their condition than telling them, until they began to believe it, that their speech, traditions, and selves, were worthless. This, he need hardly say, was one of the most important branches of Highland education, and he knew from his intercourse and correspondence with High-landers that the patriotic teaching was taking effect. Coming to the school part of education, he held that Gaelic should be so taught as to induce the children to take an interest and a pride in their language, lore, and nationality; and not be, as collectors of lore found, so many denying that they could speak Gaelic or tell a tale. The language should be assigned its proper place, by right, and not merely by permission, as an integral part of the course.

Gaelic books must be provided; and the ratepayers must return
men to the School Boards who are known to be at one with us on
this subject. In everything connected with it they must act manfully, on the understanding that this is the language, and that
these are the convictions of the Highland people. From what has
been said by Cluny, it was clear that Highland education, like
charity, must begin at home. He was glad to say that Mr Lachlan
Macbean had opened a class for teaching Gaelic; and he did trust
that those inhabitants of Inverness, whose education had been so
shamefully neglected, as not to be able to speak Gaelic, would
flock to the class, headed by the Provost, who showed himself to
be so thoroughly in sympathy with the Society. (The Provost —
Mr Jolly should go along with us.) In testimony of their entire
concurrence in what he said, he called upon them to fill their
glasses and drink "Success to Education in the Highlands," coup-
ling the toast with the name of Mr Jolly.

Mr Jolly, with whose name the toast was coupled, replied. He
was glad the subject of education in the Highlands was so largely
referred to by the Chairman, who was enthusiastic in the cause of
education—(Applause)—and by Mr Murdoch; and he wished to
speak briefly on the same matter. With regard to the demands
to be made on Government, he observed that one great point to be
kept in view while making them was to be temperate. Don't ask
too much, especially from a Government Department, or the object
might be defeated. (Hear, hear.) In recent newspaper correspondence there was much that required some comment. It was
stated that there was an impossibility of inculcating in the children
of a Highland school a love of reading, unless they were taught to
read in Gaelic. That, of course, held good in every case where a
child did not understand what it was reading; and it was not at
all peculiar to the Highlands, but common all over the country.
And the mere reading, in a mechanical way, without being
interested in it, by the teacher, could never bring about that most
desirable end of all education—the love of reading. Again, it was
stated, as if it were a peculiarity of Highland schools, that there
was among children reading without meaning. Of course, if a
child read what it did not understand, that must be the result;
but reading without meaning was not peculiar to Highland schools,
but common all over the country. The merely mechanical reading
of the past was to be regretted; but one object of the new Code
was to make children intelligent readers, by offering grants for
special results in this matter. So that, granted that there was
reading without meaning in Highland schools, it was nothing

more than was to be said of schools in every county in this country. One other point he wished to refer to; and, in bringing it forward, he spoke from experience, and after mature thought. In order to teach Gaelic-speaking children, it was not necessary to have a teacher who understood Gaelic. This might sound strange. But by resolving to have none but Gaelic-speaking teachers, they narrowed the field for selection; and it would be a great pity to narrow it too much. The most successful schools in the Highlands might be taught by Lowland men; and ample proof of this had been furnished by his own observation of facts and results. An inspector of schools made it an important point to examine the children on general intelligence. And here Mr Jolly gave five instances of Highland schools that were taught most successfully by Lowland teachers, who knew nothing whatever of the Gaelic language,* and in each of the schools instanced the speaker had noted particularly in examination the very high general intelligence of the pupils. These schools were Lochcarron and Eddrachillis, in Ross-shire; Duirinish and Portree, in Skye; Mr Gordon's (of Cluny) School in Benbecula, which was taught by a Lowland girl. Such was the result of the teaching of those entirely ignorant of Gaelic in Gaelic-speaking districts; and he had given the names in order that his assertions might be fully borne out. At the same time Gaelic had been ignored in the Government Code. Under the old Code, at the first starting of a Government system, it was not ignored to such an extent as now, for there were then grants given to teachers who passed a certain examination in Gaelic. But that arrangement had been discontinued since. They were thus worse off now than before, but he hoped that the present movement would turn out to be a happy event for the Highlands in this matter. (Applause.) Mr Jolly then referred to the meeting of School Boards which is to take place at Inverness next week, under the presidency of Sir Kenneth Mackenzie. He trusted this question of Gaelic teaching would be taken up, some practical conclusion come to with regard to it, and some definite scheme adopted for presentation to Government—to be followed up with all the influence that can be brought to bear upon it. He was sorry to differ from the previous speakers upon one important point. He should say, notwithstanding what had been said to the contrary, that Gaelic-speaking children should begin education by reading English. It should be impressed upon all that English

* These teachers have since written to the newspapers that they acquired the Gaelic language since coming to the North, and used it as a medium in teaching.

was the staple language of the country, the language which should
be acquired to ensure success in life, and that, compared with it,
Gaelic even in Gaelic-speaking parts, was subsidiary. But no good
English, with a few exceptions such as he had mentioned, could be
taught to Gaelic-speaking children, unless through the medium of
the mother-tongue. For the first two years the reading was purely
mechanical, without meaning often, and when this mechanical difficulty was got over, the teacher should bring ideas round about what
the child reads, and impress a meaning of it by his own speaking.
But the Gaelic ought to be preserved as a valuable language; and
it was thus most desirable to all that it should be taught. He
would make a practical suggestion. There were in the 4th, 5th,
and 6th standards, schedules of subjects—Latin, mathematics, even
English itself—for which grants were allowed. The speaker suggested that, in going to Government, they should ask them to add
Gaelic to this list of specific subjects that are taken up by the
teacher at his will. Thus, by making Gaelic a special subject,
joining it in a list of special subjects, to which it was quite competent to add to any extent, they would attain success. (Loud
applause.)

Cluny Macpherson was surprised to hear the sentiments just
uttered. He differed from Mr Jolly as to the teaching of Gaelic;
and pointed out that Mr Jolly had stultified his own statements
when he wished English lessons to be explained in Gaelic by a
teacher, who, he said, should not necessarily have a knowledge of
Gaelic. Teach children, he held, in the language they know, and
they will make progress. One might as well make an English-
speaking child begin education by reading Greek or French, as
make a Gaelic-speaking child begin by reading English. (Applause.)

Mr Jolly briefly explained that he was anxious to state that
the field for the selection of teachers should not be narrowed by
a resolution to appoint only Gaelic-speaking men. He would have
stultified his statements, certainly, if he wished lessons to be explained in Gaelic by those who knew nothing of it; but in Highland districts nineteen-twentieths of the teachers would be sure to
know Gaelic. In a case where a Lowland teacher was appointed,
he thought the aid of an outside individual might be called in to
teach Gaelic, as is being done at Kingussie. (Applause.)

Dr Macnee proposed the Clergy, remarking that in this age of
attacks on popular beliefs, by Tyndall, Huxley, Darwin, and
others, the clergymen should bestir themselves to a knowledge of
scientific subjects, so as to be able to meet the arguments of these

men. (Applause.) The Doctor had observed that two Yankee preachers had recently appeared in this country, on the teaching of whom the clergy seemed to be much divided—some calling them blessed messengers, others denouncing their doctrines as bad, and themselves as agents of one he would not mention. (Laughter.) Between lay preachers and the attacks of Darwin and Tyndall, the clergy would require to look to their laurels. (Applause.)

Rev. Mr Macgregor, Inverness, gave the toast of "Kindred Societies," saying :—

" Fbir-suidhe urramaich, tha aobhar taingeileachd againn gu'm bheil sinn cruinn cuideachd 'an so an nochd aig cuirm shoghail mar Chomunn Gailig Inbhirnis. Is iomadh atharrachadh a thainig air an t-saoghal o'n bha Chuideachd cheudna cruinn o cheann bliadhna air ais. Is iomadh beatha luachmhor a ghearradh as rè na bliadhna sin. Is iomadh Ard-Uasal, agus neach iosal ann an inbhè a ghairmeadh air falbh anns an uine sin. Gidheadh am measg gach caochladh muladach a thainig air an t-saoghal o'n am so 'n-uiridh, tha buidheachas againn ra thoirt do'n Ti a's Airde gu'm bheil sinn fathasd air ar caomhnadh, agus gu'm bheil sinn mar Chomunn, fathast, dian agus dealasach, chum gach cuis a bhuineas do'n Ghailig agus don Ghaidhealtachd a ghiulan air an aghaidh. Tha ruintean mor 'n'ar beachd, agus cuisean cud-thromach againn os laimh, ach fhads' sa bhios an deo anainne, cha diobair, agus cha treig sinn gach ni a ta 'nar comas a dheanamh chum na ruintean agus na euisean sin a chur air an aghaidh. Mar pheileir sneachda, bha sinn beag an toiseach, agus mar pheileir sneachda ga chuairteachadh agus a' fas mor, tha sinne air ar cuairt-eachadh, agus a' chuid 's a chuid a' fas ann am meud agus ann an cumhachd. Cha'n 'eil cuspair sam bith a ta maith ann fein, dh'aindeoin co beag suim 's a ghabhar dheth an toiseach, nach fas an an luach, ann an urram, agus ann an cumhachd, mu ghnath-aichear gu freagarrach e. Ceart mar sin tha na cuspairean a ta aig Comunn Gailig Inbhirnis 'san ambare. Tha iad 'nan cuspairibh a ta maith annta fein, 'nan cuspairibh a ta le durachd a' miann-achadh nithe a ta maith a chur air adhart, agus nan cuspairibh aig am bheil dian-dhealas chum leas aimsireil agus spioradail na Gaidhealtachd a mheudachadh. Gur i so an fhirinn air gach seol agus doigh, aidichidh gach neach a ta lathair. Chuireadh an t-urram oirnne, gu'm bheil Ard-Uaislibh treun agus tuigseach air ar taobh, daoine foghluinte agus daimheil, Cinn-fheadhna dileas agus cinneadail, Urramaich ann an lagh, ann an litrichibh, ann an leigheas, agus ann an diadhachd! Tha againn buill de Ardchomh-

airle na rioghachd, Uachdarain fearainn, agus Cinn-chinnidh aig
am bheil speis-cridhe do na cleachdan a bha ann o chein! Cha
ruig mi leas bhur n-uine a thogail le bhi 'gan ainmeachadh. Tha
Tighearna Chluanaidh an comhnuidh dileas, deas, dian, deas-chainnteach ann am fior Ghailig chum bhur leas a mheudachadh, agus
tha Coinneach Ghearrloch, le 'chabar-feidh, 'na aite, air bhur ceann.
Ach chan iad na Ghaidheil a mhain a ta agaibh mar chairdean
agus luchd-daimh, ach mar an ceudna moran de na Goill fein, aig
nach 'eil lide Gaelig nan ceann, ach focal na dha a dh' ionnsuich
iad trid durachd agus tlachd a thaobh maise agus oirdheirceas na
canain sin. A nis, a Chomuinn urramaich, gu robh bhur cairdean
a' dol a'n lionmhorachd mar a ruitheas na laithean seachad. Than
t-Ard-Albannach, le bhonait leathann, an comhnuidh deas chum
bhur lamhan a neartachadh, agus chum bhur n'eachdraidh a
sgaoileadh am fad 'sam farsuing. Chan 'eil aobhar agaibh a bhi
eu-dochasach, oir is iomadh Comunn Gaidhealach eile a tha ann an
deagh-ruin du'r taobh. Chan 'eil baile mor 'san rioghachd anns
nach 'eil Comunn aig am bheil na ceart ruintean sin nan cridhe, a
ta lionadh bhur cridhe fein, chum leas na Gaidhealtachd a mheudachadh. Uime sin, rachaibh air 'ur boinn maille rium-sa, chum
le cornaibh lana, gu'n ol sinn, leis gach urram, saoghal fad agus
deadhbheatha do gach Comunn Gaidhealach 'san Rioghachd
Bhreatunnaich air fad, agus gu robh gach cuis a' soirbheachadh leo!"

Sheriff Macdonald sung "Co bhiodh na Righ ach Tearlach,"
and various other Gaelic and English songs were sung during the
evening.

21st January 1875.

This was the annual meeting for the election of office-bearers.
There was a good attendance. The Secretary having read a letter
from Sir Kenneth S. Mackenzie, Bart., declining office as Chief
for another year, the following office-bearers were elected:—Chief
—Charles Fraser-Mackintosh, Esq. of Drummond, M.P. Chieftains—Sheriff Macdonald, Dr F. M. Mackenzie, and Chas. Mackay,
contractor, Drummond. Honorary Secretary—George J. Campbell, writer, Church Street. Secretary—Alexander Mackenzie,
auctioneer, 57 Church Street. Treasurer—Councillor John Noble,
12 Castle Street. Members of Council—John Macdonald, Exchange; Donald Campbell, draper, Bridge Street; Donald Macrae,

High School; William Mackenzie, "Free Press"; and James H. Mackenzie, bookseller, High Street.   Librarian—Lachlan Macbean, 6 Castle Street.   Piper—Pipe-Major Alexander Maclennan.

The following were elected the "Transactions Printing and Publishing Committee for Vol. III.," with full power to arrange and complete the work :— Alexander Fraser, accountant ; James Fraser, C.E.; Councillor John Noble, James H. Mackenzie, bookseller ; Wm. Mackenzie, Free Press ; and the Secretary, the latter to be Convener; after which several new members were nominated.

28TH JANUARY 1875.

The members nominated at last meeting having been duly elected, the meeting unanimously voted the sum of twenty pounds towards Professor Blackie's fund for establishing a Celtic Chair in one of the Universities.   It was agreed to request Lachlan Macbean to go on with a Gaelic class, and to afford him every assistance in the Society's power.   Several members were nominated, after which Councillor Noble read the following paper, forwarded by ALEXANDER MACKINTOSH SHAW, General Post-office, London, being a transcript of a pamphlet on the " Behaviour and Character of Samuel Macpherson, Malcolm Macpherson, and Farquhar Shaw, the three Highland Deserters who were shot at the Tower on the 18th July 1743," &c., &c.

" The pamphlet of which this is a true copy is one of a bound collection of pamphlets and broadsides in the British Museum Library, where I discovered it some six years ago.   It is of interest to Highlanders from its reference to the early history of the now famous ' Black Watch,' and of peculiar interest to Invernessians from the fact that the three men concerning whom it was written were natives of the county, and belonged to well known clans in it.

" The formation of the independent companies into a regiment, at first numbered as the 43d, subsequently as the 42d, took place in 1740, and the events narrated in the pamphlet in 1743.   In this year the Government decided, in spite of the remonstrances of Lord President Forbes,* and other warm partizans, to send the regiment to Flanders, although the men had been given to understand, on their enlistment, that their service would be confined to

---

* See Culloden Papers, No. 390.

their own country. Reports being spread that it was intended to get rid of them altogether by sending them to the West Indies, some of the men set out to return to Scotland, but were overtaken, brought back, and tried, as related in the pamphlet. Three of them were signalled out for execution; the remainder were distributed among the garrisons in the Mediterranean, the West Indies, and America.

"It is said that the rising of 1745 was accelerated by this episode, and this is very probable; for the 'decoying' of the regiment to London, and the punishment of their crime by death and transportation, would doubtless have the effect not only of impressing the clansmen in the North with a belief that the sufferers had had good reason for their attempt at escape, but of sending through them a thrill of dismay and distrust of the Hanoverian Government. The treatment of the regiment would, of course, be a powerful weapon in the hands of the Jacobite agents in the Highlands. 'The Clan Chattan,' says Henderson (p. 131), 'observing that three of their name, to whom most of them—as the other Highlanders—were related, had fallen a sacrifice for the crime of which several Grants and Monroes were equally guilty, breathed nothing but revenge; however, their resentment was smothered for a while, till it began to burn with the greater violence.' And how the Clan Chattan acted in the '45 is matter of history.

"A. M. S.

"9th Jan. 1875.

"The behaviour and character of Samuel Macpherson, Malcolm Macpherson, and Farquhar Shaw, the Three Highland Deserters, who were shot at the Tower, July the 18th, 1743; with some Observations on the conduct of a certain Stranger, who advised the Prisoners to waive any defence they had, and to plead guilty: Also, a plain Narrative of the Original Institution of the Regiment, now commanded by my Lord S—, containing an Impartial Account of the Rise and Progress of the late Mutiny in that Regiment; to which is added the Two Petitions which they sent to the Lords of the Regency, and to the Duchess of Richmond, by the Clergymen of the Church of Scotland, who conversed with them in their own language, from the time of their sentence till their execution. Nil turpe commitas neque coram alias neque tecum maxime omnium reverere teipsum.—London: Printed for Mr Cooper, in Paternoster Row, 1743. Price sixpence.

" The many inconsistent and scandalous reports that are spread about town, both in print and conversation, concerning the characters and behaviour of the three unhappy young men, who suffered in the Tower of London, on Monday, the 18th of July, make it necessary, as well for information of the public, as out of charity to their memories, to publish the following sheets.

" The author of this tract thinks it necessary to premise that he means not, in the relation he intends to make of the affair, either to justify the crime for which these men suffered, or, in the least, to arraign the justice of the court-martial in their proceedings, or tax the sentence with severity, but, from a motive of Christian charity and love for truth, means to remove from the character of the deceased such false aspersions as are cast upon them either by the malice or ignorance of some, who think it is not only necessary for the vindication of public justice to represent these unhappy men as mutineers and deserters, but must paint them as men void of every other virtue, and addicted to the grossest vices.

" In order to give the reader a just idea of this corps of men, it will not be improper to go back as far as their original institution, by which we shall be better enabled to form a just notion of their character.

" Few that are in the least acquainted with the history or constitution of Scotland but know that anciently all the lands in that kingdom were held of the Crown by military tenures or knights' service; and that the vassals of these great men held their lands of them by the same kind of tenure. By this means the nobility of that kingdom had always a number of men ready to bring into the field, either in defence of their sovereign or to decide their own private quarrels with one another, at which the Crown always connived (for political reasons) until both parties were reduced to an equal and moderate share of power.

" The practice of subjects deciding their private quarrels by the sword, obtained anciently all over Britain and most other countries, until civil polity and more wholesome laws prevailed; and still remained in the south parts and towards the borders of Scotland till near the time of the union of the Crowns in the person of King James the First, when the chief men in those parts were diverted from their private animosities by their necessary attendance on the Court, now removed at a greater distance from them. However, this spirit of family feuds still prevailed in the Highlands and more remote parts of Scotland, who, by their distance from the Court, were unacquainted with the manners of the civilised part of the nation. The inferior chieftains in those parts

still determined their mutual quarrels as usual; and in revenge
of any affront made incursions and depredations into the estates
of one another, or connived at their followers doing so, to the
great discouragement of industry and disturbance of the public
peace.

"In this situation were things in that part of the country about
the time of the Union of the Kingdoms, when the Government
very wisely, by the Act called the Clan Act, abolished these
tenures, and for preventing the depredations last mentioned, raised
several independent companies in the Highlands, the commands of
which were given to some of the most considerable gentlemen in
that corner, such as Lord Lovat, Laird of Grant, Lochnell, Fanah,
&c., all men of distinction and weight, who were willing to engage
their personal and family influence, as well as that of their companies, for suppressing those quarrels, and settling a civil polity in
the country.   When this levy was made, the officers took a special
care that none should be enlisted into that service but the sons of
the wealthiest and most respectable farmers in the country; and
the second and younger sons of some of the lesser vassals were not
ashamed to enlist in a service calculated for restoring of peace, and
establishing liberty and property in their country.   And as they
were allowed to occupy their own farms, or follow any other occn-
patiou, except upon muster days, or when they were actually
employed in pursuit of robbers or disturbers of the public peace,
they, instead of receiving bounty money, made interest with the
officer to be admitted.   In this shape they continued till they were
regimented under the command of the Honourable the Earl of
Crawford, a nobleman whose character was every way agreeable to
them, and made little or no alteration in their circumstances.
When we have taken this view of their original and history, down
to the period of their being regimented, it will be no matter of
surprise to find the private men of that regiment differing much in
their manners from those of other corps, if we consider that when
they entered the service it was impossible for them to have the
least apprehension of ever being obliged to leave their own country,
where most of them had farms or other concerns, and looked upon
themselves, and, I believe, were esteemed by the country, only as
a regulated militia, at least till such time as they were regimented,
which was only a few years ago.

"The Earl of Crawford enjoyed that Regiment but a short
time, when it was given to their present Colonel, the Honourable
Lord Semple.   They were quartered last year, the one-half of
them at Inverness, and the other at Perth. Sometime in spring

the Regiment was informed by their officers that they were to be
reviewed at Musselburgh, a village within four miles of Edinburgh, and afterwards to return to their quarters. Accordingly,
they had a route given them to that place, and arrived there; but
were told they were not to be reviewed there, but at Berwick-upon-
Tweed; when they came to this place, they were told that his
Majesty designed to review them in person at London, and that
then they would return to their families. When they arrived at
London and found that his Majesty was gone, the Regiment was
universally dissatisfied, that, after so long a march, they were disappointed of the honour of being reviewed by his Majesty. Some
time after their coming here, a report was currently spread that
the Regiment was to be sent to some parts of the West Indies,
and broke, or divided, amongst the colonies, which raised in the
private men, who believed this report, a very great animosity
against their officers, whom they groundlessly blamed for not informing them truly where they were to go before they carried
them from their own country, and not allowing them time to
settle their concerns, of which some had very considerable, which
they were obliged to leave in great disorder. They thought the
interest of the Government did no ways require that they, more
than any other Regiment in Britain, should be left ignorant of the
route they were to take, and by that means be disappointed of an
opportunity of settling their private affairs in a manner suitable
to so long an absence; that they had been so long settled in that
country without any view of being so suddenly called from it, that
it amounted to as great a hardship on them (comparatively speaking) as it would be to the militia of the city of London to be
shipped for the Indies on an hour's warning. The officers took
pains to allay this flame, by assuring the men that as soon as the
review was over they would be allowed to return home. But when
the report of their embarkation prevailed, they were out of all
patience, and looked upon the design of sending them to Flanders
only as a blind to get them on board, in order to ship them really
for the West Indies. Though their officers attempted to unde-
ceive them, yet they had been disappointed so often, and filled so
long with hopes of going home, that they had no credit with them.
Add to this, that there was another complaint pretended for the
ground of their discontent, that some small arrears were due to
them, that they had been obliged to use their own swords, and that
their clothing, especially their shoes and plaids, were remarkably
deficient—these last being not worth sixpence per yard, whereas
they used to be allowed plaids of more than double that value,

"This spirit continued after the review, when the discontented agreed, upon Tuesday night* after, to meet at Finchley Common, where a great number of them convened and waited till their number increased. In this interval some of their officers came up, and by their persuasions a great number returned. However, about 100 of them continued their first resolution of returning to their own country. Here it is remarkable that the night was so dark that they scarce could distinguish faces or make any computation of their number, and that Malcolm Macpherson, one of the deceased, had never hitherto given any consent to go away, but came within some distance of the place where the men were assembled, and, with another in company, continued irresolute what course to take until the coming up of the officers had raised some ferment, upon which he came into the crowd and allowed himself to be hurried along without knowing where he was going. Next morning, when by daylight they could discern their number, and not finding the desertion so general as they expected, Samuel Macpherson, another of the deceased, advised the whole body strenuously to return to their duty, which advice he continued to inculcate during their march to Ladywood; and in a short time after they came there, he applied to a Justice of the Peace to propose terms of surrender; and during all their stay there used his utmost endeavours to prevent things coming to the last extremity. At last, being in some hopes of a pardon by the intervention of his Grace the Duke of Montagu, to whom application was made in their behalf, they surrendered on discretion, in which Samuel Macpherson was most instrumental, as will be acknowledged by the officers to whom he surrendered. They were brought soon after to the Tower, and a court-martial appointed to try them. The first day the court-martial sat, a person, a stranger to all the prisoners, came to the grate, and, pretending a great deal of concern for their misfortunes, advised them not to mention on their trial any complaint they might have against their officers, intimating that he was certain such a plea would not avail them, and without serving them would expose their officers. That the wisest course they could follow for their own safety would be to acknowledge their guilt and plead mercy of the court-martial, which, he assured them, would effectually work their deliverance that no punishment would be inflicted on them, and, at the same time, presented them a petition which he had already drawn, addressed to the court-martial, in these terms, and they, very frankly

* 17th May.

relying on these assurances, signed and delivered the same to that honourable Court. One of the officers came next day and inculcated the same doctrine unto the prisoners that the stranger had done before, assuring them that they would all be liberate in a short time, when all justice should be done them. The prisoners were examined before the court-martial one by one. The questions asked them were to this purpose:--Was you enlisted? Have you taken the oath? Have you received your pay? Had you your clothing regularly? To all which they answered in the affirmative. They were asked if they had any complaints against their officers. They all answered in the negative, and, in general, pleaded nothing in alleviation of the crime before the court-martial but inadvertency, and that they were moved to it by a report which prevailed of their being to be sent to the West Indies, into a climate destructive of their health.

"I cannot help in this place to take notice of the remarkable officiousness of this stranger. He takes upon him, without being asked, or the least apparent interest in the prisoners, to advise them in matters of the last consequence to them, their lives, and reputations; has the rashness to prejudge the opinion of the honourable the court-martial in a point of law, which is at least a moot point amongst the lawyers themselves. How unreasonable was it for any man to pretend to determine what weight any plea would have before a Court of Judicature determining in a case of life and death; and how unjust to the prisoners to advise them to conceal any circumstance in their case that might have the smallest tendency towards alleviating their crimes, or raising the smallest motions of compassion towards them in the breasts of their judges! Suppose there had been but little weight in the plea of their want of pay, yet still it was a circumstance closely connected with their crime, without which it was impossible to form a just judgment of the heinousness of that action. For it must be granted on the one hand, that a soldier who deserts, and cannot plead want of pay, &c., is less excusable, and consequently deserves a greater degree of punishment than he who has such a pretence; this must be granted, though it should be admitted, on the other hand, that there is not so much in this plea as to screen the criminals totally from punishment. But how much or how little is in it, is a case few wise men will determine dogmatically, especially against the prisoner, since history, either ancient or modern, does not afford any one instance of capital punishment inflicted on soldiers who mutinied for want of pay. It is true, the pay they want is but small: by their own account, ten or twelve shillings, some less, some a trifle more, which I mention out of justice to the officers, because it was currently reported in town that the deficiency was much more considerable. But however trifling this and their other complaints may seem to men not concerned, yet I cannot but reckon it barbarous to have advised them to conceal these circumstances, the relation of which could not be supposed to have been capable of making the court-martial less merciful to the prisoners, if it had not the contrary effect. But, however, that plea was waived, and did not fall under the cognizance of the court-martial, who made their report, the consequence of which was that on Tuesday, the 12th, a warrant was directed by their Excellencies the Lords of the Regency to the Governor of the Tower, for the execution of Samuel Macpherson, Malcolm Macpherson, both corporals, and Farquhar Shaw, a private sentinel, all three of the number of the deserters, upon Monday, the 18th of July last.

" Having thus impartially traced this mutiny from its rise to this period, it remains that we give some account of the character and behaviour of these three unfortunate criminals, from the intimation of their sentence to their execution. Samuel Macpherson, aged about twenty-nine years, unmarried, was born in the parish of Laggan, in Badenoch, and shire of Inverness. His father, still living, is brother to Macpherson of Breachie, a gentleman of a considerable estate in that country, and is himself a man of unblemished reputation and a plentiful fortune. Samuel was the only son of a first marriage, and received a genteel education, having made some progress in the languages, and studied for some time at Edinburgh with a writer (that is, an attorney) until about six years ago he enlisted as a volunteer in Major Grant's company, where he was much respected both by the officers and private men, and was in a short time made a corporal. Malcolm Macpherson, aged about thirty years, and unmarried, was likewise born in the same parish of Laggan, was son of Angus Macpherson of Driminard, a gentleman of credit and repute, who bestowed upon Malcolm such education as that part of the country would afford. He enlisted about seven years ago in my Lord Lovat's company, where his behaviour recommended him to the esteem of his officers, and he was soon made a corporal. Farquhar Shaw, aged about thirty-five years, unmarried, was born in the parish of Rothiemurchus, in Strathspey, and shire of Inverness. His father, Alexander Shaw, was an honest farmer, but gave his son no education, as living at a distance from schools, and not in a condition to maintain him elsewhere. Farquhar lived some time by droving, but, meeting with misfortunes in that business, was reduced, and obliged for subsistence to enlist in this Regiment, where he has lived till now without any reproach.

"The sentence was intimated to them upon Tuesday before their execution. This unexpected change of their fortunes, from hopes of life and liberty to that of a short preparation for a violent death, very much shocked their resolution, but Samuel less than any of them. When the warder went to acquaint Samuel of this melancholy news, he carried with him two sentinels, for fear any accident might happen; and, after expressing his concern for being the messenger of such unhappy news, acquainted him he must die. He started with surprise: and asked with some emotion, 'How must I die?' 'You are to be shot, sir.' Then he replied, pretty composedly, 'God's will be done; I have brought this upon myself.' He then asked if he might be allowed pen and ink, and when the post went for Scotland? The warder told him the night, but that he could not live to receive any return. He said he did not want any. He very pleasantly gave the warder what weapons he had, which were only a small penknife and a razor; and, before the warder parted with him, seemed to have assumed his usual calmness of mind; and he and the other two, after some reflection, and the conversation of the clergy (who from this time attended them) were reconciled so much to their circumstances as to be able to bear the thought of death with great decency, and Christian resignation to the will of God.

"Samuel owned he had been active at the beginning of the sedition; but he could not help sometimes thinking that the great pains he took to influence the men to return to their duty afterwards, in a great measure alleviated his first crime.

"Malcolm, to the last, declared that he never advised any person to go away; on the contrary, that he never was resolved himself till the moment he joined the men in their march from Finchley Common, and then his reflection was so short that he scarce knew what he did.

"Farquhar Shaw in the same manner declared that he was no way active in raising the meeting; that he never advised any man to desert; denied that he presented his piece to any of the officers, as it was reported. He owned that he might have uttered some very passionate and indecent expressions to some of the officers who commanded him to return, but that these expressions did not import a threatening to strike any of them.

"But notwithstanding that they all three imagined themselves no more guilty than the rest of the prisoners, yet they never once uttered the least reflection against the sentence, the court-martial,

11

or the Lords of the Regency; in short, they did not attribute their death to anything else but the Divine providence of God, to which they cheerfully submitted, and acquitted all men of their unhappy end, of which Farquhar Shaw gave a lively instance. It being reported to him that one, Serjeant Macbean, had deposed before the court-martial that he (Shaw) had presented his piece to him when he commanded him to return to his duty, and that this deposition had determined the court-martial to fix upon him in particular, he sent for the serjeant, and very calmly questioned him concerning this fact; who told him that he had never been on evidence against him, but owned that he told some of his officers that he (Shaw) had threatened to strike an officer who commanded him to return to his duty; and that it was probable the colonel might receive this intelligence from the officers, and that by this means it might come to the knowledge of the court-martial. The serjeant expressed his regret that he should be any way instrumental to his misfortunes. But Shaw, in an affable manner, desired him to give himself no uneasiness on that head; that he had neither spite nor ill-will at him for what he had said, but would die in perfect love and friendship with him and all mankind; that he had sent for him on purpose to make his mind easy, and not to trouble himself with needless reflections, since he heartily forgave him; and accordingly parted with him in the most friendly and amicable manner ; and frequently after expressed to me his concern for the serjeant, lest his reflections on himself should prejudice him or make him uneasy. This behaviour of his to the man whom he was convinced had been the principal cause of his death, must argue a most charitable, forgiving, and generous temper and disposition of mind, very seldom to be met with in men of more elevated station in life.

" They all three were men of strong natural parts, and religiously disposed, both from habit and principle, the natural result of a good example and early instruction in the doctrine and precepts of Christianity; for I received from all of them a great deal of satisfaction when I examined them on the grounds of our holy religion; and even Shaw, who was perfectly illiterate, and could neither read not write, was ignorant of no Christian doctrine necessary to salvation, or from whence he could draw comfort in his present circumstance. They were educated, and died members of the Church of Scotland, though they cheerfully embraced the opportunity of receiving the Sacrament from the hands of the Reverend Mr Paterson, who officiated for the Chaplain of the Tower, after the form of the Church of England, on the Sunday preceding their execution.

"As their notions of religion were sincere, so they expressed the greatest regard for honesty and integrity, and thanked God, though they were great sinners, that His restraining grace had enabled them to avoid all vicious and profane courses, or the offering any injury to their neighbours in their persons or properties; that they hoped they had not only the approbation of a good conscience, but the testimony of their officers, friends, and acquaintances, that they have lived all their lifetime without scandal to themselves, or reproach to their friends, until this unhappy period, when rashness, without any mixture of malice, cowardice, or disaffection to his Majesty's person or Government, had brought their lives to this miserable catastrophe.

"They applied themselves diligently to the duty of prayer and reading the Scripture, from the time of their sentence, which they said they had but too much and too long neglected.

"When they were all three brought to one ward near the place of execution, about four o'clock that morning, they expressed the greatest affection and sympathy for one another, each regretting the case of the other two more than his own; at the same time encouraged one another to constancy of mind, and a dutiful resignation to the hand of God.

"Samuel Macpherson ordered three coffins to be made, of fifteen shillings value each, for which he paid; and Malcolm made a will, which he deposited in the hands of three of his own name among the Highland prisoners some days before their execution.

"These three were admitted to visit the prisoners, who told them that they thanked God they had got the better of the fears of death, and were prepared to embrace it cheerfully; that they thought their case better than that of their fellows, as they were leaving this world in hopes of eternal peace and happiness. Whilst they were to remain here exposed to new temptations and new troubles in distant and unknown countries, where they would not enjoy life, but a lingering death. They applied by petition to several persons of quality, of which the two following are true copies:—

" ' *To their Excellencies the Lord Justices.*

" ' The humble petition of Samuel Macpherson, Malcolm Macpherson, and Farquhar Shaw.

" ' *May it please your Lordships—*

" ' That whereas your poor petitioners lie under sentence of death for mutiny and desertion, and have nothing to hope (under

the Almighty) but from your lordships' favour on our behalf,
which we do most humbly entreat. And as we are sincerely sorry
for base conduct and misbehaviour, and it being our first crime,
we hope for your lordships' kind indulgence, which, should we be
so happy as to obtain, we do sincerely promise to retrieve this our
misconduct by a steady attachment to our most gracious Sovereign
King George, by defending him and his royal house with all our
power, where, and in whatever manner, we shall be directed.

> " ' SAMUEL MACPHERSON.
> " ' MALCOLM MACPHERSON.
> " ' FARQUHAR SHAW.' "

" ' *To her Grace the Duchess of Richmond.*

" ' The humble petition of Samuel Macpherson, Malcolm
Macpherson, and Farquhar Shaw.

" ' *May it please your Grace—*

" ' That, whereas your poor petitioners lie under sentence of
death for mutiny and desertion, and have nothing to hope (under
the Almighty) but from your Grace's charitable intercession to
the Lord Justices on our behalf, we do most humbly entreat your
Grace's good offices. And as we are sincerely sorry for our base
conduct and misbehaviour, and it being our first crime, we hope
for your Grace's kind indulgence, which, should we be so happy as
to obtain, we do sincerely promise to retrieve this our misconduct
by a steady attachment to our most gracious Sovereign King
George, by defending him and his royal house with all our power,
where, and in whatever manner, we shall be directed.

> " ' SAMUEL MACPHERSON.
> " ' MALCOLM MACPHERSON.
> " ' FARQUHAR SHAW.' "

" Upon the Monday morning,[*] the Governor ordered them to
put on their shrouds below their clothes, which when done, they
immediately began to pray, and continued in that exercise very
devoutly and fervently till six o'clock, when they were called out
to execution. They walked to the place, close up to the chapel in
the Tower, without expressing the least horror or despondency
in their gait or countenance, but with a Christian composure and
resignation of mind. Here Samuel Macpherson, standing on the

[*] 18th July.

plank which was appointed for them to kneel on, with an assured countenance and in an audible voice, in his own language, addressed his fellow-prisoners that were drawn up round the place of execution, in this manner:—

" ' My Friends and Countrymen—

" ' You are not strangers to the cause of my sufferings with these, my companions. I hope the anguish you must feel at the sight of this shocking scene, will be the last of your punishment, for I am convinced you must think it a punishment to see us bleed : but my blood, I hope, will contribute to your liberty; that thought affords me as much satisfaction as a soul prepared to take a flight to eternity can receive from any earthly concerns. Take example from our unfortunate ends, and endeavour to conduct yourselves so, both before God and man, as your lives may be long, and your deaths natural. Next to your duty to God, discharge what you owe your King and country ; wipe off this reproach by a steady loyalty to his sacred Majesty, and a respectful and obedient conduct towards your officers.'

. " Having uttered this speech, he, with his cousin, Macpherson, and Shaw, kneeled down, whilst the Reverend Mr Paterson and myself joined in prayer, kneeling before them on a plank. When prayers were over, their faces were covered, when eighteen soldiers, in three ranks (twelve of whom were appointed to do the execution, and the other six for a reserve, had been kept out of sight for fear of shocking the prisoners), advanced on their tip-toes, and, with the least noise possible, their pieces ready cocked for fear of the click disturbing the prisoners. Serjeant-Major Ellisson (who deserved the greatest commendation for this precaution) waved a handkerchief as a signal to present ; and, after a very short pause, waved it a second time as a signal to fire ; when they all three fell instantly backwards as dead, but Shaw being observed to move his hand, one of the six in reserve advanced, and shot him through the head, as another did Samual Macpherson. After the execution, an officer ordered three of the prisoners, namesakes of the deceased, to advance and bury them, whom they presently stripped to their shrouds, put them in their coffins, and buried them in one grave, near the place where they were shot, with great decency. The officers on duty appeared greatly affected, and three hundred of the 3d Regiment of Scotch Guards, who were drawn up in three lines, in the shape of a half moon, attended the execution, many of whom, of the hardened sort, were observed to shed tears.

"Thus ended this melancholy scene, which raised compassion from all, and drew tears from many of the spectators. They had, by their courteous behaviour, gained so much upon the affections of their warders, the inhabitants of the Tower, and others that conversed with them, that none were so hard-hearted as to deny them their pity, nay, nor hardly any had resolution to see them executed.

"What made this spectacle still more moving was, that mixture of devotion, agony, and despair that was seen in the faces and actions of the remaining Highland prisoners, who were ranged within-side the guards. When prayers began, they all fell on their knees and elbows, hanging their heads and covering their faces with their bonnets, and might easily be observed that they could not refrain from the loudest lamentations. Such a number of young men, in so suppliant a posture, offering their prayers so fervently to Heaven, with such marks of sorrow for the fate of the unhappy criminals, had a prodigious effect upon the spectators, and I am hopeful will influence the practice and conversation of all that saw them; and to the praise of these poor men (take from them the account their heinous transgression of mutiny and desertion). I believe their courteous and modest behaviour, their virtuous and pious principles, and religious disposition, would be no bad pattern for men above the rank of private sentinels, and ought to be a severer reproof to many who live here, and have all the advantages of a liberal education, and the example of a polite court; that men they esteem barbarous, inhabiting a distant and barren country, should outdo them in real politeness, that is, in the knowledge and practice of the doctrines of Christianity.

"From hence, we may remark, that those who published or propagated so many scandalous reports of these unhappy young men, must either have taken little pains to inform themselves of the truth, or must be possessed of little charity, when they load their memory with so many assertions no way connected with their crime. But, as this relation is published from the prisoners' own mouths, and attested by a person whose profession and character ought to screen him from the imputation of partiality or falsehood, it is hoped these impressions will wear off the minds of the public, and give place to sentiments of charity for their crimes, and compassion for their sufferings.

"' *Magna est veritas et prœvalebit.*' "

4TH FEBRUARY 1875.

Contributions towards the history of the Third Charge of Inverness, commonly called the Gaelic Church of Inverness, by ALEX. FRASER, Accountant, Inverness.

On looking about me hurriedly for materials for the subject of my paper of to-night, I found I had to wander a good deal to and fro, over many books and manuscripts. The more I examined, the more I found the materials were increasing, and I had to call "hold; enough!" There was not sufficient time allowed me to put these in the order I should have liked to present them here, and sooth to say, I had no time to do the subject the justice it requires. My object, in giving the present paper, was entirely to fill up a vacant evening, and if any of you feel wearied with my dry-as-dust details of bygone days, I hope such of you as so feel will come forward as I have done, at as short notice, and give something more interesting. On the spur of the moment, when urged to give a paper, I agreed, especially as I had some materials ready. Had I to do the same work over again, I should have called my subject, "The Church in Inverness since the Reformation," and then the Gaelic Church and all the other churches in Inverness might have got equal justice meted out to them, and all would be represented in their proper colour, bearing, and influence. Such a course, however, would necessitate not a paper for one night, but for at least three or four nights, and, after consideration, I have come to the conclusion that it is by such a simultaneous treatment of the Church in Inverness, that not only the position of the Gaelic Church may be best understood, but that there is no other way of appreciating its position and influence.

So much by way of introduction; and, before starting, I beg leave to add that my information is gathered from various sources. I have laid under contribution every book, rare or otherwise, that I could command. I have also had recourse to various manuscripts. The result of all and whole of which, as lawyers say, follows :—

According to one authority, the third charge, eminently the Gaelic one, was erected in 1641, in consequence of the minister of the second charge not being able to speak Gaelic. From another source we learn that in 1643 a third clergyman was engaged for a short time for the Gaelic congregation, by authority of the General Assembly. He was soon after discontinued for want of stipend—

a very natural resolve. From a third party we gather that in 1643 a third minister was appointed to preach Gaelic to two regiments that had been stationed here for some time—the one Irish and the other Highland; and in consequence of there being no room for them in the Gaelic Church, this minister addressed them every Sabbath in the Chapel-yard, but on their (the regiments') departure the appointment was discontinued. It is from the circumstance of this burying-ground becoming, as it were, a chapel-of-ease to the Gaelic Church, that it ever afterwards was called the Chapel-yard.

[This is a mistake. The Chapel-yard was so called because in it stood the original church of Inverness, of which the Abbot of Arbroath was patron.—See Chart. Morav.]

In 1706 a third minister was permanently appointed by Government, the stipend then being only £73, secured in the ancient Bishop lands of Moray and Ross. The stipend was in 1775 advanced to £110, and recently, at the general augmentation, to £150. To this permanent appointment I shall refer more fully hereafter.

From a small and scarce book by Mr Maclean, called the "Nonagenarian," I extract the following:—"In Nonagenarian's youthful days, two Gaelic congregations at one time assembled in separate parts of the Chapel-yard, listening to the discourses preparatory to the celebration of the Lord's Supper, in the open space in the centre, along which the tables are still ranged."

"One of the most eminently pious and useful ministers in my day," says Nonagenarian, "was Mr Murdo Mackenzie, connected with whose death is the following remarkable circumstance:—Lodie Ross, the head beadle of Inverness, was a perfect original in his way, of whom some amusing stories might be told. Lodie, on going one night into the High Church steeple to ring the ten o'clock bell, heard the most delightful music and singing, distinctly hearing the words repeated of the 118th Psalm and 19th verse:—

'O set ye open unto me
The gates of righteousness,
Then will I enter into them,
And I the Lord will bless.'

Finding no one was in the church, and knowing Mr Mackenzie to be in ill-health, he immediately ran to his house in Bridge Street. On arriving there, however, he found that this exemplary minister

was just departing from the scene of his earthly labour, to partake of 'the rest which remaineth for the people of God.'"

Now-a-days we don't believe in ghosts and such like stuff. The superstition of the present age lies in the belief in mediums, table turnings, spirit-rappings, and such like. Query—Are we less superstitious than our forefathers, or is ours a less ignoble **age** than theirs?

I shall now give a list of the ministers of the third charge, with some remarks—

In 1642 Duncan Macculloch was ordained, prior to 4th October, with 500 marks (£16. 13s. 4d.) of stipend.

In 1705 William Stuart, from Kiltearn, was called on 21st December 1704, and admitted after 9th April 1705. He is alluded to by Burt.

In 1720 Alexander Macbean, A.M., from Douglas, was called on 16th February, and admitted 6th December.

In 1727 Daniel Mackenzie, A.M., from Petty, was called on 10th May, presented by the Magistrates, and admitted 10th October.

In 1731 William Baillie was called on 28th April, and ordained 22d July 1731.

In 1741 Murdoch Mackenzie, A.M., from Dingwall, was called on 23d February, and admitted 13th July.

In 1752 James Grant was called, son of Mr George Grant, minister of Kirkmichael.

In 1754 Alexander Fraser, A.M., from Avoch, was called on 25th September, and admitted 13th November 1754. In order to show the regret of the Avoch people at his removal, I may state that the fishermen of that place refused to bring fish to the Inverness people, against whom they were highly incensed.

In 1763 there is mention of Robert Rose, as minister of the third charge.

In 1775 George Watson, A.M., from Kiltearn, is presented by George III., in April, and admitted 20th December.

1778 Alexander Fraser, A.M., presented by George III., and ordained 22d September.

In 1798 Alexander Rose, A.M., from Moray, is presented by George III., and admitted 18th September.

In 1801 Thomas Fraser, A.M., is presented by George III., and admitted 15th December.

In 1822 Alexander Clark, A.M., is presented by George IV., and ordained 21st March,

In 1834 Robert Macpherson is presented by William IV., and ordained 23d September.

And in the following years, I find that the following ministers were inducted—

In 1842 Simon Mackintosh.

In 1844 Donald Macconnachie.

In 1848 Hugh Mackenzie.

In 1860 Duncan Stewart.

In 1862 John Stewart.

In 18— Peter Robertson.

In 1874 Lachlan Maclachlan.

Having so far proceeded in chronological order, I shall now give some desultory observations.

The old Gaelic Church, at the bottom of Church Street, stood on the site of the present structure. The latter was built in 1792 at the expense of the heritors—the old one in 1649, at the joint expense of town and parish. The principal event connected with this building was its being converted into an hospital and prison for the followers of Prince Charles, immediately after the battle of Culloden. Among the prisoners were Provost Hossack, and the ex-Provost Fraser, of the Achnagairn family, who were supposed, from their lukewarmness to the House of Brunswick, to have been secret supporters of the Stuarts. At the intercession of the Rev. Mr Macbean, who, with President Forbes, possessed great influence with the Duke of Cumberland, on account of their known loyalty, these civic prisoners were released the following day. Numbers were taken from this prison to the Churchyard and shot, kneeling upon the stones still standing. On the south side of the church was a vault, in which I remember often having seen the large common oak coffin, or, as it was called in Gaelic, *chiste chumante*, which was used to convey the bodies of common people, or strangers, to the grave, into which they were slipped *sans ceremonie*. Although the old coffin was in existence in my day, the last time it was used was in burying those who died of their wounds received at Culloden. Connected with this church, I may mention a circumstance that occurred many years ago, which was nothing else, than the whole congregation of the Gaelic people, including, I must own, myself, being frightened out of propriety, on beholding the Rev. Mr Watson, our very pious and celebrated minister, enter the church wearing the Geneva gown, now common in other Presbyterian Churches. The reverend gentleman had always worn it in the High Church; but no sooner did he enter the Gaelic Church with it on him, than the congregation rushed out of the building, lustily crying out, "Popery! Popery!"—the minister being left with the precentor and empty pews.

The Gaelic Church was usually the place in which the bodies of drowned persons were deposited, to give time for being claimed. With one such person there is a remarkable case of second-sight connected, which I will relate as it was current eighty years ago—*i.e.*, 1762:—The Rev. Mr Morrison, minister of the parish of Petty, six miles from Inverness, was a man of remarkable devotion in his ministerial labours, and was looked upon by the people as a prophet. He had often, in vain, exhorted a wild and ungodly fisherman in his parish to attend the means of grace. Walking one evening near the manse with an elder, the Rev. Mr Morrison, naming the fisherman alluded to, said—"Well, that poor unhappy man has often been invited to attend the ordinances of the Gospel, which he will never have an opportunity of doing again, as he is at this moment drowned at the new pier of Inverness, and his body will be taken to the Gaelic Church, and remain there during the night." There are very minute particulars connected with this case of second-sight, which were verified by the fact occurring, and being mentioned in Petty, the fisherman's relations went that same evening and claimed the body.

I must, however, pass ·to the subject of Kirk discipline. Nonagenarian remembers seeing, in addition to the cutty-stool, the *brangus*, or iron collar, affixed near the entrance, and the last person said to have been exhibited as an example to offenders, was a military officer, at the instance of the Rev. Mr Macbean.

The interior of the building under description was decorated in places with black velvet, ornamented with gilded Scriptural and other devices. The pulpit and desk, at present one of the most elaborately-carved pieces of workmanship we have ever seen, is said to have been the work of a herd-boy, who resided ages ago at the Muir of Culloden, and to have been all effected with one knife, and put together with one pin. Tradition states that the Incorporated Wrights of Inverness offered him the freedom of the craft, if he would show them how he had put it together, which he refused. The seat occupied by the elders was also a piece of beautifully-carved workmanship, by the same hand. An attempt was made, at the rebuilding of the High Church in 1772, to remove this curious pulpit to that structure, but the workmen could not do so without breaking it to pieces, and the heritors being against the removal, their interference was effectual. The Laird of Macleod having contributed very largely to defray the expense of building the Gaelic Church, a seat very handsomely ornamented, having his

arms emblazoned above, was appropriated to his use. The following extract will show how the pulpit and desk came into the
possession of the Kirk-Session. It will be observed that it is
called the *little desk :—*

" At Inverness, the first day of August, one thousand six hundred and seventy-six years—The said day there was a supplication
presented by Mr William Robertson of Inches, making his humble
address to the Session of Inverness, regretting his inconvenience
for himself and family in the High Church of the said burgh, for
the reverend and incumbent attention of the said ordinances,
desiring he might be licensed and impowered to cause build and
erect two sufficient pews next to the Guildry's desk, whereupon
which application, after ripe and grave advisement, was found
very reasonable, and knowing him to be a deserving person; The
whole members of the Session did unanimously grant the said two
pews and thereby, to inherit and enjoy them peaceably and quietly
in all times coming, without any controlling, questioning, or back-
calling thereof: But to remain in his possession as an undoubted
heritage: For which two pews the said Mr William did give the
little desk belonging some time to his mother, and to be given to
Hugh Robertson, treasurer, and James Cuthbert, late bailie;
Ordaining these presents to be insert and registered in the principal Session Register of the said burgh, therein to remain for the
future security and preservation thereof. Extracted by me,
(Signed) " JOHN INNES, Clerk to the Session."

We may here remark that this pulpit will ever be connected
with the name of the late Rev. Alex. Clark, in his denunciation
of the errors of the Church of Rome, and of the first mode of
assessment under the Poor-law Act.

1719—In 1719 I meet with the name of the precentor of the
Highland Kirk of Inverness—"John Mic-Ian-dubh" (John, son
of John the Dark.)

The following document is very interesting. It has never
before seen, what I may call, day-light, and will, I hope, be so
appreciated:—

" 1720—At Inverness, the twelfth day of October 1720
years, in presence of John Forbes of Culloden, Provost;
David Fraser, James Thomson, and John Hossack,
Bailies; James Dunbar, Dean of Guild; John Fraser,
Treasurer; William Maclean, late Bailie; William

Mackintosh, Thomas Alves, and Jonathan Thomson, late Treasurer, Gilbert Gordon, Robert Rose, George Forbes, Duncan Grant, William Wilson, Robert Innes, and James Kinnaird, Councillors of the said Burgh. The Council convened anent the Town's affairs.

" The said Magistrates and Council taking to their consideration that the benefices to which the several ministers of this burgh and parish are entitled by law are not only small but also ill-paid by some in the parish, that prosecutions therefore by the ministers themselves must be vexatious and disagreeable to their inclinations, and may possibly tend to alienate the affections of their people from them, and hinder the success of their labours; and considering that it is the duty of a people, who are blest with suitable, faithful, and laborious ministers of the Gospel, to provide for their more comfortable living, and take care to have the same duly paid them, that their thoughts may be wholly taken up with the work to which they are called, by which the Gospel cannot fail, through the blessing of God, to be more successful in this corner, and thereby the glory of God advanced: therefore, and for the love, honour, and respect that are due to the merit of our worthy present ministers—Mr William Stewart, Mr Robert Baillie, and Mr Alexander Macbean—and for preserving that agreeable harmony betwixt the said ministers and them and their people, they, the said Magistrates and Council did, and hereby do, enact that from and after the term of Martinmas next 1720, and during the continuance of an Act of the 5th session of this present Parliament, laying a duty of two pennies Scots on every pint of ale or beer brewed or sold within the said burgh and liberties thereof, for the ends therein mentioned, the stipends of each of the said three ministers shall be augmented to 1600 merks yearly, attour their present manses, and of the said duty, the first year's augmentation to be paid at Martinmas 1721, provided the said ministers give a true and faithful account of the amount of their parsonage and vicarage tithes and other legal settlements, and the yearly extent of their glebes, and by whom payable, and a factory to a collector to be named by them, the said Magistrates and Council, for inbringing and receiving the saids stipends and produce of the saids glebes, which collector so to be named shall be obliged, by his accepting of the said factory, at the term of Martinmas yearly to give in a true account of the extent of the haill stipends and produce of the glebes for that year to the Council, that the sum to be payed by them out of the said duty

for making up the said sum of 1600 merks to each of the saids
three ministers may be known, and shall also be obliged to make
payment to and retire discharges from the ministers six months
after the ordinary terms of payment, and report the saids discharges, or extracts thereof, to the Council, to be kept by the
Town Treasurer : Declaring, nevertheless, that if the said factor
so to be nominated shall improve the saids glebes, or either of
them, the saids improvements, as well as the present produce of
the glebes, shall be applied to diminish the addition of stipends intended by this act; and the said Magistrates and Council, having
confidence in the fidelity and management of Alex. Baillie, Town-
Clerk of Inverness, do nominate and appoint him to be collector of
the said stipends and produce of the said glebes, in virtue of the
factory to be granted him by the saids ministers, of all years and
terms bygone resting unpaid, and in time coming, aye and until
his factory and commission be recalled by them, the saids Magistrates and Council; and they statute and enact that the sum of
200 pounds Scots money shall be paid yearly to the said collector
during his service, out of the said duty of two pennies per pint
arising by the said Act of Parliament, beginning the first year's
payment of the said salary at the term of Martinmas 1721 years,
for the preceding year : Providing, notwithstanding, that this Act
shall not be construed to extend to any minister who shall here-
after be called to, and settled in, this burgh and parish, on the
demise or translation of any of the saids three ministers above
named, without a new Act of Council entitling any such new
incumbent to the augmentation designed by this Act. And because this Act cannot take effect without the approbation of the
overseers mentioned in the said Act of Parliament, therefore they
appoint the same to be laid before them at their next meeting for
their approbation thereof. Whereupon act.   "J. FORBES, Pro."

"MEMORABILIA ANENT THE THIRD CHARGE—
"Disposition by Hugh Munro of Teaninich, 'as heir in special
served to the deceast John Fraser, merchant burgess in Inverness,
my uncle,' in favor of John Fraser, merchant in Inverness, brother-
german to James Fraser of Auchnagairn: 'That desk or piew,
presently belonging to me as heir foresaid, lying within the new
kirk of Inverness, and in the body thereof, betwixt the dask
belonging to the Laird of Mackintosh at the south, the dask
belonging to Mr David Polson of Kinmylies at the north, the kirk
wall at the west, and the common passage from the east door of
the said kirk to the north end thereof, at the east parts respectively,

.   .   .   with full power to the said John Fraser, and his foresaids, to obtain themselves confirmed in the said desk, be the Kirk Session of this burgh and parish of Inverness.'

"Witnesses, Mr David Scott, burgess of Inverness; Lachlan Mackintosh, merchant there; and Thomas Fraser, wryter there. "Dated 3d March 1713."

The following paper was kindly lent by Captain Dunbar Dunbar of Seapark, near Forres. It will be observed that there is much valuable information conveyed, and great minuteness displayed. The town of Inverness, as will be observed, is designated as the "City of Inverness," the Latin word used being *urbs*, in contradistinction to the more usual terms of *villa*, *burgum*, or *oppidum*. Places with similar royal privileges as Inverness are usually burgh; in low Latin *burgum*. *Villa* means a town, from a farm-steading and dwelling-house upwards to, say, a place like Beauly or Auldearn. The terms *urbs* and *oppidum* seldom or never occur in old charters :—

"Anne, by the grace of God, Queen of Great Britain, France, and Ireland; To all good men of her whole realm, cleric and laic; Greeting: Since we, considering the condition of the city and parish of Inverness, and parish thereof, and from information that there are therein about four thousand persons above the age of fourteen years, three thousand and more (of whom) can only speak the Gaelic language, and that said parish is very wide, and very many of the parishioners are eight miles distant from a church, whereby the ministerial duty is rendered too heavy for two ministers, especially since one of the present ministers of that parish is ignorant of the Gaelic tongue, and the other who can speak in the Gaelic is obliged to undertake the cure of one-half only of these Gaelic people, on which account about fifteen hundred of these poor Gaelic people have, to their great loss, no one to superintend them : And considering the great influence of said city and parish throughout the North Highlands of Scotland, and that the placing of a third minister at Inverness is right and necessary, which would tend greatly to the glory of God, the good of souls, and the promotion of the Reformed Protestant religion, and that it would contribute much to the preservation of peace and good order in those quarters; and also that the foresaid city and parish have been lately reduced to very great poverty through the decay of commerce and other causes; and the tiends thereof have been exhausted, and so no fixed fund can be found as a stipend for a third minister in that place; and the magistrates and heritors hitherto are agreed as to the necessity for a third minister in said city and parish, and that they have given an invitation to Mr William Stewart, minister at Kiltearn, which afterwards was considered by the National Synod of the Church of that our ancient kingdom of Scotland, and the said National Synod finding it necessary that a third minister be established at Inverness, have translated the said Mr William Stewart from Kiltearn to be one of the ministers of Inverness: And we desiring much that ministers of the Gospel have every due and requisite sustentation in the faithful administration of their office: Therefore, we, of our Royal bounty and from our maternal care for the Church and zeal for the promotion of the true Protestant religion, with special advice and consent of our very trusty and beloved cousins and counsellors, James, Duke of Queensberry, our Chief Commissioner; James, Earl of Seafield, High Chancellor; James, Marquis of Montrose, President of the Secret Council; James, Earl of Galloway; Archibald, Earl of Forfar; David, Earl of Glasgow, Lord-Depute of the Treasury; William, Lord Ross, and Master Francis Montgomery of Giffan, Lords Commissioners of the Treasury and Comptrollers of our new augmentations: And also with advice and consent, with the rest of the Lords and other Commissioners of our Exchequer, have given, granted, mortified, and disponed, and for us and our successors for ever confirmed, as also we, with advice and consent foresaid by the present charter give, grant, mortify, assign, and dispone, and for us and our successors for ever confirm, to the foresaid Magistrates and Town Council of Inverness for the time, and to their successors in office in all time to come, for the use and benefit of the said Master William Stewart upon his admission to the office of one of the ministers of Inverness, and of his successors in office in all time to come, provided always, that they be lawfully called and admitted to the incumbency of the cure, as one of the ministers of Inverness, according to the constitution of the Church as, presently established: All and whole the sum of eight hundred and eighty-one pounds one shilling and sixpence of the money of Scotland, to continue as a constant modified stipend yearly, for the foresaid Master William Stewart, and his successors in office; and which stipend we ordain to be paid yearly at the Feast of St Martin, beginning the first term of payment at the Feast of St Martin in the year of the Lord 1706, and thereafter to continue to be paid yearly in all time to come at said term, to the foresaid Magistrates and Town Council of Inverness, or to any others whomsoever having their mandate, from the rents of the Bishoprick of Moray, and particularly from those lands undermentioned, viz., from the ecclesiastical lands of the Lord of Gordonston, lying within the parish of Kinnedar, the sum two hundred and eighty-eight pounds and twelve shillings of money foresaid : *Item*—From his lands of Kirkton of Dallas six pounds thirteen shillings and fourpence : *Item*—From the ecclesiastical lands of the Lord of Brodie, in said parish of Kinnedar, £129. 12s.: *Item*—From the Lord of Muirton for his lands of Blairvie, lying in the parish of Rafford, £81. 7s.: *Item*—From the Lord of Muirtoun for his lands of Myreside, in the parish of Spynie, £20 : *Item*—From said Lord of Muirtoun for his lands of Sheriffmiln, in said parish of Spynie, £2 : *Item*—From the Lord of Bishopmiln for his lands of Bishopmiln, in said parish of Spynie, £66. 13s. 4d.: *Item*—From the Lord of Miltounbrody for his lands of Inverlochty, in the parish of Elgin, £52. 2s.: *Item* —From Master David Polson of Kylmilie for his lands of Kylmylie, and other lands formerly belonging to Hugh Baillie, in the parish of Inverness, £60 : *Item*—From the Lord of Kilravock for his temple lands in the parish of Ardclaugh, £40 : *Item*—From the said Lord of Kilravock for his lands of Kildrummie, in the parish of Nairn, £16 : *Item*—From the Lord of Dipple for his lands of Dipple, £24. 11s. 4d.: *Item*—From the Sheriff of Moray for the lands of Inchbraik, in said parish of Spynie, £15. 16s. 10d.: *Item* —From said Sheriff of Moray for his lands in the parish of Rothes, £4. 14s. 8d.: *Item*—From Abraham Lesly of Findrartie for his lands in the parish of Spynie, £36. 7s.: *Item*—From the Lord of Innes for his lands of Essell, £10. 12s.: Extending in whole to the sum of £881. 1s. 6d. of the money of Scotland foresaid, as part of the rents of the Bishoprick of Moray, which fell into our hands and came into our donation and disposition by the laws and acts of the Parliament of this kingdom, which ordained the abolition and suppression of Episcopacy, and ordained the rights, duties, and superiorities thereof, to pertain to us and our successors in all time to come, and we, with advice and consent aforesaid, give power, grant, and require the hereditary vassals, tenants, and possessors of the lands above written to make exact payment at said term, or at other terms used and wont, of the respective proportions of money to the foresaid Magistrates and Town Council of Inverness, who, for the time, may be in office, and to their successors in all time to come, or to their treasurer, or to any one having their mandate, for the use and benefit of said Master William Stewart and of his successors in office, ministers of Inverness, who have been lawfully ordained, admitted, and called to the incumbency there as said is : Declaring by the present charter that the receipt

12

of the city of Inverness or their treasurer, or of any one having
their mandate, shall be received, and be sufficient for the proper
payment of the stipend to Master William Stewart and his successors in office because of said lands, and the receipt or exoneration
shall contain the obligation of the city of Inverness, which shall be
bound to bestow the sums of money above mentioned according to
our intention, giving and delivering them to the said Master
William Stewart, or the ministers his successors in office at Inverness ; and which obligation must be immediately registered, and
an extract thereof given to said minister, and which payment
must be instructed by a registered receipt or exoneration from
the said Master William Stewart or his successors in office ; or
if said Magistrates shall neglect or procrastinate to levy the
sums foresaid for the use and benefit above mentioned, then
the foresaid Master William Stewart and his lawful successors
shall be at liberty immediately to levy them by themselves,
and to grant receipts, which shall sufficiently exoner said persons liable in payment. And that our bounty and pious intention may be more effectual, we, with consent foresaid, constitute
and ordain that in all assedations and commissions of said Bishoprick to be granted hereafter, the foresaid lands destined for payment of said third stipend shall be expressly excluded from said
assedation or commissions; and decern or ordain said Lords Commissioners of our Treasury to cause the premises so to be done and
effected; to be held and had the aforesaid annual stipend of us and
our successors as pure charity, freely, quietly, and without any
revocation; giving therefor, yearly, the foresaid Master William
Stewart and his successors in office, ministers of Inverness, prayers
and supplications to God omnipotent, both publicly and privately,
for perpetual benedictions to us and our successors in all time to
come; and this for every other burden, exaction, question, demand,
or secular service whatsoever, which can be demanded of the said
Master William Stewart and his successors in office; and in fine,
we, on the word of a prince, faithfully promise to ratify this present charter in the next session of this Parliament, if there be any,
or in the next following, or of any other Parliament of our said ancient kingdom, by requiring the States of Parliament to ratify the
same. Moreover, to the Sheriff of . . . . . and his bailies,
and also to our beloved . . . . . and to any of you conjunctly
and severally, Sheriffs of the sheriffdom of . . . . . in that
part specially constituted (we send) greeting ; and command and
order you that without delay ye cause sasine to be justly given of
the foresaid annual stipend to be levied as is foresaid to the fore-

said Magistrates and Town Council of Inverness for the time, and
their successors in office in all time to come, for the use and
benefit of the said Master William Stewart upon his admission
to the office of one of the ministers and of his successors in
office, or to their certain attorney, bearer of these presents,
according to the form and tenor of the aforesaid charter which
they have from us thereupon, under the above-written provi-
sions, and that this ye in no way omit; for the doing of which
to you and each of you conjunctly and severally, our Sheriffs
of the sheriffdom of . . . . in that part aforesaid, we commit power; in testimony of which thing to this our present
charter we have commanded our great seal to be appended : Witnesses—our very beloved Counsellors, Lord James Murray of
Philipshaugh, our Clerk of Archives and Registers; Adam Cock-
burn of Ormistoun; and our beloved Lord Charles Kerr, director
of our Chancery: At our Palace of Newmarket, the 4th day of
the month of October, the year of the Lord 1706, and fifth year
of our reign.

"This is a true copy of the principal charter above set forth,
registered in the Registers of Charters of the Chancery of our
supreme Lord the King, and from the same extracted, copied, and
collated word for word by me, Master John Russell, junior, Clerk
to. the King's Signet, and depute of the honourable man, Robert
Kerr, Esquire, director of said Chancery, under this my subscription,   "JOHN RUSSELL, Dep."

1707, Oct. 27.—"That day was read in Council a representation directed to them by Mr Robert Baillie, one of the ministers
of Inverness, mentioning that where it hath pleased some piously
devoted persons in and about the city of London, from a public
spirit and principle of zeal for promoting the knowledge of God
through the world, to bestow liberally of their substance for advancing that great end, and particularly with other things, not
only to provide their colonies in the East and West Indies with
valuable libraries, but to extend their bounty this way to the
savages and heathens in their native language, and to erect schools
to the utmost end of the earth, for the good of mankind, all being
their brethren in Adam.   In the meantime, not to forget the
Highlands of Scotland, and specially minding those bounds, as is
to be seen by the catalogue and register of books allotted to this
place, as the said petition here held as repeated, containing sundry
weighty and pregnant reasons, bears.   Therefore, craving that it
might please them to take the premises to consideration, and now

and then, by a committee of their number, to give a visit to the library, and of their bounty bestow something worthy of the honourable Court for the further providing thereof, that the inhabitants .may be encouraged to follow that laudable example; that, according to the rules, they, with the Magistrates, may have access to call for any book; for since strangers have so generously laid the foundation, your petitioner is persuaded we will not be so unnatural to ourselves as to shirk the advancing a part of the superstructure, as also that you would be pleased to advise and concur with your petitioner in some effectual method for addressing of private persons for obtaining donations from them, thus wishing that a bountiful God may enrich your Lordship and Honours with all blessings, temporal and eternal, and that your Government may be a blessing to this place. With all due respect, a favourable answer is expected by your petitioner.

(Signed) " Ro. BAILLIE."

Which representation, on being at length read and considered by the Council, and they being well advised therewith, they approve and grant the desire thereof *pro presenti,* that is, "they ordain John Taylor, their present treasurer, to pay to the said Mr Robert Baillie, petitioner, the sum of £10 sterling money, when in cash, and that for the better encouragement of the said library, and for the more promoting of the good design for which the same was appointed, and that the said sum shall be allowed to the said John Taylor in his treasury accounts."

1714.—The Rev. Wm. Stewart was one of the "considerable persons" who in December 1714 signed a petition presented to his Majesty in behalf of Lord Lovat. He also was the friend of Lady Balnagown. (See Antiquarian Notes.)

1751, Mar. 18.—Translation of Mr Murdoch Mackenzie, minister, from the signature stipends to the parochial stipend.

1752, June 27.—The vacant stipend of the third minister's living appointed to be recovered for behoof of the town.

1754, Mar. 25.—Orders given to defend the town from any augmentation of stipend.

1754, November 18.—500 merks allowed Mr Alex. Fraser, minister, for expenses of transporting himself and family from Avoch to Inverness, and one and a-half year of the signature stipend, vacant since the death of Mr Jas. Grant, appointed to be preserved for behoof of the town.

1760, Jan. 7.—One and a-half year's vacant stipend of the third minister recovered, and one year thereof ordered to be paid to the Rev. Alex. Fraser, who succeeded the late Mr Jas. Grant to that living—the other one and a-half year's stipend to be left in the treasurer's hand, but afterwards disposed of.

1766, Nov. 10.—Petition from the Rev. Mr Robt. Rose, for the interest of the town, to procure by royal grant an augmentation to his living as third minister, from the rents of the Bishopric of Moray, and application from the Magistrates and Council to Sir A. Grant, their M.P., to endeavour to bring about this desirable event. Mr Rose says there are 9000 catechisable persons in the town and parish.

Of same date, though not regarding ministers, I find a resolution passed to discountenance and discontinue the practice of meeting to drink on the evenings before and after funerals. Such resolutions were frequently made, but with little effect.

1777, April 7.—A grant is reported from his Majesty, in reply to the foregoing petition, of an additional stipend to the third minister of Inverness, of £36. 10s. per annum. The expense incurred by this grant, and in passing the seals, &c., amounting to £22. 17s. 10d., was paid by the town, and an allowance was made to Mr George Watson, third minister, of £10, for the purpose of transporting himself and family from Kiltearn, in Ross-shire.

Mr Fraser received the thanks of the meeting for his valuable paper.

11TH FEBRUARY 1875.

At this meeting the Secretary reported having sent the circular anent Gaelic Teaching in Highland Schools, prepared by his predecessor (which will be found at Page 136), to all the School Boards in the counties of Inverness, Ross, Sutherland, Argyll, Perth, and part of Moray, Banff, and Nairn shires ; and produced the following correspondence, being a letter received from the Rev. Kenneth A. Mackenzie, in reply to the circular addressed to him as chairman of the School Board of Kingussie, and the Secretary's reply thereto :—

"Manse of Kingussie, 8th February 1875.

"Dear Sir,—I received your circular anent 'Gaelic Teaching in Highland Schools,' on Friday last. From your sending such to chairmen of School Boards at this date, I take for granted that the 'Gaelic Society of Inverness' are not satisfied with the amount of aid asked from Government for the encouragement of Gaelic teaching, by the meeting of representatives of School Boards held in Inverness on the 23d ult.

"Much has of late been said and written upon this subject. No scheme or plan has been published to show how what is recommended as reasonable and beneficial can best be carried out in practice.

"Advertising for a Gaelic teacher is an easy matter; many such teachers, however, do not know how to use their knowledge of Gaelic for the benefit of their pupils, and the interest of some managers in this important matter seems to cease with the despatch of the advertisement. Will you, therefore, kindly propose a scheme by which practical effect can be given to the ideas of your Society on this subject, and, in doing so, clearly define the place which Gaelic teaching ought to occupy in the daily work of a school? This, to you, will be an easy matter, as you state that 'for some time past you have fully considered the subject of teaching Gaelic in Highland schools.' That you may be understood by all, draw out a school time-table, as is required by the Education Department. Take as your example—a not uncommon case—a school which meets for five hours on five days of the week, with an average attendance of 50, taught by a master who has pupils in each of the six standards—three Latin classes and one mathematical—and suppose that the youngest children attending know no English, with the exception of those of two families, who know not a word of Gaelic. When you do this, I shall have pleasure in calling a meeting of our School Board to consider your circular, as you request.

"I am aware that there are several managers of schools in the North who approve of your ideas, but know not how to carry them out. I shall therefore send a copy of this letter to the *Inverness Courier*, with a request to the editor to publish your reply and time-table, which I hope you can send him in time for this week's issue.

"I may add, that I cannot imagine how your Society calculate that the education of Gaelic-speaking children 'will be limited to three or four years,' when the law of the land renders eight years' instruction compulsory, and Government offer pay for 14 years. How can they fancy that members of Highland School Boards can be such traitors to their trust as this would imply?

"KENNETH A. MACKENZIE.

"A. Mackenzie, Secretary, Gaelic Society of Inverness."

"Gaelic Society of Inverness, February 9, 1875.

"The Rev. Kenneth Mackenzie, Manse of Kingussie.

"Dear Sir,—I have just received your favour of yesterday, acknowledging receipt of copy of circular issued by this Society to chairmen of School Boards in the Highlands.

"In reply to the first paragraph of your letter, I would point out that the circular is dated the '9th of January,' and that the resolution of the Society repeated therein was passed on, and is dated, the 19th of November 1874. These dates are some considerable time prior to the meeting of representatives of School Boards held at Inverness, and the circular appeared in most of the newspapers North and South, and was read by many of the representatives *before* attending the meeting. Therefore, although it may be, and probably is, true that 'the Society is not satisfied with the amount of aid asked from Government at that meeting,' this must not *necessarily* be assumed from the date on which you received the circular.

"Upon such short notice, you can hardly be in earnest when proposing that our Society should publish a complete scheme, such as you suggest, in the *Inverness Courier* of Thursday next, particularly in the face of your own remark that 'so much has been said and written already, to so little purpose,' much of which was from your own pen.

"I have not been able to submit your letter and proposal to a meeting of the Society. The first meeting at which I can possibly do so is on Thursday evening next, *after* the *Courier* appears in which you request me to publish our scheme and my reply. Under these circumstances, I cannot, meanwhile, commit the Society; but I feel sure that they will not shrink from what you propose.

"In reference to this, however, I would remark, that I do not consider it the *duty* of the Society to relieve gentlemen (members of School Boards elected for the purpose) of their unmistakable duty under the Act, to frame rules and complete schemes, and it is most clearly their duty 'to show how what is recommended as reasonable and beneficial can best be carried out in practice.'

"Your plan of removing the *onus* from School Boards, and laying it on the Gaelic Society of Inverness, is an old one, and one for which you can find precedents in higher quarters, when those in office, obliged to admit evils which they found difficult to meet and remedy, exclaimed, 'It's all very fine to demonstrate the necessity for improvement; show us how to do it.' It is admitted

on all hands that a change in the present system of teaching in
Highland schools requires attention and improvement, and I'm
afraid that the ratepayers will hesitate before they allow the School
Boards to shirk their responsibility in the matter in the manner
you propose.

"Undoubtedly a great difficulty exists about teachers qualified
to teach Gaelic in Highland schools, but this only proves that the
language has been too long despised and neglected by the ministers
and heritors who had the management of the schools in the past.
Most teachers in the Highlands are quite unable to teach Gaelic—
many of them are quite ignorant of the language, even as a spoken
tongue.   This being so, it is hardly very wise to put a high value
upon the opinion of such men as to the desirability of teaching
Gaelic in the schools.   They will naturally oppose the teaching of
a language of which they are entirely, or almost entirely, ignorant.
This is *one* of the difficulties connected with the question of teaching Gaelic in Highland schools, but it must be kept in mind that
the Education Act was not passed professedly merely for the benefit of teachers, but primarily for the education, moral and mental
improvement, of the scholars.   What most people understand by
this, is the bringing forth, cultivating, and quickening of the
natural powers of their minds, and they believe that no medium is
so suitable for attaining this as the natural and, in many cases in
the Highlands, the only tongue known to the pupils.   The system
generally practised is not education in this sense.   It is a mere
cramming in from without, and we know that often this kind of
education (?) is forgotten in a much shorter time than is taken to
acquire it.

"There is also another difficulty to contend against.   Few of
our Gaelic-preaching ministers are Gaelic scholars, many of them
cannot even spell it as it is written in their Bibles; and we know
as a matter of experience, that very few, indeed, can preach a
Gaelic sermon without mixing it up with English terms, to an
extent that appears ridiculous.   I know others who compose their
sermons in English; and translate them into Gaelic.   It is only
natural, then, that even ministers should be prejudiced against
teaching Gaelic in Highland schools.

"The Rev. Kenneth Macdonald, Applecross, boldly states in
last week's *Courier*—'I never got a Gaelic lesson, and I did not
feel the disadvantage of it.'   I know that Mr. Macdonald gives
great satisfaction to his people in Applecross, but I heard him at
Inverness using several English terms in his Gaelic sermon.   Is
it possible that any man can preach as well in a language he never

studied as a minister ought to do? If it were suggested that a
man educated entirely in French and German, but who never got
a lesson in the English language, could preach to the satisfaction
of an intelligent English congregation, the idea would be considered
simply preposterous. To be able 'to speak, and read, and write
in Gaelic as well as Professor Blackie,' is not saying much, for I'm
afraid from what I know of the Professor's Gaelic, that he would
make but a poor appearance preaching in that language in Applecross. The fact, however, that Mr Macdonald acquired such a
knowledge of Gaelic without ever receiving a lesson in it, goes far
to prove how easily *it can* be learned by the natives, without
'wasting' much time in acquiring a sufficient knowledge of it to
help them in their English.

"I have, as you requested, sent a copy of this to the *Inverness
Courier*, and to other papers.— I am, dear sir, yours faithfully,

"ALEXANDER MACKENZIE, *Secretary*."

Considerable discussion followed, and the opinion of the members was freely expressed that the rev. gentleman was barely
justified in calling upon the Society to publish such a scheme on
twenty-four hours' notice, and in sending a copy of his letter for
publication in *next day's Courier*, before the Secretary received
the original, at the same time requesting the publication of an
important educational scheme, and a public reply to his letter the
following morning; after which the following resolution was unanimously passed:—"The Secretary having read correspondence between the Rev. Mr Mackenzie, Kingussie, and himself, with reference to the circular of date 9th January 1875, issued by the Society
to School Boards, the Society approved of the Secretary's reply to
Mr Mackenzie, and find that the Society having, in that circular,
directed the attention of School Boards to defects in the present
system of teaching in Highland schools, the Society is not called
upon to formulate a scheme for remedying these defects, that being
an important part of the duties devolving upon Highland School
Boards ; and that the Secretary forward a copy of this resolution
to the Rev. Mr Mackenzie."

The Honorary Secretary read a paper on "The Highlanders,
Past and Present," which was of a very interesting character, and
highly commended.

18th FEBRUARY 1875.

The Secretary reported having forwarded to the Rev. Mr Mackenzie the resolution passed at last meeting, with the following additional remarks, which were approved : —

"In my reply of the 9th, I overlooked to notice the last paragraph of yours of the 8th, in which you say, '1 cannot imagine how your Society calculate that the education of Gaelic-speaking children will be limited to three or four years, when the law of the land renders eight years' instruction compulsory. How can they fancy that members of Highland School Boards can be such traitors to their trust as this would imply?'

"You have taken a wrong view of our meaning, or you would never have written thus. We argued from our knowledge of the present state of things what the 'limit' would be, but we certainly did not mean to imply treachery to members of School Boards. We knew, as a matter of fact, that not more than half the children of school age in many parishes in the Highlands attended school. We therefore calculated that if *some* School Boards did not enforce a better attendance than they now do, the education of children would *practically* 'be limited to three or four years.' We leave the public to decide whether your remarks are applicable to the Society, and whether they point with most force against them or against the School Boards."

The following is the rev. gentleman's reply :—

"Manse of Kingussie, 16th February 1875.

"Dear Sir,—I beg to acknowledge receipt of your letters of the 9th and 13th insts., and of the extract minute of meeting of Gaelic Society of Inverness, held on the 11th inst.

"I deem it a loss to education in the Highlands that your Society have, contrary to your own expectations, declined to grant my request. By publishing the system of Gaelic teaching you would most approve of, you could not, as you seemed to fear, relieve School Boards of responsibility, although you might aid them in improving education. No Board would adopt your system simply because it was a system recommended by an influential Society, without duly and carefully considering its merits, and coming to the conclusion that it was better than that they had in operation previously.

"I trust your Society will soon be able to look more hopefully to the future. It is impossible at this moment for any one to judge with certainty what that future may be, even as to school attendance. I, for one, believe there are bright days in prospect for our too long neglected Highland youth, and I hope these days will not be retarded by your remarks on attendance, leading parents and others to fancy that they do very well when they keep their children as long in school as the Gaelic Society of Inverness calculated they would do. You are mistaken in thinking that I have written upon the subject of teaching Gaelic in Highland schools. Could I, like your Society, say that I had 'fully considered the subject,' I would not only not grudge the trouble of doing so, but look upon myself as no friend to education in the North, did I refrain, if called upon at a time so critical and important as the present.

"My only object in writing you having been to procure, for the benefit of myself and others, a statement of your Society's views as to the amount of time and attention they would wish paid to the teaching of Gaelic under the proposed new regime, and as you have not given me any information on the point, I must now take leave of the correspondence.—I am, your obedient servant,   "KENNETH A. MACKENZIE.

"A. Mackenzie, Esq., Secretary, Gaelic Society of Inverness."

The following special committee was appointed for the collection of folk-lore, namely, Mr A. Mackenzie, secretary; Mr Donald Macrae, High School; and Alex. Fraser, accountant, with power to add to their number gentlemen outside Inverness who may be willing to collect lore in their respective districts; the Secretary to be convener. It was also unanimously decided that a sum of money be given annually by the Society to pupils in different schools in the Highlands for proficiency in the Gaelic language. The details and conditions of competition were remitted to the Council. The recommendations of the Council regarding Gaelic teaching in Highland schools was then discussed and unanimously adopted by the Society, and a copy ordered to be sent to Charles Fraser-Mackintosh, Esq., M.P., Chief of the Society, with a request that he should use his influence with the Education Department of the Privy Council, and in the House of Commons, to give effect to the views of the Society on this question. It was also resolved to send him the following petition, signed by the Chairman and Secretary on behalf of the Society, for presentation to the House of Commons :—

" To the Honourable the Commons of Great Britain and Ireland in Parliament Assembled, the Humble Petition
of the Gaelic Society of Inverness—

" Your petitioners having fully considered the present method
of teaching in Highland schools, find that it is unnatural and erroneous, in so far as it entirely ignores the native language, and
consequently, instead of facilitating, retards education, and produces most unsatisfactory results. So far as known to your petitioners, a system which, contrary to all reason, takes no advantage
of the mother tongue, as a *medium* for imparting and acquiring
instruction in a language quite unknown to a majority of the
pupils, is not adopted anywhere out of the Highlands.

" Your petitioners would therefore—*First*, Humbly pray that
your honourable House will make due provision for the teaching of
Gaelic in Highland schools, in all districts where that language is
spoken by the greater portion of the people. The natural intelligence of the pupils would thus be quickened, and they would the
more easily acquire an *intelligent* knowledge of the English
language.

" *Second*—In order to encourage teachers to qualify for teaching in and through the Gaelic language, your petitioners humbly
pray that certificates of competency in the language be granted,
entitling teachers to a small grant when placed in districts where
the Gaelic is the prevailing tongue, and where her Majesty's
Inspector of Schools reports that it is taught beneficially to the
scholars.

" *Third*—That Gaelic be recognised as a special subject.

" In order successfully to carry out the objects of, and give
proper effect to, the prayer of your petitioners, and do full justice
to the pupils and teachers, your petitioners are of opinion that it is
absolutely necessary that all inspectors of schools in the Highlands
should be able to understand, and speak and examine in and through
the native language of the scholars.

" Your petitioners humbly beg that your Honourable House be
pleased to give effect to their prayer in the revised code, and

" Your petitioners will ever pray.

"Signed in the name, and on behalf of, the Gaelic Society of
Inverness, the 18th day of February 1875, at Inverness.

" CHARLES MACKAY, *Chairman.*
" ALEXANDER MACKENZIE, *Secretary.*"

A large number of members were nominated at this meeting.

25TH FEBRUARY 1875.

Mr LACHLAN MACBEAN read an English Metrical Translation of " Gaol-nan-daoine," which was very favourably received by the meeting, and considered highly creditable to the translator.

4TH MARCH 1875.

Mr WILLIAM MACKENZIE, "Free Press," read a paper, in Gaelic, on the subject of "Teaching Gaelic in Highland Schools," which brought about one of the best discussions of the session. A letter was read from the School Board of North Uist, in reply to the circular issued by the Society, in which it was stated, "The Board concur fully in the opinion that a knowledge of Gaelic on the part of teachers in Highland districts is desirable, and renders it more easy for them to communicate explanations to their classes."

11TH MARCH 1875.

Steps were taken at this meeting for getting petitions signed throughout the Highlands in favour of teaching Gaelic in Highland schools, and for procuring information as to the number of Gaelic-speaking children in the country; after which Mr DONALD MACRAE, High School, read two very old Gaelic poems. We have only been able to procure one of them for publication.

" ORAN DHOMHNUILL DAOILIG LE A BHEAN.

"'N am dhomh ùileach 'mo leabaidh,
'N deis dhomh dùsgadh a codal;
'S ann a dh-ionndrain mi caidreamh
An t-seoid uam:
Fear foinneamh, deas, dìreach,
A dheagh shloinneadh nam biatach;
Cha bu chlagharra crion an
Tigh n-oil thu.

" Cha bu chubaire gealltach thu,
'N am togail na feachda;
Leat bu mhiannach bhi glacadh
Pìc chor-chuill:

Pìc a dh-iuthar na cr'é,
Ur fallain nach leum'adh;
Chitè faileas la greinè,
Do dhorlaich.

" Bidh cinn-iùil ort 'on t-sliosnaich,
Chuil bhuidhe 's glan sliosa;
'S dos na h-iolaire bricè
Ga seoladh:
Bidh ceir dhaithtè 'on gheilbhinn,
Chuireadh dreach air na h-airmibh;
Cinn chruadhach 'on cheardaich,
'S deagh cholg orr'.

" Slat a n-iuthair bu dirich,
Air 'bu ro-mhath cur sidè,
Agus leistear Ghleann-Libhinn
Cur smeoirn orr'.
'N aill leibh ! shealgair a chreach-uill,
A choillich 'sa ghlas gheoidh,
Fhuair thu t-fhoghlum air gaisgeachd
As t-oigè.

" 'N am direadh na bruthaich,
Cha bhi sgios na da shiubhal,
Agus plc a chuil bhuidhe
'Ad dhorlach:
Gu'm bi d-eudan air lasadh,
'S do dheud mar a chailcè;
Tha falt dubh ort, 's chan fhacas
Nis boidhchè.

" 'Nuair a rachadh tu d-eideadh,
Ann am breacan-na-feilè;
Gum bu leannan mna breid-ghìl
Bu bhoidhche thu.
Og chridhè na feilè,
Slan do thighinn gu reidh dhuit;
Bu tu m'aidhir 'us m-eibhneas,
'S mo mhor-chuis.

" Ach a nisè ma sguir thu,
'S gun do li'bhraig thu'n gunna,
Chaoidh cha dìrich thu uillinn
Na mor-bheann:

Ma choisg iad a fiadh ort,
Le àr smachd an Iarla;
Cha bhi mhanntal nan t-slias-aid
Air d-òlach."

We believe the last stanza of the song is wanting; but Mr Macrae having declined to give us the MSS. of this, or of the other read by him, we are at present unable to give the one complete, or give any part of the other. We hope, however, to be able to procure both from another source, for the next Volume of Transactions. During the evening Mr A. MACKENZIE, the Secretary, exhibited an old manuscript given him by Sir Kenneth S. Mackenzie, Bart. of Gairloch, entitled " The Blind Piper's Salute to the Laird of Gerloch, when he brought home his lady, 1730." The best authorities assert that the paper and the writing thereon are at least 130 years old, and Sir Kenneth " believes that it is the presentation copy " given by the bard to the Laird of Gairloch at the time. We may state that nine verses of this poem are given in Mackenzie's " Beauties of Gaelic Poetry." We have here fifteen; and in the version in the " Beauties" some of the stanzas are made up of two lines out of two *different* verses in ours. We give an exact copy of the original MS. (which is written phonetically), on one page, and a modern Gaelic rendering, by A. Mackenzie, the Secretary, on the opposite page.

Old Version.

" BIAUNACHK BAIRD.

1. " Chea piaunich in Teach sin Ture
   'Tie hanig ure nur keaun
   Keak honn 'holt you cliu
   Nhi puonachk Duchi gun chaule.

2. " Cheak i hanig Rhi deach uoire
   Cham bu vuochich muirne is keole
   Ho Chenich na rhune rhea
   Is ho Barron Straspe nam Bho.

3. " Who Earli Shivort in tose
   Yuchk i noi 's glan grea
   is won Teitar Halloch i riste
   Subject in Rhi aunse cach glese.

4. " Phei Grauntaich uim nach time
   Spuochach in nimort 'soach paule
   Wo spe cham bemitoch leine
   Toirt ffea de chirichin viaune.

5. " Spe won dickig an teask ear muire
   Agus ffeachach rhi tu glan
   Gu pratenach poul chom stra
   Prein vrechd du wo veine go Stra.

6. " Yout a shitt eak Clann elpan na fiach derik
   Lesh im bo vien vhi shealig cach ffree
   ffirr vashoch chast i cunchelik
   'Naum chul i shelive na stree.

7. " Saun wo na kinimn nach faune
   Hanick i noi is glan grea
   Gruoy chorkan is rask maul
   Malloch chile chaume is cule slime.

8. " Ha i sliss mur Iall i na stru
   is ha i Cru mur chanoch in iore
   Cule clechky ear chriach nan teade
   Mur aittal grene i na oire.

9. " Ha eiten gial mur' Chailk
   'Corp Sneachtive ear deach Chelive
   Mhi lennu lhe keittu Sirc
   Ear nach facis ffrich cho ferik.

(Modern Version.)

"Beannachd Baird.

1. " Dhia beannaich, an teach 'san tùr,
    'N te thainig ùr 'nar ceann ;
    Geng shona, sholt', gheibh cliù,
    Ni buannachd duthch' gun chall.

2. " Gheng i thainig rè deagh nair,
    Dha 'm bu bhuadhach muirn, is ceŏl,
    Ogha Choinnich na ruinè rèidh,
    'S ogba Bharan Sthraspè nam bo.

3. " Bho Iarla Shiphoiit an tos,
    Dhiuchd an oigh is glaine gnè,
    'S bho 'n Taoiter Shaileach i rithisd,
    'S oibid do'n righ anns gach gleus.

4. " Bha i Ghranntaich uim nach tioma,
    'S buadhach an iomairt 's gach ball,
    Bho Spè dha 'm b-iomadach linnè,
    Toirt fhiadh do dh-fhirichean bheann.

5. " Spè bho'n tigeadh an t-iasg thar muir,
    Agus fiadhach ri taobh glan ;
    Gu bradanach poll chum strn,
    Priomh-abhainn bhreac dubh, bho bheinn gu strath.

6. " Dhuit a ghibht' aig Claun Alpein na fiadh dearg,
    Leis am bu mhiann a bhi sealg gach frìth ;
    Fir mhaiseach, ghasta, gun cheilg,
    'N am dhol a sheilbh na strì.

7. " 'S ann bho na Cinnidhean nach fann,
    Thainig an oigh is glainè gne ;
    Gruaidh chorcair, 'us rosg mall,
    Mala chaol cham, 'us cùl sliom.

8. " Tha slios mar eala na strn,
    'S tha cruth mar chanach an fheoir,
    Cùl cleachdaidh air dhreach nan teud,
    Mar aiteal grein i, na òir.

9. " Tha h-eudan geal mar a chaile,
    Corp snaightè air deagh dheilbh ;
    Maoth leanabh le gibhtean seirc,
    Air nach fhacas fraoch dho feirg.

10. " Ga miall shive na hure ven oig
     Rheich Chiarloch na Corn ffiell
     She toill Chairten as cach tiere
     Go miall shive I is piaunachk chea.

11. " Go miall' shive prhe is puoy
     Go mhiall shive uoisle is eliu
     Go mhiall shive cach piaunachk i kean
     Smo vheaunoch ffene chuive ear huse.

12. " Shimug Bheaunachk agus Teiste
     Eak i noi is killi slise
     Is pheaunach eak i n Tie hug lesh
     Chanon keast cha feacht rish.

13. " Po chiole cattil i cho swone
     Is I na puochil ear i vese
     Nha cail holish ffiech do biach
     Rhealig gach neach mur came.

14. " Spuochach in Turris i vaune
     Chorte rish i nuoisle in deach hime
     Hug u lett woy vonug vianne
     Ealtichkin nach gaun chan tire.

15. " Con· in dro mish ear i vanish
     Smalliume gun drein shive deach huris
     Huk u lett I Choni vaill i
     Geak na giall Lave, Sma i Hurri.

10. " Gu meal sibh na h-ūr bhean og,
  Thriath Ghearr-loch nan corn fial ;
  Se toil chairdean anns gach tīr,
  Gu meal sibh i, 'us beannachd Dhia.

11. " Gu meal sibh breth agus buaidh
  Gu meal sibh uaislè 'us eliu,
  Gu meal sibh gach beannachd an cein,
  'S mo bheannachd fhein duibh air thūs.

12. " 'S iomadh beannachd agus teist,
  Th' aig an oigh is gilè slios,
  'S beannachd aig an ti thug leis,
  Dh-aindeon ceist dha fiachtè ris.

13. " Bu cheol codail i gu suain,
  'Us i na buachaill air a bheus,
  Na coinneal sholuis feadh a theach,
  Frithealadh gach neach mar fheum.

12. " 'S buadhach an turus a bh' ann,
  Chord ris an uaislè an deagh thiom;
  Thug thu leat bho mhonadh bheann,
  Eilteachdainn, nach gann, dha'n tir.

15. " Chon in robh mis air a bhanais,
  'S math leam gun d' rinn sibh deagh thurus ;
  Thug thu leat i chon a bhailè
  Geug nan geal lamh, 's math a h-urṛa.

18TH MARCH 1875.

Mr ALEX. MACKENZIE, the secretary, read the following paper on "The Prophecies of Coinneach Odhar Fiosaiché, the Brahan Seer":—

"The gift of prophecy, second-sight, or *Taibhsearchd*, claimed for, and believed by many to have been possessed by, Coinneach Odhar, is one the belief in which scientific men of the present day accept as evident signs of looming, if not actual, insanity. And who is not scientific in these days? I must therefore be careful, in reading a paper on such a dangerous subject, to guard against any suspicions on your part that I believe in what I am about to relate, however unsatisfactory the question may appear to my own mind, or however difficult it may be to explain away what follows. The prophecies were known in the Highlands for generations before they were fulfilled, some were fulfilled in our own day, and many are still unfulfilled. It would even be unwise to bring the Bible to my aid, as I might well do, to prove that second-sight, visions of a supernatural kind, and witchcraft were believed in of old by the sacred writers. Indeed, on more important subjects the Bible is laid aside by many of our would-be scientific dabblers, whenever it treats of anything which is not within the range of the puny mind of the reader. We have all grown so scientific, that the mere idea of anything being possible which is incomprehensible to our cultured scientific intellects cannot be entertained, even although it be admitted that in many cases the greatest men of science, and the mightiest intellects, find it impossible to understand or explain many things as to the existence of which they have no possible doubt. Those who preach and believe that angels are hovering about and ministering to the saints, would never acknowledge that the presence of the spirits was felt, or that any human being could see any signs indicating the early departure of an intimate friend. With these few remarks, I trust that you will allow me to proceed with the prophecies, without expecting me to acknowledge any belief in them, and so endanger whatever small reputation I may enjoy of possessing a small modicum of common sense.

"Coinneach Odhar was the great prophet of the Highlands, and lived near Loch-Ussie, on the Brahan estate, some 200 years ago. The Highlands are still full of his prophecies, floating about among the people. Some have been fulfilled, and others have not. It may be well that the Gaelic Society should put some of them on record, and so give an opportunity to future generations to test their faith in second-sight by comparing what may be fulfilled in their day with the unfulfilled prophecies which I am, in this paper, about to record. The Seer predicted many things which unbelievers in his supernatural powers will attribute to natural shrewdness. For instance, when, 150 years before the Caledonian Canal was thought of, he prophesied that ships would sail round the back of Tomnahurich Hill. Another of his predictions was that Tomnahurich, or, as he called it, 'Cnoc-na-Sith-ichean,' would be under lock and key, and the fairies secured in their home. Although natural shrewdness might help in predicting that ships would sail round the back of the hill, it would hardly help him in foreseeing a cemetery under lock and key, and the spirits chained within. Such as the following might also be attributed to natural shrewdness :—' That there would be a road among the hills of Ross-shire, from sea to sea, with a bridge over every stream,' and that 'the people would degenerate as their country improved.' 'That the clans would become so effeminate as to flee from their country before an army of sheep,' has only been too true.

"Another of the prophecies refers to 'Clach-an-Tiompain,' at Strathpeffer. I have no doubt this stone is well known to some of you. It is one of those pillar-looking stones standing on end, which when struck makes a great hollow sound or echo, hence the name. The prediction was that the time would arrive when ships would ride with their cables attached to it. This has not yet come to pass, and the only way by which we can imagine it to happen is by a canal being some day made through Strathpeffer, or the stone being removed to Dingwall Pier.

"There is another unfulfilled one about 'Clach-an-t-seasaidh,' near Muir of Ord. This was another upright stone, angular and sharp at the top, but I am told it is now partly broken and lying on the ground. The day would come when the ravens would, from the top of it, drink their full of the blood of the Mackenzies.

"Another is that the canonry of Ross (which is still standing) would fall when full of Mackenzies. This may happen in two ways. It is the burying-place of the Mackenzies, and the canonry may be filled with dead Mackenzies, or it may fall when a funeral is taking place, and a large concourse of the clan present.

"He also predicted that the natural arch, or 'Clach tholl,' near Storehead, in Assynt, would fall with a crash so loud as to cause the Laird of Leadmore's cattle, twenty miles away, to break their tethers.   This was fulfilled in 1841, Leadmore's cattle having strayed from home one day, to within a few hundred yards of the arch, when it fell with such a crash as to send them home in frantic fright, tearing everything before them.   'The day would come when people would be picking gooseberries on the walls of a stone bridge across the Ness.'   This happened in our own day, for gooseberry bushes grew on the stone bridge carried away some years ago by one of the Ness floods.   There is another unfulfilled one in connection with the bridges on the Ness.   He predicted that, when two false teachers came across the seas who would revolutionise the religion of the land, and when nine bridges spanned the river, 'the Highlands would be full of ministers without grace, and women without shame.'   We already have seven bridges, and we are likely soon to have the fatal number—nine.   Let us, then, watch the realisation of Coinneach's prophecy.   Another unfulfilled one is that a '*long mhaol-odhar*" would come round by Carr Point in Gairloch, and, on her first '*geum*' or boom, the six chimneys would fall off Gairloch House.   His prophecy that a white cow would calf in 'Tigh-an-Teampuill'—old Gairloch House, but now occupied by the gardener—has been fulfilled; also that a *Bo mhaol dubh*, 'a black, hornless cow,' would have a calf with two heads, in Flowerdale, happened within my own recollection.   Among others are the following:—'A fox would rear a litter of cubs on the hearthstone of Castle Downie.   A fox, white as snow, would be killed on the west coast of Sutherlandshire.   A wild deer would be caught alive at Fortrose Point.   A river in Wester Ross would be dried up.   There would be a dire persecution, by which there would be such bloodshed that one could ford the Oykel, in Sutherland, over dead men's bodies.   A raven, attired in plaid and bonnet, would drink his full of human blood on Fion-bheinn three times a-day for three successive days.'

   " I take the following from the *Highlander*, supplied by a correspondent in the district :—'About fifteen years ago there lived in the village of *Baile-Mhuilinn*, in the west of Sutherlandshire, an old woman of about ninety-five, known as Baraball Nic Choinnich, It was known that Coinneach Odhar predicted her death of the measles, but having come to such a great age, and there being no appearance of her ever having that disease, the seer was in danger of losing his credit in the district.   However, when the district was, so to speak, convalescent, the measles paid her a visit, and she departed, leaving no doubt whatever as to the trouble of which she died.'

"There are hundreds of Coinneach's prophecies floating about the country, and I hope this will lead to the recovery of more of them. I will, however, leave his general and more unimportant predictions after giving one about Fairburn Tower, when I will proceed to give you all the important prophecies which have already come to pass in the unfortunate history of the Seaforth family. The unfulfilled prophecies in reference to this family have not yet been published, but there are various people to whom they are known, and I hope yet to procure them.

"Coinneach predicted that a cow would calf on the top of Fairburn Tower. This happened twenty-four years ago, during a wet harvest. Some unthrashed corn was carried up the winding stone stair to the top room to dry. Some of the straw was dropped on the stair as it was being carried up. The cow followed, picking it up until she found herself at the very top. Being heavy in calf, it was considered dangerous to remove her, and she was left there until after she gave birth to a strong healthy calf. This prophecy was well known to my father and mother, and to many others I could mention, years before it actually came to pass.

"I will now proceed to give you those of the prophecies regarding the Seaforth family which have been literally fulfilled.

"It will be necessary to follow the history of the family somewhat closely, as it is intimately interwoven with, and is itself really the fulfilment of, Coinneach's predictions. The Seaforths were great Barons for many generations before Kenneth Mackenzie was raised to the peerage by James IV. in 1609, as Lord Mackenzie of Kintail. His son Colin was created Earl of Seaforth in 1623. Kenneth, third Earl of Seaforth, distinguished himself in the service of his king, and suffered imprisonment and privation in consequence. On the Restoration, he obtained his liberty, and married Isabella Mackenzie, daughter of Sir John Mackenzie of Tarbat, and sister of the first Earl of Cromartie. To her cruelty and violence may be traced the fearful doom which subsequently overtook her house. After the Restoration, the Earl had occasion to visit Paris. He left his Countess at Brahan Castle, while he was enjoying the gay amusements of the French capital. Lady Seaforth became very uneasy, for her lord had already prolonged his absence much beyond his original intention. Not hearing from him for a length of time, she became very anxious concerning him, and sent for Coinneach Odhar, who was famous throughout the whole North for his intimate relations with the invisible world. He was in truth a prophet of no mean reputation, consulted far and wide. It is reported that Kenneth was a

great teaze to his mistress, for he constantly expended his wit
upon her, much to her annoyance, so much so, that one day she
determined to poison his food and finish him. His master sent
him away to cut peats, and some time before the dinner hour,
having pretty well exhausted himself, he sat down on the heath to
rest, when he fell asleep. He suddenly felt something cold in his
breast, woke up, and found a round white stone, with a hole
through the middle, placed there. He examined it, and on looking through the hole, the treachery of his mistress was made clear
to him, and his life saved, for he declined to eat his dinner. Ever
after, Coinneach could foresee coming events by looking through
the white stone or *clach fhiosrachd.*

"Kenneth obeyed the orders of the Lady Seaforth, arrived at
the Castle, and presented himself to the Countess, who required
him to give her information concerning her absent lord. Coinneach asked where Seaforth was supposed to be, and said that he
thought he would be able to discover him if he was still alive.
The *clach fhiosrachd* was applied by Kenneth to his eye, when he
laughed loudly, saying to the Countess, 'Fear not for your lord,
he is safe and sound, well and hearty, merry and happy.' Being
now satisfied that her husband's life was safe, she wished Kenneth
to describe his appearance, to tell her where he was, what he was
doing, and all his surroundings? 'Be satisfied,' he said, 'ask
no questions, let it suffice you to know that your lord is well and
merry.' 'But where is he?' demanded the lady, 'with whom
is he? and is he making any preparation for coming home?'
'Your lord,' replied Coinneach, 'is in a magnificent room, in very
fine company, and far too agreeably employed at present to think
of leaving Paris.' The Countess finding that her lord was well
and happy, began to fret that she had no share in his happiness
and amusements, and to feel even the pangs of jealousy and
wounded pride. She thought there was something in the Seer's
looks and expression which seemed to justify such feelings. He
spoke sneeringly and maliciously of her husband's occupations, as
if to say 'that he could tell a disagreeable tale if he would.' The
lady tried entreaties, bribes, and threats to induce Coinneach to
give a true account of her husband, as he had seen him, to tell
who was with him, and all about him. Kenneth pulled himself
together, and proceeded to say, 'As you will know that which will
make you unhappy, I must tell you the truth. My lord seems
to have little thought of you, or of his children, or of his Highland home. I saw him in a gay-gilded room, grandly decked
out in velvets, and silks, and cloth of gold, and on his knees

before a fair lady, and his arm round her waist, with her hand pressed to his lips.' At this unexpected and painful disclosure, the rage of the lady knew no bounds. It was natural and well merited, but its object was a mistake. All the anger which ought to be directed against her husband, and which should have been concentrated in her breast, to be poured out upon him after his return, was spent upon poor Coinneach Odhar. She felt the more keenly that the disclosure of her husband's infidelity had not been made to herself in private, but in the presence and before the principal retainers of her house; so that the Earl's moral character was blasted, and her own charms were slighted, before the whole clan, and her husband's desertion of her for a French lady was certain to become the public scandal of all the North of Scotland. She formed a sudden resolution with equal presence of mind and cruelty. She determined to discredit the revelations of Coinneach, and to denounce him as a vile slanderer of her husband's character. She trusted that the signal vengeance she was about to inflict upon Kenneth as a liar and defamer would impress the minds, not only of her own clan, but of all the inhabitants of the counties of Ross and Inverness, with a sense of her thorough disbelief in the scandalous story, to which she nevertheless secretly attached full credit. Turning to the Seer, she said, ' You have spoken evil of dignities, you have villified the mighty of the land, you have defamed a mighty chief in the midst of his vassals, you have abused my hospitality and outraged my feelings, you have sullied the good name of my lord in the halls of his ancestors, and you shall suffer the most signal vengeance that I can inflict, you shall suffer the death.'

"Coinneach was filled with astonishment and dismay at this fatal result of his art. He had expected far other rewards of divination. However, he could not at first believe the rage of the Countess was serious; at all events, he expected that it would soon evaporate, and that, in the course of a few hours, he might be allowed to depart in peace. He even so far understood her feelings that he thought she was making a parade of anger in order to discredit the report of her lord's shame with the clan; and he expected that when this object was served, he might at length be dismissed without personal injury. But the decision of the Countess was no less violently conceived than it was promptly executed. The doom of Coinneach was sealed. No time was to be allowed for remorseless compunction. No preparation was permitted to the wretched man. No opportunity was given for intercession in his favour. The gallows was forthwith erected, and the miserable Seer was led out for immediate execution.

"Such a stretch of feudal oppression, at a time so little remote as the reign of Charles II., may appear strange. A castle may be pointed out, viz., Menzies Castle, much less remote from the seat of authority and the Courts of Law, than Brahan, where, half a century later, an odious vassal was starved to death by order of the wife of the Chief, the sister of the great and patriotic Duke of Argyll!

"When Coinneach found that no mercy was to be expected either from the vindictive lady or the subservient vassals, he resigned himself to his fate. He drew forth his white stone, so long the instrument of his supernatural intelligence, and once more applying it to his eye said—'I see into the far future, and I read the doom of the race of my oppressor. The long-descended line of Seaforth will, ere many generations have passed, end in extinction and in sorrow. I see a Chief, the last of his house, both deaf and dumb. He will be the father of three fair sons, all of whom he will follow to the tomb. He will live care-worn and die mourning, knowing that the honours of his line are to be extinguished for ever, and that no future Chief of the Mackenzies shall bear rule at Brahan or in Kintail. After lamenting over the last and most promising of his sons, he himself shall sink into the grave, and the remnant of his possessions shall be inherited by a white-hooded lassie from the East; and she is to kill her sister. And as a sign by which it may be known that these things are coming to pass, there shall be four great lairds in the days of the last deaf and dumb Seaforth—viz., Gairloch, Chisholm, Grant, and Raasay, of whom one shall be buck-toothed, another hare-lipped, another half-witted, and the fourth a stammerer. Chiefs distinguished by these personal marks shall be the allies and neighbours of the last Seaforth; and when he looks round him and sees them, he may know that his sons are doomed to death, that his broad lands shall pass away to the stranger, and that his race shall come to an end.'

"When the Seer had ended this prediction, he threw his white stone into a small loch, by the side of which the gallows was erected, and declared that whoever should find that stone would be similarly gifted. Then submitting to his fate, he was hung up on high, and this wild and fearful doom ended his strange and uncanny life.

"I must offer an explanation concerning the fragmentary nature of Coinneach's prophecy. He uttered it in all its horrible length; but I at present suppress the last portion, which is as yet unfulfilled. Every other part of the prediction has most literally and accurately come to pass; but let us earnestly hope that the course of future events may at length give the lie to the avenging curse of the Seer.

The last clause of the prophecy is well known to many of those versed in Highland family tradition, and I trust that it may remain unfulfilled. With regard to the four Highland lairds who were to be buck-toothed, hare-lipped, half-witted, and a stammerer —viz., Mackenzie, Baronet of Gairloch; Chisholm of Chisholm; Grant, Baronet of Grant; and Macleod of Raasay—I am uncertain which was which. Suffice it to say, that the four lairds were marked by the above-mentioned distinguishing personal peculiarities, and all four were the contemporaries of the last of the Seaforths.

" In due time the Earl returned to his home, after the fascinations of Paris had paled, and when he felt disposed to exchange frivolous or vicious enjoyment abroad for the exercise of despotic authority in the society of a jealous Countess at home. He was gathered to his fathers in 1678, and was succeeded by his eldest son, the fourth Earl. It is not my purpose to relate the vicissitudes of the family, which are unconnected with the curse of Coinneach Odhar, further than by giving a brief outline of them; and they are sufficiently remarkable to supply a strange chapter of domestic history.

" The fourth Earl married a daughter of the illustrious family of Herbert, Marquis of Powis, and he himself was created a Marquis by the abdicated King of St Germains, while his wife's brother was created a Duke. His son, the fifth Earl, being engaged in the Rebellion of 1715, forfeited his estate and titles to the Crown; but in 1726 his lands were restored to him, and he and his son after him lived in wealth and honour as great Highland chiefs; and the latter, who was by courtesy styled Lord Fortrose, represented his native county of Ross in many Parliaments about the middle of last century. In 1766, the honours of the peerage were restored to his son, who was created Viscount Fortrose, and in 1771 Earl of Seaforth; but those titles, which were Irish, did not last long, but became extinct at his death, in 1781. None of these vicissitudes were foretold in the Seer's prophecy; for, in spite of them all, the family continued to prosper. That ruin which the unsuccessful rising in 1715 had brought upon many other great houses, was retrieved in the case of Seaforth, by the exercise of sovereign favour, and restored possessions and renewed honours preserved the grandeur of the race. But on the death of the last Earl, his second cousin, descended from a younger son of the fourth Earl and his vindictive Countess, inherited the family estates and the Chiefdom of the Mackenzies, which he held for one short year, but never actually enjoyed, being slain at sea, in the south of India, by the Mahrattas, after a gallant resistance, in 1783. He was succeeded by his brother, in whom, as the last of his race, the Seer's prophecy began to be accomplished.

"Francis Humberstone Mackenzie was a very remarkable man. He was born in 1754, and although he was deaf and dumb, he was able to fill an important position in the world, by the force of his natural abilities and the favour of fortune. He may be said to have quite recovered the use of speech, for he was able to converse; but he was totally deaf, and all communications were made to him by signs and in writing. Yet he raised a regiment at the beginning of the great European War; he was created a British Peer in 1797, as Baron Seaforth of Kintail; in 1800 he went out to Barbadoes as Governor, and afterwards to Demerara and Berbice; and in 1808 he was made a Lieutenant-General. These were singular incidents in the life of a deaf and dumb man. He married a very amiable and excellent woman, Mary Proby, the daughter of a dignitary of the Church, and niece of the first Lord Carysfort, by whom he had a fine family of three sons and six daughters. When he considered his own position—deaf and formerly dumb; when he saw his three sons all rising to man's estate; and when he looked around him, and observed the peculiar marks set upon the persons of the predicted four contemporary great Highland lairds, all in accordance with Coinneach's prophecy —he must have felt ill at ease, unless he was able, with the incredulous indifference of a man of the world, to spurn the idea from him as an old wife's superstition.

"However, fatal conviction was forced upon him, and all those who remembered the family tradition, by the lamentable events which filled his house with mourning. One after another his three promising sons were cut off by death. The last, who was the most distinguished of them all, for the finest qualities both of head and heart, was stricken by a sore and lingering disease, and had gone, with a part of the family, for his health, to the south of England. Lord Seaforth remained in the North, at Brahan Castle. A daily bulletin was sent to him from the sick chamber of his beloved son. One morning, the accounts being rather more favourable, the household began to rejoice; and a friend and neighbour, who was visiting the Chief, came down after breakfast full of the good news, and gladly imparted them to the old family piper, whom he met in front of the Castle. The aged retainer shook his head and sighed —'Na, na,' said he, 'he'll never recover. It's decreed that Seaforth must outlive *all* his three sons.' This he said in allusion to the Seer's prophecy: thus his words were understood by the family; and thus members of the family have again and again repeated the strange tale. The words of the old piper proved too true. A few more posts brought to Seaforth the tidings of the death of the last of his three sons.

"At length, on the 11th January 1815, Lord Seaforth died, the last of his race. His modern title became extinct. The Chiefdom of the Mackenzies, divested of its rank and honour, passed away to a very remote collateral, who succeeded to no portion of the property, and the great Seaforth estates were inherited by a white-hooded lassie from the East. Lord Seaforth's eldest surviving daughter, the Hon. Mary Frederica Elizabeth Mackenzie, had married, in 1804, Admiral Sir Samuel *Hood*, Bart., K.B., who was Admiral of the West India station while Seaforth himself was Governor in those islands. Sir Samuel afterwards had the chief command in the Indian seas, whither his lady accompanied him, and spent several years with him in different parts of the East Indies. He died while holding that high command, very nearly at the same time with Lord Seaforth, so that his youthful wife was a recent widow at the time, and returned home from India in her widow's weeds, to take possession of her paternal inheritance; so that she was literally a white-hooded lassie (that is a young woman in widow's weeds, and a Hood by name) from the East. After some years of widowhood, Lady Hood Mackenzie married a second time, Mr Stewart, a grandson of the sixth Earl of Galloway, who assumed the name of Mackenzie, and established himself on his lady's extensive estates in the North. Thus, the possessions of Seaforth may be truly said to have passed from the male line of the ancient house of Mackenzie. And still more strikingly was this fulfilled, as regarded a large portion of these estates, when Mr and Mrs Stewart Mackenzie sold the great Island of Lews to Sir James Matheson.

"After many years of happiness and prosperity, a frightful accident threw the family into mourning. Mrs Stewart Mackenzie was one day driving her younger sister, the Honourable Caroline Mackenzie, in a pony carriage, among the woods in the vicinity of Brahan Castle. Suddenly the ponies took fright, and started off at a furious pace. Mrs Stewart Mackenzie was quite unable to check them, and both she and her sister were thrown out of the carriage much bruised and hurt. She happily speedily recovered from the accident, but the injury which her sister sustained proved fatal, and, after lingering for some time in a hopeless state, she died, to the inexpressible grief of all the members of her family.

As Mrs Stewart Mackenzie was driving the carriage at the time
of the accident, she may be said to have been the innocent cause
of her sister's death, and thus to have fulfilled the last portion of
Coinneach's prophecy which has yet been accomplished.

"Thus we have seen that the last Chief of Seaforth was *deaf
and dumb;* that he had *three sons;* that he survived them all;
that the four great Highland lairds who were his contemporaries
were all distinguished by the peculiar personal marks which were
predicted; that his estates were inherited by a *white-hooded lassie
from the East;* that his great possessions passed into the hands of
other races; and that his eldest daughter and heiress was so unfortunate as to be the cause of her *sister's death.* In this very
remarkable instance of family fate, the prophecy was not found
out after the events occurred; it had been current for generations
in the Highlands, and its tardy fulfilment was marked curiously
and anxiously by an entire clan and a whole county. Seaforth
was respected and beloved far and near, and strangers, as well as
friends and clansmen, mourned along with him in the sorrows of
his later years.   The gradual development of the doom was
watched with sympathy and grief, and the fate of Seaforth has
been, during the last half-century of his life, regarded as one of
the most curious instances of that second-sight for which the inhabitants of the Highlands of Scotland have been so long celebrated.   Mr Stewart Mackenzie, the accomplished husband of the
heiress of Seaforth, after being for many years a distinguished
member of the House of Commons and a Privy Councillor, held
several high appointments in the Colonial Dominions of the
British Crown. He was successively Governor of Ceylon and
Lord High Commissioner of the Ionian Islands, and he died,
universally beloved and lamented, in the year 1843.

"I am indebted to 'Burke's Viccissitudes of Families' for those
of the predictions referring to the Seaforth family, and have given
most of them pretty freely in Burke's own language.   The following was kindly sent me by a Lochalsh friend :—

> " Bheir Tanaistear Chlann Choinnich
> Rocus *bàn* às a choille;
> 'S bheir è ceilé bho tigh-ciuil
> Le a mhuinntir 'na aghaidh;
> 'S gum bi' n Tanaistear, mor
> Ann an gniomh 's an ceann-labhairt,
> 'Nuair bhios am Pap' anns an Roimh
> Air a thilgeadh dheth chathair.

" Thall fa-chomhair creag-a-chobh
Comhnuichaidh taillear caol odhar;
'S Seumas gorach mar thighearn,
'S Seumas glie mar fhear-tomhais—
A mharcaicheas gun srian
Air loth fhiadhaich à roghainn;
Ach cuiridh mor-chuis gun chiall
'N aite siol nam fiadh siol nan gobhar;
'S tuitidh an t-Eilean-dubh briagha
Fuidh riaghladh iasgairean Aūch.

" Nuair a bhios da eaglais an Sgire na Toiseachd
A's lamh da ordaig an I-Stian'
Da dhrochaid aig Sguideal nan geocairé
As fear da imleag an Dunean
Thig Milltearan à Carn-a-chlarsair,
Air carbad gun each gun srian,
A dh-fhagas am Blar-dubh na fhasach
Dortadh fuil le iomadh sgian;
A's olaidh am fitheach tri saitheachd
Dé dh-fhuil nan Gaidheal, bho clach nam Fionn."

"Nuair a ghlaodhas paisdean tigh Chulchallaidh
'Tha sligè ar mortairean dol thairis!'
Thig bho Cròidh madadh ruadh
Bhi's 'measg an t-sluaigh mar-mhadadh-alluidh
Re' da-fhichead bliadhna a's còrr,
'S gum bi na chotá iomadh mallachd;
'N sin tilgear e gu falamh bronach
Mar shean sguab air cul an doruis;
A's bithidh an tuath mhor mor eunlaith sporsail,
'S an tighearnan cho bochd ris na sporais.
Tha beannachd 'san onair bhoidhich,
A's mallachd an dortadh na fola!

" Nuair bhitheas caisteal ciar Chulchallaidh
Na sheasaidh fuar, agus falamh,
'S na cathagan 's na rocuis
Gu seolta sgiathail thairis,
Gabhaidh duine graineal comhnaidh,
Ri thaobh, mi-bheusal a's salach,
Nach gleidh guidhe stal-phosaidh
'S nach eisd ri cleireach na caraid

Ach bho chreag-a-chobh gu Sgir na Toiseachd
Gum be Muisean air toir gach caileag ;
A's ochan ! ochan s' ma leon
Sluigidh am balgáire suas moran talamh !

" I would give a translation of these verses, but feel the exigencies of space forbids. It will be noticed that a peculiar reference is made to the Mackenzies of Rosehaugh in the first
and second stanzas—' Bheir e ceilè bho tigh-ciùil.' · He will take a
bride from a dancing-house or saloon. And again —' Cuiridh mor-
chuis gun chiall, 'N aite Siol nam fiadh, Siol nan gobhar.' ' Foolish
pomp will put in the place of the seed of the deer the seed of the
goat.' The deer and the goat being the coat of arms respectively
of the Mackenzies and of the Fletchers. The third and fourth
verses are only too true regarding the Mackenzies and the Castle of
Kileoy.

" Having said this much of the Seer of Brahan, and of the
second-sight, it may be amusing to many to know how far the
prophecies of other seers and their fulfilments agreed. For this
purpose I select an instance or two recorded by an English nobleman in the seventeenth century, who, previous to his going to the
Highlands, was one of the sturdiest unbelievers in the second-
sight.-—

" ' Sir,—I heard very much, and believed very little, of the
second-sight ; yet its being assumed by severall of great veracitie,
I was induced to make inquirie after it in the year 1652, being
confined to abide in the North of Scotland by the English usurpers.
I was travelling in the Highlands and a good number
of servants with me, as is usual there. One of them going a little
before me, entering into a house where I was to stay all night,
and going hastily to the door, he suddenly stept back with a
screech, and did fall by a stone which hit his foot. I asked him
what the matter was, for he seemed to be very much frighted.
He told me very seriously that I should not lodge in that house,
because shortly a dead coffin would be carried out of it, for many
were carrying of it when he was heard to cry. I neglected his
words, and staying there, he said to the other servants he was
sorry for it, and that surely what he saw would come to pass.
" ' Tho' no sick person was then there, yet the landlord died of
ane apoplectick fit before I left the house. . . . I shall trouble
you with but one more, which I thought the most remarkable of any
that occurred to me. In January 1652, Lieut.-Colonel Alexander

Munro and I were in the house of one William Macleud, of Ferin-
lea, in the county of Ross. He, the landlord, and I were sitting
on three chairs neir the fire; and in the corner of the great chimney there were two islanders, who were that very night come to
the house, and were related to the landlord. While the one of
them was talking to Munro, I perceived the other to look oddly
toward me. From his look, and his being an islander, I conjectured
him a seer, and asked him what he stared at? He answered me
by desiring me to rise from the chair, for it was ane unluckie one.
I asked him why? He answered, because there is a dead man in
the chair next to me. Well, said I, if he be in the next chair to
me, I may keep mine own. But what is the likeness of the man?
He said he was a tall man with a long grey coat, booted, and one
of his legs hanging over the arme of the chair, and his head hanging dead on the other side, and his arm backward, as if it was
broken. There were some English troops then quartered near that
place, and there being at that time a great frost after a thaw, the
country was covered all over with yce. Four or five of the English
were ryding by this hons some two hours after the vision, while
we were sitting by the fire, we heard a great noise, which proved
to be those troopers, with the help of other servants, carrying in
one of their number, who had a very mischievous fall, and his arme
broke; and falling frequently in swooning fits, they brought him
into the hall, and set him on the verie chair, and in the verie posture that the seer prophecied. But the man did not die, though
he recovered with great difficulty.

    " ' Among the accounts given me by Sir Norman Maclud, there
was one worthy of special notice, which was thus:—There was a
gentleman in the Isle of Harris, who was always seen by the seers
with an arrow in his thigh. Such in the isle who thought these
prognostications infallible, did not doubt but he would be shot in
the thigh before he died. Sir Norman told me that he heard it
the subject of their discourse for many years. At last he died
without any such accident. Sir Norman was at his burial at St
Clement's Church in the Harris. At the same time the corpse
of another gentleman was brought to be buried in the veric same
church. The friends of either came to debate who should first
enter the church, and in a trice from words they came to blows.
One of the number, who was armed with a bow and arrows, let
one fly among them. (Now, everie familie in that isle have their
burial place in the church in stone chests, and the bodies are
carried in open biers to the burial place.) Sir Norman having ap-
peased the tumult, one of the arrows was found shot in the dead

14

man's thigh. To this Sir Norman was a witness. These are matters of fact which, I assure you, are truly related.

"Succinct Accompt of my Lord Torbott's Relations, in a Letter to the Hon. Robert Boyle, Esquire, of the Predictions made by Seers, whereof himself was Ear and Eye-witness.

" Armstrong says—

" ' I have seen a work on the second-sight by one who styles himself " Theophilus Insulamis," wherein is recorded a great variety of cases where these visions were exactly fulfilled, and in so satisfactory a way, that many of the Highland clergy became believers in the existence of this faculty. Either Dr Beattie must not have been aware of the circumstance, or he threw out a galling sarcasm when he said that none but the most ignorant pretended to be gifted with the second-sight.'

" These cases of shadowy prediction will enable the reader to balance the conflicting opinions entertained on the curious subject of the second-sight ; the one by Dr Beattie, of Aberdeen, and the other by the celebrated Dr Samuel Johnson. The former ascribes this pretended faculty wholly to the influence of physical causes on superstitious and uninstructed minds. He thinks that long tracts of mountainous deserts, covered with dark heath, and often obscured by misty weather, narrow valleys, thinly inhabited, and bounded by precipices resounding with the fall of torrents, the mournful dashing of waves along the firths and lakes that intersect the country, the grotesque and ghastly appearance of such a landscape, by the light of the moon, must diffuse a gloom over the fancy, which may be compatible enough with occasional and social merriment, but cannot fail to tincture the thoughts of a native in the hour of silence and solitude ; that it is not wonderful if persons of a lively imagination, immured in deep solitude, and surrounded with the stupendous scenery of clouds, precipices, and torrents, should dream (even when they think themselves awake) of those few striking ideas with which their lonely lives are diversified, of corpses, funeral processions, and other objects of terror ; or of marriages, and the arrival of strangers, and such like matters of more agreeable curiosity ; that none but ignorant people pretend to be gifted in this way, and that in them it may be nothing more, perhaps, than short fits of sudden sleep or drowsiness, attended with lively dreams, and arising from bodily disorder, the effect of idleness, low spirits, or a gloomy imagination. Nor is it extraordinary, he observes, that one should have the appearance of being awake, and should even think one's-self so, during those fits of dozing, that they should come on suddenly, and while one is engaged in some business. The same thing happens to persons much fatigued, or long kept awake, who frequently fall asleep for a moment, or for a long space, while they are standing, or walking, or riding on horseback, add but a lively dream to this slumber, and (which is the frequent effect of disease) take away the consciousness of having been asleep, and a superstitious man may easily mistake his dream for a waking vision. Beattie disbelieves the prophetical nature of the second-sight, and does not think it analogous to the operations of Providence, nor to the course of nature, that the Deity should work a miracle in order to give intimation of the frivolous matters which were commonly predicted by seers ; and that these intimations should be given for no end, and to those persons only who are idle and solitary, who speak Gaelic, or who live among mountains and deserts.

"To these objections it has been powerfully replied by Dr Johnson, that by presuming to determine what is fit, and what is beneficial, they presuppose more knowledge of the universal system than man has hitherto acquired; and therefore depend upon principles too complicated and extensive for our comprehension, and that there can be no security in the consequence when the premises are not understood; that the second-sight is only wonderful because it is rare, for considered in itself, it involves no more difficulty than dreams, or perhaps the regular exercise of the cogitative faculty; that a general opinion of communicative impulses or visionary representations has prevailed in all ages and nations; that particular instances have been given with such evidence as neither Bacon nor Boyle have been able to resist; that sudden impressions, which the event has verified, have been felt by more than own or publish them; that the second-sight of the Hebrides implies only the local frequency of a power which is nowhere totally unknown; and that where we are unable to decide by antecedent reason, we must be content to yield to the force of testimony. By pretension to second-sight, no profit was ever sought or gained. It is an involuntary affection, in which neither hope nor fear are known to have any part. Those who profess to feel it, do not boast of it as a privilege, nor are considered by others as advantageously distinguished. They have no temptation to feign, and their hearers have no motive to encourage the imposture."

Several members took part in the discussion which followed the reading of the paper (which was well received), and gave additional predictions of Coinneach Odhar. We trust to get another instalment next session, and that parties in possession of them will kindly forward them to the Secretary.

25TH MARCH 1875.

This meeting was wholly taken up with the arrangements for the competition for the Society's prizes for the best Gaelic composition, which is to be given annually in different parishes throughout the Highlands. It was unanimously agreed, " in consideration of the very active interest taken by Sir Kenneth S. Mackenzie, Bart. of Gairloch, by the School Board of which he is chairman, and by the schoolmasters of Gairloch, in forwarding the movement for teaching Gaelic in Highland schools, that the parish of Gairloch receive the *first* opportunity to compete." After which the Secretary produced a letter from the School Board of Knockbain, in reply to the Society's circular, in which "the Board agreed with the Society that it was necessary to have Gaelic taught in the schools in districts where it was the prevailing language ; and that a grant ought to be given for teaching it as a special subject."

1ST APRIL 1875.

A long paper by the late Mr GOWIE, Inland Revenue, on "The Fingallian or Parallel Roads of Glenroy," was read by the Secretary, on behalf of Mr Noble. In the paper it was stoutly maintained by Mr Gowie that the roads were made by man, but the Society unanimously held that they were the work of nature, produced by the action of water. The paper was, however, exceedingly interesting. It was agreed to discontinue regular meetings for the remainder of the session, but the Secretary was requested to call special meetings at any time if circumstances required it.

The following resolution was brought up by the special committee appointed for the purpose, unanimously agreed to, and ordered to be engrossed in the minutes:—"The Gaelic Society having learned, with sincere regret, of the untimely death of Alexander Halley, Esq., M.D., F.G.S., London, unanimously resolve to record in their minutes the high estimation in which he was held by all the members of the Society. He was one of the earliest life members of the Society, and was a gentleman who not only took a very lively interest in its proceedings and contributed to its volumes of Transactions. but also at all times gave his warm support to every movement calculated to raise the Celt, his language, and literature."

5TH JULY 1875.

This was a special meeting for the election of members and making the final arrangements for the Annual Assembly. A letter was read from the School Board of Jura, in reply to the circular regarding teaching Gaelic in Highland Schools, in which they say, "The Board approve of said resolution (embcdied in circular), and are willing to co-operate with other Boards in promoting the object in view." The Clerk of the School Board of Salen, Mull, writes, under date 4th June, in reply to the same circular—"I am instructed to state that this Board had already resolved that Gaelic should be taught in their schools." The Publishing Committee was re-elected, with full powers to print and publish the Transactions for 1875-76. Mr William Mackay, solicitor, was added to the committee, and Alex. Mackenzie, auctioneer, was re-elected Convener.

MEMBERS OF SOCIETY.

HONORARY CHIEFTAINS.

Sir Kenneth S. Mackenzie of Gairloch, Bart.
Professor John Stuart Blackie, Edinburgh University
Charles Fraser-Mackintosh, Esq. of Drummond, M.P.
Duncan Davidson, Esq. of Tulloch

LIFE MEMBERS.

Cluny Macpherson of Cluny Macpherson
Forbes, Alexander, 143 West Regent Street, Glasgow
Fraser, Alexander, 74 Church Street, Inverness
Fraser-Mackintosh, Charles, of Drummond, M.P.
Halley, Alex., M.D., 19 Harley Street, London (now deceased.)
Mackenzie, Sir Kenneth S., of Gairloch, Bart.

HONORARY MEMBERS.

Anderson, James, solicitor, Inverness
Blackie, Professor John Stuart, Edinburgh University
Bourke, Very Rev. Canon, Pres., St Jarlath's College, Tuam, Ireland
Buchan, Dr Patrick, Lancashire Insurance Company
Cameron, Captain D. C., Talisker
Campbell, George Murray, Gampola, Ceylon
Chisholm, Captain A. Macrae, Glassburn, Strathglass
Colvin, John, solicitor, Inverness
Couper, William, Highland Railway, Inverness
Davidson, Duncan, of Tulloch, Ross-shire

Davidson, Donald, solicitor, Inverness
Duff, George S., Heather Ley House, Inverness
Farquharson, Rev. Archibald, Tiree
Ferguson, Mrs, 6 Charles Street, Lowndes Square, London
Fraser, Hugh, Balloch, Culloden
Fraser, A. T. F., clothier, Church Street, Inverness
Fraser, Huntly, merchant, Inverness
Grant, John, Cardiff, Wales
Grant, General Sir Patrick, G.C.B., Royal Military Hospital, Chelsea, London
Grant, Robert, of Messrs Macdougall & Co., Inverness
Innes, Charles, solicitor, Inverness
Jolly, William, H.M. Inspector of Schools, Albyn Place, Inverness
Macalpin, Ken. Grant, A.I.C.E., F.R.G S., Pembroke, South Wales
Macalpin, Donald Alexander, R.N., F.R.G.S., Pembroke, South Wales
Macandrew, H. C., Sheriff-Clerk, Inverness-shire
Macdonald, Alexander, Balranald, Uist
Macdonald, Allan, solicitor, Inverness
Macdonald, Andrew, solicitor, Inverness
Macdonald, Captain D. P., Ben-Nevis Distillery
Macdonald, John, Station Hotel, Inverness
Macdonell, Patrick, Kinchyle, Dores
Macfarquhar, John, Douglas Row
Macgregor, Rev. Alex., M.A., Inverness
Mackay, Charles, LL.D., Fern Dell Cottage, near Dorking
Mackay, Donald, Gampola, Kandy, Ceylon
Mackay, Donald, San Francisco, California
Mackay, George F., Roxburgh, Otago, New Zealand
Mackay, James, Roxburgh, Otago, New Zealand
Mackay, John, C.E., Mountsfield, Shrewsbury
Mackay, John, of Ben Reay, near Montreal
Mackay, John Stuart, San Francisco, California
Mackay, Neil, Penylan House, Pencock, New Bridge End, Glamorganshire
Mackenzie, Rev. A. D., Free Church, Kilmorack
Mackenzie, Major Colin Lyon, of St Martins, Provost of Inverness
Mackenzie, Colonel Hugh, Poyntzfield House, Invergordon
Mackenzie, John, M.D., of Eileanach, Inverness
Mackenzie, H., Gollanfield, Inverness
Mackenzie, Osgood H., of Inverewe, Poolewe
Mackintosh, Æneas W., of Raigmore
Mackintosh, Angus, of Holme

Mackintosh, P. A., C.E., Bridgend, Glamorgan
Maclean, Rev. John, Free Church, Stratherrick
Maclennan, Alexander, of Messrs Macdougall & Co., Inverness
Macpherson, Major Gordon, of Cluny
Menzies, John, Caledonian Hotel, Inverness
Neaves, The Hon. Lord, LL.D., Edinburgh
Nicolson, Angus, LL.B., Editor of *The Gael*, Glasgow
Ross, Rev. William, Rothesay
Scott, Roderick, solicitor, Inverness
Seafield, The Right Hon. The Earl of, Castle Grant
Shaw, A. Mackintosh, Secretary's Office, General Post-office, London
Snowie, Thomas Beals, Inverness
Stewart, Charles, of Brin and Dalcrombie, Inverness
Stoddart, Evan, Mudgee, N. S. Wales, Australia
Sutherland, Alexander, Taff Brae Cottage, Cefn, Merthyr-Tydvil
Sutherland-Walker, Evan Charles, of Skibo

ORDINARY MEMBERS.

Alison, James Mackenzie, Redcastle
Baillie, Bailie Peter, Inverness
Bannatyne, W. Mackinnon, Royal Academy, Inverness
Barclay, John, accountant, Inverness
Barron, James, " Courier " Office, Inverness
Bisset, Rev. Mr, R.C., Stratherrick
Black, George, banker, Inverness
Brownlie, Alexander, rector, Raining School, Inverness
Cameron, Archibald, Auchafarick, Muasdale, Kintyre
Cameron, Colin, Polmaily Wood, Glen-Urquhart
Cameron, Donald, of Lochiel, M.P.
Campbell, Alexander, supervisor, Kyleakin, Skye
Campbell, Donald, draper, Bridge Street, Inverness
Campbell, Duncan, Polnonochan, Invergarry
Campbell, George J., writer and N.P., Church Street, Inverness
Campbell, Fraser (of Fraser & Campbell,) High Street, Inverness
Campbell, T. D. (of Cumming & Campbell,) Ness Bank, Inverness
Carmichael, Alexander A., Inland Revenue, Lochmaddy, Uist
Charleson, Hector, Railway Refreshment Rooms, Forres
Charleson, Kenneth, Inverness
Clarke, Alexander, contractor, 15 Argyle Street, Inverness
Cook, Alexander, Glen-Urquhart

Cullen, James M'C., 63 Stevenson Street, Calton, Glasgow
Cumming, James, Allanfearn, Inverness
Dallas, Alexander, Town-Clerk, Inverness
Davidson, Bailie John, Inglis Street, Inverness
Davidson, Lachlan, banker, Kingussie
Duncan, Dr George, Conobra, Lochalsh
Falconer, Peter, plasterer, Inverness
Forbes, Dr George Fiddes, of the Bombay Army, Viewfield House,
    Inverness
Forsyth, Ebenezer, " Inverness Advertiser" Office, Inverness
Forsyth, W. B., of the " Inverness Advertiser," Inverness
Fraser, A. R., British Linen Company, Kingussie
Fraser, Alexander, solicitor, Inverness
Fraser, Andrew, builder, Inverness
Fraser, Andrew, cabinetmaker, Union Street, Inverness
Fraser, D., Glenelg
Fraser, Donald, solicitor, Nairn
Fraser, Hugh, inspector of poor, Inverness
Fraser, Hugh C., Haugh, Inverness
Fraser, James, of Fraser & Mactavish, Lombard Street, Inverness
Fraser, James, C.E., Inverness
Fraser, James, Mauld, Strathglass
Fraser, James, manufacturer, 41·North Albion Street, Glasgow
Fraser, Kenneth, writer, Church Street, Inverness
Fraser, Miss, Farraline Villa, North Berwick
Fraser, Simon, banker, Lochcarron
Fraser, William, jeweller, High Street, Inverness
Fraser, William, ironmonger, Inverness
Galloway, George, chemist, Inverness
Hood, Andrew, commercial traveller, 39 Union Street, Inverness
Hood, Miss, 39 Union Street, Inverness
Keith, Charles, bookseller, Inverness
Kennedy, Donald, farmer, Drumashie, Dores
Kennedy, Neil, Kishorn, Lochcarron
Loban, Robert Cumming, Caledonian Bank, Invergarry
Macbean, Bailie Alexander, Inverness
Macbean, Lachlan, draper's assistant, Cumming & Campbell's,
    Church Street, Inverness
Mackaskill, D., saddler, Fort-William
Macculloch, Duncan, teacher, Inverness
Macdonald, Alexander, messenger-at-arms, Inverness
Macdonald, Alexander, flesher, New Market, Inverness
Macdonald, Angus, Queen Street, Inverness

Macdonald, Sheriff Andrew L., Telford Street, Inverness
Macdonald, Donald, painter, Inverness
Macdonald, Coll, hotel-keeper, Lochend
Macdonald, Finlay, Druidaig, Kintail
Macdonald, James, clerk, National Bank of Scotland, Inverness
Macdonald, John, merchant, Exchange, Inverness
Macdonald, John, Inland Revenue, Lanark
Macdonald, Robert, 48 Telford Road, Inverness
Macdonald, William, M.D., Inverness
Macdougall, Donald, Craggan, Grantown
Macgregor, Donald, 42 Glassford Street, Glasgow
Macgregor, Rev. Malcolm, F.C. Manse, Ferrintosh
Maciver, Donald (student of Aberdeen University), Church Street,
    Inverness
Maciver, Duncan, Church Street, Inverness
Maciver, Finlay, carver, Church Street, Inverness
Macinnes, John, innkeeper, Invergarry
Macinnes, Neil, hotel-keeper, Kyleakin, Skye
Mackay, Alexander, carpenter, Rose Street, Inverness
Mackay, Charles, builder, Culduthel Road, Inverness
Mackay, David, publisher, 33 Bridge Street, Inverness
Mackay, D. J., solicitor, Inverness
Mackay, George, Royal Artillery, Gun Wharf Barracks, Ports-
    mouth
Mackay, Robert, merchant, Hamilton Place, Inverness
Mackay, William, solicitor, Church Street, Inverness
Mackay, William, bookseller, High Street, Inverness
Mackenzie, Alexander, auctioneer, 57 Church Street, Inverness
Mackenzie, A. C., teacher, Maryburgh, Dingwall
Mackenzie, E. G., solicitor, Inverness
Mackenzie, C. D., 102 Linthorpe Road, Middlesboro'-on-Tees
Mackenzie, Finlay Matheson, 208 Stirling Road, Glasgow
Mackenzie, Hugh, bookbinder, Inverness
Mackenzie, Captain John, Telford Road, Inverness
Mackenzie, James H., bookseller, High Street, Inverness
Mackenzie, Malcolm J., teacher, Parish School, Lochcarron
Mackenzie, Murdoch, Inland Revenue, Tulloch, Strathdon
Mackenzie, Thomas (late of High School), Broadstone Park, Inver-
    ness
Mackenzie, William, " Aberdeen Free Press"
Mackenzie, William, draper, 19 Bridge Street, Inverness
Mackenzie, Rev. Dr, Silverwells, Inverness
Mackinnon, Charles, Back Street, Campbelton, Argyll

Mackintosh, Charles, commission-agent, Church Street, Inverness
Mackintosh, Donald, The Hotel, Glenelg
Mackintosh, Duncan, Bank of Scotland, Oban
Mackintosh, Duncan, draper, 3 Hill Place, Inverness
Mackintosh, Ewen, Roy Bridge Hotel, by Kingussie
Mackintosh, John (Divinity Student), Mauld, Strathglass
Mackintosh, Lachlan, Milton of Farr, Daviot
Mackintosh, Peter, Messrs Macdougall & Co.'s, Grantown
Maclachlan, Duncan, publisher, 64 South Bridge, Edinburgh
Maclean, Alexander, Lombard Street, Inverness
Maclean, Roderick, Alness
Maclean, John, Holm Mains, Inverness
Maclennan, Kenneth, clothier, Colchester
Macleod, Alexander, grocer, Huntly Street, Inverness
Macmillan, John, Kingsmills Road, Inverness
Macneil, Nigel, 3 Kinning Street, Glasgow
Macphail, Alexander, farmer, Cullaird, Dores
Macphater, Angus, Lintmill of Campbelton, Argyll
Macpherson, Col. A. F., of Catlodge, Waverley Hotel, Inverness
Macpherson, Mrs Sarah, Alexandra Villa, Kingussie
Macrae, Alexander M. M., Glenoze, Skye
Macrae, Rev. A., Free Church Manse, Strathpeffer
Macrae, Rev. Angus, Glen-Urquhart
Macrae, Donald, High School, Inverness
Macrae, Duncan A., Fernaig, Lochalsh
Macrae, Duncan, Braintrath, Lochalsh
Macrae, R., postmaster, Beauly
Macrae, Roderick, Island of Eigg, by Greenock
Macraild, A. R., inspector of poor, Lochalsh
Matheson, John, supervisor, Alness
Menzies, Duncan, Ness Bank, Inverness
Menzies, Rev. John, M.A., Fort-Augustus
Morrison, Robert, jeweller, Inverness
Morrison, William, rector, Dingwall Academy
Mundell, John, Scallisaig, Glenelg
Munro, John, wine-merchant, Inverness
Murdoch, John, "The Highlander," Inverness
Murray, William, chief-constable, The Castle, Inverness
Noble, Donald, baker, Muirtown Street, Inverness
Noble, John, bookseller, Castle Street, Inverness
Rhind, John, architect, Inverness
Rose, A. Macgregor (Divinity Student), 15 College Bounds, Old
    Aberdeen

Rose, Hugh, solicitor, Inverness
Ross, Alexander, architect, Inverness
Ross, James, shipowner, Portland Place, Inverness
Ross, Jonathan, draper, High Street, Inverness
Ross, —— Inland Revenue, Alness
Shaw, John D., accountant, Inverness
Simpson, Bailie Alexander, Inverness
Sinclair, Duncan, teacher, Parish School, Lochalsh
Sinclair, Roderick, High Street, Inverness
Smith, Thomas A., clerk, Waterloo Place, Inverness
Snowie, W. M., Inverness
Stewart, Rev. A., Ballachulish
Stewart, Colin J., Dingwall
Tulloch, John, painter, Inverness
Watson, William (Assistant Professor), 22 Gillespie Crescent,
    Edinburgh
Wilson, George, S.S.C., 14 Hill Street, Edinburgh
White, David, Church Street, Inverness

APPRENTICES.

Fraser, John, with Maciver & Co., Church Street, Inverness
Macdonald, Murdoch, with Maciver & Co., Church Street, Inver-
    ness
Macgillivray, William, assistant grocer, Hamilton Place, Inverness
Mackay, James John, Drummond, Inverness
Mackenzie, Alexander, assistant grocer, Hamilton Place, Inver-
    ness
Maclennan, Alexander, clerk, Goods Department, Highland Rail-
    way, Inverness
Macpherson, William, with Maciver & Co., Church Street, Inver-
    ness
Matheson, Alexander, stonecutter, Academy Street, Inverness
Noble, Andrew, assistant grocer, Bridge Street, Inverness
Ross, Donald, Union Street, Inverness
Smith, Alexander, assistant grocer, Bridge Street, Inverness
Thomson, Robert, The Grocery, High Street, Inverness

DONATIONS TO THE LIBRARY, 1873-75.

DONORS.	DONATIONS.
Maclauchlan & Stewart......	Dan Oisein (Maclauchlan's edition).
ditto	...Munro's Gaelic Primer.
ditto	...Macalpine's Gaelic Dictionary.
ditto	...Macvuirich's Duanaire.
ditto	...Munro's Gaelic Grammar.
ditto	...Orain Mhic-an-t-saoir.
ditto	...Ross's Gaelic Songs.
ditto	...Dewar's Gaelic Sermons.
D. Mackintosh, Milton	...History of the Rebellion, 1745-6.
Lauchlan Mackintosh........	Welsh Bible.
John Murdoch..............	The Dauntless Red Hugh.
Alex. Macbean..............	Grace Myer's Sewing Machine.
Lachlan Macbean............	Old Gaelic Testament.
ditto	...Adhamh agus Eubh.
ditto	...Macpherson's Ossian.
ditto	...Old Gaelic Bible.
D. Maciver...................	Philological Uses of the Celtic Tongue.
Alex. Mackintosh Shaw.....	Comh-chruinneachadh Orain Gailig.
ditto	..."The Clan Battle of Perth."
The Publishers..............	The Gael, 1873.
H. Mackenzie, Bank Lane..	Fraser of Knockie's Highland Music.
W. Mackay..................	The Game Laws.
The Author..................	Six copies of Mackenzie's Eachdraidh-na-h-Alba for the Gaelic Class.

PRINTED AT THE COURIER OFFICE, INVERNESS.

Lightning Source UK Ltd.
Milton Keynes UK
UKOW05f1819230317
297375UK00024B/637/P